Tom
Edna
1982

The
Christ Life
from
Nativity to
Ascension

2019

The Christ Life from Nativity to Ascension

Geoffrey Hodson

(1975)

A QUEST BOOK
Published under a grant from the Kern Foundation

THE THEOSOPHICAL PUBLISHING HOUSE
Wheaton, Ill., U.S.A.
Madras, India / London, England

First Quest edition published by The
Theosophical Publishing House,
Wheaton, Illinois, a department of the
Theosophical Society in America

ISBN: 0-8356-0467-5

Library of Congress Catalog Number 75-4169

Printed in the United States of America

DEDICATION

This work is dedicated to Philo Judaeus, the great Alexandrian Sage

Sometimes, when I have come to my work empty, I have suddenly become full, ideas being in an invisible manner showered upon me, and implanted in me from on high; so that through the influence of divine inspiration I have become filled with enthusiasm, and have known neither the place in which I was nor those who were present, nor myself, nor what I was saying, nor what I was writing, for then I have been conscious of a richness of interpretation, an enjoyment of light, a most keen-sighted vision, a most distinct view of the objects treated, such as would be given through the eyes from the clearest exhibition.

—Philo
Translated by W. R. Inge.

CONTENTS

PREFACE

The Gospel Story of the life of Christ is much loved and also found to be an unfailing source of inspiration by so many. The familiar story is herein considered in both its literal or historical and its allegorical significances. St. John in his first five verses, for example, indicates his intent that the Christ be regarded primarily as an allegorical account of the incarnation and evolution of both the Godhead of the universe and of the God-self of man. So skillfully have the Evangelists concealed and revealed beneath the veil of allegory and symbol the mystery of the Divine Incarnation (or Nativity) into a universe and the subsequent phases of evolution that the direct knowledge or Mystery Tradition is not always readily discernible. This book is written in the hope of providing some guidance in the discovery of the secret Wisdom contained in the four accounts or Gospels of the life of Christ.

It must ever be remembered that the wondrous story was never intended to be read merely as a record of external events but also as a revelation of the divine behind man's mortal and underdeveloped material manifestations. Indeed, the total account, written by the unknown hands of the Evangelists, is simply a record of the experiences of spirit in matter, of Monad in man, and of the ascent of both from matter and its deathly grip, back to that freedom which is the natural state of spirit and Monad in the world of divine reality.

A mystical significance must not be overlooked; for every human being has an inherent Christhood as an essential part of his nature. Eventually he comes to learn and draw upon this interior power as an unfailing source of strength and comfort for both himself and his fellowmen. The Christ within may, however, as yet be but prophesied or foreshadowed as dawning wisdom and compassion, awakening and "newly born" universal love. Gradually, through transcendental Baptism and Transfiguration, this divine love becomes directly known as a spiritual power and presence enshrined within the innermost recesses of the soul. Thereafter, the Christ Indwelling becomes an illuminant and center of undisturbable peace, just as the historical Savior enlightened and bestowed peace upon all mankind. The interior Crucifixion follows the Transfiguration, but only as an experience on the pathway leading to Ascension, when earth and all things of earth are left behind, and oneness with the Father (or Monad) becomes an unbroken experience in consciousness forever.

ACKNOWLEDGMENTS

I acknowledge with gratitude the help in the production of this work received from my wife, Sandra, who at dictation wrote out all the original interpretations of biblical passages; from my deeply appreciated friend David Hugh Chisholm who undertook the final typing of the work and the production of the index; and from Truman Caylor Wadlington, my valued literary collaborator, in editing and coordinating the successive parts of this book.

This work is founded upon the King James Bible, and all quotations and references are taken from that version.

THE HIDDEN WISDOM
AND WHY IT IS CONCEALED

The greatest degree of power which occult science can bestow is derived from knowledge of the unity and interaction between the macrocosm and the microcosm, the universe and man. "The mystery of the earthly and mortal man is after the mystery of the supernal and immortal One," wrote Eliphas Levi. Lao-tse also expresses this truth in his words, "The Universe is a man on a large scale."

The whole universe with all its parts, from the highest plane down to physical nature, is regarded as interlocked and interwoven to make a single whole—one body, one organism, one power, one life, one consciousness, all cyclically evolving under one law. The "organs" or parts of the macrocosm, though apparently separated in space and on different planes of manifestation, are in fact harmoniously interrelated, intercommunicative, and continually interactive.

According to this revelation of occult philosophy, the zodiac, the galaxies and their component systems, and the planets with their kingdoms and planes of nature, elements, orders of beings, radiating forces, colors and notes, are not only parts of a coordinated whole in correspondence or mutual resonance with each other, but also—which is of profound significance—they have their representations within man himself. This system of correspondences is in operation throughout the whole of the microcosm, from the Monad, or innermost spirit, to the mortal flesh, including the parts of the mechanism of consciousness, the vehicles and their *chakras,** by means of which the spirit of man is manifested throughout his whole nature, varying in degree according to the stage of evolutionary development. The human being who discovers this truth could enter the power aspect of the universe and tap any one of these forces. He would then become endowed with almost irresistible influence over both nature and his fellowman.

This knowledge of the relationship between universe and man is part of the secret wisdom of Kabbalism, which teaches that in the chain of being everything is magically contained within everything else. Where one stands, there stand all the worlds. What is above is below; what is inside is outside. Everything ceaselessly acts upon all that exists. Kabbalism thus stresses the interrelation of all worlds and levels of being according to exact, though unfathomable, laws. All things, moreover, possess infinite depths which from every point may be contemplated.

Such is part of the wisdom which is said to be implicit in the *Torah*. This sacred book is for Kabbalists a revelation of the laws of the cosmos, of its interrelationship with man and of the history of the Jews. All is, however, deeply concealed under successive veils of allegory, symbol and metaphorical history. Origen, in *Selecta in Psalmos, Patrologia Graeca XII*, wrote,

---

**Chakras.* Centers in man through which superphysical forces flow. See Glossary.

"The Holy Scriptures are like large houses with many, many rooms, and outside each door lies a key; but it is not the right one. To find the right keys that will open the doors, that is the great and arduous task."

This task is arduous indeed, demanding some knowledge of cosmogenesis, of the emanation of the universe from the Absolute, of the finite from the infinite, and of the successive cycles, major and minor, of involution and evolution. In addition, the knowledge of the symbolical language, its purposes, methods and classical symbols, and the faculty of analyzing and interpreting historical metaphors are necessary to open the casket of hidden wisdom—the Holy Bible itself.

Where the Word found that things done according to the history could be adapted to these mystical senses, he made use of them, concealing from the multitude the deeper meaning; but where in the narrative of the development of super-sensual things, there did not follow the performance of those certain events which were already indicated by the mystical meaning, the Scripture interwove in the history the account of some event that did not take place, sometimes what could not have happened; sometimes what could, but did not."

> *De Principiis*, Origen, Christian
> philosopher and Biblical scholar,
> famed for his teaching at Alexandria
> and Caesarea(C.185-C254 A.D.)

What man of sense will agree with the statement that the first, second and third days in which the *evening* is named and the *morning*, were without sun, moon, and stars, and the first day without a heaven? What man is found such an idiot as to suppose that God planted trees in Paradise, in Eden, like a husbandman, and planted therein the tree of life, perceptible to the eyes and senses, which gave life to the eater thereof; and another tree which gave to the eater thereof a knowledge of good and evil? I believe that every man must hold these things for images, under which the hidden sense lies concealed.

> Origen: Huet., *Origeniana*, 167,
> Franck, p. 142.

Every time that you find in our books a tale the reality of which seems impossible, a story which is repugnant to both reason and common sense, then be sure that the tale contains a profound allegory veiling a deeply mysterious truth; and the greater the absurdity of the letter, the deeper the wisdom of the spirit.

> Moses Maimonides, Jewish theologian,
> historian, Talmudist, philosopher
> and physician (1135-1205 A.D.)

Like unto a beautiful woman hidden in the interior of a palace who, when her friend and beloved passes by, opens for a moment a secret window, and is only seen by him: then again retires and disappears for a long time; so the doctrine shows herself only to the elect, but also not even to these always in the same manner. In the beginning, deeply veiled, she only beckons to the one passing, with her hand; it simply depends (on himself) if in his understanding he perceives this gentle hint. Later she approaches him somewhat nearer, and whispers to him a few words, but her countenance is still hidden in the thick veil, which his glances cannot penetrate. Still later she converses with him, her countenance covered with a thinner veil. After he has accustomed himself to her society, she finally shows herself to him face to face, and entrusts him with the innermost secrets of her heart (Sod).

Zohar II, 99a. (Soncino Ed.
Vol. III, p. 301).

Woe . . . to the man who sees in the Thorah, i.e. Law, only simple recitals and ordinary words! Because, if in truth it only contained these, we would even today be able to compose a Thorah much more worthy of admiration . . . The recitals of the Thorah are the vestments of the Thorah. Woe to him who takes this garment for the Thorah itself! . . . There are some foolish people who, seeing a man covered with a beautiful garment, carry their regard no further, and take the garment for the body, whilst there exists a still more precious thing, which is the soul . . . The Wise, the servitors of the Supreme King, those who inhabit the heights of Sinai, are occupied only with the soul, which is the basis of all the rest, which is the Thorah itself; and in the future time they will be prepared to contemplate the Soul of that Soul (i.e. the Deity) which breathes in the Thorah.

Zohar III, 152b. (Soncino Ed.
Vol. V, p. 211).

Rabbi Simeon said, "If a man looks upon the Torah as merely a book presenting narratives and everyday matters, alas for him! Such a Torah, one treating with everyday concerns, and indeed a more excellent one, we too, even we, could compile. More than that, in the possession of the rulers of the world there are books of even greater merit, and these we could emulate if we wished to compile some such Torah. But the Torah, in all of its words, holds supernal truths and sublime secrets."

Zohar III, 152a.

The shell, the white, and the yolk form the perfect egg. The shell protects the white and the yolk, and the yolk feeds upon the white; and when the white has vanished, the yolk, in the form of the fledged bird, breaks through the shell and presently soars into the air. Thus does the static become the dynamic, the material the spiritual.

"If the shell is the exoteric principle and the yolk the esoteric, what then is the white? The white is the food of the second, the accumulated wisdom of the world centering round the mystery of growth, which each single individual must absorb before he can break the shell. The transmutation of the white, by the yolk, into the fledgling is the secret of secrets of the entire Qabalistic philosophy.

The Secret Wisdom of the Qabalah,
J. F. C. Fuller

Having taken the Upanishad as the bow, as the great weapon, let him place on it the arrow, sharpened by devotion! Then having drawn it with a thought directed to that which is, hit the mark, O Friend, namely, that which is Indestructible! Om is the bow, the Self is the arrow, Brahman is called the Aim. It is to be hit by a man who is not thoughtless, and then as the arrow becomes one with the target, he will become one with Brahman.

Mundaka Upanishad, II.

And the disciples came, and said unto him, Why speakest thou unto them in parables?

He answered and said unto them, Because it is given unto you to know the mysteries of the kingdom of heaven, but to them it is not given. . .

But blessed are your eyes, for they see: and your ears, for they hear.

Matt. 13:10, 11 and 16.

"Whoso eateth my flesh, and drinketh my blood, hath eternal life; and I will raise him up at the last day. For my flesh is meat indeed, and my blood is drink indeed. He that eateth my flesh, and drinketh my blood, dwelleth in me, and I in him. As the living Father hath sent me, and I live by the Father: so he that eateth me, even he shall live by me."

John 6:54-57.

The early Genesis accounts of the creation, Adam and Eve and the Fall of man contain truths of a religious nature which do not depend for their validity upon historical or scientific confirmation. Such accounts expressed truths of a timeless nature. They were myths, teaching spiritual truths by allegories.

From a sermon by The Most Reverend
Dr. Frank Woods,
Anglican Archbishop
of Melbourne, speaking at St. Paul's
Cathedral on the 18th February, 1961

To enclose all truth in a spoken language, to express the highest occult mysteries in an abstract style, this would not only be useless, dangerous and sacrilegious, but also impossible. There are truths of a subtle, synthetic and divine order, to express which in all their inviolate completeness, human language is incapable. Only music can sometimes make the soul feel them, only ectasy can show them in absolute vision, and only esoteric symbolism can reveal them to the spirit in a concrete way.

Ay Seuil de Mystiere, S. De Guaita

PART ONE

THE GOSPEL STORY—A BRIEF SURVEY

Chapter One

Although the Christian religion came into being after Jesus the Christ appeared in Palestine some two thousand years ago, it was by no means either an isolated or a new revelation. Rather it formed a part of a long historical development established and maintained on this planet by the spiritual Teachers of the race, referred to in the New Testament as "the just men made perfect."[1] St. Augustine recognized the new religion as a continuance of an already existing religious system when he wrote in the fourth century: "The identical thing that we now call the Christian Religion existed among the ancients, and has not been lacking from the beginning of the human race until the coming of Christ in the flesh, from which moment onwards the true religion, which already existed, began to be called Christian."[2] St. Paul, in a letter to his converts in Corinth, referred to the primordial existence of a divine wisdom in the following words: "But we speak the wisdom of God in a mystery, even the hidden wisdom, which God ordained before the world unto our glory."[3]

The teachings of this Ageless Wisdom are found at the heart of all great world faiths as a group of central doctrines common to them all. This uniformity is revealed by an examination of the sacred books of various religions and the original sayings of the world's greatest Teachers. The Ancient Wisdom is indeed the oldest of all religions, consisting of *Theosophia,* the wisdom of divinely enlightened beings through the ages, in modern times called Theosophy.[4]

Evidently a worldwide resurgence of this one Wisdom Religion occurred between 700 B.C. and 300 A.D. During that period appeared Lao-tse and Confucius in China; the Lord Buddha and Shri Shankaracharya in India; Zoroaster in Persia; Pythagoras, Plato, Socrates and Aristotle in Greece; and Ammonius Saccus, Plotinus, and the other Neo-Platonists in Alexandria. All contributed to a great revival of philosophic and religious thought. In addition, the Lesser and Greater Mysteries in Egypt and Greece were still continuing to attract, teach, and initiate occultists and mystics. To these may be added those Jews who studied esoteric Hebraism known as the *Kabbalah,* and also the Gnostics (Valentinus, Basilides, Marcion, and others) who contributed the concept of the "Mystery of the Kingdom." These and other contemporary streams of thought and culture became blended in early Christianity. This synthesis was illumined and empowered by the presence, and later worship, of Jesus the Christ as a living center and source of personal inspiration, the spiritual founder of the "new" faith.

Apart from his profound effect upon the lives of millions of people, little or nothing is really known about the person, life and death of Jesus of Nazareth. His physical appearance is not recorded in the New Testament, nor is the family life of Jesus, except that he had at least four brothers and two sisters, worked as a carpenter, and grew in wisdom. Furthermore, the Evangelists' autographed Gospels have been either secretly withdrawn or lost. Later copies, doubtless much amended, are the only ones now available. Translated, edited, altered to suit changing theological concepts and dogmas, these copies falsify the original accounts in certain passages, though they are truthful in the main. In addition, no written record of the events and actions associated with Jesus was made, and the Four Gospels were written long after those events from oral tradition based on memory. Apart from a questionable passage in Josephus, no contemporary historical record of the series of incidents recorded in the Gospels is anywhere to be found. The total absence of any reference whatever in the writings of historians of the period or in the records of the Roman Empire and other countries bordering on Judea may be regarded as remarkable, if only because of the highly dramatic sequence of events which culminated in the Crucifixion, Resurrection and Ascension of the Lord.

William Foxwell Albright, in his book, *The Archeology of Palestine,* comments on the early texts of the New Testament:

> The only manuscript of the Greek New Testament antedating the fifth or sixth centuries A.D. which was known to exist a century ago was the Codex Vaticanus, a vellum (parchment) text preserved in the library of the Vatican, but it was at that time virtually inaccessible to scholars and had scarcely been utilized at all by textual critics. In 1859 a German scholar, Constantin Tischendorf, discovered a parchment codex of equally old date in the monastery of St. Catherine at Mount Sinai, and he was able to acquire this precious text for the Tsar of Russia. In 1933 the Codex Sinaiticus, having been purchased from Russia by the British Government, became the chief treasure of the British Museum, which now houses two of the three most important Greek biblical manuscripts in the world (the other being the fifth-century Codex Alexandrinus). Dating from the first half of the fourth century A.D., the Vaticanus and the Sinaiticus now represent the most valuable extant authorities for the text of the New Testament. . . .

Under the impact of the new finds, a strong reaction has recently set in, materially aided by C. C. Torrey's view that John is a translation from an Aramaic text written down well before A.D. 70. Some radical scholars (e.g. Ervin Goodenough) now consider John as the earliest of the Gospels instead of the latest.

The talks by Jesus to his disciples recorded by the Evangelists bear the marks of a combined authorship, as of a number who contributed after listening to many such talks and hearing others relate them. These remembered utterances and such records as may have existed were repeated, each one accentuating passages which harmonized with his temperament. The more objective minds were doubtless moved by and so recalled the historical teachings. The devotees and mystics, on the other hand, each contributed according to his outlook. All these repeated recollections became blended into one narrative, supposedly describing a single occasion. Actually, however, many addresses at many gatherings contributed the several ideas and sayings of Jesus, but are presented somewhat as if they were all spoken at one and the same time. It is clear that great latitude must have been allowed to the Evangelists in the compilation of their Gospels.

Indeed, no scripture of any ancient peoples is to be regarded as a straightforward and continuing narrative of events written by one man. Quite the contrary is true. All are compilations to which, through the centuries, additions have been made. Ideas differed among those who wrote allegorically concerning the extent of the occult revelation of power-bestowing knowledge, the degree of enveiling, and even the nature of the veils to be employed. All scriptures and mythologies should therefore be read and studied as compilations by many hands. Some of these were quite uninspired and even gross, particularly when the writer of a passage, in ignorance, regarded the whole narrative as history alone. The result is an undesirable mixture of the divinely inspired and humanly crude. Yet in many instances the spiritual breaks through the more material account, just as sunshine bursts through dark clouds and fills the world with light.

A critical examination of the Gospels reveals that St. Matthew and St. Luke describe the Nativity differently, and that St. Mark and St. John do not mention it at all. An immaculate conception and a virgin birth are described by the former two Evangelists, though the descent of Jesus through the male line is affirmed. While St. Luke brings the family directly back to Nazareth, St. Matthew takes them to Egypt in order to escape the danger caused by Herod, who had ordered the death of all the male children two years old or less. Herod, however, is known to have died four years before the date given for the beginning of the Christian Era. This places the natal date at some six years before Jesus is traditionally believed to have been born. The Resurrection, so vitally important to Christians, is differently narrated, as are the discovery of the empty tomb by Mary Magdalene and Jesus' later appearances. St. Paul, who wrote at least fifty years afterward, states that Jesus reappeared to over five hundred people and eventually to himself.[5] The Gospels, however, limit the number to under twenty.

Modern scholarship has carried the investigation so far that one can no longer hope for further precise information. Even the amazing and apparently accidental discovery in this century of the Dead Sea Scrolls, partly contemporary with Jesus, has not helped as yet; for as thus far assembled and translated they do not mention Jesus.

In this volume the historical approach will not be followed solely, although it is not denied. Rather, the possibility will be considered that the Gospels were written by profoundly illumined men whose purposes were less to write biographies of a great personage than to reveal, under the veil of allegory and symbol, truths which are eternal. Internal evidence indicates that the Evangelists were possessed of occult knowledge, apparently in the form of Kabbalism, which is the esoteric doctrine of the Hebrews. This is especially notable in the fourth Gospel in which St. John represents the Christ as a cosmic figure, declaring his intention to do so in the first five verses of his first chapter.

In presenting such a view, the historicity of the Gospels is not necessarily called into question. Although decisive contemporary evidence is thus far unavailable—except for the much-disputed short paragraph in Josephus —the majority of biblical scholars agree that the historical Jesus did live on earth, performed some of the acts, gave some of the teachings attributed to him, and met with a violent death.

Nevertheless, the Christian Bible, as also the scriptures of other faiths, has from remote times been regarded as belonging to a special, even unique, category of literature generally referred to as the sacred language of allegory and symbol. Exponents of oriental religious writing, the early Kabbalists, the disciples of Ammonius Saccus, other Neo-Platonists of Alexandria known as "Analogeticists" and their successors down to modern times—all these have regarded world scriptures as largely, but not entirely, allegorical. Granting a historical basis, they also looked upon them as being constructed of analogies, metaphors, parables and symbols. Literature thus produced is said to preserve for posterity, to reveal and yet to conceal, profound spiritual and therefore power-bestowing truths.

According to occult teachings, historical events were marshaled and used so far as they were known and so far as it was thought advisable to divulge them. Many supernatural events and miracles were added, some of which actually occurred, and the great drama of life, cosmic and human, was thus allegorically composed and related. For example, the young initiate, Jesus, having passed through training in Egypt and Israel, embarked on his mission with wisdom and zeal. The people followed him. Advanced souls became associated with him, but the temporal and ecclesiastical authorities feared and hated him and plotted his death. Eventually he was murdered by stoning and his body hung upon a tree, as was the custom of the time according to St. Peter.[6] This ignominious end was not readily adaptable to the cosmic and initiatory symbolism which the authors of the Gospels wanted to employ, so the account was altered.

This view leads to the conclusion that it would have been of little or no moment to the authors whether or not they recorded actual events. Thus they unhesitatingly introduced into their narratives accounts of visions of people shared by no one and, therefore, unlikely ever to have been recorded, as well as incidents which certainly were not recorded and, indeed, may never have actually happened. Yet they were not at all guilty of falsification, since their whole motive was to use the supposed history of events happening in time as a vehicle for eternal truths.

In addition, as initiates they would be under two obligations: first to reveal hidden truths, and second to lead intuitively awakened readers to occult knowledge while yet veiling it from the uninitiated. By such means and by inculcating self-training repeatedly advocated and described by both John and Jesus, they worked to prepare people for discipleship and initiation into the Mysteries. This, I suggest, was their purpose, especially that of John who did not regard himself as obliged to be an accurate historian, but far above and beyond that, a revealer of the *Gnosis* and an awakener of souls.[7] The Evangelists thus undertook the enormously important task of preserving the story of Jesus and of relating the mystery teaching, both openly and in allegorical forms, to avoid losing these during the foreseen dark ages referred to as the "wars and rumors of wars."[8] An analogical and allegorical interpretation of the Gospels—and so of many other books in the Bible—thus appears to be perfectly permissible. This approach is indeed justified by the added illumination to be gained by the use of the scriptures for this purpose. Furthermore, obscure, meaningless and even repellent passages can by these means become sources of important knowledge.

The Gospels reveal eternal truths such as the laws of being and the interior mystical experiences and attainments of nations and of men. The related incidents, in addition to temporal significance as history, have at least four timeless meanings. They depict laws and operations of the divine in nature, cosmic and solar; mystical experience of mankind in general; interior awakening in disciples or those developing in advance of the race; experiences during the great initiations that lead to the superhuman state of adeptship.[9] Below is a statement and application *to man* of four of the seven possible keys or main interpretations of the allegories and symbols of the world which help make clear the language of allegory and symbol.[10]

The first key is that all the recorded, external, supposedly historical events also occur interiorly as already stated. Each recorded event is descriptive of a subjective experience of man, whether as the race, nation or an individual. This application is essentially twofold, referring both to the experiences and attainments of those advancing by the normal, gradual, evolutionary method and to individuals who are treading "the way of holiness" in advance of the race.

The second key is that each of the persons figuring prominently in the stories represents a condition of consciousness and a quality of character. All the actors are personifications of aspects of human nature, of attributes, principles, powers, faculties, limitations, weaknesses and errors of man. Sometimes such qualities are absent, sometimes they are being born or are awakening, and sometimes they are dominant, according to the temperament and degree of development of the person being described.

The third key is that each story is regarded as a graphic description of the experiences of the human soul as it passes through the various phases of its evolutionary journey to the Promised Land, or cosmic consciousness—the

goal and summit of human perfection. The narratives relate the adventures
and particularly the tests, ordeals, defeats and victories of one person who
symbolizes mankind. Successful exploits describe interior achievements,
while partial and complete failures, defeats and surrenders are allegories of
temporary victories of the human over the divine in man, or conquests of
matter over spirit. The labors of Hercules, the voyage of the Argonauts, the
journeys and experiences of the Israelites, the lives of the Lord Shri Krishna
and of the Lord Christ (and of the prodigal son in the parable of that name),[11]
among many others, are all symbolically descriptive of the journey of the soul
and of the psychological, intellectual and spiritual exaltations passed through
on that journey. When human beings are the heroes, the life of man at the
normal stage of development is being described. When the hero is
semidivine, the accent is upon the progress of the divine Self in man after it
has begun to assume preponderant power. When, however, the central figure
is an *Avatar*,[12] or descent of an aspect of Deity, his experiences narrate those
of the spiritual Self during the later phases of evolution of the divine in man
toward the stature of perfected manhood.

The fourth key is that all objects as well as certain words have special
symbolic meanings. The sacred language of the initiates of the Mystery
Schools is formed of hierograms and symbols rather than of words alone,
their meaning always constant, as is also the doctrine which this language
everywhere reveals.[13]

Inspired allegories are always distinguishable from novels and biographies
by several characteristics, one of which is the intrusion of the supernatural,
such as angelic and divine beings, even Deity itself. When this is found, the
existence of a hidden revelation may be suspected. The reader possessed of
the keys may then penetrate the veil of symbolism to find aspects of the
hidden wisdom that are being revealed. Often the literal approach limits the
reality in question to one given plane, the physical, whereas the recognition
of a symbolical intuitive meaning underlying a narrative awakens within one
an echo which can resound through all levels of consciousness, from the
corporeal to the spiritual. Such, my own studies have led me to believe, is the
general purpose and method employed by the ancient writers of the world's
scriptures and mythologies. This view forms the major theme of this work
and also of my books dealing with the Old Testament.[14]

The revelation of the existence of a sacred language of allegory and symbol
and the real interpretation of the scriptures which this makes possible constitute the true instruments for the liberation of Christendom from the burden of
priestcraft and exploitation, and from the darkness of ignorance under which
Christians for so long have lived. What changes would such interpretation
involve? At least the following:

While Deity exists on a cosmic scale, the presiding Being within our solar
system is the Solar Logos, of inconceivable power, wisdom, intelligence and
glory, both immanent and transcendent.[15]

This active Logos is expressed as a Trinity. The First Aspect of the Deity or
Father, as the original creator or rather emanator of the universe, is as-

sociated with the beginning of the outward expression in time and space of the absolute and eternal principle which remains forever remote and yet inherent in all things. The Second Aspect is the life-giving and preserving presence at the heart of all creation which keeps all beings and all things both nourished and sustained upon their appointed pathways, without which all would fall into decay. This, indeed, actually occurs at the close of every age or "Day of Creation," when the interior life-force is withdrawn from the external, objective universe. The Holy Ghost or Third Aspect may be regarded as the *manifested* Logos, the presence and the Word of God incarnate in his universe and active as a redemptive power in man. While God the Father as original emanator withdraws after originating the procedure of manifestation, the Third Aspect of Deity as director, fashioner and energizer remains constantly in highly concentrated and immensely powerful activity in and through every atom of every world. This is the Aspect most especially associated with Jesus.

Jesus speaks as an *Avatar*, one of a long series of periodic manifestations of the divine, on whom has descended the overshadowing presence of the Third Aspect of Deity, the Holy Ghost.

In his innermost being, man is the Monad, the Immortal Germ, in which are already present limitless possibilities for development and growth. This Indwelling Christ is ever one with and in no way apart from the Solar Logos, who is the true and highest Father in Heaven.[16] Thus each man in his spiritual nature is God, being thus established in his own divine right, as affirmed by both Jesus and St. Paul.[17]

The Monad in man is expressed in his immortal soul or Ego as a trinity, the higher triad of spiritual will, love and intelligence, each of which represents an Aspect of the threefold Deity. This spiritual soul resides in a vehicle called the causal body or "robe of glory."[18]

The outer man consists of three personal vehicles, the mental, emotional and physical, which embody the full descent of spirit in man.

Each aspect of man's being has an appropriate material vehicle, whether physical or superphysical, as its means of expression. These are of succeeding degrees of fineness, from the physical which is the most dense to the exceedingly rarefied matter of the casual body. All these levels exist in the same space, as it were, and interpenetrate one another. They extend around the body of each person as a superphysical emanation or aura.[19]

Each human being can and will attain to Christhood or salvation by sole power of his divine attributes. These are inherited from the Dweller in the Innermost, the Monad in man, ever existent within the Solar Logos.[20]

The ministration of the historical Christ is not only that of Redeemer and Savior. Those two processes can be carried out by the individual himself, since he is amply endowed with an innate redemptive power. The Christ also functions as the awakening messenger, bringing into activity that redeeming principle within. The mystical Christ is the Christ nature within man, born or awakened into activity from within the spiritual intelligence, as St. Paul makes clear.[21] The central message of reformed Christian theology should always have been: ". . .Christ in you, the hope of glory."[22] As our Bible assures us, no mediator and no priest are necessary to bring about the salvation of any man.

Religion is solely concerned with each individual's discovery of his own divine Selfhood, the Christ within him, the Logos of the soul.

Abstinences are useful only when they assist the seeker in the discovery of the divine Self within.

Prayer is not directed to an external deity, but to the God within. It is simply a mode of conscious realization of unity with the Indwelling God (as is yoga).

Life must conform to what one professes, and conduct must be conducive to communion with the divine Self.[23] The discrepancy between Sunday and weekday lives must vanish; every day must be lived as a holy day, and so must ultimately become a "holiday."

Some members of the human race have already fulfilled the prophecy of the Christ, having become ". . .just men made perfect."[24] These have entered the strait gate and trodden the narrow way[25] which leads along the spiritual path to Ascension, Christhood, adeptship. Along the way they must pass through great initiations such as conferred in the Mystery Schools. These perfect ones comprise the Communion of Saints and the membership of the order of the Priesthood of Melchizedek,[26] also known as the Adept Hierarchy which governs life on the planet from within.[27]

The spiritual soul of man attains to adeptship by successive lives or rebirths on earth.[28]

Harmony and long-termed justice are assured by the operation of the law of cause and effect, or sowing and reaping, in the East called karma.[29]

A mysterious law governs enduring human happiness and fulfillment. Briefly stated it is: Give to live, share to enjoy, serve in order to unfold. Strangely, practice of the ideal of selfless giving brings not loss but gain, not death but life more abundant. Disobedience to this law, moved by desire for exclusively personal possessions and powers, brings not gain but loss, not life but death. This self-emptying (*kenosis*—Gr.) is practiced by the Logos himself who nourishes and sustains the solar system by the perpetual outpouring of his own life. This self-emptying attitude and mode of life is a central ideal in Christianity; it was enunciated by our Lord, who said, ". . .he that hateth his life in this world shall keep it unto life eternal," and, ". . .except a corn of wheat fall into the ground and die, it abideth alone: but if it die, it bringeth forth much fruit."[30]

Man is accompanied on his evolutionary road by countless members of the angelic hosts, certain orders of which are allies of mankind.[31] The ministry of angels is available in all work carried out in the service of God and humanity.

Christianity like all other faiths is a way of life, not only a theological system with which one must be in intellectual agreement. I suggest one may legitimately challenge and even deny certain church doctrines and still be worthy of the title *Christian*. Also, ideas such as those preceding may be included in a truly Christian faith.

How many nominal Christians are there? Of two hundred and fifty thousand million or more people of earth, some eight and a half hundred million—one in every three—are listed as Christian. Of these, four hundred and eighty-four million are Roman Catholic, fory-one million Presbyterian, and forty million Anglican or Church of England. Strangely enough, in the last two thousand years such a diversity of belief has developed among these and many other denominations that it is now difficult to recognize the fact that they all belong to the same faith and acknowledge the same Lord.

Modern Christian belief is perhaps best stated in the Apostles' Creed and the Lord's Prayer.[32]

"I believe in one God the Father Almighty, Maker of heaven and earth, And of all things visible and invisible:

"And in one Lord Jesus Christ, the only-begotten Son of God, Begotten of his Father before all worlds, God of God, Light of Light, Very God of very God, Begotten, not made, Being of one substance with the Father, By whom all things were made: Who for us men, and for our salvation came down from heaven, And was incarnate by the Holy Ghost of the Virgin Mary, And was made man, And was crucified also for us under Pontius Pilate. He suffered and was buried, And the third day he rose again according to the Scriptures, And ascended into heaven, And sitteth on the right hand of the Father. And he shall come again with glory to judge both the quick and the dead: Whose kingdom shall have no end.

"And I believe in the Holy Ghost, the Lord and Giver of Life, Who proceedeth from the Father and the Son, who with the Father and the Son together is worshipped and glorified, Who spake by the Prophets. And I believe one Catholic and Apostolic Church. I acknowledge one Baptism for the remission of sins, And I look for the Resurrection of the dead, And the Life of the World to come. Amen."

"Our Father, which art in heaven, Hallowed be thy name. Thy kingdom come. Thy will be done, on earth as it is in heaven. Give us this day our daily bread. And forgive us our trespasses, As we forgive them that trespass against us. And lead us not into temptation; but deliver us from evil; For thine is the kingdom, the power, and the glory, For ever and ever. Amen."

I regard the following as an ideal Act of Faith:[33]

"We believe that God is Love, and Power, and Truth, and Light; that perfect justice rules the world; that all His sons shall one day reach His feet, however far they stray. We hold the Fatherhood of God, the Brotherhood of man; we know that we do serve Him best when best we serve our brother man. So shall His blessing rest on us and peace forever more. Amen."

Let us now consider the possibility that the Gospels were written by men who knew the Ancient Wisdom; who were skilled in the language of allegory and symbol; and who wrote in that language, less to preserve a historical account than to preserve the power-bestowing knowledge throughout successive dark ages. Let us examine certain Christian dogmas and developments in the light of Theosophy, a modern statement of the Ancient Wisdom, which constitutes an esoteric synthesis of world faiths. Many biblical events become meaningful if viewed in this light.

St. John, whose first five verses affirm the Logos doctrine, accentuates the cosmos, referring to the Nativity, Baptism, Crucifixion and Ascension of the Christ in such a way that they are applicable to the emanation, involution, and evolution of the one Life of the cosmos as a whole. The Monad-bearing divine Life, personified by Christ of the universe, is emanated into matter through deepening degrees of density. If this approach is followed, then the Baptism of the Christ represents the further descent of spirit into matter, and the River Jordan is lifted out of time and space and seen by the inspired authors as a symbol of universal matter into which the divine Life (the Christ) "descends" on the involutionary arc. The temptation in the wilderness indicates that the descent continues, that the taint of matter is experienced. The Transfiguration in its turn implies that, cosmically, spirit is still consciously in touch with the Source, though the experiences in Gethsemane which follow refer to the still deeper descent of the one Life and foreshadow the "death" and later "burial" in a rock tomb (entry into the mineral kingdom). There it is metaphorically dead on the cross of matter—emblematic of four directions of space.[34] Eventually, under the impulse of cyclic law, this divine Life embarks upon a journey of return to its spiritual Source. From this densest point in matter, the process of evolution (Resurrection) begins, marking the upward turn, while Ascension is emblematic of the final completion of the cycle of forthgoing and return. Matter no longer imprisons spirit, which then transcends material limitations.

The Christ drama is also enacted within the soul of man, for every individual passes through the experiences recounted in the Gospels. All men have their conversions to idealism (however temporary), baptisms or sorrow, temptations, upliftments, dark nights of the soul, crucifixions and burials of all their hopes. These are common human experiences. The life of Christ is indeed a universal life.

Further, in a possible microcosmic interpretation, at the dawn of the emanation of the finite universe from the Absolute, the spirit of man embarks upon a great pilgrimage from pure spirit into densest matter—involution. The human Monad first projects its ray into the evolutionary field (Nativity), descends deeper and deeper into matter (Baptism), and eventually is born into a physical body, a crucifixion and burial indeed. Each minor cycle of physical birth and death, the later stages of human evolution and entry upon the path of spiritual rebirth or initiation, and the final establishment of the rule of the spirit with human entry into the superhuman kingdom of nature are described symbolically.

If the life of Christ is also interpreted as descriptive of entry upon the path of swift unfoldment,[35] then the divine Self in spiritually awakened man begins to take its evolution into its own hands, or, in biblical terms, responds to the call of John the Baptist to "repent." The neophyte becomes a disciple, embarks upon the path (the Way of the Cross), enters "the stream" (Baptism), and takes the five great initiations (Birth, Baptism, Transfiguration,

Crucifixion and Ascension). As described by St. Paul, he then comes "into the measure of the stature of the fulness of Christ," or attains to adeptship.[36] Having outgrown the natural egoism, he becomes free in consciousness or resurrected from the tomb and deadness of the flesh. The various annunciations and visions of the parents of John the Baptist and Jesus are descriptive of interior awakenings and developments of divine power in such highly advanced men. In this interpretation, the narrative is applicable to every disciple, initiate and Adept, and thus to every human being who passes through these experiences.

The events also apply to the passage of one man, Jesus, through those phases of hastened evolution. The discipleship of an adept Teacher leading to his presentation before the Brotherhood of Adepts, the resistance to temptation, the steadfast endurance of suffering, some of the secrets enacted and conveyed at rites of initiation, all these are included in allegory in one or more of the four Gospels.

The doctrine of Original Sin, important in Christianity, may be interpreted in the light of this teaching. A statement of this doctrine occurs in the Thirty-nine Articles of Religion of the Church of England: "Original Sin standeth not in the following of *Adam* (as the *Pelagians* do vainly talk) but it is the fault and corruption of the Nature of every man, that naturally is engendered of the offspring of *Adam*; whereby man is very far gone from original righteousness, and is of his own nature inclined to evil, so that the flesh lusteth always contrary to the spirit; and therefore in every person born into this world, it deserveth God's wrath and damnation. And this infection of nature doth remain, yea in them that are regenerated." Again, "the condition of Man after the fall of *Adam* is such, that he cannot turn and prepare himself, by his own natural strength and good works, to faith, and calling upon God; Wherefore we have no power to do good works pleasant and acceptable to God, without the grace of God by Christ preventing us, that we may have a good will, and working with us, when we have that good will."

The views thus officially stated are hardly acceptable to the student of the Ancient Wisdom. "Original sin," misunderstood to mean the sex relationship of Adam and Eve, is regarded as an inevitable concomitant of the involutionary process of spirit descending into matter, and definitely not as a deliberately committed wickedness for which every human being has ever since been condemned to be born in sin. Whatever stain there may have been will ultimately be left behind, its effect upon either body or soul in no way permanent. The whole process of descent, or involution, is a perfectly natural one. For a period it brings suffering and degradation, but it cannot be truthfully described as a tragic fall. The fruit will be full knowledge of and capacity to wield the mightiest of all the powers in nature and in man—the divine power to emanate universes and all they contain.

With regard to the resurrection of the body, originally it was believed that the particles of the physical body of every man magically rose from the grave, were knit into a heavenly body and went to live up in the sky. The Resurrection of Christ, on the other hand, meant that Christ himself did truly rise from death and take again the same body of flesh and bones. This body, though untouchable to Mary Magdelene, was later touched by St. Thomas.[37] Christ thereafter ascended into heaven where he remains until the day of his return to judge all men.

Taken allegorically resurrection may refer to the macrocosmic view that evolution naturally follows involution. It may also refer to microcosmic resurrection, the ascent of man from the domination of matter to freedom into full spiritual realization. In this sense the spirit of man, also personified by Christ, becomes resurrected, not bodily but in terms of consciousness—freed from the limitations both of the flesh and the egoistic principle in the mind.

The doctrine of the Atonement by Christ for the sins of mankind and for all individuals who "believe in him" is also susceptible of a theosophical interpretation. The attainment of Christhood or adeptship, for example, brings full and conscious realization of oneness with the Christ nature within every human being. The symbol of Christ as bridegroom and the allegory of the heavenly marriage are appropriately used to describe this interior unification. Oneness achieved, the ascended one pours forth and shares with every human being his own perfected spiritual power, life and consciousness. In varying degrees according to capacity to respond, this enables the human being in bodily life to resist temptation, to renounce the "world, the flesh and the devil" and, ultimately, to realize his or her own spiritual Selfhood as an immortal and eternal being.

Thus viewed, the Atonement is an interior process, an at-one-ment. It is transmission of light and an inpouring of spiritualized and perfected life rather than a transference of water and of blood.[38] It is wisdom which is shed from the wounds of the Christ upon the Cross.

One's thought is thus led to the Christ Indwelling, the interior Christ principle and nature (Atma-Buddhi[39]) in every human being, the "Christ in you" and the "God that worketh all in all" of St. Paul.[40] Our Lord Himself affirmed his unfailing presence in man to his disciples, "I am in my Father and ye in me, and I in you," and to all mankind in his words upon the Cross, "Lo, I am with you always even unto the end of the world."[41] This interior atonement does not prevent the operation of the law of cause and effect. It neither nullifies the effects of the operation of karma upon those who have deliberately, willfully and continuously sinned, nor does it "wash their souls until they are whiter than snow," regardless of evil intentionally committed.

This approach brings us near to the heart of Christianity, even of all religions, for the existence within man of the Christ presence is indeed man's assurance of "salvation" or ultimate attainment of Christhood. This divine ministration was declared by the Lord to be universal and implies in him wisdom, love and compassion for all. One remembers his words, "And other sheep I have, which are not of this fold: them also I must bring, and they shall hear my voice; and there shall be one fold, and one shepherd."[42] Thus the Lord Christ himself regards all beings as if they were his only child. His concern for all will, we are assured, never cease, nor will he depart from the earth until every human being reaches Christhood or is "saved"; for his ministration never ceases, never ebbs, but always flows, never declines, but is always at its maximum. In this sense the term *Christ* implies also a supreme wisdom and love operating as a function within the depth of man's being, Christhood pertaining to the beyond which is also within, like the moon or a flower reflected on the quiescent surface of a mirror.

This view, however imperfectly expressed here, lifts our subjects far above the limitations of dogma, doctrine and domination. One rises in thought to that level at which God and man exist as one, and where the Lord Christ is revealed, not only as a divine visitant to earth two thousand years ago, but also as an essential part of the spiritual Self of man, the Christ Indwelling.

This would seem to be supported by St. Paul who wrote, "Christ in you the hope of glory," and "I travail in birth again that the Christ be formed in you," and "Work out your own salvation with fear and trembling, for it is God that worketh in you."[43] In these and other writings, St. Paul clearly diverged from the orthodox rabbinical view of scripture as an account in the history of the Hebrew nation. Supernatural beings such as Jehovah and his antitheses played important parts in the life of the Jewish people. Throughout this work both views—the Pauline and the historical—have been duly considered, the accent however being upon the former or mystical interpretation.

Turning to Jesus himself, the significant events in his life recorded in the New Testament may be listed as follows: his preexistence;[44] the Nativity in Bethlehem; the flight into Egypt; his childhood and youth at Nazareth, followed by an absence of information until his reappearance at the first Passover at Jerusalem when he was twelve years old; Baptism when the Spirit of God descended upon him in the form of a dove; the temptation and victory in the wilderness of Judea; the calling of many disciples and the performing of many miracles; the two rejections by the citizens of his home town, Nazareth; residence at Capernaum and his delivery there of the Sermon on the Mount; the healing of many people with various diseases; the teaching by parable and the two prophecies of his forthcoming death and the Resurrection; the Transformation on a mountain; visits to his friends Mary and Martha at Bethany; triumphal entry into Jerusalem on Palm Sunday and his lamentation over that city; the plots against him by the priests and elders from whom one of his disciples, Judas, received payment for betrayal; washing the feet of his disciples; the Lord's Supper and the agony suffered in the Garden of Gethsemane; betrayal and arrest; three separate Jewish trials; the Roman trials under Pilate and Herod, followed by condemnation, scourging, mockery and crucifixion after carrying his own cross along the *Via Dolorasa* in Jerusalem; supernormal phenomena at death; the burial, the resurrection and the reappearance to many people; the Ascension into heaven and various reappearances thereafter; and the final promise, ". . .lo, I am with you always, even to the end of the world." These events will be considered both historically and symbolically in this volume.

The words of the Lord as they have come down to us are both inspiring and rich in practical guidance in the conduct of daily life. He counseled that he himself should ever be remembered as the Way, the Truth and the Life, the very heart of the world. In divine compassion he called: "Come unto me, all ye that labour and are heavy laden, and I will give you rest. Take my yoke upon you, and learn of me; for I am meek and lowly in heart: and ye shall find rest unto your souls. For my yoke is easy, and my burden is light."[45] He also taught the ideal of service, saying: ". . .he that is greatest among you shall be your servant,"[46] and of love: "This is my commandment, that ye love one another, as I have loved you. Greater love hath no man than this, that a man lay down his life for his friends."[47] Other well-known teachings for the guidance of mankind include: "Let your light so shine before men, that they may see your good works, and glorify your Father which is in heaven." "Lay not up for yourselves treasures upon the earth, where moth and rust doth corrupt, and where thieves break through and steal: But lay up for yourselves treasures in heaven; where neither moth nor rust doth corrupt, and where thieves do not break through nor steal." "Therefore all things whatsoever ye would that men should do to you, do ye even so to them; for this is the law and the prophets," and "Not every one that saith unto me, Lord, Lord, shall enter into the kingdom of heaven; but he that doeth the will of my Father which is in heaven."[48]

We can picture the great Hebrew initiate, possibly dressed in a loose but graceful white garment, somewhat taller in stature than most of the people, carrying himself very erect, with brown hair, slight moustache and beard, straight features and clear brown eyes. In manner we might suppose he was, in general, mild, winning and intimate, though capable of a great sternness, his visage seeming to change and his person to become almost kingly and patriarchal in its majesty, his eyes stern and accusing. Occasionally he would stretch forth his hand as if in denunciation, sometimes even causing the people nearer to him to shrink back as if from a burning fire.

Thereafter, he would seat himself upon rock or stone and fall into silence as if musing deep within himself. Then it would be that the humble, the sick and the anxious would approach him with petitions for healing grace and spiritual aid. These were never refused, and in some cases he would look upon the suppliant with the most winning ways, sometimes touching, sometimes affirming, always aiding to the limit of his powers, which were very great indeed. Children always evoked his tenderest love and concern, and their parents would bring them from towns, villages and little homes to be near him and to be blessed by him as he passed by.

In all this, while he knew himself as a messenger from the Adept Brotherhood and Mystery Temple wherein he had been several times initiated, he held no thought that a great world religion would be founded in his name and upon his words and deeds. The formalities of religion held no interest for him. In fact, he strongly disapproved of them as they were followed in the synagogues and among the rabbis of his time.

His sandaled feet trod the roads, field paths, lake shores, river banks and also the village and city streets. His light shone all around him and often became visible as a radiance, sometimes dazzling in its intensity. At these times, indeed, it was enough to be near him or to touch him in order to be healed, whether of the ills of the mortal soul or of the body. Within himself he was always at ease, preserving a silent contentment founded upon the knowledge of an initiated one, that indeed in his spiritual identity he was beyond the reach of all adversity and of the severest enemy, whatever his body might be called upon to endure. Ever and anon an exaltation of spirit would change his whole demeanor. He would become more remote, almost as if speaking from a great distance and across a mental chasm. These were the occasions when the spirit from on high descended upon him, such as allegorically described in the account of his Baptism. This descent did not, however, occur on one occasion only, as there suggested, but quite frequently as he became the vehicle for the embodiment of immortal and divine wisdom.

As a born teacher, as the Gospels tell, he would draw upon the human ways and experiences of his hearers for analogies, similes and metaphors with which to explain his ideas. He liked to refer to the seasons and their changes, to day and night, the sun, the moon and the stars. Himself highly sensitive to all such natural phenomena and influences, he made them symbols for his wisdom and spontaneously constructed parables based upon them and their relationship to changes and conditions of human life and personality. The simple people who gathered round and listened to him were intimately associated with the soil, with agriculture, and the procedures of planting, tending and harvesting the fruits of their labors.

Far more often than is recorded, naturally and rightly, he withdrew with his disciples into the privacy either of the countryside or the homes of one or more of them. In these gatherings he imparted to them much of the secret wisdom which he knew so well, and gently chided any of those who had perhaps fallen from the high ideals of discipleship. At the same time he encouraged and elevated them by his presence and his talks.[49]

As it appears in the Gospels, the Sermon on the Mount records some of the teachings which he gave them, especially the so-called *Beatitudes*. But there was much more concerning both the desirable practices and restrictions which a disciple must follow. For those who persisted and remained faithful, he imparted a measure of his own inner powers and linked them intimately with himself. Naturally not everyone who thus drew near to him remained faithful and stalwart throughout the mental and physical demands of the spiritual life.

Thus began the establishment, however simply and naturally, of what later came to be known as the Mysteries of Jesus. These practices were carried on and developed throughout the later years of his ministry and were continued after the untimely death of his body. The Gnostic remains give fairly accurate accounts of these Mysteries, which, as in all cases, were practiced in profound secrecy.[50] In this Jesus was acting not only on his own behalf but under the direction of the great Brotherhood of the adept Teachers on earth. A powerful, and it was hoped enduring, spiritual impulse was to be given to Western humanity and Western civilization which was at that time developing. Egypt and Greece were already declining in power. Their Mysteries were beginning to lose their pristine purity and, in consequence, their channelship for both the hierophantic power and the esoteric wisdom. The rise and fall of the Roman Empire was of course fully known and foreseen, as also were the relative barbarism and Dark Ages which were to follow.

The mission of Jesus thus assumed an even greater significance than is given to it by exoteric religion; for it included the transmission of the Mystery teachings, the initiatory power and the ceremonial rites which it was hoped would remain at the heart of the slowly growing and maturing civilizations and nations of the Middle East and Europe.

The mission of Jesus the Christ was tragically cut short, the world thereby suffering an irreparable loss. After the death of their leader, it was natural that the apostles, and all those who had accepted Christ's messages, should band together in the small community that eventually was to become the Christian Church. They formed a brotherhood in a hostile world, for only in unity could they find strength to put into practice the teaching of their Master. An account of their method of living is given in The Acts of The Apostles, 2:42-47:

The Acts 2:42.   And they continued steadfastly in the apostles' doctrine and fellowship, and in breaking of bread, and in prayers.

43.   And fear came upon every soul: and many wonders and signs were done by the apostles.

44.   And all that believed were together, and had all things common;

45.   And sold their possessions and goods, and parted them to all men, as every man had need.

46.   And they, continuing daily with one accord in the temple, and breaking bread from house to house, did eat their meat with gladness and singleness of heart.

47.   Praising God, and having favour with all the people. And the Lord added to the church daily such as should be saved.

Officially persecuted, martyred, and scorned by individuals, the early Christians thus held firm to their faith, which was transmitted through them to the world.

Unfortunately, this period of deep spiritual unity, inspiration, living experience and universality of outlook, enjoyed by the early leaders and their congregations in the first century, did not endure. Gradually these waters of living truth gave way to a process of crystallization into fixed dogmas. From the birth of theology and creed in the third and fourth centuries sprang intolerance and sectarianism. The Neoplatonic schools closed after the martyrdom of Hypatia, and Gnosticism was proscribed as heresy. Thus the esoteric wisdom, the *Gnosis* or *Theosophia*, was largely lost to orthodox Christianity, an almost irreparable tragedy, some of the effects of which have persisted right down to the present day.

However, the relative failure of this plan is more apparent than real. It is true that ecclesiasticism, orthodox Christian theology, strife within the churches, and the lust for spiritual, political, and religious domination in the earlier centuries of the era drove the esotericism which Jesus imparted more and more deeply underground. Nevertheless, research into the Mysteries of nature and of man continued, however much in secrecy and under the constant threat of arraignment by the authorities. Many initiates—reborn from earlier periods—were being incarnated in the more civilized portions of the Western world. The list of them is much larger than is historically known because they lived and worked in secret, partly for their own safety and partly in obedience to the ideal of humility. Charlatans existed among them——inevitable at the present stage of human evolution—and some of these became historically known. This was not entirely adverse since they proved to be a shield for the real Adepts at work behind the veil of initiate silence. Secret and semisecret societies and orders later arose, including the so-called Fire Philosphers, the Rosicrucians and the Alchemists. Some members of these groups were genuine initiates, while others were only beginning to be drawn toward the great quest which they would continue in later lives.

Occasionally, *Arhats* and Adepts took birth under favorable circumstances and founded centers for the pursuit of the esoteric life and wisdom.[51] Among these were Appolonius of Tyana, Christian Rosenkreutz and some of his disciples, Lord Bacon, the leading Platonists of England, and he who chose to appear under the name of the Comte de St. Germain. Far earlier than these Jesus of Nazareth not only healed the sick and instructed the multitudes, but also kept alive and refueled the fires of the spiritual and occult knowledge, and thus made much more easily available on the physical plane all the aspects of the Mystery Tradition.

REFERENCES AND NOTES

1. Heb. 12:23.
2. *Retractions* 1. 13:3.
3. Cor. 2:7 (probably written A.D. 50).
4. See Geoffrey Hodson, *The Hidden Wisdom in the Holy Bible,* Vol. 1, Ch. 6, and Vol. 2, pp. 48-9.
5. 1 Cor. 15:6-8.
6. Acts 5:30.
7. *Gnosis,* see G.R.S. Mead: *Pistis Sophia, Fragments of a Faith Forgotten.*
8. Matt. 24:6.
9. Initiation, Adepts—see Glossary.
10. See Hodson, *Hidden Wisdom,* Vol. 1, Introduction and pp.85-99.
11. *Ibid.,* Pt. 4.
12. Avatar—see Glossary.
13. For a further exposition of the keys, see Hodson, *Hidden Wisdom,* Vol. 1, Parts 2 and 3.
14. *Ibid.,* Vols. 1, 2, 3.

15. Logos—see Glossary and Geoffrey Hodson, *Lecture Notes from the School of the Wisdom,* Vol. 1, pp. 468, 474-5.

16. Monad—see Glossary and also Hodson, *Lecture Notes,* Vol. 1, Ch. 1.

17. John 10:34, 1 Cor. 3:16.

18. Causal body—see Glossary.

19. Aura—see Glossary.

20. Adam and Eve personify only the physical progenitors, the first androgynes to become single sexed.

21. Gal. 4:19.

22. Col. 1:27; I John 3:24.

23. cf. Matt. 7:21.

24. Matt. 5:48. (R.V.)

25. Matt. 7:13, 14.

26. Ps. 110:4; Heb. 5:6, 10.

27. Adept Hierarchy—see *Adept,* Glossary.

28. Mal. 4:5; Matt. 11:14; Mark 9:13. See also Geoffrey Hodson, *Reincarnation, Fact or Fallacy?*

29. Gal. 6:7; Matt. 5:18 and 7:12.

30. John 12:25; John 12:24. See also Hodson, *Hidden Wisdom,* Vol. 1, pp. 24-38.

31. See Geoffrey Hodson, *The Kingdom of the Gods,* and *The Brotherhood of Angels and of Men.*

32. Taken verbatim from *The Book of Common Prayer.*

33. From *The Liturgy According to the Use of the Liberal Catholic Church,* 3rd. ed. (London: St. Albans Press, 1942), p. 174.

34. Matt. 27:60.

35. See Hodson, *Hidden Wisdom,* Vol. 1, pp. 216-220.

36. Eph. 4:13.

37. John 20:27.

38. John 19:34.

39. See *Atma* and *Buddhi,* Glossary.

40. 1 Cor. 12:6.

41. Matt. 28:20.

42. John 10:16.

43. Col. 1:27; Gal. 4:15; Phil. 2:12.

44. John 1:1, 14.

45. Matt. 11:28, 29, 30.

46. Matt. 23:11.

47. John 15:12, 13.

48. Matt. 5:16; 7:12; 7:21.

49. Living as I have done from early boyhood in a devout love for Jesus and dwelling so often in prolonged thought of him, as for example, when writing my books on the Bible, I have found the figure I here describe forming itself in my mind. I venture, therefore, to include a description of him at this place in my text especially, as while

I was thus writing, the image of the Master seemed to become so living and so clear. (G.H.)

50. See G.R.S. Mead, *Fragments of a Faith Forgotten.*

51. *Arhat*—see Glossary and Hodson, *Hidden Wisdom,* Vol. 1, p. 227.

PART TWO

**THE ANNUNCIATION
THE IMMACULATE CONCEPTION
THE NATIVITY
THE COMING OF THE MAGI**

Chapter Two

The whole episode of the Annunciation is susceptible to interpretation in two ways. One of these might be termed the miraculous, in which parthenogenesis occurs by means of divine intervention, and a physical child named Jesus is born of Mary. While this is perhaps not wholly impossible, such a birth is better regarded as an example of the intrusion of the supernatural and the divine into a supposedly historical narrative. This contradiction may have been introduced in order to suggest to the reader a possible revelation of truth beneath a veil of allegory and symbol. In either case—the miraculous or the allegorical—conception and birth are immaculate, being wholly spiritual.

> Luke 1:26. And in the sixth month the angel Gabriel was sent from God unto a city of Galilee, named Nazareth,
>
> 27. To a virgin espoused to a man whose name was Joseph, of the house of David; and the virgin's name was Mary.
>
> 28. And the angel came in unto her, and said, Hail, thou that art highly favoured, the Lord is with thee: blessed art thou among women.

As the birth histories of other great Teachers such as the Lords Shri Krishna and Siddartha Gautama Buddha were marked by both prophetic visions and supernormal phenomena, so also accounts of the Nativity of Jesus included descriptions of not dissimilar events. Almost in contradiction—or perchance in addition—to the description of these events as recorded by St. Matthew, in Luke the angel of the Annunciation appeared, not to Joseph, the husband-to-be, but to the Virgin Mary herself. Consequently, a digression is made from the commentary upon the first chapter of The Gospel According to St. Matthew in Part II of this book in order to give consideration to the account recorded by St. Luke, which begins as follows:

> Luke 1:29. And when she saw him she was troubled at his saying, and cast in her mind what manner of salutation this should be.
>
> 30. And the angel said unto her, Fear not, Mary: for thou hast found favour with God.

In the accounts given by St. Matthew the Annunciation to Joseph was made in a dream, while in St. Luke's account, it occurred to Mary when she was evidently wide awake and, indeed, somewhat disturbed.

Luke 1:31.   And, behold, thou shalt conceive in thy womb, and bring forth a son, and shalt call his name JESUS.

32.   He shall be great, and shall be called the Son of the Highest; and the Lord God shall give unto him the throne of his father David:

33.   And he shall reign over the house of Jacob for ever; and of his kingdom there shall be no end.

34.   Then said Mary unto the angel, How shall this be, seeing I know not a man?

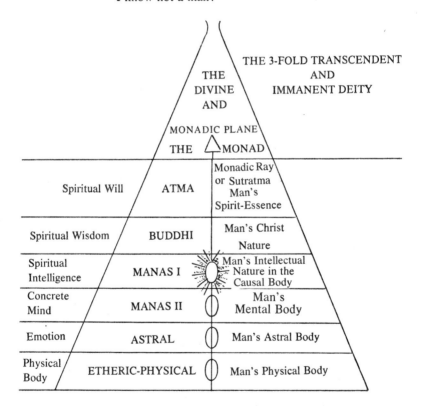

This event is so related as to make it applicable to the processes of cosmogenesis, an interpretation which is supported, even affirmed, in the opening verses of The Gospel According to St. John.[1] Allegorically, the conception and emanation of a universe are being described; for the interaction of the Holy Spirit and Mary (*mare* or sea of matter), the essential positive and negative creative potencies, are introduced into the account. Similarly, the spirit-essence in man and its "vesture of light", "the Robe of Glory" or causal body, are brought into creative, if not procreative, union.[2] From the spirit-essence a universe is born, and from the vesture of light Jesus, the Christ-to-be, personifying the Christ nature or intuitive wisdom in man, is roused from latency into potency, from the embryonic into the active condition or birth.[3]

In this view, the Annunciation, conception and birth of Jesus may be regarded less as historical events than as deeply interior changes that occur in every human on the attainment of a certain spiritual stature, partly personified also by John the Baptist. Thus, the three events may be interpreted less as having occurred in succession and thus limited in time, than as a continuing interior regeneration and enlightenment which takes place throughout the whole world of men, not only in Nazareth or Bethlehem.

Furthermore, these events may be viewed as beyond space or geographical position, less localized than global, and less occurring to only one woman than to the Virgin Mary within every human being. Although the Evangelist in his thirty-fourth verse restricts the events to a certain time and place and to one particular woman, withdrawing temporarily from an allegory of the birth of a universal being, nevertheless, the introduction of the supernatural may permissibly be regarded as also implying an allegorical intent.

> Luke 1:35. And the angel answered and said unto her, The Holy Ghost shall come upon thee, and the power of the Highest shall overshadow thee: therefore also that holy thing which shall be born of thee shall be called the Son of God.

Mary is a personification of the "vesture of light," in which the three-fold Divinity (the true man) is enrobed. She may also be regarded as a vehicle for the manifestation of the spiritual intelligence in man—the abstract mind. Mary is the interior, maternal principle, potential and later actual, within which the Christ Indwelling in every man stirs to life. Thereafter, this principle is born and gradually develops into full manhood, "the measure of the stature of the fulness of Christ,"[4] the perfected man.

Each of the participants may be regarded as a personfication of one of the three aspects of the divine Self in every human being; the generative power of the divine will is represented by the archangel and his words, the conceiving and producing capacity personified by the Virgin Mary, and the divine wisdom represented by the child Jesus. The angel of Annunciation personifies the Dweller in the Innermost, the Monad or divine spirit-essence in man. The words of Annunciation and the power of which they were an expression represent the manifestation of the positive will-force, the fructifying power, the Word by the utterance of which the seeming miracle is brought about—an immaculate conception.

In the cosmic sense, the product of this "miracle" is the universe, and in the human sense it is the conception, birth and development of the innate but hitherto germinal Christ-like nature of man.

Three names are given to the child who is to be born—Jesus, the Son of the Highest, and the Son of God. The first of these was bestowed upon the child at birth and borne by him throughout his life. The word Christ, which was added as a second name, is nevertheless no personal name; rather is it descriptive of a state of being, a degree of evolutionary stature and a condition of both body and soul. In ancient Greece the term *Christos,* "the anointed," was applied to those who had been admitted to a certain grade in the Greater Mysteries, Initiates who had attained to this grade or degree were wholly dedicated to the spiritual way of life and the service of God and their fellowmen. In this sense they were "the anointed" or consecrated.

The life history of Jesus from the time of his Baptism onward reveals that, indeed, he was in every respect and in the fullest manner an anointed one—thus his name, Jesus the Christ.

St. Luke's account goes on to describe the conception of John the Baptist.

> Luke 1:36.   And, behold, thy cousin Elisabeth, she hath also conceived a son in her old age: and this is the sixth month with her, who was called barren.

The conception and birth of John the Baptist was foretold to his father, Zacharias, by the Angel of the Annunciation, the archangel Gabriel, but there was no suggestion of an immaculate conception. The boy was normally conceived, even though his mother, Elisabeth, was advanced in years and supposedly barren. It is worthy of note, however, that although Elisabeth was only in her sixth month, the Archangel was aware of the sex of the child-to-be, namely, male. In fact, there are three elements of the supernatural included in the account of the conception and birth of John: the appearance of the angel to Zacharias in a dream, the supernormal powers of perception, and the foreknowledge of the sex of the child-to-be.

Jesus and John were thus linked by the shared events of archangelic annunciation and prophecies and quite unusual material conditions. They were also intimately associated by ancient prophecy which concerned them both. It was foretold that John would appear first as forerunner and preparer of the way and that Jesus would follow him as the Lord who would faithfully pursue that way fulfilling the prophecy and his destiny. Jesus, when questioned by his disciples, confirmed that view; he also stated that John the Baptist was a reincarnation of the prophet Elijah, or "Elias that was for to come."[5]

The suggestion may tentatively be advanced that Joseph, the putative father of Jesus, might in his turn be a reincarnation of Joseph of the Book of Genesis, since both bore the same name and were also sons of Jacob. A relationship between the prophet Elijah and John the Baptist may also be discerned by the fact of the similarity of their clothing, diet, and visits to the desert, or wilderness.

John as well as Jesus was clearly a predestined figure, allegorically described as also with the Lord Buddha and Jesus, by an annunciation, either by physically present sages, a member of the angelic hosts, or a messenger from on high. Such visitors inform the parents-to-be—and especially the mother—that a son is to be born of them who will display divine qualities and very greatly influence mankind.

In reality, though an angelic visitation is not denied, this implies that the inner Self had reached that degree of development at which the path will be entered early in life, followed through even up to death, with consequent entry on an advanced evolutionary phase. The Ego itself has determined upon a particular course of conduct in its next rebirth—the complete self-liberation from all the restrictions which bodily life applies. These include the limitation to purely rational thinking; argument and egotism born of the delusion of self-separateness; desire, the indulgence of which clouds brain-consciousness; even the necessity for further rebirth into physical life. This latter inevitably necessitates growing up, discipline, education, and the errors into which childhood and youth are prone to fall. Adult life also brings its impulses and temptations, while old age is often accompanied by a pitiful decline in the mental and physical capacities.

Advanced Egos—generally those who have achieved initiation in the Greater Mysteries in previous life—determine that an end shall be put to these and other degradations of spirit which normally are inseparable from incarnation in bodies of mind, emotion and flesh. This decision—the true Annunciation—is so strongly held by the reincarnating Ego that the mother of the child developing in her womb becomes aware of it, sensing that, parental pride apart, a wonderful, even wondrous, child is to be born to her. This she knows interiorly, but the direct knowledge may reach her from external sources also, perhaps as an annunciation by an angel.

This inner decision is, however, never taken for liberation of themselves alone. Men steeped in ignorance, and therefore falling continually into error and provoking reactions under law, must similarly be saved from the tribulations inseparable from the purely worldly life and wordly motives for living. Thus there is also a marked sense of a mission.

Symbolically interpreted the desert would represent an arid, spiritually unfruitful, even materialistic state of mind. John's arrival in the desert and his dual call to a spiritual way of life and preparation of the way of the Lord cause him aptly to be seen as a personification of the increasing influence of the spiritual Self upon the hitherto unspiritual mind, notably in the form of conscience. Thus, a change from a self-centered and materialistic mode of thought and life, "the wilderness," is brought about by the power of the indwelling spirit in man, John the Baptist. This change is necessary before admission to the Greater Mysteries and before passing through those phases of interior development allegorically described as an immaculate conception and a birth of the Christ Child, the mystical Nativity. The initiate is born anew and becomes worthy of the title *Christos,* the anointed one. Thus, John the Baptist prepares the way for the coming Lord.

The appropriateness of this symbolism as well as the human personifications of the threefold, immortal Self of man lends support to an allegorical interpretation of the events preceding, during, and following the birth of Jesus.

Luke 1:37.   For with God nothing shall be impossible.

This verse is of interest if only because it makes credible both the historical and the mystical readings of the accounts of the Nativity of Jesus. Such biblical utterances can have the effect of silencing the voice of reason, since no criteria exist by which the divine omnipotence may be measured; for even the laws of nature are made to be subservient to the divine will which, it is biblically affirmed, can set them at naught. The mind is thereby bereft of an alternative, since the will of God is claimed to be all-powerful; for the otherwise impossible and incredible occurrence of parthenogenesis in a human female (Mary) is here affirmed, if only in the special single case of Jesus, the Christ.

The demands of reason, logic and facts are ignored, even flouted, since it is presumably ordained that these pathways to knowledge may not be trodden by those who would receive divine or spiritual rather than purely material learning. If, however, the whole story is regarded as allegorical, then the annunciation, immaculate conception and miraculous birth—not only of Jesus from Mary but of the Christ consciousness within the higher intellect of every man, whatever the sex of the body—become credible because they occur within the divine nature rather than the bodily form of the human individual.

Luke 1:38.   And Mary said, Behold the handmaid of the Lord; be it unto me according to thy word. And the angel departed from her.

A certain intuitive responsiveness and passivity of mind are essential to mystical illumination and to the birth and development of spiritual intuitiveness or implicit insight. Since Mary displayed these necessary attributes, the three events gain support as being deeply interior occurrences which take place within the depths—or if it be preferred, the heights—of human nature.[6]

Luke 1:39.   And Mary arose in those days, and went into the hill country with haste, into a city of Juda;

40.   And entered into the house of Zacharias, and saluted Elisabeth.

If the term *hill country* is read as a symbol from topography for an uplifted or spiritual state of awareness, then support is gained for the mystical reading; for after being exalted by the "Annunciation," the mystic naturally withdraws into a meditative state. The company of others similarly uplifted is naturally entered, and so Mary, newly impregnated of the Holy Ghost, goes into the presence of Elisabeth, who although hitherto barren and already aged, is about to become the mother of John (at Ein Kerim or wherever that event may have occurred[7]).

Luke 1:41.   And it came to pass, that, when Elisabeth heard the salutation of Mary, the babe leaped in her womb; and Elisabeth was filled with the Holy Ghost:

42.   And she spake out with a loud voice, and said, Blessed art thou among women, and blessed is the fruit of thy womb.

Illuminati recognize each other, and thus Elisabeth, the mother-to-be of

John the Baptist, perceived the illumined condition of Mary, the mother-to-be of Jesus. All that follows is descriptive of experiences within the higher consciousness of those who reach that evolutionary stature or phase of spiritual development at which supernormal faculties and powers develop. Indeed, it may well be assumed that the mysteries of initiation and concomitant lofty exaltations are revealed allegorically in all that is described concerning the conception and birth of both Jesus and John the Baptist. If this is the case, doubts concerning the date and place of the birth of Jesus and divergencies in the various accounts sink into insignificance; for a universally occurring mystery is being described rather than, or in addition to, a historical event.

Luke 1:43. And whence is this to me, that the mother of my Lord should come to me?

44. For, lo, as soon as the voice of thy salutation sounded in mine ears, the babe leaped in my womb for joy.

45. And blessed is she that believed: for there shall be a performance of those things which were told her from the Lord.

Before the birth of Jesus, the members of the two Hebrew families of Jesus and John passed through closely similar experiences. St. Luke accentuates the supernatural aspects of both pregnancies, Mary's which was immaculate, and Elisabeth's occurring late in life. Both of these as described are so closely related that they are susceptible to mystical interpretations. Thus viewed, Mary personifies the "vesture of light," the "spiritual body" of St. Paul as already suggested.[8] Elisabeth's advanced years may indicate evolutionary age and the stage of spiritual development at which a similar, interior birth is about to occur. Both she and Zacharias were "stricken in years," signifying that in each of them the soul had entered upon a phase of development characterized by advanced maturity. This is suggested by the fact that the faculties of intuitive insight, profound comprehension of spiritual principles and the power of prophecy displayed by John, their son, are only developed after a certain evolutionary age has been attained. Both the parents were thus advanced beyond the normal and so able to give birth to a child gifted with unusual powers.

Luke 1:45. And Mary said, My soul doth magnify the Lord,

47. And my spirit hath rejoiced in God my Saviour.

48. For he hath regarded the low estate of his handmaiden: for, behold, from henceforth all generations shall call me blessed.

49. For he that is mighty hath done to me great things; and holy is his name.

50. And his mercy is on them that fear him from generation to generation.

51. He hath shewed strength with his arm; he hath scattered the proud in the imagination of their hearts.

52. He hath put down the mighty from their seats, and exalted them of low degree.

53. He hath filled the hungry with good things; and the rich he hath sent empty away.

54. He hath holpen his servant Israel, in remembrance of his mercy;

55. As he spake to our fathers, to Abraham, and to his seed for ever.

These verses known as "The Magnificat" or Hymn of the Virgin Mary, reveal and beautifully portray the highly elevated mental and spiritual state of Mary, giving support to a mystical reading of the Nativity of Jesus.

Luke 1:56. And Mary abode with her about three months, and returned to her own house.

While historically feasible, the number three in this verse may be symbolic and refer again to the threefold spiritual Self of man—divine will, wisdom, and intelligence—within its vesture of light. The house, in its turn, may symbolize the four mortal vehicles of concrete thought, emotion, vitality and flesh into the consciousness and the limitation of which the higher Self of illumined ones must return between phases of spiritual exaltation.

Luke 1:57. Now Elisabeth's full time came that she should be delivered; and she brought forth a son.

All nativities whether of the central figure of a spiritual allegory or of close associates, are susceptible to at least three interpretations. Two of these have already been discussed: the emergence of cosmos from chaos or the inception of the process of cosmogenesis (generally depicted by the Saviour himself), and the transcendence of a limitation of consciousness and entry into a more exalted state. In man, and especially in the women who become the mothers, this process generally involves the attainment of supramental states, particularly intuitive wisdom. A third interpretation is that history itself is being recorded, notably the birth of an *Avatar*, the chosen vehicle or body into which an aspect, or a group of attributes, of Deity will "descend."[9] When the miraculous is introduced into a story by annunciations by archangels and conceptions which are either immaculate or occurring beyond the normal age, the elevation of consciousness is described, but the actual physical birth of a wondrous child is also signified.

John the Baptist as a wondrous child, for example, typifies the dawning faculty in man of the power to comprehend the underlying principles of any subject, especially a subject relating to the emergence of predesigned forms in nature from divine archetypal "Ideas" (as in the Platonic sense). When this power is unfolded, the inner Self assumes increasing command over the outer man. Conscience then becomes dominant, and an almost rigid rule of ethical behavior is enforced upon the outer physical man or woman. Such in part were the annunciation, the conception and the birth of John the Baptist by his mother, Elisabeth, the elderly wife of Zacharias.

Luke 1:58.   And her neighbours and her cousins heard how the Lord had shewed great mercy upon her; and they rejoiced with her.

59.   And it came to pass, that on the eighth day they came to circumcise the child; and they called him Zacharias, after the name of his father.

60.   And his mother answered and said, Not so; but he shall be called John.

61.   And they said unto her, There is none of thy kindred that is called by this name.

62.   And they made signs to his father, how he would have him called.

63.   And he asked for a writing table, and wrote, saying, His name is John. And they marvelled all.

At this point it is important to remember that all the people in such allegories of spiritual unfoldment signify parts of the constitution of one person. In the case of the Nativity of Jesus, the father, Joseph, represents the reasoning mind of man after it has reached a certain maturity. The mother, Mary, personifies the inner Self in its vesture of light, conscious and active particularly at the level of the abstract intelligence. The newborn child Jesus portrays the new phase of development at which all that is represented by the concept of the Christ nature in man will be "born" or made manifest and developed.

Jesus and John display differing degrees of such development. John himself, the reincarnation of Elijah who was a prophet and a seer,[10] proclaimed the near approach of one far greater than he who would "baptize with fire and with Spirit."[11] He represents the power of the abstract and prophetic mind which has become active. Jesus, on the other hand, is portrayed by St. John in the Gospels as the incarnate Wisdom itself and, in addition, a veritable manifestation upon earth of the Word of God.[12] He signifies compassion and intuitive perception. If the conception is not pressed too far, then these two in their turn portray phases of development of the same individual, the first dawning and later full manifestation of the powers of the Christ nature in each and every man. The precedence in time of the birth of John the Baptist is strictly in accordance with natural evolutionary process. In other words, the expanded and illuminated state of the human intellect (John) precedes the development of the capacity for direct, intuitive insight (Jesus). This was always present, inherent, in the immortal Self, but had remained latent, unexpressed, until the requisite evolutionary time had arrived. After its awakening, truth will be known from within, and no longer only from without. The later relationship of the two boys as men, the Baptism of Jesus at Jordan supports this view; for John is still but man, however richly endowed with prophetic insight. Jesus, on the other hand, is presented as a representative and manifestation of the Supreme Deity.

The births of saviors and divine and semidivine heroes represent that special time of awakening. Hence, the insistence by Elisabeth and Zacharias that their son should be called John.[13] To name the child after his father would represent repetition and so lack of advancement, while the name John (at which the people marvelled) portrayed the birth (interior manifestation and development) of a divine power which in terms of evolutionary progress was new or newborn.

> Luke 1:64. And his mouth was opened immediately, and his tongue loosed, and he spake, and praised God.

The sudden and seemingly miraculous or supernatural display of the faculty of speech by a newborn infant indicates that, in addition to a historical account, a spiritual interpretation of the event should be undertaken. This capacity for speech shown by John the Baptist and St. John's statement that Jesus was a manifestation of the Word of God might be regarded as linking the two boys. This would give further support to the possibility that they are presented as personifications of two aspects and stages of infoldment in one individual, a highly evolved human being.

The remainder of this chapter may be read both literally and mystically, for it concerns the actions of Zacharias rather than of Jesus or John the Baptist.

> Luke 1:65. And fear came on all that dwelt round about them: and all these sayings were noised abroad throughout all the hill country of Judea.
>
> 66. And all they that heard them laid them up in their hearts, saying, What manner of child shall this be! And the hand of the Lord was with him.
>
> 67. And his father Zacharias was filled with the Holy Ghost, and prophesied, saying,
>
> 68. Blessed be the Lord God of Israel; for he hath visited and redeemed his people,
>
> 69. And hath raised up an horn of salvation for us in the house of his servant David;
>
> 70. As he spake by the mouth of his holy prophets, which have been since the world began;
>
> 71. That we should be saved from our enemies, and from the hand of all that hate us;
>
> 72. To perform the mercy promised to our fathers, and to remember his holy covenant;
>
> 73. the oath which he sware to our father Abraham.
>
> 74. That he would grant unto us, that we being delivered out of the hand of our enemies might serve him without fear,
>
> 75. In holiness and righteousness before him, all the days of our life.

The above verses, supposedly recording verbatim the utterances of Zacharias under the influence of the Holy Ghost, constitute both a repetition of the prophecy in the Old Testament and a personal prevision of its fulfillment. Yet it contains many patently false prophecies about the future of the Hebrew nation; for, in complete contradiction of the actual events, a lofty and secure position among the nations of the world was foretold. What, then, may be permissibly deduced from such profound ignorance of the future in one said to be lifted up in spirit and thereby enabled to perceive accurately the future which lay ahead for the Jewish people? If, as heretofore, a falsity recorded in a supposedly historical narrative indicates a mystical revelation rather than a historical fact, then, it is suggested, the narrative is describing a condition of consciousness of the whole human race on earth, as well as individual members of that race.

Then the experience is seen as interior rather than objective and refers to a future attainment in consciousness by humanity itself rather than a particular preeminence to be granted to one small group of people by divine ordinance. This attainment may well be described as Messianic, since it includes the awakening (or birth) and the continuing development in man—indeed in *all* men—of a mature Christ-like concern and compassion for *all* mankind.[14] The capacity to know truth directly—another sign of a Messianic state of consciousness—becomes established throughout the whole spiritual, intellectual and physical nature of man. Instead of one aspect predominating over or successfully at war with another, the total human being achieves balance in the activity and influences of all its principles. The whole man is spiritually exalted and intellectually illumined far beyond the condition normal for mankind at the time the prophecies were made (and, for that matter, tragically, even today).

Thus interpreted, these attainments are prophesied for all mankind, not only the Hebrews as opposed to all others. It is also true, however, that certain people and certain groups, such as those gathered as disciples around great teachers or Avatars, reach this stature in advance of the human race as a whole. Harmony among the nations of the world will have become established by then and, in consequence, the position of every single nation will be completely secure; each will be respected and even honored by all its fellow nations—a Messianic age indeed.

If this view is taken, then the prophetic revelations are not false prophecies but correct descriptions of the result of the vast sweep of evolutionary progress into future and higher states of being for all mankind. All of the beautiful, even poetic, descriptions of that future are thus strictly correct as foretold by prophets whose consciousness became so elevated that far-distant attainments of the race were foreseen.

John the Baptist, over whose birth the poetic and prophetic raptures of his father were uttered, is seen as a personification of human intelligence, to which humanity is evolving and will attain. The child, Jesus, and the mature Jesus the Christ to whom reference is made by Zacharias and indirectly by his forerunners, personifies a still further and greater state of human development. In this stage the divine in man and the universe are consciously realized as aspects of one divinity.[15] Indeed, this may well be described as a visitation of "the dayspring from on high."[16]

REFERENCES AND NOTES

1. "In the beginning was the Word, and Word was with God, and the Word was God." John 1:1.

2. Causal body—see Glossary. Also see G.R.S. Mead, *The Hymn of the Robe of Glory* for a Gnostic explanation.

3. "Birth." See Gal. 4:19. Before his Baptism, the Lord is referred to in this work by his Hebrew name, Jesus. Thereafter, since a descent upon him of the Holy Spirit occurred, he is referred to as Jesus the Christ.

4. Eph. 4:13.

5. Mal. 4:5; Matt. 17:10-13, and Mark. 9:13. See also Geoffrey Hodson, *Reincarnation, Fact or Fallacy?*, Ch. 4.

6. More correctly "within."

7. Ein Kerim is the reputed birthplace of John.

8. 1 Cor. 15:44.

9. *Avatar*—see Glossary.

10. Matt. 11:14.

11. Matt. 3:11.

12. John 1:1-5.

13. English form of Johanan, "Jehovah hath been gracious."

14. John 10:16.

15. "I and My father are One."

16. Luke 1:78.

Chapter Three

With the greatest skill, St. John blends these mystic and mysterious powers of both the cosmic Godhead and the God in man with the historical narrative. He creates an epic story in which these two aspects of the manifested Deity are blended with the person and life story of Jesus of Nazareth. Unless this triplicity is recognized, I submit, the three intertwined threads become confused and almost inextricably mixed in the accounts of the life of Jesus as the Son of God. It is only when the three strands are understood separately that the immortal story can become wholly comprehensible.

The strands concerning the nature and evolution of the spiritual soul of man to "the measure of the stature of the fulness of Christ"[1] is of special value to all those in whom the intuitive faculty is awakening. In these the mystic quest has begun and they seek to enter the "strait gate" and follow the "narrow way."[2] For them, the spiritually awakened among men, the life story of Jesus is replete with guidance in gaining understanding—as from the *Logia* and especially the Sermon on the Mount—and in living out their lives among men from the time of the inner event of mystical nativity to that of ascension into heaven. Immaculate Conception, Birth, Baptism, Transfiguration, Crucifixion and Ascension may all be perceived as allegorical portrayals of the passage followed by every spiritually awakened human being through the stages, degrees of illumination and initiations in the Greater Mysteries.[3]

The different Evangelists were aware in varying degrees of these deeper and more esoteric teachings, especially St. John. They were also bound by mystic vows to veil that knowledge. At the same time, these vows obliged them wisely and safely to share with their fellowmen (of whom the inn was full) that which had been revealed to them in the secrecy of the Hall of Initiation (partly symbolized as the stable of the inn).[4] This St. John does in the following verses.

John 1:1. In the beginning was the Word, and the Word was with God, and the Word was God.

2. The same was in the beginning with God.

3. All things were made by him; and without him was not any thing made that was made.

4. In him was life; and the life was the light of men.
5. And the light shineth in darkness; and the darkness comprehended it not.

The author or authors of The Gospel According to St. John begin the biography of Jesus with three general statements. First, the name of the Deity of the universe is the "Word." Second, the young Hebrew whose life story is to be narrated was a manifestation of that Word as Creator of the universe. The third statement, in the fourth verse, suggests that this same creative Word was also "the light of men."

The Latin word for the Deity thus named is *Verbum* and, in the Greek, *Logos*. This may refer to a teaching also found in the scriptures of both the ancient Egyptian religion and those upon which the Brahmanical faith is founded. This states that the process of the creation of the universe is effected by the utterance or emission of a power of the quality of sound.[5]

St. John also affirms that the deity whom he names the Word pre-existed before all things were made. This principle came into active existence as an emanative and formative power shaping the matter of virgin space into forms conceived in the divine Mind and brought to expression by the emitted sounds of the voice of God, or by the Word. Jesus, whose life story is to be related, is thus implicitly referred to as a manifestation of the Supreme Deity in human form,[6] a vehicle of the Divine, an *Avatar*.

While the fourth verse may be regarded solely as a description of the effect of the presence of Jesus upon humanity, it may also be received in an interior or mystical sense, as may so much in the Gospels, particularly in this fourth one. If this latter interpretation is accepted, then the divine Being referred to as "the light of men" is the divine presence manifest within every human being.

Adoption of this view can entirely change one's approach to and reception of the life story of Jesus, for it then appears neither solely macrocosmic nor restricted to the historical person of Jesus. Rather, as a power and a presence within the inner Self of every human being, it is both universal and microcosmic.[7] One must continually keep in mind that these are not two separate and distinct deities—the Supreme Word or creative Logos who brought the universe into being, on the one hand, and the light of men on the other. They are one and the same; for the divinity within man and that nameless power responsible for and presiding over the whole universe are eternally and forever *one*. Otherwise expressed, the light of the universe and the light of men are not two lights but one, throughout eternity.

The plural word *men* seems to indicate a repetition of the view found in other scriptures that this light not only shines upon the world solely from within chosen vehicles such as Jesus, but also shines within and from the inner Self of all mankind. This God indwelling is referred to as "the Inner Ruler immortal seated in the hearts of all beings," and the *Horus* of the Soul.[8]

The doctrine of the formation of the universe and all that it contains by "speech," "voice," or "Word" need not be especially enunciated here, since it is more fully referred to in an earlier volume of proffered interpretations of the Bible.[9]

> John 1:6.   There was a man sent from God, whose name was John.
>
> 7.   The same came for a witness, to bear witness of the Light, that all men through him might believe.
>
> 8.   He was not that Light, but was sent to bear witness of that Light.

One wonders if the immediate introduction of John the Baptist into the narrative changes its content from a blend of the macrocosmic and microcosmic into the purely historical. The possibe symbolic significance of the strange figure of John is considered in the next pages and fully treated in Chapters Six and Seven of this work.

> John 1:9.   That was the true Light, which lighteth every man that cometh into the world.

St. John here reiterates that the Logos is light, both macrocosmic and microcosmic. This light results from self-manifestation of the Logos as a shining presence and power which illumines both precosmic space and the mind of man. In this verse the human application is accentuated, every human being born into the physical world bearing an inward light.

This light is also identified with Jesus the Christ and may be regarded as a synonym for an attribute of man's spiritual soul, the divinity in him by which, according to St. John, the pathway into incarnation is illumined. This is the true "Light that lighteth every man that cometh into the world." If the narrative is taken allegorically, then man is unaware of this interior light until a certain phase of evolutionary progress has been entered, described by St. Paul as a mystical nativity.[10]

This spiritual and psychological regeneration or "rebirth," as Jesus referred to it, is preceded by a drastic if gradual change in outlook on life and conduct of the mode of daily living.[11] The human being in whom this mystical conception has occurred prepares for the resultant second birth by self-purification. John the Baptist may be regarded as a personification of the call to make this change, reaching the outer man from his inner Self through the voice of conscience. Thus this change is largely moral, and the ascetic habits of life attributed to John the Baptist as well as his call to prepare for the way of the Lord appropriately portray this influence. Otherwise expressed, the completely worldly man becomes changed from within into an increasingly spiritual man. John the Baptist is the herald of this change, the Hermes, as it were, who rescues Persephone, the incarnate soul, from the underworld.[12] Thus, it is said of him in the eighth verse that "He was not that Light, but was sent to bear witness of that Light."

The fourth Gospel begins in such a manner as to indicate that both Jesus the Christ and John the Baptist were personifications of interior powers of man. Thus read, the fourth Gospel is not only a description in allegorical form of the spiritual way of life, but also a call by the interior John the Baptist to mankind to enter upon that life.

The reader of this volume is informed that its author is not denying the historicity of the four gospels, for this is not the subject. Rather he sees in numerous, if somewhat veiled, suggestions apparent in them an account of the progress of man from a purely worldly to a spiritual life.

John 1:10.   He was in the world, and the world knew him not.

11.   He came unto his own, and his own received him not.

THE LIFE OF CHRIST

II. THE GOSPEL STORY

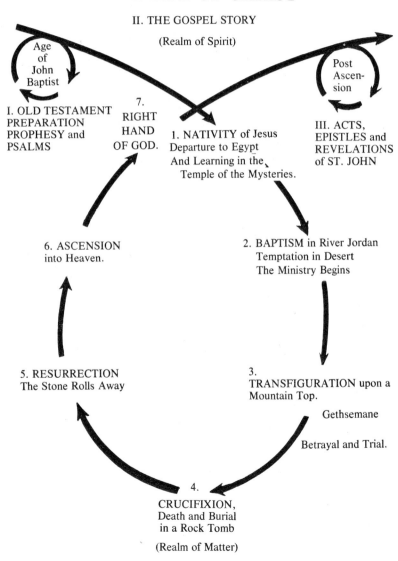

(Realm of Spirit)

Age of John Baptist

Post Ascension

I. OLD TESTAMENT PREPARATION PROPHESY and PSALMS

7. RIGHT HAND OF GOD.

1. NATIVITY of Jesus Departure to Egypt And Learning in the Temple of the Mysteries.

III. ACTS, EPISTLES and REVELATIONS of ST. JOHN

6. ASCENSION into Heaven.

2. BAPTISM in River Jordan Temptation in Desert The Ministry Begins

5. RESURRECTION The Stone Rolls Away

3. TRANSFIGURATION upon a Mountain Top.

Gethsemane

Betrayal and Trial.

4. CRUCIFIXION, Death and Burial in a Rock Tomb

(Realm of Matter)

In these two verses we see a blending of the three Christs: the creative Word, the spiritual light within man (the Savior), and the historical Jesus. The divine visitation is said to have been unperceived and unreceived by the world, doubtless meaning humanity at large. The charge is indeed true: Christ the indwelling light of every human being, the Logos of the soul, was and still is unperceived and unreceived,[13] which is perhaps not unnatural throughout the earlier phases of human evolution. Only when the mental principle in man begins to develop the faculty of abstract and intuitive thought does his spiritual or monadic light begin to be perceived and acknowledged, ultimately becoming the guiding principle of his whole life. Before this evolutionary stature is attained, whether by the human race or the individual man, it is indeed true that "the world received him not."

The recorded life of the historical Jesus mirrors these same phases of intellectual and spiritual unfoldment. Jesus as teacher, Redeemer and Savior was unaccepted by those in authority, personifying as they do the rule of the personal, formal mind with its attributes of separateness, self-satisfaction, acquisitiveness and pride.[14] Jesus was perceived and recognized by only the few, his family, his disciples and immediate friends, all of whom personify the spiritually illumined intellect.

REFERENCES AND NOTES

1. Eph. 4:13.

2. Matt. 7:13; Matt. 7:14.

3. See Hodson, *Hidden Wisdom*, Vol. I, Pt. 6.

4. Luke 2:7.

5. *Amen-Ra* and *Shabda-Brahman*.

6. John 1:14.

7. Macrocosmic, Microcosmic—see Glossary.

8. *Bhagavad Gita; Horus*. Second Person of the Triad of Edfu.

9. Hodson, *Hidden Wisdom*, Vol. II, Part 3, Introduction and Ch. I.

10. Gal. 4:19.

11. John 3:3.

12. Persephone. For a full exposition see Hodson, *Hidden Wisdom,* Vol. I, pp. 252-6.

13. Consider the condition of the world and the conduct of many human beings in this era: wars, crime, corruption, and vice being rampant.

14. The favorable qualities of this part of man's mind and the advance of science and technology to which they have contributed are by no means overlooked or underestimated.

Chapter Four

Two purposes, among others, were fulfilled by the ancient writers in the symbolical language.[1] One of these was to convey knowledge concerning the laws of being, including the fundamental principles of the emanation of universes and all that they contain,[2] their vitalization and evolution to the highest possible stage. The other purpose was to indicate the pathway of self-illumination by directing thought toward the understanding and experience of the one supreme fact of human existence, namely, that the God in man and the God in the universe are one God.[3] Both these purposes can be discerned in the Gospels.

Many other accounts of the lives of saviors are similarly descriptive of solar, initiatory and seasonal cycles.[4] The onset of winter is emblematic of old age, the darkest, coldest months referring to death. Likewise, annunciations and nativities refer to the promise and later arrival of spring. In that season the sun begins to reassume its light, heat and energy-giving power, and vegetation that has been inactive awakens into a new life. Metaphorically, nature is reborn and comes to life visibly on earth.

Each germ cell exhibits somewhat similar phases. Before fertilization it is inactive. Fructification corresponds to annunciations or promises of "birth." Active generative processes indicate prenatal life, while the ultimate product, the new organism, corresponds to nativity. All the various phases of development indicated by analogy are subject to certain dangers, as was Jesus. The events in the life of Jesus may be read with this in view.

The eighteenth verse of the first chapter of the Gospel according to St. Matthew is chosen for the beginning of my proffered interpretation of the story of the life of Jesus. The preceding verses are unused because they consist entirely of statements of the genealogy of Jesus through Joseph, the putative husband of Mary. Since, however, verse eighteen states that the child was immaculately conceived of the Holy Ghost—and not naturally of Joseph—the genealogy is entirely without significance.

> Matt. 1:18. Now the birth of Jesus Christ was on this wise: When as his mother Mary was espoused to Joseph, before they came together was found with child of the Holy Ghost.

This verse describing the generative and fructifying activity of the Third Aspect of the Trinity within Virgin Mary affirms the occurrence of an event which is a physical impossibility except by miracle. When interpreted as an allegory, however, the statement is found to be replete with spiritual truth.

One may assume that the author of this Gospel (the only one affirming the birth to be immaculate) would hardly be likely to begin relating the life story of Jesus by asking his readers to accept such an incredible statement without question or deep inquiry. On the contrary, I suggest, the authors intended to stimulate mental and intuitional research by including apparent incredibilities and impossibilities in the scriptures.[5] One is reminded of the words of Moses Maimonides quoted at the beginning of this book and those in the *Zohar*, also earlier quoted, regarding the "supernal truths and sublime secrets" hidden beneath the veil of allegory and symbol. The reader who is in search of these may wish to make use of the methods of interpretation described in the first, second and third volumes of my book *The Hidden Wisdom in the Holy Bible*. He may meditatively and intuitively apply the proferred keys to unlock spiritual meanings, the way in which all scriptures should be read.

As already discussed, Jesus the Christ can be regarded as a representation of the power and thought (Word) by which "All things were made."[5] His conception and birth are therefore first offered from this, the cosmic point of view.

A description of the beginning of cosmogenesis is given in both the verse under consideration and the second verse of the Book of Genesis. In Genesis the masculine agent is referred to as the Spirit of God and the feminine principle indicated by the symbol of water, but the meaning is the same in both accounts. In terms of occult philosophy this process may be described as follows: spirit-matter, unpolarized and therefore quiescent, preexisted in a unitary state in the Absolute.[6] When a finite universe is to be emanated from the infinite under rhythmic law, spirit and matter become oppositely polarized and interact creatively. The universe is the offspring of this cosmogenetical union. Symbolically, as in Matthew, a woman conceives of the Holy Ghost.

Otherwise stated, the divine Intelligence—the Holy Ghost in this verse —which presides over the emergence of a universe from the Absolute, projects an Aspect of its power into the circumscribed region or "sea" (*mare*) of space: "And the Spirit of God moved upon the face of the waters."[7] The seed or egg of a universe, its archetypal Idea, comes into being as a dynamic model and embryo."[8] The eighteenth verse of this chapter may therefore be read as a description of the first stage of cosmogenesis. The masculine and feminine creative potencies are personified by the Holy Spirit and the Virgin Mary respectively, while the formative activity is indicated in terms of human procreation. Thus the purely abstract is presented in a somewhat concrete form, a spiritual truth thereby brought partially within the reach of human understanding. The authors are careful to avoid a materialistic interpretation of the subject by reporting divine intervention in the most intimate circumstances in the life of an individual, thereby producing an immaculate conception.

A similar process of spiritual creativity is enacted by two potencies within the spiritual nature of man. These are the purest spirit-essence—a ray of the one Godhead—and the immortal Individuality in its "vesture of light," the spiritual body referred to by St. Paul.[9]

The faculty of spiritual intuitiveness lies dormant or seed-like within this vesture of the soul throughout the periods in which man's physical body, emotions and analytical mind are evolving. Eventually the mind reaches a degree of development at which it can begin to grasp abstract ideas. This capacity has lain dormant, virginal, being feminine in its relation to man's positive power of spiritual will. Then the universal creative process is enacted within the soul of man; the hitherto unfertilized germ of spiritual intuitiveness is fructified by the action of the innermost spirit on the virginal abstract mind, "conceived," and later "born." The fruit of this interaction, the newborn power of spiritual intuition, is called the Christ consciousness. Allegorically, the Christ is conceived within Mary by the action of the Holy Ghost. The subsequent birth of the Christ consciousness in man has been named by mystics "the Christmas of the soul." Apparently it was this event rather than the historical birth of Jesus to which St. Paul referred when he wrote to his converts, "My little children, of whom I travail in birth again until Christ be formed in you."[10] These new powers are also personified by infant saviors and their emergence protrayed as nativities—an oft-used devise in which a supposed external event in reality describes an interior experience.[11]

This is man's interior enactment of divine creative processes. Indeed, a new faculty *is* born. When developed and matured it will radically change—even completely revolutionize—a man's whole outlook upon life; for he will then see all creation, all being and all things no longer as separate from each other but as parts of one larger whole. The beginning of this phase of human evolution is allegorically described in this verse of St. Matthew and also in the second verse of the Book of Genesis.

A fourth person is introduced into the story—Joseph, affianced but not yet wed to Mary. Though later the rightful parent of her children, yet he did not participate in the parenthood of Jesus. This is meaningful if he is considered a personification of the formal, concrete mind of man. Joseph's mind was sufficiently developed to respond to, rather than deny, the apparently illogical flashes of illumination which come from the intuition; he therefore is aptly described as a just man. He cannot, however, participate in the spiritual birth or conception because the purely logical mind which he personifies by its very nature cannot be actively intuitive. Joseph, therefore, and very rightly, is only the foster father of Jesus. In this interpretation the problem of the extreme unlikelihood, if not impossibility, of a virgin birth is resolved, for a spiritual, interior development is being described. Thus, the conception of Jesus the Christ by Mary is immaculate, as the Evangelist affirms.

> Matt. 1:19.   Then Joseph her husband, being a just man, and not willing
> to make her a public example, was minded to put her away
> privily.

This action of Joseph's might be regarded less as strictly just, as the word
has been translated, than as kind, tolerant and compassionate. These qualities and their expression despite personal feelings indicate a mature person,
and this, indeed, is the character of one in whom spiritual intuitiveness is
about to show itself and ultimately develop.

> Matt. 1:20.   But while he thought on these things, behold, the angel of
> the Lord appeared unto him in a dream, saying, Joseph,
> thou son of David, fear not to take unto thee Mary thy
> wife: for that which is conceived in her is of the Holy
> Ghost.

In an interpretation as cosmogenesis, creative spirit (the Holy Ghost) and
virgin space (the Virgin Mary) unite to produce a son (Jesus Christ) who
represents the newly emanated universe and its indwelling, all-preserving,
vitalizing life-force. Universal Mind undertakes the task of fashioning and
perfecting the forms of the universe and of directing the involutionary and
evolutionary processes. Joseph may be regarded as a personification of this,
the directive Intelligence throughout all nature. The angel of the Lord who
appeared to Joseph personifies the influence or radiance of the now active
Supreme Spirit, the light of the Logos which brings knowledge of the archetypal Idea; and so, allegorically, an angel informs Joseph of the divine
plan.

In terms of purely human evolution, all prenatal prophecies concerning the
births and missions of great beings visiting the earth and all annunciations
refer to a deeply interior process. The angels signify the generative function
of the spiritual will of awakened man. The fathers who hear and respond
represent the active but disciplined mind, brain consciousness, and the
physical body. The mother is the interlinking principle between these two,
the causal body, which becomes the Robe of Glory.[12] Thus these verses
describe a ray (the angel) from the Monad or innermost divine spirit-essence
of man (the Lord) penetrating into the mind of highly developed men
(Joseph). Understanding the significance of human existence and knowledge
of the phase of human evolution upon which the inner Self is entering thus
reach the outer man (again Joseph). The fact that Joseph did not resist the
incredible announcement delivered by the angelic messenger further indicates his maturity and dawning intuitiveness.

Under the high exaltation of spirit being described, and as a result of his
evolutionary stature, the spiritually developed man becomes aware of "the
Christ in you the hope of glory,"[13] the existence of which is affirmed by St.
Paul.

The human mind, in the course of its evolution, has many warnings and
foreshadowings of this event, finding itself increasingly illumined by revealing flashes of insight and knowledge independent of the usual mental processes. Eventually, the divine spirit in man becomes so powerful, and the

evolution of his abstract mind and intuition so advanced, that he acknowledges their power. In the plant kingdom this corresponds to the mysterious formation of the new tissue that will become a bud, and out of which will develop the flower, fragrance and seed—the promise of immortality. Doubts, arguments, and discussions regarding the actuality of the records, dates, authorship, contradictory genealogies and descriptions of the method of parentage of Mary and Joseph vanish like a mist in morning sunshine when once the true nature of the message is grasped.

> Matt. 1:21.   And she shall bring forth a son, and thou shalt call his name JESUS: for he shall save his people from their sins.

Whenever a text suggests a violation of law, such statements should be viewed as a suggestion to look beneath the surface meaning for a possible revelation of esoteric wisdom. The law of cause and effect, for example, under which every human action brings its own precisely appropriate reaction, modified only by the intervening actions of the actor, can never be broken.[14] No power in cosmos, not even the Deity, can set aside the operation of this law. This thought is here introduced in order to make clear that the terms *savior*, *saviorship,* and *saving,* in relation to Jesus, imply not the slightest degree of abrogation of the law of action and reaction upon which Jesus himself so firmly insisted and the existence of which St. Paul also affirmed.[15] The idea that man can by some means escape, nullify or be saved from the operation of this law where conduct with adverse effects is concerned is thus seen to be completely erroneous. If one who is seeking truth allows the idea of a possible way of escape from the law of cause and effect to gain any hold whatever upon his mind, then that search can never wholly succeed; for there will always be a blind area, or at least a bias, in the mind that will prevent the clear perception of truth and law.

The verse under consideration is of very great importance, not only in the study of the life of Jesus, but also of Christian theological doctrine in general. The prophecy made by the angel of the Lord to Joseph in a dream, that Jesus "shall save his people from their sins," has most unfortunately been misread and misinterpreted, leading to the gradual development and insistence upon a grossly materialized view of the Vicarious Atonement as essential to salvation. This error has blurred and marred Christian thinking ever since, resulting in belief that the law of equal and opposite action and reaction does not apply to the conduct of confessing and believing Christians.

No greater harm could be done to any man, I submit, than to prevent him from reaping as he has sown, from being assessed according to his merits; for the fruits of two important processes—education by experience and the development of a high moral sense—would be lost to him. The history of Western people since the establishment of Christianity as a state religion indicates that, despite splendid examples to the contrary, these two disasters have befallen Christian nations. One has but to notice the wars and religious persecutions, including that most terrible of organized institutions, the Holy Inquisition, to perceive the demoralizing effects of this doctrine.

Nevertheless, saviors *have* visited the earth and have performed a "saving ministry." Such salvation may be briefly described as enhancement of the spiritual and moral agencies at work within a human so that he is "saved" from far greater self-debasement than otherwise by the spiritualizing and purifying influences world saviors exert, both exteriorly by their lives and teachings and interiorly by sharing their exalted spiritual powers with the immortal Self of all men. In varying degrees according to capacity to respond, the human being becomes able to resist temptation and ultimately to realize spiritual selfhood as an immortal and eternal being.

Thus, not only the "death" of the Savior but also his "birth" saves one from his sins, in at least two ways. First, the awakened spiritual powers of will and wisdom functioning through the mind reduce the tendency to transgression; second, they enable the transgressor to acquire the maximum benefit in the form of understanding gained from the reactions produced under the law. An enhanced conscience and a decision never again to act similarly are among the beneficent results.

Thus viewed, the Atonement is an inner event, an at-one-ment, which does not prevent the operation of the law of cause and effect, for it is the Christ Presence within man that assures salvation or ultimate attainment of Christhood, not obliterating karma. In this sense the term *Christ* implies a supreme wisdom and love operating as a function within the depth of man's being. So regarded, Christhood pertains to the beyond which is also within, like the moon reflected on the surface of water.

Certain Christian mystics have carried the teaching even further, saying with Angelus Silesius:[16]

> Though Christ a thousand times in Bethlehem be born
> And not within thyself,
> Thy soul will be forlorn.
> The Cross on Golgotha thou lookest to in vain,
> Unless within thyself it be set up again.

Matt. 1:22. Now all this was done, that it might be fulfilled which was spoken of the Lord by the prophet, saying,

23. Behold, a virgin shall be with child, and shall bring forth a son, and they shall call his name Emmanuel, which being interpreted is, God with us.

Spiritual experiences such as this are of an extremely private nature. It is unlikely that Joseph would have communicated his dream in which the angel's words referred to his affianced wife's purity.[17] Only "babblers" broadcast profound spiritual and mystical experiences; but Joseph, being wise and mature, would have no such inclination.

This being the case, the reader is inclined towards a more mystical interpretation of the recorded incident. In this Mary personifies the faculties associated with spiritual intuitiveness beginning to emerge from within the abstract mind. This phase in the development of the human soul consists of the promise and later fulfillment of the Christ Indwelling coming into power (being born) within man.

The same symbology appears to have been employed by the prophets of old, to whom reference is made in these verses, in describing precisely the same human developments. Emmanuel, meaning "God with us," refers to a newly developed God-power within man, the spiritual intuitiveness and pure wisdom from which Christ-like understanding and compassion are born. The word *Emmanuel* means not only "God be with us" but also "God is with us," which implies that this fact is realized. Emmanuel thus describes a state of consciousness. Though it may signify both a prayer and an affirmation, its mystical meaning corresponds to the Sanskrit word *Aum,* with all its deep interior overtones including the affirmation completely born of experience that the spirit of man is an expression or ray identical with the spirit of the universe.

> Matt. 1:24. Then Joseph being raised from sleep did as the angel of the Lord had bidden him, and took unto him his wife;
> 25. And knew her not till she had brought forth her firstborn son: and he called his name JESUS.

A newly initiated neophyte has ever been referred to as the newborn babe;[18] but it is not his bodily person that is reborn. Rather it is his immortal Self, the divine nature, which is born into a higher level of consciousness. This divine Self has received such power as to transform it into the semblance of a new being, a transfigured individuality. The angel is the agent for this creative power, conveyed symbolically as sound. This is the same sound or Word by which universes are evoked,[19] or awakened from their agelong sleep upon the couch of eternal substance, the waters of the deep.[20]

Neither substance nor human beings can ever be regarded as quite the same after this inner fructification (annunciation), conception and birth have occurred. The recipient is renewed from within, and so "newborn," "twiceborn" or "born again" in the mystical sense. Throughout the gospel narratives this mysteriously born, interior power is named Jesus Christ, just as in the Hindu scripture, *The Bhagavad Purana,* the same power is named Shri Krishna.

The obedience of Joseph in carrying out to the letter the angel's instruction portrays the maturity, self-control, flexibility and intuitiveness of the mind of the highly evolved man. No longer "a slayer of the real,"[21] the mind has become the docile yet skilled agent of the inner will. Symbolically, in a dream Joseph receives instructions from an angel which he carries out on waking.

The actual self-fertilization of the ovum may not be entirely impossible in the future. Occult philosophy includes the idea that future races of men on earth will naturally use this method of reproduction, while later still in human evolution new physical bodies into which human souls incarnate will be created by thought power. Reproductive processes themselves undergo evolutionary changes, and they exhibit obedience to the law of cyclic progression. The first physical race of men on earth, personified by Adam, was androgynous anf self-reproductive.[22] When, later, single-sexed organisms (Adam and Eve) developed, the present method of procreation became normal. This, again according to occult philosphy, will gradually give way to a resumption, at a much higher level, of self-reproduction. However, the story of the Immaculate Conception of Jesus is, I believe, best regarded in its mystical significance; for while the main outlines of the story may or may not be historically true, mystically it is entirely valid.

REFERENCES AND NOTES

1. See Hodson: *The Hidden Wisdom,* Vol. I, Introduction.

2. *Ibid.,* Vol. II, pp. 87-89.

3. Cf. Phil. 2:13; 1 Cor. 3:16 and 6:19; 2 Cor. 6:16.

4. Kansa and Shri Krishna, Devadatta and Gautama Buddha, Sat and Osiris, the Titans and Dionysius, Pluto and Persephone, Loki and Baldur, etc

5. John 1:13.

6. Absolute—see Glossary.

7. Gen. 1:2.

8. Archetype—see Glossary.

9. 1 Cor. 15:44.

10. Gal. 4:19.

11. By writers in the symbolic language. Cf. the births of Shri Krishna, Gautama Buddha and of gods, goddesses and semidivine children in mythology.

12. Causal Body—see Glossary. "Robe of Glory" is a gnostic title for the Causal Body. See also G.R.S. Mead, *The Robe of Glory*.

13. Col. 1:27.

14. Karma—see Glossary.

15. Matt. 5:18, Matt. 7:1; Gal. 6:7. "Be not deceived; God is not mocked: for whatsoever a man soweth, that shall he also reap."

16. Pseudonym for Johann Scheffler: "The Cherubic Wanderer."

17. Matt. 1:24.

18. Initiate—see Glossary

19. See Hodson: *Hidden Wisdom,* Vol. II, pg. 98.

20. In Hindu cosmogenesis, Vishnu rests upon the serpent-couch (Ananta) which floats on the Waters of Space.

21. A reference to an occult axiom: "The mind is the great slayer of the Real. Let the disciple slay the slayer." The unintuitive, overargumentative and materialistic attributes of the concrete mind contribute to "slaying" the Real, meaning eternal Truth.

22. See Hodson: *Hidden Wisdom*, Vol. II, pp. 113-116.

Chapter Five

Problems of historical accuracy, literary sources and authorships, important though they are to the student of the letter of the Bible, lose both their significance and their power to disturb the devotee when Christ's Life is interpreted as mystical experience, a birth that continually occurs as the inherent powers of the human Monad unfold. Bethlehem is lifted out of time and space as symbolic of a high level of awareness and of the vehicle through which the soul of man is active and aware at the higher mental or causal level.[1] History is of little importance to the true mystic, for he has discovered that the mysterious development of plant from seed, man from ovum and Adept from man is an expression of a universal process and is in no way confined or limited to one particular time, place or person. While critics argue and find their doubts impossible to resolve, the mystic knows himself to be in presence of God Transcendant and Immanent; he sees Deity coming to fuller manifestation as the divine in man and, in consequence, worships the newborn Christ child in its aspect of God in man and as man, a God on earth. Thus may the accounts of Jesus' earliest days be read.

> Matt. 2:1.   Now when Jesus was born in Bethlehem of Judea in the days of Herod the king, behold, there came wise men from the east to Jerusalem,
>
> 2.   Saying, Where is he that is born King of the Jews? for we have seen his star in the east, and are come to worship him.

These verses may be interpreted as referring to a spiritually advanced human being and his experiences while traveling along the way of holiness to the goal of Ascension, or perfected manhood.[1] Bethlehem (the house of bread) becomes the "vesture of light," the vehicle of the spiritual soul which is the Dweller in the Innermost. When the phase of development is entered at which the outer man chooses the way of holiness, the inner Self has begun the unfoldment (birth) of the faculty of direct intuitive perception. It is then threefold: it functions as spiritual will, typified by the angel of the Annunciation, spiritual intelligence, typified by Mary, and spiritual intuition and wisdom, personified by Jesus.[2]

The Nativity, in its turn, represents the process of awakening the Christ nature in man into active power. This extremely important stage in the evolution of the spiritual Self is assisted by highly evolved intelligences, as are so many other processes in nature. The wise men coming from afar personify these agencies, who are ministers of the Solar Logos and his official representatives on this planet.[3] They may be thought of as also assisting during the mystical or interior "accouchement."

The star which attracts their attention and guides them to the scene of the Nativity represents the additional spiritual power and light that shines from the advance soul at this phase of its progress towards perfection.[4] As the mystical "pregnancy" advances to the birth of the Christ child within, the aura becomes enlarged and displays increased luminosity. This change continues throughout the later stages of development to become the auric "clouds of glory"[5] in which the then fully grown and mature Christ-power metaphorically ascends into heaven to be seated at the right hand of God.[6]

The first of the five great initiations through which man on the threshold of superhumanity passes is also allegorically described in the accounts of the Nativity of Jesus. In this rendering, the stable becomes the hall of initiation, and the inn, which is full, typifies the wordly life, "crowded," as it were, by men of the world. In this reading the wise men are officiants in the sacred rite and the star symbolizes the presence of the One Initiator on this planet.[7] The two accounts of the Nativity[8] plus St. Paul's references to the Christ Indwelling to be born in man reveal a complete account of both the mystical and the occult in allegorical form.[9]

Allegories may also be interpreted in terms of occult physiolgy. In this sense they are descriptive of changes that occur in the physical and superphysical bodies of man during preparation for and passage through the great initiations. Before this time arrives, the divine powers resident in man are relatively inactive, and there is little or no conscious awareness of them. Chief among these is the creative life-force, the fiery power by which universes are brought into being, fashioned and perfected.[10]

This power abides in man but remains unborn, as it were, until a certain evolutionary phase is entered. Then its arousal into activity begins by the action of another divine power in man, that of spiritual will, which is quite distinct from the creative Fire. The will in man proceeds from the First Aspect of the Divine Trinity in man, God the Father, and in this interpretation the fire of creation is the Third Aspect, God the Holy Ghost. Evolution gradually brings about the active expression of man's inner spiritual will, one of whose functions is to descend into, touch and awaken the sleeping creative fire which resides at the root of the spinal cord. This process is allegorically described in the Annunciations to Joseph, Zacharias and Mary. The two men represent the mortal personality and Mary the "vesture of light," the most tenuous of man's superphysical bodies in which the spiritual Self and will of man are incarnated as unfolding immortal being.[11] The approach of the Archangel of Annunciation, and the intent and sound of his uttered, prophetic words, represent the descent of the awakening, interior spiritual will-force.

The result of this union between spiritual will and spiritual intelligence in man is in the main twofold. The sacred fire at the base of the spine is fanned into a flame or stirred into activity,[12] and the faculty of spiritual intuitiveness (the Christ child)—hitherto germinally present within the abstract mind of man—begins to become an active power. These two processes are complementary. The ascending fire renders the brain and the consciousness within it responsive to the power, the intuitive wisdom and the knowledge of the inner Self which is seeking physical expression. The intuitive faculty, including implicit insight and the capacity to realize unity amid diversity, thereby finds a vehicle which becomes increasingly responsive to it, in the veritably new life of the spiritually awakened man.

The term *immaculate conception* is not inaccurate if thus understood to apply to a deeply spiritual process of interior germination(the Annunciation). Gestation follows during which the highly sensitized neophyte lives in retreat, generally within a Temple of the Greater Mysteries or at the home of his Master, who carefully guards him. This guardianship is necessary, for dangers exist, and unless they are averted a kind of occult "miscarriage" could occur. Considerable strain is thrown upon the nervous system by the awakening of the creative fire. The brain itself may be alternately overstimulated and bedulled. The mind in its turn may become clear, powerful and illumined by flashes of penetrating intuitiveness, bringing the danger of Herod-like egoism and pride. Psychic visions may also occur, and, until he becomes accustomed to them, they may distract and mislead the neophyte. These and other experiences can cause the aspirant to turn aside from the true spiritual path, to become (for example) an embodiment of pride instead of an incarnation of humility.

These dangers avoided, the mystical Nativity naturally occurs. The creative fire ascends into the heart and the head, and spiritual wisdom and divine compassion transform the initiated neophyte into a divinely inspired servant of his fellow men. So complete is the transformation that veritably a new and Christ-like being is born.

> Matt. 2:3.   When Herod the king had heard these things, he was troubled, and all Jerusalem with him.
>
>   4.   And when he had gathered all the chief priests and scribes of the people together, he demanded of them where Christ should be born.

The dangers described above continue to threaten the newly born. Mystically interpreted, Herod personifies the interior source of all these dangers. He also represents the instinctive resistance of matter, both to domination by spirit and with regard to inertia toward activity. The mental, emotional and physical bodies of man are built of a subtle kind of matter which has inherent tendencies that resist manifestation of spiritual will, purest wisdom and unrestricted intellectual activity. The qualities of egoism, desire to retain rulership, physical appetites and habitual indulgences continue to demand gratification.

Since the rule of the divine spirit within man inevitably portends the subjugation of the bodies and the transmutation into purely spiritual channels of such of their energies as have hitherto produced undesirable results resentment and active opposition arise.[13] Just as Herod fears to lose his power as king, so the mortal parts of man's nature fear to lose their freedom and their power over his immortal Self. In consequence, Herod-like, they become bent upon the destruction of the newborn life.

> Matt. 2:5.   And they said unto him, In Bethlehem of Judea: for thus it is written by the prophet,
>
> 6.   And thou, Bethlehem, in the land of Juda, art not the least among the princes of Juda: for out of thee shall come a Governor, that shall rule my people Israel.

While this enmity may delay or mar the expression of the divine in man through his mortal nature, this cannot be destroyed, since it abides in a region beyond the reach of the formal mind. This region is the "vesture of light," or causal body, within which all spiritual nativities occur, the mother, the Virgin Mary.

Hitherto, the mind has ruled the man, as Herod ruled his kingdom. As that rule is now being threatened, cunning, guile and deceit, as described in these verses, are employed. Pretending deference may be an assumed mask concealing murderous intentions. The human mind, when imbued with possessive individualism, uses mental arts to try to discover the whereabouts of the secret power threatening its long-standing domination of the whole man. These verses indicate also that Herod knew only by hearsay of the birth of Jesus and of the appearance of the star. The symbolism is exact, for the analytical mind cannot know directly the pure wisdom and spiritual intuitiveness symbolized by the star and personified by the Christ child.

Just as adult hands aid the newborn infant, so seniors in evolution assist those who are spiritually newborn. In consequence, their inner strength is enhanced and their outer, mortal vehicles harmonized. Adepts and initiates—the wise men from the East and the shepherds of the gospel allegory—surround the newly initiated one with their protective power and, by means of stately ceremonial, invoke divine and angelic aid for him. Eventually, however, the young initiate must, like the esquire in the Order of Chivalry, "win his spurs," achieve knighthood, by the exercise of his own powers.[14]

In the meantime, as these verses indicate, interior enmity and resistance to that achievement are building up. The self-assertive and hitherto tyrannical parts of human nature—mental, passional and physical—determine upon the death of that which threatens them and the continuance of their tyranny.

> Matt. 2:9.   When they had heard the king, they departed; and, lo, the star, which they saw in the east, went before them, till it came and stood over where the young child was.
>
> 10.   When they saw the star, they rejoiced with exceeding great joy.
>
> 11.   And when they were come into the house, they saw the young child with Mary his mother, and fell down and worshipped him: and when they had opened their treas-

ures, they presented unto him gifts, gold; and frankin-
cense, and myrrh.

The wise men from afar who temporarily obeyed Herod can also be taken
to represent the more spiritual qualities and attributes of man which are
derived from his highest nature, the divine within him, which indeed is afar,
or removed from the undesirable expressions of human nature. These stimulate man to search for truth and light which, when found, are recognized and
worshiped.

The number three applied to the wise men and their gifts symbolically
refers to the higher triad of spiritual will, love and intelligence, the unfolding
immortal, spiritual soul. Each of its three aspects is a representation and a
reflection in the spiritual soul of man of an aspect of the threefold Deity, the
Blessed Trinity. Each is aroused into added activity as a result of both
evolutionary development and the solemn rite of initiation.

The newborn faculty of direct spiritual perception and compassion-
arousing vision, which reveals the indivisible unity of the life within all forms,
receives a measure or "gift" of a particular type of energy and benediction.
This energy is inherent in the three aspects of Deity as well as in the three
components of the inner Self of man. When the phase of development being
described is entered by a human soul, the divine in both nature and man is
stirred into beneficent activity. The law of correspondences brings the forces
of the macrocosm into increased activity within man, the microcosm.[15] The
Christ Indwelling, newly awakened, is the focus for the interior activity or
receipt of these "external" powers or gifts.

All nature responds in its spiritual, intellectual, dynamic and physical
forms whenever this mystical birth occurs. Members of the hierarchies of the
angels, referred to in St. Luke as a heavenly host which appeared to the
shepherds, become involved.[16] These are the Elohim or intelligences associated with the cosmic forces. They awaken into added activity the newborn God in man, his inherent divinity. They too bring their gifts which
consist of direct association with the various currents of life force represented by different orders. In electrical terms, the great generating station for
this energy consists physically of the sun and planets and superphysically of
their spiritual counterparts and regents. The initiate is placed in circuit with
this. Different types of cosmic energy or currents channeled by the angels
may be described as different wave lengths on which the one energy is
expressed throughout nature and in man, visible and invisible.

This cosmic, solar, planetary and atomic power is partly expressed as
sound, a vast chord composed of myriads of notes, each with its overtones.
Thus, the angels present at the Nativity appropriately chant their angelic
song; and since the power is one, the theme of their song is oneness, harmony, peace, and good will among men.

Matt. 2:12.   And being warned of God in a dream that they should not
               return to Herod, they departed into their own country
               another way.

The three spiritual principles at work in man's inner nature, the higher triad or trinity, increasingly influence the outer man as progress towards adeptship is made. The wise men visit and speak to Herod for a specific purpose but, symbolically, do not remain in his kingdom and what it represents, departing to their own homes by another route.

The use of speech in the sacred language symbolizes the transference of spiritual power from one level to another. Thus, angels of annunciation speak to men, as the wise men spoke to Herod, but neither angels nor wise men remain for long; they depart to their own mysterious abodes. Similarly, God is said to speak to inspired patriarchs, prophets and seers and then to fall silent. In such cases a mystical communion between the immortal and mortal parts of human nature is also being described.

> Matt. 2:13.   And when they were departed, behold, the angel of the Lord appeareth to Joseph in a dream, saying, Arise, and take the young child and his mother, and flee into Egypt, and be thou there until I bring thee word: for Herod will seek the young child to destroy him.

Experience with an angel comes to Joseph a second time, according to Matthew. After prophesying the birth of Jesus, the angel comes again and warns him of danger and tells how it may be avoided. The attainment of any true mystical experience or of any great expansion of consciousness is generally, if not always, followed by a certain conflict. When in the exalted state, the neophyte is temporarily forgetful of his body, its demands and necessities. On emerging, these seem more insistent than formerly by contrast with the uplifted state. This is because of an instinctive resistance exerted by the inertia of matter and by the instinctual fear of loss of freedom to indulge in material desires. Herod personifies this resistance set up by the egoistic mentality, the possessive and sensual emotions, and the habitual activities and pleasures of the body.

Undoubtedly, the rule of the mortal man over the life of the immortal Self in the body *is* threatened and its end *is* near. This change does not occur without a struggle or an organized attempt by the worldly mind to destroy the spiritual idealism. Two methods of defense against this resistance from within are possible. One is a frontal attack upon undesired attributes; the other is a withdrawal of consciousness from them so that they are ignored and tend to die of inanition. The latter course is advised and was followed by Jesus, who, metaphorically, fled to Egypt. Joseph, the mind, intuitively perceived both the danger and the way to avoid it. Allegorically, an angel instructed him.

Interpretation of such narratives as descriptive of interior experiences, illuminations and expansions of consciousness is, I have come to believe, both more fruitful for the reader and more applicable to that universal, human experience which, when thus viewed, the Gospels portray. However, this view of annunciations and other guidance received from angels by no means excludes either the historicity of the narrative or the possibility of the existence of the orders of the angels and of their conversing with men. Indeed, the changes of consciousness referred to in this commentary may be aided by angelic ministration.

Matt. 2:14.　　When he arose, he took the young child and his mother by
　　　　　　　night, and departed into Egypt;

　　　　15.　　And was there until the death of Herod: that it might be ful-
　　　　　　　filled which was spoken of the Lord by the prophet,
　　　　　　　saying, Out of Egypt have I called my son.

The journey of Jesus to Egypt is, I suggest, miscalled a flight, since various
other readings of the passages are possible. One of these is discernible in the
Old Testament, the authors of which used Egypt as a symbol from topography for the densest state of matter into which the divine Life descends on its
outward or involutionary journey, therein becoming severely restricted. In
the human sense, Egypt thus represented the body into which the unfolding
spiritual Self of man becomes incarnate throughout successive rebirths,
where it is indeed in a kind of bondage to the flesh and to the so-called
fleshpots of Egypt.

In the New Testament the accent is placed upon the returning arc of the
journey of the One Life, nature's evolutionary rather than involutionary
procedure. Egypt thus becomes a starting point, even a springboard, for the
journey of the unfolding human spirit, the immortal soul, back to its Source.
Thus Egypt is a symbol for the evolutionary stage and state of consciousness
at which man voluntarily and consciously embarks upon that journey which
will bring him rapidly to the illumined state and later to the fulfillment of his
life in adeptship.

In another historical interpretation of the incident in the life of Jesus, Egypt
constitutes a region on earth where sanctuaries of the Greater Mysteries
existed. Admission to these centers of initiation was open to certain sufficiently evolved men and women who withdrew from the ordinary affairs of
life and passed through certain forms of training and instruction. If at the end
of these they proved themselves able and worthy, they were admitted,
through rites of initiation, to membership of that occult fraternity known as
the Great White Brotherhood.

In consequence of such experiences, evolution was quickened, and added
intellectual and theurgic powers, as well as profound knowledge of cosmic,
planetary and human life, were obtained. The laws underlying the manifestation, involution and evolution of the divine Life in nature, the basic principles
whereby nature's processes occur, and direct contact with orders of the
angelic hosts and their archangelic heads—all these become part of the
consciousness of the initiate. When the training was completed and the
spiritual accolade had been conferred, the younger initiates were then sent
out into the world to guardedly teach the knowledge they had gained; to find
and accept disciples whom they could train for similar advancement and
service; and to lift the level of consciousness and life of humanity out of rigid
orthodoxy into higher levels of thought and direct perception of communion
with God. The inner occult life of such men is always profoundly secret, and
while undergoing their training they live in retreat. This universal and age-old
custom was evidently followed by Jesus of whom no records are given until
he appears at the age of twelve. The verses under consideration constitute a

brief and veiled reference to this part of the preparation of Jesus for his great mission.

> Matt. 2:16.   Then Herod, when he saw that he was mocked of the wise men, was exceeding wroth, and sent forth, and slew all the children that were in Bethlehem, and in all the coasts thereof, from two years old and under, according to the time which he had diligently enquired of the wise men.

While it was in the power of such representatives of Rome as Herod to order the assassinations, which may actually have occurred, history has no record of the action described in this verse. However, the terms *children* and *little ones* are used in the sacred language to designate those who have been newly initiated. Perhaps this is what is meant here. Such men and women do incur the wrath of those who wield temporal power, whether ecclesiastically or politically. The murder of initiates has stained the history of mankind, and the massacre of the innocents by Herod may be read as a reference to this unfortunate fact.

Childlikeness, purity, simplicity, spontaneity and directness are qualities displayed by initiates, indeed essential in candidates for initiation. This is in part the meaning of the saying of Jesus, "Verily I say unto you, whosoever shall not receive the kingdom of God as a little child shall in no wise enter therein."[17] The kingdom of heaven is a state of consciousness in which the unity of the spirit of man with the spirit of the universe is a continuing experience. Evolutionary progress and occult ceremonial elevate the initiate into this state so that in this sense he becomes "as a little child."

The prideful, egotistic mind (Herod) resists, often actively, forcefully and even murderously, the changes in consciousness, motive and conduct brought about by entry into the kingdom of heaven state of awareness. Thus, allegorically, Herod massacres the children.

This universal principle is revealed by means of allegory in many world scriptures and mythologies. In the Greek account of creation, Cronos, head of the state and father of the gods-to-be, was warned that his children would in their turn depose him as he had deposed his own father, Uranus. To prevent this Cronos devoured each of his children immediately after birth. By a subterfuge Zeus was saved.

In Hindu scripture King Kansa was warned that a son of Devaki and Vasudeva would depose him, and in consequence he destroyed child after child immediately after it was born. By the intervention of supernormal beings—*Mahadevas* and *Devas*, the creative hierarchies of archangels and angels—the eighth child, Shri Krishna, was saved. On growing up he became the Savior and Teacher of mankind. Herod was warned that a child would be born in Israel who would depose him. He therefore massacred the innocents; but again, as if by divine intervention, the child Jesus was saved and became the spiritual teacher of countless millions of people.

Here also, by means of allegorical narrative, are accounts of the privations spirit must suffer or endure, the inevitable forfeit, as it becomes manifest in matter. Furthermore, the deeper the density of the "material substance," the greater the deprivation of power. Shri Krishna, Jesus and Zeus being saved might possibly be regarded as portraying the victory of spirit over matter, which is inevitably achieved once the creative process has been initiated at the first "dawn." Nothing can effectually and finally oppose the forthgoing of spirit into matter or the evolution of that same spirit, a process by which a savior of men is produced or, in the case of humanity at large, adeptship is attained. Thus, I suggest, the completely irresistible power by which the emanation of universes is brought about is revealed in these immortal stories.

The human Monad similarly suffers successive privations as it becomes manifested and embodied in matter of successive degrees of density. Eventually, as is truly prophesied in the myths, the resistance of matter will be overcome and the "divine child"—adeptic power, wisdom and intelligence—be born. Repulsive though such allegories may appear when only the cover or blind is considered, the deliberately concealed principle beneath is revealed to those who know how to draw the blind aside.

> Matt. 2:17. Then was fulfilled that which was spoken by Jeremy the prophet, saying,
>
> 18. In Rama was there a voice heard, lamentation, and weeping, and great mourning, Rachel weeping for her children, and would not be comforted, because they are not.

Such breaks in the gospel narrative suggest interpolations of the words of the Hebrew prophets to support the messiahship of Jesus. Jeremiah may, however, have been writing of the interior struggle between the higher and the lower natures of candidates for initiation, making reference to the inevitable sense of loss associated with the surrender of self that accompanies realization of unity with God. If so, his words are applicable not only to Jesus but to every successful initiate.

> Matt. 2:19. But when Herod was dead, behold an angel of the Lord appeareth in a dream to Joseph in Egypt.
>
> 20. Saying Arise, and take the young child and his mother, and go into the land of Israel: for they are dead which sought the young child's life.

The second visitation to Joseph by an angel is susceptible of interpretations similar to those applied to the first (Matt. 2:13). In the historical sense, as foster father and guide of the young child, Joseph would know that the next phase of Jesus' development and training could best be carried out in his native land where his mission was to be fulfilled. Essene communities existed in Palestine at the time, and the studies and the preparations of the young initiate could well have taken place in one or more of these.

Under guidance Joseph changed the direction and objective of the family's journey to Palestine. They are thus said to have established themselves in Nazareth, supposedly in order that a prophecy might be fulfilled, for, according to ancient prophecy, the Messiah was to be a Nazarene. A reference to the occult life of Jesus may here by discerned. A Nazar is one set apart, a dedicated, consecrated man. The Nazarenes were a group of such men, celibates, who submitted themselves to an occult training and discipline somewhat similar of those of the Essenes. The hair was permitted to grow long; Jesus is traditionally described as having long hair, a mustache and beard. In this and in the life of purity and service he later adopted, he could well be described as a Nazarene.

The Ancient Wisdom holds that a hierarchy of Adepts guides life on this planet from behind the scenes. The plans of the hierarchy, which presumably include Jesus's birth and training, would be known to the hierophant of the temple in which he received his initiation. For the occult life of the planet is highly organized, a complete system of communication and collaboration between the world's initiates and Adepts having long ago been established. If the hierophant ordered Jesus's return his guidance would be so strictly private that it might be referred to only in the allegorical form of an angel guiding Joseph. The return may have been in accordance with a prearranged plan for the further training of Jesus and the fulfillment of his great mission.

A brief consideration of Jesus's mission may not be out of place here (though fuller attention will be given to it later, when for example, the Baptism of Jesus and the events which followed are interpreted). The ageless Wisdom—the one religion which underlies all creeds—includes the idea that the humanity which is evolving upon a planet is never left unguided, however little heed is paid to such guidance during certain phases, such as the present. One form of guidance consists of the continuous illumination of the minds of men by the members of the Adept Hierarchy; for these sages flood the superphysical worlds with spiritual impulses, inspiration and illumination. Also, under adept influence, their disciples—the great teachers of the world—convey aspects of their Wisdom to the minds of men through their lives, their teachings, and their writings. This process is continuous, though more evident at some periods of history than at others.

In addition, certain exalted members of the Occult Hierarchy themselves appear visibly on earth, either in their own bodies or overshadowing those of highly evolved disciples. The power and efficacy of such visitations are, on occasions, greatly enhanced by descent of one or other of the Aspects or Persons of the Blessed Trinity or Solar Logos. The mind and body of the human representative must be very carefully prepared in order to withstand the strain of the power that flows through the body when the manifestations are at their height. According to gnostic tradition one part of the mission assigned to Jesus was to serve as a vehicle for such a visitation and descent from on high, [18] beginning at the period of the Baptism in the waters of Jordan.[19] This preparation, it is assumed, had begun in Egypt and continued in Palestine.

> Matt. 2:21.   And he arose, and took the young child and his mother, and came into the land of Israel.
>
> 22.   But when he heard that Archelaus did reign in Judea in the room of his father Herod, he was afraid to go thither:

> notwithstanding, being warned of God in a dream he
> turned aside into the parts of Galilee:

Matt. 2:23.   And he came and dwelt in a city called Nazareth: that
it might be fulfilled which was spoken by the prophets,
He shall be called a Nazarene.

The dangers—interior or psychological and external or objective—arising
from the fear and hatred of self-styled enemies are again referred to in these
verses. Both kinds of danger are very real, being encountered by every
idealist and more especially by every disciple and initiate, owing to the
quickened pace of progress. No one can escape them. The Ancient Wisdom
teaches that man incarnates on earth repeatedly, and the group of successive
lives during which aspiration awakens and the spiritual path is entered are
particularly fraught with danger. As maturity brings watchfulness and wisdom in each physical life, so in the later phases of development in the spiritual
life dangers are foreseen, guarded against or avoided. Since, however, some
difficulties are compensatory reapings from adverse sowings in former lives,
and therefore karmic, they cannot be avoided altogether. Certain debts must
be paid to the full as is indicated by the adversities described in the life history
of Jesus. In addition, hastened progress brings heightened resistance from
matter itself, particularly that composing the bodies with its habits, desires
and remaining egoism. Difficulties also stem from people inflamed to hatred
by members of the Dark Brotherhood, the Lords of the Dark Face, who are
the self-constituted opponents of the Great White Brotherhood on earth and
all its agents among men.

Within the restrictions imposed by the law of cause and effect, every
sincere neophyte is guided, guarded and directed, both visibly and invisibly,
by his seniors in evolution. This is another meaning of the annunciations and
the warnings received from members of the angelic hosts or from God. The
Deity here, however, is less the Solar Logos of the whole universe than his
reproduction of himself as the Monad or divine spirit-essence in man. The
Solar Logos is occupied with vast concerns with respect to the processes of
involution and evolution in all the kingdoms of nature, and their countless
myriads of representations. Nevertheless, the possibility of intervention by
the Supreme Deity of a whole universe on behalf of one man is by no means
denied, however improbable it might seem. The ageless wisdom teaches that
the receipt of divine grace, whatever its source, is a reality in human
experience.[20]

Communion with the Supreme Deity is indeed frequently affirmed in both
the Old and New Testaments. The more highly evolved the human participant, the more deeply interior the experience becomes. The sense of unity with
God deepens to culminate in full knowledge of unity and identity with that
eternal Being who presides over the evolution and dwells within the soul of all
created beings.

REFERENCES AND NOTES

1. Isa. 35:8.
2. For a fuller interpretation, see Hodson, *Hidden Wisdom, Vol. I, pp. 198-215.*
3. Logos and Logos Doctrine—see Glossary. See also Geoffrey Hodson. *The Kingdom of the Gods,* Pt. 3, Ch. 4, and *Lecture Notes of the School of the Wisdom,* Vol. I, Ch. 16.
4. Perfection. See Hodson, *Hidden Wisdom,* Vol. I, pp. 56-74.
5. Luke 21:27.
6. Mark 16:19.
7. See Geoffrey Hodson, *Lecture Notes of the School of the Wisdom,* Vol. I, Ch. 16, Sec. 4.
8. Matt. 1:18-25 and Luke 2:1-7.
9. See Hodson, *Hidden Wisdom,* Vol. I, Pts. 5 and 6.
10. Kundalini—see Glossary.
11. Ego—see Glossary.
12. Kundalini.
13. This inner transformation of man's nature constitutes the true alchemy.
14. A representative in the outer world of the successive degrees in the Lesser and the Greater Mysteries, as also in Freemasonry.
15. Law of Correspondences—see Glossary.
16. Luke 2:13.
17. Luke 18:17.
18. See C. W. King, *The Gnostics and Their Remains.* (London: David Nutt, 1887); pp. 100-1.
19. Matt. 3:16.
20. cf. *The Bhagavad Gita,* Twelfth Discourse.

PART THREE

BAPTISM

Chapter Six

If the terms of the symbolic language are accepted, the river symbolizes that ancient "stream" approached and entered by every successful candidate for the attainment of spiritual regeneration by entry upon the narrow path which leads to eternal life. This so-called stream typifies the one all-pervading spiritual life of the universe and the indwelling presence of the Source of all life, God the Preserver. Entering the stream implies conscious realization of the presence within.[1] Crossing the stream refers to an allegory of full attainment of unity and identity with that Source, personal and universal. Thus Jesus's Baptism, as every incident described in the lives of exalted beings in inspired scriptures, has profound symbolic meaning.

> Matt. 3:1.   In those days came John the Baptist, preaching in the wilderness of Judea,
>
>   2.   And saying, Repent ye: for the kingdom of heaven is at hand.
>
>   3.   For this is he that was spoken of by the prophet Essaias, saying, The voice of one crying in the wilderness, Prepare ye the way of the Lord, make his paths straight.

A new character is now introduced into the story by St. Matthew, namely, John the Baptist. As discussed previously, his actions personify the admonitory, warning, and spiritually arousing influences exerted by the developed inner Self over the outer man. He represents the awakening of idealism, the growing power of conscience, and the foreshadowing intuitiveness, or the Christ nature in man. Until the position in evolution is reached where conscience is dominant, man remains unillumined and uninspired. This condition is symbolized by a desert or a wilderness, implying a state of spiritual dryness and mental aridity. When, however, the inner Self begins to assume overmastering power and a reformation of character and conduct is in process, this stage is appropriately described as the voice of an ascetic crying in the wilderness.

Sometimes the performance of music is used to convey a similar meaning. The flute of Shri Krishna proved irresistible to men and women from the ordinary walks of life, so that metaphorically they left all and followed him. Orpheus harmonized and subdued all beings and living things that heard the music of his lyre. Medea soothed with incantations the hissing, loathsome and immortal dragon of a thousand coils guarding the Golden Fleece,[2] and the Lord Shri Krishna overcame the enmity of the black serpent, Kaliya, by dancing upon its seven hoods.[3] In the Gnostic Fragment called The Hymn of the Robe of Glory, considered by literary critics to have been written by Bardesanes, the parable of the Prodigal Son is repeated in the first person, possibly Bardesanes himself. We read:

And I began (then) to charm him,
The terrible loud-breathing Serpent.
I lulled him to sleep and to slumber,
Chanting o'er him the Name of my Father,
The Name of our Second, (my Brother),
And (Name) of my Mother, the East-Queen.[4]

Religious chanting is an externalization of such an interior call to the spiritual heights, and by its harmonizing and elevating influence it can assist in responding to that call.

Later in life Jesus called his disciples and, on hearing his voice, they in their turn metaphorically "forsook their nets, and followed him."[5] Mystically, the divine personages in world scriptures represent the Dweller-in-the-Innermost, the Monad of man (See chart in Chapter Two), while the "call" portrays the ray of impelling power, the will-force, that the Monad sends or sounds forth into the "ears" of the outer man..

Matt. 3:4.   And the same John had his raiment of camel's hair, and a leathern girdle about his loins; and his meat was locusts and wild honey.

John's camel-hair garment and his food of the locust bean and wild honey, which do not depend on the taking of life, indicate the simplicity and vegetarian diet customary among certain sects at the time. This regimen is still followed in almost all communities and ashrams established for purposes of studying the laws and obeying the rules of hastened occult and spiritual development.[6] Such an ascetic mode of life was also chosen by Jesus, Buddha, and incarnations of other highly developed beings.

The mission of John the Baptist also indicates a psychological necessity, namely, that surrender must precede the attainment of greater power. The clothing and food of John symbolize the simplicity and ascetisim that are adopted in this phase of human evolution in accordance with this law. Indulgences, egoism, possessiveness, and habits that coarsen, must be overcome or transcended before the intuitive faculty or qualities of the Christ in man can be fully expressed. New powers demand new sacrifices. Spiritual victories demand material renunciations.

Also implied, though not here specified, is a reference to the mode of life and the mission of Elijah, who was both a prototype of John and a personification of the same interior development and the same psychospiritual law.

Matt. 3:5.   Then went out to him Jerusalem, and all Judaea, and all the region round about Jordan.

6.   And were baptized of him in Jordan, confessing their sins.

The existence and mission of John the Baptist can neither be confirmed nor denied on any available historical grounds other than the Gospels. Nevertheless, the story is meaningful in the spiritual life, for the acceptance of the rulings of conscience as complete guides to life can both remove a sense of guilt and prevent willful transgression. This attitude may well be regarded as a baptism, John representing conscience and the waters of Jordan the admonitory and purifying influences exerted upon the outer man, his character and mode of life. Ceremonial baptism without the adoption of a lofty standard of morality can be a mere sham. The interior baptism emanating from the spiritual part of man's nature can, on the other hand, be a most powerful force and elevating influence affecting the whole life of one thus truly "baptized." He then needs neither priest nor holy water, having found everything necessary within himself. Such a state of mind is, however, attainable only by those who have reached a certain stage in the unfoldment of the soul, a stage at which the spiritual is beginning to dominate the material part of man—the state of the inwardly awakened human being.

> Matt. 3:7. But when he saw many of the Pharisees and Sadducees come to his baptism, he said unto them, O generation of vipers, who hath warned you to flee from the wrath to come?
>
> 8. Bring forth therefore fruits meet for repentence:
>
> 9. And think not to say within yourselves, We have Abraham to our father: for I say unto you, that God is able of these stones to raise up children unto Abraham.
>
> 10. And now also the axe is laid unto the root of the trees: therefore every tree which bringeth not forth good fruit is hewn down, and cast into the fire.
>
> 11. I indeed baptise you with water unto repentance: but he that cometh after me is mightier than I, whose shoes I am not worthy to bear: he shall baptise you with the Holy Ghost, and with fire:
>
> 12. Whose fan is in his hand, and he will thoroughly purge his floor, and gather his wheat into the garner; but he will burn up the chaff with unquenchable fire.

The objurgation and the prophecy uttered by John to the Pharisees and Sadducees may be similarly interpreted. The voice of conscience, if heeded, can transmute hardness of heart, materialism, and selfishness into the virtues of compassion, spirituality, and selflessness. First, however, there must be a cleansing of the lower nature, a process which in these verses in symbolized by cutting down unfruitful trees and casting them into the fire. Such repentance and self-purification will naturally be followed by greater and more direct manifestations of the spirit in man. John the Baptist alludes to this process as baptism "with the Holy Ghost, and with fire."

The person of John, his works and his words, thus epitomize the prior requisites for spiritual progress and the attainment of occult knowledge and power. Self-denudation and surrender of the lower self to the higher are essential to such baptism with the spirit, meaning the manifestation within the outer mortal man of the interior, immortal God-power. The symbolism of the Elements of Air and Fire is introduced, also described as purificatory forces. Air has come to be regarded as a symbol of the intuitive faculty and Fire the discerning mind.[7] These are indeed effective, even essential, when applied together to the process of self-purification in preparation for the realized presence and manifestation of the Christ power within.

John's words spoken to the Pharisees beside the River Jordan immediately before the Baptism of Jesus are thus seen to constitute a remarkable description of the psychospiritual processes necessary for the attainment of illumination, at all times and for all people. Applied to the progress on the path of hastened evolution, they also describe the required attitude of mind and self-discipline to be adopted by the candidate for successive initiations. True, the normal processes of evolution will bring all men to this "baptized" state. Nevertheless, aspirants seeking to reach the spiritual heights more quickly in order better to serve are moved from within to deliberately bring about the necessary transformation of character and conduct.

We turn now to the Gospel according to St. John. The author, or authors, of the fourth Gospel add to our understanding of the symbolism. They evidently approached their task of recording for posterity the life story of Jesus of Nazareth with specific intentions differing in many respects from those of the authors of the Synoptics. The cosmic Christos as the creative Word or divine formative power, and the mystic presence or Christ Indwelling in every human being, were to be blended with the historic Savior of men. Jesus, the son of Mary, was to be shown as a manifestation of the Supreme Deity in both its transcendent and its immanent aspects.

In consequence, the episodes in the life of Jesus selected for inclusion were those which lent themselves to such a presentation, while much was added which is not found in the accounts of the other three Evangelists. The life story is related in such a manner that, adequately interpreted, it portrays the history of both cosmos and man. Human evolution naturally received greater attention and was described so as to reveal all stages of the unfoldment of the divine principle in man. This applies to the period when man was passing through almost primitive phases (e.g., the crowd crying, "Crucify him"[8]), through entry upon the path of discipleship, and deeply interior and external developments which culminate in the attainment of the stature of the perfect man, the veritable apotheosis of the human period of evolution (Ascension).

Readers capable of the necessary discernment were thus to be illumined concerning their own being, condition, advancement, and spiritual destination in attained Christhood. Each recorded incident—from the ministry of John the Baptist (an advanced evolutionary phase) up to his death by decapitation, and followed by selected events in the life of Jesus—was so related that both the cosmic and the mystic meanings were revealed, however symbolically.

The fourth Gospel is clearly the work of a man or a group of men who were deeply versed in the Logos doctrine. They were also well informed regarding the normal mode of life for mankind at the present epoch and for those advancing ahead of their fellows upon the evolutionary pathway. By the aid of a master or spiritual sage, such men were moving rapidly toward the fulfillment of the purpose for which human evolution is designed, described by the experiences and action of Jesus himself.

> John 1:29. The next day John seeth Jesus coming unto him, and saith, Behold the Lamb of God, which taketh away the sin of the world.

In this verse John the Baptist—whether historically, purely symbolically, or both—is said to have drawn the attention of the people to the young man who had appeared among them as being no ordinary mortal person, but a veritable incarnation of the Supreme Deity. This may be regarded as descriptive of the stage of illumination reached by a human being (John) at which he is to perceive the cosmic within the human, the divine within a man standing on the threshold of fully unfolded divinity (Jesus the Christ). Himself illumined, John draws the attention of others whose minds might similarly be opened to both the transcendent vision and the living example before them of that which they would one day become.

This is done in symbolic form, the first symbol being the Lamb of God. While generally the newborn lamb evokes the concept of unstained, unmarred, spontaneous, and playful childishness, for the Jewish people the little animal had other significations. Among these were the promise of continued tribal existence, since their forefathers were a shepherd people. Not only was the lamb the most highly prized possession they could own, but also it was regarded as the most highly valued gift and sacrifice which they could offer. Thus, for the Jews, it was a symbol of utmost self-surrender in supposed worship.

In a not dissimilar sense, the Deity in turn made a sacrifice of his only Son, divinely conceived and offered, in order that the mortality and sinfulness of mankind might be transcended and man be redeemed by the Lamb of God. Repellent though this concept of literal sacrifice of a lamb may be to some minds, it is nonetheless mystically true. God has offered a portion of himself, the living God, buried deep within every human being, to give assurance of ultimate immortality and salvation.[9] The accent here is not on the bodily person of Jesus but upon the sacrificed fragment of the divine nature as the inherent reality, the undying and ever stainless God-Presence in every human being. Thus regarded, the Lord of the universe permits a portion of himself (his "Son") to be enclosed in form, imprisoned or enthroned in matter. The word *imprisoned* may justly be used with regard to the precosmic condition of eternal life.

> John 1:30   This is he of whom I said. After me cometh a man which is preferred before me: for he was before me.

This verse is a natural continuance of the address which John the Baptist was making to the people around him. Here again the fact that he knew who Jesus was, by the exercise of superior and intuitive perception, indicates that he also may be regarded as personifying one of the vehicles of human consciousness, the "higher mind," in a highly evolved condition.

John 1:31.   And I knew him not: but that he should be made manifest
to Israel, therefore am I come baptizing with water.

32.   And John bare record, saying, I saw the Spirit descending from heaven like a dove, and it abode upon him.

Just as St. Paul wrote of the Nativity of Jesus as an interior event occurring
within the consciousness and nature of man,[10] so, it would appear, St. John
wrote of the Baptism in similar terms, making John the Baptist his spokesman.

John the Baptist by his own admission was a prophet whose powers were
but imperfectly developed since, although Jesus had earlier stood before him,
John for a time did not recognize him. Similarly, the prophetic power inherent
in the spiritual Self of man in its "vesture of light" undergoes a gradual
development and emerges as the power of direct, intuitive insight. John
evidently was on the threshold of this state and eventually recognized and
proclaimed the presence of this power within himself, since he later knew,
reverenced, and baptized Jesus and presumably "saw" the descent of the
Holy Spirit upon him in the form of a dove.

The difference in spiritual stature is also partially indicated by the further
history of Jesus and John. John spoke out fearlessly and truthfully against
wickedness in high places, and so forfeited his life, apparently without a
record of other services. Jesus healed the sick, instructed humanity in the
realities of religion, restated the gospel of selfless love, and collected and
trained disciples, after which, in his turn, his life was taken. Thus, the
Evangelists present Jesus as greater than John; and this John acknowledged,
saying that he was unworthy to latch the Master's shoes." However, both
presumably stood within the stream of all-pervading spiritual life, typified by
the River Jordan, and Jesus was baptized by John, the older man in years
assisting the younger. Thereafter, apart from verbal communications through
others and some references by Jesus, the two did not meet again. John,
however, fulfilled his dharma of calling his fellow countrymen to repentance,
baptizing Jesus, denouncing adultery, and surrendering his life rather than
paying lip service to temporal power. the splendid figures of John the Baptist
and Jesus personify every aspirant who has ever moved toward the great
attainment of evolutionary advancement.

John 1:33.   And I knew him not: but he that sent me to baptize with
water, the same said unto me, Upon whom thou shalt see
the Spirit descending, and remaining on him, the same is
he which baptizeth with the Holy Ghost.

In this verse, John the Baptist mysteriously refers to an unnamed and
unidentified being under whose direction he carried out his baptismal mission. This presumed teacher—or perchance hierophant of a mystery
temple—warned that an exalted personage would appear before him, recognizable as one upon whom the spirit could visibly be seen descending. This
exalted one was none other than the Messiah, whose appearance the
prophets of old had foretold.

No further reference is made to this mysterious person. If the suggestion is permissible, a hint may be seen of the existence of an order to which John had been admitted and in which he had received instruction—perhaps Essene.

John 1:34. And I saw, and bare record that this is the Son of God.

In this verse, the full vision is described. The actual presence of the Christ, here as throughout the Gospels, may be regarded as descriptive of that phase in the evolution of the individual at which his own Christ nature is revealed to him with all its illuminating and healing influence. Thus, when in his veritable presence, John the Baptist realized that Jesus was the Son of God.

John 1:35. Again the next day after John stood, and two of his disciples;
36. And looking upon Jesus as he walked, he saith, Behold the Lamb of God!
37. And the two disciples heard him speak, and they followed Jesus.
38. Then Jesus turned, and saw them following, and saith unto them, What seek ye? They said unto him, Rabbi, where dwellest Thou?[12]

The remaining verses of this first chapter of the Gospel according to St. John relate in almost historical form the ancient and continuing process of the discovery of his true spiritual Teacher by one who is prepared. The necessary preparation includes both the immortal soul arriving at the appointed evolutionary stature and search by the outer man for his true Master.

A senior and leader on the spiritual way is usually found first, and this is exemplified by the relationship between the aspirants and John the Baptist whose disciples and friends they had become. This intermediate leader, himself already illumined, serves as a guide or even bridge, providing the necessary aid in man's search for his Master-to-be. Once they have met, the Master accepts the suitably prepared aspirant as his disciple; symbolically, he takes him into his home. Sometimes the Master reveals that he had earlier known and watched the disciple in the mystical sense or had seen him "under the fig tree." This is a symbol of the processes of divine manifestation, its laws, growth, and fruit, as portrayed by the Tree of Life.

The responses and reactions of the newly accepted disciple, differing according to temperament and background, are indicated by the conversations related in the remaining verses of this first chapter. Not unusually on such occasions the inner sight of the disciple is opened, and either mystically or objectively or both, he perceives his Master's true spiritual greatness; his mission as a Messiah to men; and his relationship with the Deity, the archangels and angels of the heavenly hosts.

Thus, early in the life story of Jesus as narrated by St. John, he is proclaimed a veritable manifestation of the creative Word, a representative on earth of Deity, both as a vehicle or channel and as a highly evolved and illumined human being in his own right.

· · · · · ·

Returning to Matthew's account of the baptism of Jesus by John, other mystical, occult, and cosmic connotations become apparent.

Matt. 3:13.   Then cometh Jesus from Galilee to Jordan unto John, to be baptized by him.

Matthew's recording of the story signifies that when the essential conditions have been met—the mind and the heart made ready—man learns by direct experience that he himself is a spiritual being, immortal, eternal, and free. He also comes to know the further truth of the identity of his own inner spirit-essence with the same divine presence within all beings. The fruits of his past incarnations—the capacities and faculties developed while passing through them—become available for use in the present life. Symbolically, when the wheat is separated from the chaff and garnered (verse 12), the Christ nature reveals itself to the mortal man. Allegorically, Jesus comes to John from Galilee to Jordan.

Matt. 3:14.   But John forbade him, saying, I have need to be baptized of thee, and comest thou to me?

The Christ nature in man is greater than his intellect; the indwelling divinity is greater than its vehicle. In addition, pure intuition is a higher faculty than abstract intelligence. John, representing the latter, rightly recognizes this fact and humbly acknowledges it.

Matt. 3:15.   And Jesus answering said unto him, Suffer it to be so now: for thus it becometh us to fulfill all righteousness. Then he suffered him.

If Matthew's account of the Baptism of Jesus be read literally, then indeed John's objection is reasonable and just; for as an incarnation of divinity, Jesus would neither need, nor could he appropriately receive, baptism at the hand of a man such as John, however illumined and dedicated he might be. The insistence of Jesus does, in fact, seem to be inappropriate and the hesitation of John more suitable.

This anomaly suggests underlying meanings, of which many are possible. Rivers, for example, are sometimes used as symbols from topography for the spinal cord of man, particularly after "electrification" by the universal, creative force known as kundalini. This energy, symbolized in this case by the water in the river, is carefully sheathed in the spinal cord of man. When stirred into heightened activity as a result of natural evolutionary development—aided by certain occult exercise or passage through the rite of initiation—this force flows along the spinal cord into the brain, which it vivifies to produce heightened awareness in the physical body. The source of such symbolical rivers represents the center and reservoir of the creative power at the sacrum, while the recipient sea or lake refers to the head, particularly the central portions and glands near the brain. The River Nile is also used as a symbol for kundalini, with Lake Victoria Nyanza and the surrounding region as source and the delta and Mediterranean Sea as recipient. The shape of the *dadu* of *tet*, used both as nilometer and as a religious symbol, sometimes with human legs and arms, resembles the spinal column, thereby pointing to symbolical significance of the River Nile.

The stemming of the flow of the river Jordan from its source in Lebanon to its entry into the Dead Sea is also typical of symbolical usage.[13] The water of rivers flows downward from sources to estuary. But when man is erect, any force arising from his sacrum would need to flow upward against gravity to reach the brain.

In the terms of the sacred language, to be baptized in the waters of a river is to fully arouse the creative force so that it plays up into the head and out at the crown, bestowing spiritual states of consciousness upon the neophyte thus empowered (verses 16 and 17). This interpretation is supported by by the supernormal events that are said to have occurred after the Baptism of Jesus; for one of the results of such an exaltation is to become conscious of the stream of vitalizing life force by which all physical forms are sustained and preserved. Man thus illumined experiences unification with the currents of the all-pervading life, symbolized by water and the technical term "the stream." The man Jesus, as distinct from the incarnate Logos (John 1:1-5), entered the stream[14] or, allegorically, was baptized in the waters of Jordan.

> Matt. 3:16. And Jesus, when he was baptized, went up straightway out of the water: and lo, the heavens were opened unto him, and he saw the Spirit of God descending like a dove, and lighting upon him:
>
> 17. And lo a voice from heaven, saying, This is my beloved Son, in whom I am well pleased.

These verses may be read as an allegory descriptive of the expansion of consciousness and realization of unity with the Deity which baptism produces in the sense already indicated. The words in the narrative *he saw* indicate that Jesus passed through an interior state of awareness that was personal to him alone. It is extremely improbable that Jesus revealed such deeply sacred spiritual experiences to a possible recorder. In such a case when scripture describes events which could not possibly have been known to an observer, one in encouraged[15] to apply a symbolical interpretation. The experience was evidently dual, consisting of an ascent of his consciousness into a state of illumination—the opened heaven—and a descent of spiritual power and benediction—the dove and the voice of the Father.

These verses may well be read as descriptive of the interior, mystical effects of passage through one of the great initiations. Barriers that have hitherto enclosed and limited the range of awareness of the Source of being are either pierced or wholly overcome. As a prisoner escapes through opened prison doors, so during the initiatory rite the center of self-awareness in the initiate is freed from its limitations, notably those associated with a remaining sense of separated individuality and self-centered thought. These no longer bind consciousness either to earth or to the boundaries of earthly existence. Heaven opens, as it were, and consciousness is freed. Universal awareness is attained as all terrestrial limitations fall away. The whole nature of man thus illumined is empowered as if by a descent upon him of the will of God, the very spirit of Deity. The choice of the dove as a symbol for this celestial influence suggests that, while the action of threefold Logos was involved, the Second Aspect of pure Wisdom was accentuated.

The young Hebrew initiate whose life story is being told in its more occult aspects, at a certain period of his life (between the second and third initiations, Baptism and Transfiguration), was lifted up in spirit beyond the mystical realizations and expansions that usually accompany initiation; for he also became the central figure in an event of planetary significance. While he was being baptized by John in the river Jordan, his whole nature, physical, intellectual and spiritual, became the vehicle for the Supreme Deity, particularly of the Second Aspect, the *Christos;* for Jesus the man became attuned to that manifestation of Deity known as the cosmic Christ. This is described as the preserving and sustaining power, wisdom and love of the Solar Logos, a divine and completely impersonal power ever poured out upon all that lives as benediction and sustaining spiritual vitality. It is the mysterious, omnipresent life force of the manifested Deity. This benign influence should be regarded as welling up from within the inner Self of man rather than as descending from an elevated location in space.

This outpouring is all-pervasive, but it does not preclude the possibility of a direct concentration of divine wisdom and love temporarily focused in one human being. This could occur in addition to the upwelling spiritual influence of the Second Logos enhanced by passage through initiatory rites.[16]

Although the doctrine that such "descents" repeatedly occur may not be wholly acceptable to Christian orthodoxy, it nevertheless has its traditional place in oriental philosophy. The descents or *Avatars* of Vishnu and Shiva are recorded in Hinduism as means whereby the Second and Third Aspects respectively of the Solar Logos exert spiritualizing influences upon the evolving life of the planet, and particularly upon the human race. The proclamations by the Lord Shri Krishna that whenever there was a decay of righteousness, he as the Second Aspect of the *Trimurti* always came forth; of the Buddha, that he would be followed by a successor named Maitreya; and of the Christ, through the lips of Jesus, that he would visit the earth again,[17] all refer to cyclic manifestations on earth of the Supreme Deity of our universe, the Solar Logos. The more transcendent teachings and the miraculous actions of Jesus may be presumed to have taken place when such a descent was most intense. This is at least suggested in the last verse of this chapter, which records that a voice from heaven spoke, saying, "This is my beloved Son, in whom I am well pleased."

One may well quote at this point from the writings of H.P. Blavatsky who, referring to the teachings of the Ophites and the Nazarenes, says, "Therefore, Christos, the perfect, uniting himself with Sophia (divine wisdom) descended through the seven planetary regions, assuming in each an analogous form. . .[and] entered into the man Jesus at the moment of his baptism in the Jordan. From this time forth Jesus began to work miracles; before that he had been entirely ignorant of his own mission."[18]

REFERENCES AND NOTES

1. As in Buddhism.

2. Robert Graves, *The Greek Myths,* Vol. 2.

3. *Bhagavad Purana.*

4. G.R.S. Mead, *Echoes from the Gnosis,* (London and Benares: The Theosophical Publishing Society, 1908), Vol. 10, p. 23.

5. Mark 1:18.

6. Ashram (Sk.). A sacred building, monastery, or hermitage for ascetic purposes, in India.

7. cf. I Thess. 4:17. St. Paul suggests that the element of Air corresponds to the level of consciousness at which the Lord is met. See also Hodson, *Hidden Wisdom*, Vol. 1. Pt. 3, Ch. 1.

8. Mark 15:13.

9. 2 Cor. 6:16.

10. Gal. 4:19.

11. Matt. 3:11.

12. Rabbi may be interpreted as "Master."

13. See Josh. 3:13-17.

14. See Hodson, *Hidden Wisdom,* Vol. 1, pg. 3, Ch. 1. "Geographical Features."

15. *Ibid.* Vol. 1, pp. 93-98.

16. *Ibid.* Vol. 1, Pt. 6.

17. Matt: 24:6-30 and Mark 13:1-26.

18. H.P. Blavatsky, *The Secret Doctrine,* 6- vol. ed. (Adyar: Theosophical Publishing House), Vol. 5, p. 168.

PART FOUR

THE MINISTRY BEGINS

Chapter Seven

If the accounts given in the Gospels are taken literally, it is quite clear that two distinct personages were involved in the series of recorded events: the proclaimed Son of God, or Second Aspect of the Blessed Trinity, and Jesus the man. The verses following lend support to this view.

Matt. 4:1. Then was Jesus led up of the Spirit into the wilderness to be tempted of the devil.

The Gospel chronology of events, which places the temptation incident next in succession after the Baptism, is somewhat strange unless this is done deliberately; for if Jesus were the Second Aspect of the Deity on earth, as had just been proclaimed from heaven, then temptation in the ordinary meaning of the word could never reach him. If, as the ageless Wisdom teaches, the universe and its transcendent and immanent Deity are regarded as undergoing a process of unfoldment, then this Deity in each of its three aspects must in preceding universes have evolved far beyond the possibility of temptation, at least in the orthodox meaning of that word. It is, indeed, blashphemous to attribute human weaknesses of any kind to either the Supreme Deity of a solar system or his Son, and such an anomaly is one of the well recognized reasons for regarding certain passages in the world scriptures as allegorical rather than either literal or historical.

Evidently, then, it was not the Incarnate Word but rather Jesus the man who, in common with all other men, was subject alternatively to exaltation and aridity and thus became susceptible to temptation.[1] Even so, the fact that every attempt failed to lure him from his lofty idealism and the fulfillment of his divine mission indicates that he was indeed no ordinary man. Rather- —according to the theme of this work—was he a man on the threshold of attaining to the "measure of the stature of the fulness of Christ,"[2] passing through successive expansions of consciousness, with not unnatural intermediate alternations.

Many experiences contribute to positive and negative conditions in the psychology of man. In negative states material inclinations tend to become uppermost and the power of spiritual idealism declines. This latter condition, described as being in a wilderness or desert and on rocky ground in the

Parable of the Sower,[3] was overridden by Jesus despite the subtle temptations to which he was submitted. He thus personifies the state of equilibrium and harmony between the two conditions, positive and negative, or "the pairs of opposites," a balance necessary for spiritual attainment.

The devil, to whom the names Satan and Beelzebub are also given, is first introduced into the account of the life of Jesus in this verse. The devil is not regarded by esotericists as a single extremely potent and subtle being moved towards evil and in opposition to God or good. Indeed, he is not regarded as actually existing at all, particularly as an isolated embodiment of infamy, wickedness and the lust to seduce mankind into evil ways. Rather he represents both man himself in his more "devilish" aspects and matter with its materializing, despiritualizing influence and its blinding, imprisoning effect upon the human mind.

If this view is followed, then the spirit of man in conflict with its material encasements, universal consciousness versus intellect imprisoned in matter, are being described. This conflict is a very real one and no man can escape it; for the pathway of involution and evolution which the human Monad has chosen to follow is inevitably strewn with obstacles, opposition and resistance.[4] These are personified by the symbolic figure of Satan who is darkness in opposition to light, restriction in opposition to freedom, self-desire as against selflessness, and self-will in contradistinction to self-surrender to a universal Will. He has been described as "the shadow of himself which a man sees when he turns his back to the light."

The episode of the temptation of Jesus may thus be regarded as an allegory of this conflict, but more especially as a phase of the battle in which victory, ultimately to be attained, is already near. Jesus, therefore, is a man on the threshold of superhumanity, spiritually empowered, about to be self-liberated from the imprisonment of matter, flesh, desire and self-will. Although such weaknesses have been so far transcended that no real battle occurs and the devil is dismissed out of hand, final victory is only attained at the Resurrection from the tomb and the Ascension into Heaven.

> Matt. 4:2. And when he had fasted forty days and forty nights, he was afterward an hungered.
>
> 3. And when the tempter came to him, he said, If thou be the Son of God, command that these stones be made bread.

In the symbolical language, one meaning attributed to fasting is the withdrawal of consciousness from the body and its demands, while hunger, in its turn, refers to the ardent aspiration of the human soul to be merged in its Source. Mystics fast, hunger and thirst for God and for all that the Godhead implies. They also mortify the flesh, hoping thereby to obtain liberation from the bonds of matter and self, the final goal. The number forty, which by reduction may be treated as four, refers to the material aspects of human nature, and more particularly to the four mortal vehicles—physical, vital, emotional and mental[5]—that need to be refined if the limitations they impose upon the spiritual Self are to be reduced and eventually overcome. The period of the fast of Jesus in the wilderness thus signifies the denial of the demands and attributes of the fourfold mortal self. The God-Self then rules and the matter-self is ignored—hardly even existing. While such a condition is normal in the perfected man, in man still imperfect it must be brought about by the exercise of the will, the contemplation of the divine, or by the procedures of yoga, the science of the transcendence of duality and realization of unity.[6]

> Matt. 4:4. But he answered and said, It is written Man shall not live by bread alone, but by every word that proceedeth out of the mouth of God.

Materialism is here shown to be overridden. The consciousness of the mystic is made impervious to all that the devil represents, including the physical appetites.

Bread in the symbolical language stands for spiritual truth or esoteric wisdom when transformed into direct experience and knowledge. This is achieved by virtue of the "leaven" of the spiritual will in man and is, as it were, made ready by the fire of God active within him. Grain can be likened to fundamental fact or basic truth that is "ground" between the upper and nether millstones of the abstract and the formal minds. Thus prepared, spiritual truth is acted upon within the consciousness by the spiritual Self of man to become as dough containing leaven, finally made ready for assimilation—allegorically "eating"—by exposure to the fire of the intellect. The result is the very bread of life, namely spiritual wisdom or esoteric knowledge absorbed as the food of the soul. Such is the "word that proceedeth out of the mouth of God." Before this essential food can be obtained, the demands and desires of the mortal nature must be denied (fasting) and all temptations, however subtle, must be successfully resisted. In the process the devil is made into a nonentity.

A further development of the symbolism is possible. A trained occultist possesses the knowledge and power by which to produce physical objects phenomenally. The vast storehouse of nature, sometimes referred to as the "soul of the world," the *Akasa,*[7] is at his disposal, an inexhaustible quarry in which he learns to work and from which the very material of the earth itself is drawn. In this sense stones can be turned into bread by occult means.

The exercise of such power for personal gratification would constitute an occult "fall." The temptation to this, and thereby to exhibit occult powers, must be successfully resisted, or rather, overridden. Every human being who attains to knowledge which bestows power is confronted with the possibility of its use either for self alone or for humanity. The lure of power, wealth, position and prestige is exceedingly great. Many succumb, a few resist, while for a smaller number no tendency to be tempted even exists. Every aspirant to the swift attainment of perfection must meet with and successfully pass through the most searching test, which presents itself in many forms. The temptation of Jesus in the wilderness is an allegorical description of this universal experience.

> Matt. 4:5. Then the devil taketh him up into the holy city, and setteth him on a pinnacle of the temple.

6. And saith unto him, If thou be the Son of God, cast thyself down: for it is written, He shall give his angels charge concerning thee: and in their hands they shall bear thee up at any time thou dash thy foot against a stone.

These words can hardly be taken literally. The magical process of bearing a man through the air from the wilderness to Jerusalem and causing him to be poised safely on one of the pinnacles of the temple, while perhaps possible, would be extremely difficult and would certainly have created a disturbance if it had happened in the daytime. Furthermore, the text suggests that Jesus was in conflict with the devil and therefore would have resisted attempts at such magical and even dangerous transportation. The absence of any third person who could have acted as recorder of the incident also supports the necessity for an interpretation of meaning. Evidently, the holy city, the temple, and its pinnacle have symbolical meanings.

What then is intended? A condition of consciousness and a position in evolution are probably being described. The holy city is a symbol for the "vesture of light" in which the threefold immortal Self of man is robed, sometimes called the causal body. The experience of the holy city is attainment of awareness of oneself as divine, eternal, and so immune from death. This achievment in consciousness will be natural for the whole race in the appropriate evolutionary phase. It can, however, be achieved in a fraction of that time by the successful practice of yoga— and by faithfully following the "way of holiness."[9] When this way is followed and the achievement is in advance of natural development, certain dangers exist; these are exemplified in the episode of the temptation of Jesus in the wilderness. God-consciousness causes a man to feel God-like and, unless deeply and truly humble in his nature, pride may overtake him. He may be tempted to display his spiritual powers in order to gratify that pride; and this, I suggest, is symbolized in the proposition made by the devil.

A city's temple is its spiritual center; the temple in Jerusalem is a symbol for the spiritual Self of man, the Logos of the soul. The pinnacle of the temple represents the highest peak of elevation in consciousness attainable at any given time. It also represents the Dweller-in-the-Innermost, the Monad itself. A very lofty level of attainment is thus described in the allegory of the presence of Jesus upon the pinnacle of the temple in the holy city. Temptation to misuse such an achievement and its accompanying powers may seem to be at the least very unlikely. However, it can and does occur, pride being one of the last fetters outgrown by the advancing soul. Even at the very threshold of adeptship the extremely subtle forms of the allurement to display power can bring about a fall.

The nature of the test is partly described in the opening words of the tempter, "If thou be the Son of God." The initiate can at this stage so readily demonstrate supernormal faculties, even God-like powers, that any challenge can evoke such a demonstration. On this occasion and also before Pilate Jesus refrained, as must every successful initiate.

This temptation also indicates the typical demand of the analytical mind that eternal principles and abstract truths should be translated into purely logical, conceptual and three-dimensional terms. In other allegories concerning this insistent demand, knowledge of his or her name is demanded of one of the characters. Lohengrin gave his name to Elizabeth who had persisted but, in consequence, thereafter disappeared.[11] As Lohengrin warned, such particularization of the universal inevitably involves severe restrictions, so that total loss can result.

The devil also personifies the formal mind of man with all its separative, prideful and tyrannical attributes. These produce extreme expressions, and, unless the neophyte is fully emanicipated and can wholly sustain spiritual awareness, there is the danger of a fall. "Prove that divinity, eternity and immortality exist," demands the mind, also represented by those who jeered at Jesus on the Cross and called upon him to deliver himself. "Demonstrate your powers or be arraigned as an imposter," cry both mind and mob, tempting the initiate to self-justification.

A purely physical meaning may also be discerned. Dangers to the body can beset the initiate treading the way of holiness. Evil beings, agents of the Brothers of the Shadow,[12] lie in wait to seduce, injure and even destroy the bodily man. Death by apparent accident is one of the perils to be met on the path. Even the illumined man may trust too greatly in the availability of occult support and so experience injury or death.

Matt. 4:7.   Jesus said unto him, It is written again, Thou shalt not tempt the Lord thy God.

Jesus, both as a person and as representative of every successful initiate, was so firmly established in his own spiritual awareness that the material part of him (the devil) had no power to distract him from his spiritual center, for by long-continued, regular practice, Jesus had overcome the demands of his mortal nature. Spontaneously, naturally and invariably, all his responses and reactions to his tempter demonstrated he was completely established in the realm of eternal reality. Every aspirant must similarly establish himself in the "citadel" of his spiritual nature, the divine in him, and in the knowledge that the same divinity exists in all men. Then no power in heaven above or on earth beneath (or even hell as a state of consciousness) can successfully assail the self-spiritualized but also universalized, knowing that there is but one spiritual Self in the whole universe. Indeed, each human being belongs to but one spiritual race which is without division (walls) of any kind.

In this verse Jesus not only remains unmoved by the allurement and the snare set for him by the devil; he also rebukes the devil for impiety and lack of reverence. The mind (devil) is being disciplined by its user, the thinker within. This process must be continued until the spiritual response becomes habitual.

Matt. 4:8.   Again, the devil taketh him up into an exceeding high mountain, and sheweth him all the kingdoms of the world, and the glory of them;

9.   And saith unto him, All these things will I give thee, if thou wilt fall down and worship me.

Authority, power, possessions and prestige are indeed within the reach of a man who is more evolved than his fellows. By the exercise of highly intuitive and intellectual powers and by the deliberate use of magnetic forces to sway the mass mind, leadership may be gained and his endowments be acclaimed. Many of those who tread the way of holiness fall under this test. Those who thus fail are certain, eventually, to discover the transitoriness of the mundane and of the earthly thrones and support of the masses. The penetrating gaze of spiritually illumined man perceives the hollowness of material things, the instability of all temporal power, and the deceitfulness of all external glory. The shame that surrender brings acts also as both a teacher and a deterrent. Everyone who is placed in high office or attains to intellectual or spiritual eminence—the mountain top to which the devil elevated Jesus—must make his decision, this test, recurring life after life until failure has become impossible.

> Matt. 4:10.   Then saith Jesus unto him, Get thee hence, Satan: for it is written, Thou shalt worship the Lord thy God, and him only shalt thou serve.

A time is reached in the life of nations and individuals when a choice between right and wrong, even between the higher and the lower, must be made. The initiate aspiring to the attainment of adeptship in advance of the race meets with this acid test in its most acute forms, as the accounts of their varied temptations indicate.[13] Rooted in the knowledge of ultimate reality, the neophyte is protected against all allurements presented by the world of the unreal.[14] Thus, Jesus finally dismisses Satan and affirms as the only goal worthy of illumined and aspiring men, the worship of the divine principle and the service of the one Supreme Deity, transcendent and indwelling.

> Matt. 4:11.   Then the devil leaveth him, and, behold, angels came and ministered unto him.

Events in the lives of saviors and heroes which are described as single happenings are generally descriptive of long-continued and oft-repeated processes. If it is accepted that, as heretofore explained, the wilderness is descriptive of a state of consciousness and the devil is an exaggerated sense of separated selfhood and I-ness, then the so-called temptation was an interior experience that is continuous throughout many earthly lives. Conflicts, temptations, defeats, failures and eventual victories are not confined to any particular period in any particular life. They are rehearsed and practiced on the stage of life with varying results, until at last a perfect performance is achieved.

This applies most especially to the process of outgrowing the natural (and, in preceding stages, even desirable) sense of individuality, and of uprooting time and time again the inevitable egoism that it produces. As new and more advanced phases of evolution are approached and entered, these mental states and bodily impressions fade quite naturally, even though established habit must still be resisted. Eventually, full liberation from self is attained. One's existence is known as an expression of one Supernal Be-ness or All-Being. Then one experiences bliss of a highly exalted state of consciousness, unlimited and unclouded by any restrictions, and communion with the divine aspects of all beings. This development is described allegorically in the verse above, which relates that the devil left Jesus and thereafter angels ministered unto him.

> John 2:1.   And the third day there was a marriage in Cana of Galilee; and the mother of Jesus was there:

The duality mentioned above is well exemplified in St. John's account of the "miracle" of the changing of water into wine at the wedding feast in the village of Cana. The account may indeed be recognized as an example of both spiritual revelation in the form of an allegory and its concealment from the unworthy behind the veil of history and symbol. Support for this view may, perhaps, be gained from the fact that John, the most mystical of the four Evangelists and the one who identifies Jesus the Christ with the creative Deity or Word, is the only one to include the story of the marriage feast at Cana in his account of the life of Jesus.

In the mystic language in which the Gospels are written—indeed many of the books of the Old Testament as well—the purely physical event of a marriage is invested with a deeply interior significance. This has been referred to as "the heavenly marriage" and the fully conscious union of the mortal self of any mystic with his or her deeply interior divine nature.

At a certain state of evolution, and not infrequently assisted by an adept Master, the realization is achieved that the mortal, personal self—which hitherto has been regarded as the real identity—is in fact no more than a vehicle for and manifestation of the true and spiritual Self. This realization is aptly described as a marriage, since a veritable fusion of the formal mind with the spiritual intelligence of man is achieved. This description by allegory seems to have been the purpose of the author, who in the first verse of this chapter affirms that the mother of Jesus was present. As earlier stated and indicated in the illustrative diagram the feminine principle or mother in marriages and nativities personifies the spiritual intelligence in man and more especially the "vesture of light" in which it is enrobed, the so-called causal body. All the other people present personify human beings at various stages of development—from the hosts, apparently parents of the bride, who omitted to provide the necessary wine, to Jesus himself who performed the transmutation.

> John 2:2.   And both Jesus was called, and his disciples, to the marriage.

If this interpretation of the incident is continued, then Jesus represents both the adept Master and the wisdom principle or Christ nature within the immortal Self of man. The disciples in their turn personify the purified or "disciplined" physical, emotional and mental vehicle of an advanced human being in whose inner Self the supposed miracle is about to occur. This consists of the transmutation of the sensuous elements in the mortal nature—water—into the wine of pure wisdom. Thereafter, personal desire and possessive love become changed into universal, impersonal love for all beings.

> John 2:3. And when they wanted wine, the mother of Jesus saith
> unto him, They have no wine.

Recognition of the absence of or need for wine is also descriptive of that phase of human development at which a yearning for wisdom is experienced. This implicit insight is deeper than acquired knowledge and is derived from the spiritual intelligence or maternal principle in the higher Self, Mary. Thus, it is appropriate that the mother of Jesus draws attention to the need for wine.

> John 2:4. Jesus saith unto her, Woman, what have I to do with
> thee? mine hour is not yet come.
>
> 5. His mother saith unto the servants, Whatsoever he saith
> unto you, do it.

Intuitively, Mary perceives the necessity for both the external miracle—if the story is thus read—and the interior, mystical attainment. The obedient outer personality, in this case the servants, render available the means whereby the transmutation may be brought about.

> John 2:6. And there were set there six waterpots of stone, after
> the manner of the purifying of the Jews, containing two or
> three firkins apiece.

If a numerical symbol is to be recognized here rather than a mere description, then the number six may be regarded as a reference to the six principles in nature and in man as represented by King Solomon's seal or the interlaced, equilateral triangles. The triangle that points upwards represents the triple divinity, while the one which points downwards portrays its reflection and manifestation in the material universe and the mortal bodies of man. Such an interpretation is appropriate, since the elevation of the consciousness of man while awake in his threefold mortal nature would necessarily be intimately conjoined with the triple, spiritual Self.

If it is objected that too much is being made of a mere triviality, the six vessels, it may well be recalled that in inspired allegories portraying deeply mystical and therefore power-bestowing knowledge, the description is enriched by the inclusion of recognized symbols, both objective and numerical, in order to draw the attention and the intuition of the reader to the mystical revelation.

> John 2:7. Jesus saith unto them, Fill the waterpots with water. And
> they filled them up to the brim.
>
> 8. And he saith unto them, Draw out now, and bear unto the
> governor of the feast. And they bare it.
>
> John 2:9. When the ruler of the feast had tasted the water that was
> made wine, and knew not whence it was, (but the
> servants which drew the water knew;) the governor of
> the feast called the bridegroom,

The act of drinking the wine implies the full absorption into the nature of the individual of powers resulting from transmuting the sensual into spiritual wisdom and will. The "miracle" may also be regarded as descriptive of changes which are brought about within the physical brain structure when the Christ nature manifests itself as an available power in the physical world, (as portrayed by the actual presence of Jesus at the wedding feast). Various portions of the brain and their associated glands are profoundly affected by this attainment. The hitherto spiritually unresponsive cerebrum and cerebellum and the pituitary and pineal glands almost miraculously begin to transmit to the waking consciousness spiritual truths concerning the higher nature of man and the universe.

Wine in symbolic language means spiritual wisdom and powers which become available to the man or woman in whom the enlightment has become part of experience in waking consciousness. The village of Cana, and particularly the house and even the room in which the marriage feast took place correspond to the bony structure or skull in which the brain is enclosed, while the marriage ceremony which has just been performed portrays the intimate fusion of the consciousness of the mortal and the immortal parts of man. Under these conditions alone can the powers and faculties of the Christ nature become manifest, the result not infrequently appearing to be miraculous in the eyes of the beholders. The whole event, then, in these several ways is descriptive of the passage of a sufficiently evolved person through those phases of self-illumination which lead toward the fulfillment of human life in adeptship.

Passage through these phases—sometimes accompanied by both physiological and psychological difficulties—is generally aided by admission to a temple of the Greater Mysteries and by initiations at the hand of the hierophant or ruler of the temple. The seclusion and protective care which are available in such temples are designed also to help the initiate through any stresses which may arise, whether in the brain and nervous system or in the superphysical bodies and their psychological counterparts.

Wine is also a universally used symbol, both for the teachings given in the Greater Mysteries and for the condition of being wise after such teachings have been assimilated, or after the wine has been drunk. The strange words introduced into the narrative, *governor* and *ruler*, may also indicate the ruling head of a particular temple.

These interpretations of the event prove helpful in meeting the objections sometimes expressed that Jesus the Christ, representing the highest spiritual state and mode of life, would not be likely to encourage the consumption of alcohol, which when taken in excess is the cause of so much human misery and degradation. The mystical interpretation receives support from this angle also.

John 2:10. And saith unto him, Every man at the beginning doth set forth good wine; and when men have well drunk, then that which is worse: but thou has kept the good wine until now.

11. This beginning of miracles did Jesus in Cana of Galilee, and manifested forth his glory; and his disciples believed on him.

The student of occult philosophy will note with interest that in St. John's account Jesus begins his ministry by the performance of a miracle, in this case in the presence of newly accepted disciples. The closing words of the eleventh verse, if regarded objectively, may possibly indicate part of the purpose for the miracle, namely to assist the new and as yet untrained disciples to have confidence in their Master, founded upon their own observation and experience of his occult powers.

> John 4:27. And upon this came his disciples, and marvelled that he talked with the woman: yet no man said, What seekest thou? or Why talkest thou with her?

As Jesus' ministry continues, he is found talking with a woman at Samaria. The disciples had evidently not been present during this most private and personal interview, concerning which the author of the Gospel was probably not informed. The fact that the disciples asked no questions when they came upon the scene in which their Master, a Jew, was found to be in apparently close conversation with a Samaritan, suggests their immediate comprehension of the nature of the episode.

> John 4:28. The woman then left her waterpot, and went her way into the city, and saith to the men,
>
> 29. Come, see a man, which told me all things that ever I did: is not this the Christ?
>
> 30. Then they went out of the city, and came unto him.

The training Jesus had presumably received during the earlier years of his life and the overshadowing of the Holy Ghost at his Baptism enabled him to reach the mind of the woman of Samaria with esoteric teachings (the "living water") and to win her assent by the exercise of supernormal powers of perception. When she was thus convinced, she brought the great news of the physical existence of the Messiah to her own people, with the result that the numbers in his audiences were increased.

> John 4:31. In the meanwhile his disciples prayed him, saying, Master, eat.
>
> 32. But he said unto them, I have meat to eat that ye know not of.
>
> John 4:33. Therefore said the disciples one to another, Hath any man bought him *ought* to eat?
>
> 34. Jesus saith unto them, My meat is to do the will of him that sent me, and to finish his work.

The analogy of living water as representing spiritual wisdom is now extended to include the idea of a form of sustenance which, in its turn, is not physical but intellectual and spiritual. "Meat that ye know not of" symbolically portrays knowledge of the laws of Being, of Jesus' mission to humanity, and the power or will of God necessary to its fulfillment.

In this period of his life—as also until his death—Jesus is depicted by St. John as having entered a lofty state of spiritual enlightment and power as befits "the Word which became flesh and dwelt among us."[15] Under the exaltation of such interior experience, the need for physical food would tend greatly to decline, even if not completely to disappear.

> John 4:35. Say not ye, There are yet four months, and *then* cometh harvest? behold, I say unto you, Lift up your eyes, and look on the fields; for they are white already to harvest.

The seasons of the year and the natural agricultural acitivities appropriate to each of them are treated symbolically, normal seasonal limitations being overridden. Physical time and superphysical time differ from each other, so that reaping and harvesting may follow almost immediately upon the sowing of spiritual seeds; the teachings of everlasting truths and transferring of spiritual powers may awaken the intuition in recipients almost immediately. Perhaps the harvest to which Jesus referred consisted of the enlightment of the women of Samaria and the successful spread of his teachings to her people.

> John 4:36. And he that reapeth receiveth wages, and gathereth fruit unto life eternal; that both he that soweth and he that reapeth may rejoice together.

Often throughout his mission, Jesus chooses for his teachings analogies from the agricultural pursuits of most of his hearers. Sowing and reaping bring forth much fruit in the form of intuitively perceived knowledge and wisdom. In addition, the power is attained to apply them intelligently in meeting the spiritual and the material needs of mankind, these interior endowments being referred to as "wages."

> John 4:37. And herein is that saying true, One soweth, and another reapeth.
> 38. I sent you to reap that whereon ye bestowed no labour: other men laboured, and ye are entered into their labours.

Either the incidents here are misreported, or the original document is mistranslated, or deeply spiritual truths are being revealed. Unjust, unfair and contradictory though these instructions seem to be on the surface, an underlying significance can be discerned if the terms *sowing* and *reaping* are regarded as purely metaphorical. Jesus may have been speaking symbolically and yet also very directly to his disciples when he told them that they reaped or gained from the sowing or labor of other people. As disciples of a divinely overshadowed, highly evolved teacher, they had become part of the hidden life, the secret occult tradition upon earth.

Those who follow this path at any given time truly reap where others have sown. From the remotest times, even the early beginnings of human life upon the planet, men and women searched for and intuitively discovered not only eternal truths but also the methods and procedures whereby those truths could be intellectually realized and applied to life. This metaphorical sowing of the seeds of wisdom still continues with the result that every new entrant upon the path—and the disciples at that time were newly called—benefits from the researches and discoveries of his predecessors.

Thus, no sincere and selfless aspirants endeavoring to comprehend the underlying principles governing both material and spiritual life are ever alone or wholly dependent upon their own efforts; for their teacher or Master gradually reveals to them the acquired and inherited wisdom of the ages. This in its turn constitutes reapings from earlier sowings in this highly specialized "field"—the reaping of knowledge directly attained, wisdom personally acquired, and will power applicable to both the spiritual and the worldly life of highly developed man. In this sense, every disciple under adept instruction reaps where he has not sown. If these teachings of Jesus to his disciples are thus read, then no slightest injustice or infringement of the rules upon which justice is based can be discerned. This view is surely supported by the fact that a purely literal reading indicates a serious injustice.

> John 4:39.   And many of the Samaritans of that city believed on him for the saying of the woman, which testified, He told me all that ever I did.

The discourse would seem to have ended somewhat abruptly; but instruction was given to the disciples to become as laborers in the same field. The results of such labors and such a mission are thereupon described in terms of increased reception of the Ancient Wisdom and so of the number of those who would seek, find and tread the ancient way. Thus the woman of Samaria told her people of the powers and the wisdom of Jesus.

> John 4:40.   So when the Samaritans were come unto him, they besought him that he would tarry with them: and he abode there two days.
>
> 41.   And many more believed because of his own word;
>
> 42.   And said unto the women, Now we believe, not because of thy saying: for we have heard him ourselves, and know that this is indeed the Christ, the Saviour of the world.

Citizens of Samaria who came out to hear Jesus, and in consequence were illumined, represent those men and women who throughout the ages have eventually found their own light and discovered their own truth. While aided by the study of the teachings of predecessors, their ultimate conviction is due to an interior and highly intuitive illumination of the mind. Throughout the gospel story this individual spiritual power, wisdom and capacity for self-harmonization are personified by Jesus the Christ.

If a purely mystical interpretation of the whole episode is applied, then the woman of Samaria personifies the immortal, evolving spiritual soul of man in its vesture of light, while Samaria and its people personify the mortal man of mind, emotion and physical body. The meeting with Jesus at Jacob's well may then be seen as an allegorical description of the awakening into perceptive activity of the wisdom principle within the spiritual Self. This leads eventually to illumination of the mind and brain of the outer man by that wisdom, symbolized by Jesus as the living water.

In this approach, the whole story is descriptive of the interior experience of one person—or rather of every person—who seeks and successfully finds those truths which predecessors have discovered—not purely worldly wisdom but a deeply perceived, spiritual truth (water from a well) concerning the timeless Life upon which the phenomenal worlds are based.

John 4:43. Now after two days he departed thence, and went into Galilee.

44. For Jesus himself testified, that a prophet hath no honour in his own country.

45. Then when he was come into Galilee, the Galileans received him, having seen all the things that he did at Jerusalem at the feast: for they also went unto the feast.

The place of birth of the Savior and the people living there represent both the resistant tendencies of mind and brain and personal familiarity which can prevent the recognition that was granted to Jesus outside of Nazareth. These rejections and acceptances may especially refer to the attitudes of different members of a family into which a great soul is born, e.g., Osiris, Typhon, Buddha, and Devadatta.

Galilee, however, with its beautiful lake, shores, surrounding hills and its people, may also be thought of as portraying a condition of the mind which is favorable to spiritual enlightenment or intuitive perception in general. It may also signify recognition born of inward experience of a spiritual teacher and the wisdom which he or she teaches.

John 4:46. So Jesus came again into Cana of Galilee, where he made the water wine. And there was a certain nobleman, whose son was sick at Capernaum.

47. When he heard that Jesus was come out of Judea into Galilee, he went unto him, and besought him that he would come down, and heal his son: for he was at the point of death.

48. Then said Jesus unto him, Except ye see signs and wonders, ye will not believe.

49. The nobleman saith unto him, Sir, come down ere my child die.

50. Jesus saith unto him, Go thy way; thy son liveth. And the man believed the word that Jesus had spoken unto him, and he went his way.

51. And as he was now going down, his servants met him, and told him, saying, Thy son liveth.

52. Then inquired he of them the hour when he began to amend. And they said unto him, Yesterday at the seventh hour the fever left him.

53. So the father knew that it was at the same hour, in the which Jesus said unto him, Thy son liveth: and himself believed, and his whole house.

54. This is the second miracle that Jesus did, when he was come out of Judea into Galilee.

This dramatic and beautiful account describes a power attained by every Adept to override the normal barriers of place and distance and act, whether supernormally or naturally, in another part of a country or even the world. The fully unfolded spiritual Self transcends boundaries which physically separate geographical positions. Distance, therefore, offers no separation and constitutes no obstacle to either the self-manifestation of the Adept or the projection of his power.

The healing of the nobleman's son performed at a distance constitutes demonstration of this capacity, the transcendence of space. Synchronicity in time is introduced into the narrative, too, since the servants report to the nobleman that the fever departed and recovery began at the very moment at which Jesus had pronounced the words "Thy son liveth."

This story also lends itself to a mystical interpretation. The Christ nature, even though not yet active or apparent, is nevertheless present as part of the make-up of every individual. Normally man is unaware of this interior power, and, as the story tells, can even be prevented from gaining such self-knowledge by the metaphorical "fever" or excessive and rabid activity of the mind, emotions or body, symptoms of the illness of the nobleman's son. Fever is appropriate, since this very feverishness in the personality can so greatly preoccupy the mind that it is incapable of interior stillness—the return to health in the mystical sense—which is the essential precursor of illumination, a condition beyond both body and mind. Just as Jesus stilled the tempest at the height of the storm on Galilee, so in this case he reduced the fever which the nobleman's son had been enduring. Thereupon, the son was saved from a "death" of spiritual declivity.

In such a reading, the father in the story would personify both the innate intuitiveness of man and a condition of the mind resulting from evolutionary development in which truth may be sought and inwardly perceived. Joseph, the foster father of Jesus, portrays this same evolved mental stature. However, these proffered mystical and psychological interpretations of recorded incidents in the life of Jesus are in no sense intended to preclude the historicity of the four Gospels.

> John 5:1.   After this there was a feast of the Jews; and Jesus went up to Jerusalem.
>
> 2.   Now there is at Jerusalem by the sheep market a pool, which is called in the Hebrew tongue Bethesda, having five porches.
>
> 3.   In these lay a great multitude of impotent folk, of blind, halt, withered, waiting for the moving of the water.
>
> 4.   For an angel went down at a certain season into the pool, and troubled the water: whosoever then first after the troubling of the water stepped in was made whole of whatsoever disease he had.

By the shores of a lake, on the slopes of mountains or in the city streets, at this phase in his life Jesus continued his compassionate ministrations by healing the sick. In this fifth chapter the locality changes from country to town, from the fields of Galilee to the capital city of Jerusalem. Yet, in spite of the removal, the "miracles" of healing continue. The scene beside the pool of Bethesda is indeed a pitiful one; for "a great multitude of impotent folk, of blind, halt, withered," was gathered there hopefully, ardently aspiring to be made whole. Yet apparently only one of them was destined to be healed.

Though a supernormal event cannot be wholly discounted, the story is so unlikely and the incidents so unusual that symbolical interpretation is encouraged. To achieve this, both incredibility and incongruity are sometimes introduced into a supposedly historical narrative. For example, incongruously, only one person from the whole multitude was to be healed despite the presence and the action of the angel.

What then may be the meaning of this strange pool, the waiting multitude of the sick, the mysterious troubling of the waters by an angel and the failure of all save one of the suppliants to be healed? Perhaps the sick personify almost the whole human race; for are not almost all lacking in good health when judged from the condition of their minds, their emotions and the relationships of these to their conduct? To be whole in this sense implies that the dictates of conscience are followed day by day in the conduct of life. And when this practice is not followed, the "waters" of human life are troubled indeed, not so much externally by an angel as interiorly by the action of that law which St. Paul described as sowing and reaping and which the ancient Sanskritists named *karma*. [16]

John 5:5.   And a certain man was there, which had an infirmity thirty and eight years.

6.   When Jesus saw him lie, and knew that he had been now a long time in that case, he saith unto him, Wilt thou be made whole?

7.   The impotent man answered him, Sir, I have no man, when the water is troubled, to put me into the pool: but while I am coming, another steppeth down before me.

8.   Jesus saith unto him, Rise, take up thy bed, and walk.

9.   And immediately the man was made whole, and took up his bed, and walked: and on the same day was the sabbath.

Two instances of the supernormal are brought into the story. First, Jesus by means of inward vision knew that the man about to be healed had waited a long time in the hopes of being the first to enter the pool. Second, by his divine power, Jesus healed the man while he lay upon his bed. Such actions lie readily within the power of the Adept when karma permits, and Jesus may actually have performed a healing. However, the narrative also lends itself to an interpretation as an allegory descriptive of the attainment of spiritual, intellectual and personal illumination or wholeness, in this case particularly of the mind.

The paralysis of the body from which this man suffered signifies a condition of the human mind in which it becomes so rigid and so immovable as to render almost impossible the functions of reason and intuition. This is a paralysis of the worst kind, one that is all too common among the multitudes of men. However, when the inner Self becomes sufficiently evolved to cause the person to recognize the disability and desire to take action to gain freedom from it (resort to the healing pool) and when the interior Christ nature (Jesus) is powerful enough to free mind from its paralytic impotence, then the individual is healed or made whole. This essentially inward, psychological effect frees both the body and the rigid, bigoted brain-mind from their afflictions. Symbolically, the sufferer is able to respond to the inward command, "Rise, take up thy bed, and walk." Freedom of movement or mental activity is restored by the direct action of the awakened intuitive wisdom.

Further guidance may be gained from the fact that the sufferer recognized his disability and, on being interrogated by Jesus, answered with a description of his further difficulties. Thus, he both recognized the deficiency and was hopeful of recovery from a "paralyzed" condition. This may refer to what some schools regard as the first necessity in the attainment of self-illumination—a sincere and even intense yearning for that wholeness which follows knowledge of one's own divine nature and union with God. The Christ nature coming to power produces a self-correction and self-harmonization throughout the whole personality. This action is allegorically described in the Gospels by all the seemingly miraculous healings of the sick and the resuscitations of those who were pronounced to be dead. Elsewhere, Jesus himself taught of this necessity, advising all aspirants to ask, to seek and to knock at that door, which, when opened, leads into the Hall of Truth.[17]

An angel troubling the waters of the pool of Bethesda implies a state of consciousness that is no longer rigidly material but seeks and is open to the invisible or spiritual parts of human nature.

If, however, the story is read as a description of the seemingly miraculous, then the teachings of occult philosophy relating to a troubling of waters by an invisible agency may be intended. The word *troubling,* thus regarded, would imply charging the particles of the water with a special kind of energy—magnetizing them, to use another term—so that a person entering the water could be healed of a physical disease. It is further possible that the intensity of energy or degree of magnetization was sufficient for the healing of only one person, which would exhaust the power.

Thus, a literal reading of the account as descriptive of an actual physical pool within the city of Jerusalem, and of two supernormal actions—one from olden times by an angel and the other by Jesus—becomes possible only if the miraculous is allowed.

John 5:10. The Jews therefore said unto him that was cured, It is the sabbath day: it is not lawful for thee to carry thy bed.

11. He answered them, He that made me whole, the same said unto me, Take up thy bed, and walk.

12. Then asked they him, What man is that which said unto thee, Take up thy bed, and walk?

13. And he that was healed wist not who it was: for Jesus had conveyed himself away, a multitude being in that place.

14. Afterward Jesus findeth him in the temple, and said unto him, Behold, thou art made whole: sin no more, lest a worse thing come unto thee.

15. The man departed, and told the Jews that it was Jesus, which had made him whole.

16. And therefore did the Jews persecute Jesus, and sought to slay him, because he had done things on the sabbath day.

St. John here brings into sharp contrast the attitude of Jesus toward his fellowmen on the one hand, Jesus healing and helping without regard for rigid regulations or crystallized theology. The people on the other, held the regulations more important than restoring health to a suffering human being. For the orthodox, formalism inclines to come first, while for the perfected one, it can have no place at all.

Here one perceives, too, the first suggestions that enmity toward Jesus may already exist on the part of orthodox Jews, and more especially the rabbis. Eventually, as the Evangelists reveal, antagonism proved strong enough to bring about the premature cessation of his mission.

One may also discern in these verses Jesus' enunciation of two important principles governing the health or ill-health of human beings: first, the state of a person's mind—and so conduct in relation to the voice of conscience —could directly influence the condition of his body; and, second, that disease was the product of infringement of law, or "sinning." The words "go, sin no more" would indeed seem distinctly to indicate that the paralyzed condition of the man who was healed was the result of former actions under a law of cause and effect, which Jesus himself later more fully affirmed and also St. Paul.[18] Great teachers preceding Jesus repeatedly enunciated this law—that actions are followed by appropriate reactions according to a sequence under which effect follows cause, modified by intervening actions.

John 5:17. But Jesus answered them, My Father worketh hitherto, and I work.

18. Therefore the Jews sought the more to kill him, because he not only had broken the sabbath, but said also that God was his Father, making himself equal with God.

John 5:19. Then answered Jesus and said unto them, Verily, verily, I say unto you, The Son can do nothing of himself, but what he seeth the Father do: for what things soever he doeth, these also doeth the Son likewise.

20. For the Father loveth the Son, and sheweth him all things that himself doeth: and he will shew him greater works than these, that ye may marvel.

23. That all men should honour the Son, even as they honour the Father. He that honoureth not the Son honoureth not the Father which hath sent him.

Many of the remaining verses in the Book of John describe Jesus' Sonship and unity with the Father. Although Jesus may appear to have been proclaiming a specially privileged relationship with God whom he designates *my Father,* nevertheless, that which he states also applies to every human being, although few may be aware of it. An extremely advanced evolutionary stature, and in consequence, a full realization of Sonship with God, a divine apostleship, and an intimate realization of dependence upon God are reflected in the reply which St. John reports.

Jesus, himself, intimated more than once that every man is a god, and St. Paul stated that each human being has a natural body and a spiritual body.[19] These, and similar affirmations which are of the innate divinity of every human being, harmonize with the descriptions of the full nature of man found in the scriptures of other world faiths. The Second Aspect of the Hindu *Trimurti-Vishnu*—is described in the Hindu scriptures as "the Inner Ruler Immortal seated in the hearts of all beings."[20] St. Paul wrote, "Know ye not that ye are the temple of God, and that the Spirit of God dwelleth in you?" Other quotations are, "Christ in you, the hope of glory," and ". . .work out your own salvation with fear and trembling. For it is God that worketh in you. . . ."[21] Jesus, himself, affirmed his realization of this deeply interior unity with God in his words, "I and my Father are one."[22] Thus each man is defined as a god by his own nature, a Monad or unit of the one divine essence, a spark within the One Flame which in Christianity is given the name *God*. This interior divinity is the ultimate reality of every human being. Jesus was thus claiming for himself no more than what is true of all men, the difference consisting only in the degree to which this truth is consciously realized and has become a ruling principle and source of guidance and power. In spiritually unillumined men the realization unfortunately is either nonexistent or fitful, while in Jesus it was complete and continuous. One may even be moved to question whether these were actually public proclamations, since such forthright utterances seem unwise. Is it not possible that they were private instructions given to his disciples and other more intimate associates?

In the verses under consideration Jesus affirms this knowledge and its importance in the present and future lives of a human being. They therefore convey both a truthful description of man himself and the effects upon human life, present and future, of realization of kinship with the one God who is in a spiritual sense the Father of all.

REFERENCES AND NOTES

1. Incarnate Word—see John 1:1-5.

2. Eph. 4:13.

3. Matt. 1:13.

4. See Hodson, *Hidden Wisdom*, Vol. 1, Pt. 4.

5. *Ibid.*, Vol. 1, Pt. 1, Ch. 6.

6. See Geoffrey Hodson: *A Yoga of Light*.

7. Akasa—see Glossary.

8. See Geoffrey Hodson: *A Yoga of Light*.

9. Isa. 35:8.

10. Matt. 26:53.

11. Lohengrin and Elisabeth—Illustrated in Wagner's opera "Lohengrin."

12. See Geoffrey Hodson: *Lecture Notes of the School of the Wisdom*. Vol. I, p. 509 *et seq*.

13. Cf. Samson and Delilah (Judg. 13); Saul and Bath-sheba (2 Sam. 11:12); Herod and Jesus (Matt. 2:16); Peter (Matt. 26:69-74); Judas Iscariot (Matt. 26:14, 47 and 27:5).

14. Real and unreal. Cf. Hodson, *Hidden Wisdom,* Vol. 2, p. 197.

15. John 1:14.

16. Karma is sometimes likened to the ripples produced when a stone is thrown into water, these continuing until neutralized.

17. Luke 11:9, 10.

18. Matt. 5:18; 7:1, 2; Gal. 6:7.

19. 1 Cor. 15:44.

20. *Bhagavad Gita*.

21. 1 Cor. 3:16; Col. 1:27; Phil. 2:12, 13.

22. John 10:30.

Chapter Eight

As in the case of other spiritual teachers and revealers of everlasting wisdom, Jesus followed the practice of winning attention, if not assent, by performing seeming miracles. Thereby the intuition of the recipients may be opened to give credence to profoundly spiritual truths which otherwise might have been rejected and beyond the comprehension of the intellect. When credence and conviction have been gained by such a method, then an individual, or even a group, may become receptive to profound ideas concerning man's inner, spiritual life.

The miracles of feeding the multitudes and walking upon the water, occurring before the following incidents in the Book of John, are omitted here as they are fully covered in Chapters Twenty and Twenty-one.

John 6:47. Verily, verily, I say unto you, He that believeth in me hath everlasting life.
48. I am that bread of life.
49. Your fathers did eat manna in the wilderness, and are dead.
50. This is the bread which cometh down from heaven, that a man may eat thereof, and not die.
51. I am the living bread which came down from heaven: if any man eat of this bread, he shall live for ever: and the bread that I will give is my flesh, which I will live for the life of the world.
52. The Jews therefore strove among themselves, saying, How can this man give us his flesh to eat?
53. Then Jesus said unto them, Verily, verily, I say unto you, Except ye eat the flesh of the Son of man, and drink his blood, ye have no life in you.
54. Whoso eateth my flesh, and drinketh my blood, hath eternal life; and I will raise him up on the last day.

Just as a distinction was made earlier between physical water and "living" water, so in these verses a distinction is made between natural and spiritual bread. The Israelites in the desert, one remembers, had been saved from starvation by the descent of manna, and the multitude at Capernaum had recently, also miraculously, been fed by Jesus from only five loaves. In quite a long discourse Jesus identifies himself with "living" or heavenly bread.[1]

Clearly, the word *bread* is symbolic and may be interpreted as referring to the immortal nature of man (heaven) and the attributes thereof. Physical bread, on the other hand, refers to the mortal nature of man and its attributes, notably that of inevitable death. The words of Jesus may thus be interpreted as advice to eat "living bread," meaning to participate in the life of man's spiritual nature with its immunity from death. He who thinks and lives solely as a natural human being of flesh and blood is destined to die, while he who establishes himself in realization of his ever-existent, intrinsic spiritual nature, will in this, his real Self, never die. Jesus then offers himself as mediator between these two aspects of man, the divine or "Father in Heaven" and the bodily nature of which alone man is normally aware. These verses may then be read as both a teaching concerning the constitution of man and an exhortation to self-discovery.

Jesus proclaimed himself metaphorically as composed of that flesh and that blood which, when consumed, bestow immortal life. Taken literally this is almost repellent, since it suggests a form of cannabalism, and St. John states that on this account both members of the public and some of the disciples ceased to follow him. However, if Jesus is considered not only as a historical personage, but also as a personification of the "Christ in you," or the mystical power, life and knowledge of the spiritual nature of man,then the otherwise difficult-to-understand words of Jesus become comprehensible.

At this point, it may be added that knowledge of the nature of both bodily death and eternal life or resurrection were central themes of some of the teachings given secretly in temples of the Mysteries as in Egypt, Greece and earlier civilizations. A study of occult philosophy and of the brief statements on the subject of death which initiates of these temples permitted themselves to make indicates that during a ceremony of initiation, the initiate loses consciousness, becomes entranced or figuratively "dies." While his body is thus unconscious, his inner Self, freed therefrom, is fully aware of its own immortal nature, divine and eternal Being, and so of its immunity from death. On returning to the body, or being "raised from the dead," the initiate remembers the experience through which he has passed. Thereafter, death has no terrors for him, for he knows by experience that he, himself, cannot die. In the ceremonies of the Lesser Mysteries, all this is done symbolically, the death being only figurative rather than involving loss of consciousness.

As one remembers these traditions concerning the ancient Mysteries and their modern representatives and reads this sixth chapter, one notices a close resemblance between the two sources of knowledge. This supports the possiblity that Jesus' actions and the knowledge during this early part of his ministry, however symbolically imparted, may refer to the secret teachings of temples of the ancient Mysteries. This concept is supported by the incomprehensibility of a literal reading of the statements of Jesus.[2]

> John 6:66. From that time many of his disciples went back, and walked no more with him.

If it is asked why Jesus—as in the verses of this chapter—spoke of himself in terms which inevitably alienated both the public and even some of the disciples, it may possibly be answered that these are the teachings of the sanctuary and, therefore, appropriate only to certain degrees in a temple of the Mysteries. The teachings are by no means applicable to humanity at large; for while neophytes under training would understand and benefit from them, to the public present at the time they might seem meaningless verbiage or egotistic claims of a divine mission.

> John 2:12. After this he went down to Capernaum, he, and his mother, and his brethren, and his disciples; and they continued there not many days.
>
> 13. And the Jews' passover was at hand, and Jesus went up to Jerusalem,
>
> 14. And found in the temple those that sold oxen and sheep and doves, and the changers of money sitting:
>
> 15. And when he had made a scourge of small cords, he drove them all out of the temple, and the sheep, and the oxen; and poured out the changers' money, and overthrew the tables;
>
> 16. And said unto them that sold doves, Take these things hence; make not my Father's house a house of merchandise.

The very remarkable incident generally referred to as the cleansing of the temple may be regarded both literally and mystically. The former seems somewhat unlikely, since a long-established and very lucrative custom would be overthrown by one man only with great difficulty, however great his zeal. The dealers were many and therefore well able to resist the attempts of any one person to upset their tables and close down their businesses. This view is strengthened by the facts that Jesus was both a young man and apparently a complete stranger in Jerusalem and at the temple. Normally, only those officially vested with civil or sacerdotal authority would have the power to drive the traders out of the temple and upset their livelihood. Even then legal and personal resistance would likely be aroused, the traders outraged at the interference and determined to protect their way of business. However, Jesus had been newly baptized and spiritually empowered so that he could perform miracles, and some of his theurgic force may have been apparent, especially when his indignation was aroused.

If regarded as allegorical, then the incident is rich in symbolism. The temple, for example, represents the mortal man of mind, emotion and body, within which the divine presence, Shekinah or Monad, is enshrined in the Holy of Holies. The cruelty and the lust for gold, inseparable from the sale and killing of sacrificial animals, would mean a degradation of the temple. Thus, a deeply rooted evil was to be eradicated from the mortal man, and this is achieved when the spiritual Self, personified by Jesus the Christ, begins to take charge of the bodily man, as portrayed by his presence at the temple.

The incident may also describe a necessary step in preparing for discipleship as well as participation in ordinary, spiritual and religious life. Jesus had been choosing and receiving disciples, and his action describes achieving fitness for that privilege by cleansing the bodily person of established unspiritual habits and customs. The life story of Judas Iscariot, particularly in its closing months, offers a dramatic example of the results of failure to achieve this cleansing, particularly of the cupidity which brought about his downfall. Whether recording history or not, St. John was revealing certain laws of the spiritual life and particularly those which affect progress on the way of holiness.

> John 2:17.   And his disciples remembered that it was written, The zeal of thine house hath eaten me up.

This verse reveals that the newly received disciples had accompanied Jesus and so had witnessed his cleansing of the temple and the zeal with which it had been done. This zeal is also essential to success in achieving the veritable revolution in character and way of life which is necessary to success on the path of discipleship.

> John 2:18.   Then answered the Jews and said unto him, What sign shewest thou unto us, seeing that thou doest these things?
> 19.   Jesus answered and said unto them, Destroy this temple, and in three days I will raise it up.
> 20.   Then said the Jews, Forty and six years was this temple in building, and wilt thou rear it up in three days?
> 21.   But he spake of the temple of his body.
> 22.   When therefore he was risen from the dead, his disciples remembered that he had said this unto them; and they believed the scripture, and the word which Jesus had said.

If the account is accepted literally, the action of Jesus again aroused protest. His replies to the protesters are distinctly shown by St. John as indicating a mystical revelation; for the twenty-first verse makes clear that Jesus "spake of the temple of his body." Verse twenty-two carries the story forward to the Resurrection of Jesus and again seems to stress the value of a metaphorical reading of the very remarkable incident.

> John 2:23.   Now when he was in Jerusalem at the passover, in the feast day, many believed in his name, when they saw the miracles which he did.

If, as has been indicated, the divine mission of Jesus as manifestation of the Holy Spirit had actually begun after his Baptism, then miracles would be possible for him by this time and likely to be performed.

> John 2:24.   But Jesus did not commit himself unto them, because he knew all men,
> 25.   And needed not that any should testify of man: for he knew what was in man.

In these two verses, St. John writes as if he had been admitted to the private counsels of Jesus; for he describes Jesus' mental state and his reservations concerning the people around him. Yet at this time St. John, as the named author, had not been called to discipleship. Since these extremely private views, based perhaps upon prophetic insight, lay deep in the recesses of Jesus' mind and were hardly likely to be expressed verbally, some doubt arises concerning the reliability of this Gospel as a record of the life of Jesus the Christ. Indeed, as already suggested, the reader is even left in doubt as to whether the cleansing of the temple actually occurred or was only symbolic.

John 3:1.   There was a man of the Pharisees, named Nicodemus, a ruler of the Jews:

2.   The same came to Jesus by night, and said unto him, Rabbi, we know that thou art a teacher come from God: for no man can do these miracles that thou doest, except God be with him.

3.   Jesus answered and said unto him, Verily, verily, I say unto thee, Except a man be born again, he cannot see the kingdom of God.

Jesus' reply to Nicodemus indicates that Jesus spoke and John recorded his words in a mystical sense and definitely not as physical reality. The term *born again* may be read either as a reference to the doctrine of reincarnation or as an interior change which produces effects of so drastic a nature that the individual almost becomes another person. According to the records Jesus referred to reincarnation on only one occasion—Elias reborn as John the Baptist.[3] The term *see the kingdom of God* implies an interior illumination. Therefore, a mystical reading seems here to be more appropriate. Thus, to be born again, in the sense in which the teaching was given, did not imply a return to the mother's womb and rebirth therefrom, but a metaphorical rebirth into a level of consciousness higher than the normal which perceives only physical events and laws.

Just as the birth of Jesus was preceded by the call to repentance and self-cleansing uttered by John the Baptist, so also the purification of the temple (mind and body) appropriately preceded the illumination of Nicodemus and his receiving instruction from the Master. The child-state of purity, meaning spontaneity and naturalness, is elsewhere referred to by Jesus as essential to the attainment of the inward vision or rebirth. In his words, "Whosoever shall not receive the kingdom of God as a little child shall in no wise enter therein." Occult tradition refers to this profound, interior self-regeneration as an *initiation,* a word which implies both a return to first principles and a new beginning. The words of Jesus may thus permissibly be interpreted as meaning, "Except a man be initiated he cannot see the kingdom of God."

However orthodox the officials who witnessed the miracles of Jesus, the ruler named Nicodemus was personally convinced, though he chose to reveal this fact "by night." Whether an actual person or a personification of the human mind on the threshold of illumination, he makes the very natural reply in terms of logic alone. But Jesus apparently wished to elevate the thought of

Nicodemus above the limitations of the logical reasoning mind into a loftier realm of consciousness wherein unchanging principles are comprehended and underlying truths are realized. The incident is so related by St. John as to provide a most valuable description of that which is essential to the attainment of intuitive insight and purely spiritual perception, namely, the transcendence of the limitations of the logically reasoning and even argumentative mind.

> John 3:4.   Nicodemus saith unto him, How can a man be born when he is old? can he enter the second time into his mother's womb, and be born?
>
> 5.   Jesus answered, Verily, verily, I say unto thee, Except a man be born of water and of the Spirit, he cannot enter into the kingdom of God.
>
> 6.   That which is born of the flesh is flesh; and that which is born of the Spirit is spirit.
>
> 7.   Marvel not that I said unto thee, Ye must be born again.

The words of Jesus were and still are an appeal to the capacity of intuitive perception to which Jesus refers symbolically as "water" and "spirit." Here the mind is led toward the deepest and most interior part of human nature, the divine spirit, which is the reality within, that Holy Spirit said to have descended upon Jesus at Baptism,[5] but which may also be regarded as shining forth or being born within him. This is the spiritual rebirth through which every successful mystic passes, an initiation in truth, whether this is actually conferred within the sacred retreat of a temple of the Mysteries or signifies a psychological transformation of outlook and manner of life in one who has attained spiritual vision.

The very intimate instruction of Nicodemus by Jesus, recorded only by St. John, was doubtless accompanied by a full explanation and an induced elevation of consciousness, as is customary when a pupil receives instruction from a Master. Thus Nicodemus, in the very presence of Jesus, hearing his words and being influenced by the sound and power of his voice, must be presumed to have direct experience and knowledge that Jesus was indeed a divine Being, come to earth for the salvation of mankind. Belief in the Son of God externally and objectively manifested in the visible person of Jesus can proceed from an almost immediate intuitive acceptance.

> John 3:8.   The wind bloweth where it listeth, and thou hearest the sound thereof, but canst not tell whence it cometh, and whither it goeth: so is every one that is born of the Spirit.

While the whole remarkable episode may be read and accepted literally and understood according to orthodox views, it is also rich in spiritual allusions. The comparison of the apparently wayward wind with the experiences of man when lifted up in spirit is very apt indeed; for as Jesus informs Nicodemus, spiritual experience is supramental and does not necessarily conform to the demands of reason, but elevates the mind into realms where the laws of physical nature do not operate.

John 3:9.   Nicodemus answered and said unto him, How can these things be?

⟶   10.   Jesus answered and said unto him, Art thou a master of Israel, and knowest not these things?

Again, Nicodemus, as personification of the formal mind, is unable to follow the Master into the realm of awareness where the laws of objective nature do not appear to apply; for just as there are laws and processes appropriate to a single drop of water, so there are others which apply to the wide ocean as a whole with its apparent sourcelessness and boundless extensions throughout the whole earth.

Evidently Nicodemus was worthy of the title *a master of Israel,* doubtless in the religious and philosophic senses, and should therefore have become aware of the more esoteric meanings of the scriptures and by prayer have begun to enter into spiritual levels of consciousness.

John 3:11.   Verily, verily, I say unto thee, We speak that we do know, and testify that we have seen; and ye receive not our witness.

Perhaps in order to reassure and even strengthen Nicodemus's faith, Jesus affirms that he himself has entered into the highest levels of awareness of which he speaks. Therefore, presumably, he should be worthy of credence and his teachings should be received with the greatest possible respect and readiness to believe.

John 3:12.   If I have told you earthly things, and ye believe not, how shall ye believe, if I tell you of heavenly things?

If the whole account is interpreted as descriptive of an interior experience, then the physically present Jesus personifies the divine Self within man, while Nicodemus, in his turn, portrays the concrete mind with both its advantages and disadvantages. Its limitations are made obvious by the difficulties experienced by Nicodemus in understanding and assenting to the teachings of the Master.

The care with which Jesus endeavors to illumine the mind of Nicodemus is of special interest, both to those who seek the higher consciousness by meditation and to those who study the teachings of sages and Masters of the Wisdom. Preliminary difficulties can be very great, since a barrier exists—a veritable veil indeed—between the formal and the abstract mind of man. This can generally be broken through when Christ or intuitive nature in man comes to the assistance of the mind.

John 3:13.   And no man hath ascended up to heaven, but he that came down from heaven, even the Son of man which is in heaven.

The divine spirit with man existing at the innermost levels of human nature—"heaven"—is here proclaimed, as is also the possibility of ascent to those heights and of return, illumined, to the worlds of mind and body.

John 3:14.   And as Moses lifted up the serpent in the wilderness, even so must the Son of man be lifted up:

In this verse, again the language is admittedly used figuratively. The serpent raised up by Moses upon the cross in the wilderness is here stated to be a parallel to the Lord Christ himself. In the preceding chapter, the temple of Jerusalem was regarded by the disciples as a symbol for the body of the Lord. Here the serpent is somewhat similarly used.

If the teachings of occult philosophy are applied to this passage, then it refers to powers within man's body by means of which spiritual awareness may be attained. This power consists of an energy which also inheres in the Deity and in nature. In man it is concealed within the spine along which it ascends into the brain by means of a winding or serpentine path. In consequence, this power is referred to as "The Serpent Fire."[6] When this creative and procreative force is sublimated from the lower to the higer parts of the human body, the brain becomes sufficiently sensitized and its inherent mentality sufficiently illumined to enable the inner man to comprehend spiritual truths. Symbol, metaphor and allegory thereafter light up with meanings, not concerning the material and objective world, but the spiritual and subjective aspects of human consciousness. If Nicodemus had achieved this state, then the references made by Jesus to rebirth would not have evoked the concept of returning to his mother's womb. On the contrary, with his mind-brain afire and enlightened, he would have perceived instantly the more metaphysical and mystical meaning, namely, birth into an entirely new or spiritual outlook.

The Old Testament story of the brazen serpent is susceptible of a similar interpretation.[7] The supposed sickness of the Israelites refers to limitations of the human mind and mental outlook, while the elevation of the serpent may permissibly be seen as a symbol of the elevation of the creative serpent-power enabling the man to enter into supramental, purely spiritual states of consciousness. A similar use of the symbol of the serpent is found in the account of the changing of the rod of Aaron into a serpent before Pharoah,[8] in consequence of which the Israelites were permitted to depart from their bondage in Egypt. Here bondage means enslavement of the mind and emotions to the desires of the body and their gratification—the so-called "flesh-pots" of Egypt.

Thus viewed, the account of the meeting between Jesus and Nicodemus, including their conversation, may be seen as describing by allegory the normal, materialistic or objective limitations of the human mind; the super-normal, Christlike, spiritual intelligence of man (Jesus and his mystical teaching); and the means whereby the former may become responsive to the latter through the elevation of the serpent power. Unless so read, the verses under consideration are so difficult to comprehend that a full grasp of their import is virtually impossible.

> John 3:15. That whosoever believeth in him should not perish, but have eternal life.

The elevation of the Son of Man to which Jesus refers may be read as a prophecy of the Crucifixion or even of the ultimate Ascension. The latter would seem to be more appropriate in that an elevation of consciousness is implied. The affirmation by Jesus that eternal life would be possessed may also refer to the direct experience of the immortal Self of man, the spiritual soul which, in contradistinction to the body, does not die.

> John 3:16.   For God so loved the world, that he gave his only begotten Son, that whosoever believeth in him should not perish, but have everlasting life.

The term *God* would seem here to call for special consideration. It may refer to the "living God" within every man,[9] the Dweller-in-the-Innermost, the divine spark, the Monad. From here the power of initiation becomes manifest, bestowing upon the initiated one knowledge of his own eternal nature and that in his true Self he can never die. Admittedly, such reading differs greatly from that of traditional and orthodox Christian theology with its accent upon an external Deity, a visibly appearing Son, and a soul-saving ministry.

God as used here may also signify those dimensions within the cosmos over which God is presumed to preside. This includes the totality of stars, nebulae, galaxies and all that they contain, as well as a Deity more especially interested in the humanity of the planet earth. A worshipping humanity would permissibly use the term *God* to refer to a divine creative Power, an indwelling and all-sustaining divine life, and a directing, divine Intelligence. Such a concept of God is threefold in the nature of its activity, yet one in its actuality, which is both transcendent beyond and immanent within the cosmos as a whole. To this definition would doubtless be added the concept of a timeless, limitless and inexhaustible Source of all that ever was, now is, and ever will exist. Such a cosmic Deity would include within its all-embracing compassion the humanity of a single planet, particularly of the earth. With this concept of deity, the emanation of an expression on earth of the divine, compassionate love for the human race is conceivable. This partly expresses the view of Christian orthodox theology which is based upon these verses.

Yet, literally, these statements are almost without meaning. Since man as a manifestation of pure spitit, or God, and made in his image, is imperishable by his very nature, the immense sacrifice implied in a literal reading is quite unnecessary. Rather, the verse may be read as descriptive of the manifestation of the Christ nature in man with bodily or mortal consciousness. This achieved, the illumined one gains the certainty that as a spiritual being he will never die. Death may take the body in its ice-cold grasp, but neither death itself nor the fear of death is ever again possible to one who has attained to the Christ consciousness. The whole episode may be read as an allegorical description of the quickened evolution of a man or woman, either in the normal course or by finding the Master and being guided by him to the portals of a temple of the Mysteries to receive initiation. This confers direct experience of both the meaning of death and the immortality of the spiritual Self of man. Nicodemus may have been such an illumined one.

> John 3:17.   For God sent not his Son into the world to condemn the world; but that the world through him might be saved.

18. He that believeth on him is not condemned: but he that believeth not is condemned already, because he hath not believed in the name of the only begotten Son of God

19. And this is the condemnation, that light is come into the world, and men loved darkness rather than light, because their deeds were evil.

20. For every one that doeth evil hateth the light, neither cometh to the light, lest his deeds should be reproved.

21. But he that doeth truth cometh to the light, that his deeds may be made manifest, that they are wrought in God.

As stated by St. John in these verses, Jesus's birth, mission, and death supposedly had the single motive that through him humanity might be saved. The meaning of the words *saved* and *condemnation,* as well as the presumed divine intention, need to be considered.

Saved implies the existence and threat of a danger, in this case presumably condemnation of the souls of mankind. Literally read, the scriptures might be construed to mean souls are condemned for unbelief.

With all reverence, I submit that the concept of condemnation does not agree with the Deity's decision to "make man in our own image" "to be immortal, to be an image of his own eternity created he him."[10] If these scriptural utterances are accepted literally, then the human race is freed from all possibility of misconduct. Furthermore, spiritual death and eternal damnation cannot exist for man, since he is immortal and eternal by his very nature.

This apparent though unavoidable dilemma is solved if the divine intention and action thus described are accepted as mystical birth of divine power, wisdom, compassion and intelligence inherent in the nature of mankind. This view, moreover, harmonizes with the utterances of St. Paul, "Christ in you, the hope of glory," and "Work out your own salvation with fear and trembling. For it is God that worketh in you."[11] Sages, seers and prophets throughout the ages have borne testimony that their illuminations were due to realizations of the existence *within themselves* of the divine presence. In the Hindu Scripture, Yddisthira proclaimed, "Thou art not Shri Krishna. Thou art the Inner Ruler Immortal seated in the hearts of all beings."[12] Thus, the question whether the God who is said to have taken the saving action is a cosmic Being or the more personal Deity concerned with humanity on the planet earth loses its significance, since a divine power indwelling throughout all nature and therefore in the souls of men is implied.

The word *condemnation* requires interpretation in this light; for the sense of the word, as Jesus is presumed to have used it, implies, not condemnation by God for unbelief, but rather, it is suggested, for an unillumined state, a purely materialistic outlook and conduct based thereupon. Condemnation in this sense might be inferred from the scriptural words "light is come into the world, and men love darkness rather than light, because their deeds were evil."

The word which in these verses is translated as *belief* is not to be understood as credence affirmed from blind faith; for such belief, while perhaps considered worthy ecclesiastically, can have little or no power to produce the interior illumination and its effects upon conduct to which Jesus apparently refers. Thus, it is to be presumed that Jesus means a belief founded upon personal, direct spiritual experience. This is to be attained by elevation and penetration of the mind into those realms of human consciousness where the Christ nature or "Son of God" is established in man. The whole passage, thus viewed, becomes a description of the effects of such direct knowledge resulting from mystical illumination to the point at which the "Word which was made flesh" becomes directly known.[13] The result is a veritable transfiguration, both of the mind and of the conduct of life. In such a case the individual can in no sense come under condemnation, whether by God or by man. Ultimately, as the twenty-first verse indicates, deeds rather than words, conduct rather than affirmed belief, constitute the final test of an individual's worthiness.

> John 3:22.   After these things came Jesus and his disciples into the land of Judea; and there he tarried with them, and baptized.
>
> 23.   And John also was baptizing in Aenon near to Salim, because there was much water there: and they came, and were baptized.
>
> 24.   For John was not yet cast into prison.

The twenty-fourth verse may perhaps be regarded as of symbolical interest. If, as heretofore suggested, prison in the symbolical language is descriptive of a mental state of a closed and unillumined mind, then John at this time in his career was in an illumined state. This conclusion is supported by John's words as given up to the end of this chapter.

Whether or not his later imprisonment and decapitation were due to a fall from grace, as could appear to be most unlikely for one of his prophetic seership and spiritual insight, these events are of symbolic significance to inhibit the free flow of intuitively perceived ideas. The head as symbol of this state of mind is removed, and the egotistic, argumentative materialism of a preceding period is replaced by direct, intuitive perception.

. . . .

> John 3:28.   Ye yourselves bear me witness, that said, I am not the Christ, but that I am sent before him.

. . . . . .

> John 3:34.   For he whom God hath sent speaketh the words of God; for God giveth not the Spirit by measure unto him.
>
> 35.   The Father loveth the Son, and hath given all things into his hand.

These verses, as the remainder of this chapter, largely consists of a repetition of the affirmation of John the Baptist concerning himself as forerunner and Jesus as the Messiah who had come. With the utmost humility born of spiritual vision, John presents himself as a lowly human being with the mission to prepare the way of the Lord. In the veritable presence of Jesus, John proclaimed him to be the Son of God.

John 3:36.   He that believeth on the Son hath everlasting life: and he that believeth not the son shall not see life; but the wrath of God abideth on him.

The closing words of the address by John to his disciples and the people around him indicate two conditions of the human intellect, the worldly and the spiritual. This concept is extended to include the realization of the immortal nature of the divine Self in man; for this is referred to by John as "the Son (who) hath everlasting life."

John 4:1.   When therefore the Lord knew how the Pharisees had heard that Jesus made and baptized more disciples than John,

This verse, which consists of the first part of a sentence, refers to the dual nature or presence of Jesus; for a distinction is made between the Lord and Jesus. If this is intentional, as must be assumed, then St. John again affirms Jesus to be a human vehicle and representative for the Supreme Deity or Lord. Furthermore, the overshadowing divine spirit is shown to be in decisive command, since in the third verse, which completes the sentence, Jesus thereupon left the district because of the opposition of the Pharisees and went to Galilee, signifying universal consciousness.

John 4:2.   (Though Jesus himself baptized not, but his disciples,)

One is here reminded of the Pentecostal transmission of power by Jesus to his disciples and his promise that whatsoever they seek to do in his name shall be done.[14] Apparently, Jesus himself did not perform the outward, baptismal ceremony but left this to his disciples who doubtless baptized in his name.

John 4:3.   He left Judea, and departed again into Galilee.
     4.   And he must needs go through Samaria.

While geography and actual places visited have their significance, especially as regards the literal reading of the Gospels, Palestine becomes the whole world for those who perceive the symbolical meaning of the various locations. Thus, Jesus passes from Judea, where some questioning and even opposition concerning his activities had arisen, and went to Galilee.

Judea thus represents a measure of dividedness and even of conflict in the mind of an initiate while passing through the final states of progress to perfection. To avoid distraction from the central purpose of his last human incarnation, a withdrawal is made to Galilee where peace reigns. These and all other places visited represent states of consciousness through which every initiate passes, the nature of which is indicated by the attitudes of the people in those localities.

John 4:5.   Then cometh he to a city of Samaria, which is called Sychar, near to the parcel of ground that Jacob gave to his son Joseph.
     6.   Now Jacob's well was there. Jesus therefore, being wearied with his journey, sat thus on the well: and it was about the sixth hour.

Sychar thus becomes a symbol from topography for a state of consciousness which includes the strain inseparable from forcing and quickening the pace of evolutionary unfoldment. Opportunity to relieve that strain by contemplation of the Ageless Wisdom is symbolized by the water in a well. This refreshment of the soul is made available by the forerunners, sages, who preceded those now treading the path. These are personified by Jacob and his son Joseph, initiates of earlier days.

The number seven symbolizes the completion of a cycle or of one round in the spiral ascent of the soul toward perfection. The number six may be read as referring to a preceding phase, near to final fulfillment, symbolized by the Ascension of Jesus. The statement is therefore apt that Jesus rested at the well at Sychar at the sixth hour; for only some three years passed before his triumphant Ascension to the right hand of God, in its mystical meaning of both self-deliverance from separateness and complete absorption in the essential life of the univers.

John 4:7.　　There cometh a woman of Samaria to draw water: Jesus saith unto her, Give me to drink.

As was later made plain by Jesus himself, water is used as a symbol for the ever available and inexhaustible supply of the Wisdom of the ages, the water of truth.

John 4:8.　　(For his disciples were gone away unto the city to buy meat.)

This verse, inserted into the narrative parenthetically, may indicate either that a literal, historical reading of the following verses is intended, or, more mystically, that a state of aloneness is essential to self-refreshment by drinking of the "waters of life." Thus, Jesus was alone at the well where he met the woman of Samaria.

John 4:9.　　Then saith the woman of Samaria unto him, How is it that thou, being a Jew, askest drink of me, which am a woman of Samaria? for the Jews have no dealings with the Samaritans.

The question asked by the woman shows that Jesus looked like a Jew. This provides one of the rare clues, perhaps the only one, to his appearance. Evidently, physically, he was a typical young Hebrew man of those times.

The woman of Samaria was as one of almost another race inhabiting the same country. The two peoples evidently had neither commercial nor domestic association in those days. Yet to her astonishment Jesus disregarded this situation and immediately asked her for a drink, thus overriding any divisions between the two groups.

John 4:10.　　Jesus answered and said unto her, If thou knewest the gift of God, and who it is that saith to thee, Give me to drink; thou wouldest have asked of him, and he would have given thee living water.

From this verse onwards, the episode changes from the possibly historical to the definitely mystical. *Living water* evidently refers to an interior, spiritual element which can quench the thirst for knowledge, wisdom and truth. Jesus also refers to himself as no ordinary mortal man of the Hebrew race but as a hierophant, able to dispense these spiritual gifts or living water.

> John 4:11.   The woman saith unto him, Sir, thou hast nothing to draw with, and the well is deep: from whence then hast thou that living water?

As in the case of Nicodemus, one participant in the conversation represents a person normally accustomed to using only the worldly mind and the bodily senses. Failing to recognize the real presence before her, especially at first, she observed the absence of a bucket and a rope. Gradually, as the later verses show, the inner eye of the Samaritan woman begins to be open, and eventually she realizes that she is in the presence of a prophet.

This incident also may describe the attainment of self-illumination by an aspirant (the woman was seeking water) or the steps of initiation, during which the neophyte is led by the hierophant into the experience of his own divine nature (the well) and of the inexhaustible measure of its spiritual life-force (water).

> John 4:12.   Art thou greater than our father Jacob, which gave us the well, and drank thereof himself, and his children, and his cattle?

The tendencies and limitations of the objective mentality, the reasoning mind, continue to obstruct or at least defer entry into the mystic state, and so the woman asks of Jesus the very natural but purely physical questions concerning both himself and the well.

> John 4:13.   Jesus answered and said unto her, Whosoever drinketh of this water shall thirst again:
>
> 14.   But whosoever drinketh of the water that I shall give him shall never thirst; but the water that I shall give him shall be in him a well of water springing up into everlasting life.

Jesus persists, and gradually the divine vision is open within the questing mind. The use of water, used as a symbol in this incident, shifts its normal symbolic meanings—ordinary space in the macrocosm and the human emotions in the microcosm. Here, however, the term *living water* implies truth perceived by supramental and intuitional means. The affirmation is therefore completely correct that whosoever drinks of ordinary water is most certainly self-condemned to recurring and continual thirst; for emotion, save in its very loftiest forms can never either satisfy or even satiate except temporarily, as it is inevitably followed by further thirst.

Living water, on the other hand, fulfills the highest aspirations of the heart and mind of the aspirant; for as purest spiritual wisdom, it bestows unalterable truths, eternal verities and also the faculty for comprehending these. Since these derive from the principle of spiritual wisdom or Christ nature in man, the Savior speaks truly, if symbolically, to the woman of Samaria, who personifies the mortal man in search of truth.

Aptly, Jesus and the woman meet at a well, for a well is both a container of water and a source from which it may be drawn. Moreover, this particular well possessed special powers, since it had been associated with a patriarch and sage of former times. This signifies the living waters of the ageless

Wisdom discovered and delivered to mankind by sages of old. Thus viewed, the incident describes an interior process taking place deep within a human being already on the threshold of spiritual awakening. The woman of Samaria personifies all those aspirants to light and truth throughout the ages who have "thirsted" and come to a well in order to assuage their thirst.

Unfailingly according to time-honored custom, when an aspirant is ready, a teacher appears and gives instruction concerning the pathway to interior illumination, the living waters.

> John 4:15. The woman saith unto him, Sir, give me this water, that I thirst not, neither come hither to draw.

The aspirant responds and realizes that such thirst cannot be quenched at a well and that external wells need be sought no more. In the light of the Teacher's presence she observes and acknowledges that truth is within.

> John 4:16. Jesus saith unto her, Go, call thy husband, and come hither.
> 17. The woman answered and said, I have no husband. Jesus said unto her, Thou hast well said, I have no husband:
> 18. For thou hast had five husbands; and he whom thou now hast is not thy husband: in that saidst thou truly.
> 19. The woman saith unto him, Sir, I perceive that thou art a prophet.

Jesus displayed very private knowledge concerning the woman of Samaria which normally he could not possibly have known, for he disclosed to her the facts of her domestic and married life. This revelation of supernormal powers of perception fulfilled its purpose of winning attention and opening the intuition; for thereafter the woman recognized him as a prophet and not only listened to him with opened mind, but also drew many others unto him to receive his wisdom. The incident had the effect of bringing very large numbers of people to listen to Jesus and so enabled him at that time to fulfill his mission.

The husbands might be regarded as personifications of monadic potencies expressed as will, wisdom, intelligence, emotion, and physical awareness and action. However, perhaps in this case they may be better regarded as real human beings who had played their parts in the life of the woman of Samaria, as Jesus occultly discerned.

Blending of the matter-of-fact with the miraculous, as in this story, gives ground for a symbolic interpretation of both the episode as a whole and of the various speeches and actions of the participants. Whether the woman had or had not been married five times or more is of less importance than the teaching concerning the living waters; the illumination bestowed upon the woman so that she knew Jesus to be the Messiah; and the responsiveness of the people of Samaria to his teaching. As he himself later said, this last provided further opportunities to fulfill his divine mission received from his Father which is in heaven. Furthermore, it is during this incident that Jesus admitted and even proclaimed that he was the Messiah whose appearance the earlier prophets had foretold.

John 4:20.   Our fathers worshipped in this mountain; and ye say, that in Jerusalem is the place where men ought to worship.

21.   Jesus saith unto her, Woman, believe me, the hour cometh, when ye shall neither in this mountain, nor yet at Jerusalem, worship the Father.

In these verses Jesus lifts the procedures of worship beyond the limitations of either place or time. The attainment of spiritual illumination and the adoration or worship of its divine Source are independent of earthly altitude or any of the cities of the world, however holy.

John 4:22.   Ye worship ye know not what: we know what we worship: for salvation is of the Jews.

23.   But the hour cometh, and now is, when the true worshipers shall worship the Father in spirit and in truth: for the Father seeketh such to worship him.

24.   God is a Spirit: and they that worship him must worship him in spirit and in truth.

The passage reveals in a wonderful utterance that the Father in Heaven is less to be regarded as an external Deity than a spiritual Presence within the universe and every man. Jesus differentiates between a personal and perhaps anthropomorphic deity and the omnipresent Spirit-Power ideally to be worshiped. Adoring, the worshiper may draw near to and even discover within himself that which he designates by affirming that "God is a Spirit." It is there in the interior nature of things that the divine is to be discovered, worshiped and revealed.

All religion, all religious practices and ideas are thus transformed into the pursuit and the attainment of the mystic union between the spirit of man and the Spirit which is God. By these words the gospel story, and more especially the fourth Gospel, repeats and so reveals the Ageless Wisdom concerning the divine, parental Source of all that exists, Universal Spirit. This has ever been regarded and taught by mystics as the essential, though formless and illusive, truth concerning the nature of the divine.

John 4:25.   The woman saith unto him, I know that Messias cometh, which is called Christ: when he is come, he will tell us all things.

26.   Jesus saith unto her, I that speak unto thee am he.

These two verses reveal more interior, spiritual experience than its supposed historical and external confirmation. Jesus declaring himself to be the Messiah may be historically read, but the woman's illumination is mystical. Also use of the term *Christ* as a name throws some doubt upon the historicity of the passage and so supports a mystical reading. The term *Christ* or *Christos*—derived from the mystery tradition—rather than being a name, describes a condition, "the anointed" or consecrated, which would probably not be known by an apparently humble housewife of Samaria.

The manifestation of the Messiah and the elevation of the Hebrew peoples above the rest of humanity according to ancient prophecy contrasts sharply with the ignominious death of Jesus after three and a half years of ministry. It also is in contrast with the condition and place of the Jews among their fellowmen ever since his coming. The difficulty is largely overcome if the Messianic Era to come implies a state of spiritual elevation and intellectual illumination, to be achieved by all mankind in the course of the evolution of the human race. This, moreover, is not wholly limited to some future time, but is continually foreshadowed by individuals who enter into the mystic state ahead of the race and receive a revelation or visitation of the divine. The woman of Samaria, to whom Jesus reveals himself, personifies both contemporary mystics and an illumined humanity of future ages.

Jesus in his turn portrays the Source of the divine revelation within mankind, the spiritual Self, and the ancient well with its continuing supply of water stands for both a state of consciousness and a temple of the Mysteries not made with hands.

We now turn to the Gospel according to St. Matthew to continue the account of Jesus' mission.

> Matt. 4:12. Now when Jesus had heard that John was cast into prison, he departed into Galilee;
>
> 13. And leaving Nazareth, he came and dwelt in Capernaum, which is upon the sea coast, in the borders of Zabulon and Nephthalim:
>
> 14. That it might be fulfilled which was spoken by Esais the prophet, saying,
>
> 15. The land of Zabulon, and the land of Nephthalim, by the way of the sea, beyond Jordan, Galilee of the Gentiles;
>
> 16. The people which sat in darkness saw great light; and to them which sat in the region and shadow of death light is sprung up.
>
> 17. From that time Jesus began to preach, and to say, Repent: for the kingdom of heaven is at hand.

John the Baptist had been imprisoned, and thereupon Jesus repeats part of John's message, supposedly in fulfillment of certain prophetic passages in the Book of Isaiah.[15] John, as we have seen, represents the disciplinary and spiritualizing influence of the inner Self upon the outer man. His ministry describes the condition of the human soul which naturally responds to the call to live the higher, purer mode of life in order that the divine may become manifest and empower the outer man.

Humanity has not, however, reached this stage, and this applies particularly to such wielders of power as Herod. These men "imprison" the John the Baptist within themselves; they become deaf to the voice of the redemptive power within and continue to submit to the allurements of a purely worldly life. If the voice of conscience is consistently unheeded, the mind tends to become deaf to its call, until eventually the call becomes so insistent that it can be ignored no longer and at last breaks through the unresponsiveness of the mind. Thus Jesus continues the interrupted preparatory mission of John the Baptist, in his turn preaching "Repent: for the kingdom of heaven is at hand."

> Matt. 4:18.   And Jesus, walking by the sea of Galilee, saw two breth-
> ren, Simon called Peter, and Andrew his brother, casting
> a net into the sea: for they were fishers.
>
> 19.   And he saith unto them, Follow me, and I will make you
> fishers of men.

The presence of the Son of God on earth as the chief actor in this episode, his choice of two people to be admitted to the most sacred of relationships, their instant response, all suggest something more than a purely natural meeting and wordly occupation. In a mystical interpretation Peter and Andrew, the first disciples, represent the redeeming principle within man, that quality which more readily responds to a call from the inner heights. Their occupation as fishermen gives a clue to the nature of that quality, for fish is a symbol for divine, Christlike love, tenderness, compassion and the desire to remove pain. To catch fish implies that these attributes are already developed and are finding expression in those qualified for discipleship. Ministration arising from compassion and a sense of responsibility for the welfare of others is one of the highest attributes of man. The divine spirit personified by Jesus reaches and "calls" the outer man through these qualities. Aptly, therefore, the two disciples, Peter and Andrew, are described as fishermen.

All great Masters who have visited mankind, including Jesus, have followed this practice of teaching publicly to the multitude and privately to carefully selected students. It may be presumed, however, that his disciples numbered more than twelve, this number doubtless being chosen in accordance with the technique and method of the symbolic language; for the number twelve represents wholeness, totality and the full unfoldment in man of all the twelve zodiacal qualities.[16] Discipleship with an adept Master is designed by him to hasten the attainment of this twelvefold perfection.

> Matt. 4:20.   And they straightway left their nets, and followed him.

If the foregoing mystical interpretation of this incident is accepted, then the cessation of gainful employment which had enabled them to provide for themselves and their dependents is understandable. The preceding verse indicates that Peter and Andrew, in their turn, were to become increasingly wise and teachers of wisdom, symbolically "fishers of men." Their action of forsaking their nets thus indicates a definite and deliberate accentuation of spiritual over material values in the conduct of their lives. This term may also be interpreted as referring to the duty of the disciple heedfully to notice others in whom the conditions for discipleship exist, associate with these and, when suitable, present them to the Master. Symbolically, this procedure would constitute "fishing for" and "catching" those ready to enter in at the strait gate.

Forsaking their former way of life was instantaneous, indicating that they had already reached a stage of development and attained to a degree of enlightenment that made their full response interiorly and externally obvious, inevitable and therefore instantaneous; for a life of discipleship lived in the presence of the teacher is for such men and women the most desirable of all modes of living—indeed the only one.[17]

Degrees of development are indicated in the various responses to Jesus and his mission made by those who came into contact with him. The most highly developed followed and served him immediately and unquestioningly. Others listened wonderingly,[18] while some found in him an enemy to their established power and, in consequence, persecuted him. Still others scoffed and jeered at his sufferings and his apparent inability to deliver himself from them.

> Matt. 4:21. And going on from thence, he saw other two brethren, James the son of Zebedee, and John his brother, in a ship with Zebedee their father, mending their nets; and he called them.
>
> 22. And they immediately left the ship and their father, and followed him.

The net is usually interpreted as a symbol of the formal mind of man with its dual capacity for receiving wisdom (catching fish) and of collecting objective facts (catching and holding fish). It also signifies possessiveness, acquisitiveness and hoarding, arising from an accentuated sense of separated individuality. Allegorically, both this habit and that of insistent dependence upon concrete thought alone must be outgrown by those who would become disciples; for comprehension of the principles, processes, and laws underlying the manifestation of the divine in nature and in man is dependent upon a function of the abstract intellect. Self-emancipation from the restrictions of purely conceptual thinking and consequent universalization of consciousness are implied by the immediate response of the first four disciples.[19]

The ship is the symbol of the means of conveyance or action used by consciousness, represented by passengers and crew.[20] a vessel, then, is the body or vehicle, spiritual, intellectual or physical, or all of these. However useful, a ship is inevitably restrictive, since it encloses and locates its passengers in time and space. Therefore, to enter a ship is somewhat like being born into a body. Voluntarily to leave a ship, as the disciples did, indicates outgrowing restrictions and attainment of a certain freedom, in this case particularly of mental outlook or reduction to a minimum of the delusion of self-separateness. This freedom is one of the qualities which mark the man or woman who is ready for discipleship.

The father and his ship may represent the valuable conditions of being embodied and of possessing a home and security; but they also connote the restrictions upon thought and action that a habitual environment can impose. The disciple is one who is able to override the limitations of the past, of tradition, and of mental and physical habits. James and John, the sons of Zebedee, had clearly reached this evolutionary condition and, in consequence, on hearing the call of the Master, "they immediately left the ship and their father, and followed him."

A disciple is thus a person who is able to enter a new world of thought, to cross established frontiers and, while not being unscientific, think beyond the limitations of accepted and apparently proven facts into higher dimensional conditions of awareness. A particular phenomenon is for him no longer an isolated fact but an expression of a universal Idea. Principles concern him far more than fact and phenomena, and he has developed the power to perceive and comprehend fundamental laws. When therefore a superhuman being, a Master, approaches and calls him, he responds at once.

Thus in these remarkable verses, phases of human evolution, qualities in human beings, the interior, mystical life of devotees, and the coming into power of the interior, redemptive principle are all described by means of allegory and symbol.

> Matt. 4:23.   And Jesus went about all Galilee, teaching in their synagogues, and preaching the gospel of the kingdom, and healing all manner of sickness and all manner of disease among the people.

While the historical personage, the overshadowed and illumined Jesus, actually carried out his wonderful mission of moving among, teaching and healing the people, an enlightening description of a psychological development in man may also be discerned. Mystically interpreted, when the center of self-awareness has become established in the higher prophetic intellect and is open to power and wisdom from still higher levels (is baptized), then the mortal man becomes illumined, empowered, unified and "healed." The Christ nature within man harmonizes and, when necessary, heals the mortal human being, represented in this verse by the people. All of these states within an individual are influenced by the divine spirit within, the Christ Indwelling; for this principle of man passes through the same experiences as did Jesus of the Gospels. Metaphysically, the unfolding Monad of man is born, grows up, is baptized, resists temptation, and goes on to redeem the outer man. Discordances are then harmonized and weaknesses replaced by powers. Thus in this mystical sense, the healing mission of the Redeemer within is fulfilled.

Though this harmonizing, coordinating potency lies within all men, the evolution of mankind has not yet entered the phase in which the Christ nature is sufficiently developed to assume power and predominance over the purely mortal man. Some advanced people have, however, entered upon this experience ahead of the race, while a number—the "just men made perfect"[21]—have already reached the goal of evolution for earth's humanity. In the main then, there are three classes of human beings: those whose development has proceeded at the normal rate, those who are advanced, and others who have already reached perfection. Variations exist within the first two of these categories and are represented in inspired allegories by the masses of the population and heroes and disciples, respectively. The central figure in such allegories usually personifies the Adept.

> Matt. 4:24.   And his fame went throughout all Syria: and they brought unto him all sick people that were taken with divers diseases and torments, and those which were possessed with devils, and those which were lunatic, and those that had the palsy; and he healed them.

Each of these named sicknesses has its correspondence in a particular psychological disorder. To be possessed of a devil refers to the dominance in man of the material, animalistic and irrational qualities resulting from the excessive expression and indulgence of certain human desires and passions. Actual obsession by evil influences and beings, however, is not discounted. External and interior forms may be combined in one person and may produce veritable torment and even satanic attributes. Obsession by a fixed idea can render a person insane, either completely or where that idea and its expression are concerned. Psychological palsy, in its turn, might be described as a condition in which the control and direction of the body and mind are unstable, extremely variable in degree and, on occasion, absent.

While normal evolutionary progress will remove these disabilities, they can be corrected by the action of an awakened divine power, wisdom, and intelligence within the sufferer. This purifying and healing power does not become available, however, until an advanced phase of evolution is entered. Indeed, all men's difficulties, whether external or interior, are natural to him in his present condition and will so remain until he outgrows them. This process may be hastened and a man can deliver himself from evil by quickening his evolutionary progress with the aid of those who have already advanced to a further stage. This is the life of discipleship, the so-called inner life, the Way of the Cross. To call and train disciples is to bring human attributes under the influence of the divine in man, and thereby to displace ignorance by wisdom and to replace discord by accord, waywardness by control, sensuality by purity, and pride by humility.

> Matt. 4:25.   And there followed him great multitudes of people from Galilee, and from Decapolis, and from Jerusalem, and from Judea, and from beyond Jordan.

Every true reformer (and even some who perhaps are not so true) enjoys periods of public acclaim, as did Jesus at this wonderful time of his life. The enemies of reform, those who are entrenched in revenue-producing positions, are not yet aroused to a sense of danger or to jealousy accompanied by fear of the loss of prestige and power. Supporters acclaim the Christ, and apparently enemies still sleep.

Jesus, having received the descent of the Holy Spirit, was shining with its radiance, displaying complete dominance over worldly desires and the material element in human nature. He had begun to give expression to the great powers with which he had been endowed. In all this he was a perfect example of an initiate of the Greater Mysteries. The Godhead had become active within him; a manifestation of divine power for the sake of humanity was occurring. Before him was the world of men, ignorant, either because they had not yet discovered the truth or because they were deliberately maintained in that state by those in authority. Those in search of wisdom and those sick in mind or in body (or both) were drawn toward him from near and far, and he enlightened and healed them. The trials of strength had not yet begun. The great world tragedy of a sublime teacher physically to be lost to the world was still far away. The shadow of the Cross had not yet fallen upon Jesus the Christ, the anointed One.

REFERENCES AND NOTES

1. See Hodson, *Hidden Wisdom,* Vol. 1, P. 109. for further interpretation of the symbolism of mountains, numbers, bread and fish.
2. See Hodson, *Hidden Wisdom,* Vol. 1, Ch. 3.
3. Matt. 11:14.
4. Luke 18:17.
5. John 1:33.
6. Kundalini.
7. Num. 21:9.
8. Exod. 7:10.
9. 2 Cor. 6:16.
10. Gen. 1:26; Wisd. of Sol. 2:23.
11. Phil. 2:12-13.
12. *Bhagavad Gita.*
13. John 1:14.
14. John 16:23, 24, 26.
15. Isa. 9:1, 2.
16. Human characteristics represented by the signs of the zodiac.
17. Cf. *Upanishad,* "There is no other path at all to go."
18. E.g. Matt. 19:16-23, the rich young ruler.
19. Cf. Matt. 14:47-8.
20. See Hodson, *Hidden Wisdom,* Vol. 1. p. 120.
21. Heb. 12:23.

PART FIVE

THE SERMON ON THE MOUNT

Chapter Nine

The Beatitudes are statements of age-old aphorisms that constitute the heart of the teachings given by every true spiritual Master to every disciple. Progress upon the path of swift attainment, the way of holiness, or the narrow way, depends upon both the realization and the application of the lofty ideals they present. St. Matthew describes the circumstances that led to their affirmation by Jesus.

> Matt. 5:1. And seeing the multitudes, he went up into a mountain: and when he was set, his disciples came unto him:

After prolonged ministration to the multitudes, self-renewal apparently became necessary. The mount of the Beatitudes, rising from the western shores of the Sea of Galilee, has for a long time been designated as the elevation from which Jesus preached. However, the mount also signifies that he withdrew into his own higher consciousness, presumably contemplated the divine within himself and the universe,[1] drew near to himself the members of the inner circle of his friends, and shared with them aphorisms from the Ageless Wisdom which he had made his own, as his teachings clearly demonstrate.

The episode may also be regarded as an allegory descriptive of the process of spiritual alchemy, of the purification, refinement and transmutation of the whole mortal nature of man, "lead," into the fine inward "gold" of unsullied spirituality. Selfish desire is finally extirpated, self-existence is transcended, and worldly power is known to be a worthless objective—indeed a hindrance to spiritual self-empowerment. The age-old qualities of discriminative wisdom, detachment, dispassion, personal disinterestedness or even indifference, combined with a sublime and selfless love for all that breathes, all those who hope and suffer—these become living powers in the life of the savior and servant of humanity, the Adept-to-be.

Probably not the whole of the great sermon has been passed on to us, but fortunately its complete message is available both in those scriptures that preserve the teaching of other illumined beings and in their modes of life.[2] Jesus exemplified the spirit of the Sermon on the Mount throughout his life and notably in Gethsemane, when, in uttermost self-surrender, he said, "not my will but Thine be done."[3] This, surely, was the peak of selflessness, the summit of that "mount" from which, mystically, the great sermon was preached.

Matt. 5:2. And he opened his mouth, and taught them, saying,

3. Blessed are the poor in spirit: for their's is the kingdom of heaven.

These remarkable aphorisms may be regarded as descriptive of the way to full illumination and the attitude toward life of those who have followed it to its end. The word *blessed* indicates an interior state of consciousness attained as a result of the deliberate self-denudation of self. This is achieved either as a result of natural development or brought about by the practice of the science of yoga,[4] particularly the attainment of complete dispassion born of realized unity with the spirit-essence of the universe. It does not, therefore, solely imply the receipt of blessings from above or without, but also the elevated state of blessedness, immortality or liberation from earthly restrictions, the condition of those who have become fully illumined and perfect, and so immortal.

The words *poor in spirit* refer to the complete absence of either egoism or pride, and to the perfectly natural humility and modesty with which these have been replaced. Indeed, the sense of existing as a separate being has been entirely transcended, leaving only realization of oneness with universal Life. An exaggerated sense of self-existence as a named individuality which appears to give riches, inevitably prevents the attainment of universalized consciousness. But here the normal human attributes, which arise from belief in a separate self, no longer exist.

The second phrase indicates the result of this emergence from the chrysalis of egoism. Complete freedom within universal existence is attained, like the butterfly which is free in the air—the totality and the infinity of being. For man the chrysalis-state, with its temporary advantages as well as its limitations has been lost, but these are replaced by the larger, if impersonally enjoyed, freedom of a higher state of existence. In this verse this state of consciousness is described as the kingdom of heaven.

Matt. 5:4. Blessed are they that mourn: for they shall be comforted.

The affirmations of which the Sermon on the Mount consists give assurance that surrender of self brings not loss but gain from a higher point of view. This same truth shines through the pages of the great philosophic and religious literature of ancient peoples and, as stated, is particularly noticeable in that of Hinduism, Buddhism and Taoism. While aspirants to spiritual and occult wisdom have discovered this truth, the world at large is far from having done so in the present phase of human evolution, for the mind, despite its magnificent intellectual capacities, displays also the qualities of acquisitiveness, egoism and pride (*ahamkara*).[5] A selfless and nonpossessive attitude is being perpetually denied by nations and individuals, thus bringing about the root cause of the evils that trouble mankind. The application of the Sermon on the Mount to worldly and, equally, to personal affairs, is the one solution to the critical problems now confronting mankind.

While those who are bereaved (that mourn) suffer, true selflessness brings with it the knowledge that departed loved ones still live, still love, and still share the secrets of heart and mind. Death is no mystery to those who have reached the evolutionary phase described in these verses; for they have solved it by direct experience of the immortality of their own spiritual Self as well as that of all men. They are supported, therefore, less by external ministration than by interior knowledge.

Matt. 5:5.   Blessed are the meek: for they shall inherit the earth.

Translations of such aphorisms into English from any ancient language must almost inevitably be imperfect and incomplete and can therefore be misleading. Here meekness in no sense implies weakness. Rather it refers to an attitude toward life from which self-assertiveness is wholly absent. Those who are truly illumined never experience the slightest need to assert themselves. They know that only the Supreme Self, the one Self of the universe, exists, the human sense of personal selfhood being an illusion which they have transcended. The resultant approach to living and to association with others is neither hypocritically meek nor unnaturally humble and modest. Rather is it completely free from any demands, even any wishes for responses that would gratify pride or the purse. Strange and contradictory though the fact may appear, the result is the attainment of an inner royalty and a realization of interior abundance perpetualy available to meet all needs, spiritual, mental and even at times material.

Matt. 5:6.   Blessed are they which do hunger and thirst after right-eousness: for they shall be filled.

As one reads this peerless presentation of the great aphorisms and meditates upon them, one may be led back in thought to those private and exceedingly intimate gatherings in which Jesus instructed his chosen disciples in the way of the spiritual life. Such privacy is not arranged by spiritual Teachers in order to deprive the public of the divine Wisdom, but only to provide conditions under which advanced teaching may be given to a small group of chosen disciples whom the Master doubtless sees are at least on the threshold of the desired state of consciousness, and near the phase of evolution at which the ideals would become possible and practicable. This highly specialized teaching could not usefully be given by Jesus to all of the people who gathered round him. Misunderstood, misinterpreted and faultily applied by unintuitive people, the instruction could seem to imply absence of all effort, surrender to passivity, and even premature advice to forsake the world. This could only lead to disaster, frustration, sorrow and poverty. Pseudo - holy men escaping from the work of the world become drones, a drain on the community and a hindrance to their own evolution.

The text may not seem wholly worthy either of the sublime ideas or of their deliverance to the disciples unless one realizes the language is purposely cryptic, mystifying to the spiritually uninstructed, but fully comprehensible to disciples. To inherit the earth, for example, means to be master of matter, material existence, and so of one's own physical body. At a particular phase of occult and spiritual development, physical matter ceases to be a resistant opponent of the will of the neophyte. He has conquered it, wrested its secrets, and penetrated to its core which is cosmic power. Thus freed from the limitations of matter, he metaphorically inherits the earth with all its possibilities and powers.

The great discovery is by no means easy. With his whole being, heart, mind and spirit, the successful aspirant seeks the knowledge which is power. He aspires with an intense ardor; he seeks with uttermost determination; he knocks with relentless will, inwardly moved to know truth and then to apply that knowledge to perfection of living. In this sense he hungers and thirsts after righteousness, meaning pure wisdom and its perfect application to daily living. This verse assures all aspirants that this righteousness is attainable in fullest measure. Indeed, the whole sermon partly describes the attitude of mind essential to such an attainment. This attitude arises naturally from the transcendence of the idea of self and separateness. The disciples were being trained, as are all disciples, in the attainment of the consciousness of All-Existence, the one totality of Being. The verses of the Beatitudes describe the resultant approach to life. Perfection must be determinedly sought. Selfishness and egoism must be transcended. Spiritual knowledge, wisdom and power must become the goal of all endeavor.

Matt. 5:7.   Blessed are the merciful: for they shall obtain mercy.

Sermons for the general public are usually formulated and received as guidance in the conduct of life, and the Sermon on the Mount may thus be studied, even though its teachings are difficult to apply to life in the workaday world. However, it also describes the results of spiritual unfoldment. Those who have become illumined, "anointed" as it were, are naturally full of compassion and therefore merciful. They have themselves become the embodiment of mercy in the sense of compassionate love for all that lives, suffers, and is in need. Thus, this verse provides guidance in living, a statement of the law of cause and effect, and describes a state of consciousness.

Matt. 5:8.   Blessed are the pure in heart: for they shall see God.

Purity of heart is a spiritual condition—and indeed a very lofty one—particularly when regarded as a state of complete freedom from personal desire of any kind. In such a state the heart is open in one direction only, outwards, with no inflow either expected or possible. From this highest point of view the deeply embedded attribute of human consciousness which gives rise to expectation of a return or payment for every action constitutes impurity of heart.

Man is accustomed to expect a return for every effort and every action, particularly when others are benefited. This approach to life cannot justly be condemned or even criticized. Man must live. He needs food and shelter for his body, expression for his emotions, and the give and take of ideas for his mind. Even if unconsciously, people and nations found their mutual relationships on this principle of balanced outgoing and return. If there is a profit, then so much the better.

When, however, a new level of consciousness is reached, the motive of personal gain and even of just reward declines as a driving force for action. Indeed, at the new and higher level of awareness, the apparent division between oneself and all other selves is seen to be illusion; it melts away with nothing dividing living beings one from another. Self-gain becomes meaningless, self-giving a perfectly natural attitude toward one's fellowmen and the only reasonable way of living. This is true purity of heart, and those who have attained it know the one divine Self in all universes, all beings and all things. In the words of the Teacher, "the pure in heart . . . see God."

Although here placed sixth among the virtues, purity of heart is the one great essential of them all; for without unstained selflessness all others are vain. The very thought of some reward, however spiritual, sullies and in a certain measure negates the other virtues. It also bars the way to the Christ consciousness of unity with all that lives.

> Matt. 5:9.   Blessed are the peacemakers: for they shall be called the children of God.

Since spiritually all men are children of God, and justly so designated, the term as used by the Master must here have a special meaning. True peacemakers, surely, are those who have established peace within themselves. This implies two conditions: a completely harmonious relationship between the outer man and his spiritual Self, and harmony between his whole being and the indwelling Life by which the universe is pervaded, vitalized and sustained. Selfish and cruel motives, thoughts, words, and deeds are discordant. People in whom discordant conditions are habitual are neither peaceful within themselves nor at peace with the eternal life which surrounds and pervades them. They cannot, therefore, justly be called either peacemakers or children of God as far as their conduct and inner state are concerned.

Unruffled calm, inward serenity, and peace of heart and mind are essential to progress on the way of holiness. These produce patience, forbearance and forgiveness, each of which contributes to that interior equipoise which also may be described as peace. Under such conditions man may become aware of his divine nature, manifest his divine qualities and powers, and in this sense be referred to as a child of God.

> Matt. 5:10.   Blessed are they which are persecuted for righteousness' sake: for theirs is the kingdom of heaven.

Fear of persecution is natural, and few men are ready to expose themselves to hostility in support of a cause "for righteousness' sake." Occasionally, however, men and women arise who are ready to fearlessly proclaim what they regard as truth and to courageously face all consequences. Self-sacrifice and readiness to face persecution for a just cause in the name of truth are qualities that open the pathway of communion between man and the Deity

Matt. 5:11.   Blessed are ye, when men shall revile you, and persecute
you, and shall say all manner of evil against you falsely,
for my sake.

12.   Rejoice, and be exceeding glad: for great is your
reward in heaven: for so persecuted they the prophets
which were before you.

As certain plants in a garden blossom before others and as certain trees in
an orchard bear fruit early in the season, so the spiritual souls of men are at
different stages of development. Some have already produced their fruit,
others are in flower or bud, while the great majority are still in leaf. Advanced
souls have knowledge not directly available to their fellows of lesser stature.
They therefore stand out as different, are sought for as teachers by the few,
and scorned and persecuted by the many. Their outlook, their motives and, in
some respects, their conduct, are incomprehensible. Should they teach, their
teachings appear heretical and may arouse distrust, fear and, from some
people, active opposition; for the very foundations of civilization, and especially of orthodoxy, appear to be assailed and endangered. Defense by attack
may then occur, leading to persecution and even murder, as has been demonstrated throughout history. The life of the Christ as narrated in the Gospels is
an example of these tendencies and their tragic consummation.

These verses assure those suffering from persecution that their stand for
righteousness is not in vain. They are blessed, especially in the sense that
they enter into conscious union with all life, however diverse its forms. Body
and brain can imprison them no longer; the separative tendencies of the mind
can no longer shut them off from their fellowmen. Death has lost its power
over them because they have established their center of life and awareness,
not in the mortal body, but in the immortal and indestructible spiritual Self. It
is they, the wise ones and their disciples, who are the happy men on earth, for
they abide in peace even though the population around them is decimated by
war. These advanced souls are blessed indeed, as also are those who are wise
and perceptive enough to seek their counsel and sit at their feet.

Matt. 5:13.   Ye are the salt of the earth: but if the salt have lost his
savor, wherewith shall it be salted? It is thenceforth good
for nothing, but to be cast out, and to be trodden under
foot of men.

The phrase *salt of the earth* has come down through the centuries into
common usage to imply people of the finest and highest kinds, the very best.
The original saying, however, expressed another meaning: that of the very
essence of things, or the innermost nautre. If this meaning is accepted, then a
warning against insincerity is given. Though the disciple appears to his
fellowmen, particularly the unillumined, to remain much the same as before
his discipleship, actually he is profoundly changed in that his innermost
nature, his spiritual Self, has revealed itself to his brain-mind. The revelation
deepens as his discipleship continues and develops, since it is in no sense
static.

As long as this hastened evolution of the inner Self and the quickened development of the outer man continue normally, with the former gaining increasing dominance, then all is well and, metaphorically, the salt retains its savor. If, however, the outer man loses or renounces contact with his inner Self, even though the nominal status is retained, the discipleship becomes a hollow sham. Under such conditions the salt has lost its savor. The outer man no longer cares for, and may even shrink from, the inner Self. An occult failure, against which warning is given, is the inevitable result.

As these and other aphorisms were delivered to the disciples early in their occult careers, each was doubtless followed by commentaries and many repetitions. The ancient records have, however, only handed down the maxims themselves, and these in somewhat cryptic form.

Matt. 5:14.   Ye are the light of the world. A city that is set on an hill cannot be hid.

In occult training the term *light of the world* refers to the innermost spiritual essence, the spirit-Self of the universe and man. The neophyte is trained regularly to affirm and so, eventually, to know by direct experience the manifestation of universal, spiritual light within himself as the core of his own being. This is partly achieved by the method of affirmation in which the devotee affirms: "I am the Spirit-Self, that Self am I," or "I am universal light, that light am I," or more simply "I AM THAT, THAT AM I."[6] In this verse Jesus assures his disciples of this truth, doubtless encouraging and helping them to discover and fully realize the "true light" within them.

This true light is, of course, no physical source of illumination; rather it is a manifestation or mode of perception by man of the divine spirit within him. Spiritual upliftment or yogic exaltation is not infrequently experienced as entering a universe consisting only of light. There no forms, no beings are seen, no divisions exist, and shadows and distinctions are inconceivable. The sense of separate individuality vanishes or is reduced to a minimum, and only universal light subsists. The devotee knows himself and "the light of the world."

This realization of perpetual light is referred to in the incident of the prolongation of day by Joshua,[7] and in the promise uttered by Isaiah, "Arise, shine; for thy light has come, and the glory of the Lord is risen upon thee."[8]

The symbolism changes in the second sentence of this verse. Since hills and mountains in the symbolical language refer to uplifted and spiritual states of consciousness, the term "city that is set on an hill" can be interpreted as the vehicle of the spiritual Self, the *Karana Sharira* of Hindu philosophy, the causal body, the immortal vesture of the spiritual soul. While *salt* and *the light of the world* refer to the inner essence of man's being, the city on the hill designates the vehicle through which that essence is expressed at the level of the abstract and prophetic intellect. It is indeed true that the fruits of such realization cannot be hid. Moses, on descending from Mount Sinai, did not know that his face shone, although those who saw him perceived the fact.[9]

Matt. 5:15.   Neither do men light a candle, and put it under a bushel, but on a candlestick; and it giveth light unto all that are in the house.

16. Let your light so shine before men, that they may see your good works, and glorify your Father which is in heaven.

As was his custom, Jesus used homely analogies in the expression of his teachings. The further instruction was given to the disciples to share with their fellowmen that which they had discovered and received. The importance and the effect of giving full expression to intellectual and spiritual realization are affirmed. Light received must be shared for three reasons at least. The first is for the helping of humanity. Example inspires others and enables them to perceive the divine in the inspired servant of the race. The God in man so rarely shines forth through its physical encasement, is so rarely seen, that expressions of it in high and noble modes of living and demonstrations of wisdom and power are of great benefit to observers privileged to be present.

The second reason for sharing is so that truth and light may continually flow through the illumined man, vitalizing him and keeping open the interior channels through which more knowledge and light may be received. Failure in these inevitably leads to delayed progress, to a darkened mind, and to a form of psychospiritual stagnation—withering and lifeless almost as death.

Thirdly, every time the divine spirit in man shines forth through its vehicles, especially the physical one, its power over the personality increases. Channels are carved and widened each time spirituality characterizes personal conduct. As reasonable exercise causes muscles to grow, so the continued material expression of the spirit in man increases its power. The Father which is in heaven is a name for this spirit, the Monad, the empowering principle which exalts the human nature of him through whom it is made manifest.

Matt. 5:17.   Think not that I am come to destroy the law, or the prophets: I am not come to destroy, but to fulfill.

These words of Jesus to his disciples appear to be describing his mission and explaining any iconoclasm which he may have expressed. By this he sought, not to destroy the inherited wisdom of the Hebrews, the *Torah,* the law, but to free its expression from encrustations. Dogmatically asserted interpretations of the Old Testament, particularly the Mosaic books, had built up a somewhat rigid orthodoxy and had led to outright errors. The mission of Jesus was to fulfill the law by challenging the orthodoxy of the time and to free responsive minds from its severe restrictions. The destruction of false conceptions naturally occurred when he gave expression to his pure wisdom. He himself was free in this sense and had achieved continuing interior experience of the law or pure wisdom. Thus his person, his life, his words and his works were fulfillments of the law.

Matt. 5:18.   For verily I say unto you, Till heaven and earth pass, one jot or one tittle shall in no wise pass from the law, till all be fulfilled.

The overriding and omnipotent power of pure truth is here affirmed. The essential wisdom, the esoteric heart of Hebraism—as of every other religion—is above dispute, unassailable, indestructible. It lives when universes fall; it is present at their rebirth as cycle follows cycle; it is unfailing.

In another sense suggested by the verses which follow, the law of causation of especially referred to. Effect must follow cause as night follows day throughout unending series of such sequences, for the law of action and reaction transcends the limitations of time, space and substance, eternal even though quiescent during periods of creative night.

> Matt. 5:19.   Whosoever therefore shall break one of these least com-
> mandments, and shall teach men so, he shall be called the
> least in the kingdom of heaven: but whosoever shall do and
> teach them, the same shall be called great in the kingdom
> of heaven.

These verses not only convey philosophic and ethical wisdom but also enunciate the rules of yoga. As the kingdom of heaven means an exalted state of consciousness, the phrase describes the normal state of awareness of the spiritual Self of man, particularly the blending of abstract intellect and intuition. This state cannot be entered if the outer, mortal man is a deliberate transgressor. Chosen lawbreaking as a policy of life raises impassable barriers between the inner and outer man and closes the kingdom of heaven to brain consciousness. Therefore, one of the laws governing Self-illumination is enunciated in this verse.

Experience of the kingdom-of-heaven state of consciousness partly depends upon interior harmony. Mind and emotion must be reasonably attuned to each other and both of them unified with the Spirit-essence within. This entails the faithful surrender of the outer man to the indwelling God. The gateway leading from earth to heaven is then open. On the other hand, transgression creates discord and bedulls the responses of the psyche to the impulses from the higher Self, which is thereby shut out from the brain. The degree of Self-illumination, then, depends to a considerable extent upon the degree of harmony in feeling and thought which is established and maintained by right conduct based upon selfless motives.

The Noble Eightfold Path of Buddhism and the Sermon on the Mount are not only descriptions of modes of conduct; they are also, and far more, statements of law, descriptions of the impersonal action of the law of cause and effect; they define conditions of thought, motive, and action which are essential to the attainment of spiritual states of awareness. Not one of these conditions can be ignored or deliberately flouted without a reduction in the degree of Self-enlightenment.

The levels of consciousness which can be attained by man through meditation and contemplation are many, and their associated experiences are various. The very greatest, loftiest and holiest state consists of uttermost and final absorption into the rhythmically pulsing, intensely luminous, life inherent in the universe—though without complete loss of identity. This is *Paranirvana* or greatness in the kingdom of heaven in the terms used here. Such a *nirvanee,* though in a body, is stainless, sinless, perfectly attuned throughout the whole range of levels of his existence, consciousness and action. However, human beings can enter the kingdom of heaven in this sense in spite of human blemishes, though the heights attained will be far less transcendent. Such a man is here described as "least in the kingdom of heaven."

Such comparative placements are not the result of judgments by external beings, like examiners in educational systems. God is not to be regarded as a guardian of the doors of heaven or as a judge deciding the fates of different people. This occurs in accordance with impersonal law which governs not only reactions arising from human conduct, but spiritual attainments as well. Law penetrates deeply to the very heart of both universal and human life, and no level of existence is unaffected by the principle of action and reaction. Physical conditions are produced by physical conduct, truly, but teachers of the law point also to its operation upon those who seek the higher life and the higher consciousness. Man alone brings about and determines the condition of his soul by his motives and conduct and his ability or inability to enter into states of spiritual awareness.

> Matt. 5:20.   For I say unto you, That except your righteousness shall exceed the righteousness of the scribes and Pharisees, ye shall in no case enter into the kingdom of heaven.

In this verse unsurpassable barriers to the attainment of enlightenment are described: hypocrisy and its twin, insincerity. These are personified by scribes and Pharisees, members of the Jewish community of the time. Underlying both of these qualities is that impurity of heart which habitually looks for gain.

The presence of this undesirable character renders impossible of attainment the condition of interior harmony which results from obedience to the laws of right conduct. The hypocrite is continually discordant in his own inner nature and in his relationship with nature and his fellowmen. Though outwardly he may present the appearance of material well-being, inwardly he is at war. If he represses this conflict, then his subconscious self becomes increasingly burdened with the underlying discordances. Eventually these will become so prevalent and so strong as to invade his conscious mind and life. Under such conditions he is in danger of the disintegration of his personal mind. Inevitably the outer appearance of well-being will crumble before the discordant and warring forces within him. Thus self-encumbered and self-fettered, no man can attain to the state of consciousness described as the kingdom of heaven, which at its highest is *Nirvana*.

> Matt. 5:21.   Ye have heard that it was said by them of old time, Thou shalt not kill; and whosoever shall kill shall be in danger of the judgment:
>
> 22.   But I say unto you, That whosoever is angry with his brother without a cause shall be in danger of the judgment: and whosoever shall say to his brother, Raca, shall be in danger of the council: but whosoever shall say, Thou fool, shall be in danger of hell fire.

If read literally, condemnation of anyone to hell-fire merely for calling another a fool would be devoid of justice, of reason and especially of mercy. It cannot, therefore, be regarded as a divine ordinance. Rather the verses refer to the fundamental outlook and character of the individual. The Christ in these teachings penetrates far more deeply into human conduct and the character and conditions of the psyche than does any human lawgiver. What a man does depends upon what a man is, and it is the interior condition of heart and mind that the spiritual Teacher pronounces to be decisive as far as fate is concerned.

Both the kingdom of heaven and its opposite, the so-called hell-fire, are phrases describing states of consciousness and psychological conditions. The one is based upon realization of unity, and the other upon its denial in motive and conduct; they are conditions of unification and disintegration, respectively. Neither is to be regarded as an actual place having an objective existence in either the visible or invisible worlds.

Matt. 5:23. Therefore if thou bring thy gift to the altar, and there rememberest that thy brother hath ought against thee;

24. Leave there thy gift before the altar, and go thy way; first be reconciled to thy brother, and then come and offer thy gift.

In these utterances, the Lord strikes at the very root of both human nature with its hypocritical tendencies and the attainment of spiritual awareness, which is impossible for those who are deliberately separative and insincere. Harmony within and harmonious relationships with others, combined, are shown to be far more important than external acts of worship. It is of little use to approach the symbolical altar with gifts, on the one hand, and to deny that for which the altar stands on the other. When continued and ignored, a breach with a fellowman can render as naught even the greatest of outward demonstrations of moral and religious worthiness. The one cancels out the other, not only in the realm of observances, but far more in the process of gaining that spiritual realization described as the kingdom of heaven.

This results, not from a judgment by the Deity, but from the action of natural law. Indeed, this wonderful statement concerning the kingdom of heaven begins by the enunciation of law given in verse eighteen.

Matt. 5:25. Agree with thine adversary quickly, whiles thou art in the way with him; lest at any time the adversary deliver thee to the judge, and the judge deliver thee to the officer, and thou be cast into prison.

26. Verily I say unto thee, Thou shalt by no means come out thence, till you hast paid the uttermost farthing.

Morality is dynamic; the play and interplay of forces form the root of so-called moral law. Up to a certain stage of human development, man is moral in obedience to instruction and from fear of consequences. Eventually his life is naturally moral, as spiritually enlightened man lives less from conforming to morality than because delinquency has become utterly foreign. He knows the effects produced upon himself by discordant conduct. Harmony becomes prized as the richest treasure, and maintaining it within himself and in his relationship with his fellowmen is of first importance; for this is required, not only to enter, but also to perpetually abide in the kingdom of heaven.

Hostility is discordant, destructive of harmony without and within. The spiritually aspiring neophyte refrains from hostile feelings toward anyone and seeks to neutralize the hostility felt toward him by another. To agree with an adversary both mentally and verbally helps reduce his hostility. The adage that it takes two to make a quarrel expresses not only an obvious fact, but also an occult truth. One on the path is moved by natural tendencies, not only toward peace and the preservation of harmony, but also toward the prevention or modification of adverse effects of law. The counsel given by the Lord is therefore both moral and occult and is of great importance from both points of view.

The law is personified as the judge, doubtless for ease of presentation. Actually from the spiritual point of view, judge, policeman and prison exist only as natural law and the effect of its operation upon those who become lawless. The twenty-sixth verse repeats the powerful affirmation of verse eighteen; the law of cause and effect cannot be evaded, and results must follow causes until a broken harmony is restored or increased by beneficent actions. While intervening actions affect both processes, nevertheless, no one can win release from the metaphorical prison until he has paid the price to the uttermost farthing.

> Matt. 5:27.   Ye have heard that it was said by them of old time, Thou shalt not commit adultery:
>
> 28.   But I say unto you, That whosoever looketh on a woman to lust after her hath committed adultery with her already in his heart.

These verses are well known, have been the subject of many interpretations and applications, and received universal acceptance. Their truth is self-evident, especially within the context of the chapter as a whole. The teaching is elsewhere enunciated in the words, "As a man thinketh in his heart, so is he."[10] This shows that morality must not be merely skin deep; it must penetrate to the very roots of human nature, for the uncontrolled, undisciplined and, still more, the vicious mind, is indeed the source and cause of human evil. Since the mind rules the man, such mental states, among others, can lead to darkness and even to death. Under the law, the assurance of happiness as well as the cause of pain stem from the mind, for the injunction of the Lord applies equally to virtuous and vicious actions. Both originate in the human mind.

In these verses an exceedingly loftly morality is presented. The appraisal of human conduct is lifted from action alone to include intention, which is regarded as of equal weight. Though demanding, the teaching in its penetrating directness is of great importance, especially to those who aspire to transmute desire and to progress rapidly toward the fulfillment of the purpose of human existence, the development of all the faculties inherent in man. The teaching will be the accepted rule for later races in which the focus of life activities will be raised from physical to mental levels. Thus, future man will be centered in his blended spiritual and mental faculties. Thereafter, desire will have been outgrown.

> Matt. 5:29. And if thy right eye offend thee, pluck it out, and cast it from thee: for it is profitable for thee that one of thy members should perish, and not that thy whole body should be cast into hell.
>
> 30. And if thy right hand offend thee, cut it off, and cast it from thee: for it is profitable for thee that one of thy members should perish, and not that thy whole body should be cast into hell.

Here again the language is metaphorical, for it is hardly likely that any great spiritual teacher would advise self-mutilation as a means of self-purification. Again, surely, attention is drawn to the mind and, more especially, to the undesirable thoughts, plans and plots which are permitted to arise and develop therein. Error, stupidity, prejudice, pride, and ignorance can steadily increase in those minds in which they are given free expression, uninhibited activity. Outwardly moral conduct can be hypocritical, many kinds of vice existing within heart and mind. As these can fester or develop into malignancy, it is indeed essential that they be excised.

If this is not done in good time, much of a man's mental power can become perverted to base ends, leading to base conduct, which under the law brings suffering or, metaphorically, casts the evildoer into hell (a state of misery, as heaven is a state of bliss). The surgery, therefore, must be done upon every adverse mental habit or part of the human make-up. The surgeon's knife is the will of steel which excises from the mind—and so the conduct—"diseased organs" and "mental malignancies." The analogy is susceptible of even further development and application. For example, the order and technique of the operating theater and the calmness, skill and precision of surgeons may serve as examples of the ideal method.

These utterances of the Lord indicate a certain quality of character, a mental condition which may be defined as *downrightness,* completely applying oneself to the task of self-correction at whatever cost. Those who could and would follow the Lord's teaching must hold back nothing where the purification of the soul and illumination of the mind are concerned. Indeed, wholeness, fullness and uttermost sincerity are essential to success in mental as in medical hygiene.

> Matt. 5:31. It hath been said, Whosoever shall put away his wife, let him give her a writing of divorcement:
>
> 32. But I say unto you, That whosoever shall put away his wife, saving for the cause of fornication, causeth her to commit adultery: and whosoever shall marry her that is divorced committeth adultery.

These words, if correctly translated and truthfully preserved down the centuries, offer a point of view upon which each person must make his own decision, whatever advice and action may follow. The quality of the thought is again that of directness, whether or not it has always been acceptable in the changing marital attitudes and circumstances during the long period of the Christian Era. These words must have been somewhat revolutionary at the time of their utterance, for they place the responsibility in such marital circumstances squarely upon the man. This would seem to be particularly notable in an age in which the status of woman was generally that of inferiority to the male. In modern days, however, equal responsibility in freedom to act and judgment are, perhaps, preferred.

Matt. 5:33.　Again, ye have heard that it hath been said by them of old time, Thou shalt not forswear thyself, but shalt perform unto the Lord thine oaths:

34.　But I say unto you, Swear not at all; neither by heaven; for it is God's throne:

35.　Nor by the earth; for it is his footstool; neither by Jerusalem; for it is the city of the great King.

Matt. 5:36.　Neither shalt thou swear by thy head, because thou canst not make one hair white or black.

37.　But let your communication be, Yea, yea; Nay, nay: for whatsoever is more than these cometh of evil.

The great Reformer was doubtless striking at crystallized attitudes, rigid national habits of thought and customs, seeking to free men from these restrictions. In doing so he struck at the root of the error, cut through the complications, and affirmed the importance of simplicity. A man is to make his word his bond: if he says yes, he means yes in all truth, and if he says no, then the negative is entirely correct. One can well understand that such an approach could arouse hostility, and yet light–bearers must deliver the truth, come what may.

Again, the teaching can be applied to the inner life of man and to his search for truth where exactitude and directness, as well as simplicity, are essential to full success.

Matt. 5:38.　Ye have heard that it hath been said, An eye for an eye, and a tooth for a tooth:

39.　But I say unto you, That ye resist not evil: but whosoever shall smite thee on thy right cheek, turn to him the other also.

The method of teaching by antithesis is employed, and again the advice runs counter to accepted standard of conduct based upon the Mosaic law. The contrast, and even incompatibility, between the accepted and natural reaction and the guidance of the Lord are here made apparent. Considered from the point of view of worldly conduct, retaliation of any kind is not only permissible but desirable. Counterattack is the best means of defense.

The laws of the spiritual life indicate the reverse. Not only are nondefense and nonretaliation advised, but—extending the principle—it appears as if repetition of the assault invited by nonaction is recommended. The counsel is, indeed, difficult both to understand and to put into practice from the purely worldly point of view. It may, therefore, be concluded that it is not so intended. Like the maxims of the Sermon of the Mount, this group of ideas is offered to the spiritually minded who aspire to the higher consciousness, and especially to that interior and external harmony essential to its attainment.

Philosophically, no man is one's enemy; all men are instruments and agents of the law of cause and effect. The philosophically minded man does not resent attack but calmly recognizes it as produced originally by himself upon himself under that law. He knows, furthermore, that if he returns the attack, thereby increasing violence, he is only perpetuating enmity and rendering accord more difficult to reach. The individual who permits himself, not only to feel provoked but also to hit back whether mentally or physically is gravely in error. A discipline of nonreaction to outward stress and the preservation under all circumstances of interior equipoise are essential; for then perfect harmony is established and rules thought and conduct. The aspirant, therefore, remains calm, unmoved, and nonretaliatory in the fact of every assault upon the citadel of his inner consciousness. With its wall of philosophic calm maintained by nonaction, that citadel is impregnable.

This advice is, admittedly, a counsel of perfection for most people and is fully applied only by the Adept. This is because the average person has as yet neither conceived nor found his own center of existence and awareness. The neophyte makes this discovery a primary objective; and when he begins to attain success, interior calm and self-command become easier than before. Contrary to the apparent meaning of the thirty-ninth verse, this implies neither weakness nor surrender to a supposed external foe. On the contrary, strength of mind and unyielding self-command are essential to success.

In yoga the human self-center of existence is recognized as fundamentally inseparable from universal spirit, and the yogi seeks to experience this in full consciousness. Moreover, he practices maintaining that experience throughout his waking hours. This is of great assistance because the spirit of the universe is maintained in dynamic equipoise. Realization of unity with this brings about participation by the yogi in the universal dynamic calm and active harmony. Therefore, no true yogi would permit himself to introduce discord into the field of his consciousness. Hence he does not react to adverse disturbances, whether they arise in his psyche or from outside. Symbolically, he turns the other cheek.

From the purely practical point of view, also, this is the wisest procedure in the end. Harmony is truth, and assault is error. As long as error is not met with further error and so given life, it will fail, truth always ultimately prevailing, as the ancient maxim declares. Firmly established in this belief, the wise man can afford to meet discord with harmony, preserving silence.

Where the individual alone is concerned, the method is to retreat into the center of perfect equipoise immediately whenever discordance approaches, whether from within or from without, and there remain. Regular practice despite difficulties will establish this habit, until at last interior harmony and external nonreaction are natural, instinctual responses. This is the yoga ideal and one most difficult to reach.

The situation is, however, radically changed when another person or group is assailed. A new law and rule of conduct then applies. This may be described as protection and defense born of compassion, ideally free from passion. Under such conditions involving a principle or the welfare of others, the advice of Sri Krishna to Arjuna, "Fight, O Partha," indicates the correct conduct.[11] While one may be relatively indifferent and pacific on one's own behalf, one cannot ideally be pacifist before the needs of another.

> Matt. 5:40.   And if any man will sue thee at law, and take away thy coat, let him have thy cloak also.

The esotericist does not go to law in his own defense, however unjustly attacked. He knows that, ultimately, truth will prevail, whatever earthly judges may decree. He knows also that apparently undeserved adversity will always produce beneficence, even though he seeks it not. Furthermore, he is possessionless. To him, coat or cloak constitutes part of the transient apparel for the physical body, itself known to be but a garment borrowed from nature. Upon this realization, possessiveness concerning worldly goods is outgrown. When, however, the coat or cloak of another is unjustly or illegally acquired, then he recognizes the paramount duty to defend the victim, if needs be restore the property, and assist the law in the capture of the criminal.

Lord Christ himself upheld the law as when with whip and denunciation he drove from the temple those who profaned its sacred precincts by selling merchandise for profit. An important principle is herein involved; it concerns the extension of spiritual power and influence into the domain of politics and commerce for the unworthy motive of gain. All too often this principle is ignored and even flagrantly denied by those of influence in the religions of the world.

> Matt. 5:41.   And whosoever shall compel thee to go a mile, go with him twain.

In this, as elsewhere in such teachings, an attitude of mind rather than actual conduct is enjoined. Self-centeredness, self-desire and acute self-concern might well result in refusal even to "walk a mile" except for personal pleasure or profit. Training in the attainment of selflessness to which the aspirant submits himself brings about gradual dissolving of the separative mental attribute of egoism. Selflessness becomes a deeply rooted and permanent attribute of the personal attitude and conduct of man thus self-freed. Unnecessary and even undesirable though this may seem to the worldly mind, it is of the utmost importance to the spiritual aspirant from the very first moment at which he places his feet upon the ancient and narrow way.

The attitude of self-defense, self-assertion, possessiveness and aggressive insistence on supposed personal rights has been built up through hundreds of lives. It has been, indeed is, quite necessary for the preservation of individuality and personal and family life. When the path is approached, all this accretion from the past must be undone and dissolved. This is the message of the wonderful Sermon on the Mount. This is the meaning of these seemingly difficult teachings of the Lord.

> Matt. 5:42.   Give to him that asketh thee, and from him that would borrow of thee turn not thou away.

The very ideas of giving and lending depend upon a sense of personal possession, of actually having something to give and to lend. In all worldly matters this sense is well founded, but in rapid progress to adeptship the sense of personal possessiveness must disappear. At first, this is somewhat, but not wholly, an artificially adopted attitude of mine. Indeed, the neophyte needs constantly to repudiate the egoism upon which possessiveness depends. In his innermost thought, deep in the recesses of his mind, after all worldly considerations have received due attention, he denies and declines to regard himself as separate from other men and the universe in which all live. These two meet in the inner mind of the aspirant so that, in due course, the fact of spiritual identity with the inner essence of the cosmos becomes a realized truth, an obvious fact of existence. Thereafter, requests for gifts and loans are naturally responded to, though in degree according to the dictates of worldly good sense. Indeed, when this development has occurred, there is little or no sense of giving or lending anything. One who is liberated from accentuated I-ness knows himself as but a steward for those supplies which are available to all.

> Matt. 5:43. Ye have heard that it hath been said, Thou shalt love thy neighbour, and hate thine enemy.
>
> 44. But I say unto you, Love your enemies, bless them that curse you, do good to them that hate you, and pray for them which despitefully use you, and persecute you.

In these verses the ideal is raised from application to material actions and goods to an attitude of heart and mind. Through and through from his physical life into his deepest and most secret thoughts and intentions, the neophyte must be penetrated by the ideal of selflessness, of identity with all that exists. When this is achieved the teachings of the Sermon on the Mount become perfectly natural, spontaneous manifestations of the aspirant's condition of consciousness. Realization of Oneness fills the whole being of illumined man. In no artificial or hypocritical sense, he truly loves all men because of his awareness of this kinship with them. Whether they are enemies or friends in their physical encasements is largely decided by the operation of causative law. The actual truth concerning them is that they are brothers in one family and in a deeper sense expressions of the same spirit-life. Whatever the outer actions of men, in their inner selves they are intimately akin, even to those whom they may injure.

Admittedly this is a very elevated attitude, a lofty realization. For the Adept it is the only one possible. This is part of the symbolic significance of the elevation above the ground of the crucified Christ. Crucifixion and death are but bodily and symbolic representations of the dissolution of I-ness and the elevation of consciousness above all the illusions and the errors to which they lead and of which the mass of mankind is victim. The Sermon on the Mount is delivered from such a height, in this case a mountain.

> Matt. 5:45. That ye may be the children of your Father which is in heaven: for he maketh his sun to rise on the evil and on the good, and sendeth rain on the just and on the unjust.

The Fatherhood of God and the brotherhood of man are no mere dogmas of orthodox theology, though often so regarded. They are vital and dynamic truths concerning the oneness of Life, or indeed one truth manifested as twin principles. Thus, the sun as symbol of eternal beneficence shines upon all, and the rain of spiritual grace descends equally upon the just and the unjust. Upon this one truth the conduct advised in the Sermon on the Mount is founded.

Matt. 5:45.   For if ye love them which love you, what reward have ye? do not even the publicans the same?

Here a measure of reason is used to aid in understanding the lofty ideal. Progress depends, said the Lord, upon rising in conduct above the level of what is expected of those as yet spiritually unawakened, symbolically, the publicans. The counsel to "love one another" can only be adopted by those who have achieved a measure of interior harmony, sincerity and selflessness; for without these, self-centeredness and self-guarding occupy too large an area and teave little or no room even for interest in others, to say nothing of love for them.

Matt. 5:47.   And if ye salute your brethren only, what do ye more than others? do not even the publicans so?

Recognition and courtesy to all men, of whatever degree and of whatever state of sin or sinlessness, is here injoined. The recognition and interest bestowed on those of good or even lofty standard and position in the community is due to all, high or low, saint or sinner. True brotherhood is inwardly realized and outwardly expressed to all men.

Matt. 5:48.   Be ye therefore perfect, even as your Father which is in heaven is perfect.

Both the ancient mystery rituals and those of modern days deriving from them inform neophytes of the destiny of all men—perfection—and adjure them so to act in the present as to hasten its fulfillment.

The Lord Jesus Christ, it should be remembered, was speaking from direct experience of inward truth of the absolute identity of the life principle in all beings. Even while the words flowed from his lips and were caught by the ears and minds of his rapt audience upon the mountainside in Judea, he himself was seated in the eternal, rooted in realization of the spiritual oneness of everything within the universe and all that it contains. This realization bestowed upon his words not only meanings to the mind, but a fire and a conviction born of his own interior knowledge.

The scene may be pictured in meditative thought. One envisages the white-robed figure of the Lord standing in great dignity which mounted to majesty as the spirit descended upon him. Seated upon the ground, the multitude of men gaze upon him, while his closer friends, disciples, relatives and others drawing near to discipleship listen to the voice which spake as never yet man spake. The short and simple sentences uttered by that beautifully modulated voice reach through the bodily ears and worldly minds into the diviner aspects of human consciousness. However difficult of application to the experiences of worldly life, while he speaks the teachings seem easy of comprehension and even obvious to all those in the elevated state. Thus he, the Teacher of men, revealed the very heart of truth, that all men are one in their innermost essence.

REFERENCES AND NOTES

1. See Hodson, *Hidden Wisdom,* Vol 1, pp. 115–116.
2. E.g. *The Light of Asia; The Bhagavad Gita; The Crest Jewel of Wisdom* (Viveka-Chudamani); Lao-tse, *Tao-te-Ching.*
3. Matt. 26:39.
4. See Geoffrey Hodson, *A Yoga of Light.*
5. *Ahamkara*—see Glossary.
6. See Geoffrey Hodson, *A Yoga of Light.*
7. Josh. 10:13.
8. Isa. 60:1 and 60:19–20.
9. Exod. 34:29.
10. Prov. 23:7.
11. *Bhagavad Gita*

Chapter Ten

The great Sermon on the Mount is not only an ethical discourse, not only a description of a lofty ideal of utter selflessness, but also a description of the pathway which leads to realization of the Godhead within man. It is, in fact, a dissertation upon the ancient science of yoga and its qualifications.

Matt. 6:1. Take heed that ye do not your alms before men, to be seen of them: otherwise ye have no reward of your Father which is in heaven.

2. Therefore when thou doest thine alms, do not sound a trumpet before thee, as the hypocrites do in the synagogues and in the streets, that they may have glory of men. Verily I say unto you, They have their reward.

In these verses the Lord insistently places the accent upon motive. Uttermost sincerity, complete truthfulness, and singleness of mind and heart are here enjoined. Almsgiving, as all giving, must be solely for giving's sake, for love of mankind, and to help those in need. A primary, or even secondary, motive to win esteem for being a charitable man mars the purity of both almsgiving and the love by which it is inspired. Almsgiving with an eye to popularity and prestige is almost worthless from the point of view of benefit to the giver.

To give freely is to release a power from beyond mind and heart. In consequence, forces from deep within the innermost Self find channels through which to flow, thereby empowering and illuminating both mind and heart. Such giving blesses the giver and evokes a response from the "Father which is in Heaven," the Dweller-in-the-Innermost, the human Monad. This expansion and the unfoldment produced by acts of love and truly sacrificial self-giving are, indeed, the natural effects upon the giver, his reward. The receiver also benefits, not only materially, but from the harmony which is established. Such giving is, in addition, a sowing from which an appropriate reaping naturally follows under law. These advantages should ideally have no place in the heart the giver who should give for giving's sake, for love's sake, and solely to help fellowmen. Such is the lofty ideal of giving.

Since, however, modern man has arrived at his present place in nature by the exercise through many incarnations of watchfulness, careful planning, and work carried out with a view to gain—which is essential to self-preservation and the ability to fulfill obligations—the deeply established, self-centered motive dies hard. Herein lies the task and the difficulty that confronts those who would for love's sake purify themselves of self.

The key to this attainment is realization of the illusory nature of the ingrained sense of self-identity, illusory because the spirit-essence, of which each human Monad is a manifestation, is the same in all. When this is realized, even the idea that a gift is being given is changed to that of sharing from a universal supply for which man is a steward. The water carrier does not supply the water which he bestows. He who offers heat and light is not personally responsible or praiseworthy for those gifts. He only makes them available; he does not create them, and they are not his alone. In Christian terms, they are the Lord's and should, therefore, be given impersonally in his name and in his name alone. While applying this principle to almsgiving, Jesus also enunciates the ideal for every act.

> Matt. 6:3.   But when thou doest alms, let not thy left hand know what thy right hand doeth:
>
> 4.   That thine alms may be in secret: and thy Father which seeth in secret himself shall reward thee openly.

"Give and forget" has been advanced as the true ideal in all ministration whether spiritual, verbal, material or combinations of these. The alternative must consist of a system of bargaining, however much concealed even from oneself. Such concepts of *quid pro quo,* purchase of divine favors, and of doing outward good for an inward reward are, indeed, totally foreign to the ideal of which Jesus was speaking.

With regard to karma, also, underlying selfishness in performing service, giving in order to get, is quite unsound. Motive is even more influential than action where the operation of the law of sowing and reaping is concerned. Divine blessing, divine aid, and material benefits divinely bestowed cannot be purchased by any means whatever. They will, however, inevitably follow from a life of selfless love and selfless service. Reward from the Father thus indicates the reaction of law.

> Matt. 6:5.   And when thou prayest, thou shalt not be as the hypocrites are: for they love to pray standing in the synagogues and in the corners of the street, that they may be seen of men. Verily I say unto you, They have their reward.

Ostentation and meditation are mutually incompatible. If prayer is regarded as interior communion with the God within, "the hope of glory," then success depends upon wholeness of heart. If a man prays to God that others may see his devotion, "God" will neither hear nor answer, for the strong though subtle idea of self-gain will impose an impassable barrier between the outer and the inner, the human and the divine in man. The cup offered for receipt of divine grace—the wine of wisdom and love—must be empty of all else. The careful cleansing of the sacred vessels at the altar symbolizes this truth.

A law is thus enunciated, the law governing the process of self-illumination. A high yoga is described, difficult indeed to practice. A world Teacher must ever teach the highest ideals—in this case self-free service and self-free prayer.

> Matt. 6:6.   But thou, when thou prayest, enter into thy closet, and
> when thou hast shut thy door, pray to thy Father which is
> in secret; and thy Father which seeth in secret shall
> reward thee openly.

Complete privacy, one of the requisites of conscious realization of the divine within, is described in this verse. This is necessary, not only for freedom from ostentation, but also in order to free the mind from external influences and distractions. The luminous aura surrounding man must not be impinged upon by the auric forces of others. Also, the delicate process of attuning the brain-mind to the spiritual mind, and through that with indwelling spirit itself, must be unhindered and free from interference.

Silence, privacy, aloneness, and inviolate security are among the external necessities in reaching and communing with the God enshrined in man. When these and other conditions are met, that inward presence will reveal itself —perhaps as a whisper, a word, or a call, perhaps as light or a truth perceived. This is the "reward."

> Matt. 6:7.   But when ye pray, use not vain repetitions, as the
> heathen do: for they think that they shall be heard for
> their much speaking.

Silence, strange though the idea may seem, is essential in successful prayer; for prayer is neither an asking nor a verbal declaration. Rather is it silent communion between Father and son, God and man. Though a man in distress may lift up his voice and heart to the highest he knows, praying for aid, a man seeking light asks naught. He knows that he himself needs but to open his inner eyes in order to perceive the light which shines within and without all the time. Outer vision must be darkened; ears must be unresponsive to the sounds of the world; voice must be still—unless chanting the Holy Name—if the word within is to be heard. Mere repetitions will not bring about this consummation or reward, though utterly sincere verbal prayers of aspiration and adoration may serve to prepare the way. But then silence must prevail.

> Matt. 6:8.   Be not ye therefore like unto them: for your Father
> knoweth what things ye have need of, before ye ask him.

As the sun shines perpetually at its maximum power, so the divine within and beyond all nature and all men is perpetually self-manifest to the highest possible degree. Furthermore, just as clouds create veils between sun and man, inner clouds make obstructions between mind and brain. The seeming absence of sunlight, physical or mental, is an illusion; for the sun without and within shines perpetually from eternity to eternity. The problem then rests wholly with man himself, and it is within his power to dispel all clouds which veil the light from his inner eye.

As no increase in shining is obtained from prayers to the visible sun, so also no added beneficence is normally received from prayers of petition to the spiritual Sun, God the Father, the divine presence, power and light in every atom and within the inmost nature of man. Indeed, it is quite impossible for this divinity to increase the degree of its beneficent raying forth, as divine manifestation is always at its maximum.

Prayer, nevertheless, can be of value if it removes clouds from the mind and veils from the emotions and lifts the level of receptivity above these regions to heights at which the divine shining may be perceived. The most efficacious prayer, the most potent act of yoga, consists less of attempting to "bring down" additional power and light, than of opening mind, emotion and body in surrender and receptivity to the divine. As rain falls refreshingly upon the plants supplying moisture without preference to any single plant, so heavenly rain is universally provided by an all-beneficent Providence which needs no prompting from any man.

> Matt. 6:9.   After this manner therefore pray ye: Our Father which art in heaven, Hallowed be thy name.

The ancient prayer known to Christians as The Lord's Prayer is less to be regarded as a petition to an external Deity on behalf of humanity than as an upreaching of mind and heart to the divine *within* man, "the Father in Heaven," the innermost Self of man. Like the divine presence in nature, this divinity is expressed in three modes and this prayer addresses all three. The word *Father* refers to the innermost essence, the pure spirit in man, *Heaven,* as its abiding place, refers to the vehicle of its manifestation, the Christ nature in man. The *name,* indeed holy, refers to the directive intelligence within the divine Mind by the operations of which all things are fashioned. A trinity is thus addressed. In nature it is Father, Son and Holy Ghost, while in man it is represented by deific power, wisdom and intelligence. The prayer begins, then, by an address or affirmation lifting the thought of the devotee to the triple Self within him, the Father within his heaven whose name is Holiness.

> Matt. 6:10.   Thy kingdom come. Thy will be done in earth, as it is in heaven.
>
> 11.   Give us this day our daily bread.
>
> 12.   And forgive us our debts, as we forgive our debtors.
>
> 13.   And lead us not into temptation, but deliver us from evil: For thine is the kingdom, and the power, and the glory, for ever. Amen.

In the thirteenth verse in the Authorized Version in English, both the record of the words of the Lord in the first sentence and also the translation are patently at fault. No thoughtful person, no philosopher, no one who has any understanding of the nature of Deity could possibly regard that divine Being as deliberately leading anyone to evil, which is implied by the petition not to do so. Furthermore, the influence of the spiritual presence, attributes and powers within man must ever be regarded as unfailingly beneficent, inspiring and purificatory. If one believes at all in a Deity, whether within nature and man or transcendent beyond, then such must indeed be the case. The Father in Heaven, the sovereign Lord of the universe to whom the great prayer is addressed, must be conceived as always moving every man to righteousness; no prayers that God refrain from tempting man and deliver him from transgression can possibly be needed.

What, then, can be the meaning of the petition? The whole prayer may, I suggest, be regarded legitimately as an invocation to the higher Self of the devotee to draw into closer communion with his mortal nature, which in the act of prayer is lifted up in thought toward that divine Self. The kingdom of God in its microcosmic sense is the true Individuality in its "vesture of light," the Ego in the causal body. This is the instrument of universalized consciousness, agent for the operations of the divine Mind, and vehicle of the threefold Self. The prayer invokes the attributes of the inner Self, particularly in its universalized state, into the formal mind, so this may become similarly illumined.

Philosophers have agreed that the source of deliberate evil in man is to be found in the separative and egotistic tendencies of the formal mind. This is indeed the real tempter, and against its influence upon motive and conduct aid is sought from the universalized, abstract intelligence within. Until this begins and the mental outlook is changed from a basis of selfish personality to universality, the higher levels of consciousness cannot be reached during waking hours. Thus, the first invocation, following the affirmation of the existence of the triple Self, is directed toward the two aspects of the human mind. Abstract and formal mind first meet, then blend, and finally be united. This is the "Heavenly Marriage" and the coming of the kingdom of God into the active mind. In Kabalistic terms, the veil between them, the *Paraketh*, must not only be rent[1] but eventually must disappear altogether, after which illumined man has but one mind and one mental outlook and activity—that of the immortal Self.

The famous words "Give us our daily bread" refer not to wheat and bread, but to the very bread of life, the spiritual essence of the universe and man, that divine "sustenance" whereby they exist and are maintained. The prayer for daily bread may thus be interpreted as an affirmation that the inner power or will-force in man may become increasingly embodied in the corresponding mortal vehicle, the physical body. Such support may indeed be metaphorically likened to a supply of food, the very bread of life itself.

Read literally, the twelfth verse is almost without meaning, since in reality there cannot be forgiveness by an external Deity for trespasses committed by man, though one may excuse a person for offence against himself. According to the utterance of Jesus and St. Paul,[2] the operation of the law of cause and effect can in no wise and by no being ever be stayed or even interrupted save by modifying actions performed by the same actor, whether harmfully or beneficently as far as he himself is concerned.[3] Therefore, the reestablishment of complete harmony—both interiorly among the vehicles and externally with nature and men—is indicated. The invocation is directed to the ideal of harmony, goodness, and sympathy, the wisdom principle in the higher Self, that these attributes may be more fully expressed in the activities of the emotions, thereby maintaining and, if need be, restoring the tendency toward harmonization or forgiveness.

Since the pain-producing action of the law of cause and effect arises from a universal principle of perpetual reharmonization whenever necessary, establishing a natural tendency toward harmony is a great advantage. Pain-causing action by thought, feeling, word and deed will be less likely and happiness-giving action natural. Less pain and more pleasure to the actor will then accrue under impersonal law. By strengthening and enlarging the link between the threefold Godhead in man and its outer vehicles, the prayer—actually a meditation—is designed to bring about self-illumination and the ultimate absorption of the material into the spiritual parts of human nature—the underlying purpose of the great utterance. An interior process is being instituted to overcome the resistances of concrete mind, physical body and daily life—stimulated and continued by daily meditation as well as natural progress in evolution. The phrase "thy will be done on earth as it is in heaven" indicates this consummation. The threefold inner Self has been invoked into the corresponding aspects of the threefold outer man, divine will-force to the body, wisdom to the emotions and intelligence to the mind.

The mind, emotion and flesh may be represented as a downward pointing triangle, a reflection into matter of the triple higher Self, which is symbolized as an upward pointing triangle. Normally the two bases representing the two aspects of the mind are apart. A link is gradually formed between them until eventually the lower triangle moves up to blend with the higher. The symbol of the interlaced triangles well expresses both the intent and the results of this great prayer, the consummation of all yoga, which is thus seen to be geometrical in design.[4] The prayer might be translated thus: May the divine will, wisdom and intelligence which I am, manifest through my mind, heart and body, both to produce interior harmony within me and to inspire me to make restitution for all harmfulness toward that same triplicity in any other being or form.

The invocation closes with an affirmation of surrender—"For thine is the kingdom, and the power, and the glory, for ever. Amen."—and this well expresses the desired result. With the capacity for reasoning preserved and exercised, consciousness has become centered in realization of oneness with the Holy Trinity. The argumentative and individualistic tendencies of the mind have been temporarily subdued, the whole nature being thus offered unreservedly as a vehicle for the divine. The consummation is complete. Higher and lower triads are blended into one. This is finally affirmed by the closing words, "So be it," or "Amen."

Matt. 6:14.   For if ye forgive men their trespasses, your heavenly Father will also forgive you:

The heart and the feelings of man are here referred to directly. When humble and compassionate, neither harboring nor expressing resentment, the individual becomes inerrant. Under these circumstances little or no adverse karma is generated. When a harmful action is directed against one, if he neither feels nor acts resentfully, the cycle is closed. If, however, such a lofty ideal is not yet fully established in the heart, then resentment at injury can lead to resentful thoughts and deeds or even desire for revenge. Then a minor discord becomes a major conflict. The cycle is, in consequence, by no means closed, nor will it be until the interchanges cease and the pain-producing effects have followed the pain-producing causes by the action of law. Then and then only will harmony be restored, or in the terms of the prayer, trespasses be "forgiven," meaning counterbalanced. This response is not always easy to attain.

The subject has profound philosophic implications. If both the universe and human life are ruled by law, then no one can ever hurt any man unjustly.[5] In all cases the one who is hurt has acted in the past in such a manner as to make himself susceptible to an exactly proportionate attack. The inner Self, ever inerrant, can in no wise be harmed whether from without or from within. Rooted in this conviction, holding firmly to this realization born of experience, the true philosopher is personally unmoved by the most virulent attack and abuse. Wise and kind, he will regret the adversity which the attacker unfortunately is generating for himself. This concern for others is exemplified in the words of the Christ spoken from the Cross in reference to those who scorned, tortured and then crucified him: "Father forgive them, for they know not what they do."

This is valuable as a magnificent example of personal forgiveness under extreme provocation, doubtless a spontaneous prayer on behalf of his tormentors. Yet in terms of the affirmations by Jesus and St. Paul of the inevitability of the law,[6] the supplication can hardly be regarded as likely to have beneficial effects upon those responsible for the crucifixion.[7] The actions were theirs, and so upon them the appropriate reactions must infallibly be precipitated. Only so can there possibly be a principle of justice operative in the world, and so fair play for man.

Admittedly, such undisturbed calm while enduring torture and such compassion for the torturers are almost superhuman. Nevertheless, the teaching was given by the great Master and is also recognized as an ideal of the way of holiness. Indeed, its acceptance and application to life have been proclaimed by great Teachers as essential for those who would enter in at the "strait gate" and tread the "narrow way."[8] Such forgivingness, selflessness and the power to remain unmoved before a storm depend upon both evolutionary development and self-command attained through systematic self-discipline.

> Matt. 6:15.   But if ye forgive not men their trespasses, neither will your Father forgive your trespasses.

The recorders of the original teaching of the Christ and their translators have tended throughout to personify universal law as a paternal Deity. They have, moreover, presented that eternal principle in the guise of the First Aspect of the Logos in its manifestation as emanator. Thus, the term *Father* is used instead of *law* accentuating the monotheism of the Hebrews and attributing to the Lord the role of a father of a family. This must surely be seen as wholly erroneous. Impersonal, and thus incapable of choice and preferences, the law can neither reward nor forgive; for action produces appropriate reaction at the levels at which it was conceived and carried out. Personification of impersonal laws and processes may not be without its usefulness in bringing abstract ideas within the compass of the mind, but a literal reading is hardly acceptable to the philosophically minded. Nevertheless, the ideas enunciated in verses fourteen and fifteen represent high ideals of human conduct. Forgiveness is surely within the compass of all.

However, it should be remembered that the Master was addressing disciples and would-be disciples, not only those of his own time, but of all time. These are men and women on the way to adeptship when the great cycle of human life reaches its close and a complete and final balancing of karma is achieved. When the process is completed in advance of the normal time, this balancing demands self-denial and self-surrender and can be accompanied by considerably pain. The Passion of the trial and Crucifixion of Jesus exemplifies this suffering. Would-be disciples are advised to refrain from generating further adversity, lest this produce a shackle binding their feet as they tread the upward way. This particularly applies to apparently unjustified attacks, nonresentment being aided by the knowledge that these are but responses to former causative activities.

Matt. 6:16.   Moreover when ye fast, be not, as the hypocrites, of a sad countenance: for they disfigure their faces, that they may appear unto men to fast. Verily I say unto you, They have their reward.

The affirmation that a divine reprisal or "reward" would follow upon insincerity in one's religious life may at first seem somewhat extreme, but examined closely it is clear that, while hypocrisy may be of temporary benefit in worldly affairs, ultimately it is a generator of adversities in both the worldly and the spiritual life. Apart from the more immediate effects, once enacted it can become a habit. On the very first occasion, the mind is adversely affected and, through it, the character. Hypocritical actions can then follow each other without being recognized as such, and hypocrisy can creep so subtly into character and action as to be almost unrecognizable. Becoming established as a tendency in the mind. Purity of heart is then diminished, and conduct can include a series of lying maneuvers for personal gain. Thereafter, one of the most important of all qualities governing success in the spiritual life, namely, integrity, is displaced by its opposite, thereby stultifying the whole great enterprise. Doubtless this is part of the Master's meaning concerning a reward.

Matt. 6:17.   But thou, when thou fastest, anoint thine head, and wash thy face;

18.   That thou appear not unto men to fast, but unto thy Father which is in secret: and thy Father, which seeth in secret, shall reward thee openly.

The necessity for the utmost integrity, sincerity and truthfulness in both the material and the spiritual life is again enunciated. This teaching may seem unduly repeated, both in this and other sermons of Jesus. This is because sincerity and hypocrisy are so prevalent as to be uncritically accepted and even condoned. In some measure they are almost inseparable from man's external and ceremonial practice of religion. This apparently was observable then as now. Thus, the guidance and the warning could not be given too often. Neither can they be repeated and heeded too often in our day, being always applicable when religion is practiced as an external, visible and corporate activity.

The whole nature must be given up to the act of devotion. Actually as well as metaphorically, the body must be cleansed and the head shaven. Thus and thus alone may one tread the pathway from the mortal to the immortal mind and then into the divine presence which is within. Thus approached, that presence will reveal itself, and its light will shine into the mortal mind and heart of the devotee. Such, one assumes, is the response—here called a "reward."

Thus viewed, the warning given has not only ethical but also mystical implications. In the present age the veil between the inner and the outer man, between the mortal and the immortal minds, is normally almost impenetrable. Man's whole effort is required to overcome its resistance and, eventually, to dissolve it. Such hypocrisies as public worship in order to appear holy before one's fellows—outer show which is not matched, by inner integrity —constitute hindrances in the attempt to penetrate this veil.

If one may presume to comment further, this great sermon also teaches that true religion is ideally an entirely interior, private, even secret search for and union with God in nature and in man. The divine is assuredly present, intimately near, waiting, as the Master elsewhere said, but may be known only when heart and mind are utterly sincere and truthful. It is apparent, is it not, that the opposites of these must inevitably repel that which is veritably Truth itself? The untruthful mind could never recognize an inherently pure and perfect expression of truth. Throughout this part of the sermon the Master accentuates this fact.

> Matt. 6:19.   Lay not up for yourselves treasure upon earth, where moth and rust doth corrupt, and where thieves break through and steal:
>
> 20.   But lay up for yourselves treasures in heaven, where neither moth nor rust doth corrupt, and where thieves do not break through nor steal.

It is of the first importance when studying the Sermon on the Mount to remember that it is addressed primarily to those who are either approaching and aspiring toward the spiritual way of life or have already embarked upon it. Unless this is remembered, the teachings can be regarded as wholly impracticable and so ignored. This would be a great loss; for the very essence of wisdom, the heart of spiritual philosophy, is contained in the great utterance.

If applied solely to material life and wordly affairs, these verses might, indeed, appear to advise and encourage improvidence. Addressed to disciples, however, they counsel a recognition of the distinction between that which is real in the philosophic sense, meaning permanent, and that which is unreal or impermanent, transitory. The transitory with its allurement of passing pleasure and satisfactions can entrap body and mind. Thus ensnared, aspirants, particularly those newly embarked upon the "way of holiness," are caught in a net of overaccentuation of material profit and pleasure. However, once this distinction between the real and the unreal is recognized, motive and conduct are inevitably influenced. The admittedly necessary and essential concern with preservation and security in worldly matters for oneself and family no longer engages the *whole* attention, is no longer the only goal of life or purpose for living.

After security is reasonably assured, the wise man studies truths relating to the spiritual aspects of human nature and ponders the nature of his soul. Gradually the accent changes. Effective physical action still continues but becomes increasingly relegated to the concerns of the worldly life. Cultural, artistic, philosophic interest and development occupy an increasing position until, eventually, they become predominant. Contemplation of the eternal center of all that exists, including himself, occupies more and more time and thought. At last, this alone occupies the arena of the life and thought of spiritually awakened man, the accepted disciple. Thus occurs a gradual and perfectly natural progression from the worldly to the purely spiritual direction of thought and interest. In this way a man metaphorically lays up for himself "treasures in heaven."

What, then, are these treasures? They are powers of the soul as distinct from those of the body and outer personality. They include the capacity to exert a decisive control over the activities of consciousness at any level of awareness and action. Will and thought, each developed to a high degree, combine in absolute rulership and interior autocracy from which there is no appeal.

Innate wisdom is developed into inclusive insight into first truths. The intellect then penetrates automatically into the underlying principles of any situation, group of facts or, indeed, any single fact. The processes of thought begin from within the underlying principle and proceed outward to survey the varied expressions of that principle. Thus, the higher intellect of one so developed faultlessly interprets every event and every idea; natural laws and processes and items of knowledge—especially those which appear self-contradictory—are both grasped by the mind and comprehended by the higher intellect.

Perhaps the greatest of all treasures in heaven, is the capacity to perceive and at all times recognize the unifying principle in the universe, that which unites all diversities, preserves them all in harmonious interrelationship and is, in fact, the reality of their existence. When this treasure is attained, man is transfigured and his life in the world is transformed. Inwardly, he is illumined and endowed with the gifts of the spirit, while outwardly his relations with all other beings are expressions of a compassionate, if impersonal, love.

Empowered and illumined by the faculties of the soul, disciples, initiates and Adepts are rich indeed, for they recognize and seek the true wealth of man and evaluate all else accordingly. They distinguish unerringly between the false and the true, the transitory and the everlasting, the unreal and the real.

Matt. 6:21.   For where your treasure is, there will your heart be also.

The great sermon tells of the first necessity for progress in self-spiritualization, namely, interest and aspiration, both gradually developing into a fiery resolve. Without this little or no progress can be made in hastening development.

This interest can hardly be artificially developed; it is beyond pretense. Awakened from within a person, it is one of the most notable indications of evolutionary progress toward great spiritual heights. It is far more important than great intellectual power or any physical achievement.

Interest in the spiritual life is thus to be regarded as one of the great milestones or landmarks on the pathway trodden by man toward adeptship. It is only born in the personal mind when two developments have occurred within. These are fully conscious realization of the divine Self and realization of the power of that Self to reach the mind and produce aspiration toward the heights. The moment the mortal man says, "I aspire ardently to achieve hastened progress, to reach discipleship and adeptship," all things become possible, including interior unfoldment and advancement on the way of holiness. The importance of heartfelt interest can hardly be overstressed.

> Matt. 6:22.   The light of the body is the eye: if therefore thine eye be single, thy whole body shall be full of light.

Here the great Teacher begins to expound another aspect of the qualities required to tread the way of holiness successfully: wholeheartedness in character and conduct and one-pointedness in aspiration to the spiritual heights. Anything less than these will result in slow and intermittent progress on the ascent or failure.

Admittedly, these characteristics must undergo processes of development. They cannot be expected to be full-grown from the first. Quite naturally, aspirants may waver in the first life in which these new attributes of his outer nature begin to influence his thoughts and, through them, his actions.[9] Even if he fails in the conflict with his own past, his karma, and his physical demands, the will to the heights will manifest itself increasingly life after life. The inward power continues growing stronger until there comes that incarnation in which it becomes a single, all-consuming and well-organized determination to succeed. Then the demands of these verses are met. Symbolically, his eye is single and so his "whole body is full of light."

> Matt. 6:23.   But if thine eye be evil, thy whole body shall be full of darkness. If therefore the light that is in thee be darkness, how great is that darkness!

Naturally, the language in these verses is metaphorical. Here the "eye" represents the mind and the mental attitude, tendencies, habitual thinking, and the outlook upon life. More than any other principle in man, the mind with its motivations influences the character and conduct of physical man. If the mental attitude is right, then, however gradually, all else will become right. Conversely, if the mind is insincere, halfhearted, unsure concerning hastened evolution to perfection, this will erect an almost impassable barrier between the spiritual impulse and its increasing expression in daily life.

The mind cut off from the spiritual Self can be almost as a demon, tempting man to betray his conscience, both in relationships with others and in conduct. The mind in this state can also deflect interest from the spiritual toward the material, from truth to untruth, from the permanent to the transient, and from psychological unity and wholeness to diverse and conflicting desires and states. In this sense, then, the eye can be evil and, in consequence, the whole body be full of "darkness."

> Matt. 6:24.   No man can serve two masters: for either he will hate the one, and love the other; or else he will hold to the one, and despise the other. Ye cannot serve God and mammon.

Here the burden of this part of the Sermon on the Mount with regard to wholeheartedness is repeated. However gradually, the neophyte must become assured within himself that it is God and not mammon which calls to his soul. Even though he may be obliged for duty's sake to be *in* the world and concerned with its affairs, he becomes less and less *of* the world, ultimately regarding it as nothing more than a valuable school. Until then the desire for worldly wealth and power and the actions necessary to attain them will continue to tempt him from the true path and, should he fall, endanger his spiritual progress. The safeguard against this danger, as posited by the great Master, is singlemindedness, oneness of purpose, and the full adoption of a spiritual objective or goal.

> Matt. 6:25. Therefore I say unto you, Take no thought for your life, what ye shall eat, or what ye shall drink; nor yet for your body, what ye shall put on. Is not the life more than meat, and the body than raiment?

Jesus evidently perceived among the wealthier classes of his day an established custom of overaccentuating the value of material possessions to the neglect of, or greatly reduce interest in, underlying spiritual principles. Unfortunately, this error, which had long existed before his time, would, as he foresaw, continue to exist long afterward. His words may not have come down to us wholly unaltered, even though it is reasonable to assume that he would have safeguarded his teaching against misapprehension and misapplication. Since a literal reading of this verse inculcates impractical otherworldliness, laxity and neglect of the laws of physical life, and deliberate dependence upon others, it is clear that a metaphorical meaning is intended. The verse may thus permissibly be read as referring to emphasis rather than total management in certain affairs on one's life. Acute concern with the body and purely physical life is to be gradually displaced by complete self-dedication to the spiritual way of living. The normal rules of physical conduct—including practicality—must still be obeyed; but these are mere exercises in physical living or expressions of the art of earthly life. The aspirant cares for his body just as he lubricates machinery in obedience to known laws. Ideally, he performs these preservative actions to meet natural requirements. He does not become passionately absorbed in the processes of preservation, nor does he carry to extreme any self-benefiting physical action. He keeps the body in good order so that it may serve him well—and that is all. Similar instructions are given in yoga philosophy to exercise discrimination, detachment and dispassion where worldly matters are concerned.

Needs regarding the life of the spirit, the enrichment of the soul, and the sustenance of the mind with truth, can be fully met from that boundless granary and storehouse which is the spiritual aspect of nature. Just as, physically, prodigal abundance of the germs of life is seen in the seeds of plants and trees and the sperms of higher organisms, so also superphysically and spiritually the great "Father-Mother" of all provides lavishly for every need of the soul of man. Knowledge of this is part of the secret Wisdom of the ages, and when discovered, is relied upon quite naturally. Restless striving is displaced by serenity in full assurance of a bountiful supply of all the inner necessities. Eventually this becomes reflected in the conduct of physical life.

Immoderate passion for power and wealth is replaced by an orderly mode of living in which undue craving has no place. Such, indeed, is the way to peace of heart and mind.

>Matt. 6:26.   Behold the fowls of the air: for they sow not, neither do they reap, nor gather into barns; yet your heavenly Father feedeth them. Are ye not much better than they?

In accordance with his custom, the Master drew analogies from nature in order to illustrate his teachings. Whether or not in his original words he personified nature as the divine Father or paternal Deity, he here regards Deity as synonymous with nature herself, which indeed is but a manifestation of the omnipresent Source of all that exists. Generally, though perhaps not in every particular and under all climatic conditions, nature does provide prodigally for all animate life. Similarly, the self-same principal contains within itself and permeates all worlds with the necessities for spiritual and superphysical life, bountifully supplied.

When this analogy from nature grows from a mental concept to a vital experience in consciousness—as in the practice of yoga—mysteriously, the infinite Source is found to be *with* man himself. More mysterious still, he is, in fact, discovered to be identical with that Source. From this point of view, the idea of an outward flowing supply of the necessities of existence is erroneous. An example is thus provided of the difference between the functioning of the brain-mind of man and of his higher intellect. The mind *must* conceive of source and supply as two separate existences, but the higher intelligence knows them as a single state of being; for there is neither within nor without in God-consciousness, nor is there any such duality as source and supply.

The principle of unfailing supply from within is discovered by God-illumined man. This experience in consciousness banishes fear and every anxiety and bestows serenity. In this sense, only as an attitude of mind, should man "take no thought for his life."

>Matt. 6:27.   Which of you by taking thought can add one cubit unto his stature?

Here another pertinent analogy is drawn from nature—that of the growth of organic forms. This natural process is, in general, beyond the control of man and uninfluenced by his thought; indeed, the less he concerns himself with it, the better. Similarly, in all the normal processes of nature at every level, an attitude of detachment is enjoined. The great sermon may safely be regarded as descriptive of such an attitude of mind toward life. This is valuable for all and completely essential for the aspirant seeking to attain to spiritual enlightenment, to whom the Lord's teachings are especially addressed. Over-accentuation of the provision of material possessions will inevitably produce underaccentuation of the true purpose of life, which is to achieve enlightenment.

Again, the teachings must not be regarded as advice to neglect such necessities as the nutrition and care of the body, but rather to avoid the error of undue attention to these.

Matt. 6:28.   And why take ye thought for raiment? Consider the lilies of the field, how they grow; they toil not, neither do they spin:

29.   And yet I say unto you, That even Solomon in all his glory was not arrayed like one of these.

Yet another well-chosen analogy from nature is used by Our Lord in order to instruct neophytes in the attainment of a special attitude toward the spiritual life. Two approaches to life and two modes of living are contrasted: undue attention to clothing and outward personal appearance and simplicity and naturalness.

Again, the teaching cannot be taken too literally, especially by those whose circumstances oblige them to live in the outer world. The Sermon on the Mount describes an approach to living and definitely *not* a mode of life or details of application; for, of course, lackadaisical carelessness, irresponsibility, and drifting under a plea of naturalness can only lead to disaster, material and spiritual. In an incarnation which permits retirement to a hermitage or ashram, however, and where the climate permits, extreme simplicity in clothing is obviously desirable. In addition, both the withdrawal of attention from such externals and concentration upon the interior light are enjoined since, by such means, distractions of mind and body are reduced to a minimum.

An even deeper and more subtle instruction is discernible. The natural processes by which the plant kingdom is beautifully clothed, as in the case of the lily family, also occur in man; but, being endowed with mind, he can interfere with natural processes by the power of his thought, which can intrude inharmoniously upon that which should be left to nature. In order to keep up with his associates, he clothes himself, furnishes and decorates his home and provides himself with the latest mode of transportation, thereby employing time and money which could be spent more advantageously. In addition, he complicates his life and even impoverishes himself. Thus, instead of being content with the simple necessities for a dignified and cultured mode of living, he establishes conditions which inevitably distract his attention from spiritual, cultural and bodily needs.

While mental activity can produce undue complexity, right thinking concerning the conduct of life brings a much desired simplicity. Spontaneity, unforced naturalness, permits the free play of the life-forces. Spiritually illumined man knows that life itself will abundantly provide for all his needs. He leaves to the life-force the work which it is designed to perform, while he himself is concerned with the task to which he has set himself—the achievement of greater illumination and perfection.[10] Those who have already advanced ahead of the race and also those who by yoga have attained an intuitive vision of life are already applying these principles to their lives; for man is evolving. Eventually, the teachings of the Sermon on the Mount will quite naturally be applied by all.

Matt. 6:30.   Therefore, if God so clothe the grass of the field, which today is, and tomorrow is cast into the oven, shall he not much more clothe you, O ye of little faith?

31. Therefore take no thought, saying, What shall we eat? or, What shall we drink? or, Wherewithal shall we be clothed?

32. (For after all these things do the Gentiles seek:) for your heavenly Father knoweth that ye have need of all these things.

33. But seek ye first the kingdom of God, and his righteousness; and all these things shall be added unto you.

34. Take therefore no thought for the morrow: for the morrow shall take thought for the things of itself. Sufficient unto the day is the evil thereof.

He who would hasten his progress on the pathway to perfection should carefully study the words of wisdom given to mankind so long ago and almost miraculously preserved down to the present day. He should learn to recognize the laws enunciated. Then he may be trusted to intelligently apply the qualities of dispassion and detachment concerning the things of the material world with its prizes and rewards.

If the Master is charged with overaccentuating the importance of purely spiritual values and pursuits, then it should be recognized that this is far less harmful than its opposite. Furthermore, the very demands of the body and of bodily life crying irresistibly for satisfaction generally tend to restore any imbalance. Rightly understood, the whole sermon—and especially the closing verses—constitutes a magnificent utterance.

REFERENCES AND NOTES

1. Matt. 27:51.

2. Matt. 5:18; Rom. 12:19.

3. See Geoffrey Hodson, *Lecture Notes of the School of Wisdom*, Vol. I.

4. Within an enclosing circle the interlaced triangle represents the Adept, whose "sign" is the Solomon's Seal.

5. See Geoffrey Hodson, *Reincarnation, Fact or Fallacy?*

6. Matt. 5:18; Rom. 12:19.

7. See Geoffrey Hodson, *Reincarnation, Fact or Fallacy?* pp. 254-6.

8. Matt. 7:13.

9. Man's evolution to Christhood by means of successive lives on earth is here assumed.

10. Ct. "Be ye therefore perfect, even as your Father which is in Heaven is perfect." Matt. 5:48.

Chapter Eleven

Man's seniors in evolution have ever sought to offset materialism and to inculcate recognition of spiritual values. The Sermon on the Mount, a magnificent effort in this direction, is recognized as wise counsel in the true tradition of occult guidance to be studied and applied to life by those who would hasten their progress on the way of holiness.

Matt. 7:1.   Judge not, that ye be not judged.
　　　2.   For with what judgment ye judge, ye shall be judged: and with what measure ye mete, it shall be measured to you again.

The Lord, while still offering counsel concerning ideal attitudes of both mind and heart, now changes his theme. Although not at first enunciating the law of cause and effect, he nonetheless proceeds to describe its operation, showing that actions and reactions are intimately related. The accent of this verse is placed less upon conduct. A lofty moral standard is enjoined and a practical reason for its attainment is given: failure to act according to a high ethical code is to produce a corresponding adverse effect upon the actor.

The teaching is carried still further in the second verse of this chapter, which indicates mathematical exactitude in the operation of the law: the degree of adverse judgment to be strictly in accordance with the act of judging. Philosophically considered, this pronouncement is indeed remarkable, for a universal law, a natural and inevadable sequence of cause and effect, is shown to govern every experience of man in a most precise manner. If the measure of the reaction is exactly proportionate to that of the preceding action, as the Lord Christ affirms, then indeed universal law inescapably rules every particular circumstance of every man's existence. Thus, the universal and the particular meet with extreme precision—a remarkable idea.

In expounding this law the process of weighing is generally shown by analogy. In the Egyptian presentation, the heart of the actor was weighed against a feather. St. Paul used an agricultural illustration; action as the sowing of seed and reaction as the consequent reaping according to the nature of the seed sown. In all such teaching, accuracy, precision and exactitude of operation are consistently affirmed.

The Master Jesus was evidently of a practical turn of mind and one, moreover, who recognized the essential simplicity of the minds of his hearers. Whenever he taught of an abstract principle, he rarely failed to bring its application down to common human experience that could easily be appreciated and understood. Thus, he taught whatever your judgment of a man and his way of life may be, so you and your conduct will tend to be judged. Appreciate, and you will be likely to be appreciated in your turn. Condemn, and condemnation is likely to be your lot. These treatments by others are both automatic and precise.

However, if the subject is considered rather more deeply and in terms of a gradual development of character through customary modes of thought, then adverse judgments, condemnations of others, can establish discordance, resulting in increasingly strong tendencies to adverse criticism. These both color and, to that extent, falsify assessments of other people's character and conduct and build into the make-up the undesirable qualities of separativeness, superiority and the severance of the bonds of unity that should bind all men together. Thus, the Lord counsels all to establish the habit of appreciation and kindly, even beneficent, thinking about one's fellowmen, whether high or low, sinner or saint.

Matt. 7:3.   And why beholdest thou the mote that is in thy brother's eye, but considerest not the beam that is in thine own eye?

While the conduct here advised is undoubtedly the wisest and the best, intelligent recognition of good and bad qualities in others, and sane and safe thinking and action based upon it, are by no means to be discarded. Human individualities vary not only in their inherent characters but also in the expression of their qualities at different times. Obviously, there are occasions when one must "judge" others, as for example when choosing them for positions of trust or admission to degrees of intimacy. An assessment of the integrity of character, for example, is not only permissible but necessary. Watchful observance of others, particularly those with whom one is in close contact, is by no means an error. Indeed, without it a person could be befooled on every side. Condemnation, however, particularly on insufficient grounds and leading to an injustice, must be guarded against. This is not only because such action would be both unfair and unkind, but also because it would be inevitably followed by a similar adversity.

Nevertheless, the great Master warns that such assessments should begin with the person making them. A frank recognition of one's own limitations will generally either prevent or reduce the severity of criticism of adverse qualities in others. The counsel is carried further by the great Teacher. Action based upon self-observation must come first. One should look to one's own undesirable qualities and weaknesses and remove them before destructively criticizing and condemning adverse qualities in others.

This teaching in the great sermon must, therefore, be very carefully considered and nicely weighed in the balance of the mind. Thereafter it may be carefully and rightly applied to the conduct of life.

Matt. 7:4.   Or how wilt thou say to thy brother, Let me pull out the
              mote out of thine eye; and, behold, a beam is in thine own
              eye?

For many, this is a counsel of perfection. Two difficulties stand in the way
of its acceptance and application. The first is that of detached and impartial
analysis of one's own character, followed by full recognition of the less
desirable attributes which it reveals. The second difficulty arises from a
natural unreadiness to submit oneself to needed disciplines and to the surgery
which removal of faults frequently demand. Inertia, apathy, the ease and
comfort of continuing in customary motives and actions all contribute to
resistance to self-purification. However, the disciple and the would-be disciple are eager to remove interior obstacles to that hastened progress to which
they aspire. Some may even be too drastic, too severe—an error which leads
to unbalanced asceticism.

Whether applied to the life of the man of the world or of the spiritual
neophyte, the counsel so wonderfully received and delivered is equally
valuable. Indeed, it appears almost too obvious in its simplicity. As soon,
however, as the attempt is sincerely made to apply it to oneself, it is found to
be far from simple and very far from easy to adopt.

Matt. 7:5.   Thou hypocrite, first cast out the beam out of thine own
              eye; and then shalt thou see clearly to cast out the mote
              out of thy brother's eye.

Here the instruction is carried further, and support for it is advanced.
Blindness in oneself, however slight, inevitably prevents one from examining
impartially, clearly, and accurately the character of others. The outlook is
inevitably colored and so rendered partially incorrect by defects in the
observer and his means of observation. Thus, an additional reason is given
for the recognition and extirpation of one's own faults before presuming to
pronounce upon those of others.

Matt. 7:6.   Give not that which is holy unto dogs, neither cast ye
              your pearls before swine, lest they trample them under
              their feet, and turn again and rend you.

The subject of the teaching once more changes so abruptly that one
suspects a gap in the original record or in copies of it. This verse pronounces a
profound occult dictum. Secrecy concerning potent knowledge is stricly
enjoined, and a warning is given against unwise public dissemination of
power-bestowing truths. Perhaps the great Teacher had found that the more
subtle and elevated ideas which he had advanced were neither understood
nor given due consideration. They may even have been received with scorn.

Such truths are likened to pearls, swine signifying those who for lack of
progess in evolution are unable to comprehend them. The long history of
numerous attempts to instruct and guide humanity into pathways of peace
and happiness by revelations of spiritual law gives ground for the warning.
Almost inevitably the unevolved, and so ignorant, crowd fails to comprehend
either the motive of the revealer or the truths revealed. Such people tend to

judge the conduct of others in terms of their own self-preserving, self-seeking and purely selfish modes of thought and action. They are quite unable to see and appreciate in a true Teacher either a stature greater then their own or a purpose unsullied by self-interest. These disabilities and instinctual resentment can cause an uninstructed mob to turn upon and ill-treat, if not destroy, a teacher of spiritual truths and moral law beyond their comprehension.

An ever deeper significance may be discerned in the warning given in this verse. Accepted neophytes, disciples and initiates of the Mystery Schools are taught certain deeply occult truths. According to their degree of development in and passage through the grades of the Mysteries, they receive practical instruction concerning occult forces and associated intelligences and ways to employ these. In wrong hands this knowledge can be exceedingly dangerous, both for those who prematurely disclose it and for those who prematurely receive it. In Egyptian religious art, the statue of the child Horus Harpocrates, with finger to lips, portrays a newly initiated member of the Greater Mysteries, his gesture indicating the necessity for silence.

Even so, occasions can arise in which a Teacher must speak, though condemnation and punishment unto death be the result. Jesus must have known this and may even have foreseen his own experience of it when led to pronounce the words of this verse.

> Matt. 7:7.   Ask, and it shall be given you; seek and ye shall find; knock, and it shall be opened unto you:
>
> 8.   For every one that asketh receiveth; and he that seeketh findeth; and to him that knocketh it shall be opened.

The admonition to preserve secrecy concerning such truth and knowledge might seem to close the door in the face of the seeker and to close the mouth of him from whom knowledge is sought. In these verses the Master approaches the same subject from the point of view of one who is seeking for truth, for light and for admission to the deeper Mysteries of both knowledge and life itself.

The way in which barriers may be passed over and closed mouths brought to speak is described in these verses: knock persistently on the door of the metaphorical temple of truth and appeal insistently for guidance from a teacher of truth. Initiates of the Mysteries, lesser and greater, move continually among men, whether recognized or not. Each of them bears the duty to seek, to find, and to respond to would-be neophytes, sincere seekers for truth. They may not close their ears to any cry for light, nor may they refuse to teach those who ask them with ardor and with will. While always discriminating, the possessors of the keys of knowledge are under the bounden duty to use them to unlock the stores of wisdom for those who knock, seek, and ask.

Such external responses are complemented by changes within the aspirant. The inner Self responds to the cry of the outer man for light and to his determination to find it. A deepening understanding of the esoteric aspects and occult implications of existing religious teaching, a widening sympathy for fellowmen, opportunities for service and special faculties for giving it are all found within himself by the spiritually awakening man. His seeking, asking and knocking must be from a pure heart that is without thought of personal gain, and with readiness to share whatever may be useful. Thus aroused, determined, and with eyes fixed upon the spiritual heights, every aspirant is assured of eventual success in the great quest for light, truth and power.

Matt. 7:9.   Or what man is there of you, whom if his son ask bread, will he give him a stone?

In metaphorical language the great Teacher here differentiates between the bread of esoteric wisdom and the stone of mere tradition, dogma and orthodoxy. Just as no father would give a hungry son a stone wherewith to assuage his hunger, so no true teacher will merely repeat received tradition when asked to bestow the living truth.

Matt. 7:10.   Or if he ask a fish, will he give him a serpent?

The same thought is expressed by means of another analogy contrasting the edible with the inedible. The greatness of the Lord Christ as Teacher is revealed in the facility with which he thus illustrates and makes understandable somewhat abstract ideas by means of analogies based upon familiar things and natural processes and objects.

To many of his hearers the idea of a vital, living wisdom and religious teaching may have been quite new. This is because in many cases they had known none other than the doctrines of orthodoxy based largely on the Mosaic law. One part of the mission of Jesus was to widen the outlook of the people in such matters, and in so doing to break the grip of priestcraft and rigid scriptural interpretations upon their minds. The need for reform was very great, and the outlook of large numbers was, doubtless, made much more liberal, again arousing the enmity of the established institution, its chief and associated priests. The whole of the sacerdotal caste of the time rose against him and took his life. This was not before, however, this sermon had been preached and a great light shed into the minds of men.

Matt. 7:11.   If ye then, being evil, know how to give good gifts unto your children, how much more shall your Father which is in heaven give good things to them that ask him?

The Essenes of the time of Jesus were well informed concerning Hindu and Buddhist philosophy. The concept of karma was well known to them; for traders and teachers from the East were constantly traveling through Palestine in those days. Jesus, having been trained among the Essenes in his youth, must have become imbued with this doctrine. Oriental philosophy of those days, as in the present, in no such way personifies universal law. On certain occasions, however, either Jesus's words have been altered or he deliberately personified the law as a watchful Deity to make it more understandable. The Father in Heaven of this verse is, indeed, closely analogous to the function of the law of cause and effect. Reaction follows action as impersonally and naturally as all other laws and forces in nature produce their effects. Magnetic attraction and repulsion are in no sense the result of the intrusion upon or interference with nature. They occur because they are manifestations of the very law of existence, the very nature and structure of the manifested universe. So also, taught the Eastern sages, human action produces reaction under natural law, apparently personified by Jesus as a divine Father in Heaven.

> Matt. 7:12.   Therefore all things whatsoever ye would that men should do to you, do ye even so to them: for this is the law and the prophets.

Impersonality, universality, and the inevadability of such a law is here unequivocally stated. The Deity is not made responsible for the results of men's actions or the principle governing human relationships. Indeed, this verse may be decisively quoted as a statement of fundamental natural law. To help others is to find help available in times of need; to injure others is to invite, nay to receive, commensurate injury. Moreover, the finest gradations and interminglings of different types of conduct bring about exactly appropriate effects.

For example, if a man strikes another, casting him to the ground, three further actions can follow. The striker may give the victim a further blow even unto death; he may feel and express contrition by aiding, raising up, and healing the one so struck; or he may ignore him, leaving him to his fate. Each of these actions will affect the results of the first blow at whatever levels the blow was struck—mentally, emotionally, verbally, physically, or a combination of several of these.

Should a second and perhaps fatal blow follow the first, then the reaction will be still more severe. Should compassion lead to sincere reparation and the rendering of all possible aid, then the reaction from the first blow will be proportionately reduced. Indeed, it might even be neutralized, especially if the aid is continued long after all effects from the blow disappear and a permanent and successful arrangement for helping is established. In the third case in which the victim is ignored, left to suffer and even die, the full effects of the action will be felt by the actor or even increased, since, as the familiar maxim says, acts of omission producing suffering can bring adversity.[5] Such indeed is the law as enunciated by the succession of sages, philosophers, and saints who have visited and instructed mankind.

Here again, Christian orthodoxy has doubly misled mankind—by failing to pronounce this natural process to be a law of the universe, and by dogmatically affirming the opposite. According to the orthodox view, however deeply and deliberately a human being may, by vice or cruelty, transgress divine and human law, results can be prevented and the law negated by faith in the supposed fact of vicarious atonement.

A very grave disservice to humanity is inherent in the dogma of the Atonement, which in *uttermost error* has been placed at the heart of Christian theology. This is because the doctrine itself is untrue and indeed men are encouraged to indulge in every kind of wickedness by assurance that there will be no painful results whatever in this world or the next. Human minds are in consequence indoctrinated with untruth, and the incentive to self-discipline produced by knowledge that effect must follow cause is taken away from mankind. The grievous condition of the Western world since the time of Jesus, and particularly in the present era, may well be partly the result of the twin effects of the doctrine of the remission of sins.

With this law there can be no bargaining any more than a prayer to the Deity can change the laws under which planets, suns, and universes proceed in their motions through space. The death of Jesus, regardless of sincerity of belief, can in no wise and in no slightest degree turn aside even by a hairsbreadth the operation of the justice-insuring law.

Modern Christian orthodoxy is in error in placing the accent upon Atonement and remisssion of sins instead of upon the wisdom which is the *Logia* Jesus gave to the world. As for the instructed Buddhist the dharma is the Buddha's gift to mankind, so the instructed Christian should regard the teachings of Jesus, in their turn, as his great gift.

> Matt. 7:13.   Enter ye in at the strait gate; for wide is the gate, and broad is the way, that leadeth to destruction, and many there be which go in thereat:
>
> 14.   Because strait is the gate, and narrow is the way, which leadeth unto life, and few there be that find it.

Again, an abrupt change of subject occurs, suggesting either the loss of connecting passages or their deliberate deletion. Nevertheless, a connection may be conceived between intellectual realization that the law of causation operates unerringly and entry upon the way of holiness. The choice of the new and living way is born partly from a purely mental realization of fundamental natural laws and principles. This discovery in consciousness, in due course, inevitably offsets both a wordly outlook on life and, through that, the way of living. This change might be described as intelligent conformity with the laws of being and cooperation with the processes of nature now realized. The change of attitude and its implication in conduct can be exceedingly drastic, dramatic and even apparently selfish and neglectful. The impulse arising from within the mind is, however, so strong as to be irresistible. The person thus inwardly inspired literally has no choice. He must enter in at the straight gate, and he must live according to the so-called narrow way.

The impulse is not only from the intellect, however, but also from the heart—the conjoined intuition and emotion. The will, too, becomes kindled by action from the highest Self, awake, active and assuming domination over the personal, mortal nature.

In verses thirteen and fourteen certain words are used in a special sense other than the literal. The statement that entrance upon the broad way leads to destruction and the narrow way to life is worthy of close examination. Man, living amid the affairs of the world and forced continually to deal with his own concerns, cannot know of a broad way or a strait gate leading to a narrow way; neither can he understand such terms as *life* and *destruction*. For him all is life until the moment of death, and all ways concern the living of wordly life. Thus, the meaning is clearly metaphorical.

An error of recording or translation, or even a change in the text by some theologian, may have mistakenly inserted the word *destruction*. If applied to the spirit of man, his true individuality, the word in its common meaning is unacceptable; for the innermost divinity in man, his pure spirit-essence, is utterly indestructible. Nothing in the whole universe of time and space can affect adversely or ever destroy it. Even if the outer, bodily person consistently and deliberately through several lives pursues a pathway of materialism, sensuality and tyranny—typified here by the broad way—the divine Dweller within remains unaffected with regard to eternal existence and well-being. Though a man in his outer personality deliberately continues to live as if he were a mere bodily person or even pursues the pathway of wickedness, the spirit-Self in its "vesture of light" reaps whatever harvesting of faculty may be possible and carries this and the residual effects of that life into a later bodily personality.

Thus, destruction does not refer to the soul of man, but rather to two particular motives for living and ways of life, each with its effect upon those who choose them. The strait gate refers to a disciplined, if not ascetic, mode of life. The narrow way refers to the "razor-edged path" of Hinduism with pitfalls and dangers on either side, treading which a man strictly adheres to certain rules of life. Choosing such a controlled and directed mode of living quickens the evolution of those who pursue it. Initiation and adeptship are by this means attained ahead of the race, as are certain spiritual states of consciousness appropriate to those attainments. On the other hand, a purely worldly life, and more especially an overindulgent life recognizing only the bodily person, rarely leads to waking knowledge of the divine Self, the immortal soul. Aware of inevitable mortality, such a one moves on to death without realization of the immortality of the soul. For this condition the word *destruction* is used descriptively. One way is narrow and one is broad; disciples choose the former and nondisciples choose the latter. No element of either praise or judgment concerning this choice can exist in an enlightened mind. It is the result of quite natural processes. Just as the bud forms on a flowering plant at a certain time and season, so the bud of Christhood forms and later opens in the soul of man. Before that time arrives, however, there can be neither bud nor plant nor soul-awakening.

True, foreshadowings and intimations of the change may occur. Indeed, several earthly lives may pass before the decision is made. Ratification in physical conduct may be gradual and even resisted by the physical body and the habit-governed mind. This becomes less and less effective, being burned away, as it were, by the fire of the newly awakened Self. Eventually, in one life the full change occurs, often as a complete conversion, an interior revolution, even with an appearance of fanaticism. The decision is then irrevocable. The resistance of the habit-ridden body and mind, already worn thin, is quickly overcome, both being subdued. The narrow way is then chosen and trodden to its end, however great the difficulties and however serious the falls. The deeply interior formation and incipient opening of the bud of adeptship has begun.

This is a phase in human development which is watched for and readily recognized by the Master-to-be, the guardian Adept, when it is entered upon. This is typified by the actions of Jesus and the so-called fishermen. The Master recognized their awakened condition and called them to discipleship. They answered unhesitatingly; they "left all and followed him."

The affirmation that the narrow way leads to life is true in terms of consiousness for the one who treads it; for as the way is trodden, awareness of oneself as a purely spiritual being is gradually attained. Ordinarily personalities disintegrate gradually after death, while the individual consciousness, the Ego, the vehicle of the spirit, remains. The initiate comes to know himself as immortal and eternal, as a purely spiritual identity, a ray of the Supreme Self. The death of the body means but little to those thoroughly established in this realization born of direct experience, gained by following the rules of life expounded in the Sermon on the Mount. He realizes that death is but the loss of name and form; for the spiritual soul lives on continuously, evolving throughout the long series of earthly lives, each with its physical birth and death. In the sense, at least, entering in at the strait gate and treading the narrow way "leadeth unto life," meaning eternal life or conscious immortality.

An exception to the natural processes at death occurs in those men and women who progress upon the way of holiness to a phase at which the emotional and mental natures and vehicles do not disintegrate. This is one of the effects produced by passage through the rite of initiation into the Greater Mysteries; for the touch of the thyrsus in the hands of an adept hierophant pervades these vehicles with a sufficient measure of the fire of spirit to render them immortal. Thereafter, they do not die, being retained at least until adeptship is reached. In this deeply occult sense, the initiate attains to life eternal, relatively speaking.

Still deeper implications can possibly be found in the term *life*. Those Adepts who voluntarily decide to retain a physical body are able to bestow upon it unusual longevity. The body does not appear to age; it continues in youthful maturity and efficiency far beyond the normal span, for many centuries in fact, and is laid aside solely according to the Adept's own decision and will. Even though their bodies die, no decline occurs in the full spiritual awareness to which, as divine and immortal beings, they have attained. This may also be included in the term *life,* for two meanings can be given to the word, namely, fully conscious realization of the deathlessness of the spiritual soul and the attainment of extreme longevity of the body.

As a trained Essene and an initiated member of the Greater Mysteries as practiced in Egypt at the time, the great Hebrew Reformer who has come to be known as Jesus Christ must have known these facts. His instructors taught them, and he himself—great Gnostic that he was, using that term in its highest significance—would have learned these mysteries by direct experience. From these considerations it seems abundantly clear that, while many have heard it, the Sermon on the Mount was delivered chiefly as guidance for candidates for discipleship and initiation, those who in fact had passed through the strait gate and were treading the narrow way. Indeed, it is true that there are but few that find this way.

> Matt. 7:15.   Beware of false prophets, which come to you in sheep's clothing, but inwardly they are ravening wolves.

One of the many pitfalls along the narrow way is to be misled by those of impure, selfish motives claiming to be spiritual teachers. This danger is very real and arises from contact with two different kinds of people. One of these consists of men or women who desire to attain prestige and thereby power by assuming spiritual wisdom, making occult pretensions, and claiming to be appointed guides. The other kind is still more dangerous because it represents the forces to darkness. This consists of evil men and women who deliberately set their wills against the evolutionary process, who seek to debase human beings so that they readily fall victim, and who attack especially neophytes on the narrow way. Indeed, "they are as ravening wolves."

Fortunately, the true teachers and their guidance also exist and are available. This guidance, such as the Sermon on the Mount, consists not only of a revelation of the laws of the spiritual life, but also of a warning against the pitfalls, including those here named false prophets.

> Matt. 7:16.   Ye shall know them by their fruits. Do men gather grapes of thorns, or figs of thistles?

Guidance is here given in discerning the false from the true teacher. The neophyte should examine closely the inner motives, the character, and the mode of life of anyone who proposes to reveal spiritual truths. In addition, his or her intuition should be allowed full play, so that, guided by the intellect, sincerity of purpose may be perceived and insincerity uncovered. Where there is the slightest sign of pretense, the neophyte should be strictly on guard, always applying pure reason to every item of instruction.

As was his custom, the great Master here again uses a simile from nature, from horticulture. As grapes do not grow on thorn trees, and as figs are not gathered from thistle plants, so truth cannot be found in the hypocrite nor safe guidance from those who deliberately deceive.

> Matt. 7:17.   Even so every good tree bringeth forth good fruit; but a corrupt tree bringeth forth evil fruit.

When pure spirituality is under consideration and the qualifications of a professed teacher of spiritual truths are being evaluated, singleness of purpose—in this case the highest purpose—constitutes the acid test. The true teacher has but one motive for teaching and, indeed, for living, namely to teach the highest and the deepest truth as he knows it. Wherever a second motive, a duality of purpose, is discerned, doubt should exist in the mind of the would-be pupil. The secondary purpose should then be investigated; only if it harmonizes with the ideal has a true teacher been found.

Motive is here accentuated; for the term *good* means genuine, sincere, truly enlightened, and free from self-desire. The term *corrupt*, on the other hand, means the opposite of these and, even more, their absence in the characters of those who seek to exploit their small amount of understanding for their own benefit. While this latter is permissible or even necessary in worldly matters, it is definitely an evil within a system of spiritual guidance, whether by a single teacher or an organized group.

The element of self-gain—personal benefit of any kind—is deeply ingrained in every human being, and naturally so. The necessity to sustain life and freedom forces upon man this motive. Even a genuine counselor of men, a teacher of spiritual truths, may fall under the spell of personal reward, whether of goods, finance or prestige.

The motive of self-gain corrodes purity of heart. Every pupil comes to be regarded, not only as a recipient of instruction, but also as a source of wealth. Choice of the rich, mental influence to give generously, and other subtle machinations then mar the purity of motive; single-mindedness has then been lost. Wisdom intuition, and delicate and precise comprehension begin to diminish, and the feeling of unity with the pupil is reduced to a minimum. Even those men and women who come from the hands of their own true teacher pure of heart can, in time, become self-degraded into businessmen with the supposed official status and wisdom as their wares.

Deeper and more harmful errors may also afflict the soul of the would-be teacher and, more especially, the self-styled *guru*. He or she may attack and erode the honor, probity and morality of those in his charge. A spiritual relationship thus becomes degraded into a sensual one, bringing very grave harm to a trustful and therefore vulnerable pupil. Indeed, as this verse indicates, such false prophets come in sheep's clothing but inwardly are ravening wolves.

Those who search for wisdom and for guidance in entering in at the strait gate should therefore take special care in the choice and acceptance of a teacher, with the above-mentioned tests in view. Signs of deterioration should also be discerned and the teacher repudiated immediately if unworthiness is found. This is not ingratitude, nor is it excess of criticism. Rather is it wise caution concerning matters involving not only the present but also future lives and the speed and directness of progress toward deliverance.

In the darkened era of the present historical period, selfishness and self-seeking inevitably predominate. Indeed, they are virtually forced upon mankind by the difficulties, necessities, and dangers inseparable from bodily life. In consequence, true teachers tend to be rare and false ones many. Wise, therefore, is the guidance of the Master against them. Since this is especially true today when many are awakening to the search for truth, the warning is even more appropriate than it was in the period at which it was given.

Matt. 7:18.   A good tree cannot bring forth evil fruit, neither can a corrupt tree bring forth good fruit.

An underlying truth is here presented, again with an analogy from nature. Even though at times well intentioned, the insincere, self-seeking exploiter of occult knowledge can never serve as a bringer of enlightenment to a seeking mind. He may teach certain laws, but the interior illumination of the mind depends upon an influence from higher levels. This the corrupt teacher cannot bring about.

In the case of the genuine, pure-hearted and humble shepherd of souls seeking only to give aid, beneficial results are virtually assured from his ministrations. Not only can he share his acquired wisdom, but he can also be used as a vehicle for higher influences. In this matter of channelship, sincerity of purpose and purity of heart are of the first importance.

> Matt. 7:19. Every tree that bringeth not forth good fruit is hewn down, and cast into the fire.
>
> 20. Wherefore by their fruits ye shall know them.

A brief summing up closes the strongly worded and precisely stated warning against false prophets addressed to those seeking inner light and spiritual truth. The Lord was very decisive about these, their evil ways, and their potential danger to the world and spiritually awakening men and women in particular. The method for discovering their true nature is stated in this verse, namely, to see the effects of their activities, to judge them by their fruits. No room is left for compromise. Unless the fruits are good, then society must be guarded against evil agents, even to an extreme degree; they must be eliminated or "hewn down, and cast into the fire."

> Matt. 7:21. Not every one that saith unto me, Lord, Lord, shall enter into the kingdom of heaven; but he that doeth the will of my Father which is in heaven.

By the method of antithesis a fundamental principle of the truly spiritual way of life is here enunciated—that of self-surrender. This law of the higher life is among the most difficult to obey because self-surrender cannot be artificially attained. One of the most deeply interior states, it cannot be presumed or pretended. The slightest artificiality in the matter declares and reveals falseness, as is indicated in this verse. Merely to say "Lord, Lord" will not induce the state of consciousness implied and expressed in surrendering to the Will of God.

Interior upliftment, inspiration, and bliss consciousness, or the kingdom of heaven state, unfoldment and the practice of yoga, combined; it will be reached by all men when passing through the appropriate evolutionary phase. Negation of self-will and disinterestedness in self and self-desire also comes to birth in a man quite naturally, marking the arrival at a certain stage of development. Enlightenment and bliss can be attained in advance of the natural time as far as the race as a whole is concerned.

Similarly, nature will produce a bud on a rosebush and, in due season, that bud will unfold in color, shape, dimensions and fragrance strictly according to its kind or species. The horticulturist, however, can, by forcing advance the time of flowering and seed or fruit-producing in a plant. Nevertheless, flower, seed, and fruit will be strictly according to species. Similarly, in the evolution of human consciousness, though interior exaltation is capable of being forced, it will be essentially natural, true to the human species and the particular person who thus attains.

> Matt. 7:22.   Many will say to me in that day, Lord, Lord, have we not
> prophesied in thy name? and in thy name have cast out
> devils? and in thy name done many wonderful works?

The same theme is here continued. Self-proclamation and self-praise which
are not based upon the true interior light and experience are condemned as
worthless, being sheer hypocrisy. This affirmation penetrates deeply into the
heart of human nature, beyond words and beyond mind, into that living truth
which is an expression of the God in man.

> Matt. 7:23.   And then will I profess unto them, I never knew you:
> depart from me, ye that work iniquity.

While the great Teacher here speaks of his own presence before an unjust
and untruthful claimant, he also stands for Truth itself. The false prophet and
the self-proclaimed seer who has no vision inevitably fail by the sheer force of
events and the nature of Truth.

A man who has not attained to spiritual awareness cannot, for long,
successfully claim to have done so. Sooner or later his life, his bearing, his
glance, his words, and his works will reveal him for what he is and show what
he is not. Truth and truthfulness are among the strongest powers. Their
presence is self-revealed, needing no claims. Their absence inevitably leads
to defeat, whether in this world or the next, in this life or in a future
incarnation.

It is surely most fitting that the great sermon enunciating the laws of the
spiritual life should close by presentation of, and insistence upon, uttermost
truthfulness. Such a life demands complete sincerity in everything which
concerns that life and its impact upon others.

Yet the element of expediency and the desire to stand well before one's
fellows—almost natural in the worldly life—are most difficult to eradicate
and outgrow. They can creep in insidiously pervading thought and motive
until the man himself fails to recognize them for what they are, thinly veiled
untruths. Unless they are checked, they can turn an otherwise good man into
a hypocrite.

> Matt. 7:24.   Therefore whosoever heareth these sayings of mine, and
> doeth them, I will liken him unto a wise man, which built
> his house upon a rock:
>
> 25.   And the rain descended, and the floods came, and the
> winds blew, and beat upon that house; and it fell not: for
> it was founded upon a rock.

These verses and this summing up clearly express the idea by analogy. Just
as the stability of any building depends upon the firmness of its foundations,
so also the stability of man's inner life, and the sureness and safety with which
he treads the narrow way, depend upon an unstainable sincerity, an unassailable truthfulness and genuineness in his heart and his life. Without these
the winds of doubt and the floods of fear, desire, and human weaknesses will
cause his footsteps to falter. Unless eradicated, untruth and falseness will
cause him to halt, making no further progress, or to turn back, his last state
being worse than his first.

Those who lightly embark upon the path—particularly those still governed by the rules of worldly life with their acceptance of expediency—can hardly be expected to realize its difficulties and dangers. This will inevitably lead to a serious fall. Temporary failure through lack of control under the stresses of both the inner and the outer life are to be expected. But deliberately and flagrantly denying ideals throughout life after the pretense of accepting them is much more serious. Long-continued and regularly applied choice of purely worldly standards after the path is entered constitute foundations of sand, as the opposite constitutes a foundation of rock.

This conflict is waged in the innermost depth of the human heart throughout many lives before, at last, the inner divine Self attains victory over the outer mortal man. Simply put, the task of the aspirant to the way of holiness is to blend the two aspects of human nature—the bodily and personal and the divine—so that the god rules the man. This dominion of spirit over matter in a human being shows itself in the choice of the life of the path. Even though domination by spirit will steadily increase where truthfulness reigns, it will not be complete until adeptship is attained. This cannot be otherwise, and there is no expectation that it should be. There will inevitably be falls and failures along the way. The secret of ultimate success consists of the inner, irrevocable, and determined decision to attain and the spirit of sincerity and truth underlying motives for the conduct of life.

> Matt. 7:26.   And every one that heareth these sayings of mine, and doeth them not, shall be likened unto a foolish man, which built his house upon the sand.
>
> 27.   And the rain descended, and the floods came, and the winds blew, and beat upon that house; and it fell: and great was the fall of it.

Simply put, the rock is sincerity and the sand is hypocrisy. Where the former exists *all* things can be achieved, despite the limitations of humanity. Where the latter persists, failure continually threatens or is inevitable.

Despite the clear-cut and sharp distinction drawn by the great Teacher, the issue is not, in fact, as final as might appear. A human being living in the world has to live out his or her life, and this process is characterized by variability. Clear-cut and final decisions permitting no variation and suffering no change are very rare in human thought and conduct. Intentions may be extremely good and fully adhered to for many years and even lives. However, the well-intentioned structure can be temporarily distorted by influences from former lives (often quite remote), astrological changes reflected within the person, ill health, frustrations, and disasters. Similarly, a ship may veer from its course when influenced by strong currents, winds, the inattention of the steersman, or the vagaries of the compass. Discovered, the error may be soon corrected and indeed lead to greater care and watchfulness on the part of navigator and steersman. Such deviations need in no wise imperil either the safety of the ship or its arrival at its destination.

Similarly, temporary deviations while ascending the mount by the steep and direct route in no way endanger the safety of the climber or the success of the expedition. He may choose the less steep and easier pathway temporarily or totally. Or the steep path may be chosen under the impulse of interior experiences or the impact of outer events.

To return to the simile used by the Lord, even a rock-like foundation can display weaknesses that can be repaired; and a sand-like foundation, when its weaknesses become evident, can be replaced by rock. In human nature beings below the rank of Adept, decisions and their ratification are rarely, if ever, final. Moreover, the spirit in man is resistless; its victory over matter is assured.

> Matt. 7:28. And it came to pass, when Jesus had ended these sayings, the people were astonished at his doctrine:
> 29. For he taught them as one having authority, and not as the scribes.

Here defined in a phrase that has come down from remote times is the difference between an official speaking according to orthodoxy and an illumined man speaking from his own experience and knowledge. The original personage, partially and imperfectly revealed by the Jesus of the Gospels, indeed spoke from the authority of his own experience. He was an agent and representative of the Brotherhood of illumined men and women who have been initiated into the Greater Mysteries, a small company. He was a great exponent of its esoteric wisdom.

From these verses an image, almost a portrait, of the great Reformer can be obtained. He was a young man moving among the masses with the assurance of one in the possession of profound knowledge and the power which it bestows. In addition, he was obviously trained to live precisely according to those principles and laws of the higher life enunciated in his great sermon. Every word and gesture, the expression of the face, the motion and carriage of the body, would all have revealed both his position as a man among men and his status in evolution as a superior being. The authority with which he spoke, born of personal experience, the purity of his life, and the power which he radiated attracted the populace.

Inevitably, this aroused the acute jealousy and hostility of the entrenched priesthood: for here was an outsider, a man of the people, successfully claiming to know more and teach more wisely than the doctors of the Hebraic law and religion themselves. When, in addition, he seemed to flout age-old beliefs and established religious dogmas and laws, this antagonism assumed great proportions.

He doubtless knew that the deliverance of this sermon at once placed him in danger; for no man may safely attack orthodoxy, especially in religion, without drawing the attention and exciting the hostility of those pledged to defend it. When, in addition, their offices and revenues are threatened, the antagonism becomes active and dangerous indeed. The deliverance of the sermon may, therefore, justly be regarded as an action that contributed greatly to the official hostility which surrounded Jesus and eventually brought about his premature death.

Nevertheless, the great sermon lives on, as does the person of Jesus, in the hearts of countless millions, while those who brought about his murder are either forgotten or execrated. Unhappily, within history, the same fate from the same sources has threatened and still threatens those who follow in the footsteps of Jesus as a deliverer of the Ageless Wisdom and its applications to the conduct of life, both spiritual and secular.

PART SIX

MIRACLES OF HEALING

Chapter Twelve

Nearly all the incidents recorded in the biographies of great world Teachers and divine visitants to the earth are susceptible of interpretation as various kinds of mystical experience. Some of them may have a factual, historical basis, while others do not. In either case, all the incidents are true if regarded as events, scenes and acts in the drama of the soul. This is true also of the miracles and healings performed by Jesus. In so many other places in the Bible, and especially in the accounts of the miracles of the Christ, the almost omnipotent power of the divine presence in man as personified by great beings, is referred to, and the advice given to seek, find, and place in power or enthrone that inmost presence, thereafter becoming whole. Indeed, in its more mystical aspects the Bible might justly be regarded as an exposition of a special form of spiritual exercises and attainment which could well be named "the yoga of the presence."

> Matt. 8:1.   When he was come down from the mountain, great multitudes followed him.

Interpreted in terms of the symbolical language, this verse implies that the truths and laws of the Sermon on the Mount were given when Jesus was in a state of uplifted consciousness in which the very laws of being are perceived.[1] Their application to the conduct of human life and to the end of both human happiness and hastened attainment of fully unfolded Christhood is also perceived and delivered to men by the great Teacher.

His hearers also had been lifted up so that they, in their turn, not only heard the Teacher's voice but realized interiorly the truth of his words. Thus, in mystical terms the experience of both teacher and hearers occurred within a state of elevated consciousness. Pure spiritual intuitiveness, personified by the Christ, revealed fundamental truths beyond the limitations of time and space. The mind thus illumined, portrayed by Christ as Teacher, conveys the resultant wisdom and guidance to brain and body, thereby giving perfect guidance in the conduct of life. The multitude in the allegory—if the account of the incident may be so regarded—represents the great variety of human beings and of qualities and characteristics of each single man.

In terms of the universal religion, the yoga of knowledge is described, and the fruits of its successful practice are clearly defined. The story of the Sermon on the Mount may thus be regarded as an exposition of *jnana yoga,* the way of enlightenment through the illumination of the mind from supramental levels of awareness or mountain heights.

This way of looking at the event in no wise detracts from it as history. Doubtless, the great Teacher, during his all-too-brief ministry, did draw many people to the slopes of the hills as well as in towns and cities where he talked to them, sharing the wisdom he had perceived and received. Not once but many times this scene must have been enacted, as also during the ministries of other members of the immortal race of the Teachers of mankind, the divine ones, who successively visit the earth and mankind.

> Matt. 8:2.   And, behold, there came a leper and worshipped him, saying, Lord, if thou wilt, thou canst make me clean.
>
> 3.   And Jesus put forth his hand, and touched him, saying, I will; be thou clean. And immediately his leprosy was cleansed.

Unless arrested, leprosy is a mortal disease corroding the flesh and terminated only by death. It is, therefore, a symbol of mortality. The divine Self of man, on the other hand, is immortal and by its intimate blending with the mind, emotions and bodily consciousness can bestow upon them extreme longevity if not full immortality. Regarded as an allegory, the miracle recorded as following immediately upon Christ's descent from the mountain describes the state of wholeness or complete unification of all aspects of human nature, spiritual and material, so that disease is defied and death driven away.

There is also a leprosy of the mind, the harboring and expression of corrosive, hypercritical, hostile and angry thoughts as a mental habit. This, too, is eliminated when once the unifying and illuminating influence of the spiritual Self reaches, floods and pervades the whole mentality of man. This, it would appear, can only be brought about as a result of an expressed desire for aid in outgrowing and eliminating the corrosive evil. Thus, the leper sought the Christ who touched and healed him. The search or quest, based upon a sincere and humble confession of fault, enabled the innermost Self to act outwardly, reaching or symbolically touching the mind. That direct contact was sufficient, as it ever is, to heal the dread disease.

> Matt. 8:4.   And Jesus saith unto him, See thou tell no man; but go thy way, shew thyself to the priest, and offer the gift that Moses commanded, for a testimony unto them.

On more than one occasion Jesus instructed those for whom he had performed a miracle to preserve silence. This is in accordance with universal custom observed by those great ones who come as Teachers to men. Pure wisdom is their gift, and in delivering it they seek no fame, knowing that it is not their own, though perceived within themselves.

Miracles may be performed chiefly out of compassion for those who suffer, or in some cases to serve as evidence for the possession of the power which wisdom bestows. Notoriety as a wonder-worker, another reason for performing miracles, is the least of the objectives, while the illumination of the minds of men is the greatest.

In the Sermon on the Mount, Jesus had encouraged modification, if not contravention, of the Mosaic law, particularly in respect to retaliation in reaction to injury. The multitude followed and acclaimed him. He was doubtless aware that the anger and the jealously of the priesthood would be thereby aroused. Wishing naught for himself and perhaps seeking to heel the breach, he instructed the leper to present himself to the priest and follow the Mosaic law of recognition and material offering for spiritual favors gained. After this inevitably fatal disease of the soul as well as of the body had been cured, the outer life should conform to natural, ecclesiastical and spiritual law, both psychological and physical. Hence, the admonition to go to the priest.

Matt. 8:5.   And when Jesus was entered into Capernaum, there came unto him a centurian, beseeching him.

6.   And saying, Lord, my servant lieth at home sick of the palsy, grievously tormented.

While this record of the second great miracle of healing has doubtless a true, historical basis, a mystical reading of the story is also possible. When the Christ nature in man reaches maturity and becomes a self-evident power within him, *wholeness* and therefore health is one of the results. The external Christ walking among the people, teaching and healing them, personifies the awakened or manifest and mature Christ principle in a spiritually evolved man. When this phase of evolution is entered, apparent miracles can well be performed, astonishing to the eyes of the world. The greatest of all miracles also becomes possible: the transmission of spiritual power to the outer personal man who thereby becomes "anointed," a healer and savior of men.

Such an illumined one becomes naturally healed in the sense of the establishment of complete harmony throughout his whole mortal nature; he is whole, healed through and through. In consequence, neither discord nor disease can any longer exist in him. So, precisely, was Jesus himself; so also is every other similarly anointed one. Thus viewed, each miracle may be read as descriptive of a manifestation in power of the true spiritual Self, as a result of which various disorders—leprosy, palsy, paralysis, blindness, and even death itself—are overcome.

Furthermore, each such illness is descriptive and typical of a false state of mind and mistaken outlook upon life. A man can suffer from the leprosy of hate, the palsy of indecisivenss and unreliability, blindness to spiritual light. While external guidance and therapy can help in overcoming these difficulties, the real cure must be drawn from within.

Writers who used the allegorical language were well aware of the existence of interior and psychological wounds and diseases, as also of their effective cure. They revealed this knowledge as guidance to mankind by means of allegories and symbols. Whether or not this approach is acceptable to all students of world scriptures, such mystical readings can provide illumination to the mind and even hints, if not full revelation, to means of self-cure.

Matt. 8:7.   And Jesus saith unto him, I will come and heal him.

The means of cure is revealed in the account of this incident and especially in this verse. The centurion who approached the Lord represents a mind which has reached a phase of human development in which it begins to realize and seek the spirit within—a stage at which imperfection is recognized and greater stature and understanding are sought. If the applicant had been but a common soldier, he would represent normal, unillumined man. He is, however, a superior soldier in command of those still in the ranks, representing one somewhat in advance of the race as far as his evolutionary development is concerned.

The servant typifies the physical body with its natural appetites, attitudes toward life, tendencies and limitations. When the brain-mind is unillumined, the body is sick in the sense of lacking the full expression of spirit in mental states and physical conduct.

Upon the scene, whether regarded historically or mystically, there enters a divine personage, the Lord Jesus Christ. He recognizes the centurion's nationality and position in the army, or, in the mystical sense, in evolution. As in this verse, Jesus, personifying the Christ nature within every man, answers the centurion with a promise to visit his servant; the ever present divine nature within man responds at once to the aspiration and call of the mortal personality through the mind. Thus Jesus was readily available, as was the physical Jesus who walked at a leisurely pace throughout Judea.

> Matt. 8:8.   The centurion answered and said, Lord, I am not worthy that thou shouldest come under my roof: but speak the word only, and my servant shall be healed.

Faith born of deep interior illumination and recognition of divine power and presence is indicated in this verse. Humility is also suggested, as is recognition of the power of the hidden interior Self to transcend earthly limitations. Omnipresence is indeed an attribute of the divine in nature and in man. The centurion realizes this in the dramatic story and demonstrates his belief by stating that no physical movement in space is required of the Lord.

Surrender is implied in the humility of the centurion and his readiness to seek aid from a member of a supposedly inferior race, the defeated Hebrews. In this state of mind and heart, understanding is born, intuitive perception is awakened and developed, and the Christ consciousness becomes manifest in the outer personality which, in consequence, is unified and illumined. Symbolically, the servant is cured by the exertion of miraculous power; at a distance the body is made whole.

The phrase "speak the word" may indicate realization of the potencies of sound, particularly the voice of the God within, to produce outward effects. While this phrase may have been only a manner of speech, it is nevertheless significant from the occult point of view. A form of communion and transmission of power and wisdom comparable to speech occurs in certain mystical experiences and transformations. The phrases "the still small voice," "the divine voice," and "The Word" all refer to this manifestation of the inward spirit to the mind and heart of the mystic. The Logos doctrine may also be implied or inferred. According to this, in the fashioning of universes Universal Mind manifests as the formative agency through a spiritual power of the quality of sound.

> Matt. 8:9.   For I am a man under authority, having soldiers under me: and I say to this man, Go and he goeth; and to another, Come, and he cometh; and to my servant, Do this, and he doeth it.

By statements regarding his complete faith in Jesus and his own temporal power, the centurion contrasts the condition of his mind with that of his wordly affairs. Pride in military and personal power resulting from his office had not been allowed to invade his mental and spiritual life. In these he was humble and self-surrendered, which gave him the ability to recognize Jesus as a Master among men and to place his whole trust in Jesus's spiritual powers. This provides a valuable lesson to all who seek spiritual illumination and its consequent healing of the outer nature.

In this story, as in so many others in the Bible, the laws of the spiritual life and the necessities for spiritual illumination are enunciated by means of stories describing supposed, and in some cases actual, events. The centurion thus personifies an ideal. As a man invested with the authority which he describes, he is, nevertheless, both humble and discerning in his mind and heart. Therefore, symbolically, his servant was healed at a distance. In terms of mystical experience, the Christ nature within him was enabled by a conducive attitude of mind to reach and illumine or make whole his mortal nature, including especially the brain-mind.

Readiness to receive is reflected in the material circumstances of those to whom mystical revelations occur. Humble origin may indicate by analogy humility of mind and freedom from pride and ostentation. At the other end of the social scale, kingship—though having little or no relevance in matters spiritual—may indicate pride of birth and position which have become adequately controlled. In both cases, as in all possible intermediate states, conditions of heart and mind are to be discerned. When the mind turns toward the hidden Master of the soul, as with the centurion, the reply is always the same: "I will come and heal . . ."

The Roman Empire was the power behind the centurion, who held his office in its name. Rome, therefore, represents the higher mind wherein are contained the principles and fundamentals upon which mind and body are founded. The emperor is the Lord of all those and represents the divine intelligence functioning through inner Self and outer man.

The processes of colonization in their mystical meaning imply the attainment of dominion by the inner Self over mind and body with its myriads of cells and parts—subject peoples.

> Matt. 8:10.   When Jesus heard it, he marvelled, and said to them that followed, Verily I say unto you, I have not found so great faith, no, not in Israel.

This equilibrium between pure spirituality and wordly power and responsibility is indeed rare, not only in Israel, but in all the world of men. In its long evolutionary development, the human race is passing through a phase in which the individualistic—and so prideful—attributes of the mind are being unfolded. Unfortunately, these qualities tend to prevent expression of the intuitive faculty. While mankind thus spiritually sleeps in mental darkness, individuals here and there break through the screen erected by such mental habits into the larger life and spiritual outlook. Since these are rare (happily, their number increases) contact with them can produce a response which St. Matthew describes as the amazement of Jesus. Actually, he would not have been amazed in the ordinary meaning of the word. Rather, endowed as he was with a divine perceptiveness, he would instantly discern the rare spiritualized condition of the mind of the centurion.

Very large numbers of people must have heard of his presence in the land, a smaller number must have seen him, and still fewer approached and sought his aid. A minority went further and became his pledged disciples. In these gradations of approach to Jesus, the Evangelists also present phases of man's mental and spiritual evolution. The worldly and worldly wise are either unaware of, or disinterested in, any presumed spiritual presence within them. The seekers are those who have received intimations of the mystical character of that presence. Those healed or raised from the dead represent the regenerated ones for whom the quest of the spiritual life has become gradually an inevitable way of life. Disciples are those who know the divine within themselves and are irrevocably pledged to its ever fuller realization and to the ever more complete surrender of their outer lives to its perfect expression.

> Matt. 8:11.   And I say unto you, That many shall come from the east and west, and shall sit down with Abraham, and Isaac, and Jacob, in the kingdom of heaven.

The universality of spiritual illumination is here referred to, insofar as these verses correctly record the Master's words. The centurion was a Roman, a representative of a hated race of conquerors and oppressors. Moreover, he was himself an officer in the army of occupation. Yet he was illumined.

Strictly orthodox Hebrews would have difficulty in accepting, even after such demonstration, the possibility that a Roman soldier could possess and display such wisdom as to amaze the Teacher. Jesus, however, affirmed that wisdom knows no barriers of nation or class, of East or West. Any man from anywhere on earth, belonging to any religion or none, can become illumined, and would, after death, achieve beatitude. Metaphorically, he would sit down with Abraham, Isaac and Jacob in the Kingdom of Heaven.

> Matt. 8:12.   But the children of the kingdom shall be cast out into outer darkness: there shall be weeping and gnashing of teeth.

The opposite is also stated to be true in this verse. Those born into the "chosen" race may, nevertheless, fall into darkness, just as may members of any other nation or race. Pure wisdom is no respecter of persons; and also unwisdom, ignorance and sin can be manifest in any man anywhere, even in Israel. This must have been a very striking doctrine to his hearers as Jesus enunciated this theme.

Matt. 8:13.   And Jesus said unto the centurion, Go thy way; and as
thou hast believed, so be it done unto thee. And his
servant was healed in the self-same hour.

The conclusion of the episode demonstrates the truth of the teaching of
Jesus. The centurion's complete trust and faith in Jesus resulted in the healing
of his servant. Many such physical healings were doubtless brought about by
the great Teacher in Palestine. The Evangelists may well have been recording
fact, though dependent upon memory and oral repetition of events half a
century or more in the past.

Nevertheless, the story contains certain elements which indicate a mystical intent and the use of the symbolical language. Among these are the
application for healing by a Roman officer to a member of a defeated race, a
people despised by some Romans; the supposed wonder of Jesus who, as a
divine person, would at once perceive the state of consciousness to which the
centurion had attained; and the healing at a distance as if by miraculous or
magical power. Divine interventions, it may well be remembered, in scriptural accounts of supposedly normal affairs of mortal men, generally indicate
the author's intention to apply a moral or mystical significance.

.Matt. 8:14.   And when Jesus was come into Peter's house, he saw his
wife's mother laid, and sick of a fever.

15.   And he touched her hand, and the fever left her; and she
arose, and ministered unto them.

The symbology changes, but the revelation is the same. Recognition of
one's interior divine power and presence quiets the fevered mind, cools and
calms excited or strained emotions, so that body and mind acquire equipoise.

Once again a mystical interpretation is suggested by divine intervention
and magical means. Despite the inclusion in the story of relatives, Peter, who
had already attained to discipleship, is the subject of the allegory if the
incident is so regarded. Peter's house is his body, the dwelling place of the
spiritual Self expressed as mind and emotion. His wife is the psyche or mental
and emotional nature and attributes, a manifestation of the power of the
indwelling spirit at those levels. Her mother is the nervous and psychological
condition, in this case disturbed, fevered, heated.

Incidents are related in the life of the apostle Peter which indicate that he
may have suffered from disequilibrium. Such reactions as his ardent protest
at the prophesied passion and death of the Lord and his denial and inability to
walk on water to meet the risen Christ may possibly be interpreted as
indications of some imbalance still remaining in his nature, great disciple
though he proved to be.

The remedy for such a condition is indicated in this incident. It is to enter
the presence, symbolically to invite into his house the divine aspects of his
own nature, his highest spiritual Self. In this exalted state of consciousness,
symbolized by the presence of the Christ in the home, equilibrium and
normality are restored. The disturbance in the home, the anxiety of the wife,
and the disability of her mother—each with its mystical significance—are all

successfully treated. Harmony resulting in smooth running of the home is restored.

> Matt. 8:16.   When the even was come, they brought unto him many that were possessed with devils: and he cast out the spirits with his word, and healed all that were sick.

Such afflictions are susceptible of interpretation in the terms referred to above. However, some mental and psychological diseases may be caused or intensified by the presence of obsessing evil forces or beings. The divine power within man brought into full personal consciousness can exorcise or eliminate the disturbing agencies. This does not negate the ability of any adept physician readily to cure either of the two conditions. In the exorcism of undesirable obsessing entities the situation is carefully examined, somewhat as a doctor diagnoses a case of sickness. The intimacy which has developed between the invader and its victim is assessed, and the nature of the unwanted being, whether human or non-human, the most effective means of driving it out, and finally, means of its disposal thereafter.

In certain cases the intimacy is so close that occult surgery might endanger the life of the sufferer. In such a case the exorcism is performed gradually. If this is not so, then the necessary amount of will-force is instantly applied to sever the psychic connection and drive out the offending and unwelcome invader. If it is only a temporary thought-form brought into being and vitalized by human, rather than divine, creative activity—as by magical ceremonial for example—then it can be exploded or otherwise destroyed. This would not constitute an act of murder, since no evolving spiritual principle is present. However, a disembodied human obsessing agency may not suffer the destruction of its astral or superphysical form. It must be forcibly driven out and forbidden to return, the aura of the victim being also sealed against it. Another procedure is to force a different embodiment or condition upon the obsessing being. This generally consists of some subhuman form of life and substance such as swine, as in a later verse.

The agency for this curative power is indicated by the statement that Jesus cured the sick by his word. The occult potency of sound uttered with knowledge and intent by the voice is here suggested. The mantra yoga of oriental philosophy and the Logos doctrine accentuated by St. John and the authors of Genesis are related.

> Matt. 8:17.   That it might be fulfilled which was spoken by Esaias the prophet, saying Himself took our infirmities, and bare our sicknesses.

While the words and the works of Jesus in Palestine are sufficient to establish him as a divine visitant endowed with supernormal powers and wisdom, the Evangelists or later writers sought to strengthen this position by showing it as the fulfillment of ancient prophecy. It must be remembered, however, that the prophets themselves wrote mystically as well as historically. They also may be read as describing interior developments occurring in spiritually awakened man.

The prophet Isaiah describes certain mystical experiences: interior illuminations as by perpetual light, transcendence of death, realization of immortality, and the complete harmonization of all aspects of human nature. Some parts of man's nature may be in conflict with, and even a threat to, the higher qualities. Isaiah refers to these as beasts of prey and other dangerous creatures. His famous statement that "the lion shall lie down with the lamb" describes the complete harmonization of all powers and attributes of the higher and lower natures of man.[2]

Great seers write for all people and all times, even though using one person or one age as exemplification. Isaiah thus wrote, not only of the coming of Jesus, the Messiah, but of everyone who enters into true mystical experience and is initiated into the hidden wisdom and Mysteries. The Evangelists also combine the mystical with the historical, using the language of symbols for this purpose.

> Matt. 8:18. Now when Jesus saw great multitudes about him, he gave commandment to depart unto the other side.
>
> 19. And a certain scribe came, and said unto him, Master, I will follow thee whithersoever thou goest.
>
> 20. And Jesus saith unto him, The foxes have holes, and the birds of the air have nests; but the Son of man hath not where to lay his head.

This interpretation is borne out by the answer of Jesus to the scribe; for indeed at a certain stage of spiritual unfoldment, or when a certain grade in the Mysteries is entered, the mystic is figuratively homeless and generally without possessions. Sometimes this is a physical condition as in the state of the forest-dweller of Hindu philosophy. Sometimes it may refer only to a state of mind characterized by complete freedom from possessiveness or any earthly desires. The initiate then becomes a wanderer, a teaching sage whose home is in the hearts of his fellowmen.[3] These inner and outer conditions are well described in the words of the Master recorded in the twentieth verse.

> Matt. 8:21. And another of his disciples said unto him, Lord, suffer me first to go and bury my father.
>
> 22. But Jesus said unto him, Follow me; and let the dead bury their dead.

In the symbolical language the dead are those in whom no living spark of spirituality and pure idealism as yet burns to influence the conduct of daily life. These people are figuratively dead from the purely spiritual point of view, which largely concerns the degree of illumination and control which the inner Self brings to the outer man.

Such people must be helped in general rather than individually as particular persons with whom disciples are mostly concerned. Orthodox religion is provided for them; its ethical counsels such as the Ten Commandments meet their spiritual needs reasonably well. Doubtless they are admirable and good people, but as yet they are not likely to benefit from either the esoteric wisdom or the esoteric life.

Such rather trenchant utterances of the Christ—and a number of such are recorded in the Gospels—may also be regarded as descriptive of a certain approach to the pathway of discipleship and hastened attainment. This attitude is one of complete purposefulness, single-minded and almost exclusive preoccupation with the great spiritual quest, the tasks and duties of the disciple, and the attainment of pure wisdom. Material considerations and even family ties take second place in the thought and life of the disciple who, nevertheless, skillfully fulfills necessary duties. Pursuit of any worldly objective, if it is to be successful, requires this quality of single-mindedness and therefore exclusiveness, particularly with regard to matters and people not concerned with the enterprise. If this is true and necessary in the worldly life, it must be far more so in the spiritual life. The endeavor to hasten evolutionary processes occurring within the spiritual soul and to attain ahead of the race a state of spiritual illumination inevitably makes great demands upon him who would succeed.

This necessity for one-pointedness may be implied by the apparently stern admonition of the Christ to the disciple. In this reading the guidance might well be thus interpreted: "Keep your mind wholly upon the spiritual life and the Master. There are others whose task it is to perform the more worldly and material duties. All communities have officers and their subordinates for the performance of interments. Leave that task to them and concentrate upon your own lifework which is to be the perfect disciple."

This aspect of the esoteric life must seem rather severe to those whose motives are formed from worldly and more personal considerations. Whether or not Christ's statements are correctly reported and translated, one may be completely assured that neither callousness nor neglect of filial duty would ever be inculcated by a true Master and Teacher of men.

> Matt. 8:23. And when he was entered into a ship, his disciples followed him.
>
> 24. And, behold, there arose a great tempest in the sea, insomuch that the ship was covered with the waves: but he was asleep.
>
> 25. And his disciples came to him, and awoke him, saying Lord, save us: we perish.
>
> 26. And he saith unto them, Why are ye fearful, O ye of little faith? Then he arose, and rebuked the winds and the sea; and there was a great calm.

According to esoteric tradition, such a manifestation of thaumaturgic power is well within the capacity of a fully attained Adept. When in addition, his power is enhanced by a manifestation within him of an Aspect of the Godhead, then all nature is obedient to his will. This relative omnipotence applies to the Elements of Earth and Water, as well as Air and Fire. These, with the minor and major intelligences intimately associated with both their physical and their superphysical expressions, are under the direct control of the Adept; for these so-called Elements together with a fifth are manifested powers or *shaktis* of the one Godhead and therefore directly obedient to the divine Will. Since the will of the Adept is now consciously surrendered to, merged in, and identified with the one Will, every expression of that Will and its objective powers are readily directed by him, less from without than from within.

The trained occultist knows himself to be permeated with and surrounded by these unseen manifesting powers, forces and agencies; for him the universe teems with them. Indeed it could almost be said that the universe in its more subjective existence consists of unseen forces being built of and by them, a product of their operations.

The essential substance of the Element Earth with all its variety of components, each with its own molecular constitution and design, is one of five major manifestations of one energy emanating in a group of varied frequencies from one power station. From the occult point of view, every physical atom, in the true meaning of the word as *indivisible,* is itself a localized generating station. The atom performs a dual function, relaying the one energy from levels above it into those below, in the process itself becoming a kind of generating station. This is also true of the substance, constitution and ultimate units of the four Elements of Earth, Water, Air and Fire. This tremendous activity occurs throughout a universe which in this sense is electrically alive, being both charged with energy and a vehicle or conductor.

Atomic physicists from the remotest times have known that the ultimate *substans* of the universe is energy, constantly flowing force. This produces innumerable effects which, entering into various combinations, impinge upon the senses of animals and men producing the lighted, audible, tangible, odoriferous, taste-producing objective universe that they experience. Whereas the chemist partially discovers and realizes this fact, the adept scientist knows it as a continuing experience in consciousness. This intimate knowledge, combined with virtually irresistible will and thought, enables him to affect all these appearances, either by influencing the senses of observers or controlling the elements themselves. If, therefore, the account of the stilling of the tempest by the Christ, who exercised his power vocally, is to be read literally as the record of a miracle, then it is both understandable and acceptable as such to the student of occult science.

The devotee whose religion is founded less upon understanding then faith and cares little or nothing for the *modus operandi* readily accepts such remarkable manifestations as solid facts, well within the capacities of his adored spiritual Lord and Master. Others less interested in either occult dynamics or manifestations of pure devotion may read the account as descriptive of mystical experiences, particularly changes brought about within the inner and outer consciousness of man. Thus viewed, the incident so briefly and concisely related may be regarded as a description of the evolution of man. The mind of man becomes the true scene of both storm and miraculous intervention by a higher power. One particular and all-important phase is accentuated, namely, that of spiritual awakening and its more immediate results.

Long ages of evolutionary development pass. The bark of man's outer life sails on. The captain, the mind, commands the vessel according to established rules which suffice for the fulfillment of his task. The bodily life of man continues race by race and life after life. The waters of life bear upon its journey the vessel of its interior Godhead—the material universe. Natural law preserves both universe and mortal man.

The storm consists of winds of doubt and waves of desire and the danger with which these threaten the bodily ship of man's life. He recognizes the uncertainties and the instability of a purely material basis for living. Unavoidable stresses and uncontrollable events indicate the existence of forces and laws hitherto unperceived and unknown. Gradually, however, a figurative storm begins to brew in the human mind. Symbolically, variations of the compass are observed.

The mental storm gathers momentum as the mind becomes determined to find stability amid the instability of mundane affairs. Familiar concepts and accepted ideas increasingly lose validity, and many of them are cast aside. Man develops a determined will to know and through knowledge to attain unshakable stability, unassailable peace. This phase is characterized by two insights: recognition of the instability and insecurity of a life dependent solely upon material support and emotional satisfaction, and intuitive perception that stability and security are to be found only in supramental and spiritual realms. Dependence upon the material world, material knowledge, and material power alone cannot solve the riddle of existence; neither can these reveal the truth which serves as unshakable foundations for thought and action.

The disciples in their stress represent aspiration, determination and awakening intuition, as a result of which the great discovery is made. The key phrase in St. Matthew's account is the cry of the disciples, "Lord save us: we perish." When once this cry metaphorically arises from within the heart and mind of a man, a new evolutionary phase for that individual is entered. The formal mind deliberately throws itself open to light and truth from deeply interior sources hitherto unknown and untapped. The manifestation of the spirit in man and its dominance over matter in him is depicted by the Lord Christ's emergence from sleep in the interior of the vessel. As the latter is asleep and apparently unaware of the crisis until awakened with an appeal for aid, so also the spirit-power in man abides in its own world, fulfilling only automatic, life preserving functions. Symbolically, the hitherto sleeping Christ is awakened by the endangered disciples attempting to navigate their vessel in a storm. The disciples realize one Being alone can save them in their grave emergency, the divine Master when awakened from sleep. He responds to this appeal and demonstrates complete command over the aerial and watery Elements. A meeting occurs followed by a union; spirit, mind and brain become one entity of consciousness. Mental storms of doubt, of revolt against ignorance and impotence and instability, all die down. Peace reigns, the true peace of the eternal.

Although the response is immediate in the story, many lives may be needed for the transference of interest and security from material to spiritual thought and standards of conduct. This change cannot normally be initiated or enforced by an outside agency. Temporary awakenings generally foreshadow the great event, but their influence is not at first sustained. Life follows life, each with its tests and its storms as well as its victories and joys. Gradually the great transference occurs. Occult and spiritual truths, laws and moral standards become accepted. In consequence, the storminess and insecurity of life are replaced by mental tranquillity and discovery within of an unshakable spiritual power, a rock of ages indeed. This corresponds to the presence of the Christ as the Master and accepting his call to discipleship.

The question as to whether the authors themselves recorded the incident of the stilling of the tempest with the intention of also describing such mystical unfoldments and attainments receives at least the suggestion of an affirmative answer; for the introduction of a divine presence and miraculous and magical power to produce supernormal effects may be taken as indications of such an intent and as justification for such an interpretation. If this is not the case, if no personal application of the story was intended, then the value of the account is greatly reduced, to say the least; for it becomes only part of the biography of Jesus and the history of the Jewish people of some two thousand years ago. However, there is much internal literary evidence that, like the authors of certain books and passages in the Old Testament, the Evangelists were instructed Kabbalists and therefore well versed in the occult lore of esoteric Hebraism.

> Matt. 8:27.   But the men marvelled, saying, What manner of man is this, that even the winds and sea obey him!

This verse, in which the incident is closed, reveals the element of wonder which, blended with others, characterizes the state of mind of the successful seeker for spiritual light and truth as the very basis for living.

> Matt. 8:28.   And when he was come to the other side into the country of the Gergesenes, there met him two possessed with devils, coming out of the tombs, exceeding fierce, so that no man might pass by that way.
>
> 29.   And, behold, they cried out, saying, What have we to do with thee, Jesus, thou Son of God? art thou come hither to torment us before the time?

In the incident in the life of Jesus which followed that of the stilling of the tempest, men possessed of devils were contacted and a miracle of exorcism was performed. Admittedly, such exorcism is readily within the power of the Adept, and Jesus must have possessed it. A literal reading is both interesting and instructive, although lacking guidance in the personal application by any others than the actors involved. Regarded as an allegory, however, much may be learned of direct value to all men of all times and especially to those who are symbolically "possessed with devils." To receive this illumination —it must be remembered, as always when interpreting inspired allegories —one must regard the whole incident as descriptive of one person alone, not two and not three, each actor personifying that person's attributes and actions.

Thus the two men represent mind and body. The past with its incidents, trials, memories and resultant karma are not inappropriately represented by obsessing devils from the tomb. The tomb is a condition of consciousness, particularly of mind, in which a man is totally unaware of his spiritual Self. In this state he is as one dead and buried.

Thus, bereft of the light and power of his own inner nature, man is indeed at the mercy of his own past, of which he is so largely the product. This condition does not, however, last forever. Evolution continues and life unfolds perpetually. As in the story, the time of the true Self declaring itself to the mind eventually draws near. In the allegorical terms of this passage, the Christ crosses over to the other side of the lake and comes into the presence of the two men possessed of devils.

Extremely critical action is then taken by these men. They approach and speak to Christ, questioningly, but with apparent hostility. One aspect of the human mind resents the incursion into it and the intervention of spiritual power and light. This is partly born of fear arising from instinctual realization that when once the light of intuition illumines the brain-mind, domination of the personality by the acquisitive, supercilious, materialistic mind will cease forthwith. The scoffing of one of the thieves crucified beside the Lord is descriptive of this resentful and jeering mental attitude.

Resistance on the part of the outer man may continue through several lives. There will inevitably come, however, that life in which the inner Self proves more powerful than the materialistic mind and sensual emotions—the two possessed men—and their domination is at an end. Allegorically, the Christ appears on the scene and exorcises the devils. The fact that the two men recognized Jesus as the Son of God indicates the development of a measure of spiritual perceptiveness and so of evolutionary progress toward the state of pure spirituality and self-exorcism of past restrictions and error.

> Matt. 8:30.   And there was a good way off from them an herd of many swine feeding.
>
> 31.   So the devils besought him, saying, If thou cast us out, suffer us to go away into the herd of swine.
>
> 32.   And he said unto them, Go. And when they were come out, they went into the herd of swine; and, behold, the whole herd of swine ran violently down a steep place into the sea, and perished in the waters.

The process of self-cleansing and the result of its successful conclusion are here described. The coarser, cruder undesirable attributes of human nature are represented by devils. Also symbolized by the swine, they belong to the animal aspect of man. The substance of the subtler vehicles by which they are represented is the coarser type of astral matter, inbued with an instinctual vicious tendency—swinish indeed.[4] This type of matter is also exorcised from the human aura, leaving it pure. The substance itself, however, joins the coarsest and densest types of free astral matter, suggested by the swine rushing down a steep decline. The obsessed swine are rightly made allegorically to rush into the sea, since in the symbolical language the sea and water generally are emblems of human emotion and the emotional plane or astral world.

Whether in the natural course of evolution or by taking strict measures as in the practice of yoga, egoism and sensuality are transcended and sink out of the sight of normal consciousness. They may abide for a time in regions below the threshold of full consciousness in a subdued condition, but they will eventually be completely extirpated, leaving the self-purified person free from them. When the inner Self or Christ nature of man enters upon the field of human consciousness, these evils are gradually displaced by spirituality and self-mastery. When that final stage is reached, liberation or salvation has been attained. The liberated human being is then stainless and unstainable.

Such an interpretation does not preclude the fact of the objective existence of obsessing, evilly disposed entities; neither does it deny the possibility of their being cast out by anyone endowed with the necessary knowledge and power. Ceremonies performed by those who have been vested with this power or who have developed their own will to the necessary degree can exorcise such demons by will-thought and words of power.

The exorcist who is still but a man must generally employ both sentences and symbols or signs of power, as a study of rituals of exorcism and healing shows. The Adept, if he decides to use audible language, needs but to pronounce a single word commanding departure. Thus, Jesus achieves the exorcism by pronouncing the command, "Go." Uttered by an Adept and expressive of his will, this word is irresistible, representing a final command.

Whether the entities thus driven out are thought-forms or disembodied human beings, they must obey, thereafter returning to the lower levels of the astral world where by their nature they belong.

A literal reading of the account is unacceptable on the grounds that no Adept destroys life unnecessarily. Indeed, the so-called devils could easily have been disposed of in a manner which would not be harmful or death-dealing to a subhuman form of life. From these considerations, the mystical interpretation of this dramatic narrative and application to oneself as reader is more acceptable. This is particularly so when the aptness of such a view is perceived.

> Matt. 8:33. And they that kept them fled, and went their ways into the city, and told every thing, and what was befallen to the possessed of the devils.
>
> 34. And, behold, the whole city came out to meet Jesus: and when they saw him, they besought him that he would depart out of their coasts.

When the human mind becomes aware of the divine presence within and invites its fuller manifestation, then both inborn evil and developed evil proclivities lose their hold and eventually are driven out. This restores the illumined individual to purity and wholeness.

The majority of people on earth are as yet incapable of understanding such a mystical and interior approach to God. Many instinctively shrink from its revelation and the renunciations which they mistakenly suppose must follow. Some self-purification and self-discipline are necessarily involved; some determination is required to overcome undesirable habits. But the impulse to do this arises from within the spiritually awakening devotee, so that elements of darkness and decay are rather outgrown than painfully renounced.

At the present stage of human evolution upon this planet, however, humanity is unready for such spiritual illumination and personal surrender. When, therefore, a call reaches the ears of such men and the first interior, spiritualizing impulses begin to be felt, resentment can arise. Thus the disturbing pressure or call can be denied access to the life and conduct of the man in his body and bodily concerns. This may be the psychological and mystical reference contained in these two verses, which tell that a whole city besought Jesus to "depart out of their coasts."

REFERENCES AND NOTES

1. See Hodson, *Hidden Wisdom,* Vol. 1, pp. 130-1.
2. Isa. 11:6-9.
3. *Parivrajaka*—Wanderer.
4. Astral—see Glossary.

Chapter Thirteen

The ministry of Jesus as recorded in the Gospels was evidently unique in the world's history of the appearances of spiritual visitants to mankind. He alone made physical healing of the sick a constant and characteristic part of his mission. The Lord Buddha renounced his princedom and his kingdom after seeing with his own eyes various forms of human suffering. His response was, however, not so much to heal individuals as to attain illumination concerning the true causes and permanent prevention and cure of human suffering.

Worthy of note is the fact that the three other Evangelists make no reference to many events recorded by St. John, possibly for one or other of the following reasons: lack of knowledge on the part of the authors; deliberate withholding of information for fear highly secret occult knowledge might be revealed; or recognition of the dangers of the misuse of power-bestowing truths. Any of these may have contributed to the incompleteness of the life story of Jesus during this and other periods.

> Matt. 9:1. And he entered into a ship, and passed over, and came into his own city.
>
> 2. And, behold, they brought to him a man sick of the palsy, lying on a bed: and Jesus seeing their faith said unto the sick of the palsy; Son, be of good cheer; thy sins be forgiven thee.

The Adept in occult science is virtually omnipotent as regards the physical world, physical life, and the play and interplay of natural forces. In degree according to his rank, he can appear to transcend and override the restrictions imposed upon life by form and to suspend the operations of certain apparently fixed laws. No being however high can abolish natural law; the Adept is able temporarily to inhibit its operation, chiefly upon himself but also upon others. The faculty of levitation is one example of this power.

In affecting others, the person's own relationship with Nature is a decisive factor. No one can, for example, be relieved of sickness if he or she is still in a condition of discordance with the life principle. Some relief may be brought about, but only in strict accordance with the extent of the discord.

The man healed of the palsy had passed through the phases of retribution which follow discordant action before final liberation from the debt. Had it not been so, even Jesus could not have healed him wholly.

If, however, the historical saviors represent an interior power, a spiritualizing agency within man, then its action may so modify the subsequent attitude and discordant conduct of the actor as speedily to bring about a neutralization of adversity. Interior illumination may be produced, enabling the transgressor to reharmonize himself with nature and the people against whom he has transgressed. This too is an action which would produce its results, one of which could be to hasten healing.

Apart from this, time itself eventually brings about a restoration of harmony. Discordant forces eventually exhaust themselves, whereupon such harmony, quite naturally, supervenes. Healing, whether miraculous or medical, is dependent upon this restoration of accord. The penetrating gaze of a true seer enables him to perceive whether or not this has occurred. The term "thy sins are forgiven thee" may thus simply mean that cause and effect are almost balanced, that the adversity is naturally near or at its end. A wisely directed and powerful act of spiritual harmonization is then sufficient to bring the sufferer back to the right road and so to freedom from adversity.

If the account of the miracle given in these verses is taken historically, then the words of the christ may be read as affirmations that this reharmonization was in this case complete. While ordinarily there may be delay before a living organism reassumes normality, whether of environment or of interior condition, an Adept is able to bring about restoration very quickly.

The terms *faith* and *forgiveness* used in the text may properly be read as reharmonization. This applies both externally in relationship with other people and interiorly with the man's relationship with his own soul; when the debt is paid, harmony obtains, externally and interiorly. This principle applies equally to harmonious and harmonizing conduct which result in personal and environmental well-being, as well as interior psychological and spiritual harmony and peace. Thus regarded, the account of the miracle may be read as an illustration of the existence and operation of the law of cause and effect and of an Adept's power to discern the condition of any human being in relation to that law.

If, however, the incident is regarded as an allegory, then other truths are revealed. Palsy is an uncontrollable movement of the whole body or a trembling of certain members. Thus regarded, a palsied life is one which is not directed from within, a heedless, wholly material, unbalanced and unstable mode of living. This indeed is the condition of the majority of men in this present phase of human development, so that the race may be regarded as palsied.

However, for a minority this is not so. Those in advance of the race become increasingly moved from within, lighted by idealism, disciplined and constrained in body and mind according to a set of ideals. They voluntarily recognize the rule of law and respect for law. Though the majority may see benefits from civil law and may obey its decrees, they are not yet thoroughly imbued with the ideal of right action for its own sake. History reveals that this is indeed the condition of humanity in the mass. One sign of evolutionary advancement is the acceptance of right for its own sake rather than for personal benefit. This comes from the Christ nature within man, whether consciously realized or not. Gradually realization dawns, the living God reveals itself to sensitize mind and heart. Uncontrolled and ill-directed action cease, and the person is spiritually and psychologically whole.

> Matt. 9:3. And, behold, certain of the scribes said within themselves, This man blasphemeth.
>
> 4. And Jesus knowing their thoughts said, Wherefore think ye evil in your hearts?
>
> 5. For whether is easier, to say, Thy sins be forgiven thee; or to say, Arise, and walk?
>
> 6. But that ye may know that the son of man hath power on earth to forgive sins, (then saith he to the sick of the palsy,) Arise, take up thy bed, and go unto thine house.

Jesus had divined the thoughts and had become aware of the words of the scribes. In answer, he points to the miracle of sudden healing itself, suggesting that the words of forgiveness and the healing were, in fact, the same thing. Objectively, this is indeed the case, since the miracle could not have been performed unless the effects of the actions causing the illness had been fully worked out, bringing a return to harmony. Seeing this, Jesus pronounced the healing words, whereupon the man, being cured, arose and went to his home.

This miracle occurs in Christ's own city. In the language of symbols, the city typifies the "vesture of light" in which the indwelling spirit is incarnate. When the indwelling spirit in this vesture is actively realized by the mind-brain, the outer man becomes transformed, integrated and so "healed."

The instruction to the man healed of palsy is susceptible of a similar interpretation. To go to one's home is, in this sense, to withdraw into one's inner Self, to establish oneself there in consciousness and to be motivated and act from that position and that Self-manifested vehicle of awareness. Thus, the Christ nature within man manifests itself to the outer personality, unifies its hitherto diverse elements, bestows upon it cohesion, intelligent direction and control of movement. The palsied state is then replaced by a measure of self-control, purposeful self-direction and wholeness.

The account of the sequel to the miracle begins in the third verse of this chapter, wherein the scribes are said to have declared the proclaimed forgiveness of sins to be blasphemous. They represent the envious, materializing, scornful, cynical, and destructively critical attributes of man's analytical mentality.

The human mind includes the two distinct faculties of abstract and concrete or critical thought. The power of detached, critical analysis and estimation of any idea or plan for the direction of the practical affairs of life is both natural and valuable. Thus used, no fault can be found with either the capacity itself or its consistent, detailed and precise application to the solution of material problems and the conduct of life.

If, however, abstract ideas and intuitive perceptions are submitted to undue analysis, particularly with a bias of hostility, then the deeper understandings and their eventual application to thought processes and experiences can be stultified. This is especially true in the early phases of self-illumination, whether regarding mundane or spiritual levels of understanding. Mental silence, or at best a waiting mental attitude, is most conducive to the dawning of new and creative ideas and the function of spiritual ideation. These cannot take root, develop, and flower in the mind if they are critically analyzed from the beginning.

In St. Matthew's account of Jesus's healing of the man stricken with the palsy, the scribes and their combined action personify this mental attribute. This hostility is born of the fear that the admission of the emergent ideas would lead to a loss of power, influence and directive agency in the conduct of physical life. In this sense, the formal mind resembles a dictator in an authoritarian state. Such an official cannot, dare not, brook any interference or suggestion of control of his dictatorship by others, for should this develop, his dictatorship would eventually come to an end. Narrow and entrenched religious orthodoxy is in precisely the same position with regard to maintaining its system and control over the unreasoning minds of its members. All dogmatism in religious matters arises from this fear and this impulse to power and its preservation.

Jesus, on the other hand, personifies the completely fluid, untrammeled pure wisdom from levels beyond the analytical, individualistic and power-seeking mind. The whole drama of the Christ life may be read as an allegory of the conflict between these two aspects of human nature. The inner spirit of man, whence pure wisdom reaches his outer self, leads ever to newness, new birth and the reception of new ideas. Since these inspire new concepts of life and modes of thinking and acting, they inevitably threaten established forms of thought and religious orthodoxy. The enemies of saviors and heroes in the great allegories personify the resistance, while the saviors and heroes themselves personify ever new spiritual impulses and ever fresh spiritual illumination and creative ideas. Devadatta, Kansa, Set and Herod, as also Satan in certain aspects, represnet these mental attributes and actions, as has been stated heretofore. Conflict is inevitable, and all battles in the world's allegories—including the war in heaven, *Kurukshetra, Armageddon,* the more personal combats between representatives of light and darkness, men and predatory beasts—typify this continuing conflict.

While for the thaumaturgist the demonstration of miraculous healing itself was conclusive leaving no room for further argument, for the philosopher this may not actually be so. The two approaches belong to two differing though interconnected levels of consciousness and action. From the philosopher's view, the apparent assumption by Jesus of the power to forgive sins brings into question the correctness of the record itself, for no illumined sage would be guilty of claiming power to abrogate this law, as the whole universe itself is founded upon the principle from which it is derived. The original document, the various translations through which it has passed in process of copying, and—most especially—the honesty and integrity of copyists and translators came into question. Unfortunately, theologians and even ignorant men have tampered with the text of the Bible and nowhere more so than in the words of the four Gospels. Records of events and statements, therefore, can be very misleading or at best incomplete. Statements which offend reason and deny unchanging principles should be read with discrimination if comprehension is to be achieved.

Since the Bible, in common with other scriptures, contains many such incongruities, the mystical interpretation possesses great force, providing, as it does, the only possible reconciliation.

Matt. 9:7.   And he arose, and departed to his house.

Physically, this is but the continued description of the miracle of healing. Mystically, when a spiritual aspirant goes home, he returns to his Source. An Adept can aid him greatly in this, both by guiding him along the pathway of return and sharing intimately his own illumined state. Indeed, the true adept healer not only initiates curative action in the body which is sick, but makes the dweller in the body realize unity with the spiritual Self. After action and reaction have been equalized and counterbalanced, or nearly so, these two procedures unite to restore interior harmony and bodily health.

The action of Jesus, to be considered later, in mixing clay with his own spittle and placing it as pads upon the eyes of one who was blind, restoring sight, is an example of the recourse by the adept healer to material measures, placing substance from his own person in effective contact with a suppliant for healing.

Spirit and matter are coexistent, coeternal and coactive. Spirit is dependent upon matter for its manifestation. In sickness the matter in the human bodies is in an abnormal condition and, therefore, obstructs the full and harmonious manifestation in and through it of spiritual influences, forces and power. This applies also to mystical experiences in the waking state. Brain substance and brain cells are involved in heightened awareness, as is also the matter of the subtler bodies. Genius, inspiration and interior illumination are dependent upon heightened receptivity of the mind-brain, which involves a condition of their substance. Yoga, prayer and contemplation involve, not only expansion of consciousness, but also the condition and function of molecules and cells in the physical body and energies in the superphysical vehicles. The action of will and thought through the pronunciation of words of power in the preliminary phases of self-exaltation affect both consciousness and the matter of its vehicles.

This also applies to spiritual healing in which correction of abnormalities in the condition and function of the substance of the vehicles affected is brought about. A so-called, miscalled, miracle of healing, though to all appearances a simple operation, can be in fact quite a complicated one. Matter of varying degrees of density in the mental, emotional, etheric and physical bodies of man is involved. In deep sickness such as a palsy or paralysis the abnormality may be present in all of these vehicles; it must therefore be corrected in them all. This requires great occult knowledge and the application of force according to occult principles in which initiates are instructed.

Pathology can exist deep within the psyche of man, involving an abnormal state of the matter of which the astral and mental bodies are built. An actual molecular deviation from the normal may exist, and it is this, the material aspect of disease, which the occult healer must correct. While some of the healing miracles of Jesus, as of other sages, appear as simple or single acts, in reality quite complex procedures must have been involved. Naturally, recorders could hardly report these or even know of them since the inner processes are invisible.

So-called miracles are miraculous only because of ignorance of the laws under which the effects are produced. Scientific achievements in this age would have appeared miraculous in former times; yet they are the result of the application of knowledge gained more recently. The analogy is, however, not exact since the causes of such happenings as spiritual healing are not, and can never be, perceived and known physically. Humanity will eventually cognize and learn to use these forces, as Adepts can, just as physical energies of increasing potencies are being tapped by modern man. When this occurs, effects produced by their use will appear no more miraculous than the many uses of electricity appear today.

Matt. 9:8.   But when the multitudes saw it, they marveled, and glorified God, which had given such power unto men.

An act of magic can demonstrate the magician's power, serve to illustrate a philosophic truth, and attract those who may be skeptical to a consideration of that truth. Here it is said to produce exaltation and worship on the beholding of the performance of the miracle of healing, which is perfectly natural and doubtless occurred.

If, on the other hand, the Christ of the Gospels is in large measure, if not entircly, a personification of the spiritual power and Presence within man, then all the miracles which are performed can be interpreted as the effects of spiritual realization upon a meditating devotee. There is indeed a sickness of soul as well as of body. The power, the voice and the realized presence of the interior Godhead within man, the Word made flesh, restores the soul to clear vision, purifies and controls emotion and sanity, and produces effectiveness of bodily life. The complete correction and resultant alignment and sensitization of man's vehicles and of the matter of the physical brain are certain to produce an upliftment of spirit. Such realization brings exaltation of an inward joy, worship of the interior Godhead, and psychospiritual wholeness. This remedial and beneficent action of spirit upon man is the greatest of all miracles and the most powerful of all magic. It can mount to an intoxication of joy in the experience of God-consciousness.

Matt. 9:9.   And as Jesus passed forth from thence, he saw a man, named Matthew, sitting at the receipt of custom: and he saith unto him, Follow me. And he arose, and followed him.

The age-old and continuing process of the selection by an Adept Teacher of a disciple is here described. From the childhood of the human race upon this planet, its evolution has been guided, its progress through periods of danger and difficulty guarded by both invisible and a visible ministration by man's seniors in evolution. Invisible, the fraternity of Adepts has exerted a directive and protective influence upon the mind and the emotions of man. Visibly, lofty beings from among them have physically visited the earth and appeared in certain restricted regions and to chosen peoples.

In addition, two particular types of men and women have been selected for acceptance and training as disciples. One type consists of those who have attained to stages of development in advance of the normal for their time. Since these are potentially very useful to both the race and the Adept Brotherhood, special aid is offered them in the form of close association with a spiritual Teacher. The other type consists of those who have felt stirring strongly within them an aspiration for spiritual experience and a determination to gain knowledge about, and know directly, the underlying principles and laws of universal, planetary and human life. The latter, whether deliberately or not, have uttered a call from within their minds for understanding and spiritual guidance. Such a call is never left unanswered. When it proves to be both genuine and persistent, an Adept Teacher takes note of it and with great wisdom chooses a method of response. This may at first be wholly mystical, or it may be quite objective, as the calling of the disciples of the Buddha or of the Lord Christ.

The brief description of the call to Matthew contains the significant statement that on hearing the words "Follow me" he arose and followed. Herein is portrayed the instant response of spirit to kindred spirit and the immediate recognition of the Teacher by the disciple who at last found his Master. When the search is sincere and the discovery a true one, the response is unhesitating. The life of dicipleship becomes the only true and desirable one thereafter. Thus Matthew, with his fellow disciples of the Christ, entered upon the ancient way, having heard the call, and knelt at the Master's feet.

> Matt. 9:10.   And it came to pass, as Jesus sat at meat in the house, behold, many publicans and sinners came and sat down with him and his disciples.

When greatly advanced men and superhuman beings visit the world of ordinary humanity, they display disregard for certain conventional attitudes of mind and modes of conduct. Since the achievement is in advance of the normal, this attitude arouses resentment and resistance. Doubts, criticisms and condemnations arise in minds that are either too ignorant to understand or fearful for their own prestige and position. This hostility matters not in the least to the divine visitant, whose sole purpose is to come into intimate contact and communion with mankind. This is symbolized by entry into a house and partaking of food in a mixed company.

Two opposing attitudes are displayed in the account of this incident. One is the single-minded purpose of the teacher, whose objective is quite independent of associations of caste and social standing. The other attitude is adopted by those who, unaware of the existence of such spiritual purposes, are self-imprisoned and spiritually lost in their own artificial concepts concerning society and human intercourse. Illumined ones who come and minister to men care naught for artificial distinctions, for they are concerned with the unfolding spiritual presence for which the bodily encasement is as a temple—though all too often it proves a tomb.

Herein, also, the whole nature of a human being is portrayed by means of personifications. The Christ is the divine principle; the disciples are the higher and more noble attributes, qualities and capacities, chiefly intellectual. The so-called publicans and sinners represent the desire nature, and more particularly those aspects of it which are as yet unreformed and unregenerated. The house is the physical body, and the aura, the enclosing field or envelope of force within which all these aspects of human nature are gathered together.

The process of regeneration is allegorically portrayed. The divine principles, the Christ, the nobler and more disciplined attributes, and the lower more animal-like nature of man enter into close relationship, partaking of the same food. Interpreted, this implies that a stage of development has been entered at which the inner Self is illuminating and spiritualizing the outer man. The mystical Christ Presence is noticeably felt; its influence is recognized and acknowledged. The material and spiritual aspects of human nature are becoming intimately blended and a spiritual mode of life is about to be entered.

> Matt. 9:11. And when the Pharisees saw it, they said unto his disciples, Why eateth your Master with publicans and sinners?

Entrance upon an increasingly spiritual mode of life always meets with resistance both from within the aspirant and from family, friends and the members of society amid which he lives. The Pharisees personify these resistances. Interiorly, habit, custom, apprehension lest valued positions and pleasures be lost can pose a considerable barrier. In this reading, the Pharisees are within all men. Such challenge, complaint, and questionings do arise and must be met and overridden.

> Matt. 9:22. But when Jesus heard that, he said unto them, They that be whole need not a physician, but they that are sick.

The actions and the words of Jesus on this occasion and throughout many of the recorded events of his life indicate his attainment and habitual use of a level of consciousness which was not normal in his day and has not yet been attained by the mass of mankind. This attainment is supramental and marks entry and advance upon a stage of evolution which may legitimately be described as new. Until this stage is entered, the mind is the sole arbiter and judge of the fitness of conduct. Two mental attributes, rigidity and separativeness, make difficult this "new and living way"; for these must be overridden, as also must other mental restrictions of outlook. While the majority of mankind in this age is limited mentally by certain restrictive attributes, the more advanced among men are free of these. Flexiblility and universality of consciousness mark the development of the wisdom principle in man, which is personified by the Christ. Advanced men begin to see the world as a whole, humanity as one family, all men as brothers. The picture or account of the Christ seated at table with publicans and sinners represents the developed power of perceiving unity amid diversity and of being totally unaffected by the illusory divisions of cast and convention. There are racial leaders among men of today who also exemplify this outlook and are forerunners of a race now being born.

One part of the function of those great beings who periodically visit the earth and mankind is to stimulate and quicken the growth in the world mind of the wisdom principle or Christ nature in man. Their very presence has this effect, thereby helping those who can respond to a state of consciousness which sees men and nature from within and observes the unfolding, interior life principle at work. Their vision is not limited to external forms with their temporary difference and divisions.

Wisdom, pure and direct, takes such a sage to the heart of human problems and solves them. This is evinced in the reply of the Christ to the Pharisees given in this verse, "They that be whole need not a physician, but they that are sick."

> Matt. 9:13.   But go ye and learn what that meaneth, I will have mercy, and not sacrifice: for I am not come to call the righteous, but sinners to repentance.

Christ's reply not only answers the criticism of the Pharisees but bids them discover truth for themselves. The ideal of human kindness and compassion is called for, being above formal sacrificial offerings in temple worship. As in the parable of the lost sheep, the Christ describes one part of the mission of a divine being who visits the world of men. This, he said, is to aid especially those in dire need, those falling by the wayside of evolution, whose strength is failing, virtue declining, and spiritual insight being lost. Such men and women evoke, not judgment and condemnation, but divine compassion and divine aid.

Just as the physician and the reformer can and do minister more especially to those who are sick in body and in mind, so an inspired sage comes to aid those who are sick in soul, wounded and weary at heart under the stresses and temptations of bodily life.

Mystically interpreted, this implies that the inner will and inspiration of the fainthearted and the falling can be restored by a manifestation of the Christ nature within them. The injunction "Go ye and learn what that meaneth" constitutes a call to that inward search for the spirit of divine compassion and love. This spirit lies buried within all men and shines forth resplendent in a savior of the world, particularly on behalf of the fallen among mankind.

> Matt. 9:14.   Then came to him the disciples of John, saying, Why do we and the Pharisees fast oft, but thy disciples fast not?
>
> 15.   And Jesus said unto them, Can the children of the bride-chamber mourn, as long as the bridegroom is with them?

> but the days will come, when the bridegroom shall be taken from them, and then shall they fast.
>
> 16. No man putteth a piece of new cloth unto an old garment, for that which is put in to fill up taketh from the garment, and the rent is made worse.
>
> 17. Neither do men put new wine into old bottles: else the bottles break, and the wine runneth out, and the bottles perish: but they put new wine into new bottles, and both are preserved.

The spiritual and bodily discipline of fasting is here shown as a means and not an end. Since the disciples were with the Master and intimately united with him, the goal of realization of his presence had been attained. Fasting, therefore, was no longer necessary for them. The rules which govern training in any walk of life and for any human endeavor apply also to the spiritual life. When a particular goal has been attained, the methods of training which brought about the success no longer need rigorously be applied. Nevertheless, a certain flexible asceticism and a strict adherence to principles still obtains.

The principle of single-mindedness and completeness of intent and action is inculcated by two analogies. Attempted patchwork and the endeavor to mix a little of the new way of life with the old can but lead to failure. The surrender must be complete, the heart wholly pure. The pathway to self-liberation gradually becomes the whole and the single motive for living. This is one of the most difficult of the laws of the higher life for the aspirant, particularly the neophyte. Fortunately, the change may be made gradually. The very aspiration indicated that the inner Self is active within the outer man. In consequence, the difficult necessity for wholeness of heart, mind and bodily life can be met.

In many phrases in the Bible this law is enunciated. Lot's wife became petrified because she looked back while walking away from the past. The tendency is quite natural and in the early stages the life of a neophyte does not assume undue importance. Eventually, however, the old claims die, former tendencies to indulgence are outgrown, and the whole being becomes an embodiment of the will to attain. Single-mindedness, as the Christ implies, is the only way to the spiritual heights.

> Matt. 9:18. While he spake these things unto them, behold, there came a certain ruler, and worshipped him, saying, My daughter is even now dead: but come and lay thy hand upon her, and she shall live.

Indeed, as one reads the accounts of the miracles of Christ, one can readily be transported in thought to the actual scene. The wandering Teacher accompanied by his entourage encounters those who are suffering from various disorders. By his spiritual and occult powers he heals some of them, whether by his touch, his words or a silent manifestation of healing power. The man Jesus, a highly trained occultist, a seer and a *magus,* had attained to high evolutionary stature and initiatory degree. It was therefore well within his powers both to discern root causes of diseases or even death and under certain conditions to correct them.

Resuscitation from death is possible for an Adept by two means. Where death is only apparent, because the body is sunk into a very deep coma, the spark of life not actually extinct, the physical cause of the condition may be corrected and inner consciousness restored, the mind again becoming operative in the body. Thereafter the person will wake up, either gradually or immediately, the full functioning of the mechanisms of consciousness at every level having been restored. It is almost exclusively under such circumstances that an Adept will perform the seeming miracle. The karma of the patient, as also of the family and others more immediately concerned, is the decisive factor, both in the decision of the Adept to resuscitate and the degree of immediate and later functioning of the inner Self in the body. Before acting, the Adept ascertains the karmic situation, as he is well able to do, and then acts accordingly.

If death has actually occurred, however, and the link between the inner Self and the body has been finally severed, then action of an altogether different kind becomes necessary. Again the adept seer must study the physical and superphysical conditions, note the karmic situation and act accordingly. If he decides to proceed, the magnetic link between the Ego and the outer man, the "silver cord," is restored and the original inhabitant returns to the abandoned body. Sometimes another Ego might become attached to the body. Intricate karmic conditions and relationships enter into such a procedure, and an official of the Inner Government of the World may have to be consulted. He is one whose tasks include supervising the administration of karmic law and is himself in collaboration with still higher authorities, the Lords of Karma revealed in occult literature.

In both cases the brain itself must receive a powerful stimulation from an enforced uprush of the creative life-force, the *Kundalini-Shakti,* into the head. At the same time the force center at the crown of the head must be reopened at etheric and physical levels, and the whole mechanism of consciousness at all levels be reactivated. The degree and positions at which this is necessary depend upon the condition of the person, which the adept operator is careful to ascertain. When these two processes have been successfully completed, the inner Self in induced and drawn by a certain magnetic affinity with the body to take up physical life in it again. When a new Ego is introduced, one is chosen which has lost its own body prematurely in terms of years, as for example by "accidental" death.

Scriptural accounts of such events may have a psychospiritual significance; In the cypher of the Bible the word *death* is used to describe a state of complete unawareness of anything but the physical surroundings, ignorance of spiritual experience and the consequent denial of its existence. Coma and sleep refer to the temporary eclipse, as far as bodily awareness is concerned, of its inner Self, its radiance, and other influences. In both cases it is the mind of man which is really dead and so remains until natural death occurs, unless illumination restores spiritual awareness and "aliveness."

This can come about in more than one way. The natural processes of evolution through long ages will sensitize the very matter of which the brain and the mental body consist so that the indwelling spirit becomes known by direct experience. On occasions, a racial, national or personal disaster or shock can so shake the foundations of a purely worldly and material faith as to bring about by desperation, as it were, its renunciation and an admission of its unreliability and untruth. This provides the inner Self with an opportunity to bring about a revelation of spiritual realities within the brain-mind, as if by an act of divine grace. The sufferer then turns inward to the only possible source of aid.

A third way in which the deadness of the mind-brain can be overcome is by the practice of yoga, consistently incorporated into the daily life. This includes both meditation upon the divine at certain hours and the permeation of the daily life with spiritual and utterly unselfish motives for every action, particularly those in which others are involved. This practice brings about forcibly, as it were, the sensitization of brain and mind to the constantly transmitted will-force and intuitive understanding of the inner Self.

Still another way to renewed life results from utter failure or worse due to desperate deeds. In this case the Christ principle, the divine Atma, forces its way, as it were, into the consciousness of the personality, which then becomes illumined and spiritually alive. Allegories of a savior responding to a prayer to intervene and raise one who is dead generally describes this latter.

Whatever the cause or causes, the effect is veritably to raise the outer man from a condition of spiritual deadness, of living death. The resultant mystical experiences and the way by which they are obtained are described by key words used as symbols of conditions of consciousness. The house of the deceased, for example, refers to the physical body and its normal state of physical awareness. The deceased person represents the formal mind in a state of total ignorance of underlying spiritual laws and of the true user of the mind, the hidden spiritual Self.

A divine visitant then appears, whether in the guise of a healer or a messenger who, Hermes-like, raises a Persephone from the underworld.[1] The spoken word in such allegories represents the transmitted power, which, as a vitalizing influence, awakens the mind to a realization of the spiritual content of universe and man. This, indeed, is as a resurrection from the dead, a miraculous resuscitation and restoration of life.

> Matt. 9:20. And, behold, a woman, which was diseased with an issue of blood twelve years, came behind him, and touched the hem of his garment:
>
> 21. For she said within herself, If I may but touch his garment, I shall be whole.
>
> 22. But Jesus turned him about, and when he saw her, he said, Daughter, be of good comfort; thy faith hath made thee whole. And the woman was made whole from that hour.

In the larger cosmic sense this refers to a phase in the evolution of a universe at which earth touches heaven and heaven touches earth—the spiritualization of matter has proceeded to the stage where spirit (Jesus) and matter (the woman) were becoming unified. The constricting, tainting and even degrading influence of matter upon spiritual beings (the sickness) then becomes reduced to a minimum.

The loss of the physical life-sap, the blood, doubtless through the generative organ, describes the condition before this phase is entered; for then the creative life-force is wasted. Throughout this earlier phase matter in general and the physical body of human beings are bereft of the regenerative coordinating influence of spirit. This condition is typical of the so-called dark ages, major and minor, through which in cyclic progressions universes and their components inevitably pass. At the stage described in the incident, this adverse condition is outgrown, left behind, its symbolical ill effect no longer felt. Allegorically, the woman is healed.

In terms of purely human evolution, the sick woman represents humanity, self-degraded, accentuating the material and the sensual to the neglect and even denial of the spiritual and intuitional. Fortunately for mankind, this condition, though long-lasting, is eventually outgrown. In due course normal evolutionary processes bring the inner and the outer man into intimate relationship, such as is indicated by the symbol of Solomon's Seal. The inner Self in which spiritual will and wisdom have become sufficiently developed reveal themselves to the mortal man, causing him to aspire to spiritual wholeness. Thus the sick woman seeks to be healed by realization of the divine Self.

At that stage of unfoldment in the personal life of a man or woman, a regeneration of the outer is brought about by the power and realized presence of the inner Self. Then and then alone, the human being, self-surrendered, is really whole, a total being in whom spirit and matter are consciously united and mutually interactive or whole. Then the outer man becomes illumined, purified and integrated by the touch and words of the inner Self, personified by Jesus the Christ.

Occultly interpreted, the stage at which the aspirant meets the Master and is illumined by him is described by means of this allegory. The woman's sickness refers to the divine discontent which impels a human being at this stage in evolution to purify and control his outer person and mode of life and to dicover both the inner presence and the Master who will guide him on the path of spiritual life.

As the story tells, such aspiration is always answered. The very confession of error due to overaccentuation of material motives—the sickness—and the determined search based upon intuition, or even the influence of the Master himself, lead to their meeting. At first this is somewhat limited, the woman only touching the garment of the Christ from behind. But in response the Master turns full face and exercises the power of the Word. The sentence expressing his full assent to the aspirant's request indicates the establishment of an intimate relationship between Master and disciple as well as between the ego and personality.

The garment of the Christ is a symbol for the radiant vesture of light in which the divine presence is incarnate at spiritual levels of consciousness. To touch this is symbolically to enter the outer levels of that state of being and thereby to release the power of the dweller within, to become aware at the fringe of divine consciousness. This leads later to full awareness and mutual interchange between the immortal and the mortal man, who in consequence becomes whole.

The bridge between the mortal, personal man and the Adept Teacher is thus allegorically described as consisting of the realization of imperfection and sickness and the aspiration to reach his feet. The woman's search, her intuitive knowledge that he exists and when found will heal her, the touching of his garment, a humble receptiveness to his influence, hearing his words and being thereafter accepted into his consciousness, all these are descriptive of changes which occur within the aspirant and of the expressions in conduct to which they will lead.

This is the unchanging pathway for which there is no alternative, leading from the normal work-a-day life and world of man to the supernormal, supersensual worlds of perfected men. He (or she) who in the fullness of his heart treads that path or crosses that bridge linking the two worlds unfailingly arrives at his destination, which is the presence of the Master and the receipt of his wisdom and integrating power.

If that story is carefully studied in its application to the practice of the science of yoga, the woman who is sick also represents the mind and the brain as its physiological organ. Unillumined and therefore wasting both time and life-force as the evolutionary pathway is very slowly trodden, they urgently need the illuminating and enlightening presence and influence consciously received from the spiritual will, wisdom and intelligence, the Christ nature. The search for the healer corresponds to intuitive perception that the source of perfection and of healing lies within, consists in fact of the interior divine presence. This presence must be found and "touched," lightly at first—the woman only touches the hem of his garment. The brain is as yet insufficiently illumined, sensitized and responsive to enable its possessor to realize the Christ power in waking consciousness. Thereafter, though, the Master "turned him about" and spoke to her; the Christ power is known face to face; the yogi hears the word of the divine within. This culminates in the full revelation experienced within the brain while wide awake of both the presence of the eternal spirit which is the true man and of identity therewith.

This realization can only be attained by an active search which takes the form of practicing the art and science of self-illumination. By the mastery of dwelling in thought upon the source of inner light with the purpose of becoming identified with it, a steadily increasing flow is produced of both the vital fluid (prana) and the universal procreative energy and fire which rise and flow from the body into the brain (kundalini.) This improves capacity for metaphysical thought and sensitivity to the influence of the divine Self within. Another result consists of "descent" of that Presence realized by the yogi in various ways according to temperament and other basic characteristics. The God-Self may become known by the meditating yogi as an over-whelming interior power and will force; as a steadily increasing spiritual intuitiveness and wisdom; as a deepening compassion and tenderness for the embodied divinity in all others, especially in those suffering and those engaged in a similar search; as experiences of unity and identity; as light and enlightment within the mind and brain. One or more of these—eventually all—assume increasing power in the inner and outer life of the devotee who, in consequence, is harmonized, whole, or in terms of the story, is healed by faith.

Thus, as in other instances, scriptural accounts of miracles, notably those of miraculous healings, are found to be descriptive of interior experiences and illuminations which come to people, particularly to those who recognize and confess their limitations and sincerely seek to overcome them. The sick ones, who in their great need search for and trust in a divine healer, find him and are healed.

> Matt. 9:23. And when Jesus came into the ruler's house, and saw the minstrels and the people making a noise,
>
> 24. He said unto them, Give place: for the maid is not dead, but sleepeth. And they laughed him to scorn.
>
> 25. But when the people were put forth, he went in, and took her by the hand, and the maid arose.
>
> 26. And the fame hereof went abroad into all that land.

The Gospel of St. Matthew has here been mutilated as in certain other places. Indeed, the copies of, and references to, the original documents have been much changed by passage through many and various hands. In some cases the changes have been inadvertent, in others, made with good intentions to improve literary form. Unfortunately, there have been other cases of deliberate forgery, deletion and addition.

The account of the raising of the ruler's daughter from apparent death was originally preceded by an introductory verse now lost, so that the transition from the story of the woman healed is abrupt.[2] Nevertheless, the incident even as related is full of interest from both the occult and the mystical points of view. In the former, Jesus, as a trained occultist, would perceive readily that the girl was only apparently dead, the silver cord not yet broken and the brain still alive.

Although reference to it may not be made, the law of cause and effect plays an almost decisive part in such a seeming miracle. In this, both the members of the family and the entranced person are concerned, for the condition and the experience for all result from that law. In a former life, probably, all had generated the adversity, possibly by bringing about the death of another. The entranced person may have actually delivered the death dealing blow.

If the act was a purely personal one deliberately performed to satisfy hatred, a desire for revenge, or other murderous instinct, then resuscitation from trance would be unlikely. Karma would not permit occult intervention;[3] the hands of the healer would be tied, so to speak. If the murder was an official act performed at the instance of a higher command but with some personal satisfaction, or the karma was almost worked out, then occult intervention might occur, being within the great law.

If read as a description of the recovery of temporarily lost idealism and spirituality, then the verbal call to arise and the action of taking the maiden by the hand refer to the effective and intimate interior contact between the inner and the outer selves. The voice is an expression of the inmost spirit and the handclasp represents its manifestion in the body. As a result, a restoration of spiritual awareness and of Egoic control and illumination to the personality are achieved.

In both the literal and the mystical applications of the story, the essential influence is that of the awakened and empowered Christ Presence, whether as a physical visitant or as an interior spiritual power.

Matt. 9:27. And when Jesus departed thence, two blind men followed him, crying, and saying, Thou son of David, have mercy on us.

28. And when he was come into the house, the blind men came to him: and Jesus saith unto them, Believe ye that I am able to do this? They said unto him, Yea, Lord.

29. Then touched he their eyes, saying, According to your faith be it unto you.

30. And their eyes were opened; and Jesus straitly charged them, saying, See that no man know it.

31. But they, when they were departed, spread abroad his fame in all that country.

In the mystical interpretations of all Christ's miracles, Judea with its varied scenery, places and people, represents Egoic consciousness and its numerous attributes. The presence of Jesus the Christ in the land portrays the divine power indwelling, the innermost spiritual essence which is the radiance from the Monad. The suppliants for healing portray the mortal, personal nature in various difficulties and limitations, particularly lack of spiritual illumination.

In this instance, the two blind men represent the conjoined mind and emotions on the one hand and the physical body on the other. A phase of evolution has been entered in which the existence of spiritual light is recognized and its absence from the mind and brain realized and regretted. Man as seeker for spiritual light is thus portrayed—man who has realized that all earthly light is but darkness, and that those who know no other light are blind indeed. Intuitively awakened to this blindness and impoverishment, the human being in this stage determines to seek and find the spiritual light, to become personally illumined. Thus the two blind men cry out to Jesus as the Son of David, the divine principle, for mercy on them and their mentally shadowed condition. The recognition of the kingly lineage of Jesus may possibly be a reference to the Monad itself as the original source, and so the progenitor of the Christ power.

The entry of Jesus into the house of the blind men indicates entry upon that phase in man's mystical life at which the inner, royal Presence is partially realized in waking consciousness; for the house in this case implies mind, brain and body as the physical house of the inner Self.

Jesus's direct question concerning faith in him indicates the necessity for an intellectual and intuitional recognition of the existence within oneself of a divine power and presence. Both men affirmed their full recognition of the inner light and complete trust in its power to illumine. This is critical if enlightenment is to be gained. Without this as basis for spiritual aspiration and discipline, the quest will be difficult of fulfillment. The search must be founded upon a real contact between the inner *Atma,* or spirit, and the outer man, despite the fact that the full effects are not yet realized.

The eyes are symbols of the mind, abstract and concrete, and when blind, the unillumined state. The touch of Christ's hand which brought about the healing refers to the nearness of the inner power to the mind and describes the result of full contact, which causes enlightenment. Thus, symbolically, the eyes of the blind men were opened.

The fact that Jesus charged the two men not to reveal their experience and his action refers to a profound spiritual law: interior and occult experiences lose a measure of their efficacy and power when unduly revealed and unadvisably discussed. Mental illumination is the result of a mysterious process of nature—of a secret working of man's inner spiritual essence, the Christ—in the laboratory of the human mind. Success demands a measure of stillness, secrecy, and silence since the process itself possesses those attributes. Thus silence best becomes those in whom the process is occurring. This applies especially to casual acquaintances, but less to intimate friends who are similarly seeking and have begun likewise to be illumined.

Matt. 9:32. As they went out, behold, they brought to him a dumb man possessed with a devil.

33. And when the devil was cast out, the dumb spake: and the multitudes marvelled, saying, It was never so seen in Israel.

The sufferer in this case exhibits symptoms of two disorders, speechlessness and a degree of insanity. Possession by a devil was offered and accepted as an explanation of such psychological disorders among the ancients, but, in fact, rarely had foundation. Though such a diagnosis may not be entirely ruled out, acute emotional distress from the inability to speak, or a form of schizophrenia is also possible and perhaps more probable.

Whichever may have been true, the account of this miracle, brief though it is, suggests that its inclusion in the narrative is for historical rather than symbolic purposes. The language in which St. Matthew reports the incident suggests that he regarded it historically. In the mystical sense, however, dumbness indicates inablility to give physical expression to the dictates and inspiration derived from the spiritual part of human nature. Such a person may actually be able to speak and yet be dumb in this sense, his thought and language being wholly mundane. There are indeed all too many, even in these days, suffering from this limitation, which may arise from conditions in the home, companionships, early environment and its effect upon the mind and outlook of life. Immaturity is another possible cause for this limitation. In the course of evolution, however, the more spiritual part of man, personified by the Christ, increasingly influences the mentality and so the mode of life. In consequence, that spiritual "dumbness" gives place to spiritual self-expression.

Possession by a so-called devil constitutes another and quite distinct pathological condition of the mind-brain. The invasion of the mental or emotional vehicles of man by a hostile superphysical being is a possibility and when it occurs can cause physical disabilities including lunacy. Discarnate human souls or their "shells," victims of sudden death, whether by suicide, a decree of justice, or a mishap, do remain for a time in areas of the underworld, are in close spatial proximity with the surface of the earth and may have a psychological affinity with distressed or weak-minded people. Such entities can attach themselves to the psyche of those who are mediumistically inclined. An occultist possessed of the necessary perception and power, such as Jesus, is able to dislodge such an intruder, whereupon the physical ailment may speedily be cured. Dumbness may be regarded as a very unusual effect of such obsession, the term "possessed of a devil" being rather descriptive of an abnormal psychological condition. Mystically regarded, the closer contact of the inner spiritual Self with the mind-brain of the person would automatically decrease unreasonableness and increase the degree of intelligence in the conduct of life.

While the ingredients of historical fact and primitive superstition are recognized in this brief account, the psychophysical conditions of dumbness and obsession may be viewed as results of past misdeeds. Dumbness, for example, a condition of inexpressiveness, of inability to convey thought by means of speech, may result from silence imposed by karmic decree. Physical dumbness can be associated with and even caused by various forms of psychological restrictions to full Self-expression. One of these affects the expression of feelings of love, in which case the loving person is tongue-tied, severely restricted, shut in, as it were, in a psychological prison of sheer physical inability to express love. This might, perhaps, be the karma of undue promiscuity in former lives.

There is also a psychological conditon characterized by a mental blockage which renders the sufferer incapable of self-expression where metaphysical ideas are concerned. This may be a karmic reaction from broken vows of silence in former lives. As a member of a Mystery temple or school, certain vows of silence had been taken and ultimately broken. So-called sacred knowledge and even occult truths received under the vow had been either willfully or carelessly repeated. In the former case, more especially, a peculiar restriction of personal self-expression is part of the karmic result. Other aspects of such nemesis can be inability to find and be admitted to an occult school, or a mental blindness which prevents the mind from recognizing both the school itself and the wisdom which it teaches. In addition, there is a more or less natural condition of inexpressiveness where metaphysical ideas are concerned.

In this incident the dumb man represents the severely restricted personality, while the Christ personifies the inner spiritual Self, particularly in its aspect of power. The realized spiritual will (the recognized presence of Christ) exercises such a power upon the bedulled mind and brain that the obstacles to Self-expression gradually become less effective and finally disappear. Thus, as spiritual power declares and reveals itself within the individual, a full and free expression of the inner Self through the outer is achieved. Symbolically, a dumb man is healed by the occult action of the Christ.

> Matt. 9:34. But the Pharisees said, He casteth out devils through the prince of devils.

Human nature is well described by the statement that the multitudes marvelled while the Pharisees charged that Jesus performed healing and exorcism through the agency of the devil. There is an attitude of the human mind which reacts, sometimes quite violently, against that which is beyond its comprehension and domination. Demonstration of occult and spiritual power can arouse this type of mentality into self-protective hostility. Those who perform seeming miracles by the capacities beyond the reach of such materialists are, in consequence, often charged with doing so by evil agencies.

Such enemies of man can be either exterior or interior. Both represent resistance, restriction and in extreme cases the desire to destroy. If external, these are hostile men; if interior, they are attributes, qualities of character, habitual modes of thought and action which distort and constrict the expression of the spiritual Self of man through his bodily nature.

The Pharisees, as other avowed enemies in the inspired scripture, can represent both of these. The Pharisees in the New Testament personify resistance to change, determined assertion of the superiority and final truthfulness of established modes of thought and religious dogma. These are the Pharisees of all ages, all scriptures, myths and allegories, in which they never fail to appear; for the initiated authors know full well this attribute of humanity and its more general modes of expression.

The pharisees are made in this verse to try to besmear Jesus's reputation and so to undermine his influence. The spirit in him is in conflict with them and may for a time be defeated, partly by fear of public contempt and partly by the lack of the evolutionary stature which bestows courage and steadfastness in the cause of truth. This verse, short though it is, expresses all these considerations, many of which are summed up with the word which has become part of some languages, namely, *pharisaical*.

Jesus represents regions of consciousness as yet beyond the range of comprehension and attainment. The suppliants for healing and those who recover are symbolic of such people outgrowing, but still limited by, bigotry and materialism. By the aid of the inner Self, the interior Christ nature, they become liberated from their intellectual limitations. Light dawns upon their minds, understanding reaches their mental ears, and their mental paralysis concerning spiritual truths is overcome. Rigidity of mind is replaced by flexibility and open-mindedness concerning metaphysical ideas.

These most beneficial changes generally come about gradually, though the final stages of self-illumination can occur with dramatic speed. Illumination can come in an instant, as it were. In the sacred language these interior experiences are described in the form of the dramatic actions of visiting saviors.

> Matt. 9:35.   And Jesus went about all the cities and villages, teaching in their synagogues, and preaching the gospel of the kingdom, and healing every sickness and every disease among the people.

As in all human experiences there are periods of maximum fulfillment as also of restriction and decline, so in the recorded history of Jesus there were times when his mission reached great heights of success. This verse records one of such times. Here we see Jesus at the height of his power and his success. Although darkness threatens and the forces personified by the Pharisees plot destruction, the great Savior of men continues his divine ministrations unconcerned and unaffected. The festival of Palm Sunday is based upon experiences of such epochs. Indeed, the tide of Jesus' mission was at its flood.

This law applies also to the interior, spiritual life of man. Indeed, there is not one incident in the immortal story of the life of Jesus which does not have its expression in the life of every human being as also of every nation. There are months or years in the lives of human beings when spiritual aspiration, idealism and their determined application to daily life are strongly felt and sucessfully achieved. These are the times, following the example of Jesus and other great ones, to grasp such opportunities and give full rein to the highest influences then at work. Fortunate are they for whom this verse is a truthful description of both their inner and their outer lives.

> Matt. 9:36.   But when he saw the multitudes, he was moved with compassion on them, because they fainted, and were scattered abroad, as sheep having no shepherd.
>
> 37.   Then saith he unto his disciples, The harvest truly is plenteous, but the labourers are few;
>
> 38.   Pray ye therefore the Lord of the harvest, that he will send forth labourers into his harvest.

These words, apparently uttered after a series of acts of spiritual healing, while applicable to the time when they were uttered, have an almost timeless truth. They constitute a diagnosis of a long-continued and still-continuing world need.

Thus far throughout the present phase of man's intellectual development—which has lasted at least a million years and will continue for thousands more—accentuated individualism has brought sin and sorrow to mankind. The dimensions of both have long been enormous and unhappily are increasing today. The mind of man may be thought of diagrammatically as consisting of layers or strata of types of mentality. When one of these becomes more active than the others, it tends to obscure their light and produce mental imbalance. The remarkable technological progress of modern man is achieved at the great price of the obscuration of the light of morality, conscience and spirituality. Mechanical and so-called scientific achievement fills the mental vision to the exclusion of the sense of moral responsibility for the right use of the products of such developments. This is a contributory factor in the condition of mankind on earth today.

Humanity is indeed faint for grievously lacking spiritual wisdom and knowledge, esoteric and exoteric, of the purposes and laws of human life on earth and how they may be applied to the processes of human living. *Avidya,* or ignorance, causes humanity's grievous errors, and knowledge is both antidote and cure. Yet, despite the wealth of teaching which its elders, the laborers, have continuously made available, the need is still pressing.

In this interpretation, the harvest is humanity itself and particularly suffering nations and individuals: the oppressed, the imprisoned, the tortured, the criminal element, and all who suffer from mental and physical diseases, including the evil of crowd psychology.

Fortunately, illumined men and women also exist on earth and are exerting their beneficent influence and raising their voices in a call to replace such evils as the destructive use of the products of scientific advance with their application to constructive purposes and goals. Everyone who can become articulate, who will raise voices and use pens in calls to humanity to recognize other and wholly constructive objectives and achievements, serves the race mightily in this critical time in history. These harvesters are the wise, self-illumined, dedicated and compassionate men and women. They range from the "just men made perfect," the planetary Adepts, through inspired teachers, educators and statesmen dealing with multitudes and large issues, to all those in every walk of life who, often unnoticed, dutifully serve their fellowmen. The words of wise men can illumine the mind, and the lives of dedicated men can touch and inspire the heart.

Happily, these numbers increase as, unhappily, does the need for more and more of them. Seers, saints and Adepts, or perfected men, have always arisen from the ranks of mankind. They continue to arise but still are all too few in proportion to the enormous and mounting demand for their influence and services. The "way of holiness," the narrow path leading to eternal life, is open, is being found and trodden, even if as yet by a very small minority of human beings. These, however, are of great importance to the race, out of all proportion to their numbers. Their effectiveness comes from advancing out of the condition of being only learners into that of self-illumination, and by deepening penetration, knowing truth direct. Since the Christ was addressing his own disciples, it seems reasonable to assume that he was referring to the occult life of mankind upon the earth and to the neophytes, disciples, true initiates in the Greater Mysteries, and Adepts who are the flower of the human race.

Thus interpreted, the words of the Christ constitute a call sent out to all mankind, not only for service and sacrifice in their lives, but also—using another analogy—to seek and find the Master and by him to be made "fishers of men." So the great chapter closes with a call from the Master of Masters for increasing numbers of men and women to embark upon a mode of life motived by selflessness and characterized by self-purification, self-discipline, service to humanity, and especially the search for the Master and the spiritual wisdom of which he is the embodiment. It is profoundly true today as two thousand years ago that the harvest is ready but the laborers are few.

REFERENCES AND NOTES

1. See Hodson, *Hidden Wisdom,* Vol. 1, p. 81.
2. Mark 5:22. (Jairus)
3. See Hodson, *Lecture Notes,* p. 180.

PART SEVEN

CHRIST AND HIS APOSTLES

Chapter Fourteen

Jesus, the wondrous embodiment of divine love in human form, grew to manhood, exhibited supernormal power, wisdom and intelligence and drew round himself a group of disciples. To these he both imparted his wisdom—as in the Sermon on the Mount—and taught the secret knowledge. This he kept hidden from the multitude beneath the veil of allegory and symbol referred to as *parable*. He also imparted to them a special measure of his divine power and grace so that after his physical departure they were able to continue his mission, with the result that the Christian religion came into being and has continued to exist.

Certain words of Our Lord to his disciples which affirm the duality of his message may well be remembered as this chapter is considered; for when asked by his disciples why he taught the people in parables, he replied, "Unto you it is given to know the mystery of the kingdom of God: but unto them that are without, all these things are done in parables."[1] This duality of method—direct and allegorical—is nowhere more apparent than in the verses of which interpretations are about to be proffered. In them—assuming that the Lord is correctly reported—the naked truth, the unveiled wisdom, is delivered to the disciples whom he regarded as among those "given to know the mystery of the kingdom of God." It is all-important that this duality —direct and allegorical—in the teachings of Our Lord be kept in mind as these verses are studied.

> Matt. 10:1.   And when he had called unto him his twelve disciples, he gave them power against unclean spirits, to cast them out, and to heal all manner of sickness and all manner of disease.

When a solar system or any of its components reaches the phase of evolution at which pure spirit or *Atma* becomes the dominant power and presence, with all denser planes and vehicles subservient to it, evil vanishes. Every form of discord is replaced by harmony and the whole purified of the taint of matter, completely ruled by spirit. Symbolically, the Christ is present as the acknowledged Master, and the disciples receive the Christ power, each of them representing a vehicle and an attribute of human consciousness.

On every occasion when a Monad-Ego reaches this phase of development in advance of the normal time, the same phenomenon occurs. The great initiations powerfully enhance the Atmic presence. During the phase of discipleship, silently and unseen the Master has exerted a spiritualizing influence upon the disciple's consciousness and vehicles at all levels, thereby preparing the disciple as a candidate for initiation. The work of the guru[2] in its highest sense as expressed by the great Rishis includes such preparatory ministration, which is also promoted by the teachings and the tasks given to the disciples. Thus aided and empowered from within, the disciple gradually brings about, as interior states of being, the conditions described in this verse.

While the regular and normal training given by Adept Teachers to their disciples is here partly described, the verse may also be interpreted in a mystical sense. Such disciples are drawn from those human beings in whom the spiritual aspects of human nature are beginning to predominate over their material tendencies. The Christ power has awakened or been born in them as a result of both evolutionary development and the regular practice of contemplation as a meditative procedure and a mode of life.

When this phase is entered, the conditions in the personal nature described as unclean spirits, sicknesses and diseases are automatically reduced, eventually to disappear. The Christ within, awake and active, banishes impurity and harmonizes discordances. This is less a deliberate act than the natural result of added spirituality in thought and life and increased manifestation of the God-Self in the bodily person. Indeed, no room is left for that which is unspiritual and discordant in a personality which is becoming filled, as it were, with the incarnate divine presence.

In addition, every occultist, meaning one touched by the fire of *Atma* and studying occult science, eventually becomes endowed with the power to drive out actual obsessing entities from people and places. The faculty and techniques of exorcism and healing involve a transmission of power from teacher to disciple and instruction in its effective use. As implied, unclean and unpleasant inhabitants of the superphysical worlds do exist and can obsess living people. They are generally, but not always, discarnate persons who were evil during their physical lives and continue to be so after death, at least for a time. Such beings can fasten themselves onto the superphysical vehicles of their victims, the emotional nature being chiefly used as a kind of residence. Trained occultists are able both to see such an invading entity and to drive it out, thereafter sealing the aura of the victim against further intrusions. Similarly, sicknesses and diseases caused by such obsessions, as also by other physical and psychological influences, can be both diagnosed and cured by the disciples of an adept Teacher.

Such training is both mystical and occult. The interior spiritual nature of the disciple, the Dweller in the Innermost, is discovered and called into activity, and a measure of the Master's own far greater spiritual power is made available to the disciple by means of a mystical fusion of their individualities. In addition, definite occult training in the application of the resultant power to both self-purification and spiritual healing in general is received.

Intimate relationship between the Adept Teachers and their chosen disciples thus form one part of the ever-continuing, though secret, spiritual and occult life followed by a small minority of human beings on this planet. In earlier epochs in which the material propensities in man were stronger than the spiritual ones, special training was needed to enable those who were advancing ahead of the race to understand and live the path of hastened unfoldment.

The power to cast out that which is unclean and to heal are carried to fulfillment in a solar system at its close, in a disciple when he reaches adeptship, and in the world of men at the corresponding phases of racial evolution.[3]

Those readers who may be interested in astrology will perhaps take special notice of the following attempted application of this science to an aspect of the life of Christ. In the cosmic sense, the twelve apostles represent zodiacal powers, forces, influences which affect man as individual and race, and the cosmic intelligences associated with these centers of power.[4] These are a profound mystery, especially since the stars of each of the signs of the zodiac have no apparent spatial or electromagnetic relationship with each other. Their combinations into supposed units have no basis of astronomical fact, save that they may appear to move synchronously.

The occult doctrine suggests that this knowledge was part of the contribution of man's earliest teachers and spiritual progenitors. This receives some support from the fact that similar, though not always identical, forms, names and emanating influences are attributed to each of the signs by peoples widely separated both in time and the locations of their civilizations. The system would have been well-known to instructed Kabbalists of the period when the Gospels were written.

When the science of astrology is correctly used and aspects are rightly interpreted, strong evidence—if not proof—is given for the reality of influences supposedly emanating from the named groups of stars. Astrological aspects can be related to various conditions such as human characteristics, tendencies toward actions of a particular kind, freedom from or resistance to the general trend of events, whether concerning individuals, nations or the race as a whole. The subject is at least worthy of investigation and has indeed won the attention and respect of great minds.

Interchanges of electromagnetic forces are occurring throughout the whole cosmos. Certain of these can be detected by modern instruments. Occult science teaches that, in addition, superphysical forces are radiating from heavenly bodies, including the earth and every object upon it, whether organic or inorganic.[5] Adepts of earlier epochs were aware of these facts and possessed of organized knowledge concerning their nature and sources. This knowledge of the interplay of stellar influences was organized by them into a science, a fragment of which was revealed to the initiates of earlier times. These in their turn conveyed the more material aspects of the science to the populace, partly to preserve knowledge in the racial mind of the fact that the universe and man consist of far more than mere physical matter and material forms. Astrology is indeed one of the most effective ways of bringing this truth home to receptive minds.

The disciples numbering twelve suggests both a solar and a cosmic significance with regard to the person of the Christ. In the first place, he would not necessarily have limited himself to only twelve disciples, but almost certainly would have chosen a larger number from the men and women of the Hebrew nation who were drawn to and followed him. The several occult communities active at the time, such as the Essenes, the Ebionites and the Nazarenes, would all contain members who were already living the life of discipleship. These would very likely be in attendance upon Jesus, particularly after the descent of the spirit upon him at the Baptism. In addition, there would probably be others newly drawn to the inner life and even some from distant lands who would come to receive the blessing and be for a time in the presence of the great living Master.

The disciples of Jesus numbering only twelve, the twelve tribes of Israel and their patriarchs, the twelve labors of Hercules, and other twelvefold classifications in ancient literature—all these constitute references to the twelvefold physical and superphysical influences and their corresponding characteristics within the human race on earth.[6] For example, Judas Iscariot, who brought about the capture, trial, death and ultimate Ascension of Jesus, personifies the planet Saturn and the sign Scorpio. He represents the influence of the analytical mind with both its favorable and adverse characteristics. He also personifies the imprisoning and deadening effects of matter upon the spirit of man. Evolutionary development leads eventually to man's mastery of, and resurrection from, this dominion of mind and matter.

In terms of planetary and racial evolution, the twelve signs and their varied personifications in allegorical literature represent phases and stages of the unfoldment of human consciousness. These processes follow a series of twelve cycles in which the supposed influence of each sign follows the previous in predominance and typical events. These cycles are repeated many times throughout racial evolution, as a close study of history with this key would reveal. The Christian Era, for example, represents and has been characterized by the qualities of the sign Pisces and its two planetary rulers. Aquarius is now thought by some astrologers to be replacing the apparently waning influence of Pisces.

Man in his total nature contains—and is intimately in rapport with—the forces and intelligences of the twelve zodiacal signs and their planetary rulers. In his interior unfoldment he draws out from latency into activity these twelve capacities and powers. The twelve disciples personify these interior attributes of every man, while the Lord Christ himself, who is their Master, represents the sun, the innermost spirit, source of light and truth.

The incidents recorded in the Gospels are susceptible of a threefold interpretation with a triple revelation of truth—historical, cosmic and mystical. They reveal three Christs, as it were, the historical visitant to earth, the solar Logos, and the Monad of man. Just as the privilege of discipleship is chiefly—but not entirely—granted in order to quicken the development of disciples, so the great twelvefold allegories may be regarded as descriptive of the development of solar systems, races of men on earth, and of particular individuals. The evolution of these three orders of creation is described in the terms of the sacred language as the underlying significance of the supposed adventures and experiences of the people concerned.[7]

Christ in the midst of his disciples, guiding and leading them by example, teaching, dancing, chanting, and revealing himself spiritually, mirrors on earth the Logos of a universe in relationship to its components. Similarly, the Lord Shri Krishna as divine musician in the center of the circle of dancing *gopis* and as mystical partner to each of them in the *Rāsa-Lila* is an allegorical portrayal of the same phenomenon. So also, with varying symbolism, are Master and disciples in every authentic world scripture. Inspired authors thus link heaven and earth and describe celestial principles in the form of earthly happenings, thereby bringing these within the reach of man's minds.

> Matt. 10:2. Now the names of the twelve apostles are these: The first, Simon, who is called Peter, and Andrew his brother; James the son of Zebedee, and John his brother;
>
> 3. Philip, and Bartholomew; Thomas, and Matthew the publican; James the son of Alphaeus, and Lebbaeus, those surname was Thaddaeus;
>
> 4. Simon the Canaanite, and Judas Iscariot, who also betrayed him.

In the presence of the adept Master both the deeply interior qualities of the inner Self and the basic and finest characteristics of the disciple's personality become revealed. The Master with his piercing and perfect vision turned upon the disciple sees these attributes completely. They also tend to emerge and become apparent to the disciple himself. In consequence, the Master knows and understands the disciple thoroughly and completely and the disciple begins to know himself.

This true nature of both the innermost and the outer man has its own self-expression, or in occult terms, *name*. The Master knows this name and may inform the disciple at a certain stage of his spiritual progress of its character. Symbolically, and sometimes actually, the disciple is also given a mystic name.

In a more deeply occult sense, this name serves as a means of communication, particularly from the Master to the disciple. The Master causes the vibratory frequencies of the name to sound out in himself when directing his thought to the disciple, particularly when physically absent. Thus through uttering the name, whether mentally or physically, he places himself in the most intimate relationship possible with the disciple, arresting the attention of the outer man, strengthening all that is highest and best in the disciple, and calling out his real Self. In occultism even a person's given and family names are regarded as important and are used carefully, partly for the above-mentioned purposes. In these verses the mystic names of twelve of the disciples of Jesus are given.[8]

> Matt. 10:5.   These twelve Jesus sent forth, and commanded them, saying, Go out into the way of the Gentiles, and into any city of the Samaritans enter ye not:
>
> 6.   But go rather to the lost sheep of the house of Israel.
>
> 7.   And as ye go, preach, saying, The kingdom of heaven is at hand.

These verses may be regarded as of dubious authenticity. In their surface meaning, they seem out of character, contradicting the universality of the mind of Jesus as exemplified in other verses. He himself, at any rate, regarded his mission as worldwide and definitely extending beyond the restrictions of any race or time, including his own.[9] However, the regeneration and revivification of the Hebrew faith, the drawing back into its fold of those who had withdrawn or lapsed from its practices or beliefs, may well have been regarded as of first importance. Nevertheless, the disciples and the apostle Paul did carry the message which Jesus delivered to them far and wide throughout the Mediterranean world, and in truth without distinction of race or religion.

As both a state of consciousness and an interior condition of the spiritual Self of man, the kingdom of heaven is always close at hand; for it is, in fact, a continuing attribute of the consciousness of man's spiritual soul. This state of being includes bliss-consciousness and complete and undisturbable serenity based upon absolute certainty of the eternity and so the immortality of the inmost Self. Also, an abiding and perpetual realization of oneness with all life and its innumerable embodiments characterizes spiritual awareness. This implies the absence of the slightest sense of division or separation from any of these embodiments—a condition which is untranslatable and indescribable in terms of conceptual thought. God as the innermost essence and core of all existence, including man's own nature, it ever present without and within. Moreover, spiritual awareness knows no darkness, since another of its attributes consists of perpetual light. These conditions are not argued as reasonable conclusions, not are they challenged by the opposite point of view; for the latter cannot exist for the inner Self.

The heart of the teaching of Jesus, as of every other great esotericist, consists of an affirmation of the existence of the divine Self, reference to its state of being, and exhortation to become aware of it and ultimately to abide in it forevermore. In these terms, it is truly taught that the kingdom of heaven is indeed "within you."

> Matt. 10:8.   Heal the sick, cleanse the lepers, raise the dead, cast out devils: freely ye have received, freely give.

Disciples are taught first the rudiments and then the deeper truths and revelations of occult science. The regular application to thought, motive and conduct of these ideas and ideals gives them a validity and reality which thereafter can never be lost. In addition to such oral teaching, Teachers who accept and train disciples initiate and accelerate certain evolutionary processes. Furthermore, the Master establishes an interactive spiritual and magnetic—connection—indeed identification—between himself and each of his disciples in the spiritual aspects of their natures, between Master and disciple. This assures intercommunication and renders the disciple effective as an outpost of the Master's consciousness and a vehicle for the Master's power. One result is to make the disciple a channel for the occult forces of the Master which flow through and about the devotee as a radiant and divine effluence, a benediction which accompanies him wherever he goes.

The disciple can also perform adeptic deeds by such powers. These include healing the sick, whether present or absent, cleansing lepers, raising the dead, exorcising or casting out devils, whether actual or only psychological. The Master can and frequently does intervene in the disciple's work to use his vehicles as channels for healing and corrective forces. Furthermore, the disciple can deliberately invoke and become a channel for the healing grace and power of the Teacher. He may establish such conditions in himself and then invoke the Master's aid in a particular case, whether for an individual or a group of people. This power of mediation is bestowed upon the disciple by the Teacher, who uses an occult procedure for the establishment of the required rapport and the transmission of power. The words of this verse suggest that the Lord Christ bestowed these particular occult and spiritual faculties upon his disciples when instructing them in the work indicated by his words, so that the disciples bore and represented his presence as they carried out the mission to which he called them.

Another method of healing results from the training in occult science which forms part of the relationship between disciple and Adept Teacher. Occult physiology is taught and the flow of vital energies and electromagnetic forces in the physical body are studied by means of clairvoyance which the pupil has developed. In addition, the anatomy of the superphysical bodies under normal conditions and with pathology are studied, again directly by means of trained, positive clairvoyance. Diagnosis of physical, vital, and psychological conditions then becomes possible. Not infrequently, an intuitive grasp of the total situation rather than of details is obtained.

In addition, corrective procedures are taught. These include the projection of certain occult forces by means of will-thought in order to clear away discordances and restore harmony, both in organs and their functions. In cases of invading and obsessing superphysical entities—whether elemental and thought-produced discarded superphysical bodies or deceased human beings in full consciousness—the psychic intruders are dislodged.

The term *freely give* may be interpreted as meaning, not only to serve others whenever called upon, but also to minister to humanity without thought of self. The latter is an important consideration, as discrimination must always be used in all physical actions, especially those of ministration, lest the body should be weakened or even destroyed. An attitude of self-forgetfulness can serve as a protection.

An occult and spiritual law is also indicated. The pupil who becomes a recipient of the Master's power and blessing must in his turn relay these in ministration to his fellowmen. If such powers are, as it were, stored or hoarded for personal use, instead of being poured out through open hearts to relieve the suffering of mankind and illumine darkened minds, then the supply and inflow diminish, eventually to cease altogether. This injunction may thus be regarded, not only as an immediate instruction, but also as both a warning and a statement of law.

Matt. 10:9.   Provide neither gold, not silver nor brass in your purses,
10.   Nor scrip for your journey, neither two coats, neither shoes, nor yet staves: for the workman is worthy of his meat.

This counsel represents the age-old ascetic ideal for every disciple, namely, complete renunciation of worldly possessions, referring especially to a mental attitude of complete detachment from the objects of sense and dispassion concerning personal possessions. Poverty, when deliberately chosen by the disciple, expresses both a state of consciousness and a state of evolution in which desire has been reduced to a minimum and possessiveness and acquisitiveness displaced by an increasing degree of disinterestedness concerning his person and his own personal life. Indeed, these are essential conditions for discipleship, and more especially for the later stages of the pathway of swift unfoldment. They culminate in total indifference as far as one's own person is concerned.

The true disciple has divested himself physically, and especially mentally, of the delusion that possessions of themselves can give either power or pleasure. The only realm over which the truly spiritual individual desires to rule is his own human nature, particularly his mind. He is content to leave all else in the world to the direction and the possession of others whose lot it is.

Though it may seem strange to the uninitiated, he may possess property and wealth. However, he will use these for the benefit of others and to provide himself with the necessities for his work and his chosen mode of life. There eventually comes a period in a particular incarnation at which possessions become both irksome and hindrances in the attainment of interior illumination and final liberation from the chains of self and selfishness. Then all is surrendered, display gives way to simplicity, external demands are reduced to a minimum, and quite often the solitude of a retreat is sought and found. Thereafter the injunction of Jesus to his disciples is followed literally. In the East such seekers may become as beggars and maintain their lives by the use of the begging bowl and water pot.

Discriminative wisdom is of the utmost importance in all such planning to forsake the world and worldliness and to reduce oneself almost to the status of a mendicant, possessing only the barest necessities. The body, for example, must be fed, clothed and sheltered. Unless endowed with supernormal powers, the disciple must first of all ensure these necessities for the continuance of life, even if reduced to the merest minimum.

The occult law has ever been that renunciation, born of realization of spiritual reality, must find expression in all the habits and the visible aspects of the disciple's daily life. While every true disciple has reached indifference concerning the effects of his appearance upon others, he does recognize a responsibility personally to uphold before the world the ideals which he teaches. The worldly mind judges according to worldly standards and appearances. Since the ideal includes recruitment of others, consideration of this very natural trend is also part of the life of discipleship. New aspirants must be attracted rather than repelled, as they could be by hypocrisy or discrepancy between doctrine and personal practice. In this important matter the disciple's outer life must be just, sincere and true, not only in order to influence the minds of others, but for truth's sake.

Thus, personal possessions, clothing and finance are maintained at a sensible minimum, discrimination always being employed in obeying this rule. The yellow robe and the begging bowl of the buddhist monk, the saffron robe, rosary, crutch and culinary and ceremonial vessels of the Hindu *Sannyasi* (holy man), and the simplicity of Elijah and John the Baptist all exemplify obedience to these ideals of detachment and dispassion.

This rule could also have been designed to be a safeguard against that cupidity into which Judas Iscariot fell. The spiritual power and the magnetic aura of an accepted disciple can prove attractive to others. The bestowal of gifts constitutes one natural reaction, and a thirst for lucre can be awakened by the receipt of them. Conscience can be dulled as funds accumulate beyond the needs of the present and future years of the disciple and his dependents. Any tendency to miserliness excited by inflowing gifts must be strictly avoided. The objects referred to in these verses may thus be regarded as both actual and symbolic of the ideal state of mind.

> Matt. 10:11.   And into whatsoever city or town ye shall enter, enquire who in it is worthy; and there abide till ye go thence.

The secret spiritual and occult life of this planet has its devotees, aspirants and more advanced followers living unsuspected in many parts of the world. While in the eyes of the world these may seem unremarkable, even somewhat eccentric according to popular standards, they do nevertheless represent both oases in deserts of materialism and selfishness and centers where shelter and seclusion are available to adept Teachers and their traveling disciples. As the disciple travels in the course of his ministry to mankind and in response to his Master's calls to service, he is either previously informed of or quickly discovers such fellow devotees. In some cases these are forewarned of his arrival. In others he must make discreet enquiries, seek out his brothers, and when suitable place himself in their care.

Apart from observing each other's mode of life and personal characteristics, both visitor and host recognize the other's worthiness or lack of it through the use of spiritual senses which have become acute in the course of training.

> Matt. 10:12.   And when ye come into an house, salute it.
>
> 13.   And if the house be worthy, let your peace come upon it: but if it be not worthy, let your peace return to you.

A state of discordance inevitably exists in some degree where human beings congregate and live together. Part of the mission of the occultist is by his presence and his actions to reduce this and increase the harmony.

While every truly accredited and occultly accepted disciple of an Adept Teacher is naturally and sometimes unconsciously a center of peace, its potency is increased by a conscious act to invoke and establish a deep interior peace. The Adept is an incarnation of that completely harmonized state of being and consciousness which is aptly described as "the peace of God, which passeth all understanding."[10] When a disciple performs the occult act of harmonization, his Master's peace is transferred and conducted through him and his aura to his surroundings. Such deliberate ministration affects both the neighborhood and the inhabitants of the house, according to their degree of responsiveness, their natural state, and the condition of their psyche at the time of the invocation of salutation.

The instruction to restrict the benediction of peace and the spiritual salutation to the house which is worthy and to withhold it from one which is unworthy calls for some explanation. *Worthy* in this context might be translated as a condition of responsiveness to spiritual influences. since the amount of peace-giving, harmonizing and healing energy available to the disciple is limited, he is advised to use it with discrimination and with an eye to its probably effectiveness; for it is a law of the spiritual life that such forces and capacities must always be used to obtain maximum results from minimum exertion.

> Matt. 10:14. And whosoever shall not receive you, nor hear your words, when ye depart out of that house or city, shake off the dust of your feet.

Though in the realm of spirit the innermost Self in all men is part of one Self, physically mankind is divided into separate and diverse personalities. Disciples are spiritually aware of that unity which underlies diversity. Still, as practical men and women they also recognize, not only differences of person, but of degrees of development, goodness of heart and receptiveness to spiritualizing influences and philosophic instruction. Since many people are still materialists in their personal lives, and only the few are seeking for and receptive to spiritual and philosophic wisdom, rejection of such ministration is far more widespread than reception and gratitude. The disciple is, in consequence, counseled to employ great discrimination in the choice of those to whom he offers the treasures of spiritual wisdom. The principle of the necessary conservation of energy must be applied. Waste of energy must be avoided and strength conserved for those generally seeking guidance and ready to respond to it. If correctly translated, the last sentence of this verse may be regarded in this light.

In this sense only, never in a spirit of condemnation and dividedness, does the disciple carefully select recipients of his Master's blessing and wisdom. Under no consideration would he ever adopt an attitude of disunity from any of his fellowmen nor fail to aid the lowest whenever that aid is likely to be of benefit.

Matt. 10:15.   Verily I say unto you, It shall be more tolerable for the land
                of Sodom and Gomorrha in the day of judgment, than for
                that city.

There may be some legitimate doubt as to whether the Lord Christ was actually the source of this verse; for in its present form the injunction would seem both too severe and philosophically of doubtful verity. It does not appear to be in keeping with the rules of the spiritual life which are founded on unity with all that lives, or their practice with discrimination born of love. Doubt of the authenticity of the passage is somewhat strengthened when it is compared with Christ's words concerning his torturers while on the Cross, "Father, forgive them, for they know not what they do."[11]

No man can be condemned for declining, even with contumely, to receive a spiritual visitant and his message; for the most part, his blindness is but a mark of present evolutionary stature. No man may be either justly condemned or committed to severe punishment because of evolutionary youthfulness. Similarly, a young scholar is unlikely either to respond to the teachings of higher mathematics or to welcome a professor in that branch of science. This is due less to unworthiness than to youthfulness and to his stage in the processes of education.

Matt. 10:16.   Behold, I send you forth as sheep in the midst of wolves:
                be ye therefore wise as serpents, and harmless as doves.

In the sacred intimacy to which disciples of an adept Master are admitted, the protective aura of their Master enfolds them. All are elevated to some extent, their normal states of consciousness transcended in the degree to which they are responsive. The powerful electromagnetic and spiritual radiations and the forces of the intensely luminous aura of the Adept raise the frequency of the bodies and auras of the disciples when they are in the presence of the Master. However, when departures occur, there is a tendency in most cases to revert toward the previous state. Unless meditation and prayer are regularly and successfully practiced, the physical and superphysical vibratory rates of the disciple's personality are considerably slowed down. He always retains, however, heightened sensitivity in a number of directions and to specific impacts. When he is out in the world, these conditions render the disciple extremely vulnerable.

This verse may thus be regarded as guidance to disciples concerning both their own interior states of being and the impacts of the world upon them. Metaphorically, they are as sheep among wolves, among men who are undisciplined in their modes of life and rapacious in their greed for power and wealth. Sensitized spiritual aspirants could become easy prey to such men. Attempts could even be made to use for selfish ends their apparent simplicity and the appeal of their spirituality.

The Master places the disciples on guard against such dangers, warning them to be wise and to refrain from every form of violence. His watchful, protective influence will, however, be extended toward them; for such is part of the meaning of the most sacred of all possible relationships—that of

Teacher and disciple. Nevertheless, leaving the Master can constitute a severe test and, in consequence, produce the danger of a spiritual fall.

These words of Jesus are as applicable today as when they were spoken. The greatest seduction to which a disciple living in the outer world may succumb is that of wealth and the worldly freedom and power which wealth seems to give. Indeed, many are those members of spiritual sanctuaries who have gone abroad on missions and succumbed to the lure of riches, that most subtle of temptations. The possession of material goods can produce the illusion that financial security can compensate for the loss of occult and spiritual integrity. This is a profound error, as those have discovered who abandoned the path of righteousness for the ways of luxury provided by money, that "picklock which never fails."

> Matt. 10:17. But beware of men: for they will deliver you up to the councils, and they will scourge you in their synagogues;
>
> 18. And ye shall be brought before governors and kings for my sake, for a testimony against them and the Gentiles.

A warning is here given. A liberator of the minds of men is everlastingly in conflict with those who would imprison him within the bonds of prescribed thought, methods of worship, and even the daily conduct of his life. A great and remarkable change is produced in the consciousness of disciples of an Adept Teacher. In consequence, they see and know increasingly the spirit of the scriptures and the mystical significance of doctrines and ceremonials. As they teach this to others, an interior realization of the essence of religion inevitably finds expression. For such illumined ones the inward truth has been made clear, and they deliver it as saints and seers have ever done, albeit with a certain wisdom and cautious reserve.

The difference between the teachings of one who speaks within the freedom resulting from spiritual experience and those who are restricted to the dead letter of scripture can be very marked.[12] The soundness of a doctrine appears to be assailed by the truly illumined person who has transcended its restrictions. Unless his language is most carefully chosen and his words restrained, he can appear to be directly attacking religious orthodoxy. Indeed, he may even feel himself called upon deliberately to do so, as Jesus did.

In addition, adept wisdom and understanding—particularly of the spiritual needs of men and how they may be met—are so deep and penetrating as to overshadow those not possessing such attributes and capacities. Nevertheless, the true, spiritual teacher must fulfill his liberating mission, since it was for this that he was sent forth into the world.

The Master is in these words warning his disciples against anger and enmity, advising them to be cautious and when necessary to speak the truth.

> Matt. 10:19. But when they deliver you up, take not thought how or what ye shall speak: for it shall be given you in that same hour what ye shall speak.

Argument and debate, and even success in both, are without value in such circumstances. This is because neither priest nor governor usually approaches either mystical experience or philosophic truth with an open mind.

It is impossible therefore to convince them, or to change those attitudes of mind in which from their youth they have been educated. Furthmore, argument can arouse heat, if only in one's adversary, and heat stirs up the emotions, causing confusion. The disciples were advised to avoid these errors, to refrain from the undue exercise of the analytical mind. However, the inspired and illumined teacher on his or her part acquires skill in the use of analytical thought, lest its lack should inhibit the fulfillment of his function as awakener of spiritual intuition.

> Matt. 10:20.   For it is not ye that speak, but the Spirit of your Father which speaketh in you.

The Father whose voice speaks from within refers to the indwelling, divine spirit in man, the living God for which the outer man is a temple, as was written by St. Paul.[13] This interior self-illumination in full physical awareness must in no sense be confused with the practice of spiritualistic mediumship, which is anathema to the occultist and the true disciple. The two differ profoundly, since mediumship involves surrender of self-command to another, while interior illumination involves full self-command and so self-enlightenment.

However, the thoughts of the Adept Teacher may be projected into the mind of the disciple and find expression in his words as he teaches; for the Teacher has blended his own consciousness with that of the disciple so that interplay between them can always take place. When pure of heart and with untroubled mind, the disciple attunes himself to his teacher. In consequence, he may in varying degrees be aware of his teacher's thought and thus test his own ideas concerning subjects under review.

The four Evangelists refrain from describing in any detail the psychological and spiritual training which the disciples of Jesus received at his hands, for this is intensely private and is always guarded as an almost divine secret, except by renegades. In these verses, however, some reference is made to this part of the relationship between disciple and Master.

> Matt. 10:21.   And the brother shall deliver up the brother to death, and the father the child: and the children shall rise up against their parents, and cause them to be put to death.

Every spiritual neophyte, every true disciple, every initiate who has surrendered to the one Life or entered "the stream" must be prepared for the adversities referred to in these verses. Each is developing a state of consciousness and entering an evolutionary phase far beyond the normal for his time. In consequence, the very atmosphere which surrounds him, as well as his words, his works and his whole attitude toward life, appear even to his own family to be in conflict with those of the world. Successful mystics and occultists tend to appear in the eyes of their fellowmen as either fools to be scorned or utterly unreliable, impractical dreamers of no value in the world of men. Further, the doctrines which they inevitably preach, however true, can appear as mischievous and even dangerous to the community, especially to those who have been set in authority and power and are determined to remain so.

In some ways there may seem to be justification for these attitudes. Disinterestedness in material concerns, whether great or small, and unreadiness to make an effort to succeed in them can give the impression of ineffectiveness, or even mental instability. To a person who has come to regard certain attributes and powers as completely essential, an attitude toward living in which these are of negligible value inevitably arouses antagonism. Yet the spiritual neophyte has found other regions of consciousness and action to be of far greater importance than those of the world; for these he knows bring the prizes of peace and happiness, while the cut-and-thrust inseparable from purely worldly objectives can bring only war and misery, as recorded history so clearly demonstrates.

Unfortunately this opposition between spiritualized men and worldly men can and does occur in otherwise intimate relationships, as this verse indicates. Father, mother, brother and sister, despite family love, are nevertheless men and women of their day and age, while the spiritual neophyte belongs to another era altogether, one that lies in the future for the so-called average person. Jesus, knowing this well, thus warns his own disciples before they go out into the maelstrom of sin, sorrow and worldliness. Forewarned and so forearmed, they are sent out upon their missions.

Despite this admonition, two of the designated disciples failed, one of them temporarily and the other finally, Peter denied his Lord in the nighttime, but he recovered when the day dawned and the voice of the inner Self as conscience, was heard and answered by sincere remorse and self-recovery.[14] Judas, on the other hand, becoming the prisoner of his own avarice as yet uncured, failed and ultimately took his own life.[15]

Such, indeed, are some of the tests and dangers inevitably to be met by all men who, interiorly inspired, deliberately embark upon the way of hastened progress and find themselves moved by ideals of life associated with that narrow way.

> Matt. 12:22.   And ye shall be hated of all men for my name's sake: but he that endureth to the end shall be saved.

The Christ continues to teach and warn his disciples in preparation for their misssion as messengers of his wisdom and aspirants to his state of Christhood. The teaching is deeply esoteric, though also applicable in lesser degrees to all who seek to break away from conventional and established modes of living. In the case of the disciple deeply pledged and already spiritually awakened, the separation between himself and his fellowmen so widens as ultimately to become a veritable chasm. He can, in consequence, come to be regarded as an alien, a foreigner, even by those who otherwise love him best. This is almost inevitable in the case of those disciples who, not called into the seclusion of spiritual retreats or their Master's home, go forth and mingle with their fellowmen out of love for them. While so doing, their otherworldliness and apparent incompetence in worldly matters can arouse enmity and even contempt. Though these experiences inevitably cause pain, they do not deter the disciple who has made his irrevocable resolve; for he has been impelled to do so in response to an interior illumination. This is produced in the brain-mind by the action of his unfolding, immortal Self, the influence of which is enhanced by his Master.

> Matt. 10:23. But when they persecute you in this city, flee ye into another: for verily I say unto you, Ye shall not have gone over the cities of Israel, till the Son of man be come.

Israel here represents the world throughout which, as spiritual messengers, accredited disciples continually make their way, teaching as they do so. The world's population is very large, the cities of the world very numerous, while gross materialism and sensuality are rife in almost all of them. Initiated teachers and their pledged disciples are, on the other hand, comparatively few. Success in spiritualizing the life of mankind on earth in this age is not, therefore, likely to succeed. This activity must, however, continue; for it is one part of the ministration on behalf of the whole human race of the "just men made perfect," the adept Brotherhood.

Evolution continues throughout the whole period of such service and will eventually bring the majority of men on earth to the condition already attained by disciples. The Christ nature, hitherto asleep in mankind, stirs in its slumber and will eventually awaken and assume command of outer men.[16] This is one possible interpretation of the words of the Christ recorded in this verse, "till the Son of man be come."

While the coming of an actual visitant, an *Avatar,* is also referred to and presumably will occur, reference to this change of consciousness is also included in the utterance. The presence of a divine being visibly on earth as a Teacher among men is supplemented by the awakening and development of the interior divinity within every human being. The advent and ministry of a Teacher, however great, must inevitably be restricted to the period of time during which his body is kept alive. Even though profound effects are produced and a lasting influence exerted by his presence on earth, the real and certainly the most valuable coming or Nativity of the Son of Man occurs *within* human nature and is therefore unrestricted as to time and place. Not only does this interior spiritual illumination thus begin and endure, but it also increases in fullness as the ages pass. Eventually, the majority of mankind will have reached such a designated level of development, the advent of the Son of Man will have occurred as a mystical experience entered into by a large proportion of humanity. Such an attainment is independent of the presence or absence of a Teacher, personal or racial, however valuable such presence must always be.

> Matt. 10:24. The disciple is not above his master, nor the servant above his lord.
>
> 25. It is enough for the disciple that he be as his master, and the servant as his lord. If they have called the master of the house of Beelzebub, how much more shall they call them of his household?

These two verses indicate the intimate relationships which are established between a true Adept Teacher and his disciple. Just as a teacher is vilified and attacked because of the liberating teaching which he represents and gives, so also the disciple is certain to receive the same hostility, even if in reduced measure. The analogy is that of the servant's reputation in the eyes of his fellowmen depending upon the position of the master. Naturally, the intimacy is far greater in the case of the disciple and the Master because that relationship is not only physical, but also of the mind and the spirit.

This whole speech also refers to the phase of evolution when spiritualizing influences gradually begin to assume dominance over the matter and forms of the universe as well as the mortal personality of man.[17] The unfolding divine Life in nature on the upward arc becomes manifest in vehicles of decreasing density (see diagram 2, p. 46). Similarly, in man the inner spiritual principle, the immortal Self, begins to enter upon the self-conscious manifestation of the Christ nature. This gradually and increasingly makes itself felt by the man in his physical body and can produce an uneasiness, a sense of remorse and guilt concerning undesirable actions performed before enlightenment began. At the same time, both a sudden if brief illumination and a deeply interior longing to escape from the trammels of the flesh may be experienced.

When this phase first appears in a nation, a divine visitation generally occurs. A member of the hierarchy of perfected men, one who has attained a lofty stature, takes upon himself the burden of the flesh and lives among the people, teaching and inspiring them by both his words and his example, thus quickening the evolution of the race. In the case of the individual human, the Master reveals himself, either directly or through an authorized disciple, to the awakening aspirant. The path of discipleship is then entered upon, and the attempt is made by the disciple deliberately to increase the degree of spirituality in his daily life and to free his mind from the illusion of self-separateness.

Whether these phenomena occur universally, racially—as in the visits of Gautama Buddha to the Hindus or the Christ to the Hebrews—or personally to a single human being, an intense resistance is always aroused. This obstruction takes many forms, external and interior. In occult science it is referred to as "The Dweller on the Threshold" who is both guardian of the portals and cruel and constrictive obsession to deny onward progress, to slay the burgeoning idealism.[18] It occurs throughout the normal evolutionary process, during discipleships, and especially during passage through the first three initiations.

Externally, the very aura of the spiritually awakening person may irritate those who pay attention to him, while his mode of life and his speech, expressive of high idealism, may antagonize people. This antagonism can take violent forms, as is shown in the history of every *Avatar* and spiritual teacher who has visited the earth.[19] Interiorly, the very cells of the neophyte's body demand, may even clamor as if in panic, for continuing former indulgences to excess. The mind in its turn automatically, as also consciously, resists universalization, and clings determinedly to its dominant attitude of separated, personal individuality.

The teaching concerning resistance and hostility, more particularly, was later to be exemplified in the life of the Christ himself; for he was vilified, attacked, betrayed, tortured and killed. In this the resistance of matter to spirit and of the mortal personality of man to the influence upon him of his own divine nature are dramatized with very great insight, skill and wisdom. Indeed, the Gospel story is a revelation of spiritual and occult knowledge in the very first rank among all the many allegorical revelations.

Matt. 10:26.   Fear them not therefore: for there is nothing covered, that shall not be revealed; and hid, that shall not be known.

The eventual triumph of light and truth—and therefore of light-bringers and truth-bearers—is here assured by the Lord who promises that the most secret wisdom will one day be known by all. That which is now esoteric will become the recognized, and therefore exoteric, truth for all mankind, however distant the day of such universal acceptance and understanding. The concealed knowledge is hidden only for man's own safeguarding. Power prematurely attained is inevitably dangerous. When mind and heart are disciplined and illumined with realization of oneness, the danger of accident or misuse no longer exists. The Lord assures his chosen ones that this day will inevitably dawn, thereby comforting and sustaining them in preparation for the trials to come.

Matt. 10:27.   What I tell you in darkness, that speak ye in light: and what ye hear in the ear, that preach ye upon the housetops.

The order is then given by the Master to the disciples fearlessly to carry out their mission, even at the risk of life itself. The teaching revealed to them as chosen and accepted messengers must be handed on to their fellowmen; for this is part of the bounden duty of the dedicated servant and hearer of truth—esoteric and exoteric. The Lord would seem to have been warning and at the same time supporting his followers, lest in the face of the antagonism of the multitudes they might withhold or unduly water down the teaching they had received.

Matt. 10:28.   And fear not them which kill the body, but are not able to kill the soul: but rather fear him which is able to destroy both soul and body in hell.

Their Master has already assured his disciples of his unity with them and of his protection. In this verse he forewarns them against those dark lords of evil who are self-constituted enemies of mankind. They are cunning and skilled in the arts of deception and in the destruction of the soul by leading it into wickedness. Disciples become the special target of their enmity and attack, and Jesus places his own apostles on guard. He himself successfully passed through all temptations and knew well all the natural dangers and the subtle wiles with which evil men seek to bring down and destroy the world's light-bringers.

Matt. 10:29.   Are not two sparrows sold for a farthing? and one of them shall not fall on the ground without your Father.

30   But the very hairs of your head are all numbered.

The greatest safeguard against evil from without and from within consists in realization of the divine Omnipresence. Such widespread and lowly creatures as sparrows are used to indicate that even in them the spirit of God is manifest. Smaller and far more numerous than sparrows are the hairs on the human head. Yet, says the Master, even in them, God is enshrined. He might have added that God is present in every atom of every form throughout the whole of nature. How much more so then, he says, is God made manifest in every human being as the light and the life of his existence. Realization of this truth, both intellectually and mystically, is the sure safeguard and shield against the powers of evil, whether from without or from within.

> Matt. 10:31.   Fear ye not therefore, ye are of more value than many sparrows.

In the scale of existence and amid the multitude of creatures and beings, man stands at the head of the known kingdoms of nature. He is the highest product—a self-conscious, self-directing individuality; the divine is more fully manifested and expressed in him. Nevertheless, God is present in the subhuman kingdoms of nature also and protects and cares for them, metaphorically noting each sparrow's fall.

The record of this long speech of counsel and comfort to the disciples is almost certainly incomplete. Written down from memory, perchance long after its delivery, it must have suffered in both the remembrance and the recording. While given by St. Matthew as one continous address, it may well be made up of the remembered portions of a number of talks such as every adept Master from time to time gives to his disciples.

One may rest assured that in homes and upper rooms, shaded groves and by lake shores and little streams, perhaps by the River Jordan itself, Jesus drew his disciples intimately near and counseled them. His words must have been deeply impressed upon their minds, so that the written memory of them may be reasonably accurate. Much, however, must also have been either forgotten or regarded as unnecessary to record. In addition, there must also have been profound esoteric teachings which they were enjoined to keep secretly within their hearts, truths to be lived rather than to be repeated. Wisdom teachings deeper than those anywhere revealed may be presumed to have been given concerning physical and psychological experiences arising from entry upon the path of hastened development.[20]

> Matt. 10:32.   Whosoever therefore shall confess me before men, him will I confess also before my Father which is in heaven.

This assurance of complete spiritual support and sustaining power promised to those who are faithful to him and loyal to his mission is also susceptible of deeply inward interpretation. In this passage Jesus the Christ as Teacher becomes blended with the Christ principle in man. Thus viewed, the Father-in-Heaven becomes the Monad.

The essential link between the outer man living the life of the world and the innermost existence or Monad is, indeed, the Christ nature in each individual, the influence of which increasingly, if gradually, becomes outwardly manifest in those at the evolutionary stage of discipleship. This is revealed as ardent aspiration, deep devotion, divine compassion, and an overflowing love for all humanity. The outward effect of the Monad is increased by the fact that the Master has intimately blended his own Christhood with that of the disciple.

Matt. 10:33.   But whosoever shall deny me before men, him will I also deny before my Father which is in heaven.

A literal reading of this verse would seem to be hardly acceptable. Mystically regarded, however, a profound truth is revealed. The man in whom the Christ principle is inactive is unable for the time being to contact or to be reached by the spiritual power and intellectual illumination of his innermost Self. Thus an evolutionary phase and the experiences and possibilities associated with it are described rather than the personal action of a Master.

Matt. 10:34.   Think not that I am come to send peace on earth: I come not to send peace, but a sword.

35.   For I am come to set a man at variance against his father, and the daughter against her mother, and the daughter in law against her mother in law.

36.   And a man's foes shall be they of his own household.

37.   He that loveth father or mother more than me is not worthy of me: and he that loveth son or daughter more than me is not worthy of me.

A literal reading of these verses, especially if applied to men and women living their ordinary, daily lives, presents the Lord Christ as a sower of discord even among members of the same family living in the same home. Indeed, it would show Jesus describing himself as a fighter and even destroyer, armed with a sword and bringing to mankind suffering and death. Since this is entirely out of character, totally contrary to the incarnate spirit of love that is the Lord Christ, a dead letter reading becomes impossible. He—as every other spiritually illumined teacher—would be incapable of deliberately disrupting family life and of setting himself up as of greater importance and more worthy of love and loyalty than father, mother, sister and brother.

Esoterically, however, the verses may be read as enunciations of most profound truths. Indeed exoteric and esoteric interpretations are nowhere more sharply contrasted than in these verses. The student is in consequence advised to read below the surface in search for the hidden truth.

Jesus was at the time speaking directly to his disciples—wholly and deeply dedicated men—and was preparing them for their calling. In these instructions Jesus fulfilled his own description of his office and his relationship to the two types of men, teaching disciples "the mystery of the kingdom of God," and speaking to others in parables.[21] The mystery of the kingdom of God includes knowledge of the supernormal and spiritual nature, powers and faculties of man and their enforced development, and also the motives and modes of living.

When read in this view, then a quality of character is found to be described. This is one-pointedness, complete single-mindedness expressed as determination to allow no person, however near and dear, no undesirable quality of character, no personal desire and no circumstance which can be controlled, to come between the empowered and enfired aspirant and his goal. As success in every great material enterprise demands a similar concentrated exclusiveness, so the far more difficult spiritual enterprise of attaining perfected manhood in advance of the race demands a similar total commitment.

It can be understood that an unswerving pursuit of the specialized mode of life of a disciple could cause occasional variance with family members. Even so, the passage needs to be read and applied with great discrimination. In addition to one-pointedness, discriminative wisdom is an attribute of developed man,[22] as also are impersonal love and consideration for others. The extreme of tactfulness would therefore characterize the expression of the disciple's irrevocable choice in his relationships with his nearest and dearest one. Inwardly, however, and where great principles are involved, he is beyond the possibility of compromise.

Personal detachment from all worldly concerns and rewards and from all human relationships which could intrude upon the chosen objectives is also indicated in these verses. Complete dispassion concerning personal affairs and possessions is presented as an essential ideal.[23]

The recorded words of Jesus may not express his complete statement; for he, like other spiritual Teachers, would likely make less drastic his enunciation of principles, even while rendering them with unmistakable clarity. Nevertheless, the terse and powerful utterance recorded in verse thirty-four remains strictly true; for the process of stepping out of a life based upon worldly interests and purely material objectives does necessitate a clear-cut, almost surgical, operation. This "severance" may appear more drastic to observers not similarly moved than to the person actually undergoing the operation; for mentally and psychologically it has become a perfectly natural, indeed inevitable, procedure. The world falls away from him as also does interest in the things of the world. He has seen the glory of the inner light. He has experienced the bliss of unity, of oneness revealed to his mind from the innermost parts of his nature. Thereafter, as an ancient scripture says, "There is no other path at all to go."[24] The attitude of increasing single-mindedness is also quite naturally adopted. Indeed, it might be said that it takes possession of the man rather than the man adopting it from personal choice.

In truth, no external agency whatever can bring about in any human being the decisive change from the life of the world to one dedicated to spirituality and the service of mankind described in the remaining verses of this chapter. Such a change and such choices, when sincerely made, come from within, and are the perfectly natural results of entry upon an advanced evolutionary phase. The Monad at that stage empowers and illumines the unfolding inner Self which, in its turn, takes possession of the outer man. Thus, the Lord may be regarded as describing less a mode of conduct than an inner attitude of mind.

If, however, it be argued that ordinary men and women of the world will be the chief readers of such works as the Gospels, and that the disruption of family life might result or at least family love endangered, then two possibilities must be considered. First, the Lord was addressing only his disciples. Second, the Gospels may be inaccurate as they were written down perhaps a century or more after the events. Since initiated allegorists participated in the production of the four Gospels, the former of these two possibilities may safely be given the greater weight for as an enunciation of both the ideal attitude of mind the disciple and the laws governing hastened evolution, the verses are to be regarded as veritable jewels of wisdom, masterpieces—even in translation—describing and giving guidance in the occult life. Precisely similar laws are laid down in the scriptures of other world faiths notably Hinduism, Buddhism, Taoism and Sufism—[25] descriptive of the almost iron self-discipline and extreme one-pointedness said to be essential to success in the attainment of high evolutionary stature in advance of the race.

> Matt. 10:38.   And he that taketh not his cross, and followeth after me, is not worthy of me.

The cross which every true disciple and initiate must bear is descriptive of the isolation, obloquy and scorn which Jesus endured and which every disciples must receive and endure with him. The modern Golgotha is the world itself, the crucifixion upon it is rather of heart and mind than of physical flesh. Whips, crown of thorns, nails and spear are nonetheless real and agonizing. They partly symbolize the effects of the thoughts, words and deeds of unillumined mankind, on whose behalf alone the great ascent is embarked upon and the summit eventually attained.

The words of the Christ are but echoes of the "words" of the innermost Self taking charge at last of its hitherto wayward, time-wasting, self-indulgent, mortal personality. The process occupies a number of earthly lives for its fulfillment.[26] Eventually, the inner control is established, the outer man tamed and mastered into willing obedience, because by then enfired with the aspiration and will of inner Self.

> Matt. 10:39.   He that findeth his life shall lose it: and he that loseth his life for my sake shall find it.

In nature outer coverings, shells, skins, and enclosing membranes are broken when the seed-germ hitherto safely enclosed within begins to reproduce its parent. This also occurs within spiritually reborn man. The enclosing shell of self-reliant, self-protective and acquisitive individuality loses power over the spiritually fructified and expanding divine consciousness within. Quite naturally, such a man begins to care less and less for his former self-centered personality and more and more for the larger divine Self embodied in the human race as a whole and the one Life embodied in all kingdoms of nature; for he now experiences oneness with all.

When, however, this change of attitude first begins to affect his outlook, the neophyte suffers from the tendency to revert to former motives and modes of thought. This is the evolutionary phase at which the true spiritual

Teacher appears, giving counsel and strengthening the inner impulse to selflessness. These two influences, the interior change and the help of the Master, eventually bring the disciple to a state of mind in which the "loss" of the enclosed self-separateness upon which he had hitherto relied is completely outweighed by the interior spiritual "gain." He discovers within himself that the very renunciation of self-interest leads, not to loss, but to a fulfillment for which he can conceive neither horizon nor limit; for he has universalized his center of self-awareness.

This gradual and remarkable transformation of outlook ultimately brings the disciple to adeptship. Having thus attained, he becomes consciously merged in the limitless ocean of the indwelling Life of the universe. Thereafter, he can say with the Lord Christ, and with equally full realization, "I and my Father are one." His human existence is then ended in the attainment of perfected manhood. He has become a superhuman being, a "just man made perfect," having attained to the "measure of the stature of the fullness of Christ."[27]

Thus, the teachings contained in this pregnant verse, which reveal the inmost secret of progress on the path of swift unfoldment, have become fully manifest in him who once was man and has now become perfected man. The secret is that the formerly existing man, as he through long ages of evolution has known himself, must die in order that the new man may live. All allegorical and figurative deaths recorded in scripture and enacted in solemn initiatory rites refer to this great truth.

> Matt. 10:40. He that receiveth you receiveth me, and he that receiveth me receiveth him that sent me.

In such utterances, Jesus is speaking as manifestation of the one Life, an *Avatar* in fact, on whom has descended as an overshadowing presence an Aspect of the Solar Logos. He is also speaking as an adept Master to his disciple; for when once that sacred relationship is fully established, the unity between them is close and intimate indeed. They are in fact one, not only in their sharing of the one Life, but because of the blending of consciousness and subtle vehicles in an intimate rapport. Such disciples carry their Master's presence with them wherever they go, while they in their turn participate as far as they are able in the Master's life and work. As he goes everywhere in the outer world with them, so to speak, they also are with him in all he does. Thus in the literal sense, when a disciple is received, whether mentally, physically or both, the Master is received also.

This interior adeptic presence can and does on occasion become manifest, whether as an atmosphere or an action, an influence or spoken words, perhaps changing the life of the recipients.

> Matt. 10:41. He that receiveth a prophet in the name of a prophet shall receive a prophet's reward; and he that receiveth a righteous man in the name of a righteous man shall receive a righteous man's reward.

A distinction of a deeply occult character is here made between a prophet, seer, or disciple of an adept, on the one hand, and a righteous man on the other. The word translated as *prophet* may be taken to mean *trained occult seer,* one who is consciously associated with an adept Teacher and serving as his agent in the world of men. In such a man, self-centeredness and self-interest as influencing motive for action have greatly declined. He lives less and less for self but for the world. The law of cause and effect brings back reactions on the levels from which the actions are performed.[28] The disciple is moved spiritually in all he does, so that while physical reactions occur and affect his physical life, the major responses—rewards as they are erroneously translated in the text—accrue to his spiritual nature and through that to the spiritual Self of all mankind. Therefore, the reactions from his deeds and words among his fellowmen will affect his inner immortal Self rather than his outer material nature. Simply put, the good which he does will benefit his immortal soul rather than his bodily self.

The normally good citizen, while living morally and bearing in mind the welfare of the community, sees and knows little more than the material world. In his case reactions will tend to reach and influence him chiefly at the level, bringing material welfare which will benefit him personally. Although such a man is at least beginning to be spiritually awakened, he is as yet but little aware of the source of his good fortune. Nevertheless, he finds himself becoming increasingly concerned for the public good.

Further distinctions between the two types of human beings also exist. The so-called prophet lives a secret life shared only by fellow disciples. He is in communion with his Master, whether physically present or not. As we have seen, he is under direct training by his Master, as is exemplified in the Sermon on the Mount. In addition, with varying degrees of awareness, he is acting under his Master's orders. Without thought of self, in his Master's name he is a helper, healer and teacher of his fellowmen.

This inner life is exceedingly private and sacred to him, not even his closest relatives being permitted—or even able—to share in it. Indeed only those who, like himself, have entered in at the "strait gate" and are treading "the narrow way" can participate in and comprehend a state of consciousness and a mode of life appropriate to discipleship.

REFERENCES AND NOTES

1. Mark 4:11.

2. Guru—teacher.

3. For an exposition of racial evolution thus regarded, see Geoffrey Hodson, *Lecture Notes of the School of the Wisdom,* Vol. I, Ch. 14.

4. Cosmic Intelligences, or Regents or Planets—see H. P. Blavatsky, *The Secret Doctrine,* Vols. 2, 3, 4, and 5 (consult Index).

5. Occult Science—see Glossary.

6. See Hodson, *Lecture Notes,* Vol. I, Ch. 13.

7. See Hodson, *Hidden Wisdom,* Vol. 1, p. 89.

8. Boanerges, was a mystic name given to James and John, for example. Mark 3:17.

9. John 10:16.

10. Phil. 4:7.

11. Luke 23:34.

12. Cf. Matt. 7:29.

13. 2 Cor. 6:16.

14. Matt. 26: 69-75.

15. Matt. 27:5.

16. The Christ nature is already stirring and awake in an increasing number of people. Hence the League of Nations, United Nations, the International Red Cross and all world movements for the help of mankind without the notice of national or personal gain.

17. See Hodson, *Lecture Notes,* Vol. I, p. 359.

18. Dweller on the Threshold—see H. P. Blavatsky, *The Secret Doctrine,* Vol. 5, pp. 501, 512, 567.

19. Cf. Shri Krishna and King Kansa, Gautama Buddha and Devadatta, and Jesus and King Herod.

20. See Hodson, *Hidden Wisdom,* Vol. II, Pt. VI.

21. Mark 4:11.

22. The Sanskrit word *Viveka* expresses this ideal. See Sankaracharya, *The Crest Jewel of Wisdom.*

23. *The Sanskrit word Vairagya,* expresses this ideal completely. See Sankaracharya, *The Crest Jewel of Wisdom,* and *Bhagavad Gita.*

24. Upanishads.

25. *The Brahmasutras, Yoga Sutras, The Bhagavad Gita, Viveka Chudamani (The Crest Jewel of Wisdom),* are examples from Hinduism; Sir Edwin Arnold, *The Light of Asia* and other works; Lao-Tse, *Tao-te-Ching,* partially translated in Hodson, *Lecture Notes,* Vol. I, Ch. 15, Section 6; Field, trans., *Confession of Al Ghazzali.*

26. See Geoffrey Hodson, *Reincarnation, Fact or Fallacy?*

27. Eph. 4:13.

28. Matt. 5:18, 7:1-2, 7:12, Gal. 6:7.

Chapter Fifteen

The possibility of hastened self-unfoldment, the way of its outworking, and the life lived by those who have succeeded are as a threefold golden thread of wisdom running through the mythologies and scriptures of the world. One recalls, for example, the labors of Hercules, the voyage of Ulysses, the rape and rescue of Persephone, the slayings of the minotaur and Medusa, the rescue of Andromeda, the lives and deaths of Balder and Siegfried, the bondage and the exodus of the Israelites in Egypt and Babylon, and the lives of Joshua, Samson and Job. Although thus portrayed in many ways, it is in reality the one interior pathway, treading which human limitations are transcended and Christlike perfection becomes manifest. Many verses of the Gospels refer to this pathway.

> Matt. 11:2. Now when John had heard in the prison the works of Christ, he sent two of his disciples,
>
> 3. And said unto him, Art thou he that should come, or do we look for another?
>
> 4. Jesus answered and said unto them, Go and shew John again those things which ye do hear and see:
>
> 5. The blind received their sight, and the lame walk, the lepers are cleansed, and the deaf hear, the dead are raised up, and the poor have the gospel preached to them.
>
> 6. And blessed is he, whosoever shall not be offended in me.

As messenger and forerunner sent to prepare the way for the Messiah, John is presented as both a historical figure and a reincarnation of Elijah. In his mode of life, his dress, his food and his gospel of self-purification, John does indeed closely resemble the Old Testament prophet. The imprisonment by Herod and the later decapitation are, however, not wholly in harmony with the view of the prophet Elijah presented in the Old Testament; for Elijah was the preserved and protected man of God who ascended into heaven in a chariot of fire, allowing his mantle to fall upon his successor, Elisha.[1] Such a man, endowed with theurgic powers, would not be overcome by a temporal Roman governor. The anomaly is resolved, however, if the story is taken allegorically.

John the Baptist in prison represents the restrictive and spiritually darkening influence upon man of the excessively analytical, critical and prideful mind—a potential prison indeed; for under its influence, spiritual wisdom is shut out and the intuitive faculties "imprisoned" or even paralyzed. Needless to say, not only undesirable qualities of the mind restrict the influence of the higher Self upon the mortal nature, but also the emotional forces in man—passion and desire—when granted undue expression. These, and the vehicle in which they arise and through which they are primarily expressed—the so-called astral body[2]—are in their turn personified by Salome, the dancer who aroused and gratified the sexual instincts of the king. The disciples represent the disciplined and dedicated mental and emotional nature of man, while the unillumined multitude, their cities, and even the land itself typify the physical body and purely material states of consciousness.

In the sacred language of allegory and symbol, the drama of initiation with its trials, ordeals and triumphs is presented as if on the stage of life—in the present instance in Judea of some 2,000 years ago. The story is however timeless, the events being perpetually enacted as self-trained and inspired men and women pass through the figurative death and resurrection by which experiences associated with passage through grades of the Greater Mysteries are described. Objective though the scriptural account may seem, the experience is wholly interior, the drama being enacted *within* the soul of spiritually awakened man. These regenerated human beings, the initiates of all time, are no longer spiritually blind, lame, leprous, deaf, dead or impoverished. As is indicated in the fifth verse, all these limitations fall away. They appertain to the restrictions of mortal manhood during the phase which precedes spiritual regeneration. When this latter occurs, the Christ presence is mystically experienced, and thereafter all suffering ceases.

Matt. 11:7.   And as they departed, Jesus began to say unto the multitudes concerning John, What went ye out into the wilderness to see? A reed shaken with the wind?

At this point in the remembered and recorded account of the mission of Jesus, he begins to prepare the minds of his hearers for a deeply occult pronouncement concerning John the Baptist. In this verse the Lord proclaimed that the appearance of John was no normal phenomenon such as a reed shaken with the wind, but possessing a supernormal significance.

Matt. 11:6.   But what went ye out for to see? A man clothed in soft raiment? behold, they that wear soft clothing are in kings' houses.

The teaching is accented by means of rhetorical questions, the purport of which is to show the marked difference between John the Baptist and a man or woman of the world, particularly one endowed with wealth and belonging to aristocracy. John was like none of these, said the Lord, referring to the fact that he chose to dwell in the wilderness, to wear simple raiment, and live on the products of plant life around him, as holy men have done from time immemorial.

> Matt. 11:9.   But what went ye out for to see? A prophet? yea, I say unto you, and more than a prophet.

The lofty spiritual stature of John the Baptist is here affirmed, as is also the truth of his declaration concerning his mission in the world. Despite the simplicity of the language, these verses possess a dramatic quality. One may almost envisage the scene and hear the words of the divine speaker as he first clears away misconceptions and then affirms the truth. John was indeed a prophet, and even more than a prophet, an actual forerunner.

> Matt. 11:10.   For this is he, of whom it is written, Behold, I send my messenger before thy face, which shall prepare the way before thee.

Here, as on other occasions, the Master refers to the Hebrew scriptures, particularly the *Torah* or Law.[3] He also acknowledges the prophecies; for the prophet Malachi had written of the reappearance of Elijah to prepare the way for the Messiah, the long reasured hope of the Jews.[4] Jesus affirms that in its more personal meaning the prophecy of old was at that very time being fulfilled. In truth, John was both the expected messenger and the preparer of the way for the coming of the Lord.

> Matt. 11:11.   Verily I say unto you, among them that are born of women there hath not risen a greater than John the Baptist: notwithstanding he that is least in the kingdom of heaven is greater than he.

This somewhat mysterious and even apparently contradictory utterance is explainable if one admits of the existence of human and superhuman kingdoms of nature. John exceeds even the greatest man in stature. Yet compared with those "just men made perfect" who abide in the spiritualized state of consciousness described as the kingdom of heaven, John is "least in the kingdom of heaven"; for although very great, he still was but man. The perfected men who have arisen from mankind and have attained the stature of spiritual kings are incomparably greater than even the greatest genius, seer and prophet; for these are as yet members of the human kingdom and are still men among men.

> Matt. 11:12.   And from the days of John the Baptist until now the kingdom of heaven suffereth violence, and the violent take it by force.

He who reaches adeptship in advance of the race does indeed take the kingdom of heaven by force, even by violence. The inner will of man, the power of divinity within, has become awakened and brooks no denial. The individual becomes absorbed with a single idea—swiftly to kill out all that is imperfect in himself and thus attain perfection.

> Matt. 11:13.   For all the prophets and the law prophesied until John.
>
> 14.   And if ye will receive it, this is Elias, which was for to come.
>
> 15.   He that hath ears to hear, let him hear.

Needless to say, the teaching which Jesus secretly gave to his disciples was not included in the gospel story. We may safely assume, however, that it consisted partly of the esotericism which is only revealed by word of mouth and in the seclusion into which great teachers and their disciples always withdraw. There parables are used no more; symbology is left behind. The mighty powers by which universes are built—the laws in obedience to which they are constructed, evolve and eventually withdraw—are no longer personified by gods, goddesses, heroes, patriarchs and their wives. Directly, and with vision imparted as the words of power were spoken, knowledge was bestowed upon the chosen few. Nevertheless, in these verses and in passages elsewhere recorded in the Gospels, some of the direct *Logia* or words accepted as having been spoken by Jesus were remembered and handed down from disciple to disciple many years after the Teacher himself had departed.

The disciples were instructed of the lesser cycle of birth, death, and rebirth, by which the indwelling spirit of man unfolds its powers to the highest degree.[5] The disciples were also fully informed that the material forms of self-expression are in their turn ultimately to be developed into instruments of perfect responsiveness and fullest beauty.

Thus Jesus, at least on one occasion (verse fourteen), pronounced to the disciples that in obedience to this law, John the Baptist was indeed a reappearance in a new body, a reincarnation of the spiritual Self which earlier had been embodied and known as Elijah. As far as the record has been transmitted, this process refers solely to the great prophet and his later incarnation. However, the disciples were given objective evidence of the operation upon all men of the universal cyclic law. Although to Hebrew orthodoxy this was plain heresy, to followers of the secret teachings of the Kabbalah the operation of the cyclic law was, and still is, quite well known.

The appeal of the Master was, however, not only to the mind, but also to the intuition, the wisdom of the heart. The last of these three verses call upon the hearer to receive, not just the words, but the truth itself behind and within the words; for all mystery teaching is addressed, not to the intellect alone—valuable though it is to the mind—but even more to those deeper intuitive perceptions and responses which arise from the wisdom aspect of the indwelling Self.

The doctrine of rebirth had reached the Mediterranean countries from the East and Far East, having been brought by merchants, missionaries, and those instructed in the Secret Doctrine as they traveled westward from their homelands. The Essenes were aware of it, as also the initiates of the Egyptian Mysteries. Jesus, as one of them, was therefore well instructed in the idea and so able to impart it to the chosen few, whom he trusted never to betray either himself or the more esoteric and unorthodox teachings which he gave. Among these was the full doctrine of cycles, universal and human, taught only in the sanctuary.

The need for secrecy was very great at that time and place. It was perilous to reveal anything not taught in the *Torah,* as Jesus later found, death being the penalty; for Jesus taught, not only the law of rebirth but, far more heterodox, the innate divinity of man himself, that each is a veritable manifestation of the pure spirit known as *Adonai*.

Matt. 11:16.   But whereunto shall I liken this generation? It is like unto children sitting in the markets, and calling unto their fellows.

17.   And saying, We have piped unto you, and ye have not danced; we have mourned unto you, and ye have not lamented.

The Lord proceeded to compare the true seekers for wisdom, the disciples of the Master, with the men of the world, the multitude at its normal state of development, the latter being viewed very unfavorably. This contrast is most marked in this chapter; for Our Lord trusts his disciples with secret wisdom and upbraids those who neither know nor care about it. He portrays the latter as seated in the market places, indicating that their major concern was, perhaps necessarily to some extent, with money-making and money-getting. They also call to each other for collaboration, but without avail since each is preoccupied with his own concerns. What was true in those days is true also today. This is part of the world tragedy in the *Kali Yuga* of the fifth root race;[6] for in this cycle the mind is beginning to both dominate the heart and to obscure the light of intuition.

The Master discusses and reveals to his disciples in private the world situation and the condition of the mass of humanity as seen with his all-encompassing vision. Nevertheless, to the people in the world at large, he was all love, as the wonderful closing verses of this chapter demonstrate.

Matt. 11:18.   For John came neither eating nor drinking, and they say, He hath a devil.

19.   The Son of man came eating and drinking, and they say, Behold a man gluttonous, and a winebibber, a friend of publicans and sinners. But wisdom is justified of her children.

The inability of matter-blinded and mind-darkened mankind to perceive the superior stature and enlightened wisdom of the world's light-bringers is here referred to. Thus, the asceticism of John the Baptist was misunderstood and derided, being in such marked contrast with the general, rather indulgent mode of life. Yet when the Lord himself outwardly behaved in closer conformity with those standards, he was branded and even condemned as being over-luxurious. The fate of John the Baptist and of the Lord himself is that of almost every other great Teacher and initiated messenger who has visited the world, particularly in the Western world.

The peoples of the East whose minds have become saturated with the metaphysical ideas of their ancient scriptures—including especially the existence on earth of superior beings, *Rishis* and *Mahatmas*—were less ignorant and so more respectful of their heavenly visitants, the Avataras. Shri Krishna, Buddha and Shri Shankaracharya lived out the chosen period of their lives in relative peacefulness, and their teachings were truly valued and preserved. The material drive characteristic of modern man, the scientific spirit with its determination to find out and reveal the innermost secrets of matter, the accentuation of activity rather than contemplative poise, to which is added the almost slavish acceptance of the letter of the scriptures—all these render western man unready to take heed of those who speak from supramental levels, revealing a wisdom and an ethic more lofty than their own.

Nevertheless, as this chapter and the Gospels generally reveal, seekers, neophytes and disciples existed at that time and sought the Master's feet. Today, happily, their number is greater, as also is their power to influence world conditions and world thought. The ideal and to a considerable extent the practice of world cooperation is one of the results, while the increase in esoteric movements, valid and otherwise, is another example of the change which is gradually leading to a world search. At the time of the Lord such movements were all too few. Among the seekers are here and there one or more who discover and embrace the Wisdom Religion and find the Master's feet. This will continue and increase as the tide of progress sweeps on.

Matt. 11:20. Then began he to upbraid the cities wherein most of his mighty works were done, because they repented not:

21. Woe unto thee, Chorazin! woe unto thee, Bethsaida! for if the mighty works, which were done in you, had been done in Tyre and Sidon, they would have repented long ago in sackcloth and ashes.

22. But I say unto you, It shall be more tolerable for Tyre and Sidon, at the day of judgment, than for you.

23. And thou, Capernaum, which art exalted unto heaven, shalt be brought down to hell: for if the mighty works, which have been done in thee, had been done in Sodom, it would have remained until this day.

24. But I say unto you, That it shall be more tolerable for the land of Sodom in the day of judgment, than for thee.

25. At this time Jesus answered and said, I think thee, O Father, Lord of heaven and earth, because thou hast hid these things from the wise and prudent, and hast revealed them unto babes.

26. Even so, Father: for so it seemed good in thy sight.

These verses are among many in the scriptures which may justly be taken in general at their face value. In a proper spirit born of recognition of his greatness, certain cities of Judea received with due respect the presence of the Lord, his teachings and his manner of life. These he praised. Other cities, even while appearing to respond to his counsels, in reality continued in their former undesirable ways. The Lord unbraided them and furthermore prophesied their downfall, which was later to come.

If, however, the verses are lifted out of time and space and read in a more universal sense, then cities and their peoples symbolize both certain types of human beings and characteristics common to almost all men. As is often the case, the sophisticated and apparently erudite become so preoccupied with their own intellectualism that they are unresponsive to the revelations of intuitive wisdom and the simple ethics which it reveals. The apparently unlearned, on the other hand, frequently referred to as babes, by the very quietude and even emptiness of their minds are able to respond to the whisperings from the deeper wisdom of their souls. The ideals of purity of life and of self-restraint where the appetites are concerned make great appeals to them. For these the Lord prophesied good fortune.

This division of humanity into two distinct types—the lettered and the relatively unlettered—must not, however, be carried too far; for, of course, deep learning can be valuable. Intellectual grasp born of profound studies and the continuing search for truth by inquiring minds need not necessarily be barriers to the perception of Truth itself. Neither need eruditon render the well-informed mind unresponsive to supramental illumination. Similarly, of course, illiteracy is not to be regarded as a prerequisite to spiritual illumination. Humility and a spirit of selfless and dedicated inquiry into the mysteries of life may well be added to the deeply interior probing toward the innermost secrets of the human soul and the discovery of the true Self of man.

> Matt. 11:27.   All things are delivered unto me of my Father: and no man knoweth the Son, but the Father; neither knoweth any man the Father, save the Son, and he to whomsoever the Son will reveal him.

That world scriptures consist of compilations by many hands becomes revealed by somewhat abrupt changes of both subject matter and style. This verse may possible be an example of such changes in both authorship and subject matter, evern though a certain sequence of ideas is discernible. Interpolations in support of theological dogmas of a given period in ecclesiastical history may also have been added by later hands.

One of the most profound of all exoteric teachings is referred to here, though unfortunately christian orthodoxy has tended to misinterpret and misrepresent the inner meaning of the words attributed to the Lord. This error, constantly repeated, arises from the custom of applying essentially impersonal ideas to persons. The phrase "neither knoweth any man the Father, save the Son, and he to whomsoever the Son will reveal" illustrates this practice. These words and others occurring in the New Testament have been taken to suggest that the Lord Jesus Christ was and remains the only mediator between man and God, and furthermore that all born and living outside the Christian faith are bereft of this mediation and so cannot know the Father. The very opposite, of course, is true. All men of all times and races are spiritual beings by their very nature and existence. The one Spirit known in Christianity as God dwells in each and every man, is, in fact, the Source of human existence and the assurance of salvation, meaning evolution to "the measure of the stature of the fullness of Christ."

In this verse the Son is far less a personage, however great, appearing in time, place and human form, than the impersonal and omnipresent divine wisdom, life and love of God. In man this presence serves as mediator between the material and the spiritual in him, his mind and the eternal light. The divine pronouncement repeated in this verse may be received as truth if the word *Son* is read as the divine voice, the interior Christ nature, the Christ Indwelling which is the true revealer and savior for all mankind. As St. Paul so frequently insisted, this is the "Christ *in* (italics mine) you, the hope of glory."[7]

Matt. 11:28. Come unto me, all ye that labour and are heavy laden, and I will give you rest.

29. Take my yoke upon you, and learn of me; for I am meek and lowly in heart: and ye shall find rest unto your souls.

30. For my yoke is easy, and my burden is light.

The transition is continued from the upbraiding of earlier verses to the utterance of a spiritual truth. No longer is the Lord warning and calling to certain human types to repent of their evil ways. Now he offers himself in words of sublimest beauty as a refuge and a rest to all mankind.

Herein speaks the voice of one who truly is the Anointed, the Christos, abiding in unity with the spiritual Self of every member of the human race. Here also speaks the more personal, but nevertheless wondrous and perfected, Teacher who visited the earth two thousand years ago as Jesus the Christ. Both manifestations, the cosmic and the superhuman, reveal a divine and almost maternal compassion and realization of suffering and of need. Thus moved, the true, interior Christ ever offers himself as consoler, Teacher and unfailing source of rest and strength to all the men and women who have lived and ever will live on this our earth.

The perfected man or woman who is self-emancipated from the limitations of purely human nature—who has transcended all human limitations and weaknesses and entered into full expression divine power—indeed finds that the burden of life has been lifted from his shoulders.[8] Such a being is free, is a master of life and death, and so endowed with divine omnipotence that the tasks normally carried out by man are effortlessly fulfilled.

Such an illumined and exalted one is, however, not far removed and withdrawn from the common life of men and women of all ranks in society. On the contrary, this very attainment causes him to be constantly aware of and alive to the needs, the struggles and the sufferings of those as yet younger in evolution than himself. They are as his children and he loves them all, whether sinners or saints. Furthermore, he offers himself to all as the true and unfailing refuge, elder brother and sharer in all the burdens of human life.

A mystical significance must not be overlooked, however, for eventually every human being comes to lean and draw upon his inherent Christhood as an unfailing source of strength and comfort, for both himself and his fellow men.

Those who translated, edited, and arranged into chapters and verses the ancient manuscript did well, it would seem, to close this chapter of stern disapprobation with words descriptive of Christlike good counsel, self-offering, and all embracing love.

REFERENCES AND NOTES

1. 2 Kings 2:11, 13.

2. Astral—see Glossary.

3. The Pentateuch.

4. Mal. 4:5.

5. See Geoffrey Hodson, *Reincarnation, Fact or Fallacy?*

6. *Kali Yuga* (Sk.)—Dark Age. According to Brahmanical and Buddhist teachings, each root race passes through four ages, golden, silver, copper and iron, the last named being referred to as *Kali* or dark. See Hodson, *Lecture Notes,* Vol. I, Ch. 14.

7. Col. 1:27. See also 1 John 3:24 and John 14:20, "I am in my Father and ye in me and I in you."

8. See Hodson, *Lecture Notes,* Vol. I, Ch. 16. According to occult philosophy adeptship can be attained by those in both male and female bodies.)

Chapter Sixteen

Rabbinical authorities pretended to find Jesus guilty of almost unlimited self-praise. He never claimed to be King of the Jews, as he was charged. His claim to be Son of God was twisted, distorted, and made personal. It was taken as a proclamation that he was indeed a representative of Deity, a Son of God, bringing God's power and truth to mankind. This supposed self-glorification was among the earliest of his utterances which, together with others, were built up to support with apparent legality the charges later made against him.

While the words of Jesus were perhaps susceptible of such an implication, they held a different twofold significance. One meaning consisted merely of the completion of a syllogism; the second may be presumed to refer to the fact that Jesus, in common with all men, was a Son of God by virtue of the divine presence within him and of its origin, namely, the Deity Itself. Thus regarded, all men are Sons of God. However, this idea ran counter to the purely exoteric and rigidly orthodox Hebraism of the time. Apart from Kabbalists and members of other secret occult communities, the rabbis taught of Jehovah as an external Deity and knew naught of his Self-manifestation as the innermost soul of every human being. To them the words of Jesus either sounded blasphemous or could be so turned against him if and when he should be arrested and brought to trial. The Master was, however, in a special category since, during the time he lived, taught and healed among his own people in Palestine, he knew by direct, interior experience that in his true nature he was divine. On occasion this realization was either unintentionally revealed or deliberately expressed in word.

The following verses recorded by St. Matthew reflect both the beginnings of the plot against him and the divinity shining through him.

Matt. 12:1. At that time Jesus went on the sabbath day through the corn; and his disciples were an hungered, and began to pluck the ears of corn, and to eat.

2. But when the Pharisees saw it, they said unto him, Behold, thy disciples do that which is not lawful to do upon the sabbath day.

3.   But he said unto them, Have ye not read what David did, when he was an hungered, and they that were with him;

4.   How he entered into the house of God, and did eat the shewbread, which was not lawful for him to eat, neithei for them which were with him, but only for the priests?

5.   Or have ye not read in the law, how that on the sabbath days the priest in the temple profane the sabbath, and are blameless?

6.   But I say unto you, That in this place is one greater than the temple.

7.   But if ye had known what this meaneth, I will have mercy, and not sacrifice, ye would not have condemned the guiltless.

8.   For the Son of man is Lord even of the sabbath day.

This episode, even in the somewhat imperfect translation, exemplifies the difference between the letter which kills and the spirit which gives light and life. Rightly understood this is of great importance, indicating the nature and attributes of the two aspects of the human mind. One of these is primarily concerned with the material world and the purely material aspects of human life. In consequence, attention is directed to the literal meaning of the spoken or written words. This tendency is valuable when used with discrimination. It can be very helpful, especially in all secular affairs. It has the disadvantage, however, that concentration upon the material and the literal renders the mind unresponsive, even closed, to an intuitive response, as the above verses indicate.

Insofar as they were genuine and sincere rather than a deliberate trap, the criticisms of the priests in these verses were justified according to the literal reading of the Ten Commandments and other injunctions contained in the Torah. Even the scriptures of the world can, however, become barriers to spiritual illumination when their dead-letter reading is exclusively accepted and applied. The reply of Jesus employing the idiom and the outlook of the more abstract aspect and activity of the human intellect makes it clear that a literal reading can be carried too far. The need for nourishment must be met whatever the day of thc week, no sin being committed on such occasions. This was the broader view which Jesus supported by biblical references.

If the incident is interpreted mystically, then the priests who criticized, at the same time setting a trap, personify the material characteristic of the analytical and cunning mind of man. There is evidence that these priests feared and even hated this young compatriot of theirs; for his influence and his apparent miracles were freeing the people from the possessive grip of orthodox religion, which the priests and their actions also personify. Jesus, in his turn, represents the divine nature of man, while the hunger of the disciples typifies the yearning of spiritually awakened minds for truth, symbolized in its turn by "corn." Spiritual and intellectual nourishment was being eagerly sought, and this is ever so when the inward awakening causes a turning away from—even a revulsion toward—the exotericism of religions and their scriptures.

The formal mind can resist the esoteric teaching and produce arguments in support of its resistance. The more spiritual and prophetic synthesizing nature of the human intellect takes and "eats" the golden grain of truth. The divine within, the mystic Christ, in its turn, both commends and acts as an arouser of the hunger for spiritual light and life. The picture of the disciples, old and young, walking with their Master through a sunlit field of ripened corn, is indeed a beautiful one and, moreover, in the terms of the symbolic language, mirrors forth the beauty and the freedom of the intercourse between mind and spirit, man and God, disciple and Master.

The episode closes with an affirmation by Jesus that he was indeed more than man, being a conscious incarnation of the Spirit of God and therefore assuming the mystic title "Son of man." We may be sure that this declaration was made solely in an endeavor to open the minds of his hearers. He sought to penetrate with his wisdom and truth the density and darkness with which orthodoxy had for so long blinded the rabbis who should have been sources of spiritual light.

Matt. 12:9. And when he was departed thence, he went into their synagogue:

10. And, behold, there was a man which had his hand withered. And they asked him, saying, Is it lawful to heal on the sabbath days? that they might accuse him.

11. And he said unto them, What man shall there be among you, that shall have one sheep, and if it fall into a pit on the sabbath day, will he not lay hold on it, and lift it out?

12. How much then is a man better than a sheep? Wherefore it is lawful to do well on the sabbath days.

13. Then saith he to the man, Stretch forth thine hand. And he stretched it forth; and it was restored whole, like as the other.

14. Then the Pharisees went out, and held a council against him, how they might destroy him.

Historically read, the entrapping question forms part of the plot frequently recorded in the Gospels designed to prove Jesus to be a breaker of the Law of Moses, the Hebrew *Torah*. If the enemies could but prove that this had been done openly in the light of day, then they could hail him before their council and have him condemned. Thus recorded, the motive was less to preserve the Mosaic and traditioal law co cerni g the Sabbath than to catch Jesus before witnesses in its infringement, if at first only verbally. It might even be assumed that the sufferer was deliberately sought out and brought before Jesus on a Sabbath day in order both to confuse him and to allure him into a violation of the law. His wisdom proved superior to this cunning; for, by means of the famous analogy of the shepherd and the lost sheep, he completely confounded his adversaries.

Then followed the miracle itself, namely, the instantaneous restoration of a man's paralyzed and withered hand, so that it was "like as the other." Evidently, the actual restoration of vitality and of the capacity to transmit signals can be returned to human tissues by means of adeptic, theurgical power. The dead cells can be brought back to life and active function. Thus, the incident may be read as a threefold revelation. First, a historical event in the life of Jesus is related. Second, the fact is demonstrated that pure wisdom as personified by Jesus can illumine and, where necessary, confound the analytical mind, despite its attributes of cunning and determination to retain dominant power, as in priestcraft. Third, it is clear that occult science, as studied and practiced by a perfected man, enables him to achieve therapeutic effects far beyond the capacity of medical science of that or later days, even up to the present time.

If furthermore, a mystical interpretation is sought and an attempt made to perceive and apply spiritual significance to such an event, then it should first be remembered that the dramatic incidents all occurred within a synagogue. What then is the significance of this particular setting? In the sacred language, the temple is a symbol for the body and bodily nature of man, as St. Paul affirmed,[1] and its surrounding influences, holy indeed, since, however deeply enveiled, the indwelling Deity in man is enshrined. Within the synagogue were people of various types and in differing conditions, each personifying both a part of the make-up of man and also various human attributes, evolutionary stature and states of mind and heart.[2] Again, Jesus represents the divine in man and his immediate disciples and trusting followers the intuitive intellect, as the cunning priests and the Pharisees represent the power-seeking, dishonest and intriguing attributes of the mind. The man with the withered hand, in his turn, typifies those illusions and sensual indulgences which inevitably lead to irrational and erroneous conduct and to the misuse of the subjective faculties.

In greater detail, he also represents man at that stage when he is as yet unable to carry out in action or put into practice the ideals which he has conceived. The hand that would serve his fellowman is impotent to do so, symbolically withered. He is the idealist full of splendid dreams which his limitied development prevents him from carrying out. Nevertheless, he is spiritually awakened (in the presence of Christ) to a certain degree and needs but an additional spirituality as far as his bodily consciousness is concerned. He meets Jesus the Christ, meaning that from within him occurs the additional outpouring of divine power, compassion and healing grace. He hears the words of Jesus, "the still, small voice" within. He obeys its command, stretches forth his hand, and immediately is healed. He has attained to that evolutionary stature at which he is then able to live out in his daily life the principles and ideals which he has intellectually conceived.

The incident thus regarded reveals that when once and at last the Christ nature and presence become active within man—symbolized by the physical presence of Jesus—low cunning fails of its objective and delusion is dispelled and replaced by true perception. In consequence the conduct, typified by the hand of the man thus illumined, becomes perfect, healed or whole.

Such readings of incidents described in sacred books give to them a perpetual and enduring significance, while at the same time conveying valuable counsel to those who read receptively. Such counsel may be stated as follows: Pure spirit is within you; seek it out by placing your mind in a condition of spiritual receptivity as in a synagogue; acknowledge wholly your infirmities or errors, or stretch forth your withered hand. Self-illumination will in due course follow, will correct your errors, give effectiveness to your conduct, and make you whole again.

The fourteenth verse further indicates that the practice of withdrawal into the sanctuary of the soul by means of prayer and contemplation must be regularly maintained. Adverse human attributes are not rendered powerless by a single experience of exalted awareness; for they have become established through many years, even many lives, of not unnatural expression and development. Metaphorically, the Pharisees will continue to seek ways in which they may destroy both the enlightening and liberating experience and its interior Source. Restrictive habits can only be extirpated slowly with effort and by living symbolically in the synagogue or temple wherein the divine is recognized and worshipped.

> Matt. 12:15. But when Jesus knew it, he withdrew himself from thence: and great multitudes followed him, and he healed them all;
>
> 16. And charged them that they should not make him known:

As recorded in the Gospels, the life of Jesus reveals many examples of wise and desirable conduct, particularly by those who would attain to enlightenment. One example is shown in avoidance of open conflict as much as possible with the enemies of truth. Another is making no parade of occult and adeptic powers; Jesus "charged them that they should not make him known." Progress upon the path of Self-regeneration is always accompanied by the development of added faculties and an increase of spiritual power and benediction. Acknowledgment and even praise of these constitute a temptation to feel and display egotism and pride. Such errors, especially that of pride, must be most carefully avoided, as is inculcated by the actions and words of Jesus recorded in these verses. He healed many, charged that they should not make him known, and then withdrew.

> Matt. 12:17. That it might be fulfilled which was spoken by Esaias the prophet, saying,
>
> 18. Behold my servant, whom I have chosen; my beloved, in whom my soul is well pleased: I will put my spirit upon him, and he shall shew judgment to the Gentiles.
>
> 19. He shall not strive, nor cry; neither shall any man hear his voice in the streets.
>
> 20. A bruised reed shall he not break, and smoking flax shall he not quench, till he send forth judgment unto victory.
>
> 21. And in his name shall the Gentiles trust.

Whether or not the quoted words of Isaiah are to be regarded as prophetic descriptions of the character of the Messiah, the guidance given in these verses is of the utmost value to all who would attain lofty spiritual and intellectual stature.

Wisdom, when wisely presented by conduct and counsel, by example and precept, is of itself all-compelling. There is, however, in the human make-up a strange tendency to resent and even powerfully to resist teaching that conflicts with preconceived and established ideas. This tendency becomes accentuated when fear is also aroused, as for example, that some valued possessions or prestige may be lost if the received counsel becomes a ruling power in the conduct of life. Jesus, indeed, always exemplified the wisest possible method of enlightening of human mind and of destroying ignorance and the errors to which it inevitably leads. He was gentle, persuasive, and wherever possible harmonious in the presenting of his ideas, even while firm and forceful as occasion demanded. In consequence, as the twenty-first verse indicates, he and his name, however much resented by the Jews, were trusted by the Gentiles.

> Matt. 12:22.   Then was brought unto him one possessed with a devil, blind, and dumb: and he healed him, insomuch that the blind and dumb both spake and saw.

The account of this miracle, brief and direct as it is, may be read both historically and mystically, as may those of other miscalled miracles.[3] A mystical interpretation becomes possible if the accounts are read as effects produced upon the mind or emotions by the realized presence of the Christ-Self within one who has hitherto been mentally blind or excessively opinionated, or has suffered from long-continued depletion or efflux of psychic end vital energies. As earlier explained, dumbness in this sense may correspond to a mental deficiency in regard to processes of meditation upon the divine within, or mystical "dumbness." The soul is mute, as it were, before the indwelling spirit. In consequence, the body is bereft of communication between the outer and the inner man.

This absence of contact may be due either to the long-continued cessation of prayer and meditation so that the faculty of inner communion is lost, or to the lack of the necessary evolutionary development of the inner Self. In this latter case, under normal circumstances there would be little or no desire, no aspiration, toward mystical experience and the elevation of bodily consciousness beyond ordinary thought of mundane affairs. When, however, the spiritual Self personified by the Christ becomes stimulated from various causes, whether permanently or temporarily, he who has been interiorly mute attains to "speech" with the inner God. Eventually evolution will bring the inner Self naturally to a condition in which it is powerful enough to reach and influence the brain-mind. Thereafter, in response to the interior impulse, the meditative life is entered upon. In either or both of such cases, the illumined state of consciousness is allegorically described as a miraculous healing—a restoration of sight, for example—by the physical presence of a divine being.

When karma permits, a high initiate of the Greater Mysteries such as Jesus is presumed to have been, especially when overshadowed by the Spirit of God,[4] is able to exorcise an obsessing entity and to heal blindness and dumbness and many other bodily afflictions as well. The aura of such an exalted being and the influence of the power for which he is always a vehicle can so illumine a sufferer's mind and heart that psychological and physical obstacles are removed, resulting in the restoration of perfect health. Moreover, when other conditions permit, the magnetic aura of such a one is potent to heal without conscious effort, as is exemplified in the incident of Christ healing the women who had suffered for twelve years from an issue of blood.[5] In this case only near presence and contact with his clothing was needed to heal her where all efforts of physicians had hitherto failed. It is of interest that the Christ did become aware of the flow of healing force resulting from the touch upon the hem of his garment, since he exclaimed, ''Somebody hath touched me.''[6]

Karmic results from former discordant actions of a serious character, as for example, extreme cruelty or wanton abuse of the body, could be overriden under karmic law, one may assume, if the Adept saw that the individual who was suffering at the time would receive great Egoic benefit by restoration of the full use of the body for the rest of that particular incarnation. The fulfillment of destiny and the accomplishment of actions likely to contribute to the welfare of the human race would be examples of causative conditions under which barriers to ''miraculous'' healing might be forcibly overridden. Such cases are rare, one would imagine, and normally the role of law is decisive in all circumstances.

Apparent miracles of healing performed by an Adept such as Christ, though beneficial and helpful, are purely mundane and, therefore, temporary. Healing from interior awakening is spiritual and so enduring.

> Matt. 12:23.   And all the people were amazed, and said, Is not this the son of David?
>
> 24.   But when the Pharisees heard it, they said, This fellow doth not cast out devils, but by Beelzebub the prince of the devils.

The bibles of the world might truthfully be regarded as descriptions by means of allegory and symbol of the nature of men and superhuman beings. Man is made to display almost all the typical attributes of human nature in general and to perform the actions arising from them, revealing the human race, both national and individual. By contrast, the counsel and conduct of superhuman beings indicate qualities far beyond those of mankind in general. It is partly this combination of allegorical descriptions of the actions of man and superman which gives their special characteristics, value and interest to religious writings from the very earliest records to the latest, namely, the Koran.

Representing a common human weakness, the defeated Pharisees, unable themselves either to explain or perform the marvels of healing achieved by Jesus, attempted to discredit him by attributing the results to demonic power or possession. By these means they hoped to reduce the admiration and acclaim of the populace for the newly arisen Teacher who threatened to undermine their authority and so reduce their power and their wealth.

The present commentary is not intended to exclude the possibility that agencies could, and even do, exist in nature which appear to function as opponents of the evolutionary progress of man. On the contrary, they admittedly exist, consisting largely of human beings who have metaphorically sold themselves to the "devil" of personal power and its unlimited indulgence. Indeed, in human character opposites and oppositions are continually encountered. The will to act on behalf of others is all too frequently opposed by the will to act wholly for self; for these are the two great antagonists, the basic pair of opposites. The verses under consideration present examples of each of them in the persons of Jesus and the Pharisees, respectively.

> Matt. 12:25. And Jesus knew their thoughts, and said unto them, Every kingdom divided against itself is brought to desolation, and every city or house divided against itself shall not stand:

The presence upon earth of a divine being and its manifestation through a human form—as is assumed to have occurred—has always produced two opposite effects. One is to arouse the enmity of those who, for their own purposes, determine to preserve the status quo; the other is to evoke favorable recognition followed by appropriate conduct. These two are personified, first by the Pharisees who determined to destroy Jesus, and second, by the multitude who followed him. The former were left in the outer darkness of their hatred, while the latter were illumined and healed, whether metaphorically or actually.

The hostility of the priesthood is understandable for priests are steeped in orthodoxy. Jesus, thus early in his career, constituted a threat to their dominion, spiritual, mental and material. Here was a man of humble origin—the son of a carpenter—with no ecclesiastical rank or title and claiming none, who consorted with the populace in general. The remarkable directness of his replies to every accusation and his obvious possession of spiritual powers which none of them possessed must have aroused apprehension.

Indeed, Jesus unfailingly met them on both their own religious grounds and those of dialectical reasoning, and these two verses offer examples of the latter. In them Jesus is shown to have demolished by sheer reasoning the absurdity of the rabbinical argument and accusation that he performed the beneficent act of healing the sick as an agent of the lord of flies, Beelzebub. Thus brought into juxtaposition, beneficent deeds and demoniacal power are obviously contradictory; if the devil healed the sick and taught wisdom to the multitude, then he could no longer be classed as evil. One may readily understand that public defeats increased the anger and aroused the irritation of those who set themselves up as his opponents, further increasing hostility and the determination to defeat Jesus and destroy his work.

> Matt. 12:26. And if Satan cast out Satan, he is divided against himself; how shall then his kingdom stand?
>
> 27. And if I by Beelzebub cast out devils, by whom do your children cast them out? therefore they shall be your judges.

28. But if I cast out devils by the Spirit of God, then the kingdom of God is come unto you.

The great Teachers who visit the world do not usually proclaim themselves
for what they are, nor did Jesus. But there must surely have been occasions
when such a revelation occurred. Clearly, his disciples knew him for what he
was and, in consequence, unhesitatingly answered his call. Here is recorded
one of the rare occasions when, by hint rather than direct statement, Jesus
may be regarded as revealing his true Self and the real source and purpose of
his mission. Placing oneself intuitively at the scene of these events, one may
imagine that as he spoke the words "the Spirit of God" a light may have
shone from within and all about him. The more simple and mentally open
people may have seen that light and have been still further moved to believe in
him as a messenger from on high.

Matt. 12:29. Or else how can one enter into a strong man's house,
and spoil his goods, except he first bind the strong man?
and then he will spoil his house.

Whether on field paths, roadsides or in village streets, Jesus proved
himself able almost instantly to call upon the remarkable capacity for healing
which he so obviously possessed. In order to heal by a glance, a word or a
touch, as Jesus did, one must have already become possessed of both knowledge
and power, not merely traditional or scriptural, but directly perceived
and consciously applied. Indeed, all argument against the existence and
possession of a spiritual power is demolished in the face of demonstration by
the actual exercise of that power. As was his custom, Jesus drew attention to
this truth by use of a most appropriate analogy—that of a strong man and his
house.

Matt. 12:30. He that is not with me is against me; and he that gathereth
not with me scattereth abroad.

It is impossible to be quite certain of the actual language used by Jesus in
proclaiming his teaching of the divine presence within man and of his own
direct knowledge of that presence within himself. Apparently, the record
included his affirmation that this teaching was ultimate truth and that all those
who declared otherwise were in error. Hence his statement, "He that is not
with me [as the personification of truth] is against me."

In this episode one may discern a part of the special teaching which Jesus
would seem to have imparted—or at least offered—to the people of his time.
He came to awaken them to the fact of their own divinity and that it was
possible for them to be aware of this truth, as was he himself. Indeed, his
miracles may thus be regarded as demonstration of the fact that he exorcised
and healed by the power of God within him and not by the power of the devil,
as he had been charged. That he was indeed a Prince of Light is also
demonstrated by the fact that his influence has endured for two thousand
years and still shows no sign of weakening. Whatever the modern representatives of the rabbis of old may say and do, countless numbers of his people
have entered into direct relationship with him, experiencing a mystical union

or "heavenly marriage." Only a great and illumined Lord of Light, one may reasonably assume, could have so charged the world with spiritual power as did the Lord Jesus Christ.

> Matt. 12:31. Wherefore I say unto you, All manner of sin and blasphemy shall be forgiven unto men: but the blasphemy against the Holy Ghost shall not be forgiven unto men.

This verse and indeed each of the four Gospels portray the Master in a threefold light—occultist performing seeming miracles; mystic affirming the spiritual unity of man with God; and reformer insisting that it is by a man's thoughts, words and deeds that his real nature is revealed. Again and again throughout his ministry, as far as the records provided by the Evangelists indicate, Jesus determinedly and continually cut through the deceitful, outer pretenses and formalized procedures of both society and religion and revealed the deep, true and decisive standards by which a human being and a nation are to be judged. Even in matters of religion which ought to elicit absolute sincerity, he evidently found that hypocrisy was prevalent at that time—and unhappily still is.

In the midst of his relentless probing to the heart and truth of the subjects upon which he speaks, there, almost as if deliberately inserted, is the verse under consideration. His words therein recorded almost seem to teach that while sin and blasphemy in the usual meanings of the words might be condoned, blasphemy against the Holy Ghost must remain forever unforgivable. Man lives in the active presence of the Holy Ghost, an Aspect of the Self-expressed cosmic and solar Deity, the manifested Logos active as a redemptive power. The Lord Jesus appears to accentuate and underscore the significance and importance of this sacred and glorious presence, which is both without and within all men. Thoughts and words which blaspheme against this apparently provoke a retaliation, however impersonal, which produces profound and longlasting adverse effects. As philosopher, Jesus may be assumed here to be speaking, not of divine judgment, but of the impersonal operation of the law of cause and effect.

What can be the nature of such injury to one who blasphemes against the Holy Ghost? As the divine Mind and its inherent, highly spiritual driving force are comprised in the term *the Holy Ghost,* so it is upon the corresponding human mental structure and capacity that the result of deliberate blasphemy are precipitated. The effects must reach and severely restrict the intellect or mind of the blasphemer, causing obstacles to his illumination from within and self-expression through word and deed.

The human mind is expressed at and from various levels. Some words and deeds are very largely physical, others contain and derive from emotion, while still others are deliberately planned within the mind. Karma is far more complex than the simple description of it might indicate. Effects are always appropriate to the actions themselves, but are affected by the level from which the impulse or decision to act arises. When an action is an expression only of the mortal part of human nature, then the reactions are restricted to those levels. When the immortal and spiritual nature of man becomes involved as a driving force and motive for words or deeds, then the effects, favorable or adverse, penetrate far more deeply. The deepest level is that of the pure spirit-essence, the Holy Ghost in man. When this Third Aspect of Deity is deliberately reviled, scorned and blasphemed against with full intent, then the effects are always most serious indeed. Not only do such acts and words of blasphemy affect the mortal man and even the Ego in the causal body, but also penetrate toward the innermost Self. Admittedly this God within is beyond all adversity. Nevertheless, its opportunity of self-expression and therefore of unfoldment can be increased, decreased, or even entirely prevented.

Condemnation for blasphemy apart, it is philosophically unsound to suggest that any action, even if constantly repeated, will be *forever* unforgivable and unforgiven. One may be pardoned for questioning the early writers, translators and editors responsible for the records of his words, though of course not Jesus. The time must arrive when under compensatory law the effects produced by causes must express themselves. Eventually the blasphemer will become enlightened and so cease to blaspheme. The effects of preceding errors will find compensation, and thereafter a harmonious return to equipoise will be established, however deep the transgression may have been.[7]

The immediate and even longtime effects of the blasphemy referred to by Jesus are evidently expected to be both severe and prolonged. Mankind is therefore most seriously warned against them and the errors from which they arise. Sin in ignorance, error during experimentation, and temporary enmity against nature's processes and human society may be natural, but deliberate, far-reaching and penetrating blasphemy against the divine power and presence within which man lives and moves and has his being is a "sin" from which only through long ages man can redeem himself.

> Matt. 12:32. And whosoever speaketh a word against the Son of man, it shall be forgiven him: but whosoever speaketh against the Holy Ghost, it shall not be forgiven him, neither in this world, neither in the world to come.

In this age and among civilized people, this deep sin of so-called blasphemy which includes the deliberate denial of all that is holiest and highest in nature and humanity is becoming less and less a known characteristic. It does occur, however, the so-called "Black Mass" being one example. Another consists of thoughts, words and deeds which deliberately divert the purest spiritual influences and aspirations to the fulfillment of devilish or satanic purposes, designed to injure and even destroy the best in human nature. Black magicians of all times, *dugpas* and demon worshippers, belong to the class of utterly self-degraded, erstwhile men who have embarked upon this dark path. The so-called blasphemy against the Holy Ghost which was so deeply condemned by Jesus must be assumed to include such perversions, wickednesses and deliberate descents into the darkest and blackest forms of evil machinations and activities.

When once a person aspires to the spiritual heights, a speeded evolution begins to occur within him. He or she unfolds, expands, grows. Inversely, when once a person seriously and with conscious intent embarks upon a path of selfishness, without regard to either moral principles or the effects of their actions upon others, then what might be termed "devolution" begins.[8] Contractions, inhibition of development, and progressive hardening of the heart are some of the results. These can become so far-reaching as to influence the condition of the Ego throughout the rest of the *Manvantara*.[9] In this sense, then, blasphemy against the Holy Ghost might be described as an unforgivable sin, especially when a very serious warning is being uttered.[10] The legendary figure of Mephistopheles partly personifies this evil and indicates the manner in which the evil ones seek to spread their own moral disease. On the other hand, every genuine aspirant toward spirituality and the discovery of the true Self moves with hastened speed, winged feet, along the pathway of swift unfoldment to the summit of the evolutionary mount, whether called Olympus or Kailas.

> Matt. 12:33. Either make the tree good, and his fruit good; or else make the tree corrupt, and his fruit corrupt: for the tree is known by his fruit.

The immovable rock upon which the objective and finite cosmos is established consists of an unbreakable chain of causation, each link of which is both an effect of preceding causes and cause in relationship to the effects which must follow. All individuals are both held safe and secure and educated by the operation of this principle.

Jesus, in this verse, is explaining how deeply into the interior nature of man the law of causation penetrates. As he says, a person with a truly good heart, acting with the best motives he or she can conceive, consistently moved by love and sheer goodness, produces effects which manifest themselves in that interior region whence motives arise. Thus good, kindly, and honorable motives for actions consistently followed build the character of the person throughout the years, mentally, psychologically, and physically. He or she becomes a good, kindly and honorable person. Nobility and even holiness of nature are developed. This is quite apart from resultant actions and their effects in the arena of physical life, where only harmonious and helpful conditions are generated.

According to the records, the great Teacher went on to say the converse is also true. Cruel, selfish, crooked and dishonorable motives when consistently followed, inevitably build corresponding qualities into the character, the mentality and outlook of the actor, however fair they may seem in their external personality. Furthermore, every time the good or the evil practice is followed, then human character, innate selfhood, is correspondingly affected more deeply. Ultimately, the real individuality inevitably emerges. From an evil and wicked soul, evil and wickedness come forth. From a pure and wise soul, purity and wisdom emanate. Hence his words which have come down to the present day as have so many others, "By their fruits ye shall know them."[11]

The problem of the extent or degree of effect needs also to be studied. Naturally the frequency or habitualness with which a motive finds expression in thought and conduct governs the effect upon character. Moral laws may infrequently be broken and this intermittence influences both the reactions under the law of cause and effect and development of character. Furthermore, such occasional errors may be interspersed with good and noble deeds inspired by the inner Self. They may also be performed without motives of personal gain. Both of these reduce the adverse effects of oppositely motivated actions. Thus in its interior operations, *karma* becomes a kind of equation which is continually changing, even day by day, hour by hour.

The horticultural simile—one among many used by Our Lord—is valuable since up to the moment of its death a tree can recover from disease and limitations of development. The virus can be eradicated; the conditions of the roots can be improved with beneficial surroundings and a ready supply of food and water. So it is also with the wondrous living "tree" which is man. Up to the last moment when evil has been so consistent as to have become almost ineradicable, the most degraded human being can still gain reprieve. Unless the voice of conscience has been so consistently disregarded and even flouted as to produce spiritual deafness—which may be described as "personal death"—the still living spark of the One Flame can once again be fanned into an effective fire.[12] In rare cases where this self-salvation is not possible, then effects inevitably follow causes, and the round of involution and evolution into the human kingdom must be trodden over again.[13]

Matt. 12:34. O generation of vipers, how can ye, being evil, speak good things? for out of the abundance of the heart the mouth speaketh.

35. A good man out of the good treasure of the heart bringeth forth good things: and an evil man out of the evil treasure bringeth forth evil things.

The complete falseness of the position of the Pharisees must have been evident in both the tones of their voices and their well-known conduct. The term *pharisaical* has come down as descriptive of uttermost hypocrisy, particularly in words and falseness of speech. Whether or not the simile is just or unjust to the ancient ruling sect of priests, the Master evidently found himself continually in the presence of people for whom intention and speech were but slightly related, with little or no regard for truth and every regard for trickery, deceit and smooth words which veiled evil intentions. In their very presence and before all the people, he both tore the mask of deceit from them and pronounced the self-created doom which awaited them as a result of their conduct. Yet the penetrating analysis of human nature contained in these two verses was neither wholly condemnatory nor limited in time, place and application to particular people. On the contrary, the Lord was revealing a profound wisdom which applies to all mankind, particularly in the present *Kali yuga.*[14]

It behooves all, and particularly spiritual neophytes, to watch carefully and to work on their characters so that virtues developed are not merely on the surface but also become established as part of their whole being. This implies truthfulness, sincerity, and the complete belief in virtue for its own sake, not only as a quality displayed for expedience; for such a path endangers the soul, which can be corroded by insincerity, inconsistency, double-dealing and double-speaking. The instruction is also necessary because it is possible to drift half unconsciously into these errors, particularly when pressed by the adverse conditions of daily life.

All attempts to live the spiritual life and to progress upon the way of holiness will ever be completely abortive under such conditions of dishonesty; for all apparent virtues, even good deeds, lose their significance and their weight when they mask a deeply rooted and deliberately pursued deceitfulness. On another occasion the Lord gave those so unfortunate as to fall into this error the title "whited sepulchres."[15]

> Matt. 12:36.   But I say unto you, That every idle word that men shall speak, they shall give account thereof in the day of judgment.
>
> 37.   For by thy words thou shalt be justified, and by thy words thou shalt be condemned.

The Master here holds up a very high standard of human conduct. At the same time he is uttering a warning concerning the importance for the speaker of the spoken word, not only in the present but also in the future. In this he himself speaks as an occult philosopher, one who knows, for example, that the power which distinguishes man from animals—and indeed all other creatures—is the capacity to express thought in words. Such attainment resulting from aeonic evolution carries with it very heavy responsibility; for while lightly spoken words uttered in play, as it were, are of little or no importance, as earlier stated, every seriously spoken word and sentence carries a power and an energy, from which significant effects must inevitably result.

In this sense a word is evidently to be regarded as of equal potency to a deed, and speech as an action which will produce its own reaction, appropriate to both inner intent and presumed meaning. Evidently destiny and character are molded, not only by visible, objective conduct and its effects upon others—potent indeed—but equally by the conclusions of the mind, the formulated thoughts and their associated words. As we read the immortal story we are in the presence of a science of life itself and are being taught some of the principles upon which human happiness and unhappiness in varying degrees are based.

The term *the day of judgment* is mistakenly thought to refer to a particular time—and even moment—when the end of this world shall come. In the divine rulership of the universe and judgments concerning the fate of man, it is mistakenly believed that trial, judgment and sentence are to be postponed until some vaguely conceived termination of objective life. This is one of the fallacies of Christian orthodoxy, and a very harmful one indeed.

The truth is that every day is as a judgment day, and one might almost add that every hour is an hour of destiny. No *external* magistrate sits in judgment, or will ever do so, over man as individual and as a race. He is forever his own judge, and by his inner intentions, his words and his deeds he, *and none other than he,* pronounces his sentence. However, just as prisoners may have sentences commuted and be liberated on parole, so when later conduct generates such causes, decrees and sentences change, becoming harsher or gentler accordingly. These subtleties were apparently left unuttered by the Master who taught central truths and, according to the records which have come down to us, delivered relatively simple and easily understood teachings.

As one pictures such scenes recorded in the gospel stories, one visualizes also the presence of the neophytes and disciples whom Jesus was collecting around him—his inner circle of pupils, so to say. All maxims, all standards which apply in general to the man and woman of the world, have special meaning and deep significance for the spiritual aspirant; for interior powers are developing which bestow added significance to both motive and conduct. Thus, together with the great utterance of the Sermon on the Mount, these ideals of the spiritual life and teachings concerning the so-called razor-edged path give additional essentials and guides for the spiritual aspirant. This was interfused with general guidance and even remonstrances delivered to the people at large.

Matt. 12:38.   Then certain of the scribes and of the Pharisees answered, saying, Master, we would see a sign from thee.

39.   But he answered and said unto them, An evil and adulterous generation seeketh after a sign; and there shall no sign be given to it, but the sign of the prophet Jonas:

40.   For as Jonas was three days and three nights in the whale's belly; so shall the Son of man be three days and three nights in the heart of the earth.

Kabbalistic interpretations and Gnostic interpretations apart, it must be remembered that the accounts of the life of Jesus in the four Gospels were pieced together from memories orally transmitted to an original historian. People would come to him with stories remembered by them or handed down within groups and families. Nothing was actually written down at the time when Jesus was alive, and the first recorder of the events of his life was completely dependent upon such sources for his material. This is one explanation for the apparent breaks in sequence to be found in the different Gospels, even though a certain continuity is evident. This is discernible, if not explicit, in the reply attributed to Jesus to the request for a sign. Though his questioners were seeking either to confuse or to trap him, he was by no means ensnared; for he spoke in a deep mystic sense concerning his own death and reappearance three days afterwards. His words, therefore, constitute a prophecy of physical events.

Other meanings may be read into the Lord's mysterious utterance. The story of Jonah's entry into the interior of a large fish,[16] as well as Jesus's reference to it, is susceptible of at least two interpretations comparable to Jesus's death. It may therefore be useful to refer to this allegory.

In one interpretation Jonas and Jesus personify the major life cycle of the manifested conscious and evolving Life Principle in the universe, characterized by passage through seven phases of descent and ascent. The third, the fourth and the fifth of these involve the deepest penetration into solid physical substance on its involutionary journey, reaching the most solid condition of the substance of space—physical matter itself, symbolized by the fish. This process may be hinted at as the descent into the center of the earth by the so-called "Son of Man." The evolutionary pathway is then entered upon, the Life Principle arises from submergence in the deepest depth of matter, and its sentient embodiments become aware in mental and supramental levels. This phase is symbolized by the air or space above the dry land upon which the body of Jonah was cast up, and into which Jesus was resurrected three days and three nights after his burial, according to scriptures. Thus, an abstract Life Principle is represented in concrete form by personification as the central figure in a drama. Such an interpretation is supported by the language used by ancient writers on these subjects; for they referred to periods of objective activity as days, and periods of subjective manifestation and relative rest as nights.[17]

The second possible significance of the story as applied to both Jonah and Jesus constitutes a revelation by means of symbol and allegory of one of the secrets of initiation, as previously suggested. In earlier days and in older civilizations the Lesser and the Greater Mysteries were public institutions, however secret the Mystery revelations themselves remained and still remain unto this day. In the Greater Mysteries wherein allegory gave place to reality, the candidate himself or herself was made—in the brief space of three days and three nights, or some other chosen time period—to enact a portion of the involutionary and evolutionary process in nature. He or she was made to lie upon a cross, symbol of the physical universe with its four quarters of space represented by arms of the cross of matter. This was the ceremonial crucifixion enacted upon the body of the candidate who represented the One Life itself, rendered unconscious in the lowest depths of the material universe, the physical world. The candidate was not nailed but rather bound upon the cross and thereafter thrown by the hierophant into a physically unconscious condition—entranced in fact. Symbolically, the divine Life sleeps in the mineral kingdom of nature, the densest condition of universal substance and planetary matter, also represented by the rock tomb in which Jesus was buried.[18] As this period closes, Life develops sentiency, eventually becoming self-conscious and capable of mystical experience in man. Thus the initiate is awakened and arises from the cross. Thus also Jonah and Jesus were resuscitated and freed from their figurative deaths. So an occult interpretation of the Nativity and Baptism indicates Jesus had actually passed through this sacred rite and was destined to do so again, the story of his Transfiguration, Passion, Crucifixion and Resurrection being an allegorical description of the final ceremonial which preceded—and still precedes—self-initiation into adeptship.

An even deeper significance may be discerned in many allegories in which the fish symbol is employed—that state of spiritual awareness in which absolute and forever unbreakable unity is realized. This is referred to as the fish state of awareness, and initiates and saviors are designated as "fishers" of other human beings. Jesus called his disciples to this office and so to that training under him which would bring them in their turn to the Mysteries and entry into fish-consciousness.[19]

Realization of unity leads to ministration on behalf of mankind, born of compassion for its sufferings. This also is portrayed by the symbol of the fish, Jesus being its perfect representative. As he revealed in these verses, he himself was destined to experience again, and still more deeply, the spiritual exaltation of absolute blending or dissolving into the infinite ocean of the Life of the universe.

Matt. 12:41. The men of Nineveh shall rise in judgment with this generation, and shall condemn it: because they repented at the preaching of Jonas; and, behold, a greater than Jonas is here.

42. The queen of the south shall rise up in the judgment with this generation, and shall condemn it: for she came from the uttermost parts of the earth to hear the wisdom of Solomon; and, behold, a greater than Solomon is here.

43. When the unclean spirit is gone out of a man, he walketh through dry places, seeking rest, and findeth none.

44. Then he saith, I will return into my house from whence I came out; and when he is come, he findeth it empty, swept, and garnished.

45. Then goeth he, and taketh with himself seven other spirits more wicked than himself, and they enter in and dwell there: and the last state of that man is worse than the first. Even so shall it be also unto this wicked generation.

Again an apparent lack of continuity is presented. From the sublime heights of prophecy of spiritual exaltation, Jesus is made straightway to embark on an oration condemnatory of the orthodoxy and malpractices of the people of his time. He censures them and almost seems to foretell the destruction of Jerusalem and the dispersion of the Jewish people, destined to occur shortly after his own departure.

Jesus, it must be remembered, was fulfilling at least three physical functions. First, he delivered to the Hebrew people, and through them, the eternal Wisdom, concentrating on certain of the principles of cosmic and human existence of which that wisdom consists. These are chiefly to be found in the so-called *Logia* such as the Sermon on the Mount and other divine utterances. Secondly, he was a reformer, and he warned the people against the evils so prevalent in his nation at that time. Indeed, he would seem veritably to have castigated his people with words of condemnation and prophecy of disaster, even doom, as in these verses under consideration. Quite evidently he also foresaw the progress of events which were to bring about the dispersal of the Hebrew people. Very shortly the temple was to be destroyed,

Jerusalem captured and occupied, Palestine to become a Roman province, and the Jews to be homelessly scattered throughout the world. Jesus linked together, as cause and effect, the low moral state of the middle and upper classes on the one hand and the oncoming disasters on the other. In this phase of his ministry must be included the softening of the old Mosaic law of an eye for an eye and a tooth for a tooth, the so-called *Lex Talionis*; for this he substituted perfect justice tempered with mercy and stressed the importance of love for one's fellowmen leading to active charitable concern for all.

The Master's third function was to select from among the general mass of people of his time those in whom he discerned loftier evolutionary stature. These were the more evolved members of the human race, some of them pupils from a former life, and all offering conditions which rendered them susceptible to spiritual training and occult development under him. The last defines his role as divine Teacher, ministering in general to all, but selecting the few to be received as his disciples.

In various utterances Jesus used the metaphorical method, as in these verses, wherein the people of Nineveh and the Queen of Sheba (the South) are emblematic of both retribution and the oncoming Roman armies.

Matt. 12:46. While he yet talked to the people, behold, his mother and his brethren stood without, desiring to speak with him.

47. Then one said unto him, Behold, thy mother and thy brethren stand without, desiring to speak with thee.

48. But he answered and said unto him that told him, Who is my mother? and who are my brethren?

49. And he stretched forth his hand toward his disciples, and said, Behold my mother and my brethren!

50. For whosoever shall do the will of my Father which is in heaven, the same is my brother, and sister, and mother.

Harsh and unfilial though these recorded words may sound, they nevertheless reveal a deeply esoteric truth which is realized both as a state of consciousness and an ideal appropriate to the life of every spiritually developed human being, whether neophyte, disciple, or initiate. The state of consciousness is entirely universal. All things and all men are equally regarded as being vehicles for the one divine Life incarnate within them. The accent is upon the indwelling life rather than upon the differentiated substances and varied forms through which it is physically expressed. Indeed, when one is elevated in spirit into conscious experience of union with the Life of the universe, then all-pervasiveness and indivisible unity are so completely realized as to obliterate both memory and awareness of separated forms. The illumined one has himself virtually disappeared as an isolated entity. Somewhere deep in his consciousness there may remain a remote and faint experience of I-ness. Nevertheless, this knowledge does not in the very least intrude upon or prevent the ever-deepening experience of oneness as of an infinite ocean without even atomic structure. Thus, physical family relationships tend to fade in comparison with the universality of the exalted state. The utterance of the Lord should indeed be regarded as comparing the two states—purely spiritual and purely physical, placing so great an accentuation upon the former that the latter virtually, but not entirely, disappears.

The ideal of obedience to the counsel, ''Be ye therefore perfect'' must give increasing importance to the concept of humanity as a whole and a reduction in the significance of one's own family, nation, and race.[20] Especially, purely bodily attachments must never be allowed to come between the servant of the race and the race as a whole. Each disciple becomes a citizen of the world, taking all mankind into his heart without reservation.

Generalizations on such subjects can sound cold and unfeeling, even harsh and forbidding. The larger state of mind is very far from that. The preceding verses indicate that Jesus was in an exalted state, highly prophetic and full of spiritual power. The interruption in his discourse would in no wise be allowed by him to cause a descent. One may, however, be sure that when the address to the people was completed and the normalities of physically embodied existence resumed, family love would find its full expression. In times of relaxation and bodily ease, Jesus, as also all illumined ones, must have been tender and kind to everyone, and especially to the members of his family. There would, however, always be a tendency for him to fall into a state of meditative thought in which he would be temporarily withdrawn from his surroundings. Those of his entourage would learn to appreciate and respect these silences and to take care that he should not be disturbed.

A seeming paradox is involved in the incident of the apparent rejection of parents and brothers on the one hand, while on the other Jesus consistently taught the importance of love, which he exalted into a lofty ideal of human relationships. Another example is the inculcation of universal love without personal preference, as opposed to righteous indignation on the part of great Teachers against evil men and the evil for which they are responsible. In this, however, the innermost spiritual Self of even a very wicked man is held to be as dear as the innermost Self of any other being. Such love is impersonal and without demands and so partakes of both spiritual and universal qualities.

REFERENCES AND NOTES

1. I Cor. 3:16.

2. See Hodson, *Hidden Wisdom,* Vol. 1, Pt. 3, Ch. 1.

3. While phenomena produced by supernormal powers may seem miraculous, they are nevertheless, always the result of the conscious exercise of will power combined with knowledge of the superphysical forces of nature, under laws not yet discovered by science. They are, therefore, not rightly to be called miracles.

4. As at the Baptism. See Matt. 3:15-17.

5. Matt. 9:20-22.

6. Luke 8:43-8.

7. See Hodson, *Reincarnation, Fact or Fallacy?*

8. Devolution. Occult philosophy does not include the possibility of retrogression. It is conceded, however, that very serious delay can occur.

9. Manvantara—see Glossary.

10. Throughout the commentaries of which this book largely consists, the English translation used in the Authorized King James Version is considered. Mistranslations, mistaken memories, records, and even deliberate falsifications are, however, recognized as possibilities. See Introduction.

11. Matt. 7:20.

12. Spark—the Monad; One Flame—the Supreme Diety.

13. See Hodson, *Lecture Notes,* Vol. I, Ch. 2.

14. *Kali Yuga* (Sk.)—the dark Age.

15. Matt. 23:27.

16. Jonah 1:7.

17. See Hodson, *Hidden Wisdom,* Vol. 2.

18. Matt. 27:60.

19. "Come ye after me, and I will make you to become fishers of men." Mark 1:17.

20. Matt. 5:48.

PART EIGHT

THE PARABLE OF THE SOWER,
ITS INTERPRETATION,
THE FEEDING OF THE FIVE THOUSAND,
AND CHRIST'S COMMANDMENT

Chapter Seventeen

While a spiritual Teacher is relating a parable, he is at the same time holding in his mind and projection the hidden wisdom clothed by the parable. A dual process is thus carried out. A story is told to the multitude by means of the Teacher's voice and at the same time an appeal to the intuition and mind is made. The ideal result of this method is that hearers grasp the inner significance of fables, myths, and parables while the Teacher is telling them. The Gospels record that, in addition, Jesus actually expounded the underlying doctrine, probably more deeply than the written record reveals. There is much to be learned from such parables as those recorded in this chapter by St. Matthew.

Matt. 13:1.   The same day went Jesus out of the house, and sat by the sea side.

2.   And great multitudes were gathered together unto him, so that he went into a ship, and sat; and the whole multitude stood on the shore.

3.   And he spake many things unto them in parables, saying. Behold, a sower went forth to sow;

4.   And when he sowed, some seeds fell by the way side, and the fowls came and devoured them up:

5.   Some fell upon stony places, where they had not much earth: and forthwith they sprung up, because they had no deepness of earth:

6.   And some fell among thorns; and the thorns sprung up and choked them:

8.   But other fell into good ground, and brought forth fruit, some an hundredfold, some sixtyfold, some thirtyfold.

9.   Who hath ears to hear, let him hear.

The parable of the sower is not only a perfect exposition in allegory of profound truths, but also a classical example of the use of the sacred language for this purpose. His interpretation or translation which followed will later receive consideration.

The scene evoked is both authentic and beautiful; for the reader is enabled to visualize a large gathering of the people of Palestine amid the hills and plains, dressed in the clothing of the times, having drawn nearer to Jesus in order to see him, to hear his voice and receive his teaching. As so often, Jesus drew his similes and analogies from nature and from the pursuits of the people who were gathered around him. How easy it must have been for them to picture the scene which he described and follow the actions of the story which began with the words, "Behold, a sower went forth to sow." As he spoke, therefore, they all felt perfectly at home in the mental atmosphere into which he drew them and in listening to what was for them a story of their own lives and familiar experiences. In this a glimpse, if not more, is afforded of the remarkable capacity of Jesus to draw near to his audience and to draw them near to himself. Indeed, the authenticity of this portion of the gospel story seems to be fully established as one reads.

Actually, however, no physical actions were being described. Rather, as his later interpretation demonstrates, stages of evolution and appropriate conditions of mind were being depicted in symbolic form. Indeed, the Master may even have been drawing upon his own experiences of the types of people whom he had met and upon their varying reactions to the wisdom which he sought to impart to them. There must have been many who were totally unready for, and therefore completely disinterested in, both the homely truths and the profound and esoteric wisdom which formed part of his conversations and addresses. Others, perchance, may have listened, rather idly and found their interest only lightly aroused and their curiosity but slightly awakened. The real teaching would mean little or nothing to them, particularly after his voice had become stilled and the hearers had returned to their daily activities. The words were above them and the ideas abstract in comparison with the hard facts of their daily lives and largely material interest. These are the people referred to by St. Mark: " . . . unto them that are without, all these things are done in parables."[1]

A few must have gained full comprehension and response, and to them the inner meaning of the parables and other teachings were revealed. From among these Jesus would draw disciples, discovering their readiness, both by direct spiritual vision of their inner stature and from their responses to his person and his message.

Matt. 13:10. And the disciples came, and said unto him, Why speakest thou unto them in parables?

   11. He answered and said unto them, Because it is given unto you to know the mysteries of the kingdom of heaven, but to them it is not given.

This reply to the question which the disciples very naturally asked gives rise to an inquiry concerning the difference between a disciple and a nondisciple, a pupil of an adept Teacher and a normal citizen. A disciple is both spiritually awakened as manifested in both consciousness and action, and has pledged himself irrevocably by a solemn oath to loyalty, to truth, to his Master, and to secrecy.

Discipleship concerns evolutionary stature, not only in the life in which it is attained, but also in a series of lives in which the advancing and unfolding spiritual Self has increasingly expressed spirituality as an underlying characteristic. Worldly attainments and positions, pleasurable pursuits where the senses alone are involved, and tendencies to act selfishly—all these decline in the series of lives which are to culminate in the discovery of the Teacher and acceptance by him. While at first an interior struggle, a mystic Armageddon, is experienced, gradually all sense of renunciation declines, to be replaced by perfectly natural and spontaneous choices of cultural, intellectual and spiritual soures of happiness. The world in its obvious and material aspects loses its hold upon the mind and heart of such an individual, while at the same time humanity's need for happiness, well-being and spiritual development increasingly occupies his interest and activity. The aspirant becomes a servant of his fellowmen. This is indicated by the statement that before they were called some of the disciples of Jesus were fishermen, and one was a physician. Being a fisherman, symbol for the human attributes of compassion, impersonal love and service, leads to saviorship and eventually to the stature of the perfect man. The occult physician heals not only bodies but souls, by training, teaching and guiding into the pathway of discipleship those who are seeking the sacred light of truth. He strives to bring about wholeness in those who seek his aid or are directed to him for guidance in living the perfect life. These interior unfoldments, changes in interest, motive and character, and the beneficent actions to which they lead constitute the mark of those who are approaching the evolutionary stage of discipleship and, still more, those who have reached and passed beyond it—the initiates among mankind

The Master with his piercing insight generally knows when these aspirations are felt by the outer man. When the aspirant can be trusted to keep his word, especially to preserve secrecy, a certain pledge is asked for and given. The nature of this obligation includes the promise to endeavor to pursue the way of holiness to its end in adeptship, to keep holy the things which are holy, guarding them from the profane, and as far as human nature permits to live a life of purity, selflessness, harmlessness and wisely directed service on behalf of one's fellowmen.

Such men and women are selected, taught and trained by adept Teachers according to a very ancient and universal custom. As they progress and prove reasonably faithful, occult teachings are revealed to them. They learn the secrets of the hidden powers, processes and component parts of both the universe and man. or, as Jesus said, "unto them it is given to know the mysteries of the kingdom of heaven."

Matt. 13:12. For whosoever hath, to him shall be given, and he shall have more abundance: but whosoever hath not, from him shall be taken away even that he hath.

13. Therefore speak I to them in parables: because they seeing see not; and hearing they hear not, neither do they understand.

The reader might be forgiven for regarding the twelfth verse either as a serious error in reporting and translating or as an utterance so cryptic as to be beyond ordinary human understanding. Truly, whatever the meaning may be and the idea which Jesus intended to present, the sentences do appear to be almost entirely self-contradictory. Even so, beneath the cryptic language a meaning of great significance may possibly be discerned.

The verse may permissibly be taken to refer to spiritual perception, intuitiveness, and the wisdom which results from the correct functioning of these two faculties. In this sense it is true that wisdom leads to further wisdom. Spiritual perceptiveness acts like a catalyst which induces more rapid change of knowledge into wisdom. Pure intuitiveness enables those who possess and wisely use it to penetrate deeply into the hidden mysteries of life, the underlying purposes of nature, and the deeply rooted influences and motives behind human conduct and personality. The sage knows Truth itself rather than a collection of separate truths alone. He comprehends the processes by which the emanation of universe, solar systems and all their components gradually occurs; and there exists a stillness amid his ever-deepening understanding within which further knowledge continually grows. Thus it is true to say of wisdom that the more one has the greater the increase.

On the other hand, the mind which is largely absorbed in the gathering of factual knowledge, which values this above ever widening and ever-deepening comprehension of those principles of which facts are but a temporary manifestation, gathers but little of the eternal wisdom, the true riches of the soul. Furthermore, the human mind can become so concentrated upon objective nature and upon arguable and even demonstrable facts as to lose the modicum of wisdom which might have begun to develop. In this sense possibly the verse may be read, especially its closing sentence.

Analogies and metaphors are necessary in order to draw attention of the uninstructed or learned men and women absorbed with outer events to the hidden laws and processes of nature in operation in human evolution and even in daily life. Metaphors, analogies, allegories and parables have a dual function. They both refer to potent truths and initiate processes in the mind of hearers which will lead to comprehension of the natural laws which are being revealed. A symbol can become a dynamic force when meditated upon with a view to the discovery of its significance.

One of the oldest methods of arousing into activity the inherent wisdom of the inner Self of man is to administer a shock of miscomprehension, mental confusion and obfuscation. It is strangely true that when the formal mind is thus shocked into emptiness and stillness, even if only for a moment, illumination may suddenly dawn. One of the essentials of such self-illumination is temporary mental silence, an active stillness—if the term may be permitted—in which peace is found to pervade the whole region of human consciousness. This in itself is a valuable fruit of the practice of absorbed contemplation. It is also the condition in which the light of wisdom is afterwards found to have dawned. This occurs less as a dazzling, suddenly blinding moment than as a quiet and continuous illumination as if from an eternal flame.

Disciples are men and women in whom the perpetual flame of wisdom has become alight. This "lamp" can never be lit in oneself by any external hand. It is a natural and deeply interior shining of light from the one eternal Light of the univese within the inner Self of truly enlightened man. The disciples of Adepts are thus distinguished from their fellows and are therefore able to perceive truth direct, to receive from their Masters knowledge which they can comprehend and are not likely to misuse. True, a Judas can always arise among them, while others may fall away from the disciplined life perhaps for the remainder of an incarnation. These are risks which every Master and Teacher must take and guard against as far as possible.

Matt. 13:14.   And in them is fulfilled the prophecy of Esaias, which saith, By hearing ye shall hear, and shall not understand; and seeing ye shall see, and shall not perceive:

15.   For this people's heart is waxed gross, and their ears are dull of hearing, and their eyes they have closed; lest at any time they should see with their eyes, and hear with their ears, and should understand with their heart, and should be converted, and I should heal them.

16.   But blessed are your eyes, for they see: and your ears, for they hear.

It is evident from these verses that they record, however symbolically, part of the Mystery Teaching which Jesus imparted to his disciples in complete privacy. One of the secrets of this teaching must, in consequence, be regarded as having occurred in the supposed original Gospel from which later versions were derived. Jesus clothed the revelation in mystic secrecy, especially in the two verses under consideration, where the eyes and the ears referred to are not those of the body but of the mind.

Mental perceptiveness—not only to direct verbal instruction, but also with regard to experiences and realizations in consciousness—is shown to be prerequisite for the reception of the Mysteries of the Kingdom of God. Without this, esoteric teachings inevitably appear to be the sheerest folly, the uttermost stupidity. Even deliberately misleading falsehoods are sometimes perpetuated for the protection of others against harmful misunderstanding, leading to grave misconduct. Personal anger aroused by a humiliating sense of inability to understand, or mystification, can lead to adverse actions.

The ignorant who "having eyes see not and ears hear not" totally misunderstand the words of the Teacher and his motives for uttering them. The fifteenth verse gives one of the reasons for this dullness of perception, namely, fear lest established religious concepts, customs and habits be upset and a new way of worship be found. Unwilling thus to be converted, the ignorant close their mental eyes to the light of truth and their ears to the words of the wise. Indeed, they hardly dare do otherwise, and so their reactions are understandable. Later in their ascent on the evolutionary ladder they will seek ardently and develop the capacity to find and comprehend the wisdom which in earlier phases was beyond their understanding. Egoic youthfulness which withholds them from the Mysteries will one day be outgrown. Thereafter a willing hand will guide them to the doorway of the sanctuary. The disciples, on the other hand, had already reached that stage and it is this which permits them to receive the Mysteries of the Kingdom of God face to face.

Matt. 13:17.   For verily I say unto you, That many prophets and righteous men have desired to see those things which ye see, and have not seen them; and to hear those things which ye hear, and have not heard them.

Again, the references are less to the organs of sense and more to conditions of the human mind, particularly those resulting from the open-mindedness and intuitive wisdom of evolutionary maturity. In the mind of the spiritual Teacher, there is no element of condemnation or even criticism of younger souls, only recognition of the different stages of the unfoldment and development of man and the characteristics associated with each.

Matt. 13:18.   Hear ye therefore the parable of the sower.

19.   When any one heareth the word of the kingdom, and understandeth it not, then cometh the wicked one, and catcheth away that which was sown in his heart. This is he which received seed by the way side.

20.   But he that received the seed into stony places, the same is he that heareth the word, and anon with joy receiveth it;

21.   Yet hath he not root in himself, but dureth for a while: for when tribulation or persecution ariseth because of the word, by and by he is offended.

22.   He also that received seed among the thorns is he that heareth the word; and the care of this world, and the deceitfulness of riches, choke the word, and he becometh u fruitful.

23.   But he that received seed into the good ground is he that heareth the word, and understandeth it; which also beareth fruit, and bringeth forth, some an hundredfold, some sixty, some thirty.

Four successive phases in the evolution of the human mind and general development are described here by means of allegory and symbol. The allegory of the ordinary activity of the farmer must have been familiar to most of those present from their early childhood, Jesus thus masterfully reaching his hearers with the ideas he wished to present. In those days, doubtless, sowing was done by hand, and a clear picture of a man performing this familiar action would at once arise in the minds of those present. Harmony and communication were thus established between speaker and audience.

"Seed" is interpreted by the Master as Truth or the Word, and the "wayside" is descriptive of man's natural interests and capacities, namely, the ordinary affairs of physical life with their limitations of understanding and interest, in consequence of which philosophic ideas evoke no interest whatever. The well-trodden path, the wayside, most aptly represents the state of mind which is heedless, careless and unappreciative of wisdom and the words of the wise. There can even arise within such minds a scorn of higher ideas and a tendency to refuse them the slightest place in thought or the slightest value in themselves. This almost exclusive interest in material existence and its demands is personified as the wicked one, presumably meaning Satan or the devil—a well used reference to the materialistic workaday mind. A profound truth is advanced—that scorn of and resistance to spiritual and philosophic illumination exist only within that part of man's mind.

Next described are the numerous persons unable to publicly stand for ideas and ideals which are both unpopular and partly heretical. Such individuals have not yet evolved to that position at which they are ready and able to hold to spiritual wisdom in the face of the world. The habit and security of conformity prove too strong. The apparent heresy—in reality esoteric wisdom—is forsaken and replaced by an insincere and hypocritical adoption of the orthodox position. Nevertheless, such people have at least received a measure of spiritual truth and understanding, have begun to awaken mentally to abstract and intuitional ideas. Later when once again the hidden wisdom reaches their minds, it will take deeper root and become so strongly established within them that it can no longer be denied.

Indeed, no mental state, undesirable or desirable, is ever final. The human mind is itself undergoing an evolutionary development which will bring it to the condition at which truth received will be sustained and eventually supplemented by direct experience of its verity. Thus the stages described in the parable may be regarded as successive in all human beings, the disciples of Jesus having reached an advanced degree of mental receptiveness and perception.

The "thorns" constitute the numerous distracting influences which so strongly grip the mind that the individual is unable to pay attention to the delicate and growing fruits of interior perception. The Master refers to the possession of riches as one of these distractions, and indeed worldly possessions can so preoccupy the mind as to make it unreceptive to and even oblivious of wisdom intuitively perceived.

Riches in themselves are not despised. Indeed, they can be useful if only for helping the less favored of the world. They can also provide freedom from toil so that receptiveness and perception may be developed by meditation and in consequence comprehension of spiritual laws attained. Wealth is only harmful where it comes between the mind and the spirit of man, where it produces an extreme preoccupation with worldliness to the exclusion of right-minded otherworldliness, mystical experiences and revelations of truth. Those human beings who have not yet evolved beyond this stage are described in the reference to the seed which was received among thorns.

The ideal state to which the minds of all mankind will one day evolve is described as receiving the seed of truth into good ground and, on hearing the word, understanding it. Even when this degree of receptiveness is reached, differences of mental capacity to comprehend abstract ideas still remain. Perfected manhood and those closely approaching it bring forth fruit an hundredfold, others sixty, and still others thirty, according to evolutionary position.

Although not directly stated as far as the record based on memory and oral tradition reveals, the doctrine of the evolution of man as it affects the development of the human mind is almost entirely described in this wonderful parable. Since, however, all conduct springs ultimately from the intellect and every action can eventually be traced there, then the total development of man is included in the revelation. All men pass through those degrees of development referred to allegorically as the wayside, stony, thorny and fertile ground. As suggested, each of these indicates the extent to which human beings are growing out of an almost primitive stage of development toward the "measure of the stature of the fullness of Christ." This teaching of man as an evolving being could be presented only allegorically to the people, but the disciples would be well able to perceive the underlying significance of the parable and to comprehend and be illumined by the wisdom concealed within it.

Esoteric truth is not deliberately withheld because of secretiveness or a system of favoritism. The guiding principle concerns the hearers' ability to comprehend and benefit from revealed truth.

Matt. 13:24.   Another parable put he forth unto them, saying, The kingdom of heaven is likened unto a man which sowed good seed in the field:

25.   But while men slept, his enemy came and sowed tares among the wheat, and went his way.

26.   But when the blade was sprung up, and brought forth fruit, then appeared the tares also.

27.   So the servants of the householder came and said unto him, Sir, didst not thou sow good seed in thy field? from whence then hath it tares?

28.   He said unto them, An enemy hath done this. The servants said unto him, Wilt thou then that we go and gather them up?

29.   But he said, Nay; lest while ye gather up the tares, ye root up also the wheat with them.

30.   Let both grow together until the harvest: and in the time of harvest I will say to the reapers, Gather ye together first the tares, and bind them in bundles to burn them: but gather the wheat into my barn.

This parable describes basic conditions and temporary states of the human mind, and also a method whereby mental difficulties may be overcome. In this view, the good seed which is to be successfully grown and harvested represents truths concerning the underlying principles of the emanation, evolution and perfection of the universe and all that it contains. The tares represent mental processes and associated contents which tend to inhibit comprehension of principles and, if permitted, deny their validity. The enemy responsible for such tares is interior rather than external, consisting of those attributes of the human mind which, if surrendered to, keep man in a state of ignorance, of unwisdom and even downright error. Thus Truth and resistance to it can exist side by side, as it were, in the same mind.

The parable indicates how the difficulties which result may best be resolved by a careful separation of the two opposing attitudes and concepts. This cannot be achieved in the early stages of human evolution before the ideas become sufficiently developed to be recognized for what they are, namely, truth and untruth or partial truth. The advice given, therefore, is to follow the only method which is likely to succeed: divide the wheat from the tares-—truth from error—and burn or eradicate the latter. Thus, the parable of the wheat and the tares signifies the progress of the human mind from ignorance toward full perception of truth, and of interior experiences which naturally accompany that progress.

Indeed, this, as other truly inspired portions of world Scriptures, actually describes man himself, the race and the individual, and records the history of his development from the primitive state to Christhood and Buddhahood. The total constitution or make-up of man, spiritual, intellectual and material, is also revealed, while at the same time wise guidance is given as to how the sorrows of life may be avoided and the pathway to perfection successfully trodden.

Matt. 13:31.   Another parable put he forth unto them, saying, The kingdom of heaven is like to a grain of mustard seed, which a man took, and sowed in his field:

32.   Which indeed is the least of all seeds: but when it is grown, it is the greatest among herbs, and becometh a tree, so that the birds of the air come and lodge in the branches thereof.

The Teachers of old did not, of course, expound the whole doctrine on each and every occasion and in each of the allegories which they inspired. Rather they selected for their expositions particular aspects of cosmos and man and special difficulties with which human beings are naturally confronted.

This parable of the grain of mustard seed may be interpreted as a symbol of the Monad of both universe and man. From this unit of pure spirit-essence, both a Solar Logos with his solar system and a human Ego with all its vehicles eventually are emanated and come into objective existence. As the mustard seed contains within itself the full potentiality of all that will be produced from it, so the Monad contains within itself all that will eventually emerge and evolve. As a seed of the Godhead it will be the source of deities unmanifest and manifest, in their turn emanators of universes.

The passage of time is also indicated, the seasonal growth of a plant to fruition corresponding to the aeonic evolution of the soul of all things and the almost immeasurable evolutionary ages. One cycle of seasonal growth in the plant kingdom brings to a close the mysterious development from a small seed. The plant itself thereafter dies, but not before large numbers of new seeds have been produced. Each of these in its turn, if planted, can become both the infinite reproductive source and the beginning in time from which the process will be repeated. This seeming miracle continues throughout all eternity.

A hint is given, doubtless expounded in private to the disciples, that members of other kingdoms of nature than the human both participate and assist in the continuous and ordered procedure occurring in cosmos and man. These are the *Elohim,* the numerous orders of angelic hierarches, symbolized by the birds of the air.

Thus, in an utterance which requires but a few lines for its recording, Jesus opens up the mind of the genuine seeker for truth to realms of divine knowledge which may thereafter be explored. It is clear that the kingdom of heaven referred to in the parable is that state of divine existence and spiritual consciousness at the very loftiest level, from which all things emerge and of which all universes and men are the ever-evolving products or fruits.

If it is contended that the interpretation which Jesus later offered to his disciples did not extend as far as is here suggested, it should be remembered that the real interpretations, the deeply esoteric teachings, were given in complete privacy to pledged disciples alone. None of those present would be likely to reveal the nature and content of interpretations thus offered, particularly in writing. In conformity with custom, Jesus himself wrote nothing, and it is reasonable to assume that both the canonical and the apocryphal books of the New Testament—especially the Gospels—give very incomplete and sometimes incorrect accounts of all that occurred. The authorships of the Gospels and the dates on which they were first compiled are unknown to biblical scholars, as also must remain the full description of all the events of the life of Jesus, and especially the full record of the secret teachings which he gave. However, much additional teaching can be permissibly inferred, particularly where classical symbols are used, and events and conversations are recorded which appear to carry with them implications of an esoteric wisdom.

> Matt. 13:33.   Another parable spake he unto them; the kingdom of heaven is like unto leaven, which a woman took, and hid in three measures of meal, till the whole was leavened.

A numerical key is here used, namely, the number three. Among its many significances, this number refers to the three component parts of the mortal personality of man while alive in the flesh—the mind and the mental faculties, the feelings and the capacities for emotion, and the physical body through which mind and emotion find expression in waking consciousness.

Under normal circumstances, and up to a certain phase of evolution, these three are limited in function to their own level of consciousness and being. The mind carries out mental processes with more or less logic and reason; the emotions express both thought and feeling combined, with the latter usually predominating; the body is the instrument of awareness and action on its own plane of existence. Rarely does an intrusion from a higher and more spiritual part of man's nature reach and noticeably influence these three functions in average and normal human being.

As a later phase of development is approaching and subsequently entered, subtle changes begin to occur: comprehension of the laws underlying physical phenomena, idealism, charity, an increasing sense of a fraternal relationship between men, a search for deeper understanding, and a religion of interior experience. These are all due to the intrusion of the spiritual Self of man from a supramental level; they come from and through the region of the abstract intelligence in which that Self abides. The *kingdom of heaven* is the symbolical term for this level and state. The parable may be interpreted as an allegorical description of the quickening effects of this manifestation with the mortal man.

Leaven or yeast as used in bread-making is the very apt symbol used for the influence upon human thought and action of spiritualizing, intellectually stimulating and purifying radiations of power from the inmost Self of man; for when once this so-called leaven reaches, or becomes "hid in" the threefold outer man, his very nature begins to be changed, just as the meal rises and expands when yeast is kneaded into it. The woman in the parable may personify Dame Nature herself; for quite natural processes are described, even though spiritual assistance from either the God within or Adept Teacher from without may quicken the whole leavening procedure and so hasten the general evolution of the individual thus assisted.

Evidently during the period of his ministry from which these parables are drawn, Jesus spoke oracularly, as is the habit of great Masters of Wisdom when addressing a mixed audience. Clearly the above-suggested meaning of the short parable would hardly be perceived by uninstructed people. It may safely be conceived, however, that among those who heard the teachings of Jesus there were many who belonged to one or other of the occult communities of the time and would, in consequence, recognize the teaching delivered. On other occasions when he was alone with these, he would doubtless interpret more and more deeply, thereby revealing such layers of esoteric wisdom as they were able to comprehend.

Matt. 13:34.   All these things spake Jesus unto the multitude in parables; and without a parable spake he not unto them:

35.   That it might be fulfilled which was spoken by the prophet, saying, I will open my mouth in parables; I will utter things which have been kept secret from the foundation of the world.

The author or authors of the Gospel according to St. Matthew reveal in this chapter their decision to record the fact that an allegorical language was used in Israel by its initiates to reveal and at the same time conceal certain layers of the esoteric Wisdom. The Hebrews were natural heirs to this Wisdom, even though at certain periods of their history it receded into the background of their religious life, thereafter becoming known and studied almost exclusively in occult communities. Thus, the author interpolates his own affirmation and belief that Jesus followed the ancient custom referred to in the Book of Psalms, revealing the secret wisdom to his disciples alone. While the profane mind, not without justification, may view the practice with disfavor, nevertheless the possession of esoteric knowledge, particularly concerning the psychical and spiritual components of both man and universe, can bestow very great powers for good or evil upon its possessor.

> Matt. 13:36.   Then Jesus sent the multitude away, and went into the house: and his disciples came unto him, saying, Declare unto us the parable of the tares of the field.
>
> 37.   He answered and said unto them, He that soweth the good seed is the Son of man;
>
> 38.   The field is the world; the good seed are the children of the kingdom; but the tares are the children of the wicked one;

Even in these published interpretations of the parables, it is clear that the same secrecy was observed. One may reasonably conceive that the expositions supposedly given by the Lord to the disciples within a house were not the truly deep and innermost aspects of the wisdom enshrined in the parables. This interpretation is itself hardly acceptable, unless indeed within it also a deeper wisdom is to be found.

The wheat may be regarded as the permanent, spiritual aspects of human nature, while the tares typify the temporary and mortal bodies of man. Perhaps this concerns the revelation of a distinction between the eternal spirit and its material clothing or embodiment in both nature and man; for the former, like the wheat in the parable, endures forever and continues to evolve or bring forth fruit, while the latter inevitably perishes or is cast into the flames. As so often is the case, the revelation is less of events and actions than of natural law.

> Matt. 13:39.   The enemy that sowed them is the devil; the harvest is the end of the world; and the reapers are the angels.
>
> 40.   As therefore the tares are gathered and burned in the fires; so shall it be in the end of this world.
>
> 41.   The Son of man shall send forth his angels, and they shall gather out of his kingdom all things that offend, and them which do iniquity;
>
> 42.   And shall cast them into a furnace of fire; there shall be wailing and gnashing of teeth.
>
> 43.   Then shall the righteous shine forth as the sun in the kingdom of their Father. Who hath ears to hear, let him hear.

The guidance offered to the disciples may well have been to fix their consciousness, hopes and aspirations upon the divine presence which constitutes the real Self, and to withdraw increasingly from its mere bodily encasement and the concerns of bodily life; the eternal spirit is the reality while the perishable body is unreal. Indeed, this is ever the call of all the Teachers of men, whether given allegorically or directly. If this view is accepted, then the supposed action of the Father in separating the wicked from the virtuous and casting the former into a furnace of fire really describes the inevitable disintegration of all forms while the spirit by which they had hitherto been animated exists eternally. The Son of Man and his angels who winnow out all that is gross and cast it into the fire stand for the perfectly natural course of cosmic events. The spirit ascends to greater and greater heights of self-expression, and its material encasements lose their hold. Indeed this happens not only in the closing phases of universal and planetary evolution, but repeatedly every time a human being dies.

Occult teachers assure their disciples that by becoming aware of themselves in their spiritual nature, maintaining their center of awareness at that level, they will become immortal. Their self-consciousness will persist unaffected by bodily death or even by the dissolution of planets and the central sun around which for ages they have traveled. As ever, in the human sense, immortality is the grand theme, and the way of its attainment is the guidance given by Teacher to disciple. Yet even the multitude, unaware of aught but the physical world around them, have the right to hear the wisdom and receive the call, clothed though both may be in symbol, allegory and parable.

> Matt. 13:44. Again, the kingdom of heaven is like unto treasure hid in a field; the which when a man hath found, he hideth, and for joy thereof goeth and selleth all that he hath, and buyeth that field.

It is to be understood that Jesus used the term *the kingdom of heaven* for both the divine, immortal part of man enshrining purest spirit-essence and also its associated state of consciousness. This is indeed the supreme treasure within the field of awareness. Blessed are those who discover the Self and enter into its state of abiding bliss; for they have found the treasure of treasures, the veriest "jewel-in-the-lotus." In the symbolical language of this chapter, Jesus exhorts all who hear him to seek first this inward Self and to know its reality. Then, though having its place and purpose, all else fades into comparative insignificance. Symbolically, the man who finds this treasure within the "field" of his day-to-day activities rightly buys that field or takes total possession so the hidden treasure may be his.

Doubtless to his chosen and dedicated disciples Jesus unveiled the allegory and revealed the hidden truth. For those who could respond, he awakened the inward vision. Apart from all his other great gifts of wisdom to the world—some, but far from all, of which are preserved in the Gospels—he stressed the supreme value of attaining direct and living experience of the divine presence and its condition of being. He taught, not only its present importance, but far more its infinite possibilities deriving from the seed of the Godhead enshrined within it. For this he chose the symbol of the mustard seed.

> Matt. 13:45. Again, the kingdom of heaven is like unto a merchant man, seeking goodly pearls:
> 46. Who, when he had found one pearl of great price, went and sold all that he had, and bought it.

A new most beautiful and most apt symbol is here chosen for the treasure of treasures—the pearl of great price. Indeed, the hidden, spiritual Self of man is of great price, nay priceless, for it is the eternal itself. Truly, when the man of time and space discovers the time-free and immortal Self, then so great is the wonder that he gives up *all* for this treasure.

> Matt. 13:47. Again, the kingdom of heaven is like unto a net, that was cast into the sea, and gathered of every kind:

> 48.   Which, when it was full, they drew to shore, and sat down, and gathered the good into vessels, but cast the bad away.

In these collected discources, probably made at different times, Jesus by way of symbols teaches about the causal body, its state of consciousness and its functions. The cup is also used as symbol for this vehicle of the soul and the allegories and symbology of the Holy Grail were largely derived from this system. The early Christians, particularly those admitted to the Mysteries of Jesus and the Gnostics, received and shared teachings upon this most important subject.

The fishing net is very well chosen, for it was a veritable part of the life of those who dwelt in the valley of the Jordan and other rivers and near the seashores of Judea. If the net symbolizes the causal body and its function, then catching fish and later sorting represents assimilating the fruits of life's experiences. All of these which have in them the qualities of spirituality and capacity to endure are indeed "caught" in and by the higher Self, into which they are incorporated as powers of the soul. Fish which are cast forth as unusable represent the results of experiences of a gross and purely material nature. These cannot be translated to the spiritual levels of consciousness and existence and so cannot be absorbed or grafted into the subtle vesture which, like an arc, preserves all enduring qualities. Metaphorically, the unusable fish are cast out after careful sorting. Thus the symbology is indeed perfect.

In an extended interpretation, the fish also represents the most divine attributes in spiritually awakened man: selfless and impersonal love, all embracing compassion and ever-ready service arising from it. To these may be added the overpowering urge to protect and to save, and a penetrating spiritual intuitiveness.

> Matt. 13:49.   So shall it be at the end of the world: the angels shall come forth, and sever the wicked from among the just,
>
> 50.   And shall cast them into the furnace of fire: there shall be wailing and gnashing of teeth.

While some theologians have been willing to accept these two verses in their literal sense and as correctly recorded utterances of Jesus, the philosopher is unable to do so. He tends, as always, first to look below the surface meaning in search for a concealed wisdom, and second to question the veracity of the recorder and even the translator, to uncover the error, either deliberate or accidental.

What, then, may be drawn from so drastic a pronouncement, and how may the words be understood with some propriety? The answers primarily depend upon which level of consciousness and aspect of human nature is thought of. If mortal man rather than the indwelling eternal spirit is considered, then the operation of the law of cause and effect is described.

After each physical death the conduct of the life then closed is automatically weighed or judged against the conscience.[2] As a result of this, all that is noble and idealistic in the character of the deceased is preserved within the inner Self to be added to the qualities and the powers already developed during preceding existences. All that is gross and deliberately wanton and materialistic is separated from the individuality or Ego and gradually disintegrates. The selection is made under a law of attraction and repulsion, the noble and idealistic being drawn into association with the spiritual man, while the gross is left behind as residue. The substance through which such grossness was expressed, and by which it was represented in the psychology and superphysical bodies of the deceased, then returns to its appropriate source in nature's reservoir, drawn by affinity, as it were, into those strata of superphysical substances of which the world is partly built.

This procedure of division after selection occurs regularly during the early post-mortem period of every human being. While it is true that the process occurs automatically, certain nonhuman intelligences—the angels of these verses—are involved. Certain orders of angels are agents of divine law; for indeed no law, no process of nature, is ever administered without the directive presence of appropriate members of the angelic hierarchy.[3] There are orders of the angels whose naturally assumed duty and task is concerned with both the construction and the dissolution of forms, and also with the induction of consciousness and life into forms, followed in due course by withdrawal.

In a more occult interpretation, during the great cyclic swing of conscious life—"downwards" in terms of deepest density and "upwards" in terms of purest abstraction—some beings inevitably become too heavily enshrouded in the deeper degrees of density. In consequence, when the upswing begins they are unable to participate in it fully at the appointed time. They are left behind, as it were, while beings in the main body of evolving life sweep on to more lofty levels.

It is of first importance, however, to realize that neither punishment nor neglect is involved. Even weeds are composed of substance which contains life. Although the gardener may uproot and discard them, he can neither destroy the indwelling life nor prevent the transformation of the substance from one condition to another. Indeed, life and matter are both eternal; and although the matter of human bodies may be separated from the indwelling spiritual soul, as at death, that soul is by its very nature indestructible and eternal. Separation is necessary in such cases of relative failure—possibly symbolized by the grief referred to—but this in no sense implies expulsion from divine consciousness, concern and care. On the contrary, special pains are taken to protect such cases, to assist them to progress at their own speed and even to catch up with, join and move onward with the "main body."

Doubtless the great Teacher concealed this profound occult knowledge under a veil of allegory, although it also seems very likely that the scribe from whose writing the Evangelist drew his biography of Jesus incorrectly recorded the words.

Matt. 13:51. Jesus saith unto them, Have ye understood all these things? They say unto him, Yea, Lord.

> 52. Then said he unto them, Therefore every scribe which is instructed unto the kingdom of heaven is like unto a man that is an householder, which bringeth forth out of his treasure things new and old.

In all life, life processes, and teachings concerning them, there must ever remain a hidden mystery, so deep that neither thought nor words can compass it. So, also, all attempted expositions of the Mystery Teachings are inevitably incomplete. Each student can only enter into the incommunicable truth which lies behind and beyond the realm of the mind.

For this reason, perhaps, the Master asked these questions of his disciples, seeking to probe into the depths of their responses to his words and evaluate the degree of their understanding. Here he makes a clear distinction between the uninstructed and the instructed scribe or student. He would then be better able to carry their instruction to further and further stages and nearer and nearer to that direct illumination which is the goal.

The disciples answered his question by clearly saying that, having understood his interpretations, they had grasped the inner and deeply veiled teachings. While none of them would consciously answer him untruthfully, nevertheless their affirmations must have been founded upon differing degrees of illumination. The disciples—not only the official apostles but many others whom he drew near to himself—had been drawn chiefly from the members of the Hebrew race and religion. Some of them were in quite humble circumstances, while others were educated according to the standards of the time. Among these latter there would have been a few instructed Kabbalists, and these would have received the deepest illumination and attained to the greatest understanding of the Mysteries that he was teaching by parables.

The householder who brings forth treasures new and old personifies the listening intelligence, the perceptive capacity, of a pupil. Whatever the stage of egoic development or degree of personal education, outer and inner, the words of a Master spoken face to face with the pupil do more than instruct. This is part of the wonder and magic of teaching by an Adept. Though he may engage in conversation concerning affairs which are more or less worldly and therefore normal, when he imparts spiritual and occult information, he not only gives knowledge but—often more importantly—draws from the inner depths of the pupil's mind his own innate wisdom and new thoughts, evoking responses from the inner Self. Thus the Master refers to the treasures new and old which the supposed householder brings forth. Indeed, this should be the ideal for all teachers, and especially for those who give philosophic instruction and present spiritual ideas.

> Matt. 13:53. And it came to pass, that when Jesus had finished these parables, he departed thence.
>
> 54. And when he was come into his own country, he taught them in their synagogue, insomuch that they were astonished, and said, Whence hath this man this wisdom, and these mighty works?

55. Is not this the carpenter's son? is not his mother called Mary? and his brethren, James, and Joses, and Simon, and Judas?

56. And his sisters, are they not all with us? Whence then hath this man all these things?

57. And they were offended in him. But Jesus said unto them, A prophet is not without honour, save in his own country, and in his own house.

58. And he did not many mighty works there because of their unbelief.

A literal acceptance of the phrase *in his own country* is, of course, quite permissible, and it is a peculiar fact that physical familiarity blinds the eyes and mind, as for instance to members of one's physical family and acquaintances from childhood. However, symbolically the proverb refers less to one's homeland than to the state of mind of the recipients of spiritual wisdom. In these verses the differentiation between the spiritually awakened and unawakened, previously referred to, becomes marked; for although the Master taught most wisely according to his custom, the people of his own district—a symbol for the unawakened mind—failed to recognize either his true stature or the wisdom of his words.

Those who criticize, scorn and scoff do so because they have not yet reached the degree of development nor, perhaps, passed through the suffering which enables the mind to perceive the impersonal truth, the hidden wisdom, and the revealed knowledge.

The phrase *in his own country* may also be interpreted as meaning those whose minds are restricted to knowledge of the merely personal and material garb of both teacher and imparted ideas. They see the flesh that is like unto their own and penetrate no further, being unable to do so. Underneath this blindness is the unawakened state which is the real barrier to response to wisdom, whatever its source may be.

REFERENCES AND NOTES

1. Mark 4:11.

2. Cf. The weighing of the heart of the deceased against a feather in the Hall of the Goddess Maat in Egyptian allegory.

3. See Hodson, *The Kingdom of the Gods.*

Chapter Eighteen

One may presume that a part of the mission of saviors is to perform an enlightening function. Somewhat as catalysts, their very presence speeds up human unfoldment and brings out the finest qualities in those who can respond. With all reverence, Jesus may perhaps thus be regarded as both a great Teacher of mankind and a quickener of human evolution. His advent and his mission, visible and invisible, speeded up the pace of natural unfoldment in general, as in those whom he healed, and produced enlightenment in those able to respond, as did the disciples. These two functions were of far greater importance than healing individual cases of sickness or performing miracles, for they struck at the root of all evil and removed causes of sickness of both soul and body.

The following incidents concerning John the Baptist, healing and miracles, as others throughout the Gospels, may be read as occurring within one individual, the various persons in the stories representing various human characteristics.

Matt. 14:1. At that time Herod the tetrarch heard of the fame of Jesus.

2. And said unto his servants, This is John the Baptist; he is risen from the dead; and therefore mighty works do shew forth themselves in him.

3. For Herod had laid hold on John, and bound him, and put him in prison for Herodias' sake, his brother Philip's wife.

4. For John said unto him, It is not lawful for thee to have her.

5. And when he would have put him to death, he feared the multitude, because they counted him as a prophet.

6. But when Herod's birthday was kept, the daughter of Herodias danced before them and pleased Herod.

7. Whereupon he promised with an oath to give her whatsoever she would ask.

8. And she, being before instructed of her mother, said, Give me here John Baptist's head in a charger.

9. And the king was sorry: nevertheless for the oath's sake, and them which sat with him at meat, he commanded it to be given her.

10. And he sent, and beheaded John in the prison.

11. And his head was brought in a charger, and given to the damsel; and she brought it to her mother.

12. And his disciples came, and took up the body, and buried it, and went and told Jesus.

In these verses the authors of the Gospel use a possibly historical event as a vehicle for the transmission of wisdom under the veil. These episodes in the life of John the Baptist are pregnant with occult significance. Each of the participants in the great drama of his life and death is a personification of one of the seven principles of man, and his or her conduct expresses an attribute of that principle. Every action indicates a law which governs success in living the spiritual life and making progress on the path of occultism, as well as pertaining to initiation.[1]

The innermost spiritual presence, the Monad, is represented by the Lord God, the inspirer of Jesus. Christ, himself, typifies the purest spiritual wisdom as shown forth in his ministry to men, born from compassion for the sufferings of which their lack of knowledge is the root cause.[2] John the Baptist, preaching self-purification and repentance for past errors, portrays man's spiritual Self in its ''vesture of light'' from where the voice of conscience is heard, if not always heeded. The baptist within ever seeks to win the outer, mortal man away from the purely sensual and material life into that spirituality by which the indwelling presence may be realized and the Messianic Age dawn for all mankind.

Herod stands for the separative, prideful, power-hungry activities of the human intellect. Herodias, the Mother of Salome, represents the same characteristic manifested as desire. Salome herself typifies sensual indulgence as both emotion and physical sexuality, in their turn used for the sake of prestige, power and wealth.

All these are present within human beings and tend to influence human conduct until spiritual awakening opens the mental eyes to their essential evil. Even then there may still remain that deeply seated characteristic of the human mind which seeks to force truth to be subservient to preconceived notions, personal concepts, and modes of expression which will preserve personal power and identity. This is the great evil in the world, the great source of almost all the sorrows of men, namely, insistence upon separate self-identity and that intellectual pride which will yield only to those ideas which conform to established patterns of thought. Cleverness and skill in argument may be thus attained, but self-illumination and direct perception of truth in its purity will always be lost in the welter of argument and verbose insistence that one's own ideas are the only true and worthwhile ones.

This characteristic of human nature, which had its usefulness in an earlier phase of human development and civilization, must be completely eliminated if pure Truth is to illumine the human mind. This is accomplished by a determined interior assault against them and eventually their elimination from the character of self-illumined man. This very great achievement is symbolized by decapitation, which is an apt portrayal of the death of the power of the separative and intolerant intellect, the wearing out of the tendency to argue and debate concerning that which is beyond the power of both. These are analytical, while full perception of Truth itself may be described as a transcendent synthesis.

The symbol of decapitation then allegorically describes the final breaking free of the abstract and prophetic intelligence. Goliath, for example, is represented as a giant in armor arrogantly challenging his enemies, but David, fresh from the fields and having entered a stream to attain a white stone, slew him and cut off his head.[3] Perseus similarly cut off the Medusa's head, while Hercules decapitated the nine-headed hydra of Lerna. The spirit of John is freed from the prison of both the flesh and the formal mind, with its past limitations and fixed ideas, including those of oppression and domination represented by Herod; for the mind must be stilled—figuratively slain —if the free flow of intuitively perceived ideas, the Christ nature, is to be realized. Indeed, I suggest, in all accounts of the decapitations of important members of the casts of symbolical dramas, each beheading signifies the end of an evolutionary epoch over which the mortal mind of the man had hitherto ruled, rightly save in extremes.[4]

Since the soul of man is undying and bodily death has no effect upon it, John the Baptist passing away from the visible and all-too-often ugly circumstances and activities of worldly life—also symbolized by death—reached "the further shore." In this he typifies every initiate who has passed through the sacred rites of successive initiations.

In the historic rather than the initiatory interpretation of the story, Herod's favorable response to Salome's demand for the head of John the Baptist on a charger may be interpreted as bringing about the end of his mission by the murder of his body. The philosopher, in his turn, would see in this event the operation of the law of karma under which John the Baptist was reaping as he had previously sown. Herod's fear, like the hesitation of Pilate when judging Jesus, indicates a dawning intuition of the true meaning of life, the real purpose of human existence, the ideal of human conduct, and the beginning of realization that the men they held captive were living examples of these virtues. All tyrants have these fears but tend to drown them in their cups for fear of losing their power, as they well might. The prick of conscience will, however, continue to harass them until it becomes as the voice of John the Baptist calling for repentance in the wilderness of mere worldly existence. Self-reform eventually will follow, and debts built up by evil deeds will be paid in sorrow and agony; for this is the Passion of the Lord through which every initiate must pass on his way to adeptship.

Matt. 14:13.   When Jesus heard of it, he departed thence by ship into a desert place apart: and when the people had heard thereof, they followed him on foot out of the cities.

14.   And Jesus went forth, and saw a great multitude, and

was moved with compassion toward them, and he healed
their sick.

That region of consciousness and that state of being and mind to which
Jesus withdrew was so lofty as to be incognizable to the uninitiated. Therefore it was to them—but not to him—as a desert. This is ever so since that
which is either unreachable or unattainable must appear dark and unproduc-
tive.

Nevertheless, so great was his power over the people and so marked was
their perception of his true stature as well as of his beauty and goodness that
they followed him even unto the so-called desert places. The incidents which
followed clearly show, however, that far from being wasteland the "country" was richly, if magically, productive.

Matt. 14:15.   And when it was evening, his disciples came to him,
saying, This is a desert place, and the time is now past:
send the multitude away, that they may go into the villages, and buy themselves victuals.

16.   But Jesus said unto them, They need not depart; give ye
them to eat.

17.   And they say unto him, We have here but five loaves, and
two fishes.

18.   He said, Bring them hither to me.

19.   And he commanded the multitude to sit down on the
grass, and took the five loaves, and the two fishes, and
looking up to heaven, he blessed, and brake, and gave
the loaves to his disciples, and the disciples to the multitude.

Quite evidently the desert place was only metaphorically so described; for
Jesus commanded the people to sit down on the grass. The narrative then lifts
the incident out of the purely material into the mystical, out of earth, as it
were, and into heaven.

The words chosen by the narrators cause the great feast to assume the
character of a sacred meal, a veritable Eucharist; for it is said that Jesus lifted
his eyes up unto heaven, "brake" the bread, and gave it to the disciples and
they to the multitude. The performance of such an act of duplication and
multiplication of physical objects is well within the capacity of every occult
sage, of every Adept who has been initiated into the Greater Mysteries. The
miracle may therefore be justly accepted as produced by one to whom such
apparent miracles were possible.

The two kinds of food, bread and fishes, are also used as symbols by those
who write in the symbolical language. Bread is interpreted as both knowledge
itself and the kind of nourishment to the mind which enables it naturally to
perceive and appreciate metaphysical ideas. Fish, on the other hand, stands
for the condition in which the oneness of all life in the universe and the
consequent spiritual unity of all beings are realized as experiences in consciousness. Furthermore, from this realization there arises a divine compassion leading to a kind of beautiful spiritual tenderness which is expressed as
wise and loving ministration to those in need.

The food, so miraculously multiplied and given to as many as five thousand, may also be regarded as mental and spiritual nutriment—the infusion into the minds of the people of that spiritual influence which rendered them responsive to illumination. Upliftment of soul was thus given the vast gathering of people rather than physical nourishment alone. A further discussion of the symbology used occurs in the following chapter under another version of the incident.

Matt. 14:20.   And they did all eat, and were filled: and they took up of the fragments that remained twelve baskets full.

21.   And they that had eaten were about five thousand men, beside women and children.

It would seem unlikely that an account of an event which had occurred some years before the story was written down would record the actual number of basketsful of fragments, even if these were counted at the time, which is also improbable. An esoteric significance may therefore be sought, even though the possibility of the production of such a superabundance from so small an original source is accepted as possible. The number twelve suggests totality, wholeness, completion. Baskets may indicate containers, vehicles or carriers, while physical food may be here interpreted as nutriment to the soul. If this view is taken, then the body of spiritual wisdom, of esoteric knowledge, was made available to the consciousness of the multitude, which in turn represents humanity as a whole. The act of the Lord typifies the ministration to mankind by the "just men made perfect" in making available that spiritual wisdom which they have discovered and preserved throughout the ages.

To some minds this interpretation of the remarkable incident may be more acceptable than its reading as a narrative of actual events. Indeed, for the vast majority of people the Lord is made out to have performed an action which to them was totally impossible. Faith, however, enables those who believe in the Bible as the inspired work of God to accept the narrative as an account of one of many miracles performed by the Lord. Even such faith, termed blind because no action of the intellect is involved, can be preferable to outright rejection; for this latter involves a closing of the mind, in consequence of which the impress and import of the account are erased and the hidden wisdom lost.

There is no inherent reason why an Adept should not multiply any physical object almost indefinitely, particularly when overshadowed and empowered by an aspect of the Divine. The Baptism of Jesus accompanied by a descent upon him of the Holy Spirit caused him to be no longer man in the ordinary meaning of the term but a divine man, unified with the supernal Lord of the universe and, in consequence, a Master of the material substance of which the universe consists. In truth all Adepts who emerge from their seclusion and enter the world of men, by their very presence as also by their words, shed abroad that pure wisdom which is not of this world. Wisdom, moreover, is infinite and therefore inexhaustible; both actually and symbolically, there is always more than that which has been made available. This closing incident which the Evangelist describes offers a clue to the understanding of the story, since it introduces the miracle or wonder that implies the inexhaustibility of that which has been provided.

> Matt. 14:22.   And straightway Jesus constrained his disciples to get into a ship, and to go before him unto the other side, while he sent the multitudes away.
>
> 23.   And when he had sent the multitudes away, he went up into a mountain apart to pray: and when the evening was come, he was there alone.

A sense of proportion and a high degree of discrimination are essential to the wise and effective expression of the results of illumination in daily life. Two of the necessities for these, as well as the restoration of both psychical and physical energy and the upliftment of the soul, are symbolically referred to in these verses. They are solitude or seclusion—both multitudes and disciples were sent away—and interior exaltation, or the ascent to the spiritual heights symbolized by the mountain. Through the regular practice of contemplation in solitude and quietness, the mind communes with the divine presence without and within. Thus evening fell and Jesus prayed alone.

> Matt. 14:24.   But the ship was now in the midst of the sea, tossed with waves: for the wind was contrary.
>
> 25.   And in the fourth watch of the night Jesus went unto them, walking on the sea.
>
> 26.   And when the disciples saw him walking on the sea, they were troubled, saying, It is a spirit; and they cried out for fear.
>
> 27.   But straightway Jesus spake unto them, saying, Be of good cheer; it is I; be not afraid.

The phenomenon of self-levitation—implying freeing oneself from the power of gravity—can be readily performed by those who are advanced on the pathway of occult unfoldment. Except as an interesting account of such wonder-working in a past age, the story in its literal form might be regarded as of little if any, direct spiritual value to modern man.

If, however, the passage is interpreted as an allegory of spiritual illumination and self-empowerment of mankind, both individually and collectively, then Jesus personifies the innermost spiritual nature of man, the Christ Indwelling, and the stormy sea refers to the emotional nature when lacking adequate control. On occasion almost all men become storm-tossed as the events of their lives disturb their peace and calm. The ship, in its turn, exemplifies the mortal man and especially the physical vehicle which conveys the soul over the so-called waters of life or material existence. The disciples on the ship represent the varying attributes of both the innermost Self and the outer man at somewhat advanced stages of controlled discipline in both motives and conduct of daily life.

Jesus's absence in the beginning indicates unconsciousness of the divine presence within, while his later arrival and reception on board (verse thirty-two) typifies recovery of awareness of the divine and self-subjection to its power in thought, word and deed. Thus, Christ and his disciples on board a ship symbolically represent the self-illumined man with his varied characteristics.

The disciples also portray the need arising from emotional disturbance; namely, safety and calm. The need may be met by the discovery or revelation of the divine presence within both body and mind. The quieting of the storm and the safe voyage of the ship to the appointed shore describe the effects of the consciously realized spiritual power of the inmost Self, and the calmness, even stillness, of mind and emotion which is then experienced. Furthermore, any danger to the welfare of the mortal man, suggested by a shipwreck, no longer poses a threat because the controlling power of the God within stills all storms in the external, mortal nature of man. This Dweller-in-the-Innermost is in no sense subservient to outer conditions, is indeed master of them, particularly of their perpetual, wave-like motion.

The incident also indicates that after a certain degree of development has been reached, symbolized by the Baptism of Jesus, desire (the waters) is outgrown. The energy which hitherto found expression through emotional outlets becomes transmuted into spiritual power, notably that of greatly enhanced will-force. Metaphorically, the indwelling spiritual Self safely "walks upon"—uses as an aid to movement—the human desire nature which hitherto possessed the attribute of danger.

The disciples aboard the ship fail to recognize Jesus until he speaks to them. This may be an allegorical reference to the voice of the divine within man, the Logos of the soul. The word *voice* in this context is also descriptive of the intimate communication which is established during mystic experiences between the divine and the mortal in man. This communion is immensely power-bestowing and therefore potentially dangerous, hence couched in allegorical language.

The words of Jesus are neither limited to him nor restricted to the time and date at which they are supposed to have been spoken. The experience may be passed through by anyone at any time; for it is timeless and universal. The God within man continually walks upon the water, enters the ship of man's bodily consciousness and thereafter stills the storms of desire. Otherwise expressed, Jesus is always walking upon the water toward mankind. Disciplined men continually witness his approach, hear his voice, and then accept him as a passenger, if sleeping at first, aboard the ship of their mortal life and minds.

Cosmically, Christ personifies the positive creative potency, divine spirit, while the water corresponds to the vast sea of hitherto Virgin Space. The authors of the first verses of the Book of Genesis used the same metaphor, which is also to be found in other cosmogonies. When the "spirit of God" moved upon the "face of the waters,"[6] precosmic quiescence gave way to generative and form-producing activity—by contrast a storm. The later domination of matter by spirit and the initiation and maintenance of the orderly evolutionary processes may also be portrayed by Christ on board the ship—the outer form of the universe—stilling the tempest.

Matt. 14:28.   And Peter answered him and said, Lord, if it be thou, bid me come unto thee on the water.

29.   And he said, Come. And when Peter was come down out of the ship, he walked on the water, to go to Jesus.

30.   But when he saw the wind boisterous, he was afraid; and beginning to sink, he cried, saying, Lord, save me.

31.   And immediately Jesus stretched forth his hand, and caught him, and said unto him, O thou of little faith, wherefore didst thou doubt?

32.   And when they were come into the ship, the wind ceased.

Impulsiveness is a typical human atrribute, and on various occasions Peter displayed it, generally with unfortunate consequences. He had not fully attained to that stage of development at which desire had no further claims upon him. This is evidenced in incidents which are later recorded in the Gospels, notably his declared outrage against the passion and death which the Lord foretold of himself, as also denial during the judgment scene. Though elevated by enthusiasm and devotion so that he could walk some distance on the water to greet his Lord, when the excitability and undue enthusiasm of his emotions intruded, he was in danger of drowning. This did not occur since, very wonderfully, the Lord stretched forth a hand and saved him.

Without in the least discrediting the power of the Adept both to walk on water and still a storm, a revelation of human nature, mortal and immortal, and of the respective conditions and powers of each, is made by means of symbol and allegory. The message of the story is in part to form the regular habit of daily contemplative prayer, thereby attaining to that inward power and peace which, when realized, will sometimes miraculously carry one safely over the turbulent waters of life. Prayer, less of petition and far more of contemplation, induces realization of this inward divinity. This in its turn elevates the man with calm mind above the storms of life.

Matt. 14:33.   Then they that were in the ship came and worshipped him, saying, Of a truth thou art the Son of God.

34.   And when they were gone over, they came into the land of Gennesaret.

35.   And when the men of that place had knowledge of him, they sent out into all that country round about, and brought unto him all that were diseased;

36.   And besought him that they might only touch the hem of his garment; and as many as touched were made perfectly whole.

This chapter closes with descriptions of events which also may be read both historically and allegorically. Indeed, much in the Gospels is historically reliable, despite differences between them, and it may be safely assumed that Jesus did sail upon the Sea of Galilee, cross from one part of its shores to another, evoke adoration from his disciples as his divine nature became revealed, and heal and teach large numbers of people. Apparently minor references, such as those to healing by touching only the hem of his garment, suggest a possible attempt at revelations of truths which are time-free; for when man with his various imperfections (diseases) elevates his personal consciousness into union with his divine Self (the presence of Christ), then his mortal nature becomes purified and spiritualized (healed of diseases).

In this process of self-elevation beyond the activities of the reasoning mind, even the earliest contacts with the synthesizing and unifying intelligence (the hem of his garment) can and do produce most remarkable effects. This truth is recorded in various ways in the scriptural and mystical literature which man has produced. Knowledge of the divine, experience of the omnipresent Life, and of being oneself a manifestation of it, can draw down as if from the fringe of the divine nature floods of inspiration and reintegrating and harmonizing influences. This fact may well be discovered at the very outset and commencement of mystical experiences.

> Luke 8:2.   And certain women, which had been healed of evil spirits and infirmities, Mary called Magdalene, out of whom went seven devils.

● ● ● ● ● ●

> John 8:3.   And the scribes and Pharisees brought unto him a woman taken in adultery; and when they had set her in the midst,
>
> 4.   They say unto him, Master, this woman was taken in adultery, in the very act.
>
> 5.   Now Moses in the law commanded us, that such should be stoned: but what sayest thou?
>
> 6.   This they said, tempting him, that they might have to accuse him. But Jesus stooped down, and with his finger wrote on the ground, as though he heard them not.
>
> 7.   So when they continued asking him, he lifted up himself, and said unto them. He that is without sin among you, let him first cast a stone at her.
>
> 8.   And again he stooped down, and wrote on the ground.
>
> 9.   And they which heard it, being convicted by their own conscience, went out one by one, beginning at the eldest, even unto the last: and Jesus was left alone, and the woman standing in the midst.
>
> 10.   When Jesus had lifted up himself, and saw none but the woman, he said unto her, Woman, where are those thine accusers? hath no man condemned thee?
>
> 11.   She said, No man, Lord. And Jesus said unto her, Neither do I condemn thee: go, and sin no more.

The woman taken in adultery—presented apparently for her condemnation before Jesus—personifies the blended emotional and mental bodies of man passing through phases of evolution during which complete sublimation and sanctification of the creative energy are allegorically portrayed. Thus, there is a Mary Magdalene in every human being, indulged in at first, but eventually transcended as the higher levels of the pathway leading to the summit of the mount of perfection are trodden. Her attainment of discipleship, her presence at the empty tomb and meeting with the risen Jesus signify her successful conquest.

REFERENCES AND NOTES

1. Initiatory interpretation—see Hodson, *Hidden Wisdom,* Vol. 2, pp. 32-3.
2. Matt. 5:18, 7:1, 2.
3. Cf. Goliath, I Sam., Ch. 21-22.
4. See Hodson, *Hidden Wisdom,* Vol. 2, pp. 289-90.
5. Gal. 6:7.
6. Gen. 1:2.

Chapter Nineteen

A literal reading of the miracles of Jesus is acceptable; historical facts may well be recorded. However, writers of the sacred language are able to record incidents in such a way that mystical overtones are also revealed, this being one of the main purposes for the invention and use of that category of literature. If a reader asks the question "which is the truth?" the answer is at least dual. A historical basis may exist and be on considerable interest, but the revelation of spiritual wisdom for which it is a vehicle is of a far greater significance and value. The authors of the world scriptures, humanity's greatest treasures, write with this intention and with this knowledge in view. The verses of the Gospels should be so read.

Matt. 15:1. Then came to Jesus scribes and Pharisees, which were of Jerusalem, saying,

2. Why do thy disciples transgress the tradition of the elders for they wash not their hands when they eat bread.

3. But he answered and said unto them, Why do ye also transgress the commandment of God by your tradition?

* * * * * *

7. Ye hypocrites, well did Esaias prophesy of you, saying,

8. This people draweth nigh unto me with their mouth, and honoureth me with their lips; but their heart is far from me.

9. But in vain they do worship me, teaching for doctrines the commandments of men.

10. And he called the multitude, and said unto them, Hear, and understand:

11. Not that which goeth into the mouth defileth a man; but that which cometh out of the mouth, this defileth a man.

* * * * * *

18. But those things which proceed out of the mouth come forth from the heart; and they defile the man.

19. For out of the heart proceed evil thoughts, murders, adulteries, fornications, thefts, false witness, blasphemies:

20. These are the things which defile a man: but to eat with unwashen hands defileth not a man.

Whether or not it is hygienically advisable to wash the hands before eating is not in question here; for the whole episode is metaphorical and thereby teaches the great importance of simple honesty and straightforwardness in the matters under consideration. It is truly said "the letter killeth but the spirit giveth life."[1] Such is the more general lesson of these verses in which people—the scribes and Pharisees in this case—are made to personify the insincerity, hypocrisy and priestcraft practiced by those who should by precept and example be teaching the living truth.

Every religious reformer who appears after the faith has become encrusted with mere formalities—the repetition of ancient formulas without their recognition in heart and life—has the difficult, if not dangerous task of removing the encrustations and revealing once more truths as originally taught and in their pristine purity. Jesus was such a reformer. In consequence he did find himself confronted by the tremendous power of established orthodoxy.

With great skill and address, he not only answered the charges brought against his disciples, but also carried the war into the enemy's camp and brought discomfiture to those who sought to ensnare and defame him and his followers. This attribute of Jesus, this trait in his character of great intellectual skill combined with penetrating insight, lawyer-like in its logic, is not generally recognized. Nevertheless the four Evangelists never once present him as himself discomfitted by any verbal attack. On the contrary, unfailingly he is presented as highly skillful in such forms of debate.

Of course, he was in an especially favorable position in relationship to his accusers. First, he could see into their hearts and note the hypocrisy behind their words. Second, he had at his command a complete grasp of the subject upon which the charges were based and, third, he was not of the common rank of men, being far above them, a high initiate or Adept. Verbally, therefore, he could never be entrapped.

Matt. 15:21.   Then Jesus went thence, and departed into the coasts of Tyre and Sidon.

22.   And, behold, a woman of Canaan came out of the same coasts, and cried unto him, saying, Have mercy on me, O Lord, thou son of David; my daughter is grievously vexed with a devil.

23.   But he answered her not a word. And his disciples came and besought him, saying, Send her away; for she crieth after us.

24.   But he answered and said, I am not sent but unto the lost sheep of the house of Israel.

25.   Then came she and worshipped him, saying, Lord, help me.

26.   But he answered and said, It is not meet to take the children's bread, and to cast it to dogs.

27   And she said, Truth, Lord: yet the dogs eat of the crumbs which fall from their masters' table.

28.   Then Jesus answered and said unto her, O woman, great

is thy faith: be it unto thee even as thou wilt. And her daughter was made whole from that very hour.

In this episode, Jesus is made to use a simile from animal husbandry. Humanity, it is suggested, is to the Masters of compassion as a flock of sheep, and they the shepherds, chiefly of souls. Very deep concern for all is felt by the perfected ones, but especially for those who have fallen into evil——symbolized here as becoming possessed of a devil.

At the beginning of the encounter with the mother Jesus seems to have been unresponsive, even harsh. The reason is that, whether for the healing of a bodily disorder or the cleansing of the soul from sin, success depends very largely upon the faithfulness or sincerity of the aspirant. Thus Jesus puts the woman to the test, applying a mental problem. Triumphantly she solves it and passes the ordeal, even answering him in his own terms with the effective analogy of the dogs. She at once becomes flooded with full intuitional realization. Thereafter the way was clear and the miracle of healing, whether external or interior, was performed symbolically. The daughter possessed of a devil may well have been either obsessed or epileptic. Esoterically she is part of her mother, since all people in allegories personify aspects of the total individuality of man, as also of the universe.

Of all the would-be recipients of the Lord's healing power, only those whose words or condition exemplified totality of surrender—or as the Gospels say "faith"—received miracles of healing. Faith in this purely psychological sense means that the mind is able to rise above the normal limitations of mentality, which are useful in material and purely intellectual matters but a hindrance to illumination by the intuition. In faith the mind can maintain openness and instinctual receptivity in matters beyond the reach of the mind. While this may appear in some cases and to some people to be either simplemindedness or credulity, it can indicate an advanced evolutionary position.

This allegory as well as other parables also describes delicate and subtle mental processes: the duality of the human intellect; the junction or meeting place of the two aspects of the mind; the peculiar and special barrier which exists there known as the "veil," useful and purposeful up to a certain stage of development; and the means whereby that barrier may be passed through. Faith in anyone is a sign that the barrier is wearing thin and that an interchange is already occurring to some extent, though not wholly. The person knows but for a time cannot mentally justify. Even so, in spite of objections, belief or faith is adhered to. Ill health indicates a psychological state under which the illumined condition cannot pass through the barrier and be received by either the argumentative mind or the brain.

The decisive factor in fully opening the portal or gate between the two aspects of mind consists of the actively applied spiritual will. This essential power is personified by the Christ successfully healing the sick. The Dweller-in-the-Innermost projects its ray—the sound of the Master's voice—into the mind;[2] for this influence on high is able to penetrate and open ever more widely the veil between the immortal and mortal self of man.

This is the true healing of the sick by miracles; for in all of the cases recorded in the Gospels it is the *mind* which is sick, whether paralyzed, blind, lame, deaf, dumb, possessed of a devil, or in a metaphorical sense dead. The action of the inward spiritual power (*Atma*) upon the diseased is to override normal mental conditions and limitations. Truly, as the ancient sages spoke, "the mind [the sick one] is the slayer of the real."[3]

Those cities wherein Jesus performed no mighty works because of unbelief refer to those human beings in whom the mind had not yet evolved sufficiently to make them responsive to the touch or word of the divine presence within them. At that stage direct intuitive perception of abstract and spiritual truth is impossible. Allegorically, the Master is not present. Prayer, attending church, and worship are valuable insofar as they aid in this desirable development. When these are followed by the study of philosophy and, still more important, the practice of yoga, the veil may be "rent in twain" even in advance of the evolutionary time. This is portrayed in scripture and myth whenever a being—divine, semi-divine or human—"calls upon the Lord," and this is exactly what the woman of Canaan did. Moreover, she called persistently, refusing to be denied.

The devil in this story simply personifies all the attributes of mind and brain which, largely by materialism, scorn and argument, shut out the light of the intuition. While generally it is the mind which is sick, in the two episodes in which Jesus cast out devils, physical and emotional disorders, deficiencies and excesses may also have contributed to the sickness. Again the true cure is the discovery of, surrender to and invocation of the spiritual Self (the Lord)—the three essentials to successful illumination. Thereafter, false and acquired attributes (the devil) which are untrue to the original nature disappear or are exorcised and driven away.

> Matt. 15:29. And Jesus departed from thence, and came nigh unto the sea of Galilee; and went up into a mountain, and sat down there.
> 30. And great multitudes came unto him, having with them those that were lame, blind, dumb, maimed, and many and cast them down at Jesus' feet; and he healed them:
> 31. Insomuch that the multitude wondered, when they saw the dumb to speak, the maimed to be whole, the lame to walk, and the blind to see: and they glorified the God of Israel.

Evidently, accounts of Jesus's first healings spread throughout the land so that he came to be regarded in a dual guise of teacher and healer. It is not difficult to understand and imagine the consequences of these reports, and the verses under consideration tell of popular response. As he traveled much of the length and breadth of his native land, sick people came themselves or were brought by relatives.

One may also assume that, while the sick received apparently miraculous restoration physically by Jesus out of compassion for their sufferings, greater receptivity to the message which he brought was a compensatory result, bringing about an illumination and clarification of the minds of the sufferers. Thus Jesus is shown as bringing light to the minds of men, particularly of those in darkness. The mentally lame, blind, dumb and maimed were restored to clear mental vision and even illumination by intuition, as personified by the Master himself. If this is true, then, both permanent cures and prevention of future mental ills would have been achieved.

Because of the remarkable spiritual manifestation which occurred at his Baptism, it is to be assumed that Jesus performed his mighty works both in his own person and as vehicle for an Aspect of Deity.

The twenty-ninth verse tells of a withdrawal from the seashores of Galilee and, accompanied by his disciples according to St. John,[4] an ascent to a mountain. Possibly secret wisdom was given them while "upon the mount," whether this elevation is regarded literally or symbolically. In either instance, Jesus evidently followed the custom of all spiritual Teachers of conveying to selected disciples occult knowledge and direct experience of the more spiritual levels of human awareness. The truths verbally conveyed would also be perceived directly because of the sensitized and uplifted conditions into which disciples are raised when in the presence of their Master. The absence of any statement descriptive of events occurring or actions performed on the mountain may well be the result of the imposed secrecy typical of such occasions.

The path of discipleship is beset by many trials, tests and ordeals under which temporary failures mar that perfection of conduct which is the ideal for every disciple. Perhaps the greatest of these dangers arises from remaining but hitherto latent prideful attributes. Very great care is therefore exercised in training disciples and revealing to them power-bestowing knowledge, the possession of which could elevate them above their fellowmen. such knowledge includes the power to perform those seeming miracles of which Jesus himself proved capable. This ability could indeed bring to life certain latent seeds of egoism and so lead to danger, if not failure, upon the path undertaken during a particular incarnation. Such error would not necessarily be final, however, since return to essential humility could always occur, either in the same life or a later one.

These and other considerations may have led Jesus to withdraw to a mountain and there sit with his disciples. Mental withdrawal into an elevated state of consciousness and practice of prolonged contemplation of the divine are among the objectives of an adept Master when teaching disciples.

Matt. 15:32.   Then Jesus called his disciples unto him, and said, I have compassion on the multitude, because they continue with me now three days, and have nothing to eat: and I will not send them away fasting, lest they faint in the way.

33.   And his disciples say unto him, Whence should we have so much bread in the wilderness, as to fill so great a multitude?

34.   And Jesus saith unto them, How many loaves have ye? And they said, Seven, and a few little fishes.

35. And he commanded the multitude to sit down on the ground.

36. And he took the seven loaves and the fishes, and gave thanks, and brake them, and gave to his disciples, and the disciples to the multitude.

37. And they did all eat, and were filled: and they took up of the broken meat that was left seven baskets full.

38. And they that did eat were four thousand men, beside women and children.

39. And he sent away the multitude, and took ship, and came into the coasts of Magdala.

The famous miracle of the duplication and great increase of a small food supply possesses a certain naturalness, since the gathering of a multitude about him, their hunger, his compassion, and its expression by means of a miracle are very likely to have occurred. If the whole account is to be read in the purely historical sense, then it possesses both charm and the element of the wonderful. The element of absurdity is also present in the episode. This plus the introduction of the supernatural into the tale provides ground for its interpretation in the mystical sense. The use of classical symbols supports this view.

The level of his consciousness is indicated by the physical scenery where the miracles occur. Sitting on the grass or ground indicates the physical body of man, and mountains uplifted states of consciousness. The hillside above Galilee, the shores of the lake and the mountains beyond represent the world itself, and those who followed Jesus and were healed and fed by him represent those aspiring souls, awakened and enlivened from within, who have become seekers for light and truth.

The number four suggests the transformation of the spiritual into the material.[5] A "descent" of spiritual power and wisdom from on high into material manifestation to feed four thousand people represents humanity on earth in its physical body, normally restricted to awareness at the physical level, receiving spiritual inspiration. In this case, the multitude had been three days without food in a relative wilderness so that they became hungry. Of these symbols, the wilderness is a state of mental aridity, while hunger indicates that an aspiration for knowledge is aroused. The three days suggest that not only mind but also the heart and the brain—the threefold man——hunger after wisdom and truth.

These latter are introduced into the story by means of their classical symbols. Bread refers to knowledge of truth concerning the underlying principles of divine existence and manifestation in nature and in man, and fish signifies that pure wisdom from the Christ nature which alone can nourish the whole man spiritually.[6] Thus fasting, thus hungering—meaning eager for spiritual wisdom—they were drawn into the presence of a spiritual Teacher, Jesus the Christ. The apparent miracle indicates that possession of wisdom and awakening of the Christ nature are sufficient to provide the necessities for both spiritual and material levels of life. The disciples who were also present indicate a condition of disciplined character.

Again a numerical symbol—seven—is employed by the Evangelist. As heretofore observed, the number seven refers to the sevenfold nature of man and to an advanced phase of development, a stage of unfoldment involving the "higher" triad and the "lower" quaternary. One epoch has come to an end and a new one has begun. Materialism and worldliness have lost their hold. Symbolically, as well as actually, a mountain has been ascended. Knowledge, however great, which is of the earth only has ceased to satisfy the mind.

The whole grouping of symbols suggests arrival at the stage in which the inner spirit has become sufficiently empowered and developed to arouse in the outer man the will to self-discipline and aspiration to acquire wisdom and the power it bestows. While the mass of humanity is as yet far from having attained to this state, numbers of individuals have continued to reach it and set forth upon the great quest for spiritual enlightenment, which is never denied. From within the spiritual soul the needed light shines forth, and the necessary nutriment for mind and heart (bread and fish) is abundantly supplied.

Jesus being responsible for the abundance of food personifies the Christ Indwelling sufficiently evolved to affect the whole fivefold nature of man.[7] His action throughout implies both a condition of highly developed spiritual wisdom, Christlikeness, and its active expression natural in an Adept's conduct of life. The whole episode may also be regarded as encouragement to aspirants concerning progress upon the inward pathway leading to "the measure of the stature of the fullness of Christ;"[8] for the Adept is not only completely sustained from interior, inexhaustible supplies, but also has at his command a spiritual abundance beyond his own needs. He is therefore able to share, and does share, with the world in general (the four thousand) and especially with those who have attained to discipleship.

This superabundance derives, not only from the spiritual Self of man, but also from the Source, the universal spirit-essence with which the Adept is consciously identified. In consequence, when a man discovers his own divine selfhood, the God-presence within him, then the power of the universe and even of the total cosmos is at his disposal. So great is the potential influence of such a highly illumined human being that for safety's sake his potency would only be revealed to humanity under a veil of allegory, as in this case.

Thus read, the incident describes less an event of nearly two thousand years ago than a continuing process, an unfoldment within the soul of man——and even of nature herself. In this sense Jesus, surrounded by his ministering disciples, is always seated upon a high mountain and ever ready to feed all those who have found the world to be as a wilderness, have ascended the mountain, there to receive the ardently sought and strongly desired spiritual wisdom and truth, the food of the soul.

This interpretation does not, however, preclude the possibility of the exercise of adeptic power by Jesus; for the ability to perform the phenomenon of multiplication, as it is technically called, is possessed by every Adept.

Meanwhile, as the immortal story goes on to tell, the Hebrew nation of the times and the scribes, Pharisees and priests who lie in wait to entrap the Lord are living their lives in their own mundane way, all heedless of the beauty and the wonder in their midst in the person of Jesus.

REFERENCES AND NOTES

1. 2 Cor. 3:6.
2. It is noteworthy that in almost all cases this theurgic act is performed by word of mouth or by the power of the word—the influence of the Logos within the soul.
3. H. B. Blavatasky, *The Voice of the Silence,* Fragment I, p. 17.
4. John 6:3.
5. Physical, etheric, emotional and mental.
6. See Hodson, *The Hidden Wisdom in the Holy Bible,* Vol. I, Quest ed., p. 109, for further interpretation of the symbolism of mountains, numbers, bread and fish.
7. See diagram, p. 46.
8. Eph. 4:13.

Chapter Twenty

The visible form of Jesus was not, as some have taught, entirely phantasmal. He was a historical personage, a physical man, some of the incidents of whose life are recorded in the Gospels. However, it will be appreciated that both the Gospels, particularly the Synoptics and St. John, are far more mystical than historical documents. This is the missing idea in all Christian expositions of the gospel story. The accent is erroneously placed upon history when it should be placed upon the mystical Jesus, the chosen vessel, the wonderful young Hebrew around whose life, imperfectly recorded, the whole structure of Christianity is founded. The many passages recording the deeply esoteric teachings of Jesus, including the Sermon on the Mount, are among the precious jewels of wisdom which he bestowed upon mankind in general and especially upon all aspirants to that full spiritual experience and attainment which the story of his life is made to describe. Thus regarded, historicity, important though it is in one sense, gives place entirely to recognition of the priceless pearl of wisdom which the gospel story contains.

Matt. 16:1.   The Pharisees also with the Sadducees came, and tempting, desired him that he would shew them a sign from heaven.

2.   He answered and said unto them, When it is evening, ye say, It will be fair weather: for the sky is red.

3.   And in the morning, It will be foul weather to day: for the sky is red and lowring. O ye hypocrites, ye can discern the face of the sky; but can ye not discern the signs of the times?

4.   A wicked and adulterous generation seeketh after a sign; and there shall no sign be given unto it, but the sign of the prophet Jonas. And he left them, and departed.

The tendency, sometimes perversely sustained, to judge physical matters according to visible exterior indications alone is referred to in these verses. The true causes of the condition of the human race or of any particular country, Jesus informed the inquirers, lie beneath the outer surface and in the hearts and minds of the people. Allegorically, man scans the skies when he should be scanning his own conduct and the motives for his deeds. This, of course, does not apply to disciples who have already learned to study and interpret the secret purposes and clandestine motives of men.

Doubtless the Sadducees and Pharisees were hoping that Jesus would answer them in terms of their inquiry, specially designed to entrap him. Possibly they were also hoping to tempt Jesus into producing some observable occult phenomena, since they had known of the miracles of healing and of the feeding of the multitude. Whatever their purpose, however, they not only failed to entrap Jesus, but his answer demonstrated that, as always, he saw through their veiled designs. In making this clear he also gave them valuable counsel concerning the ways and destinies of men, as the verses indicate.

The reference to the sign of the prophet Jonas may be interpreted as implying that a scapegoat, possibly some public figure, would be found, accused of causing disaster, and executed. Thus Jonas was charged with being responsible for the danger to the ship and cast overboard, just as Jesus himself was to be crucified.

From Jesus's reply it seems evident that a certain decadence had set in among the Jewish nation, and that Jesus, observing this, knew that it would inevitably lead to downfall. The worldliness of mankind at large and the waywardness of unillumined men are well portrayed by the historic incidents which followed. Roman power was at that time both growing and extending. Later under the Emperor Titus, Jerusalem was to fall, the temple to be sacked, and the Hebrew people to be dispersed throughout the world. All this, doubtless, Jesus foresaw, and in his reply unbraided those people who were responsible for the decadence. Indeed, his birth and his mission may well have been so timed as to forewarn, awaken morally and spiritually, and by this means save the Jewish people.

Though this did not result, a great spiritual impulse was nevertheless released. Not only the immediate disciples of Jesus, but countless millions of other people have foresaken worldliness and self-indulgence and set their feet upon the way of holiness in consequence of the message, the mission and still-enduring power which Jesus brought to the world.

Summed up, these four verses may bring a message to all men of all time, which is never to look at externals alone but to perceive, meditate upon and comprehend interior signs as well.

> Matt. 16:5.   And when his disciples were come to the other side, they had forgotten to take bread.
>
> 6.   Then Jesus said unto them, Take heed and beware of the leaven of the Pharisees and of the Sadducees.

Jesus may have brought this teaching more intimately home to his disciples somewhat later on. Bread was probably used by him as symbol for knowledge of truth or spiritual understanding. This fact that the disciples had forgotten to bring bread when they set sail with the Master for Magdala may be interpreted as an allegory of their temporary lack of this quality; for they too were looking at the external aspect of the above incident. Jesus evidently perceived this and warned against the materialistic point of view, which he symbolized as the leaven of the Pharisees and the Sadducees.

Matt. 16:7. And they reasoned among themselves, saying, It is because we have taken no bread.

8. Which when Jesus perceived, he said unto them, O ye of little faith, why reason ye among yourselves, because ye have brought no bread?

9. Do ye not yet understand, neither remember the five loaves of the five thousand, and how many baskets ye took up.

10. Neither the seven loaves of the four thousand, and how many baskets ye took up?

11 How is it that ye do not understand that I spake it not to you concerning bread, that ye should beware of the leaven of the Pharisees and of the Sadducees?

12. Then understood they how that he bade them not beware of the leaven of bread, but of the doctrine of the Pharisees and of the Sadducees.

These verses indicate that mental insight was opened in the disciples and that they discerned the mental and spiritual meaning of bread, leaven and fish, namely, that they were all symbols of knowledge of truth and spiritual wisdom. Herein one may perceive the true mission of those members of the Great Brotherhood of the Adepts, "the Just men made perfect," whenever they visibly visit and teach mankind. They come less to perform wonders—used largely to attract attention from purely material concerns—than to awaken the conscience and the consciousness of mankind to spiritual truths and spiritual values.

Leaven, the yeast which causes dough to rise in the sense in which bakers use the term, is indeed a most appropriate symbol for the secret doctrine —the esoteric wisdom and insight—which reveals hidden truths behind and within the veil of exoteric teaching. In these verses Jesus seems to give the symbol even a thaumaturgic significance, suggesting that the miracle of the feeding of the multitude was performed by means of the knowledge gained from spiritual understanding. Indeed, this is profoundly true. Laws, forces and the intelligences associated with them, as well as the secret knowledge concerning these and their workings and interrelationships, are symbolized aptly by leaven. All so-called phenomena produced by Adepts and their highly developed disciples are actually brought about exactly by these means, namely, knowledge of the secret procedures of nature, and that knowledge directed and correctly applied under the awakened will.

Pharisees and Sadducees, as the disciples are said to have realized, personify the purely exoteric in its traditional and somewhat rigid presentations. The Master warned his disciples against these and through them humanity at large. If these episodes and teachings are interpreted in the human sense, then traditional and encrusted doctrine rigidly adhered to by ecclesiastics represent the tendencies of the formal mind of man. Unleavened bread may be regarded as unsymbolic, literal literature. The Christ personifies that highly intuitive perception which, when sufficiently developed, "leavens" or illumines the intellect of man so that he both understands the literal and comprehends the significance of allegorical teachings.

If the analogy is carried further, the countryside itself represents the bodily man, the multitude and their natural hungers, bodily needs and desires. The disciples represent those same desires refined and transmuted into will, while the Lord Christ refers to the Dweller-in-the-Innermost, which, when active in a man, satisfies both heart and mind, body and soul.

While such use of analogy and metaphor do not readily commend themselves to the formal mind, especially that of purely Western people, those of the East and Near East habitually use such imagery, lightly in normal conversation and deliberately when considering and expounding spiritual truths and spiritual laws. The Gospels reveal that Jesus followed this practice.

> Matt. 16:13.   When Jesus came into the coasts of Caesarea Phillippi, he asked his disciples, saying, Whom do men say that I the Son of man am?
>
> 14.   And they said, Some say that thou art John the Baptist: some, Elias; and others, Jeremias, or one of the prophets.
>
> 15.   He saith unto them, But whom say ye that I am?
>
> 16.   And Simon Peter answered and said, Thou art the Christ, the Son of the living God.

As a literary production, this Gospel reads somewhat as a collection of remembered incidents rather than a connected narrative. Thus, naturally, the moods of Jesus change somewhat abruptly—tender, as when saving and healing; expressive of power when performing "miracles"; condemnatory when rebuking; highly elevated when teaching, as on the Mount; and almost challenging, as in these verses. The authors of the Gospels would seem to have drawn upon an original composed of a collection of many remembered journeyings, visits, differing relationships with people, and the teaching and training of his disciples. The residue must have been pieced together without much regard for relationships in time and place. Thus the verses under consideration are inserted without reference to the preceding passages.

As a divine visitant Jesus would not need to inquire of others of the way in which people were regarding him; for this he would know by his own direct perceptions. These read almost like a part of some ritual of question and answer designed to arouse the intuitive perceptions of his immediate followers.

The first answer suggests much confusion of thought in the minds of the populace. Jesus could not possibly be identified with John the Baptist who was his contemporary. The second answer—that Jesus was a reappearance of Elias, Jeremias or one of the other prophets—implies the Jewish expectation of the coming of a Messiah to usher in a Messianic Age and a knowledge of the doctrine of rebirth.

After this, without assent or denial, even without comment, Jesus addressed the disciples asking them for their opinion. Simon Peter answers almost as one who experienced a sudden spiritual revelation, whose inner perceptions were aroused into heightened activity. Whatever his original reply may have been,the verse expresses his direct knowledge of the real identity of Jesus as more than man, "the Christ, the Son of the living God."

A duality is here proclaimed: that Jesus was Christ, an "anointed one,"[1] an initiate of the Mysteries, and also "the Son," a vehicle on earth for the Second Aspect of the Trinity. Jesus is thus affirmed by Simon Peter to be both the compatriot of them all and a manifestation on earth of the Supreme Deity. He realized that the body of Jesus of Nazareth was frequently occupied by a transcendently wonderful being, a very high initiate member of the Great While Brotherhood of the Adepts. His realization reminds one of the similar expansion of consciousness attained by Thomas, surnamed Didymus.[2] Mary the Mother of Jesus held this same knowledge in her heart, the Annunciation really describing her entry into the elevated state in which the spiritual truth became known.[3] Although exoteric Christianity has neither realized nor recognized the deep significance of the affirmations of Peter and Thomas, they are among the most revealing statements in the four Gospels concerning the real nature of their Master, Jesus "the Christ, the Son of the living God."

Whether or not any or all of the other disciples enjoyed the same experience, or whether Jesus evoked the elevated state in them, is not revealed. The account restricts the proclamation to Simon Peter. However, the scene evoked in the mind as one reads the verses under consideration is quite remarkable. The disciples may have been gathered around their Master upon whom, possibly, there had descended a special radiance from the supreme Light. This may have been visible to them all, and each may have been questioned, despite the absence of any record of the fact. Perchance a form of initiation was being enacted with Jesus as hierophant and Peter as candidate. The question concerning the true nature of the Master and Peter's instantaneous and exalted response may have been due to an elevated state caused by the deliberate application of hierophantic power by Jesus upon Peter, as was customary in the Mysteries of old. While in the literary and historical senses the words used are of importance, as a description of the divine they are of less significance than the mystical experience which they imply.

> Matt. 16:17.   And Jesus answered and said unto him, Blessed art thou, Simon Bar-jona: for flesh and blood hath not revealed it unto thee, but my Father which is in heaven.

The response of Jesus is, in its turn, quite remarkable. Evidently, he receives precisely the answer for which he hoped. He blesses Simon Bar-jona and assures him that his realization of his own true nature comes from spiritual levels of consciousness rather than through the agencies of his eyes and his mind—that the knowledge of his own real identity was bestowed by "My Father Which is in Heaven."

The prophecy which follows must also be carefully considered, the whole remarkable incident standing out, as it were, against the background of the record of his life among the people of his time.

Matt. 16:18. And I say also unto thee, That thou art Peter, and upon this rock I will build my church; and the gates of hell shall not prevail against it.

19. And I will give unto thee the keys of the kingdom of heaven: and whatsoever thou shalt bind on earth shall be bound in heaven: and whatsoever thou shalt loose on earth shall be loosed in heaven.

It is a grave misfortune that this Gospel has been compiled from a number of sources, some of which are imperfectly reproduced. Words and ideas attributed to Jesus were never uttered by him, and even those which are more truly reported contain errors. The difficulty is increased by the intermixing of the cosmic, the mystic and the historical teachings and unexplained transitions from one to another. In consequence, Jesus makes prophetic utterances which were entirely false on the material plane, but entirely true in terms of the elevation of the minds of the disciples and others into the state known as the Christ consciousness.

The continuance of the benediction, which took the form of prophecy, presents certain difficulties as recorded. No church was at that time either in existence or even contemplated as far as the gospel story reveals. Therefore, Peter could hardly have been named the "rock" upon which the supposed church was to be built. As events turned out, however, the prophecy seems to have been fulfilled in a certain limited way, for according to its claims, Peter played his part in the much later founding of the Church of Rome. The tradition has been preserved, and Peter is today venerated as the rock upon which the Christian Church is built. Since this notion still exists, no adversary has been able to destroy it. Nevertheless, modern scholarship as well as history and the Pauline epistles proclaim Paul as the human founder of the Christian faith. In this connection it is of interest to note that Paul never met Jesus physically as far as the confused chronology of the New Testament indicates.

Jesus's promise to Peter of the gift of the keys to the kingdom of heaven is susceptible of several interpretations. The keys themselves refer to knowledge of those underlying principles, causative forces, powers and intelligences by the agency of which the universe is fashioned according to the divine idea. This includes knowledge of the divine order upon which universes rest and by which all objective beings and things—down to the atom itself—fit into an ordained position in the vast conception and manifestation of cosmos. Veritably, such comprehension implies an intellectual possession of the metaphorical "cup of heaven," or the plan and its cyclic expression and fulfillment throughout unending ages.

It is worthy of note that this promise by Jesus to Peter followed his perception of the real nature of his Master. Thus, his self-illumination and spiritual awareness led to intellectual illumination concerning the causes and the courses of all things. The results of initiation, which Peter may have been experiencing, consist severally of a profound spiritual regeneration, an unveiling of the spiritual eyes, so to speak, and an expansion of the intellect into knowledge of causative powers.

The nature of the resultant spiritual and occult faculties may well be allegorically described in the closing sentences of this verse concerning loosing and binding. Certainly they can by no means be accepted in their purely literal reading. The very laws of being and the operation of cause and effect—both fundamental and personal—place very great limitations upon illumined ones in the exercise of their attained powers. No man, however lofty his spiritual stature, can interfere with the basic situations and conditions of either the universe or another human being. If, however, the whole verse is read as descriptive of interior changes and of the harmonious interchange between the outer and the inner Self of an initiate, then the pronouncement may be regarded as perfectly true.

> Matt. 16:20.   Then charged he his disciples that they should tell no man that he was Jesus the Christ.

The suggestion that a ceremony of initiation had been performed in privacy receives some support for this command of Jesus to his disciples. Every initiate into both the Lesser and the Greater Mysteries is asked to take and keep a solemn oath never to reveal the secrets imparted. The great revelation to the disciples referred to here was that the beloved Master was indeed a manifestation on earth of an Aspect of the Supreme Deity, an *Avatar*. They both saw for themselves and were informed by him that through him the power, wisdom and love of the Lord Most High were being poured forth into the world. This, and especially the direct experience of it, is indeed a great and mysterious secret not to be bandied about among the unheeding populace. Even so, the knowledge must have become public, for it was largely because of it that Jesus was condemned.[4]

This outpouring, it may be presumed, was not only on behalf of humanity alone but also for all the kingdoms of nature for which this world is a home. Whenever such a descent of the Godhead through a human being is brought about, a quickening impulse reaches the unfolding life in mineral, plant, animal, human, superhuman and angelic levels.

Throughout the Gospels several such direct revelations and personal discoveries are recorded. The first of these consists of the Annunciation to Mary and her humble acceptance borne of interior realization of its verity.[5] A further experience came to the shepherds, both when with their flocks and when worshipping before the newborn Christ-child, who thus stands for newly attained spiritual illumination and spiritual perception.[6] A third revelation was received by the Magi and was symbolized by their vision of a star and correct interpretation of it as, metaphorically, shining over the Christ Child in Bethlehem, followed by their presence with the holy family.[7] A descent of the Holy Spirit upon Jesus occurred at his Baptism when the heavens opened and sounded forth the great pronouncement that he was an *Avatar*.[8] Peter's direct realization, Mary Magdalene's recognition of Jesus in the garden after his Resurrection and the declaration by Thomas—surnamed

Didymus—in the upper room in which they met[9]—all these constitute veiled references to the spiritual illumination which the presence of Jesus produced in those who drew near to him.

Matt. 16:21.   From that time forth began Jesus to shew unto his disciples, how that he must go unto Jerusalem, and suffer many things of the elders and chief priests and scribes, and be killed, and be raised again the third day.

This prophecy referring to Jesus may also well be read as a reference to the cosmic Life passing through the involutionary phase of its cyclic pilgrimage, reaching death and burial in a rock tomb, followed by the evolutionary arc, allegorically portrayed by the Resurrection, reappearance, and Ascension into heaven in clouds of glory. Jesus may have been making a revelation of this profound truth concerning that spiritual Life and Lord, of which he allowed the disciples to know he was a manifestation. Herein the cosmic and the mystical ingredients in the Gospel story are united. The authors appear to have decided to veil the truth in an allegory of personal imprisonment and death, not only in this verse but in the later chapters of the Gospel.

Matt. 16:22.   Then Peter took him, and began to rebuke him, saying, Be it far from thee, Lord: this shall not be unto thee.

23.   But he turned, and said unto Peter, Get thee behind me, Satan: thou art an offence unto me: for thou savourest not the things that be of God, but those that be of men.

Regarded historically, the two verses provide a natural sequence. Jesus, as a highly developed occultist and mystic, foresaw that his teachings so much ran counter to accepted rabbinical opinion that they were certain to provoke resistance and even assault. In spite of this no other course than fulfillment of his mission at whatever cost was open to him. Highly crystallized orthodoxy, priestly power, and the reduction of religion to mere traditional beliefs and practices had to be shaken if not broken, and Jesus felt himself called to the task. He therefore continued, winning much popular support and even acclaim because of his person, miracles and teachings. The authorities, however, fearing his apparent claim to divine origin and kingship, and the rabbis, foreseeing a weakening of their power and position felt bound to move against him, first covertly and later openly. Mystic power apart, the result could almost have been told on the grounds of reason. Eventually, the people were aroused and stoned him to death, thereafter hanging his body on a tree, according to St. Paul.[10]

Mystically, Jesus also foresaw by precognition both the triumph of temporal power and the ultimate victory of the intellectual freedom and the spiritual influences which he liberated upon the world. Quite probably he was talking these matters over with his disciples and sharing with them his view of his own future as a man. Peter, possibly as spokesman for the group, expostulated. After his recent vision, he was unable to conceive of and bear mentally and emotionally the idea of his Master's death. His protest seems perfectly natural and hardly justifying the severe rebuke which it evoked.

If, however, the symbols of interpretation are applied to the incident, then the interaction between the spiritual intelligence and the formal mind in man is presumably being described. The former is fully illumined by the light of truth and comprehension of law, while the latter tends to argue against and even to deny the outworkings in the physical world, especially concerning matters of an unpleasant, undesirable nature. The analytical mind blended with desire, personified by Peter, seeks to argue against and even denounce as untrue the insights of the intuition. Thus, Peter rebukes Jesus. This break in the process of self-illumination cannot be allowed to prevent its eventual culmination in full understanding, perfect comprehension. In this sense, both the protest and the rebuke which it evoked are descriptive of stages of self-illumination and of interior obstacles to its completion.

This view seems to be more acceptable than a purely natural and historical reading, for the interchange is made to follow far too abruptly after the description of Peter's exaltation of consciousness and the high praise and promise which it evoked from the Master. Indeed, the two episodes are mutually contradictory, while also the condemnation of Peter as comparable to Satan was surely excessive.

Matt. 16:24.   Then said Jesus unto his disciples, If any man will come after me, let him deny himself, and take up his cross, and follow me.

25.   For whosoever will save his life shall lose it: and whosoever will lose his life for my sake shall find it.

As descriptive of an interior mystical experience, Jesus personifies spiritual wisdom, and his presence indicates that this was being attained. In these verses Jesus carries the teaching still further, for in them he describes the attitude of mind which is essential to success.

The phrase "let him take up his cross" refers to a valiant acceptance of the ardors, stresses and strains inseparable from the effective quickening of evolutionary progress, with its concomitant of liquidation of debts incurred by preceding conduct in which self and self-gain at cost to others predominated.[11] Reactions from such conduct, especially that which caused pain and loss to others, must be intelligently accepted and endured. The closing phases of the life of Jesus exemplify this dictum; for the cross which he carried to Golgotha and upon which he was said to be crucified may be regarded as a figurative burden, and his acceptance of it metaphorically descriptive of the voluntary payment of all just debts in order that they may no longer oppose rapid progress to adeptship or Christhood.

The twenty-fifth verse is also a remarkable exposition of that law of the spiritual life under which self-interest, self-desire, self-seeking and all cling- ing to material existence and possessions must be completely outgrown before the transcendent realization affirmed by Jesus, "I and My Father are One," can be experienced. The unit of consciousness which is man must override and outgrow all sense of what might be described as separateness or accentuated individuality before attaining complete mergence in the All, the totality of the spiritual principles and life of the universe. Everthing which hitherto had been associated with the sense of self-separative existence must be outgrown, laid aside, or "lost."

In conveying this central truth to his disciples, Jesus—if his words are correctly reported—refers to himself as a personification of this attitude and its acceptance; for the great ideal of selflessness is an entirely universal necessity and is not limited to Jesus the man. One is reminded of precisely similar injunctions given by the Lord Shri Krishna to Arjuna, which were similarly cast in personal terms even while inculcating the very essence of universality. Interpreted impersonally, the divine Teachers personify universal Life, and their counsel exhorts all men to mergence therein.

Thus the candidate for initiation does not reach the state of complete renunciation of self and of life tainted by self-interest for the sake of the Master. Rather it becomes natural, inevitable and inescapable as the only mode of life.

> Matt. 16:26. For what is a man profited, if he shall gain the whole world, and lose his own soul? or what shall a man give in exchange for his soul?

Jesus here makes a comparison between the temporary and the eternal, the worldly life with its common, often necessary, motive of profit, and the spiritual life with its ideals of selflessness, renunciation and transcendence of desire. The relative values in his eyes are put before the disciples; the worldly life, however materially successful, is of little worth compared with the spiritual whose treasures far outweigh all earthly possessions.

Furthermore, it would appear that Jesus warned against excessive preoccupation with material wealth and the objective of obtaining it. This motive can so preoccupy the mind as to leave no room for the idealistic and spiritual goals of equipoise between the two modes of life with accentuation of the latter. The Master draws the attention of his disciples to a decision which every neophyte must make, namely, the gradual withdrawal of interest from purely objective life and its rewards to the subjective life with its immeasurable riches. Since these are neither visible nor tangible, guidance in making the choice is necessary, especially for beginners. This is in fact the acid test, both of a person's position in evolution—the age of the soul—and of his uttermost sincerity in embarking upon the spiritual life.

In the long series of earthly lives the time at last arrives when the inner Self is sufficiently developed to be able to inspire its successive personalities with the spiritual ideal. During the first life in which this occurs, the physical and personal response may be weak; but as life follows life, the power of the inner Self grows stronger and the mortal personality more responsive to it and to its call to idealism. Ultimately, however, a final choice must be made—and ultimately is made—that worldly possessions are attained for purely practical purposes and never for power, prestige and self-indulgence or ostentation. That pathway is forsaken quite naturally, finally and forever, less by deliberate choice than because no alternative is worth consideration. Jesus was putting these most important considerations before his disciples and doubtless far more, so that they might be unmistakably aware of the unavoidable and essential choice. Fortunately his words are recorded for every aspirant. Wealth as stewardship is permissible. Wealth as an obsessive objective is impermissible; for the former leads to spiritual light and the latter to spiritual darkness.

> Matt. 16:27.   For the Son of man shall come in the glory of his Father with his angels; and then he shall reward every man according to his works.

This deeply occult utterance must carry great weight for every sincere student of occult philosophy. It may be received and regarded from various points of view. The first of these for some will be as historical prophecy or promise of the coming, or rather return, of the Son of God in human form upon earth.

The succession of divine visitations at critical epochs in the life of humanity is destined to continue, the Master said to his disciples. On some future occasion, when the time is ripe and the need is great, the Second Aspect of the Blessed Trinity, the Christos or Son, will again appear before man, assuming visible human form. Again he will teach, give the keynote for a new age, gather around him selfless ones who are capable of discipleship, and train and initiate them so that a new world order may be ushered in. The eyes of the wise will be sufficiently open in the mystical sense to enable them to see, not only his shining radiance, but also the companies of angels who minister unto him, execute his orders and respond to the call of his will.

According to occult ethnology, which teaches of the evolution of both the human body and the condition of the mind which uses it, eventually spiritual perception or intuition will illumine the mind with knowledge of oneness of the Life throughout all creation, the basis for the Brotherhood of Man. This ideal will by then have attained to such command in the hearts and minds of men as to bring about a world government based upon the true family relationship of all men, both interiorly and externally enabling them to coordinate the governments of nations according to the recognized relationship of brotherhood. In this sense also, figuratively, the Son of Man will have appeared in glory upon earth accompanied by the hosts of ministering angels, also perceptible by that time to the more advance members of the human race.

In yet a third way the prophecy is destined to be fulfilled; for the time will also come when not only the more advanced but *almost all* mankind will have attained the "vision splendid," and the underlying principle of unity will have become known, honored and accepted as the sole guide in all human relationships.

In each of these phases of evolution, a certain balancing of cause and effect will have naturally occurred, and in this sense each man is judged according to his needs. A still deeper layer of occult wisdom may be perceived in the great prophetic utterance. Not on this earth but in a very much later period the Monads of men will be gathered into their innate state of oneness. Then they will continue their aeonic unfoldment to still greater heights and depths of knowledge, wisdom and power upon another man-bearing globe. At that time will come both spiritual illumination and a kind of divine shepherding, as if by him who is called the Good Shepherd.

Far off in the future, the real "judging" or assessment or spiritual and intellectual development will tend to provide the best possible conditions for further unfoldments for those in advance of or behind the standard set. The former will be aided in quickly attaining the stature of perfected manhood, while the latter will in due course receive special care and guidance to bring the same attainment nearer in time.

This is the deeply occult truth underlying the misunderstood separation of the sheep from the goats and the casting of the latter into eternal torment——gravely misunderstood indeed, for no such condition or supposed punishment by divine authority was or will ever exist. Every man at each stage of development simply reaps as he has sown. This is the sole authority and arbiter which determines the conditions of the series of lives and the bodies of men.

Such are some—by no means all—of the implications of the words of Jesus, doubtless spoken to his disciples in secret and probably followed by unrecorded commentaries; for only a portion of the secret wisdom which Jesus imparted to his disciples has ever been made available to the public at large.

> Matt. 16:18.   Verily I say unto you, There be some standing here, which shall not taste of death, till they see the Son of man coming in his kingdom.

In this verse, as in all similar statements from inspired writers and teachers, is revealed the difference between purely historical and purely spiritual utterances. When an illumined sage decides to refer to advanced phases of evolution and to their associated experiences in human awareness, he not infrequently uses historical metaphor, describing interior mystical experience in terms of supposed external and historical events. When this is done, a Master is nearly always addressing disciples who know of this method, have heard the teacher use it many times before, and so without difficulty translate the historical into the mystical.

This is one explanation of the profound error into which almost the whole Hebrew nation fell in believing in the immediate arrival of a Messiah who would establish a Messianic Age. The people at large, unaware of these distinctions and this method of teaching, grasp at the promise, the hope, and the expectation of national exaltation in the historical sense, thereby misleading both themselves and others associated with them. This is one answer to the riddle of the Hebrew—indeed every other—expectation of the coming of a Messiah never to be fulfilled; for the prophets who foretold such events were largely referring, not to a historical event, but to the arrival by their disciples—and eventually by mankind—at a "Messianic" state of consciousness. Moreover, in the occult sense these verses describe passage through the great initiations and their associated experiences in consciousness. When entered, this state both externally transfigures and interiorly illumines, so that those in whom it occurs feel filled with glory.

Nevertheless, even in the prophetic sense, mankind will eventually far in the future enter upon world conditions born from a state of consciousness in which the majority of men have become as Messiahs. Race follows race and nation follows nation, each achieving, however gradually, an enlargement and deepening of capacity for spiritual illumination. This will certainly culminate in humanity's entry into both an interior Messiah experience and the consequent establishment of a Messianic Age in the world.

Even though faultily repeated, misreported, taken out of context and included in a Gospel which would be publicly perused, the verse under consideration is profoundly true in its mystical meaning. The very language seems to indicate that the Master had gathered his disciples apart from the populace, had spoken of the pathway of initiation and its successive conditions of consciousness, and revealed that some of them were on the threshold of these experiences. The disciple John "whom Jesus loved" may very well have been such a one, while doubtless there were others whom he succeeded in bringing to the gateway of initiation.

One of the great discoveries as this phase is entered is one's own deathlessness. The initiated man differs from the preinitiate in that he has been, however temporarily at first, united with the eternal spirit which in reality he is. At the onset of the physical death of the body, this knowledge fills his mind and heart, and as his body dies he enters swiftly and directly into mystic union with his everlasting soul, knowing in full illumination and in great exaltation that he is an imperishable unit of the consciousness of the Most High God. The greater the number of initiations achieved before death, the greater the exaltation and realization of deathlessness. This is the meaning of the mystic phrase that "Initiation teaches one how to die."

REFERENCES AND NOTES

1. The use of the word *Christ* as a name rather than a title suggests the later interpolation, since the Greek word *Chrestos* meaning *the Anointed* was not used.
2. John 20:28.
3. Luke 1:46-55, *The Magnificat.*
4. Matt. 26:64, 65.
5. Luke 1:28-38.
6. Luke 2:8-15.
7. Matt. 2:2.
8. Matt. 3:16-17.
9. Mark 9:2, 5; John 21:7, 15; John 20:15-17; John 20:28.
10. Acts 5:30; 10:39.
11. Matt. 5:18; Luke 16:17; Matt. 7:1-2, 12.

Part Nine

**TRANSFIGURATION,
TEACHING AND MIRACLES**

Chapter Twenty-One

Threats and acts of excommunication and the terror evoked by the stated certainty of burning forever after death, affirmed in theological dogmatism, have all contributed to the decision to withdraw the Greater Mysteries from public gaze, and especially from the reach of Christian orthodoxy. This is a tragic and deplorable necessity. Men, women and even very young people (re-born initiates perhaps) are experiencing interior spiritual awakening with little or no guidance in their churches, either in its application to their daily lives, or to its meaning and its pathway to fulfillment.

The emphasis, however, is shifting, and modern man is less and less dependent upon external aid and more and more responsive to interior awakenings and superphysical assistance than in the days of the ancient Mysteries. The adept shepherds of souls secretly aid and even personally appear to certain advanced and illumined human beings. These they conduct to the outer and inner courts and thence to the halls of initiation, still existent and still functioning in both the psychospiritual and the actual material senses. Thus, no one whose evolutionary progress has brought him to candidacy for discipleship and initiation is ever either overlooked or neglected. Those daring and aroused souls who determine upon both self-discovery and the successful search for a spiritual teacher, obliging their personal lives to conform, are assured of the fulfillment of both aspirations, as were certain disciples in the verses that follow.

Matt. 17:1. And after six days Jesus taketh Peter, James and John his brother, and bringeth them up into a high mountain apart,

2. And was transfigured before them; and his face did shine as the sun, and his raiment was white in the light.

3. And behold, there appeared unto them Moses and Elias talking with him.

The almost abrupt change from an account of purely physical, visible, and audible deeds and words into that of mystical experience suggests that this Gospel may have been compiled from several literary sources fitted together as consecutively as possible but with a break in the Gospel narrative. This view is supported by the fact that in other accounts the succession of events is not always the same, even in the Synoptics. The six-day period of the first verse occurs without reference to preceding periods and events which do not include the succession of days. This also suggests either a deliberate omission of intervening events or the absence of information concerning these six days in the life of Christ.

In these verses descriptive of the Transfiguration of Christ, the purely historical record is elevated into an account of the spiritual experience passed through when an illumined state is entered, here by the Christ and, to a lesser degree, by the three disciples. Christ's selection of Peter, James and his brother John for participation in the Transfiguration scene suggests that these three disciples may have attained to varying degrees of enlightenment and were more advanced than the other members of the group. They may have already passed through preceding degrees and were thus permitted to enter the temple where the higher degrees were being celebrated, in order to perceive something of the great event. As recorded by St. Matthew in the apparently simple and certainly brief account, the experiences of Jesus himself are not given, but only those of the three disciples. This could indicate that he ascended to levels of consciousness and passed through an initiatory degree to which they had not yet attained.

The phenomenon of Transfiguration is a recognized experience passed through in the fullness of time while the higher initiations are being conferred.[1] To observers the initiate seems to almost disappear before their eyes, to be replaced by the radiant presence of the exalted spiritual soul. The whole person, even the physical body, appears to shine from within, as Moses is said to have done on Mount Sinai and Jesus on the Mount of Transfiguration.[2] So great is the power being expressed and so brilliant the inner light that even the clothing can appear to be lit up.

These verses also record an interior radiance beyond what is observable to those present. During the initiatory rite here being described in allegory, the center of consciousness of the initiate is united with that of the universe and its presiding Deity. This produces the experience of an intense illumination of the whole nature, as also of empowerment of both the immortal and the mortal selves of the initiate.[3]

Such major interior psychospiritual regenerations and expansions of consciousness are not passed through entirely in solitude. Those who have already attained to them, Adepts, sages of earlier times, are present and watch over the inner immortal Self—freed from its bodily encasement —while these great changes are occurring. At the Nativity of Jesus, for example, these advanced onces are allegorically referred to by the inclusion of the shepherds, one of the titles for the Adept as a shepherd of souls. Here two great Hebrew sages, Moses and Elias, were most probably present and also included in the narrative as personifications of members of the Adept Fraternity.

The "sacred way" which led from the Acropolis in Athens to the temples of iitiation in Eleusis may also be regarded as an external symbol of an interior pathway open to all those who persevere. The initiations bestowed, especially those in the Greater Mysteries, were of the same character as those allegorically described in the New Testament. Furthermore, although veiled in secrecy, these ceremonies are still being enacted in halls and crypts, symbolized by the stable, to which the profane are not granted admission.[4]

Matt. 17:4.   Then answered Peter, and said unto Jesus, Lord, it is good for us to be here: if thou wilt, let us make here three tabernacles; one for thee, and one for Moses, and one for Elias.

5.   While he yet spake, behold, a bright cloud overshadowed them: and behold a voice out of the cloud, which said, This is my beloved Son, in whom I am well pleased; hear ye him.

6.   And when the disciples heard it, they fell on their face, and were sore afraid.

An indirect reference to the custom of establishing centers, temples, or as Peter called them, tabernacles of initiation may be discerned in these verses. The mystical experience which is said to have followed, namely a bright cloud and a voice, doubtless also refer to that interior expansion of consciousness which is produced by passage through the great initiations. The fifth verse may indicate that Jesus himself had successfully achieved this, as the voice of the unnamed speaker, presumably the Lord God, proclaimed this fact.

In Egyptian days the applicant was tested and proven or disproven as ready for initiation. *The Book of the Dead,* at least in certain passages, may thus be read as an allegorical description of initiatory rites, the weighing of the heart against a feather being the test of worthiness, and the voice proclaiming success being that of Tehuti who uttered the words *"Mer Kheru,"* meaning true of voice. This judgment in the hall of the goddess Maat occurred only after the death of the physical body.[5] Entry by the soul into the fields of Aanru may however refer to the attained state of consciousness at which the candidate is metaphorically dead to the attractions and rewards of the worldly life.[6]

Matt. 17:7.   And Jesus came and touched them, and said, Arise, and be not afraid.

8.   And when they had lifted up their eyes, they saw no man, save Jesus only.

The disciples themselves may have been so elevated in consciousness by receipt of the privilege of witnessing the exaltation of Jesus, their Master, that they became temporarily endowed with extrasensory perception. The supernormal sights and sounds thereby revealed to them may well have excited an awe, referred to as fear. After the ceremony or interior experience was concluded, the heightened awareness would tend to be reduced, which, with the visible presence and the touch of Jesus, would restore them to normality.

Matt. 17:9.   And as they came down from the mountain, Jesus charged them, saying, Tell the vision to no man, until the Son of man be risen again from the dead.

The words *mountain, Son of man,* and *risen from the dead,* found in this verse, are fraught with profound significance, particularly in the context of the Transfiguration. The mountain, as has been stated, indicates the exalted state of consciousness of the mystical experience. If correctly translated, the term "Son of man" by which Jesus named himself may indicate one who has arisen from the human kingdom of nature (its "son"), a superhuman being. Since Jesus spoke within the privacy of intimate association and bound the disciples to secrecy, he may well have thus revealed to the chosen three his evolutionary position as an Adept.

The reference to resurrection from the dead may indicate that portion of the mystic experience associated with the next great initiation, allegorically described as crucifixion and resurrection. Those passing through these lofty phases of evolution may thereafter have been permissibly entrusted with knowledge of the Transfiguration. Whether or not this is so, such records as are available indicate that all the initiations in the Ancient Mysteries were shrouded in secrecy. Even today the mystical significance and actual experiences through which the initiate passes remain entirely unknown.

> Matt. 17:10.　And his disciples asked him, saying, Why then say the scribes that Elias must first come?
>
> 　　　　　11.　And Jesus answered and said unto them, Elias truly shall first come, and restore all things.

These two verses appearing almost as interpolations may be regarded from both the mystical and the historical points of view. Historically, it is credibly reported that both Isaiah and John the Baptist preceded and prophesied an event which could be interpreted as the coming of the Messiah, also prophesied by Malachi.[7] Mystically, Elijah and John the Baptist as forerunners who prepared the way of the Lord personify developments and conditions in the consciousness and character of a person who is on the threshold of a major illumination such as an initiation. The voice of conscience has become compellingly powerful, so that the outer nature and conduct of the candidate will have come into complete conformity with spiritual and moral ideals. Thus the prophets personify the powerful influence of the inner man over the outer personality.

> Matt. 17:12.　But I say unto you, That Elias has come already, And they knew him not, but have done unto him whatsoever they listed. Likewise shall also the Son of man suffer of them.[8]
>
> 　　　　　13.　Then the disciples understood that he spake unto them of John the Baptist.

This incident consists of somewhat philosophic instructions by Jesus in answer to questions from the disciples, and a seeming affirmation that the theory of reincarnation definitely applied in the case of Elijah and John the Baptist; for these two men were stated by Jesus to be reincarnations of the same interior spirit, manifestations of the God-Self of Elijah and John.

This seventeenth chapter of the Gospel of St. Matthew is also remarkable in that Jesus is twice made to prophesy his own death. In the twelfth verse

Jesus foretells that he will be submitted to the same treatment as was meted out to John the Baptist. In verses twenty-two and twenty-three, as will be seen later, Jesus foretells his own betrayal, murder and resurrection on the third day. The first forecast was historically inaccurate, in that John the Baptist was imprisoned and beheaded at the whim of a dancing woman. Jesus was, however, put to death. The second prophecy concerning himself was quite true; for the Ressurrection did take place three days after his death upon the Cross.

> Matt. 17:14. And when they were come to the multitude, there came to him a certain man, kneeling down to him, and saying,
>
> 15. Lord, have mercy on my son: for he is lunatic, and sore vexed: for ofttimes he falleth into the fire, and oft into the water.
>
> 16. And I brought him to thy disciples, and they could not cure him.
>
> 17. Then Jesus answered and said, O faithless and perverse generation, how long shall I be with you? how long shall I suffer you? bring him hither to me.
>
> 18. And Jesus rebuked the devil; and he departed out of him: and the child was cured from that very hour.

Though this might have been a case of actual obsession which Jesus, but not his disciples, could exorcise, the narrative may also be read as an allegory describing the correction of a distorted state of mind, the restoration of a temporarily lost mental control. At earlier stages of evolution the outer, mortal personality tends to be out of the control of the immortal Self and therefore mentally and even morally deficient, acting irrationally srom the egoic point of view. In so doing, it not infrequently becomes absorbed in self-gain at the cost of others, even dishonestly, if not cruelly. Such conduct evokes the "adverse" operation of the law of cause and effect and so brings suffering into the personal life.

This condition, as also the tendency to suffer from it, disappears when a certain stage of evolution is attained. Thereupon the Christ principle (personified by Jesus) has become sufficiently developed (Jesus is present) to bring order to the whole life of the personality. The conjoined will power and intuitive perception have become strong enough to cross the bridge into the mortal nature, or to use another simile, the veil between the inner and the outer man is rent or passed through.[9] The mind is then not only correctly oriented concerning worldly matters and the handling of the body and bodily life, but is also illumined by the light of wisdom and directed by full comprehension of the meaning and the purpose of human existence and the ways in which that purpose is naturally fulfilled.

The father who comes to Jesus on behalf of his son is also a significant figure in the story. He personifies the more intellectual aspect of the immortal Self, the abstract intelligence. The disciples in this case represent attributes of the mortal man which though developing, are not yet fully unfolded. In consequence the disciples fail to achieve a cure, apparently earning a rebuke in consequence. However, when with increasing measure, the power, the intuitive wisdom and intellectual insight (Jesus) are brought to bear upon the outer man, the way he conducts himself both in living his life and in his relationship with other men, becomes normalized. Indeed, before the illumined state is entered, so unintelligent, so inordinately selfish and so senselessly cruel can these relationships be that individuals and even nations may justly be described as being possessed of a devil. Only spiritual will and spiritual wisdom conjoined and fully operative, as represented by Jesus the Christ, can render man and nation free of error. At the present phase of racial evolution, many human beings have already passed—and many are now passing—beyond the stages referred to into the increasingly conscious use of the inspired and intuitively illumined abstract intelligence. It is these, the idealists among men, who become the geniuses in many walks of life and the leaders of movements designed to ameliorate the unfortunate general conditions of mankind.

Matt. 17:19. Then came the disciples to Jesus apart, and said, Why could not we cast him out?

20. And Jesus said unto them, Because of your unbelief: for verily I say unto you, If ye have faith as a grain of mustard seed, ye shall say unto this mountain, Remove hence to yonder place; and it shall remove; and nothing shall be impossible unto you.

21. Howbeit this kind goeth not out but by prayer and fasting.

These three verses may be regarded as granting partial insight, if only a glimpse, into the teaching received by a disciple from his Master. The terms *faith* and *mountain,* if correctly translated from the original, may be taken to be metaphorical. Faith in the sense of bestowing occult power implies absolute assuracce founded upon the successful application of the will under repeated tests. Every disciple who has reached a certain phase of development while in direct training under a Master achieves this assurance. The essential factor in success in any theurgic practice consists of the development and effective use of the innermost will force—in Sanskrit *Atma*—which is a manifestation of monadic power. Not only can physical phenomena be produced by the application of this power directed by perfectly clear thought, but both matter and denizens of the superphysical worlds also become obedient to the force of spiritual will.

The term *mountain* may also be regarded as metaphorical, conveying the idea of very considerable influence over both matter and psychological states. The mountain is also a symbol for varying states of consciousness, the summit meaning exaltation, the upper slopes and the foothills referring to the pathway to that state as traversed by contemplation. The base of a mountain and the level ground surrounding it are metaphors which indicate the workaday normal waking state. A trained disciple eventually attains that degree of self-mastery which enables him, not so much to move a mountain, but to transcend material states of awareness.[10] This achieved, both the restoration of those who are mentally deranged and, where necessary, the exorcism of an invading entity are well within the power of the experienced occultist. The episode and the teaching which followed the act of healing may also describe the power and its application to correct one's own interior limitations and errors (sickness), whether due to a psychic disorder or an established misconception.

As part of his training a disciple is encouraged to achieve and maintain self-command, accuracy and realism in both his personal philosophy and his way of daily living. The twenty-first verse indicates both directly and by implication the nature of this self-discipline, namely, that it brings the bodily appetites under complete control and includes a very moderate way of life, particularly where food is concerned.

> Matt. 17:22. And while they abode in Galilee, Jesus said unto them, The Son of man shall be betrayed into the hands of men:
>
> 23. And they shall kill him, and the third day he shall be raised again. And they were exceeding sorry.

Without apparent introduction or reason for the foretelling, Jesus in these verses prophesies his own betrayal, death and Resurrection at the third day. This is reported to have occurred during residence in Galilee when doubtless many private communications were received. The appellation which Jesus applies to himself, "the Son of man,[11]" suggests that he regarded himself as a preordained messenger and also that the adeptic faculty of correct precognition had revealed to him the manner of his death.

Though the young Hebrew teacher and prophet, being still human, would inevitably die naturally the Gnostic tradition favors interpretation figuratively as initiation, when the delusion of self-separateness dies.[12] From this point of view, Jesus, the human vehicle of the divine Wisdom, foresaw, prophesied and then passed through death, Resurrection and Ascension, the overshadowing Christos having withdrawn. The closing remark in the twenty-third verse would seem to indicate the latter conclusion.

While the gospel narrative may thus permissibly be regarded as partly allegorical, those who accept the story in its literal meaning may well find themselves drawn into the charmed circle of Jesus and his chosen disciples whom he had called apart for private instruction.

In purely human terms, Jesus may have been forewarning his disciples of his premature death, perhaps in order that its distressing effect upon them should be reduced to a minimum, particularly since Resurrection was also promised. Naturally the disciples who loved their Master were grieved at the possibility of his premature death.

> Matt. 17:24. And when they were come to Capernaum, they that received tribute money came to Peter, and said, Doth not your master pay tribute?
>
> 25. He saith, Yes. And when he was come into the house, Jesus prevented him, saying, What thinkest thou, Simon? of whom do the kings of the earth take custom or tribute? of their own children, or of strangers?

26. Peter saith unto him, Of strangers. Jesus saith unto him,
Then are the children free.

27. Notwithstanding, lest we should offend them, go thou to
the sea, and cast an hook, and take up the fish that
first cometh up; and when thou hast opened his mouth,
thou shalt find a piece of money: that take, and give unto
them for me and thee.

The juxtaposition in this story of the natural with the miscalled "super-natural," of the material with the spiritual, lifts the narrative out of the realm of history and takes it into that of revelation by symbol and allegory. Even though the power to perform the apparent miracle exactly as narrated in these verses is possessed by every Adept, such a method of obtaining the tribute money would be intricate and moreover involve the impermissible, unnecessary exercise of occult power, the practice of cruelty, and the killing of a sentient creature. Since these acts are not usually performed by fully spiritualized people, and since the episode itself is of doubtful validity, and existence of an underlying message beneath and within the narrative may justly be inferred.

The fish appears in many places in the world's great allegorical literature. Vaivasvata Manu was guided through the great dangers of the "flood" by the Lord Vishnu in the form of a fish.[13] Jesus, as manifestation in human form of the Christos, chose his disciples from fishermen, fed the multitude with a few fishes, obtained tribute money from within a fish, and aided his disciples to obtain a miraculous draft of fishes in water previously fished without avail. The fish, moreover, is associated in world scriptures with the Second Aspect of the Trinity, and so with the life-preserving and wisdom-bestowing attributes of the Deity indwelling in the universe of man.[14] Place should ideally be left for the exercise of this function of the Life-principle in human affairs and also for the receipt of direct guidance therefrom. If this is done, then both of the stories related in these verses may indicate that even the necessities for living will become available. This idea is very important for all mankind, and especially for modern man who has so greatly accustomed himself to turn outward to obtain the necessities for both his intellectual and his material life.

REFERENCES AND NOTES

1. Transfiguration—see Hodson, *Hidden Wisdom,* Vol. 1, pp. 226-7.
2. Exod. 34:29-30.
3. See *The Minor Works of St. Teresa* (of Avila) and *St. Clare and Her Order.*
4. See Hodson, *Hidden Wisdom,* Vol. 1, Pts. 5-6.
5. Maat is the incarnation of Truth and Justice.
6. Aanru, the immortality of the blessed.
7. Isa. 10:17; John 1:27; Mal. 3.
8. Elias, the same as Elijah.
9. Matt. 27:51.

10. See Hodson, *The Pathway to Perfection.*

11. Possibly meaning, of humanity.

12. See C.W. King, *The Gnostics and Their Remains.*

13. See Hodson, *Hidden Wisdom,* Vol. 1, p. 65.

14. See *ibid.,* Vol. 1, p. 109.

Chapter Twenty-two

It is almost inevitable that changes, additions and omissions may have substantially altered the actual story of the life of Christ. No one wrote at the time, least of all Jesus. Nevertheless, much that bears the mark of true greatness in the person and teachings of the Master has come down to mankind through both canonical and apocryphal "books." This chapter contains one of the great jewels of scriptural literature, not only in the Bible and the New Testament, but in the whole volume of received teaching concerning the way of the spiritual life.

Matt. 18:1.　At the same time came the disciples unto Jesus, saying, Who is the greatest in the kingdom of heaven?

2.　And Jesus called a little child unto him, and set him in the midst of them,

3.　And said, Verily I say unto you, Except ye be converted, and become as little children, ye shall not enter into the kingdom of heaven.

4.　Whosoever therefore shall humble himself as this little child, the same is greatest in the kingdom of heaven.

The question that the disciples asked of their Master and his reported answer would appear to deal with two entirely different levels of existence, which he referred to as heaven and of earth. The disciples may have been debating among themselves as to which of their number was the greatest or the most highly evolved. Jesus answered in both purely human terms (childhood) and in reference to a mystical state of consciousness (childlikeness). Admittedly, the practical men or women of affairs cannot live their lives like helpless little children. Wise and conservative planning, careful provision for family and state, and a certain long view into the future must necessarily have their places in human thinking and human life, whether exoteric or esoteric, man or disciple.

In the fourth verse, however, Jesus definitely advances the ideal of a certain childlikeness, its adoption and practice as essential to progress and supreme position in the kingdom of heaven, presumably meaning on the path of discipleship. This signifies the character should be simple, straightforward, spontaneous and open. Humility is taught as a supreme virtue, not the pharisaically assumed humbleness of a man with his eye upon observers, but rather the utterly true and direct humility of one who is conscious of his or her faults and limitations. Such total absence of pridefulness is evidence of clear-eyed recognition of evolutionary stature, of capacities developed and of those which as yet are not unfolded.

However, due and proper self-appraisal are far from being the only ingredients of meekness, for such could hardly be described as childlike. True humility is an innate quality of a person of advanced stature, of a developed human being in whom instinctively and perfectly naturally the virtue of genuine and sincere modesty is deeply established and unthinkingly expressed. Spiritual Teachers throughout all ages have similarly inculcated this ideal as a touchstone and test of greatness, particularly concerning hope and assurance of progress and fulfillment in the spiritual way of life. It is therefore particularly applicable to discipleship.

> Matt. 18:5.   And whoso shall receive one such little child in my name receiveth me.

In this verse as on other occasions, the Master identifies himself with all mankind. He implies the treatment meted out to another human being of whatever age and walk in life is actually and veritably meted unto him, the Lord Jesus Christ. In this verse, however, not an adult but a child is taken as an example, conforming with the previous answer.

The phrase to *become as little children* might perhaps be regarded as a reference to the doctrine of reincarnation, but in the present context may more properly be applied to those who have become spiritually reborn and in that sense are as little children, whatever the age of the body. These have experienced the inward Nativity for which St. Paul yearned for his converts. Such ones have dedicated their whole being to the life of discipleship, have begun life anew—*ab initio*—as initiates. In the eyes of Jesus, they were far greater than anyone whose life is lived amid supposed pomp and glory of worldly wealth and attainment. All these have to be renounced, which is a perfectly natural process because these outward signs have been assessed at their true value. Indeed, they appear as nothing compared with interior illumination and the far greater riches of perfect wisdom and compassionate love.

> Matt. 18:6.   But whoso shall offend one of these little ones which believe in me, it were better for him that a millstone were hanged about his neck, and that he were drowned in the depth of the sea.
>
> 7.   Woe unto the world because of offences! for it must needs be that offences come; but woe to that man by whom the offence cometh!

A purely literal reading of this verse would suggest extravagance of attitude. However, this reply is assuredly one of the true *logia* of Jesus, a revelation in very truth of a profound principle, if it is read as counsel in the spiritual life. When the terms *little one* and *child* are applied to those newly entered therein, then understatement rather than exaggeration might possibly be assumed. Precious beyond price—to the whole human race in its progress toward its true objective of spirituality—are those genuine and sincere idealists in whom a spiritual rebirth has occurred, for these are the hope of the world. These awakening idealists aspire both to serve their fellow men and to achieve the spiritualization of their whole lives. It is they and they alone who may by example and by precept lift humanity out of its self-degradation, its indescribable cruelties to animals and fellow men, and its ruthless individualism.

Throughout this whole passage, deeply significant as it would appear to be, another law is also being expounded: the law of cause and effect. Terrible indeed, said Jesus, is the reaction upon those nations and individuals who destroy—whether psychologically, physically, or both—the "little ones which believe in me" (are spiritually illumined), and so render as naught their further progress in the particular life when enlightenment came to them. In modern times, and especially in the present era of advances in science, technology, and intercommunication, there are those who are all too ready to scoff at purely spiritual and objectively undemonstrable ideas and ideals. Such scoffers can—and all too often do—turn newly inspired and dedicated men and women away from their chosen mental and physical way of life. In addition, humanity is deprived of the presence of the spiritually illumined ones and their ministrations by voice, pen, and personal example. While realism can be valuable and newly acquired knowledge must become so firmly established as to be impregnable, idealists can be especially vulnerable in the early days after mystical illumination and true and deep conversion. Unfortunately, there do exist among men certain kinds of people who take an almost devilish pleasure in such attacks, and it is against these and their conduct that Jesus may have been giving warning.

In the seventh verse the emphasis is changed from the little ones to the world to all mankind. The utterances of Jesus recorded in this verse show him as warning humanity against actions which give offence under impersonal law, by which the experiences of all men are decided.

> Matt. 18:8. Wherefore if thy hand or thy foot offend thee, cut them off, and cast them from thee: it is better for thee to enter into life halt or maimed, rather than having two hands or two feet to be cast into everlasting fire.
>
> 9. And if thine eye offend thee, pluck it out, and cast it from thee: it is better for thee to enter into life with one eye, rather than having two eyes to be cast into hell fire.

The drastic nature of these injunctions, and particularly the references to parts of the body—surely not to be read literally—suggest that they apply especially to the life of discipleship, the Way of the Cross. This view would appear to be supported by the opening statement of this chapter which indicates that Jesus is not addressing the people at large, but rather his own chosen disciples. Clearly the words of the Master do not refer directly to parts of the human body such as the eyes and the hands, but were mentioned rather as symbols for parts of human nature in general.

In this voluntarily chosen mode of thinking and living, totality of self-purification and the adoption of the highest moral standards are essential to progress on that steep and narrow way. Truly, is it called in Eastern philosophy "the razor-edged path;" for psychological, mental and even physical dangers threaten those who would mistakenly attempt to achieve self-purification in motive, word and deed while still granting to themselves former indulgences and sensual gratifications. Terrible indeed may be the fate of one who, having adopted the ideal of childlike purity, spontaneity and personal humility, later becomes a victim of the lust for power and pride of place. His downfall is utterly certain, and this has unfortunate effects upon those influenced by such a failure. As before mentioned, injury or temptation to those who have embarked upon a purely spiritual way of living is a deeply serious crime, certain to be followed by equally serious "punishment" or suffering. All great teachers have similarly warned aspirants to the spiritual way of life of these dangers, and history supports the warnings.

The words *hell-fire* may be similarly interpreted as descriptive of the acute and long-continued suffering which the above-mentioned harmful conduct will inevitably bring upon those who perform it. Occult philosophy finds no place for the existence of a perpetually burning superphysical fire into which sinners may be cast after death. Fire is a physical element which could not possibly burn those who, on release from their bodies, are vestured in non-physical vehicles; for such would be an absurdity. The whole, then, is a metaphorical way of teaching, easily understood by trained disciples.

Matt. 18:10.   Take heed that ye despise not one of these little ones; for I say unto you, That in heaven their angels do always behold the face of my Father which is in heaven.

In answering the question of the disciples as to who was greatest in the kingdom of heaven, Jesus had drawn from those about him a little child. The verses under consideration may therefore be read as referring only to children and as giving warning of the very adverse reactions under law to harmful actions against "these little ones." However as already suggested, this title also signifies those newly initiated, and so, metaphorically, "youthful" in the initiate life.

The warning applies especially to attacks upon the mind, such as the attempted destruction of intuitively acquired knowledge of the laws of life in general and of the spiritual life in particular, as for example, by cunningly and even divisively worded attacks upon admittedly other worldly rules of the spiritual way of life. Such injuries can indeed be most harmful in their effects, especially when the victim loses faith in himself, his newly chosen way of life, and in his aspirations to reach swiftly the evolutionary heights in order more effectively to minister to his fellowmen.

Room must be lift for imperfections—possibly quite grave ones—in the traditional accounts. This might apply to the tenth verse in which Jesus, when talking of children, makes references to their angels. The term may be taken to apply to that part of human nature referred to by St. Paul as the "spiritual body,"[1] for this body abides perpetually in realized unity with the Godhead. This is true of every human being, not only of children. Such a statement may be regarded as strengthening the idea that Jesus was using the terms *child* and *little one* in a special sense, namely, that of a human being newly touched in his mortal body by the power, light and fire of the Inner Ruler Immortal or the Monad.

Matt. 18:11.   For the Son of man is come to save that which was lost.

12.   How think ye? if a man have an hundred sheep, and one of them be gone astray, doth he not leave the ninety and nine, and goeth into the mountains, and seeketh that which is gone astray?

13.   And if so be that he find it, verily I say unto you, he rejoiceth more of that sheep, than of the ninety and nine which went not astray.

14.   Even so it is not the will of your Father which is in heaven, that one of these little ones should perish.

Many of Jesus' hearers were doubtless farmers and hardsmen and naturally responsive to such references. The shepherds would be deeply concerned for a single lost sheep and devote all their efforts to its discovery and return to the fold. Similarly, Jesus taught, every human being is as dear to Deity as a lost sheep to its shepherd. Such an utterance must have brought the idea of the Godhead very close to those who listened, thus conveying to them a deeply comforting sense of divine protection and of God's paternal love for all mankind.

In verse fourteen, however, Jesus again refers to the little ones as if it were their safety which evoked so great a concern, here again suggesting a special meaning for that term. In a certain measure the future of mankind —especially the spiritual and cultural future—can be profoundly affected by their successful progress in the spiritual life. Every single one who finds the Master, kneels at his feet and is taught by him, helps onward each of his brother men.

The Mystery Schools and temples of ancient days, their initiate members and their hierophants were ever open to such aspirants. These were then led by their Masters up to and through the gateway of initiation—a new beginning indeed. Thence they ascended that steep and narrow way which leads to adeptship and ultimately to the office of hierophant, not only in the temples of old, but also, if more secretly, those of today.

Although always secret as far as their revealed Mystery teaching was concerned, such spiritual centers did exist and could be found and entered, even from the most ancient days. Indeed, long before the time of Christ, during his time and ever since—and so today—the pathway, the spiritual Teacher, the outer and the inner courts leading to the adytum have always existed, can be and are found and passed through to the great goal. The condition of both body and consciousness of those who thus found and successfully trod the ancient way are necessarily extremely sensitive. Aspirants are, in consequence, very vulnerable—mentally, psychically and physically—to disturbance during the delicate process of self-establishment in the new mode of life. This is partly the reason for the seclusion which was granted within the Mystery Schools and ashrams of the world to those who could profit by it.

> Matt. 18:15. Moreover if thy brother shall trespass against thee, go and tell him his fault between thee and him alone: if he shall hear thee, thou hast gained thy brother.
>
> 16. But if he will not hear thee, then take with thee one or two more, that in the mouth of two or three witnesses every word may be established.
>
> 17. And if he shall neglect to hear them, tell it unto the church: but if he neglect to hear the church, let him be unto thee as a heathen man and a publican.

These verses also are susceptible of interpretation as guidance to his disciples and so, one may add, to disciples of all times. In an even wider sense, the instruction contains wise directions for the restoration and the maintenance of harmonious relationships with all one's fellowmen. A form of mental self-training is thus described, namely, ease and harmony in human relationships. The disciple must acquire these abilities, especially if living away from the ashram. He must everywhere be a man of peace which is founded upon justice and truth. Hence the almost legal nature of the guidance given.

While being trained, the disciple is submitted to various interior and psychological strains; for the life-energy of the Master is being shared with him, and the associated energies are playing upon the nervous systems and related areas in the etheric and subtler vehicles. His own spiritual Self is also directing both ideas and forces into the four personal vehicles when the body is awake, and the pervading psychic atmosphere and thought streams play upon him from without. These three, to which certain astrological forces may be added, all tend to set up in the disciple conditions of stress. In consequence, and in order to obtain the greatest benefit from these energies, the disciple needs greatly to attain and maintain associations which shall be as free from disturbance as possible. Quarrels and the distress caused by them, and also by deep misunderstandings, can definitely hinder and delay the disciple's progress and development, as he is especially susceptible to them while under training. For these and other reasons, doubtless, Jesus gave the advice contained in these verses.

> Matt. 18:18. Verily I say unto you, Whatsoever ye shall bind on earth shall be bound in heaven: and whatsoever ye shall loose on earth shall be loosed in heaven.

This verse may be similarly interpreted. The instruction can hardly be taken literally, since heaven is not a place. Rather is it a state in which happiness mounting to bliss founded upon perfect freedom is a permanent and unalterable condition. In consequence nothing can ever be bound in heaven, a fundamental characteristic of which is unlimited and eternal freedom and the forever unfading happiness of conscious union with God. This verse must, therefore, be read as a possible description of the powers which are developed in a disciple within whom psychic and occult forces and agencies (such as invading entities) are brought under complete control. The interrelationship is affirmed between the outer and the inner circumstances and states of being of the disciple under training.

Matt. 18:19.   Again I say unto you, That if two of you shall agree on earth as touching any thing that they shall ask, it shall be done for them of my Father which is in heaven.

This view gains force if this nineteenth verse is similarly interpreted: the term *my Father which is in heaven* referring to the divine Self of the disciple whose powers are enhanced by realization of unity with the divine presence (Father) within all nature and all beings.

Matt. 18:20.   For where two or three are gathered together in my name, there am I in the midst of them.

If, as is to be assumed, the pronoun *my* is a correct translation from the original, then Jesus here identifies himself with the omnipresent power, life and consciousness of the Supreme Deity or Father. Thus, theurgic powers are affirmed to be attainable, not only by calling upon God, but by functioning in the name of Jesus the Christ. Even if only two or three people thus gather in his name, he is assuredly present, and this may be taken to mean not only mystically but operationally or in terms of occult power. These assurances were doubtless given to the disciples in order to support and sustain them after their Master had been physically withdrawn from them by his death. This consolation was also granted in order to uphold them whenever doubt and danger should assail them.

The teachings of occult philosophy include this idea, affirming that every fully accepted and initiated disciple is intimately linked with his Master, more particularly at spiritual and intellectual levels. Because of this close association which is arranged by the Adept, he can readily reach and use the disciple as a channel for both ideas and influences, while the disciple in his turn has open access to the Master.

The most intimate of these unifications concerns chiefly the divine Self—inmost Being, or the Father which is in heaven—of both Master and disciple. The intimacy implied in verses eighteen, nineteen and twenty suggest that they belong to a series of instructions which Jesus, like every adept Master, gave secretly to his disciples at different times.

Matt. 18:21.   Then came Peter to him, and said, Lord, how oft shall my brother sin against me, and I forgive him? till seven times?

22.   Jesus saith unto him, I say not unto thee, Until seven times: but, Until seventy times seven.

Herein, the exceedingly lofty extension of the virtue of forgiveness is presented. This ideal was fully exemplified in the recorded life of Jesus, who may be seen as the veritable incarnation of forgiving love. Even while enduring such great agony as crucifixion could inflict, Jesus asked the Father to forgive those who crucified him because they did not realize what they were doing by applying such torture upon him. Thus, for the disciples and even all humanity, a great and truly Christian ideal was inculcated through the apostle Peter.

The virtue is, however, almost superhuman, and its acceptance could hardly be expected of the populace in general, although the disciples were called upon to apply it to their lives. Such instruction may, therefore, again be regarded as having been given in secret as part of the training by the Master of his disciples. Even in the conduct of business, the disciple must act with greater leniency than would be permissible for a non-disciple.

These words would be so arresting as to have been indelibly imprinted upon the memories of both those who heard them directly and others to whom they were later repeated. When, therefore, the life story of Jesus came to be written, these teachings among many others would be recalled and included in the gospel story.

Matt. 18:23. Therefore is the kingdom of heaven likened unto a certain king, which would take account of his servants.

24. And when he had begun to reckon, one was brought unto him, which owed him ten thousand talents.

25. But forasmuch as he had not to pay, his lord commanded him to be sold, and his wife, and children, and all that he had, and payment to be made.

26. The servant therefore fell down, and worshipped him, saying, Lord, have patience with me, and I will pay thee all.

27. Then the lord of that servant was moved with compassion, and loosed him, and forgave him the debt.

28. But the same servant went out, and found one of his fellow servants, which owed him a hundred pence: and he laid hands on him, and took him by the throat, saying, Pay me that thou owest.

29. And his fellow servant fell down at his feet, and besought him, saying, Have patience with me, and I will pay thee all.

30. And he would not: but went and cast him into prison, till he should pay the debt.

31. So when his fellow servants saw what was done, they were very sorry, and came and told unto their lord all that was done.

32. Then his lord, after that he had called him, said unto him, O thou wicked servant, I forgave thee all that debt, because thou desiredst me:

33. Shouldest not thou also have had compassion on thy fellow servant, even as I had pity on thee?

34. And his lord was wroth, and delivered him to the tormentors, till he should pay all that was due unto him.

35. So likewise shall my heavenly Father do also unto you, if ye from your hearts forgive not every one his brother their trespasses.

While the ideal of forgiving is in this parable applied to business debts, the results of failure to forgive—torture by "the tormentors"—are presented as most serious indeed. Herein is a further example of the method of instruction by means of an allegory in which an unacceptable idea is advanced. The economic and industrial machinery upon which humanity relies for the just and safe procedures of civilization would break down if all debts were forgiven and those who failed to do so were delivered to the torturers. The difficulty of giving assent to the idea is made even greater when in the last verse it is stated that God himself will inflict the torture.

One possible interpretation of the allegory may be that Jesus is giving his disciples direct instruction concerning the existence and operation of the law of cause and effect. As before stated, he himself enunciated this doctrine most forcibly as did the apostle Paul.[2] The same teaching is to be found in the Old Testament, as in all world scriptures.

Occult philosophy also includes this doctrine but, except by the deliberate use of allegory, it does not teach of any personal agency, divine or human, as responsible for its enforcement. On the contrary, the principle of cause and effect is presented as an automatic, impersonal sequence. This process is said to be based upon an equally impersonal procedure of harmonization or attunement which is ceaselessly in operation throughout the universe. The deification of the procedure, if correctly attributable to Jesus, may have been his way of indicating the universality and inevitability of the law under which appropriate reaction follows every action. St. Paul also introduces his enunciation of the doctrine by a reference to the omniscience of Diety, saying, "God is not mocked."[3]

REFERENCES AND NOTES

1. Cor. 15:44.
2. Matt. 5:18; Luke 16:17; Matt. 7:1-2; Matt. 7:12; Matt. 5:7; Gal. 6:7.
3. Gal. 6:7.

Chapter Twenty-three

The story of the travels of Jesus throughout the countryside, sea and lake shores of Galilee is continued. The Sea of Galilee with its surrounding hills, notably those to the west of the lake, were left behind, doubtless in order to reach another group of people. As in so many places, those who were sick were brought to him, and in his divine compassion and power he healed them.

He also taught both the populace and his disciples such truth as they could receive. While a spiritual teacher must give heed to the conditions and needs of those living normal lives, Jesus here chiefly addresses those who have become inwardly moved to seek and adopt the spiritual way of life—as indeed do all great Teachers. Thus, almost all his utterances are intended to serve as guidance for those who have become aspirants to discipleship.

> Matt. 19:1. And it came to pass, that when Jesus had finished these sayings, he departed from Galilee, and came into the coasts of Judea beyond Jordan;
>
> 2. And great multitudes followed him; and he healed them there.
>
> 3. The Pharisees also came unto him, tempting him, and saying unto him, Is it lawful for a man to put away his wife for every cause?
>
> 4 And he answered and said unto them, Have ye not read, that he which made them at the beginning made them male and female.
>
> 5. And said, For this cause shall a man leave father and mother, and shall cleave to his wife: and they twain shall be one flesh?
>
> 6. Wherefore they are no more twain, but one flesh. What therefore God hath joined together, let not man put assunder.

In a land and at a time when women were granted only inferior status, Jesus spoke in support of them, particularly stressing their equality in the eyes of God as well as their unity with their husbands. This passage has been accepted as authentic and applied to the institution of marriage by one Christian denomination for which it is still regarded as a final decree. Although thus accepted at that time by a very large number of modern Christians as an ideal for the protection of women, these words of Jesus are today both challenged and disregarded.

Matt. 19:7.   They say unto him, Why did Moses then command to give a writing of divorcement, and to put her away?

8.   He saith unto them, Moses because of the hardness of your hearts suffered you to put away your wives: but from the beginning it was not so.

9.   And I say unto you, Whosoever shall put away his wife, except for fornication, and shall marry another, committeth adultery: and whoso marrieth her which is put away doth commit adultery.

10.   His disciples say unto him, If the case of the man be so with his wife, it is not good to marry.

11.   But he said unto them, All men cannot receive this saying, save they to whom it is given.

12.   For there are some eunuchs, which were so born from their mother's womb: and there are some eunuchs, which were made eunuchs of men: and there be eunuchs, which have made themselves eunuchs for the kingdom of heaven's sake. He that is able to receive it, let him recieve it.

The reference to "eunuchs for the kingdom of heaven's sake" is definitely directed toward disciples at a certain advanced stage of progress where chastity and continence become necessary ideals and practices. They render themselves as eunuchs, meaning sexless, the thought and the aspiration of a disciple having become centered in and devoted to a purely spiritual mode of life. Through meditation and sublimation they have entered upon a phase of development at which sexual desire has been transcended.

Matt. 19:13.   Then were there brought unto him little children, that he should put his hands on them, and pray: and the disciples rebuked them.

14.   But Jesus said, Suffer little children, and forbid them not, to come unto me: for of such is the kingdom of heaven.

15.   And he laid his hands on them, and departed thence.

Doubtless, out of a natural love for them and what they represent, Jesus was always especially tender toward children. As is elsewhere apparent, he also used certain attributes of children as examples to all who would enter the higher life, the kingdom of heaven. The disciples, not as yet being sufficiently advanced, failed to perceive either the inner intent or the affection for children characteristic of their Master, and so tried to protect him from undue intrusion.

Certain awakened ones newly "reborn" may also be the children alluded to by Jesus. Association with a great teacher and the touch of his hands upon them can be of great value particularly in aiding them to resume the mode of life which they had followed in former incarnations.

The advanced human being, whether high initiate or Adept, becomes naturally possessed of a certain charm which is felt by many. Thus, we read of Jesus that multitudes of people came to him and followed him. Among these, children are likely to have been especially responsive to this almost indefinable influence, and so fearlessly drew near him from whom it radiated.

Strangely, for such is the perversity of human nature, upon some people the opposite effect is produced. These are the world's haters, their hate being chiefly born of resentment against those who are both "greater" than themselves and who inculcate a morality which they are either not willing or not able to accept. For those, the attractiveness which draws many people toward a teacher also becomes a source of offense; hence their hostility. Those who arrive in the world before it is ready for them, who exert an influence and hold up a moral ideal higher than is normal for the time, inevitably evoke this adverse response. If they continue in their self-chosen task, then the enmity increases until its effects actually become mortal, as proved to be true in the case of Jesus.

> Matt. 19:16. And, behold, one came and said unto him, Good Master, what good thing shall I do, that I may have eternal life?
>
> 17. And he said unto him, Why callest thou me good? there is none good but one, that is God: but if thou wilt enter into life, keep the commandments.
>
> 18. He saith unto him, Which? Jesus said, Thou shall do no murder, Thou shall not commit adultery, Thou shalt not steal, Thou shall not bear false witness.
>
> 19. Honour thy father and thy mother: and, Thou shalt love thy neighbour as thyself.

The distinction becomes clear between the normal, worldly life, however honorable, and life of discipleship as is later shown in the twenty-first verse. A rich young ruler came to Jesus seeking guidance in entering upon and living the spiritual life.[1] At first, Jesus with that impersonality and realistic modesty characteristic of truly great men, disclaimed all right to be called good. Doubtless unerringly discerning the stature and attitude toward life of the young man, he counsels him to keep the commandments; namely, to be a good citizen and a good Jew. In response to a request for specific guidance, Jesus thus refers him to certain of the Ten Commandments.

> Matt. 19:20. The young man saith unto him, All these things have I kept from my youth up: what lack I yet?

In asking this question, the young man displayed both the earnestness of his purpose and an intuitive sense that there existed an inner life with its own special rules governing progress toward what he at first named *eternal life*

> Matt. 19:21. Jesus said unto him, If thou wilt be perfect, go and sell that thou hast, and give to the poor, and thou shalt have treasure in heaven and come and follow me.

Small though this verse is, it yet contains almost the whole essence of both the philosophy and the attitude toward life which must be accepted in order successfully to embark upon and to live a purely spiritual mode of existence.

The first sentence, "If thou wilt be perfect," refers to a doctrine found to be almost universal in world religions namely, the perfectibility of man. The underlying purpose for living as evolution to the stature of perfected manhood or Christhood is enunciated.[2] When this goal is attained—and even as it is closely approached—the devotee discovers his true identity as a spiritual being, and therefore his deathlessness in eternal life. The pathway of swift attainment is also proclaimed and its essential mental outlook and resultant conduct described. On this path, dispassion concerning worldly possessions is naturally developed. Should the aspirant be rich, his riches are shared always with reasonable discrimination, and he himself serves as but a steward.

Matt. 19:22.   But when the young man heard that saying, he went away sorrowful: for he had great possessions.

The young man was evidently still self-imprisoned by both his possessions and his characteristic of possessiveness. In consequence he was at that time unable to follow the guidance given and to adopt the attitude of stewardship of his riches which Jesus had inculcated. The statement that he was sorrowful may perhaps indicate reason for the assumption that the turning away was regretted and so not likely to be final. The fact that he had actually sought the Master's guidance and even pressed for a statement of the true and binding conditions for the attainment of eternal life would seem to show that he was already advanced beyond the stature of the people amid whom he lived. Perhaps of him it might be said that he was awakening but not yet fully awake. The chick was pecking at the shell of its egg, but it had not yet escaped from it. Fortunately, the opportunity will occur again, if not in the same life, then in a future incarnation when success will be attained.

Indeed, if one may so comment, judged by their conduct, many of the members of the human race do not appear even to be pecking at the shell as yet, being still—and necessarily perhaps—self-ruled, self-willed and acquisitive. Idealists abound, however, and eventually a majority will both peck at and liberate themselves from the shell of self, whereupon—and not before —peace will reign on this war-torn earth.

Matt. 19:23.   Then said Jesus unto his disciples, Verily I say unto you, That a rich man shall hardly enter into the kingdom of heaven.

24.   And again I say unto you, It is easier for a camel to go through the eye of a needle, than for a rich man to enter into the kingdom of God.

The terms *kindom of heaven* and the *kingdom of God* have at least a dual significance, particularly when used in relation to the incident of the young ruler. First, a heaven-like state while conscious in the causal body, in which the immortal Self of man normally abides, is indicated. The second term refers to evolutionary stature at which—by contemplation of the divine—the mortal man is able to enter or attain this state. As elsewhere enunciated, this is an interior condition of consciousness and not an eternal realm. This mystical elevation can, and in varying degree not infrequently does, occur to certain people quite spontaneously. By the practice of one or other of the arts or by continual contemplation people can become susceptible to this communion with the inner Self. Thereupon genius renders the artist immortal among his fellowmen, while the devotee, by perpetual, exploratory consideration of divine ideas and attributes, opens up for himself a pathway into the consciousness of his own God-Self. The artist need not necessarily be a particularly evolved individual, but the mystic may legitimately be so described; for the impulse to override the limitations of ordinary sensory and mental awareness and discover truth can effectively arise only in a well-developed man or woman.

The incident of the rich young ruler led to Jesus's affirmation that intense possessiveness, especially applied to worldly goods, is a state of mind in which the selflessness characteristic of the so-called kingdom of heaven cannot be attained and enjoyed. Possessiveness implies that the natural mental attitude of "I and mine" forms a barrier to entry into a state in which these distinctions can have no place whatever. Universality of consciousness implies the complete absence of self-separateness, grasping acquisitiveness and so possessiveness. This is the state in which the divine Self of man, the "God which worketh in you,"[3] perpetually abides. These words of Jesus refer to this fact, the Master employing his remarkable faculty of teaching by analogy and simile as he enunciates this truth.

It is worthy of note that the Master neither spoke adversely of the young man nor condemned him. Here, as elsewhere in the Gospels, some of the teaching is inapplicable to those still living a worldly life. He merely stated the law governing self-spiritualization and then enlightened his disciples—for whom such teachings are primarily intended—concerning its operation. Doubtless he left each one to apply the teaching to and for himself.

> Matt. 19:25. When his disciples heard it, they were exceedingly amazed, saying, Who then can be saved?
>
> 26. But Jesus beheld them, and said unto them, With men this is impossible; but with God all things are possible.

In the first of these two verses, the disciples appear to equate the experience of entering into the kingdom of God with being saved. If poverty is essential to this attainment as they apparently thought, then a very great number of people fail to provide this essential condition. If the text is a correct record of the conversation, then the disciples were in error in concluding from their Master's words that men and women still living in the world could never be saved. However, if entering the kingdom of God refers to a mystical state of consciousness, an exaltation of spirit, then union with God can be attained whatever one's circumstances.

The word *saved* on the other hand, if correctly translated from the original, would seem to imply the eternal security of soul for those who have been saved according to the orthodox religious point of view. However, Jesus would here seem to have corrected this error by explaining that while the mortal man must die, the eternal Self lives forever beyond all theological notions of eternal damnation, and in this sense is saved. If this view is adopted, then the remark that "with God all things are possible" refers not only to a supposedly external Deity, but far more to the God-Self within every man (the two being One) the presence of which assures his salvation throughout eternity.[4]

The essential difference between the divine Self of man in its spiritual body[5] and the temporary physical garment of flesh and bone which serves as a vehicle at the level of physical daily life is a theme upon which spiritual teachers have laid great stress and given profound significance. Disciples are trained, not only to distinguish mentally between the two, but by specially designed, ordered and regularly performed meditation, to know the difference by direct experience. It is surely this mystical awareness of one's own divinity which is stated by Jesus to be so difficult of attainment by one who is still held prisoner by, still in the grip of, worldly possessions.

It seems reasonable to assume that the brief statement made by Jesus concerning this supremely important fact about man was only a part of the instruction given, the remainder having been either forgotten by the compilers or left unreported, perhaps because of its deeply esoteric nature; for without this fuller instruction, the disciples would be justly "amazed" by the sweeping affirmation made by their Master.

Matt. 19:27. Then answered Peter and said unto him, Behold, we have forsaken all, and followed thee; what shall we have therefore?

28. And Jesus said unto them, Verily I say unto you, That ye which have followed me, in the regeneration when the Son of man shall sit in the throne of his glory, ye also shall sit upon twelve thrones, judging the twelve tribes of Israel.

The apparent expostulation by Peter—or perhaps the natural question—is appropriate to his occasionally impetuous temperament. The reassuring answer may reasonably be regarded as having been couched in highly metaphorical terms.

The word *regeneration* is of special interest; for if it is applied to the whole nature of man, it signifies effective response by the mortal man to an interior, irresistible and spiritual awakening. The result of such an experience is to bring about a complete reversal of character from selfishness to selflessness, as also complete change of the motive for living as applied to daily life. As mystics proclaim, this conversion is one of the indications of readiness for discipleship, while its complete application to daily life is the eventual result of successful response to the Master's instruction.

While the Adept fully comprehends nations, tribes and individuals, he judges them rarely if ever, since he is able to perceive the evolutionary trend and position which bring people to act in certain ways, whether adverse or beneficial. He can and often does know completely both the spiritual stature and the resultant physical conduct of those whom it is his duty to assist. This knowledge ensures that his help is so wisely given as to prove effective under almost all circumstances.

The use of the idea of thrones and enthronement to describe the ultimate height of spiritual attainment and "reward" would seem to be drawn from a symbology prevalent among the Jewish people of those day; for there developed among them what has been called *throne mysticism.*

Matt. 19:29. And every one that hath forsaken houses, or brethren, or sisters, or father, or mother, or wife, or children, or lands, for my name's sake, shall receive an hundredfold, and shall inherit everlasting life.

30. But many that are first shall be last; and the last shall be the first.

If the highest degree of interior illumination is to be attained, then uttermost and complete renunciation of all external relationships with the world which could bind the devotee must be transcended. In a statement recorded by Luke, Jesus also said, "If any man come to me, and hate not his father, and mother, and wife, and children, and brethren, and sisters, yea, and his own life also, he cannot be my disciple."[6] In order to demonstrate this complete one-pointedness and totality of surrender, Abraham on Mt. Moriah prepared to sacrifice his son Isaac, but an angel stayed his hand.[7] A substitute was then found—a ram in a thicket. Jesus himself, however, admitted his own mother, Mary Magdalene and his disciples to the closest relationships and showed deep concern for his mother's future after his death; for while still alive on the Cross he commended her to John, the disciple whom he loved, and John to his mother. Evidently then, the extreme nature of the demand for total single-mindedness—even at the expense of family and friends—is to be regarded as analogy and metaphor, and not entirely in the strictly literal sense. In these verses this necessity is metaphorically translated into the realm of a human being's private life, responsibilities and duties.

Another justification for a metaphorical reading is that a strictly literal adoption of the Lord's statement of necessities and of the extreme demands upon the devotee would lead to conduct which would be the very opposite of another essential quality. This is tenderness, extending to a deep concern, not only for the members of one's family, but for the happiness of all creatures and all men.

The disciples—perhaps with the exception of Judas—are all presented as having no obligatory relationships of any kind. They were, in consequence, able literally to forsake all and follow the Master. They may therefore be seen as prototypes of those human beings whose evolutionary position and way of life (*dharma* and *karma*) have provided for them the freedom to adopt a wholly spiritual way of life. This enabled them to assume the role of mendicant or monk, whether within or without an institution, and so to be completely free to follow that path which had become their heart's true desire. One's thought is thus led to the true significance of the universal ideal found throughout Eastern and Western mysticism. It may be described as arrival at that state at which one is able to fulfill quite naturally the sole and overriding longing of the heart. The mind aspires and the will determines to find a spiritual Teacher and under his guidance to reach the evolutionary heights as soon and as fully as possible. This eventually becomes the one absorbing and even driving idea which dominates the mind and heart of the individual who is thus spiritually awakened. Thus viewed, the searching and even "cruel" (in the purely physical sense) demands made by Jesus in this twenty-ninth verse refer, not to artificial response to the orders of another, but far more to a state of consciousness. As the *Upanishad* says, "there is no other path at all to go."

The final verse of this chapter may be read as descriptive of the difference between purely temporal and spiritual appreciation of value. The one whom the worldly mind may value most and regard as first, when spiritually examined and evaluated, may be found to be less worthy than someone hitherto regarded as of lesser significance. A younger disciple might, for example, eventually outstrip his fellows, while an older and apparently more evolved brother could exhibit weaknesses which place him on a lower rung of the evolutionary ladder.

REFERENCES AND NOTES

1. Luke 18:18.
2. Eph. 4:13; Heb. 12:23.
3. Phil. 2:13.
4. See Hodson, *Lecture Notes,* Vol. I, pp. 18-19.
5. Spiritual body. See Glossary—Ego.
6. Luke 14:26.
7. Gen. 22:1-13.

Chapter Twenty-four

It is highly probable that Jesus had more than twelve disciples. Perhaps the number varied from time to time throughout his ministry. There must have been advanced souls in his day, as now, who, to use Brother Lawrence's description, were "possessed by the gale of the Holy Spirit" and in consequence went "forward even in sleep." These verses are primarily addressed to them.

Matt. 20:1.   For the kingdom of heaven is like unto a man that is an householder, which went out early in the morning to hire labourers into his vineyard.

2.   And when he had agreed with the labourers for a penny a day, he sent them into his vineyard.

3.   And he went out about the third hour, and saw others standing idle in the marketplace,

4.   And said unto them; Go ye also into the vineyard, and whatsoever is right I will give you. And they went their way.

5.   Again he went out about the sixth and ninth hour, and did likewise.

6.   And about the eleventh hour he went out, and found others standing idle, and saith unto them, Why stand ye here all the day idle?

7.   They say unto him, Because no man hath hired us. He saith unto them, Go ye also into the vineyard: and whatsoever is right, that shall ye receive.

8.   So when even was come, the lord of the vineyard saith unto his steward, Call the labourers, and give them their hire, beginning from the last unto the first.

9.   And when they came that were hired about the eleventh hour, they received every man a penny.

10.   But when the first came, they supposed that they should have received more; and they likewise received every man a penny.

11. And when they had received it, they murmured against the good man of the house.

12. Saying, These last have wrought but one hour, and thou hast made them equal unto us, which have borne the burden and heat of the day.

13. But he answered one of them, and said, Friend, I do thee no wrong: didst not thou agree with me for a penny?

14. Take that thine is, and go thy way: I will give unto this last, even as unto thee.

15. Is it not lawful for me to do what I will with mine own? Is thine eye evil, because I am good?

16. So the last shall be first, and the first last: for many be called, but few chosen.

It is not my purpose here to write a homily on this parable, which is peculiar to say the least if it is correctly remembered, reported and written down. An underlying purpose may, however, be discerned, namely, to distinguish between the purely temporal sense of propriety and fairness on the one hand and an ultimate spiritual fact on the other; for these two—the transient and the eternal—at first sight do not always appear to agree. On the outward plane the laborers were not unreasonable in their demands, even though as servants they perhaps had little right coercively to express them, as their master pointed out. He in his turn, as he said, did have a perfect right to spend his own money in his own way.

If, however, the parable, particularly its closing verse, is applied spiritually, then Jesus in this parable makes clear that neither evolutionary position nor readiness for discipleship (period of employment) depend alone upon that which is purely temporal and external; for the wellsprings of the spiritual life-force are deeply hidden within the depths of the human soul, and only a true seer or prophet can correctly either discern them or appraise their degree of activity. These may have little or no relationship to years or hours of work in the outer world. Disconcertingly at times, as almost every disciple eventually learns, a silent observer or a newly joined member of a group of aspirants may prove to be spiritually more evolved and more fully awakened—and so be worthy of at least equal "wages" (spiritual advancement)—than even the oldest and most faithful disciple. In the field of education, for example, it is not years of service alone, but far more academic attainment, which decides appointment.

The Master, however, sees unerringly into the very depth of the nature of every aspirant who comes within his purview, observes his or her true stature, whether long ago accepted or newly arrived, and accords to each the place which is justly due. While this may not seem quite fair to those without discernment, this acknowledgment of spiritual status is perfectly just according to appraisal by true values. Doubtless the Master enlarged upon these standards of judgment, not only on the recorded occasion, but frequently as he trained his disciples to judge by spiritual values and not only by material ones.

Matt. 20:17.   And Jesus going up to Jerusalem took the twelve disciples apart in the way, and said unto them,

      18.   Behold, we go up to Jerusalem; and the Son of man shall be betrayed unto the chief priests and unto the scribes, and they shall condemn him to death.

      19.   And shall deliver him to the Gentiles to mock, and to scourge, and to crucify him: and the third day he shall rise again.

Here also Jesus is said to be speaking to his disciples alone, whether they were twelve or, more likely, a greater number, a possiblity explored earlier. Jesus may have actually spoken these prophetic words. As recorded, they are taken to refer solely to himself as a historical personage. Nevertheless, the possibility does exist that a deeper metaphorical meaning was taught, particularly as some of the sayings of Jesus which the compilers have placed in this chapter were spoken to the disciples during times of that almost sacred intimacy which is characteristic of the relationship between Master and disciple.

A dual purpose may perhaps be discerned for the foreshadowing of the dramatic and tragic experiences so soon to be passed through. One of these purposes may have been to prepare the disciples' minds before the events actually occurred, in order to reduce pain and shock. The other purpose may have been to reveal certain truths and to indicate certain ordeals through which, not only Jesus, but also everyone approaching adeptship in advance of the race must inevitably pass in successive initiations into the Greater Mysteries. This reading is supported by the reply of Jesus to the sons of Zebedee, later to be considered.

In advance of the fuller interpretations which will follow, it may be here said that all disciples must be prepared to pass through ordeals comparable to those through which Jesus passed. Only those of very strong spirit would be able to pay the price demanded by nature for forcing her hand, as it were, and reaching perfection before the appointed time, this under normal circumstances being decided by the cyclic laws which govern racial evolution. In these sayings, then, Jesus was presenting himself to the disciples as an exemplar for all who, in the words of St. Paul, "come unto a perfect man, unto the measure of the stature of the fullness of Christ."[1]

Students of mystical Christianity may be interested in the theory of docetism advanced in the early Christian Church.[2] This idea sprang from the same roots as Gnosticism and was characteristically upheld by the Gnostic writers. This was a theory that Christ during his life had, not a real or natural body, but only an apparent or phantom one. The origin of the heresy is to be found in Greek, Alexandrine and oriental speculations about the essential impurity of matter. The doctrine differed much in its complexion according to the points of view adopted by different authors. The more thoroughgoing docetists assumed the position that Christ was born without any participation in matter and that all the acts and sufferings of his human life, including the Crucifixion, were only apparent. They attributed to Christ an ethereal and heavenly instead of a truly human body, and they varied in their estimation of the share this body had in the real actions and sufferings of Christ.

Matt. 20:20. Then came to him the mother of Zebedee's children with her sons, worshipping him, and desiring a certain thing of him.

21. And he said unto her, What wilt thou? She saith unto him, Grant that these my two sons may sit, one on thy right hand, and the other on the left, in thy kingdom.

22. But Jesus answered and said, Ye know not what ye ask. Are ye able to drink of the cup that I shall drink of, and to be baptized with the baptism that I am baptized with? They say unto him, We are able.

23. And he saith unto them, Ye shall drink indeed of my cup, and be baptized with the baptism that I am baptized with: but to sit on my right hand, and on my left, is not mine to give, but it shall be given to them for whom it is prepared of my Father.

As in the case of the rich young ruler who sought aid from Jesus in living the spiritual life,[3] the two sons of Zebedee are also submitted to the "acid test" of preparedness, both to embark upon that great endeavor and to sustain it to the triumphant end. In answer, Jesus refers to himself as an example of the qualities of character needed and to his own experience as indicating the ordeals through which every such aspirant must be prepared to pass. In so doing Jesus elevates his own foreknown and forthcoming Passion far above the limitations of his own personality in time and space, and presents it as a universal experience.

Unlike the rich young ruler who felt himself unable at that time in his life to meet the tests, particularly that of dispassion, the sons of Zebedee proclaimed their own readiness. They were immediately received into the company of the disciples of Jesus. He pointed out to them, however, that the position which they would ultimately occupy was not of his choosing but would depend upon the choice of his Father, who may be regarded as either eternal law or the divine presence within both himself and each of the new disciples.

Of interest to the student of symbology are the recorded facts that it was the *mother* of the sons of Zebedee who presented them to Jesus and made the request on their behalf, and the *wife* of Pilate who sent him a warning by messenger concerning his dealings with Jesus.[4] These two, as well as other women in the Bible, may be regarded as personifications of that spiritual intuitiveness which develops in advanced people and enables them to perceive both ideas and opportunities which might otherwise not be grasped, particularly by the analytical mind. Two different phases of development are portrayed. The mother of the sons of Zebedee was actually present. This signifies that the developed intuitive faculty had become an actual and active power, a *present* guide, in the life of the aspirant, enabling him to perceive, meditate upon, and respond to the awakened Christ principle within. Pilate, on the other hand, as his described conduct shows, was not so far advanced.

Allegorically his wife was *absent* and, in consequence, had to send her warning—actually an interior, intuitive misgiving—by means of a messenger. If the story is thus interpreted, the formal mind unfortunately was not sufficiently developed to be responsive to the intuitive message.

Matt. 20:24. And when the ten heard it, they were moved with indignation against the two brethren.

25. But Jesus called them unto him, and said, Ye know that the princes of the Gentiles exercise dominion over them, and they that are great exercise authority upon them.

26. But it shall not be so among you: but whosoever will be great among you, let him be your minister;

27. And whosoever will be chief among you, let him be your servant:

In the incident under examination when two entirely unknown and apparently unqualified men were admitted, a not unnatural resentment was felt by the members of the specially chosen group of the disciples. The human tendency to be unjust under such circumstances is also revealed; for the disciples temporarily forgot that the two sons of Zebedee had in fact been submitted to the severest tests—readiness to persist in the arduous life demanded of a disciple in the face of all ordeals including martyrdom. Jesus thereupon used the incident—as also does the inner Self of a developed man—to draw attention to those true values by which the worthiness of a human being may be measured. As the rightly famous verses indicate, this consists both of readiness to serve humbly and impersonally and of the act of service itself when carried out in that spirit. Dedicated selfless service performed without thought of recompense is indeed both a trustworthy revelation of human character and the true test of greatness, as Jesus is reported to have said.

Matt. 20:29. And as they departed from Jericho, a great multitude followed him.

30. And, behold, two blind men sitting by the way side, when they heard that Jesus passed by, cried out, saying, Have mercy on us, O Lord, thou son of David.

31. And the multitude rebuked them, because they should hold their peace: but they cried the more, saying, Have mercy on us, O Lord, thou son of David.

32. And Jesus stood still, and called them, and said, what will ye that I shall do unto you?

33. They say unto him, Lord, that our eyes may be opened.

34. So Jesus had compassion on them, and touched their eyes: and immediately their eyes received sight, and they followed him.

The period of time has evidently passed during which Jesus and his disciples were alone together and during which in privacy he had guided and illumined them. The receipt of instructions concerning humility, self-subordination and service to others brought to a close this part of their life together. Henceforth, Jesus was to move onward and meet the dire events preceding the great tragedy. Even so, whether as a great Adept who was visiting the world of men or as a mystic power awakening in man, he performed the "miracle" of the restoration of the sight of the two blind men.

The verses may be read literally as a description of the exercise of adeptic power for the two men who hitherto had been blind. Mystically regarded, a dramatic change of consciousness may be implied. The two men personify two parts of one individual on whose behalf spiritual vision is to be restored. At first, the mind and the heart are unillumined, unenlightened by any gleam of spiritual light, any capacity for intuitive wisdom or implicit insight—a blindness indeed. Since all men are evolving, in the course of time as the Christ nature unfolds such blindness naturally decreases. When the time is ripe, the divine presence and power of the inner Self, personified by Jesus, "enters upon the scene" of daily life and brings to bear the miraculous, mystic power by which mind and heart are illumined and the outer man becomes inwardly enlightened. Symbolically, sight is restored by the apparently chance presence of a spiritual Teacher. The "blindness" of a materialistic and self-centered mentality almost immediately disappears. The understanding heart and the open eye replace the preceding visionlessness of both heart and mind. Mental darkness diminishes and a selfishness changes into loving-kindness.

This reading is somewhat supported by the cries and supplications of the two blind men. Prayers for spiritual light, knowledge and understanding are similarly uttered, or rather arise spontaneously, within both darkened mind and heart.

Even after this change has occurred, a further step forward in evolution may be taken. This, as earlier described, is marked by a profound dissatisfaction with existing limitations, a determination to override them, to find a spiritual Teacher and, ever afterward, to follow in his footsteps. This view is supported by descriptions of the subsequent conduct of those in receipt of such ministrations. In the present case, it is stated that the two blind men whose sight had been restored by Jesus "followed him."

REFERENCES AND NOTES

1. Eph. 4:13.
2. Docetism, *Gr.,* "to seem."
3. Matt. 19:16-23.
4. Matt. 27:19.

PART TEN

**PALM SUNDAY
CLEANSING OF THE TEMPLE
FURTHER PARABLES
BETRAYAL**

Chapter Twenty-Five

The triumph which is celebrated on Palm Sunday is later followed by the disaster—however figurative—of the Crucifixion. Jesus, having twice foretold his premature death, prepares to go forward into these two opposing experiences, namely, acclamation and rejection. Furthermore, he is described as going quite willingly and without any recorded preparations for either his defense or his escape. In the eyes of the populace and of his mother, disciples and friends, he goes to defamation, torture and most cruel death after prolonged agony. Events, even the minor ones, were foreknown and so irrevocable. For Jesus there is to be no escape, and naught can and will prevent the prophecy from being wholly fulfilled. To his own knowledge, however, after the dread ordeal he is to rise again and later ascend into heaven.

Such is the portion of the narrative of the life of Jesus which begins with this twenty-first chapter. As thus related in bare outline, it is hardly credible. Furthermore, it lacks in any historical support whatever, save the admittedly interpolated sentences in Josephus.[1] The story may therefore be examined as an allegory with Jesus representing the one divine Life as it pursues both the normal pathway (in his childhood) and also that of hastened attainment (Baptism and onward). Thus viewed, the minor and major events in the recorded life of Jesus are seen to be replete with significance for the student, and with guidance for all those spiritually awakened and inwardly regenerated human beings who decide to follow him and tread the Way of the Cross.

> Matt. 21:1. And when they drew nigh unto Jerusalem, and were come to Bethphage, unto the mount of Olives, then sent Jesus two disciples,
>
> 2. Saying unto them, Go into the village over against you, and straightway ye shall find an ass tied, and a colt with her: loose them, and bring them unto me.
>
> 3. And if any may say ought to you, ye shall say, The Lord hath need of them; and straightway he will send them.

In symbolic writings such apparent incongruities as knowledge of the existence of the ass and the colt and of the owner's willingness to send them to a completely unknown person and for unknown purposes are sometimes included as a clue to the existence of any underlying meaning. Read literally, this story can be accepted as history only if one believes in the exercise of supernormal powers and development of the faculty of supernormal vision, which is naturally acquired as the narrow way is trodden. Surprising though the faculty and the results of its use might seem, they are nevertheless quite normal for one approaching adeptship, which Jesus is portrayed as doing, particularly in these later episoees of his life which culminate in his Ascension to the right hand of God.

The ass is a symbol of both proverbial stubbornness and, when tamed, placid and uncomplaining obedience to the orders of its master. The fourfold mortal nature of man—mind, emotion, vitality and flesh—stubbornly resistant to the will of the spiritual triad within,[2] becomes entirely obedient to the razor-edged path. The glyph of Jesus riding upon the ass aptly portrays this situation. Thus, viewed as an allegory, the story is found to be perfectly reasonable.

Matt. 21:4.   All this was done, that it might be fulfilled which was spoken by the prophet, saying,

5.   Tell ye the daughter of Sion, Behold, thy King cometh unto thee, meek, and sitting upon an ass, and a colt the foal of an ass.

If read literally, the story now tends to become even more difficult to accept, since it postulates the supposed fulfillment in this extraordinary way of prophecies uttered centuries earlier. The text bears the marks os either an interpolated account or a fortuitous and not very convincing reference to an ancient foretelling.[3]

The virtue of humility is, however, fully and very instructively exemplified in the lowly manner in which Jesus chose to enter the city of Jerusalem. According to worldly standards (but not those of the spiritual life) this is indeed remarkable in view of his own statement of his true Selfhood as the Son of God and the affirmation by St. John that he was actually a manifestation in human form of the creative Logos or Word.[4] This attribute of humility is also portrayed by the birth of the Son of God as a feeble, helpless, wholly dependent little babe; while in the Sermon on the Mount, Jesus himself stressed the importance—doubtless to disciples and aspirants to that relationship—of humility and meekness.[5]

Matt. 21:6.   And the disciples went, and did as Jesus commanded them.

7.   And brought the ass, and the colt, and put on them their clothes, and they set him thereon.

Foreknowledge of the incident concerning the ass imposes an element of incredibility. Scriptural statements which may seem to offend reason, logic, common sense and even propriety may be viewed, not only as errors into which authors have fallen, but also—and sometimes even far more—as signposts pointing to deeply occult revelations. Such passages may even be regarded as deliberately placed in religious writings in order, by means of mental shock, to direct attention to a hidden meaning in both the story as a whole and the particular part which is allegorically symbolic. It is even proclaimed, as by Maimonides and others, that this practice is deliberate. Intellectually or morally offensive portions may thus both conceal and also draw the reader's attention to profoundly significant ideas, thus hidden because potentially power-bestowing.

Indeed, critics might say that the complete story upon which Palm Sunday is founded is so extraordinary as to be almost beyond belief—precisely, perhaps, the effect at which the author aimed.

> Matt. 21:8. And a very great multitude spread their garments in the way; others cut down branches from the trees, and strawed them in the way.
>
> 9. And the multitudes that went before, and that followed, cried, saying, Hosanna to the son of David: Blessed is he that cometh in the name of the Lord; Hosanna in the Highest.

Viewed allegorically, a walled city such as Jerusalem conveys at least two ideas. First, a city symbolizes the world of men. Jesus is represented as voluntarily entering the world in order to teach mankind, to heal those who were sick, and to look for and select here and there those who displayed readiness for discipleship. In this, Jesus follows in the footsteps of every spiritual Teacher and of every *Avatar* or "descent" of the Godhead into a human body for the enlightenment of mankind.

In a more deeply symbolical and mystical reading, the city of Jerusalem, with its walls, its temple and its very ancient tradition, is emblematic of a spiritual state of awareness, that of the hidden or "walled" Self of man, the inner sanctuary in which the Holy of Holies is enshrined. In order to know this, one must be lowly, meek, and humble in heart and mind as was Jesus; for then only may the resistant matter of the mortal vehicles (the ass) be completely overcome or obedient. The rejoicing and acclamation of the inhabitants of the city refer to the exalted state of consciousness and the spiritual bliss which are experienced as the uplifted condition is entered upon.

> Matt. 21:10. And when he was come into Jerusalem, all the city was moved, saying, Who is this?
>
> 11. And the multitude said, This is Jesus the prophet of Nazareth of Galilee.
>
> 12. And Jesus went into the temple of God, and cast out all them that sold and bought in the temple, and overthrew the tables of the money-changers, and the seats of them that sold doves.
>
> 13. And said unto them, It is written, My house shall be called the house of prayer; but ye have made it a den of thieves.

While this action would be quite typical of a great reformer as previously discussed, it is susceptible of interpretation as a further description of the state of consciousness and of the purified way of life typical of all spiritually advanced human beings, as also of those aspiring to that state. It also has cosmic significance.

As a material object, the temple is conceived, designed and built as a place of seclusion wherein the devout may worship the Deity. As a symbol, the temple represents the shaped, material aspect of the universe and the physical and superphysical bodies of man. The temple is a symbol of the universe and man, both of which are profoundly complex, each being built and used according to the numerical design underlying its formal construction.[6]

The universe is sevenfold, as also is man, each being temple-like in that they contain a shrine, an altar and conditions under which the divine Dweller within may become manifest to those who worship therein. The fourfold shape of the temple, mosque and church is a fourfold material container for altar and shrine. This represents the field of divine Self-manifestation in the universe. In man it signifies his powers of thought, emotion, physical action and that vital fluid which is both bodily preserver and halfway house, as it were, between the dense and the less dense bodies. In his higher nature man also contains an "enshrined" divine spirit-essence, an altar-like connecting link between his innermost and outermost manifestations. The divine presence is established in the Holy of Holies—variously expressed as the Ark of the Covenant, the Robe of Glory, *Augoeides*[7] or Causal Body, or the Shekinah or Glory of the Lord[8] shining on the Mercy Seat between the Cherubin.[9] The temple, thus described, is seen as an appropriate symbol designed upon that numerical order which is the basis for the manifestation of the divine within material forms and the assurance of increasingly closer communication between them. Here symbolically both spiritual awareness and concern with the necessities of physical life can and do become conjoined. This union and communion is dependent upon the purity of motive and conduct, since impurities obstruct the interrelationship.

Those who enter and those who officiate in the temple personify qualities of character of the mortal man. If spiritual advancement is to be attained and the kingdom of heaven to be entered, then the whole lower nature of man must be purified, and the tendency to desecrate the approaches to the divine within by commercialism born of cupidity must be wholly eradicated. When, however, the Christ nature in man becomes sufficiently evolved and externally manifest in the outer self, cleansing by its power naturally takes place. Such mystical awakening and its effects are portrayed in the story of the cleansing of the temple of Jerusalem by Jesus Christ, present and active within it.

Man it is, then, who desecrates the temple of his body, emotions and mind, while the awakened and increasingly potent divine power which is his real existence, in one of its effects upon him, purifies the temple of his outermost mortal nature. Thus, in the sacred stories of the life of Jesus, history and allegory are blended into one account susceptible of being read in both its temporal and eternal significance.

In the literal sense when tragically, the desecration continues for too long a period and when worship becomes increasingly traditional and rigid, the temple loses its validity, even as temples crumble to the ground or are destroyed by conquerors. These outer, temporal falls are less a tragic loss than a means for the liberation of man from hidebound, tortuous theology, the evils of priestcraft, and domination of human beings by threats of extermination in the hereafter.

> Matt. 21:14.   And the blind and the lame came to him in the temple: and he healed them.

Only after self-purification can the essential self-healing of all mystical sickness—tendencies toward the commissions of unspiritual conduct—be achieved. Thus, symbolically, with the resultant spiritualization and coordination of all the parts of man, Jesus healed those who were sick, whether of mind, body, or both.

> Matt. 21:15.   And when the chief priests and scribes saw the wonderful things that he did, and the children crying in the temple, and saying, Hosanna to the son of David; they were sore displeased.
>
> 16.   And said unto him, Hearest thou what these say? And Jesus saith unto them, Yea; have ye never read, Out of the mouth of babes and sucklings thou hast perfected praise?

These verses, while possibly historical, both draw attention to and warn against a very human tendency. Resistance by entrenched powers to cleansing, healing and liberation is inevitable, as this verse reveals when read symbolically. If, as already suggested, the temple is regarded as representing the fourfold nature of man, then the resistance of matter to spirit—generally exerted by the mind—is personified as the chief priests and the scribes. Ever jealous of an intrusion upon their traditional position and power, these officials in their turn oppose the influence of a freedom-giving approach to life and established religious dogma. This is the almost continuing conflict, the interior Armageddon which is waged between the spirt of man (Jesus) and the lust for power and the determination to retain it once it has been acquired (the priesthood, Pharisees and scribes).

In the temple of the universe, also, the very matter of which the outward forms are built and the instinctual consciousness evolving therein tend continually to resist both the increase of sensitivity to the creative plan and the molding effect of the Archetype. Similarly, at a certain stage of man's evolution, the human mind is unwilling to permit the entrance—and especially the liberating power—of new ideas. The history of dogmatic Christian theology, with its account of self-defending proscription of supposedly heretical ideas, provides an appropriate example of this tendency—the Holy Inquisition, for example.

However, naught can perpetually stay the evolutionary progress and the changes and discoveries which it brings. Eventually, however long delayed the consummation, the ceaseless pressure of spiritualizing and molding power overcomes both the instinctual and the deliberate opposition. Ultimately the resisting instincts and attributes of the human personality are obliged to give way. Dogmas pronounced on the basis of infallibility in one age are sometimes found to be completely untrue in a following era, and so must be abandoned—the geocentric system, for example. The babes and sucklings referred to by Jesus when quoting from scripture personify the newborn, newly discovered approaches to life which are founded upon intuitively perceived truths. Thus Jesus himself may be regarded, not only as the long-awaited Messiah, but also as an exemplar of a new age of intellectual and spiritual unfoldment.

> Matt. 21:17. And he left them, and went out of the city into Bethany; and he lodged there.
>
> 18. Now in the morning as he returned into the city, he hungered.
>
> 19. And when he saw a fig tree in the way, he came to it, and found nothing thereon, but leaves only, and said unto it, Let no fruit grow on thee henceforward for ever. And presently the fig tree withered away.

While such theurgic faculty as is here described is within the power of the perfected man, the action of Jesus in withering an innocent living creation is, to say the least, unlike him, for he proclaimed that his mission was to bring life and so not to cause premature death. This incongruity suggests that the incident is allegorical, alluding to a law of life discovered by man as his spiritual nature unfolds. Under this law, stagnation unfailingly awaits individuals or nations which do not share their attainments and riches with their fellows. The fig tree which bore no fruit typifies this law in operation and especially in its final effect, fruitlessness.

It seems reasonable to assume that Jesus himself would either have interpreted or explained his action. One might be forgiven for assuming that he might restore life and vigor after having used it as an example to the withered fig tree. Nothing to this effect, however, is included in the account given by the Evangelist. Indeed, the whole narrative must be regarded as very incomplete, many things having been said and done by and to Jesus which were either forgotten by the first narrators or perhaps excluded from the account as being unnecessary.

> Matt. 21:20. And when the disciples saw it, they marvelled, saying, How soon is the fig tree withered away!
>
> 21. Jesus answered and said unto them, Verily I say unto you, If you have faith, and doubt not, ye shall not only do this which is done to the fig tree, but also if ye shall say unto this mountain, Be thou removed, and be thou cast into the sea; it shall be done.
>
> 22. And all things, whatsoever ye shall ask in prayer, believing, ye shall receive.

Jesus's comment upon the apparent miracle refers to the occult power by which the phenomenon was produced rather than to its possible spiritual significance. The word *faith* refers to knowledge from direct experience resulting in the absolute interior conviction that, when allied to directly perceived knowledge, the human will is virtually omnipotent. Such knowledge appears to be translated in the King James version as *faith*. Blind faith and wholly unsubstantiated beliefs have little or no permissible place in either occult philosophy or the practice of occult science, both of which are, above all, realistic.

This knowledge born of research and experience includes direct understanding of the fact that all outer phenomena, the whole visible universe and all nature, are the products of combined energy and thought emitted at superphysical and so supersensory levels of awareness and existence. If this force of the "Word" can be perceived and its formative effects changed, then a corresponding change will naturally follow at the solid physical levels. This is the secret whereby apparent and miscalled miracles are produced, as far as words can reveal it.

Although possibly inopportune and at variance with the purpose, intent and method of the Evangelists, the suggestion may here be offered for consideration that the phenomenon apparently produced by Jesus was an appearance only, *maya* in Sanskrit.[10] produced upon the minds of those present by the very great power with which Jesus was endowed. In any case, the message of the incident remains, namely, that he who gives lives, and he who shares enjoys, while he who retains dies, and he who hoards loses, this being the law of life itself. It is obeyed by all spiritually illumined ones and even by the Solar Logos who pours out his Life in abundance from the dawn of his objective manifestation to its eve.

Matt. 21:23. And when he was come into the temple, the chief priests and elders of the people came unto him as he was teaching, and said, By what authority doest thou these things? and who gave thee this authority?

24. And Jesus answered and said unto them, I also will ask you one thing, which if ye tell me, I in like wise will tell you by what authority I do these things.

25. The baptism of John, whence was it? from heaven, or of men? And they reasoned with themselves, saying, If we shall say, From heaven; he will say unto us, Why did ye not then believe him?

26. But if we shall say, Of man; we fear the people; for all hold John as a prophet.

27. And they answered Jesus, and said, We cannot tell. And he said unto them, Neither tell I you by what authority I do these things.

The incident here recorded is evidence of the great skill, often dialectic, with which Jesus outwitted his adversaries. John the Baptist was evidently regarded as a prophet and in consequence his Baptism of Jesus as an acceptable and spiritual fact. To accept John and to reject Jesus involved the priests in an indefensible position, and to this Jesus drew attention with consummate skill.

Jesus, it will be noted, paid little if any heed either to Jewish orthodoxy or its upholders—the priests and their official organization. Furthermore, he performed apparent miracles, and, in addition to the power which radiated from him, these manifestations of spiritual power drew the populace toward him. Officials saw this as a threat to established belief, practice and even the very existence of the priesthood itself, which eventually led to his death.

• • • • •

(Interpretations of Verses 28-46 of this Chapter 27 and of Chapters 28, 29, 30, and 31, are omitted chiefly because they record for the most part conversations, avoidance of traps, and parables. They do not contain many such incidents as lend themselves to a mystical interpretation. This omission in no sense implies that they lack either importance or instructiveness, but rather that for the most part they speak for themselves.)

REFERENCES AND NOTES

1. As pointed out by many biblical scholars.
2. Spiritual will, spiritual wisdom and spiritual intelligence.
3. Zech. 9:9.
4. John 1:1-5.
5. Matt. 5:3-27.
6. See diagram on p. 32   of the Annunciation.
7. Augoeides (Gr.)—The self-radiant divine fragment. See Glossary.
8. Skekinah—"The Glory of the Lord." the visible symbol of God's glory which anciently dwelt in the tabernacle and in Solomon's Temple. Num. 14:10; Kings. 8:10, 11.
9. Cherubim—Exod. 25:19.
10. *Maya* (Sk.), Illusion.

Chapter Twenty-Six

Before continuing the account, it may be useful to review the doctrine of the involution of spirit into matter and its subsequent evolution, as this teaching provides a background against which events in the life of Jesus, particularly in his last day, may be interpreted. In offering this interpretation of this chapter, an even more deeply metaphysical approach to the life story of Jesus is presented for consideration. Admittedly this view does not harmonize with the accustomed reading of the account of the experiences through which Jesus passed from his betrayal to his death and burial.

According to occult science, spirit remains forever unchangeable and so unchanged in its own essential nature, as throughout his life did the Lord Christ. Its embodiment in matter of deepening degrees of density and inertness reduces the freedom of spirit at each level and also imposes on its vehicles particular material characteristics. At the solid, physical degree of density, the resistance of such matter is so great that for a time the manifestation of spirit almost ceases to be expressed. The material aspect of the universe predominates greatly over the spiritual. In world allegories, spirit is figuratively betrayed, wounded and killed. It is as if the sun became enshrouded in clouds of physical dust of deepening density so that, viewed externally, its light is no longer visible. The Christ personifies the sun and Judas, as well as Christ's enemies, the enveloping clouds of matter.

This development is only temporary, however. Eventually, the infinitely powerful light of spirit not only overcomes and shines through the darkness of matter, but matter itself becomes refined and self-radiant with solar light, as it were. Thus, allegorically, Christ is resurrected from the tomb and eventually ascends into heaven, while Judas commits suicide.

Precisely similar natural processes occur when universal spirit becomes manifested as the innermost Self of a human being. Thus, in man, the Monad becomes associated with matter of deepening density. This forms itself into individual vehicles through which spirit manifests and unfolds. In consequence, the inherent and, at first latent, properties and powers of spirit are developed. When the most dense of the vehicles, the physical body, is assumed, the Monad is at first almost powerless therein.

This incarnation of spirit in matter and of the human spirit in a material body is described in the sacred language not inappropriately as a death and an entombment. The life story of Christ lends itself particularly well to such an interpretation, as do the manner of the death and resurrection of Osiris and also of Persephone. The accompanying restrictions and more particularly, the resultant sensuous and selfish tendencies, are so contrary to the sensitivity, light and beauty of the inner Self as to be worthy of descriptions as betrayals. Nature's involutionary procedure does indeed culminate in so complete a deadening of spiritual impulses as to justify figurative references to them as crucifixion and death.

Man, as Monad, eventually overcomes the limitations of matter; he sensitizes and molds his vehicles so that they are no longer restrictions but obedient, illumined instruments of monadic Self-expression. The Judas of the bodies temporarily betrays or despiritualizes consciousness, but in due course the restriction of death is conquered, and the Christ accomplishes his own Resurrection and final Ascension into heaven. This paradise includes fully conscious realization of unity with universal spirit. The Christ, having long ago achieved this, says, "I and my Father are one."[1] These processes are both natural and inevitable. Once emanation has begun, naught either in heaven or in earth can prevent the fulfillment of the cycle of forthgoing and return of the Life of both cosmos and man, each with its twelvefold potentiality. Viewed as an arc of the complete cycle of forthgoing and return, betrayal, death, and burial are both beneficial and, in fact, essential to the fulfillment of the procedure of emanation.

This view of the process of involution and evolution underlies much of the proffered interpretation in the following verses. The necessity for such blinds is not difficult to perceive since such knowledge of the deeply occult processes of the despiritualization of both cosmic Logos and Monad of man could place in the hands of evil men dangerous power which they could well use adversely.

Matt. 26:1.   And it came to pass, when Jesus had finished all these sayings, he said unto his disciples,

2.   We know that after two days is the feast of the passover, and the Son of man is betrayed to be crucified.

3.   Then assembled together the chief priests, and the scribes, and the elders of the people, unto the palace of the high priest, who was called Caiaphas,

4.   And consulted that they might take Jesus by subtilty, and kill him.

5.   But they said, Not on the feast day, lest there be an uproar among the people.

In these verses, Jesus once again foretells his betrayal and Crucifixion, thereby revealing his foreknowledge of future events, particularly those in which he himself will be the central figure. Since the foretelling would appear to be entirely without point or purpose and no suggestion made for the avoidance of the catastrophe, a mystical meaning may perhaps be inferred.

As elsewhere advanced, the apparent allies and enemies of central figures in the great allegorical dramas represent spirit and matter, life and form, the eternally opposite poles which are ever at war. All enemies represent both the materializing influences of the involutionary process upon life and those orders of angels and archangels whose task it is in the economy of nature to aid in the process of the involvement of spirit in matter macrocosmic and microcosmic. In Kabalistic terms, Judas Iscariot, Pilate, the multitude, and the soldiers all personify the Inverse Sephiras, those agencies somewhat deceptively referred to as the satanic hierarchies, whose task it is to bring about the metaphorical death which assuredly is followed by Resurrection and Ascension.[2] All the principals in the great drama—Pilate, Caiaphas and the members of the Sanhedrin for example—may in their turn be seen as the more advanced of such angelic intelligences and the subordinates as officials of lower rank. The enmity thus considered is only apparent, a blind indeed, veiling a profound occult truth. Actually, the opposition is not real when seen from the evolutionary point of view; for the aid given on the descending arc is in every way as valuable and as necessary as that provided on its opposite —the pathway of return.

Matt. 16:6.   Now when Jesus was in Bethany, in the house of Simon the leper,

7.   There came unto him a woman having an alabaster box of very precious ointment, and poured it on his head, as he sat at meat.

8.   But when his disciples saw it, they had indignation, saying, To what purpose is this waste?

9.   For this ointment might have been sold for much, and given to the poor.

10.   When Jesus understood it, he said unto them, Why trouble ye the woman? for she hath wrought a good work upon me.

11.   For ye have the poor always with you; but me ye have not always.

12.   For in that she hath poured this ointment on my body, she did it for my burial.

13.   Verily I say unto you, Wheresoever this gospel shall be preached in the whole world, there shall also this, that this woman hath done, be told for a memorial of her.

The narrative changes abruptly, perhaps, due either to the absence of further information or to a failure of memory on the part of the author of the Gospels according to St. Matthew and St. Mark. Since the Gospels were written from memory, supported by a collection of many accounts assembled in one document, it is not surprising that recollections and ways of writing could differ. However, discrepancies need not be disquieting if the accounts are viewed allegorically. According to St. John the incident of the ointment occurred, not in the house of Simon the leper, but in that of Martha, Mary, and Lazarus where Jesus was partaking of food.[3] This latter account is preferable for the student of symbology, if only because it depicts Mary as remaining quiet near Jesus while Martha is busy with the work of the house. Mary is thus shown as both mystically inclined, even illumined, and aware of the importance of the divine command to the Psalmist, "Be still and know that I am God."[4] She expresses her true character when both historically and allegorically she anoints the head of Jesus with precious and fragrant ointment.

History apart, the act of anointing may be interpreted as the provision of conditions under which the divine and the human in man are mutually harmonized so that communion between them may readily occur. Mystically interpreted, the divine principle in man, personified by Jesus, and the human mind, personified by the head of the recipient of anointment, are brought into harmony with each other. Thus regarded, Mary's action portrays a procedure which successfully causes a human being—and especially the human mind—to become aware of the interior Godhead, the Logos of the soul of man. Jesus is indeed as described in the Gospel according to St. John.[5] In Eastern terms, Mary's action may be regarded as an allegory of the practice of yoga and its effects upon the body, the brain and the mind of the yogi.[6] In consequence of this figurative anointing, he becomes aware of himself as a manifestation of the spiritual essence of the universe.

The whole scene is a beautiful portrayal of this procedure, with house representing the body, its inhabitants as qualities of character, Martha, Mary, Lazarus and the disciples, including Judas, all typifying the rich and varied complexity of human nature. The divine visitor is the God within man, the Christ Indwelling. The provision and the partaking together of food indicate the seclusion and intimacy necessary for interior illumination, as also does the harmonious relationship; for Jesus was a beloved friend of the family. All the conditions necessary to self-illumination having thus been achieved, communion between the inner and the outer selves takes place, symbolically described as the anointing of the head of Jesus. The friendliness which Jesus always found in the home, so that he visited and received hospitality there, indicate those more advanced human beings who already, and almost naturally, express in their ways of life spiritual idealism born of a deepening realization of unity. As in so many other cases, this incident with its beauty and its ugliness may thus be regarded as one of many instructive "cameos" allegorically portraying spiritual truths and mystical experiences.

Matt. 26:14.   Then one of the twelve called Judas Iscariot, went unto the chief priests,

15.   And said unto them, What will ye give me, and I will deliver him unto you? And they covenanted with him for thirty pieces of silver.

16.   And from that time he sought opportunity to betray him.

The somewhat meager account of the life of Judas Iscariot constitutes another such "cameo," and indeed a most instructive one. Those human beings who contain no Judas Iscariot-like attributes within them are rare indeed. Under what is regarded as the normal day-by-day mode of life, the presence of the interior Judas may or may not become revealed. The attributes of cupidity, grasping acquisitiveness, consciencelessness, disloyalty, deceitfulness and readiness to betray may not be evoked into either secret or obvious action, though some trace of them will be discernible to clear-eyed students of human nature. But in some measure, the Judas quality is likely to be present in most people, being part of the "stain of matter" consequent upon the descent of the Monad into generation. It represents errors into which man can fall while passing through those phases of evolution which precede enlightenment.

When the path of discipleship is entered a Master submits aspirants to tests that will reveal the degree of their worthiness. Only those who in both their deeper and their outer natures pass such profound and unerring security are admitted to one of the most—if not the most—sacred of human relationships. All qualities, both favorable and adverse, receive stimulation and are brought to the surface by close association with and instruction by an Adept. Thus undesirable characteristics are revealed. Though seemingly harmful, this emergence of characteristics is ultimately beneficent; for only when they become obvious and recognition of them is forced upon their possessor can they be recognized, admitted and so eradicated from human nature.

The Judas of the Gospel story, whether he was historical or symbolic, must be destroyed, must in fact destroy himself as Judas is made to do. Thus allegorically, Judas hangs himself, meaning his Judas-like characteristics. Many battles must be fought before final victory is won. Eventually, the disciple's aspirations increase until they become that deathless resolve which is essential to complete conquest. Some battles are secretly waged, only the fighter himself knowing about them since they occur in the arena and battlefield of his own private life. The secrecy is indicated by Judas' going privately to the enemies—in this case the priests.

The priests who paid the price, thereby purchasing the dishonor of another, in their turn portray cupidity, domination, and an instinctive fear that if the "new life" (Jesus) gained hold among the populace, their priestly power and all their prestige would be lost. Thus the "priests" within mankind are ready to resort even to the meanest measures to save themselves, namely, bribery, corruption and the kind of underground duplicity characteristic of some members of their caste. The thirty pieces of silver supposedly received in payment for the betrayal by reduction in the symbolism of numbers become three. This may be interpreted as a reference to the three densest levels of matter: mind-stuff, the substance of desire, and physical matter itself. These three offer the greatest degrees of resistance to spirit in this particular solar system and on this planet. In man they comprise the three personal vehicles wherein the almost fatal flaws exist—the mental, the emotional and the physical, represented by Judas himself. These vehicles embody the full descent of the spirit of man throughout each of his successive bodily incarnations.

Silver is in vibrational resonance with the moon, as gold is in mutual harmony with the sun. In occult terminology they are said to correspond. The moon represents the personal nature of man; his mortal bodily self and its capacities for physical generation and regeneration, emotion in all its phases, and the capacities of the formal, reasoning mind. The choice of this metal for the reward is at least suggestive of such an interpretation.

The spiritual Self of man is also three-fold in its constitution. Divine will, wisdom, and intelligence are temporarily focused into an individualized ray to form the spiritual soul of every man. Since this triple Self manifests in physical matter at each new incarnation, such matter may be said to receive a threefold benediction or payment, as in the allegory Judas receives thirty (three) pieces of silver.

> Matt. 26:17. Now the first day of the feast of unleavened bread the disciples came to Jesus, saying unto him, Where wilt thou that we prepare for thee to eat the passover?
>
> 18. And he said, Go into the city to such a man, and say unto him, The Master saith, My time is at hand; I will keep the passover at thy house with my disciples.
>
> 19. And the disciples did as Jesus had appointed them; and they made ready the passover.

Clear knowledge of a house and an owner at a distance where the Last Supper could be eaten, constituted a display of occult power as well as an indication that the narrative should be read allegorically. However, the allegorical interpretation is not to be regarded as denial, or even doubt, of its historicity.

Eating together has long been an indication of an intimate relationship. Such sacred meals antedate Christianity by many ages; for it was an ancient ritual custom. It is comparable to the relationship existing between the indwelling divine Life (Jesus) and the substance of Cosmos.

The number twelve assigned to the disciples refers to the totality of the powers and intelligences of the universe and man, portrayed from very ancient days by the twelve signs of the zodiac. Seated at table, eating together with Jesus in their midst, the assembly appropriately represents the Solar Logos with "his" twelve major zodiacal attributes in the process of becoming more and more intimately associated with matter of deepening density.[7] Man, too, goes through this process. As pure spirit-essence he enters into and evolves through subhuman and human kingdoms of nature, each with dense material bodies and so, in their turn, reducing spiritual awareness and power to a minimum. Allegorically he goes down to bondage in Egypt,[8] to exile in Babylon and betrayal and death in Jerusalem.

The oft-pictured scene described in these verses introduces the reader who possesses and uses the keys of interpretation to that phase in the process of forthgoing which immediately precedes final entry into solid physical matter, since only the ethereal part of the physical universe or human body is as yet referred to in the immortal story.[9]

If the allegorical method may be still further applied to the scene, the preparation and the serving of the food refer to those servants of the One Life known as the archangels, angels, and nature-spirits by whose aid creative power, evolving life and directive intelligence are incarnated in material vehicles. This ministration supplied to the Monad of man makes available vehicles of increasing density into which he is inducted. By experience in the use of these and by eventual victory over their resistances, he brings his germinal spiritual powers from latency into potency. Symbolically, mysterious and unnamed men ("such a man," verse eighteen) provide an ass for the journey into Jerusalem and a room and servants wherein the Last Supper may communally be eaten.

Applied to the Universe, the scene portrays the Logos, personified by Jesus, his twelve solar and zodiacal powers, personified by the twelve disciples, with their archangelic regents, or agents, for increasing the fullness of divine manifestation as emanation continues. The room is the enclosing principle or Ring-Pass-Not; the fourfold table represents the four densest levels of divine manifestation—mental, emotional, vital and physical. Since Jesus' death and burial were very near at hand at the time of the Last Supper, the closing phases of the Emanation are being allegorically portrayed. Within a few hours, as Jesus foretold even to Judas himself, he would be betrayed, condemned, cruelly murdered and buried. Thus, the deepest degree of darkness and the densest degree of material incarnation were about to be entered upon.

Matt. 26:21. And as they did eat, he said, Verily I say unto you, that one of you shall betray me.

22. And they were exceeding sorrowful, and began every one of them to say unto him, Lord is it I?

23. And he answered and said, He that dippeth his hand with me in the dish, the same shall betray me.

24. The Son of man goeth as it is written of him: but woe unto that man by whom the Son of man is betrayed! it has been good for that man if he had not been born.

25. Then Judas, which betrayed him answered and said, Master, is it I? He said unto him, Thou has said.

The dark figure of Judas enters upon the stage. Historically, the conduct of Jesus was heroic in that he knew by means of adeptic insight of the dangers inherent in Judas at his present stage of development. Even after his inclusion of Judas in his group, he saw and even prophesied the result of the conflict, both within Judas himself and as it would eventually affect himself as Jesus. Even so he proceeded, an action which, dispassionately regarded, seems entirely unreasonable, even suicidal.

Already the price of betrayal was agreed upon; nevertheless he attends and is admitted to that communal meal which proves to be the last one partaken of together before the death of Jesus upon the Cross. If, then, it be asked—as well it might—why Jesus had accepted so unworthy and potentially dangerous a disciple when presumably so many better men were available and why, without plans for his protection he continued to submit himself to a procedure which would certainly bring his earthly career and so his great mission to an end, the answer given by the Evangelist is "in order that a prophecy would be fulfilled."[10] Again, such obvious incongruity indicates meaning, concealed and yet hinted at. Truth thus lies both deeply concealed within and nearer the surface of the great and classical allegories descriptive of both Divine and human life. In many of these a traitor is introduced, whether Cain, Set, Devadatta, Loki, or the traitress, Clytemnestra.[11]

As discussed previously, the betrayal of Jesus by the disciple Judas may be considered as a portrayal of the involutionary procedure of nature and its assistance by the angelic hosts, possibly personified by Judas himself. Just as orders of angelic beings play their parts in inducting spirit-life into matter, so also the Monad-Ego of man is born into bodies built of matter of increasing density, culminating in the completion of the foetal intrauterine growth of the body. Although invisible to the physical eye, intelligences are present and actively at work, both as builders of vehicles and as directors of those creative forces of which the mechanism of consciousness linking Ego and brain is constructed. Moreover, the deprivation is progressive—mental, emotional, and physical—each stage bringing its own form of restriction, crucifixion, and death from which resurrection or liberation is, however, eventually attained.

Thus, in the allegorical reading, the Christ as personification of spirit had no choice. When once the process of the externalization and localization of spirit has been initiated, all else must follow according to universal law. This law is also revealed in the parable of the prodigal son.[12]

If such philosophical considerations are applied to the story of Judas Iscariot, then the tragic figure is not to be wholly abhorred or deplored. He plays an essential part in the drama of the Christ life. Judas and his associates are presented as evil and intensely cruel men. Nevertheless, the Resurrection and Ascension of Jesus are shown in the Gospels as direct results of the supposed apostasy of Judas and the determined assault of the judges and their soldiers who executed their decrees. Without them and what they represent, both matter and mankind would, in consequence, have been deprived of the redemption and spiritualizing influence both of spirit and of every ascended Adept. Although Judas is presented as an enemy, according to the language of allegory and symbol he actually personifies an agency which is both essential and eventually beneficial.

Since this view is advanced in certain of my earlier books, at this point I quote pertinent passages from them.

> Lofty Intelligences, *Dhyan Chohans,* the Archangels and Angels of Kaballism, direct both the involutionary and the evolutionary processes and ensure their "success." Those assisting on the downward arc tend to be regarded by man as Satanic. Those active on the upward arc are regarded as redemptive. Scriptural allegories present them as antagonists and man looks upon them as devilish and divine respectively. In reality, they are mutually equipoised powers working for temporarily opposite objectives. *The Kingdom of the Gods,* p. 177.

The Irish poet, James Stephens, intuited and expressed this profoundly occult teaching in his poem, "The Fullness of Time."[13]

On a rusty iron throne,
Past the furthest star of space,
I saw Satan sit alone,
Old and haggard was his face;
For his work was done, and he
Rested in eternity.

And to him from out the sun
Came his father and his friend,
Saying, — Now the work is done
Enmity is at an end —
And he guided Satan to
Paradises that He knew.

Gabriel, without a frown;
Uriel, without a spear;
Raphael, came singing down,
Welcoming their ancient peer;
And they seated him beside,
One who had been crucified.

One Order of Inverse Sephiras, possibly the second and third Numerations, are Intelligences who fashioned the mental, emotional, and etheric—physical bodies of the first three Races of men to inhabit this earth in this world period. These *Pitris,* as they are called in Hinduism, also fulfilled the office of "inducting" or "luring" the Monad-Egos of those Races into the bodies which they had constructed for them. Since this materialising function appears evil from the point of view of the evolutionary arc which tends toward spiritualisation, these Intelligences are sometimes referred to as the Satanic Hierarchies.

. . . Whilst the enshrouding, burying, embodying function of certain of the Inverse Sephiras does impose temporary limitations upon the life within, it cannot truly be regarded as evil. Neither can the Intelligences concerned with these processes be regarded with any truth as Satanic; for descent is essential to ascent, temporary embodiment to the development of latent powers. (*The Kingodm of the gods,* p. 172, last par. and on to p. 173, up to line 5).

Pneumatology apart, Satan as the personification and incarnation of pure evil has, in occult philosophy, no existence by himself. Evil is but the absence of good. It exists only for him or her who is made its victim. *Demon Dues Inversus est.* The Devil is the shadow of himself which a man sees when he turns his back to the light. Nature is neither good nor evil, and manifestation follows only unchanging and impersonal law. (*The Kingdom of the Gods,* p. 178, par. 3).

. . . The story of Joseph, who is presented as an historical character, is also—as are other narratives in the *Pentateuch*—an allegory descriptive of the law of cycles, one major cycle being composed of almost innumerable minor ones.[14] The major cycle of the outpouring of creative life, the emergence of Creative Officials, the building of the cosmos, its densification and the entry of the indwelling life into the deepest depths, are all revealed in that part of the story which states that Joseph was out in the field with his brethren, and culminates in the supposedly enforced descent of Joseph into the pit. Incarceration in a pit which had been dug down into the earth—as also the entombment of the Christ "in a sepulchre which was hewn out of a rock"[15]—may be taken as indicating that in the process of involution the emanated Monad-bearing life-wave had reached the deepest level of embodiment in solid physical substance, the mineral kingdom of the earth itself.

The ultimate victory of Spirit over matter, of life over form, is allegorically described in the account of Joseph's rescue from the pit and his later high attainment . . ." (*The Hidden Wisdom in the Holy Bible,* Vol. III, p. 183, line 4, *et seq.*).

The recovery of freedom at the attainment of "the measure of the stature of the fullness of Christ" is a transcendent benefit.[16] The actions of Judas according to a literal reading, which were responsible for it, were in fact only temporarily adverse. The benefits on the other hand are retained throughout all time, since the Adept is forever afterwards "above care, above sorrow, above sin and worldliness, a mendicant, a sage, a healer, the King of Kings, the Yogi of Yogis."[17]

> Matt. 26:26. And as they were eating, Jesus took bread, and blessed it, and brake it, and gave it to the disciples, and said, Take, eat; this is my body.
>
> 27. And he took the cup, and gave thanks, and gave it to them, saying, Drink ye all of it;
>
> 28. For this is my blood of the new testament, which is shed for many for the remission of sins.

The institution of the Eucharistic Feast is here described, if in its very simplest form. Although the partaking of food together is universally regarded as an indication of shared interests and communal values, the physical presence of the Christ evidently bestowed upon this "Last Supper" a profound, intrinsic moral and spiritual character. Indeed, three symbols and three actions are combined in this account of the Last Supper which Jesus and his disciples shared. The symbols are the cup, the wine which it contained, and the bread which was eaten. The three actions were the breaking of the bread, its blessing, and its administration to all who were present. Viewed macrocosmically, wine is the preserving and unifying spiritual life-energy with which the worlds are to be filled. Bread represents those Logoic principles by which the process of divine Self-manifestation is carried out. The underlying, ever-unchanging laws—such as divine Self-manifestation by means of "sound" or word and the cyclic forthgoing and return of the seed-bearing Life of the Logos—constitute the ultimate Truth which is symbolized by bread in this macrocosmic interpretation.

In the macrocosmic sense, the breaking of bread implies the action of the one Logos in becoming manifest within innumerable forms, ever in obedience to fundamental laws. Its blessing refers to the outpouring of divine power with its unfailingly spiritualizing effect and the stimulation of the tendencies toward the evolutionary process. Microcosmically viewed, bread is a symbol for esoteric knowledge. It is made from nutritive grain, a fundamental product of nature. When ground—mentally analyzed—it is combined with yeast as a leavening agency, referring to the interior leavening function upon the mind of spiritual intuitiveness. The two together—grain and yeast—imply fully understood laws of being. Partaking of bread symbolizes the intuitive and mental absorption of divine knowledge, or self-unification with the mentally nutritive grain of truth.

The cup is man's vehicle of abstract intelligence or causal body of man which receives the wisdom distilled from life's experiences. This interior wisdom is the wine with which the cup is continually refilled. It is the "wine of life" which is administered to the outer man throughout the successive incarnations. Consecrated wine symbolized for man the divine wisdom inherent in the Monad and increasingly expressed within the through its immortal Self in its "vesture of light" or the cup. The inner Self as interior priest in its turn administers this spiritual influence to successive mortal personalities as wisdom and its applications to the conduct of life.

In the twenty-eighth verse, Jesus bestows upon the wine an even more deeply symbolical significance; for after his blessing, it was to be regarded no longer as wine alone but as representative of his own blood "shed for many for the remission of sins." What, then, may be meant by such a symbology, such a sharing of a consecrated wine as symbol of the blood of Christ?

One of the functions of a lofty, spiritual being when visiting mankind is to provide vicariously on man's behalf that which as yet he is unable to provide for himself. This is the fully awakened Christ nature (*Buddhi*) which is one part of the threefold spiritual Self of every man. In humanity for this age, this vehicle and the function which it should perform are as yet normally unawakened, inactive and therefore unavailable. In the Adept it is fully unfolded, fully active, especially in its capacity as a vehicle by means of which the highest spirit may reach the outer mortal man. Wine, especially consecrated wine, is a physical symbol for this deeply interior part of the inner nature of man and of its role as a conveying medium for highest Spirit (*Atma*) into lowest matter.

When offering the cup and saying "this is my blood of the new testament," Jesus presumably referred to that New Age, the future Age, at which aided by his interior ministration—At-one-ment—the evolution of man will have brought this vehicle and power into full manifestation within him.

As blood is the essential fluid by which the life of the body is maintained, so the blood of Christ becomes a symbol for that which is essential for the sustenance and preservation of man's spiritual and mortal soul. As blood flows throughout the physical body of man, so the life-force of the Logos pervades and thereby sustains the whole universe, material and spiritual. Saviors and Redeemers themselves serve as vehicles for this inner life and hidden wisdom. They therefore prevent man from falling into deeper degradation than would otherwise occur, and awaken into life in him the hitherto sleeping Christ nature and its capacity for channeling the highest spiritual power into his daily life.

This awakening and stimulation of all that is spiritual in man cannot logically be regarded as cancelling the effects of adversity-producing actions which have already been performed. It can, however, greatly reduce the tendency to repeat these and at the same time quicken the spiritual evolution of all who are responsive to the outpoured life (or who symbolically drink of the blood of the Christ). The remission of sins which is theologically associated with the Atonement would seem to demand for those of philosophic intellect a certain symbolic interpretation. Indeed the Lord Christ's own words so potently affirming the existence and function of the law of action and reaction, cause and effect, would seem to constitute an absolute denial of such a possibility.[18] Unfortunately, the spiritual idea has been materialized into a mistaken theological concept of forgiveness of sins, thereby making it more difficult for those on the verge of sinning to resist the temptation to do so; for both the voice of conscience and the fear of later retribution are reduced in power by the acceptance of the idea that Christ will bring about forgiveness or the remission of their sins.

Symbolically, the action of Jesus becomes less an objective, sacramental rite and far more a deeply interior sharing of his own very life with all who would receive it—metaphorically drink of the cup. This is the most deeply esoteric meaning of the Atonement.

> Matt. 26:29.   But I say unto you, I will not drink henceforth of this fruit of the vine, until that day when I drink it new with you in my Father's kingdom.

The mystery drama of the life of Christ, and especially of his Last Supper, betrayal, passion, and cruel death, is also a revelation by allegory of a truth of Cosmic, superhuman and human significance, for all that is said above also applies to the action of a Logos of the universe.[19] This transcendent Being pours out perpetually his own spiritual life-force—blood in the symbolic sense—into every world and every being in the solar system. The degree and extent of this perpetual oblation increase as solar and planetary ages pass and evolution renders the spiritual principles of the system[20] increasingly receptive and responsive to this radiated, quickening power. Ultimately as the close of the solar *manvantara*—or evening of the seventh "day"—approaches, all that exists becomes saturated through and through with the celestial life-blood of the transcendent and indwelling Solar Deity. This is the cosmic oblation, sacrifice and fulfilled renunciation which also finds expression in Avatars and in those perfected human beings who "don the *Nirmanakaya* vesture"[21] Every *Avatar* or divine descent is so filled with all-encompassing love for humanity that the great renunciation of individual bliss is affirmed and carried out by them.

The statement of Jesus that he would not himself participate in this mystical Eucharist until all of his disciples were with him in his Father's Kingdom, is in conformity with similar statements by other World Teachers. This decision and this affirmation not to enter into the eternal bliss of oneness with God, of life lived wholly in union with the Logos, (*Nirvana*[22]) is also characteristic of all divine personages who visit mankind. So deep is their love for humanity that they decide to remain at one with its hidden life, in continual performance of the functions of "bridge" and awakener, thereby renouncing for themselves entry into a peace and a bliss which are beyond description. Jesus in these verses therefore utters the selfsame vow, even if apparently concerning his disciples alone.[23] The decision and the action are, however totally universal, being born of a divine love for all that exists.

Even men and women as yet not spiritually illumined make personal sacrifices for the welfare and happiness of others, and in this people rise to their greatest heights. Such acts of self-surrender and acceptance of personal loss by human beings may be regarded as one of the effects of the outpourings of spiritualizing life-force by Adepts, World-Saviors and the "Word which became flesh and dwelt amongst men."[24]—the Solar Logos. Martyrdom, in its highest form and according to the truest and most spiritual motives and ideals, is a supreme expression of this divine influence, and his life story portrays Jesus as rising to the greatest heights.

The Blessed Sacrament bestowed upon congregations during Christian church worship portrays and ultimately refers to this divine sacrifice. Intelligent recipients receiving this sacrament find themselves more and more moved toward a response to those ideals which may be described as the Good, the True, and the Beautiful.[25]

Such, I suggest, is part of the mystery enacted in Christian churches during the ceremony of Holy Communion. Such also is part of the mystical significance of the verses under consideration.

Matt. 26:30. And when they had sung an hymn, they went out into the mount of Olives.

31. Then saith Jesus unto them, All ye shall be offended because of me this night: for it is written, I will smite the shepherd, and the sheep of the flock shall be scattered abroad.

32. But after I am risen again, I will go before you into Galilee.

While the historicity of the thirtieth verse is not here doubted, it is nevertheless susceptible of interpretation as a description of entry into the higher consciousness by the group of disciples. This may have been achieved by the dual means of specially chanted sounds referred to as hymns (Mantra Yoga[26]) and a form of meditation directed by the Master. The sound of the human voice has universally and from time immemorial been recognized as an aid to the attainment of God-consciousness. Even in exoteric congregational worship, the singing of hymns is employed as a means of elevating the mind into a state of spiritual awareness—thought combining with the sound of the voice—to produce this effect.

In communities for spiritual training and among disicples of advanced teachers, this method has long been developed to a very high degree. When chanted in the correct rhythm, certain words—each expressive of a spiritual truth such as the oneness of the spirit of man with the spirit which is God—can produce predetermined effects upon both the brain cells and the condition of the mind. Gnostic literature offers examples of such practices.[27] Evidence exists that Jesus trained his discples in this highly occult art, not only in his lifetime, but even during his reappearances after death.

The ascent of the Mount of Olives by Jesus and his disciples and their arrival at the summit symbolically describe the attainment of an exalted state in which all the attributes and qualities of human nature are transformed into a spiritualized condition. When knowledge is attained by such means, universal laws are comprehended. The limitations of past, present, and future begin to be transcended, to be seen as part of a continually flowing tide of events. The power of prophecy is one of the resultant faculties. What is past and future in the time-worlds becomes the ever-present, the absolute NOW. Thus, these three time-states are placed intimately together, the past being the prophecy, the present including the almost immediate betrayal, and the future the coming reunion in Galilee.

The consciousness of such exalted personages as Jesus does in fact transcend time. On occasion, mystics and devotees among mankind enter this state and become aware of past, present, and future as an intimately related procession of events. Thus, Jesus is presented as not only knowing the future, but also being capable of deciding his own actions and their geographical location; for in a future which was to be at least four days in advance of the time at which he spoke, he named Galilee as the place of reunion.

The events which are here related do not need to have actually occurred. Indeed, the whole gospel story is so skillfully written that it reveals experiences of human consciousness, changes, developments, and progressive advances as the Christ-life is lived—wholly lived, it must be said—by any human being. This applies equally to Gentile, Jew, or member of any other racial or religious grouping.

The abrupt change from reference to a past biblical prophecy[29] to the designation of a district (Galilee) to be visited in the future gives some support to the idea that the gospels partly consist of compilations by different authors founded upon remembered or reported incidents in the life of Jesus.

Matt. 26:33.   Peter answered and said unto him, Though all men shall be offended because of thee, yet will I never be offended.

34.   Jesus said unto him, Verily I say unto thee, That this night, before the cock crow, thou shalt deny me thrice.

35.   Peter said unto him, Though I should die with thee, yet will I not deny thee. Likewise also said all the disciples.

The full experience in waking consciousness of this transcendence of the limitations of time depends upon the subjugation of mental and emotional tendencies resulting in complete equilibrium and a measure of peace of both heart and mind. As certain of his actions indicate, Peter had not up to that time attained to this condition; both his forceful affirmations of fidelity and his later denial of his Master demonstrate that he had almost totally failed in this respect. He, therefore, is a personification of that impetuosity which is part of the make-up of certain people. Jesus, on the other hand, had risen above such tendencies and was therefore in possession of foreknowledge of future events. His prophecy that Peter would deny him thrice was, in fact, completely fulfilled.

This incident provides examples of the method of revelation by the use of symbolic language. The stories are used, but only as a substratum, a basis on which to erect what might almost be designated a temple of revelation; for this is a permissible description of all inspired scriptures and, in this case, of both the Old and the New Testaments. Undesirable characteristics of the human personality (Peter) and of their transcendence by a perfected man (Jesus) are portrayed by means of a dramatic allegory.

In pursuance of this approach, denial of Christ by a human being is an allegorical method of portraying that human quality which leads a man to betray not only moral principles, but also and far more deeply his own true spiritual instinct and intuition; for it is from these that the highest idealism arises and reaches the mortal mind. In the present instance, Peter exemplifies that particular human weakenss, while Jesus personifies every noble ideal and, indeed, the faculty of spiritual intuitiveness possessed by highly developed human beings. While man is but man—still far from complete mastery of circumstance and his own nature—he is prone to fall into the error symbolized by Peter's denial of the Christ, an interior betrayal of the highest within him.

The symbol of the crowing of the cock, also employed, is not without its possible occult meaning as may, perhaps, be more fully expounded when the event itself is described, rather than in its present foretelling. It is later revealed that at cockcrow Peter experienced that remorse which can be a first step toward rectitude, as was so proved in his case.

REFERENCES AND NOTES

1. John 10:30.

2. See Geoffrey Hodson, *The Kingdom of the Gods,* Part 3, Ch. 5.

3. John 12:1-3.

4. Ps. 46:10.

5. John 1:4.

6. Cf. The Tranquil State.

7. The masculine is used for convenience only. See Glossary: God, Logos and Logos Doctrine.

8. See Hodson, *Hidden Wisdom,* Vols. 3 and 4.

9. See Glossary—Chain. Please read carefully both paragraphs and also Hodson, *Lecture Notes,* Vol. 1, Ch. 14.

10. Luke 24:44.

11. Set, Egyptian religion; Devadatta, Buddhist scriptures; Loki, Norse mythology; Clytemnestra, Greek mythology.

12. See Hodson, *Hidden Wisdom,* Vol. 1, Pt. 4.

13. James Stephens, *Collected Poems,* (London: 1931) Macmillan & Co. Ltd.

14. The rotation of a planet on its axis while itself circling round the sun partially illustrates this idea, although the number of such related cycles and sub-cycles is far greater than two.

15. Mark 15:46.

16. Eph. 4:13.

17. *The Mahatma Letters to A. P. Sinnett,* 3rd ed., Letter No. 31, p. 238.

18. Matt. 5:18; Luke 16:17; Matt. 1:2; Matt. 7:12; Gal. 6:7.

19. John 1:1-5.

20. Manifestations of divine Will, Wisdom and Intelligence.

21. *Nirmanakaya,* An Adept who instead of going into "selfish" bliss, chooses a life of self-sacrifice in order to be able to help mankind. Cf. *The Theosophical Glossary,* H. P. Bavatsky.

22. *Nirvana*—see Glossary. Also see H.P. Blavatsky, *The Voice of the Silence,* verse 145.

23. Matt. 28:20.

24. John 1:14.

25. Geoffrey Hodson, *The Priestly Ideal.*

26. Mantras (Sk.)—see Glossary.

27. *Gnostics*—see Glossary. Also see G.R.S. Mead, *The Hymn of the Robe of Glory.*

28. Cf. "And now, O Father, glorify us with thine own self with the glory which I had with thee before the world was." (John 17:5). "Jesus said unto them, Verily, verily I say unto you, Before Abraham was, I am." (John 8:58). "I am Alpha and Omega, the beginning and the end, the first and the last." (Rev. 22:13).

29. Zech. 13:7.

Chapter Twenty-Seven

From this point onward, the life story of Jesus, while still of both macrocosmic and microcosmic significance, more definitely portrays the interior experience of every man and woman who attempts to quicken the pace of his or her evolutionary progress. Since this is abnormal from the point of view of the regular periods of time during which man can become superhuman, the resistance of matter and of human nature increases in proportion to the rapidity of the advance.

The greatest task before the aspirant is first to reduce to a minimum, and eventually to transcend completely, the ingrained sense of self-separate identity, of I-ness. Motives, feelings, and physical conduct have hitherto been directed toward self-gain, naturally and rightly so. Henceforth, however, the whole nature must be turned away from self, and this is the message, not only of the Passion of Jesus, but also of every truly spiritual symbol, whether pyramid, sphinx, temple, church, or cross; for all of these and many others, pointing upward as they do, call to man to forsake self and to surrender unto the all-encompassing Self of the cosmos as a whole. These deeply mystical experiences can only be revealed to others by means of allegories. The life story of Jesus—especially from this phase onward —portrays deeply interior travails, trials, and triumphs, for the innermost Self must deny and completely override the customary demands of the outer man.

Ascent to adeptship takes place outside of the limitations of geographical areas, is indeed worldwide and continually occurring at both physical and superphysical levels of consciousness. Almost from the beginning of human habitation of the earth, some men and women have advanced in unbroken succession along the evolutionary pathway ahead of their fellows to whom they ever beckon as if saying, with Jesus, "Come ye after me and I will make you become fishers of men."[1] Within the historical era, Buddhas and Christs have arisen from among men. In the ancient Mysteries, initiates withstood the dreaded tests and passed through the great ordeals—at first largely physical, but later psychological—and received the touch of the thyrsus.[2] Thereafter they conquered death, learned how to tread the pathway of liberation from the body, and ascended out of one of nature's realms into its successor. The initiates of the Mystery temples of old, thus advanced beyond humanity and became superhuman in developed power, wisdom, knowledge, and in their skillful application to the art of living. Though they may have apparently died, actually they withdrew voluntarily from the world. Thus, mystically regarded, Gethsemane, Jerusalem, Golgotha, and the events associated with them are both spaceless and timeless. Fortunately for mankind, they will continue so to be.

Matt. 26:36.   Then cometh Jesus with them unto a place called Gethsemane, and saith unto the disciples, Sit ye here, while I go and pray yonder.

37.   And he took with him Peter and the two sons of Zebedee, and began to be sorrowful and very heavy.

38.   Then saith he unto them, My soul is exceeding sorrowful, even unto death: tarry ye here, and watch with me.

Jesus in Gethsemane, although shrinking at first from this ordeal, quickly recovers and attains to those spiritual heights which are represented by the complete submission of the personal to the divine Will.

Again, three disciples from among the twelve are chosen to accompany and watch with Jesus in Gethsemane. These three may well personify the mental, emotional, and etheric-physical bodies of man which, as vehicles of consciousness, had become controlled, tamed, or disciplined. Like everything mortal, they are unable to participate in the experiences of the immortal Self. Metaphorically, they fail to watch and on three successive occasions are found to have fallen asleep. This number underscores the above reading concerning the three disciples as representing the lower triplicity, symbolized by the downward-pointing triangle of King Solomon's Seal.[3]

The other nine disciples, as also at the Transfiguration, were not called to accompany Jesus into Gethsemane. Apparently this was because they were not sufficiently developed. Thus, the famous garden is less a place than a state of consciousness, or even an inner arena wherein the great battle against Self-separateness must be fought and victory won.

Matt. 26:39.   And he went a little farther, and fell on his face, and prayed, saying, O my Father, if it be possible, let this cup pass from me: nevertheless not as I will, but as thou wilt.

40.   And he cometh unto the disciples, and findeth them asleep, and saith unto Peter, What, could ye not watch with me one hour?

41.   Watch and pray, that ye enter not into temptation: the spirit indeed is willing, but the flesh is weak.

42.   He went away again the second time, and prayed, saying, O my Father, if this cup may not pass away from me, except I drink it, thy will be done.

43.   And he came and found them asleep again: for their eyes were heavy.

44.   And he left them, and went away again, and prayed the third time, saying the same words.

If the story is regarded as descriptive of the cosmic Christos which reportedly descended upon Jesus at his Baptism, then certain difficulties concerning its literal acceptance as history undoubtedly exist. The glorious and glorified "Person" or Being, described by St. John as the Word, must long age—doubtless in earlier ages—have passed beyond the possibility of shrinking from such a physical ordeal or praying to the Creative Logos—the Father—that he be saved from the Passion and the Cross. Furthermore any suffering whatever resulting from adverse conduct under the law of cause and effect[4]—intentional cruelty, for example—would long ago have produced its effects and a state of complete harmony, and therefore invulnerability, have been attained. Difficulties also exist if Jesus is considered as the Word made flesh, the Christ Indwelling in Man. Such incongruities[5] serve as hints given by the inspired and deeply informed authors of an underlying significance concealed within a story of supposed external events.[6]

This approach leads to a consideration of the narrative of the Hebrew initiate, Jesus, as experiences every initiate passes through on the pathway to "the measure of the stature of the fullness of Christ."[7] In such a reading the Initiatory—Jesus the man—approaches his great attainment of perfected manhood.[8] Since Jesus was still human, such ordeals, whether actual or symbolic, psychological or physical, would be unavoidable, and every one of the world's Adepts who has thus attained in advance of the rest of humanity has passed through them.

According to the Mystery Tradition no one can accompany the initiate when he enters into those depths of darkness in and by which his soul is tested and assayed. Evidently, uttermost aloneness is an inevitable and even essential part of the experience of which crucifixion is the climax, and of which the symbolic death of the body (the lower self) is the triumph. As this dread hour is experienced, even the nearest and the dearest are symbolically asleep. Aloneness, loneliness, and the total absence of any external aid or presence are inseparable from passage onward by the initiate, who with sheer determination is forcing his way ahead of the human race to adeptship. The erstwhile man is completely left behind. The threefold nature of the purely mortal man—mind, emotion, and body—must be wholly and completely cleansed of every trace of the egoism of the mind, the desires of the emotions, and the appetites and possessiveness of the body. The suffering of Jesus in Gethsemane portrays this experience. Thus, the initiate stands before the portal leading to the fourth initiation[9] and when it opens, he passes through. Therefore, the experience of finding the disciples asleep in Gethsemane is triply passed through and triply recounted.

At the Transfiguration, Jesus and his two associates were said to be enveloped by light, thereby indicating an experience within the threefold spiritual Self of man, described as occurring on the summit of a mount. The Gethsemane ordeal occurs in darkness at the foot of a mountain. This time, three people besides Jesus occupy the stage, indicating that, not the highest Self, but the mortal man played the chief part in this great drama of human self-deliverance and self-liberation. The darkness of the evening hour, the aloneness, and the necessity for the fulfillment of his self-chosen destiny reveal the essentials and the inescapable concomitants of self-enforced deliverance from the bondages by which humanity is bound.

> Matt. 26:45. Then cometh he to his disciples, and saith unto them, Sleep on now, and take your rest: behold, the hour is at hand, and the Son of man is betrayed into the hands of sinners.
>
> 46. Rise, let us be going: behold he is at hand that doth betray me.

The great drama moves on to its climax. It is noteworthy that the action is initiated by sources outside of him who occupies the center of the stage. Inwardly Jesus is completely prepared, the great sacrifice of self having been wholly, indeed triply, made. All that remains are the fulfillment to the uttermost degree unto death of the vow of self-surrender and the payment of all karmic debts incurred while passing through the human kingdom.

The whole nature of the initiate—personified by Jesus as the spiritual Self and by the disciples as the disciplined mortal nature—is fully prepared to enact the final scenes upon the stage of the world itself.

> Matt. 26:47. And while he yet spake, lo, Judas, one of the twelve, came, and with him a great multitude with swords and staves, from the chief priests and elders of the people.

Oftentimes inconsistencies in the recorded accounts add force to a symbolic view. Jesus and his disciples are presented, for example, as harmless followers of the ancient way, he as a Teacher and they as his disciples, none of whom exhibit warlike tendencies. Nevertheless, the crowd which approached this small assembly is said to have been armed with swords and staves.

One of the ultimately unbreakable laws of nature is that balance shall be preserved and, when temporarily disturbed, must be restored. In the realm of human action this law is inescapably enforced. Every intentional action produces its own appropriate reaction, however long delayed the readjustment and the compensation may be. Before final liberation from the shackles which man places upon himself, every cause must be balanced by its own natural effect. All good, noble and selfless deeds win their due rewards which take the form of benefits received and pleasures enjoyed, while every pain-producing and selfishly inspired deed must be matched by its own self-produced response as limitation and pain. The human kingdom may not —indeed cannot—be left behind until this quite natural process has been followed to the uttermost, as the Egyptian allegory of trial and judgment in the Hall of Maat portrays.

These closing scenes in the life of Jesus now to be considered, in their turn reveal the enactment of these same laws and the exaction of the same karmic retribution, however allegorically the experiences may be described. If, for example, betrayal of trust has marred the conduct of either a trusted public servant or one wholly loved within the circle of domestic life, then the offender will himself experience betrayal, however long ago the faithlessness occurred. Not during incarnation as Jesus of Nazareth of the Gospel Story but in some former life of the same spiritual Self, a betrayal must have occurred. If not wholly balanced as life followed life, then in the final human incarnation, the debt must wholly be paid. Thus, a trusted disciple betrays his Master and in consequence stands as a shameful example of faithlessness, even today.

The Garden of Gethsemane wherein the great betrayal—as it is outwardly regarded—took place may thus be discerned as the scene wherein was taken a decisive and deliberate step toward everlasting deliverance and eternal bliss and peace. Such a reading should not, however, reduce the force of the person of Judas as an example of the degradation into which a man may fall when he permits excessive cupidity to silence his conscience. Judas also stands as dread warning against faithlessness in every walk of human life. This especially applies to those in whom the desire for power and the determination to gain wealth dishonestly, lead to the betrayal of every social and moral virtue. Jesus himself warned not only the Judas of the story but all Judases throughout all time, that a temporary gain thus acquired would inevitably bring such suffering that they would wish they had never been born. Whether Judas existed as a human being or not, his greatest betrayal was not of Jesus but of himself.

Evidently, the possibility exists that a trace, at least, of this tendency, this weakness, could be present even in the noblest and the best among men, since Judas was not only admitted to the Last Supper but was allowed to place his hand in the same dish that the Master was using. It is hardly to be supposed that so profoundly adverse a quality as the faithlessness exhibited by Judas could escape detection and his acceptance as a disciple accordingly be delayed. Jesus shows a remarkable forbearance and compassion since he had proven that he knew full well that Judas was about to betray him. Another quality of highly evolved man shone out in Jesus of the Gospels; for never once did he condemn or in the least declaim against either Judas or Peter when the one betrayed and the other denied him.

Matt. 26:48. Now, he that betrayed him gave them a sign, saying, Whomsoever I shall kiss, that same is he: hold him fast.

49. And forthwith he came to Jesus, and said, Hail, Master; and kissed him.

One of the most intimate expressions of love is here employed as the means chosen by the betrayer to identify Jesus to the chief priests and others. Intimacy if thus underscored, particularly since the necessity for so personal a sign was unnecessary; pointing of the hand would have served as well. However, in a cosmic interpretation, when the spirit-essence of the universe enters into close association with the matter of virgin space, the kiss is an appropriate symbol of the relationship. The entry into matter is indicated by the authors of scriptures and myths by means of such allegories as the expressions of love.

The air of unreality which is discernible in such narratives and their unacceptability by the reasoning mind are all solved if the incarnation and death of the Logos within his solar system are regarded as the actual theme, the esoteric revelation of the numerous and almost universal stories. The Logos does not really die, of course, nor is is divine glory in the least reduced by his Self-manifestation in matter. The vast plan underlying and gradually (according to earthly time) being fulfilled may be described as the emergence and development of germinal potentialities to ever-increasing capacities, faculties, and powers; for the power, of which the plan is an expression, is deeply hidden within spirit and age upon age becomes impressed upon matter. From the moment when the spirit of the universe becomes embodied in finite matter and forms, and the spirit of man becomes incarnate in material vehicles, this mysterious process occurs within nature. Substance itself thus becomes permeated and even charged with this cosmic decision, whether of a Being or the state of "Be-ness." The impulse toward the ceaseless unfoldment of innate and latent powers is thereafter completely irresistible, as if it were the fulfillment of a continuously enunciated and irrevocable decree.

Although no individualized, divine Intelligence may be discernible, the existence of design, pattern, and archetypal purpose becomes apparent, whether in the organic kingdoms of physical nature or in man, when changes from the seed-like to the fully developed states are observed. Involution (or planting) and evolution (or growing), are far from chaotic, haphazard or based upon mere chance; on the contrary, plan, purpose, and design are everywhere visible. Thus, by inference it may be assumed that the "designful-ness" apparent in the organic kingdoms of nature of this earth is extended into all other cosmic realms, visible and invisible, near and far. This is one of the secret truths imparted to initiates of the Mysteries of old, or discovered directly by illumined seers. It is, in fact, the great key by which alone life processes become comprehensible. These are then found to be intelligent and directed, however invisible as far as the uninitiated and the unillumined are concerned. Once gained, this knowledge is directly power-bestowing and therefore capable of grave misuse, particularly when turned to such human purposes as dictatorship and domination. Hence the enveilment beneath symbol, alleogry, and myth.

If these ideas are applied to the life story of Jesus as told by the four Evangelists, then the Master himself may be regarded as a manifestation in human form of both nature's will to bring forth seed-bearing flowers from seeds and ascended men from "babes." His experiences thus describe the interaction between spirit and matter in general, and between the Monad of man and his bodily person in particular.

The betrayal by a kiss and following events portray with remarkable aptitude the results of such interplay.

> Matt. 26:50.   And Jesus said unto him, Friend, wherefore art thou come? Then came they, and laid hands on Jesus, and took him.

Throughout the centuries the narrative has been read literally as if it were a history of events which actually occurred. Symbolism apart, the story is sufficiently dramatic and the account of the Passion of Jesus which these verses describe tragic enough to evoke profound responses from the reader.

Among the many notable occurrences during these closing hours of the life of Jesus, his complete submission appears to be most remarkable. This is especially so since he proclaimed his power to free himself at will by an invocation of available angelic aid,[14] as will be further discussed under later verses.

As heretofore suggested, this so-called descent of spirit into matter is aided and even brought about by successive orders of the angelic hosts, personified by the various and successive enemies of Jesus. Each of these orders conveys the emanated spirit-essence into and through that degree of density of matter at which its own consciousness is established and functions. This procedure culminates in the embodiment of the divine presence within physical substance in its three states of solids, liquids, and gases. The approach of Judas and the attackers during the darkness, leading to both contact (the kiss) and verbal indication as means of betrayal, correspond to the incarnation of spirit in physical matter at the level of air, the medium of sound. The subsequent interrogations, and more especially the flagellations and the crowning which induces a flow of blood, would correspond to the liquid degree of density, while nailing to the cross, death, and entombment, might be read as divine immanence within matter of deepening density until the physical (mineral kingdom) is reached, symbolized by the rock-tomb.[10] Thus, the deepest point of the descent of the divine principle and presence is portrayed, almost step by step. The words of Judas to his associates, "hold him fast," may also be read as a description of the unyielding grip which physical matter maintains upon the incarnated spirit.

This view answers the question which might naturally arise concerning both the foreknowing of and the submission of Jesus to these enemies, and explains his frequent quotations of prophecies in the Old Testament. The surrender must have been voluntary; for he had already demonstrated that he could render himself invisible.

The problem may arise in the mind of the student whether the reference by Jesus to twelve legions of angels upon whom he might call for deliverance if he so wished and yet did not,[11] may be a hint to regard the narrative as largely, if not wholly, allegorical. This possibility is underscored by his use of the number seven which in occult philosophy, including Kabalism,[12] is the number of orders of angels concerned with involution. In such a reading, Jesus is indeed seen as a personification of the threefold Deity, and the closing scenes of his life as allegories descriptive of the "eternal oblation," the divine sacrifice leading to the symbolical death of God himself.

Matt. 26:51. And, behold, one of them which were with Jesus stretched out his hand, and drew his sword, and struck a servant of the high priest's, and smote off his ear.

This verse has been quoted as indicating the presence of armed men in the company surrounding Jesus. This is supported by the earlier statement that one of the disciples was a zealot. Although there is no means of either proving or entirely disproving this, the possibility exists that a political motive for the arrest of Jesus as a zealot himself resisting Roman rule provides another possible reason for the attack upon him by the authorities. The narrative, however, rather presents him as a reformer of the Hebrew religious customs of the time and, particularly, as a liberator of the people from both Pharisaical methods of worship in public and the evils of priestcraft at their worst.

The event described in this verse both supports the idea that some armed men were included in the entourage of Jesus and contravenes the teaching of meekness, mildness, and "offering the other cheek" which Jesus gave to his disciples during his Sermon on the Mount.[14] The armed man is elsewhere referred to as Simon Peter, who was one of the twelve and therefore well acquainted with the teaching which Jesus had given.[15] The severence of the ear of the servant of the high priest may possibly have happened in a kind of melee which followed the arrest, although this is a somewhat strange part of the body to suffer injury; a defensive action would have been directed toward a more vital part. If symbolical, then the cutting off of the ear could refer to the unreadiness of the people to listen to the words of the Teacher.

In occult philosophy, however, the right ear of man corresponds to the ratiocinating mind, the analytical and argumentative faculty which, used in excess, can prevent the receipt of illuminating wisdom from deeper levels of human nature, the Christ Principle.[16] The act of cutting off the right ear may thus refer to the removal of this inhibition, which occurs when the Christ nature draws near to or is able to reach the formal mind. This is possibly indicated by the actual presence of the Christ, who personifies an aspect of the divine wisdom in man, one of his disciples being the agent. St. Luke, who is referred to as a physician, records that Jesus healed the wound,[17] which act, in its turn, may symbolize the attainment of the faculty of acquiring knowledge by the exercise of the intuition.

Whether this episode is presented by the four Evangelists as historical or as one of those numerous hints of a psychological and spiritual truth cannot easily be decided. The student of occult philosophy is nevertheless able to perceive possible revelations of a deeply veiled wisdom by means of allegory.

Commenting upon this possibility, one might well receive direct, personal guidance from such an interpretation, namely, to remove or temporarily reduce the activity of the restless and argumentative aspects of the mind. Thereafter one becomes susceptible of response to that wisdom which is contained within the spiritually illumined intellect or intuition, personified by Jesus.

Matt. 26:52.   Then said Jesus unto him, Put up again thy sword into his place: for all they that take the sword shall perish with the sword.

Despite the tense and dramatic nature of the situation, the words of Jesus suggest that intellectually he is high above the strife, abiding, not in the passing incident however dangerous to his person, but in the realm of everlasting law. This condition is exemplified both by his command that the sword be sheathed and his enunciation of the law of cause and effect by which human conditions are created and ruled. The opposite affirmation is implied by the utterance, namely, that he who lives by love shall be surrounded by love during his life and when that life draws to a close; for such, indeed, is the unavoidable law of cause and effect under which, as the words of Jesus indicate, every human action is followed by appropriate reaction.

> Matt. 26:53. Thinkest thou that I cannot now pray to my Father, and he shall presently give me more than twelve legions of angels?

Herein again Jesus affirms his ability to obtain deliverance by divine aid, his foreknowledge of the future, and his ready submission to all that was about to occur. His possession of this power was more than once evidenced during his lifeitme by his action of "disappearance from their midst."[18] Doubtless in the Garden of Gethsemane, particularly since it was dark, he could have again repeated this occult phenomenon of rendering his body invisible to all those who were present.

This he refrained from doing, stating that his purpose was to fulfill the scriptures. That fulfillment of prophecy being the sole reason advanced by Jesus is the only motive for his surrender, despite his power of self-deliverance.

Down the ages, Jesus has come to be regarded as veritably a divine Being, the Son of God in truth, who voluntarily appeared on earth and submitted himself to the multitude and the authorities in order that by his death mankind might be redeemed from the otherwise ineffaceable stain of original sin left upon it by the Fall of Adam and Eve in the Garden of Eden. The Gospel according to St. John enunciates this view which may also be found in the Synoptics. Yet Jesus does not state this as his purpose. Indeed, such a possibility would have been a denial of his statement that the affairs and experiences of men are self-produced by those who performed the actions of which they are a perfectly natural and exactly appropriate reactions. If his utterance is true—no reason for doubt existing—then no one, not even the Lord Jesus Christ, whether as the creative Word of St. John[19] or the divine principle in nature and in man, can possibly abrogate this law.

> Matt. 26:54. But how then shall the scriptures be fulfilled, that thus it must be?

If the thought be permissible in the case of so lofty a personage, then this repeated statement of motive for willing—even willful—self-surrender could almost be seen as a subterfuge. True prophecy automatically demonstrates its truth by the foretold events and not by a deliberate—a critic might even be tempted to say perverse—performance of abnormal and personally harmful actions purely in order to prove that prophecy.

If Jesus's words are taken literally, then all guilt is removed from the perpetrators of the crimes against him; for he proclaims that he himself arranged and permitted these, despite the fact that he could easily have prevented them, as this verse shows. In consequence, it was not the murderers who were responsible but Jesus himself. If this view is accepted, then accusations that both the Jews and the Romans murdered Christ are largely, if not wholly, negated. He must have voluntarily submitted in order that the scriptures should be fulfilled. These prophecies, however, may be regarded as indirect to say the least, since no mention of the name of Jesus as the future sufferer is to be found.

If the experiences through which he is made to pass in the narrative are less historical than allegorical, then such apparent incongruities lose their incongruity. Thus viewed, such professed motive is seen as a hint, a clue or advice to seek an interior revelation rather than to be carried away, as it were, on the tide of narrated events.

Another possibility is worthy of consideration, namely, that the memories of those who provided the descriptions of the events and the records of statements made were imperfect, if not wholly at fault; for, be it remembered, the compilers of the Gospels were dependent upon the accounts of eyewitnesses.

Matt. 26:55.   In that same hour said Jesus to the multitudes, Are ye come out as against a thief with swords and staves for to take me? I was daily with you teaching in the temple, and ye laid no hold on me.

56.   But all this was done, that the scriptures of the prophets might be fulfilled. Then all the disciples forsook him, and fled.

Jesus affirms his power to obtain the aid of twelve legions of angels and almost immediately thereafter attempts to reason with his attackers on purely material grounds. Such blending of the supernatural with the purely natural, as in these verses and in many other places in the Bible, inevitably lifts the narratives out of the historical and into mystical and occult realms of thought. As heretofore suggested, the life story of Jesus is susceptible of interpretation as a revelation of the law of the manifesting spirit-essence in universe and man, its enclosure in matter of ever increasing density, and the pathway of return. The incidents describe the effects produced at different stages of the great journey of forthgoing and return.

Jesus's reference to his presence in the temple and his teaching of the people there describe by allegory both universe and man. Cosmically, Jesus personifies the divine immanence, and the temple is a symbol of the material universe, rendered holy by that presence. In man the spiritual presence is portrayed by Jesus, while the temple is a symbol of the mortal nature with its numerous attributes, themselves personified by the members of the congregation. The God-Presence having the same name in both interpretations —cosmic and human—underscores the ancient teaching that the two are identical; the Christ in all nature and the Christ in man are not two divinities, but one and the same. The truth is indeed aptly portrayed by the glyph of Christ in the temple and his teaching the people there.

His presence in the temple, a place of worship, may also refer to a stage on the pathway of forthgoing which precedes descent into the deepest levels where resistance will be at its greatest. In the temple Jesus is still on holy ground and so as yet immune. Jesus in Gethsemane and advancing rapidly toward Calvary is in contact with the matter of the universe at its greatest density, portrayed by the enmity shown in the attack on his and by the betrayal by Judas. He is symbolically murdered or given a figurative death, later to rise again. Thus, one concludes, the surrender and death of Jesus were not that an ancient prophecy might be fulfilled, but rather that the law of the descent of spirit into matter followed by its return to its Source is inevadable, a process which governs all manifestations of spirit in matter, divinity in nature, and the Godhead in man.[20]

As spirit thus becomes incarnate in dense physical matter and the divine principle in man becomes embodied in a physical body, with its appetites and its substance as yet unspiritualized, divine attributes are expressed with increasing difficulty, eventually to disappear. Thus, "all the disciples forsook him and fled."

This action is difficult to accept in a literal sense, especially in the case of the disciple John, who loved his Master and whom Jesus loved. However faithless even the majority of the chosen ones may have proved to be, it is reasonable to assume that some of the disciples must have followed their Master at a distance. Indeed, the statement is contradicted in the fifty-eighth verse which states that "Peter followed him afar off . . . ."

These inconsistencies in the story also draw attention to the trials, tests, and ordeals through which an initiate passes when treading the pathway of hastened attainment of adeptship. At a certain stage all external aid appears to have been withdrawn, all support, moral and physical, to have failed at a time of greatest need. This must be so, since the Dweller-in-the-Innermost must become fully realized and thereby known as the only unfailing assurance of salvation, as indeed the only real, eternal identity in universe and man. This ordeal and this ultimate realization are also confirmed by the words of Jesus upon the Cross and his affirmation, "I and my Father are one."[21]

Matt. 26:57. And they that had laid hold on Jesus led him away to Caiaphas the high priest, where the scribes and the elders assembled.

58. But Peter followed him afar off unto the high priest's palace, and went in, and sat with the servants, to see the end.

The direct confrontation between two orders or levels of consciousness is here allegorically described. Caiaphas the high priest represents the old order, the established custom, the routine, the hard-and-fast method developed through centuries of use. Jesus, on the other hand, personifies the fresh, indeed the ever new. Jesus before Caiaphas thus portrays dramatic epochs in the history of man concerning both the unfoldment of his intellectual and intuitive powers and his methods of government.

In the history of the development of the human intellect, the intrusion of an entirely new, fresh and even spring-like intuitive faculty by which truth is known direct, instead of by means of prolonged comparison and observation, inevitably evokes resistance from existent standards, buttressed by self-gain as they generally are. With regard to government, the acquisition and maintenance of positions of power, prestige and financial gain by means of dictatorship and force are never relinquished until evolutionary processes demonstrate their unreliability. History records that, for a time in this battle between the outworn and the newborn, the old temporarily vanquishes the new. However, dogmatism and control by threat and fear eventually bring about their own defeat and disappearance, as is evidenced at the present time. Colonialism maintained by force, for example, has given way to the demand for freedom and self-rule. Even nature in the plant kingdom displays this procedure as season follows season and that which has become old dies out to be replaced by forms which are new.

Thus, while the enemies of Jesus conquered and destroyed him materially, he himself lives on as an influence for good and an embodiment of freedom long after his ancient foes have departed from the world. Although Jesus stands apparently powerless before his foes, victory is eventually accorded to the developing order of consciousness and democratic form of government.

The apostle Peter, who followed his Master, thrice denied him, and thereafter repented, personifies that attribute of the human mind which even while newly grasping a truth, nevertheless fights against it, denies it in fact even as Peter denied his Lord. Eventually truth prevails as Peter both relented and repented. As the personal and apostolic basis for the Christian faith, he eventually become recipient and transmitter of the very truth which, in a moment of human weakness, he had betrayed. In the phase of his life described in this and the following verses, Peter is made to display the human weakness of self-saving at the expense of truth. He is thus presented as performing an act of cowardice in order to save himself from being arraigned beside his Master. At that time he could not accept the ignominy inevitably associated with followers of one who, after trial, was condemned as both an enemy of the state and as a heretic. In consequence, he denied the association.

Mystically interpreted, the incident portrays the effects upon the human mind, motives, and conduct of being dissociated from one's higher Self. Thus regarded, Peter is not in the actual presence of Jesus but among the servants, the menials in fact, however worthy such servants may personally have been. This metaphorically describes a state of consciousness in which a person is for the time being—as under great stress for example—uninspired by his spiritual Self (Jesus) but rather is concerned with less desirable attributes of human nature (servants). These are the conditions under which a man may fall far below the best that is within him and in moments of crisis fail himself, his Master, and his cause.

Against this, however, must be placed the possibility that Peter was under very great stress. The events in Gethsemane, the prophecy by Jesus of his own death, the advance of the enemies led by Judas, and the act of betrayal by a kiss, the surrender by Jesus who might have been expected to display supernormal powers, and the incident of the cutting off of the ear followed by the Lord's rebuke—may well have deeply disturbed a man such as Peter, who on occasion was capable of a certain impetuosity as part of his character. Furthermore, the disciples must have hoped that Jesus would justify their faith in him—possibly as Messiah—and confound his own enemies by means of a demonstration of spiritual power. This hope, it may be assumed, had begun to fade.

Peter then may well be forgiven, even as history forgives him, since when day dawned he repented. A certain inevitability is associated with his act of denial, almost as if it were an irrevocable fate since Jesus himself had earlier foretold it.

Peter, be it remembered, personifies the mortal nature of man—mental, emotional, and physical. In conformity with the practice followed by allegorical writers, his actions portray both the illumined and the unillumined state, particularly of the mind by which emotion and body are directed. Thus Peter in exultation proclaims his loyalty and in the unillumined state denies it. So also man himself before self-illumination is permanently established is subject to alternations of many kinds, which are contributory causes of his many sufferings and downfalls. Indeed, the story of the apostle Peter may be interpreted as both warning and advice to acquire by regular contemplation that personal equilibrium which assures continuity of spiritual experience and a certain steadiness under all circumstances, particularly under the added strain of treading the path of discipleship. When the episode is over, however, Peter repents and is present in the upper room when Jesus reappears. He ultimately justifies the prophecy of Jesus who, translating his name into "rock,"[22] affirms that his Church will be built upon him. Whether later interpolated or not, this prophecy and its fulfillment indicate that man, being essentially a spirit, can always recover however great the fall, even from denial of his own self-existent spiritual nature personified by Jesus in the Gospels.

Matt. 26:59.   Now the chief priests, and elders, and all the council, sought false witness against Jesus, to put him to death;

60.   But found none: yea, though many false witnesses came, yet found they none. At the last came two false witnesses,

The enemies of truth, knowing that its full revelation will bring an end to their domination, always seek by every means to bring that truth to naught, not hesitating metaphorically to utilize false witnesses. These attempts are always foredoomed to ultimate failure, even though they may achieve some temporary success, as the life story and the early death of Jesus reveal.

Matt. 26:61.   And said, This fellow said, I am able to destroy the temple of God, and to build it in three days.

As previously suggested, Jesus's claim that he could rebuild the temple in three days had symbolic reference to his own body and Resurrection.[23] His accusers' literal interpretation of the statement as meaning an actual building is here used against him.

Matt. 26:62.　And the high priest arose, and said unto him, Answerest thou nothing? what is it which these witness against thee?

The silence of Jesus before his accusers is an indication of both his remarkable self-control and his wisdom, since he knew full well condemnation had already been decided upon. His silence also shows that, in a more mystical reading, the inmost Self, the source of wisdom, does not reach the mind of one who is absorbed in deliberately chosen error and is giving expression in action to that untruth. The hall or room in which the accusations and questionings were carried out represents the physical body; the priests and their false witnesses personify the wilfully untruthful and unlawful state of the emotions and the mind; while Jesus in the midst portrays the higher Self, inevitably silent under such circumstances.

Admittedly, however, the historian may question the actuality and the accuracy of the account of the proceedings given by the Evangelists, since no records were made at the time of the trial and no completely reliable account of the incidents was likely to be available. The authors of the supposed original document were presumably dependent upon the memory of those present and the accuracy of their accounts. This encourages acceptance of the view that the gospel story is an allegorical description of the drama of the soul of man. Jesus is the chief actor in such a presentation and personifies the spiritually inspired and empowered higher Self which presses onward along the age-old pathway to perfection, the so-called "Way of the Cross." His eleven disicples represent developed and controlled qualities in the character of the initiate, while one of them—Judas—and all those arrayed against Jesus, personify the interior enemies of the soul—the remaining purely human attributes. The lives of all those other great Teachers who have visited mankind are susceptible of similar interpretations. In the macrocosmic view, as already discussed, the life of the universe as it enters into deeper and deeper depths of incarnation in matter is portrayed.

Matt. 26:63.　But Jesus held his peace. And the high priest answered and said unto him, I adjure thee by the living God, that thou tell us whether thou be the Christ, the Son of God.

64.　Jesus saith unto him, Thou hast said: nevertheless I say unto you, Hereafter shall ye see the Son of man sitting on the right hand of power, and coming in the clouds of heaven.

An interior drama is being related by means of an allegory. In the microcosmic view—granting accuracy of record, translation, and final form in the King James Bible—the outer man (high priest) is beginning to realize his true nature, his own interior divinity. His mind typically seeks verification, even demonstration, of the presence within of a godlike being, a veritable deity, the Christos of the soul.

The mortal man enters the stage, as it were, sees upon it his own divinity as personified by Jesus. Surprised, he questions the reality of the vision as later did Thomas. A dramatic revelation occurs, an interior light shines from within upon the mind and brain of the mortal man, who finds himself, perhaps unprepared, on the brink of the greatest of all discoveries, namely, his own immortal soul. Thomas Didymus exclaims, "My Lord, my God."[24]

Beyond all expectations, the great revelation occurs. Jesus as the immortal and eternal Self gives positive answer and, moreover, foretells the assured attainment of the evolutionary goal. Every man who thus earnestly turns inward toward the depth of his being assuredly finds that which he seeks. Speaking in these terms, Jesus uttered but the simple truth when he answered his judges.

"The clouds of heaven" refer to the radiance of many hues with which the perfected man is surrounded in the spiritual or heaven worlds by which those who have eyes to see may recognize his stature.

The supposed—even imagined—Messiah to be expected in the future is in reality the perfected man of every age, and such human beings do continually attain and so "arrive." The purest bliss and most perfect wisdom in which every perfected human being abides—and to which every man will one day evolve—may also be the condition to which the prophesy of a Second Coming refers. Perchance a state of consciousness, rather than the arrival of a particular divine personage, is being described. This hidden wisdom concerning the evolution and the future of man—and so of Jesus himself—was revealed in the reply and the affirmation of Jesus to the high priest.

> Matt. 26:65.　Then the high priest rent his clothes, saying, He hath spoken blasphemy; what further need have we of witnesses? behold, now ye have heard his blasphemy.

The phrase "what further need have we of witnesses?" is rich with spiritual significance; for once the direct interior vision has been attained, no external affirming voice is needed, as Thomas was made to indicate. Very different, however, are the reactions of the two people upon this selfsame stage, doubtless caused by the difference in their position upon the evolutionary path. Thomas was evolved to that degree in which he not only recognized his own divine Self, but openly proclaimed the fact. This means that thereafter the vision splendid was accepted and wholly applied to the life of the outer man. Such wholehearted, even exalted, response rarely occurs, particularly when the implications of the interior experience run counter to the desires of the temporarily illumined one, to his pleasure-giving opportunities, and to his position among his fellowmen. Pilate-like, he denies the truth—washes his hands metaphorically of the whole experience—and surrenders, not to the highest, but to the lowest elements in human nature. Unable at this time to pass the test—admittedly a very severe one—he reassumes the associations, the mode of life, and the position of power to which, as a worldly man, he had attained. To his fellow "priests," also sitting in judgment, he proclaims the Christ to be a blasphemer and the vision splendid of proclaimed spiritual stature to be a blasphemy.

Few indeed are those who enter the living presence of the Master —whether as a hidden light or as a personage who has reached adeptship —and emerge from that vision steadfast and strong. Fewer still are those who turn away from the temptations of the worldly life with its outer pomp, its prestige and its power, and embark upon that which Isaiah called, "the way of holiness."[25]

Within those who temporarily fail, the Christ nature, the very Self, is "crucified" as the life story of Jesus thus interpreted allegorically portrays.

> Matt. 26:66. What think ye? They answered and said, He is guilty of death.

Even in the terms of the literal reading of the text, no blasphemy whatever had been committed by Jesus when he admitted himself to be "the Christ, the Son of God," for this is also true of every human being. Every well-read Hebrew, and especially every priest, must have known the affirmation, "For God created man to be immortal, and made him to be an image of His own eternity."[26] Thus, the admission of Jesus that he was the Son of God, was—and forever is—perfectly true, as it was also true of the high priest himself. Quite evidently, therefore, a plot against Jesus had been conceived and, with the connivance of Judas, was then being carried out.

The translation of this verse would appear to be faulty, since a prisoner may be judged to be guilty of sin and, according to law, therefore worthy of being sentenced to death, but he cannot be said to be "guilty of death."

> Matt. 26:67. Then did they spit in his face, and buffeted him; and others smote him with the palms of their hands.
>
> 68. Saying, Prophesy unto us, thou Christ, Who is he that smote thee?

History apart, the inevitable degradation which spirit must suffer when becoming incarnate in and surrendering to the deeper densities of matter is also here allegorically described. Similarly, as heretofore suggested, the selfsame spirit in man becomes subject to the limitations and even debasements imposed upon it by incarnation in vehicles of thought, emotion and flesh. This must indeed be so, since only by these submissions may the innate powers in Deity and man become aroused into activity and thereafter evolve into consciously and objectively employed faculties and capacities.

Jesus the Galilean—not the overshadowing Avatar—differed from those who arrested, insulted and ill-treated him since his inner powers were highly evolved. Approaching quite nearly, as he was, to the ascended or perfected state, he knew by virtue of continual living experience that indeed he was the Son of God and would very shortly ascend in "clouds of glory."

The blindness of the high priests, the Roman officials and the multitude to this truth concerning the young Hebrew whom they were degrading and planned to destroy is also typical of the effect upon consciousness of incarnation in bodies of successively increasing density.

> Matt. 26:69. Now Peter sat without in the palace: and a damsel came unto him, saying, Thou also wast with Jesus of Galilee.
>
> 70. But he denied before them all, saying, I know not what thou sayest.
>
> 71. And when he was gone out into the porch, another maid saw hin, and said unto them that were there, This fellow was also with Jesus of Nazareth.
>
> 72. And again he denied with an oath, I do not know that man.
>
> 73. And after a while came unto him they that stood by, and said to Peter, Surely thou also are one of them; for thy speech betrayeth thee.

74. Then began he to curse and to swear, saying, I know not the man. And immediately the cock crew.

75. And Peter remembered the word of Jesus, which said unto him, Before the cock crow, thou shalt deny me thrice. And he went out, and wept bitterly.

The triple denial of Jesus by Peter, as the betrayal of Judas, depicts aspects of the mind of a man who is as yet imperfect. Peter also is everyman at a certain stage of development, such as that at which a convenient lie is made to replace the actual truth. So Peter lied, three times, mentally, emotionally, and verbally, as Jesus the Christ *in him* had foretold.

The prophecy proved to be only too true, although in Peter's case dawn brought repentence as the cock crew thrice. Peter was afraid that he too might share his Master's fate, and this fear caused him to deny, not only the historical Jesus, but also the very highest in himself, the God within.

The introduction into the two stories of the number three indicates the three densest levels of matter and the three mortal vehicles of man. Judas accepted—doubtless bargained for—thirty pieces of silver, while Peter thrice denied any association with his Master. In the former case, cupidity and faithlessness caused the fall; in the latter, fear even stronger than both vows and the love of the disciple for his Lord was chiefly responsible.

The fall of Judas is complete, ending in suicide. Peter, on the other hand, while filled with remorse manifested by tears, recovered his integrity and, since no record to the contrary exists, is assumed to have been accepted again into the company of the disciples of Jesus. The actions of Peter were designed only for self-protection and in no way seem to have contributed to the condemnation of Jesus by the authorities. His error, therefore, was far less serious than that of Judas, who gained financially and was responsible for the identification and arrest of his Master, as also of all that followed.

The grave misconduct of both Judas and Peter and Pilate's surrender of Jesus to the crowd occurred during the darkness of night, and this in itself is significant, for blindness, darkness, sleep, death, and night when applied to man are symbols of reduced activity of the spiritual Self. They represent the darkened mind and the despiritualized condition of the whole personality of man. This condition is further indicated by the fact that neither Judas nor Peter was physically in the presence of Jesus when the plans for betrayal were made and the denial occurred. This absence from the Master may be interpreted as a state of consciousness in which the more spiritual aspects of human nature (Jesus) were out of touch with the mortal personalities (Judas and Peter).

Day, on the other hand, implies the full influence and expression of the immortal soul in and through its mortal vehicles. This symbolism is apparently employed in the story of Peter whose remorse was so deeply felt at the dawn of day. The crowing of the cock introduces the additional element of sound and certian sounds correctly uttered—mantras—are said to have the power to dispel darkness from the human mind, however deep that darkness may have been. Thus the vibratory effects—such as the sound waves emitted by the cock when crowing—may awaken darkened minds to the interior light of idealism, good judgment, and high moral standards. Symbolically, the cock crow both heralds and brings about the dawn of a condition of "daylight" or the sun-illumined intellect. Of interest also is the fact that both men used the voice during the two episodes, although the words of Peter are of greater significance as, on the third occasion, he gave support to his denial by the use of curses, which may have been blasphemous.

Since Peter was the only disciple present in the guard-room, no indication is given of the presence there of a recorder of the incidents. The question arises as to how the recorded events could have become known to any observer, especially to the later compilers of the Gospels. If this doubt has weight, then an interpretation of the incident as allegorical is further justified.

In cosmogenesis, spirit is regarded as of positive polarity, the masculine potency in the creative process, while matter, on the other hand, is of negative polarity, the feminine potency. These two are not infrequently represented by male and female beings respectively, the goddess Nut and the god Seb in Egyptian symbology, for example.

In man, the higher triad (soul) is referred to as male and the lower quaternary (outer man) as female, and it is this latter which is made to be at enmity with the former in scriptural and mythological symbology. In conformity with this method of writing, a damsel is made to challenge Peter and evoke his threefold denial, perhaps representing the more material part of the constitution of man and therefore the initiator of his falls from grace. The episode of Samson and Delilah is one among many in the Old Testament to which this interpretation could be applied.

Exceptions to this rule do, however, exist. On occasion, the higher nature of man is represented by a female and the outer nature by a male. Hence, the Goddess Athena was the inspirer and protectress of heroes, and it was the wife of Pilate who warned him concerning his relationship with Jesus, an episode which will be considered later.

REFERENCES AND NOTES

1. Mark 1:17.
2. Thyrsus—the rod of initiation.
3. See diagram no. 4, p. 154.
4. See Hodson, *Lecture Notes,* Vol. 1, p. 185.
5. John 1:4 and 14.
6. See Hodson, *Hidden Wisdom,* Vol. 1, p. 93.
7. Eph. 4:13.
8. See Hodson, *Hidden Wisdom,* Vol. 1, p. 198.
9. See Hodson, *The Pathway to Perfection* and *Hidden Wisdom,* Vol. 1.
10. In Greek Myths: Zeus coming in the form of a cloud signifies air and water. His entry into Danae in the form of a shower of gold signifies mineral. The capture by Hephaestus of Aries and Aphrodite and their entrapment in a net indicates mental and emotional.

The bull upon which Europa was carried away and all which is presumed to have followed symbolizes the cosmic, generative power of Godhead (Zeus).

The Minatour may be somewhat similarly interpreted as both a realized union of the generative and procreative powers (bull) of Deity and illumined man, while Pasiphae, urgently driven by desire for the Minatour and united therewith, represents both matter itself (the feminine principle in nature and the awakened intuitive faculty in man) ardently aspiring to unity with the Divine, or *Buddhi* united with and vehicle for *Atma*.

The Christ (Logos nailed upon the Cross of matter) is perhaps the most perfect symbol of the procedure of the incarnation of spirit. Indeed, the Cross itself with its intersecting vertical (spirit) and horizontal (matter) arms portrays the same idea.

The ceremonial procedure known as Holy Unction—apart from its immediate significance—also portrays the imposition upon and penetration of spirit (Consecrated oil) into matter—the body of the recipient.

11. Matt. 26:53.

12. See Hodson, *Hidden Wisdom,* Vol. 2, Appendix, The Sephirothal Tree.

13. Matt. 26:53.

14. Matt. 5:7; Luke 6:20.

15. John 18:10.

16. See Hodson, *Lecture Notes,* Vol. I, Ch. 13, Chart. Right eye—*Buddhi*; left eye—*Manas* 1; right ear—*Manas* 2 (rationcinating mind); left ear—astral; right nostral—*prana*; left nostral—etheric double; mouth—*Atma*.

17. Luke 22:51.

18. Luke 24:31, 51.

19. John 6:63.

20. See Hodson, *Hidden Wisdom,* Vol. 1, Part IV.

21. John 19:28; 10:30.

22. Matt. 16:18.

23. John 2:19.

24. John 20:28.

25. Isa. 35:8.

26. *Wisd. of Sol.,* 2:23.

PART ELEVEN

TRIAL, CRUCIFIXION, RESURRECTION, REAPPEARANCES AND ASCENSION

Chapter Twenty-Eight

The great drama of the life, ministry and death of Jesus, the Christ, now moves on toward its closing phases, of which the four Gospels sufficiently reveal the historical account. This may be taken at its own face value. It may also be somewhat exoterically read as descriptive of the natural and apparently instinctive reaction of mankind during the present phase of human evolution to influences which would bring about change. When such changes involve the destruction of outworn methods and ideas in order to make room for new and improved approaches in both religion and daily life, then man resists, not hesitating to use the most cruel means of self-protection against undesired elements of change. Unfortunately, such history as is available reveals that enmity has been aroused, generally directed with force against great Teachers and the new vision of which they teach. Individuals who personally benefit by existing regimes fear for the loss of both prestige and financial gain. They also take sides with those forces which fear and resist new ideas and their applications to human living.

In the case of Jesus, the material forces arrayed against him, including as they did the occupying Roman regime, proved to be far too strong. Since he refrained from drawing upon the spiritual and occult powers which were at his disposal, the bodily vehicle of the Avatar was condemned and died upon the Cross. Truth, however, is indestructible, however mortal its verbal expressions in given eras. Times change and every epoch inevitably gives place to a succession in which the resisted and resented powers, truths and ideas new in former times are given prominence in the minds and ultimately the governments of mankind, and new regimes are founded as means for their expression. Thus, Jesus eventually ascended into heaven.

If, however, the great story is read as allegory, then the condemnation, death, and burial of Jesus very aptly portray cosmic and universal phases in the emanation into matter and consequent evolution of divine power, life, and intelligence. The story may also be read as descriptive of monadic involution and evolution through matter and kingdoms of nature until superhumanity is attained. Furthermore, it may possibly be adduced that certain men who became disciples of the Master, and so were endowed with supernormal powers, successfully directed the spiritual impulse initiated by their Master to bring into existence the Christian faith.

Whichever of these three views is given consideration, it becomes clear that the story of the life and death of Jesus is immortal; for the involution and evolution of the divine spirit-essence within the universe and man are still continuing and are destined to do so until the end of the epoch. Furthermore, other Masters of life and death have arisen during the intervening two thousand years; other men have become their disciples and have been trained to become agents for the powers, blessings and ideas their Masters have revealed to them.

Thus viewed, the narrative assumes a universality which lifts it out of the limitations of time and space, and bestows upon it the quality of a revelation of truths which are eternal. The axioms of Euclid such as "Things which are equal to the same things are equal to one another" remain true whether applied before or after the Christian Era and whether in the Northern or the Southern Hemisphere. Neither time nor place can deny or default them. So also the emanation, involution, evolution and steady improvement in manifestation of the indwelling spirit of universe and man are also philosophically axiomatic and thus independent of time and space.

Since the life story of Jesus related in the Gospels is a dramatic presentation of the above-mentioned processes, then neither the accuracy of the record nor the time at which Jesus is said to have lived are of special moment to the philosophic mind. Even so, the English translation of the original Gospels is so rich in symbolical, philosophical and occult allusions written in the mystery language that a study of the narrative can prove to be highly rewarding.

Matt. 27:1.   When the morning was come, all the chief priests and elders of the people took counsel against Jesus to put him to death:

2.   And when they had bound him, they led him away, and delivered him to Pontius Pilate the governor.

Directly interpreted in the terms of occult philosophy already advanced, orders of angelic hosts unite to induce and induct universal spirit into deeper depths of matter, performing the same function for the Monad of man. This highly important, spiritual and occult function—like all others in objective universes—is fulfilled in strict obedience to the laws governing the emanative procedure. Having themselves severely restricted the forthgoing or "descending" spirit, personified by Jesus, these intelligences recognize the rulership of spiritual law. Thus, Jesus is bound by the chief priests and delivered to Pontius Pilate, the governor.

Matt. 27:3.   Then Judas, which had betrayed him, when he saw that he was condemned, repented himself, and brought again the thirty pieces of silver to the chief priests and elders.

4.   Saying, I have sinned in that I have betrayed the innocent blood. And they said, What is that to us? see thou to that.

5.   And he cast down the pieces of silver in the temple, and departed, and went and hanged himself.

In these verses, Judas is presented as a tragic figure indeed. Repentance came with the dawn, as in Peter's case. Unlike Peter, however, Judas, who had actually sold his Master for gain and perchance a place of honor, realized the worthlessness of the price of his treachery. So deep had he fallen into self-degradation that the repentance and the return of the price of betrayal offered no hope of future happiness. For him, self-tortured by remorse, there was no place either among the disciples of Jesus or the high priests. In his hopelessness he added to his errors the further crime of suicide. In so doing he deprived himself of all possibility of recovering his own sense of honor and of rehabilitation among his fellowmen. Judas thus stands before mankind as a tragic figure indeed and a warning to all would-be traitors, whether to an ideal, a cause, or a person.

As an allegory, the influence of matter upon spirit and of desire and depravity upon the conduct of a human being is depicted here. If, however, such an approach to the last phases of the life of Judas is carried somewhat further, then self-murder may possibly indicate victory over the evil within himself, or the "killing out" of the elements of cupidity and disloyalty which he personified.

Cosmically interpreted, Judas's suicide represents the grip of matter over spirit eventually becoming loosened, ultimately to disappear or die, as it were, by its own hand. The ascended Adept has freed himself from the restrictions imposed upon will and consciousness by matter at all degrees of density. The triple attributes of activity, rhythm and inertia no longer influence him against his will, while he is completely self-harmonized in relation to all the pairs of opposites.

The view is not overlooked that Judas deliberately sought to play a beneficent part by giving his Master the opportunity to display his godlike powers before the high priests and the multitude. Indeed, some such hope would seem to have been held by the other disciples who expected Jesus to free himself, thereby demonstrating his Messiahship. Evidently Judas, as also the two disciples walking along the road to Emmaus,[1] found this expectancy to have failed, especially if some spectacular demonstration of divine power had been anticipated. This deep disappointment and even dejection must have remained with the disciples and the three Marys until the Resurrection of Jesus became known to them. Reillumined and with renewed spiritual faith, they proceeded to form that nucleus from which the Christian faith developed. In addition, Gnostic fragments, if accepted as historical rather than symbolic, indicate that Jesus personally taught and inspired them for some years after his Resurrection. But this experience was personal and largely private, and so in no wise did it fulfill hopes founded upon prophecy of a public and world demonstration of Messiahship.

Matt. 27:6.   And the chief priests took the silver pieces, and said, It is not lawful for to put them into the treasure, because it is the price of blood.

7.   And they took counsel, and bought with them the potter's field, to bury strangers in.

8.   Wherefore that field was called, The field of blood, unto this day.

The mental attitude and the action of the priests concerning the returned thirty pieces of silver hardly seem logical; for, in the first place, they were ready to pay money from the treasury as a bribe for the betrayal unto the death of Jesus, yet they were unready to pay it back again into the treasury after their purpose had been fulfilled. Their ultimate use of the money to buy and use a piece of land as a burial ground and their naming of it "the field of blood" bestow upon the record of the incident the possibility of a further symbolical interpretation as the loss of control over the mortal man by the inner Ego. Indeed, the story of Judas from his acceptance as a disciple to his suicide may be seen as descriptive of the conflict between two aspects and characteristics of the human mind. This war occurs at a certain stage of evolution when the spiritual Self is not as yet sufficiently developed to illumine and control the motives and conduct of the mortal man. Because every man is both divine and human, the waging of this interior way—the true Armageddon—is inevitable.

Judas, whether he ever existed or not, accurately portrays a man at a certain phase of development when the inner Self, the divine in him, is beginning to attain the power of spiritualizing the whole mortal man, his conscience, his motives, and his conduct. This is evidenced by the fact that he was drawn within the circle of the associates of Jesus as a chosen disicple. Jesus personifies the inner Self seeking to purify and to elevate the outer man, while Judas is that outer man with his spiritual aspirations and his still remaining human weaknesses and possibilities of self-degradation. The unfoldment of the spiritual Self of Judas, as of all those men of whom he is a prototype, was not yet sufficiently powerful to eliminate or reduce to impotence these qualities; and so the man Judas was defeated in the interior war.

The remainder of his story tells only of the result of failure upon the mortal man who, despite a temporary return of conscience, by his own hand died to the possibility of passage through "the strait gate" and entry upon "the narrow way," the way of holiness.[2] Occult philosophy, which is replete with teaching upon these and cognate subjects, gives assurance that no such experience as final defeat is ever possible to any human being, all men being a combination of an eternal and undying spirit and a mortal individuality, the two united by the presence and activity of the intellect.

Judas as an incarnated Ego—as also the rich young ruler—will live again, will once more aspire, and most certainly will ultimately become trustworthy disciples, for the spirit of man contains within itself the assurance of complete victory.

Matt. 27:9.   Then was fulfilled that which was spoken by Jeremy the prophet, saying, And they took the thirty pieces of silver, the price of him that was valued, whom they of the children of Israel did value;

10.   And gave them for the potter's field, as the Lord appointed me.

Again, the reference to the fulfillment of ancient prophecy would seem to become intelligible only when the life story of Jesus and the writings of the prophets of old are interpreted as descriptions of the descent of spirit into matter.

The number thirty, as heretofore suggested, is susceptible of interpretation as the incarnation of the threefold human Monad in man's mortal bodies of mind, emotion and flesh, the zero being ignored in such a case. Cosmically, the threefold Logos, in its turn, objectively manifests as triplicity when mirrored in matter. These two triplicities found in both man and nature —spiritual and material—are presented as interlaced in their ancient symbol known to the Hebrews as Solomon's Seal.[3]

The number three, to which the number thirty is reduced by the elision of the zero, may also refer to the three attributes of matter—activity, rhythm and inertia. In addition, the hidden energies in matter are threefold in terms of their polarization, namely, positive, negative, and neutral; it may well be that the biblical authors were referring to these attributes of matter whenever they introduced triplicities into their allegorical revelations. Such views also gain support from the statement that the thirty pieces of silver were used for purchase of a potter's field. The word *field* is a term employed for the matter of space, whether virginal or impregnated by spirit. The process of the shaping of all the forms of nature and the bodies of men by spirit resembles by analogy the work of a potter, as is indicated in the cosmogony of the ancient Egyptians.[4] Indeed, Judas himself may be said to personify the influence of matter upon spirit, which is symbolically to "betray," as already suggested.

If it should be charged that too much is being deduced from too little, then it may well be remembered that the ancient inspired writers were deliberately concealing profound and highly significant truths in their works, which would eventually become available to the public in general. The true seeker for light, moreover, is ever prepared to watch for both hints and symbolic declarations of the truth which he or she is determined to discover. Such students, while always submitting their findings to the ultimate test of reasonableness and concordance with the secret wisdom, are prepared to inquire after the treasures of truth, however deeply they may be buried in the rich mines of that literature which is written in the mystery language.

The Pythagorean quaternary, upon the value of which so much was placed, does not negate the existence of the eternal triplicities inherent in both spirit and matter. As the great sage knew so well, the fourth element is supplied by their continual interaction, positive and negative, forever entwining themselves, as it were, round the central or neutral polarity. This is the cosmic caduceus, the triple serpentine power in the Logos, in nature, and in man. The initiate and the Adept learn to use this triplicity as their means of self-liberation from the imprisoning grip of otherwise unyielding matter. Hence we have the caduceus in the Greek Mysteries, other serpent symbology in the Egyptian Mysteries, and the supposed fertility rites of Hinduism. The coiling form of the Ying and the Yang of ancient Chinese philosophic thought, with their harmonious interaction as essential to liberation, is based upon the same idea.

> Matt. 27:11.   And Jesus stood before the governor: and the governor asked him, saying, Art thou the King of the Jews? And Jesus said unto him, Thou sayest.

If this verse is truthfully historical, and if the reply of Jesus is to be interpreted as both an admission and an affirmation, then according to law Jesus was guilty of treason and rightfully subject to the penalty of death. Although Jesus is described as being descended from a king of the Jews, namely David, the Hebrews at that time possessed no royal house and so could not legitimately claim to have a king. Jesus was therefore deeply and voluntarily in error if his reply is indeed to be regarded as claim to royalty. In such a case the infliction of the penalty of death was virtually assured. Doubt of the historicity of the incident arises from the fact that Jesus must have known this and in so replying actually and deliberately condemned himself to death. Furthermore, the total absence of any historical record—apart from an admittedly doubtful reference in Josephus—of the existence among the Jews of Jesus, his heresy, and his claim to kingship, with all that is said by the Evangelists to have followed, cannot but throw grave doubt upon the historicity of the gospel story.

If, however, the Evangelists and others who testified were Magi, wise men steeped in the hidden wisdom, and were writing a wondrous allegory as revelation to mankind down the centuries, then their story is most exact indeed.

Both Logos and Monad are as kings and do quite voluntarily become incarnate in matter of the deepest density in order that their innate life may become increasingly manifest and shine forth resplendently as royal powers indeed. Doubt of the historicity of the incident arises from the fact that Jesus must have known this and in so replying actually and deliberately condemned himself to death. The apparent mystery of the self-condemnatory reply is solved by the realization of the fact that in very truth both Logos and Monad are indeed as kings among men.

Thus Jesus is made virtually to condemn himself to death (at the hand of matter and its attributes) but always with the full knowledge, as he proclaims, of the ascent which must and will follow, allegorically portrayed by Resurrection and Ascension.

> Matt. 27:12.   And when he was accused of the chief priests and elders, he answered nothing.
>
> 13.   Then said Pilate unto him, Hearest thou not how many things they witness against thee?
>
> 14.   And he answered him to never a word; insomuch that the governor marvelled greatly.

The silence of Jesus before his accusers thus becomes inevitable. Indeed, if the story is as much or even more allegorical than historical, spirit in its self-chosen submission to matter has naught to answer. Similarly, the Monad of man on its self-chosen pilgrimage through incarnation can have no complaints against the restrictions which are the inevadable price of that long cyclic journey from unconscious, innate divine powers toward their development and full manifestation.

Historically viewed, the arraignment was so serious and the forces arrayed against him so powerful that any attempt at self-defense would be unlikely to succeed; for his enemies were determined upon his execution, and this he knew full well. In either reading the silence of Jesus is understandable.

> Matt. 27:15.   Now at that feast the governor was wont to release unto the people a prisoner, whom they would.
>
> 16.   And they had then a notable prisoner, called Barabbas.
>
> 17.   Therefore when they were gathered together, Pilate said unto them, Whom will ye that I release unto you? Barabbas, or Jesus which is called Christ?
>
> 18.   For he knew that for envy they had delivered him.

Foreknowledge of Jesus's fate was evidently shared by Pilate who, as the eighteenth verse makes clear, put up but a show of fairness. Hebrew custom was, however, duly recognized and Barabbas, a condemned thief, was offered as substitute for Jesus.

> Matt. 27:19.   When he was set down on the judgment seat, his wife sent unto him, saying, Have thou nothing to do with that just man; for I have suffered many things this day in a dream because of him.

At this point the narrative once again becomes descriptive of interior experiences, evolutionary stature and consequent actions taking place within the mind of a human being. Certain men in their evolution find that duplicity is almost natural to them.

Pilate himself personifies the stage of a man deliberately acting through self-interest and those lower elements which can lead man to contravene any dawning idealism and realistic conscience. He owes his honorable position as governor to the Romans, a position which he was not ready to place in jeopardy by setting free to the people a man who claimed to be the king of the Jews. Also, he was acutely aware of the pressure put upon him by the people themselves, represented in the narrative as rabidly demanding the death of Jesus. The narrators, whoever they may have been, would almost seem to have recognized and decided to portray a certain element of goodness and high principle in Pilate, who must thus have been at war within himself. The story is richly informative if thus regarded.

His wife represents the best in him, the higher instincts, even the intuitive faculty. This intrudes upon his tortuous mentality, as can so often occur, even if disregarded, deep within the mind of a man determined upon dishonesty or at best duplicity. Such a reading is supported by the wording of the message which Pilate's wife sent to him, namely, that her misgivings were entertained "this day," an allusion to an enlightened and even uplifted, clear-seeing state of mind. However, she was not present, meaning that the faculty was not sufficiently developed to be continuously operative. Instead of being an active part of Pilate's character, who was absent and was obliged to send her warning by a messenger.

Thus viewed, the life of Jesus is the story of the life of everyman, and each of the incidents reveals truths concerning the nobler and baser attributes of human nature and, with great skill, that interior conflict which must be waged between them until victory is won.

Matt. 27:20.   But the chief priests and elders persuaded the multitude that they should ask Barabbas, and destroy Jesus.

21.   The governor answered and said unto them, Whether of the twain will ye that I release unto you? They said, Barabbas.

22.   Pilate saith unto them, What shall I do then with Jesus which is called Christ? They all say unto him, Let him be crucified.

Continuing the preceding approach to the story, the rabid multitude represents those qualities in human nature which make almost irresistible demands for the gratification of passionately felt desires to which man succumbs until a certain stature is attained. Thus, the multitude refused the substitute named Barabbas, a condemned thief, and demanded the death of Jesus who had moved harmlessly among them as teacher and healer.

In the macrocosmic and the monadic interpretations of the story, Pilate and the multitude personify the degrading and temporarily blinding effects of the attributes of matter upon spirit. In occult philosophy, these attributes are described as threefold—namely, activity, harmony and inertia.[5] When the first and the last of these are controlled and evenly expressed in a human being, then harmony is destroyed. While the relatively less evolved people around him displayed the excesses referred to, Jesus throughout the narrative is seen as a perfect embodiment and personification of the perfected man.

Matt. 27:23.   And the governor said, Why, what evil hath he done? But they cried out the more, saying, Let him be crucified.

24.   When Pilate saw that he could prevail nothing, but that rather a tumult was made, he took water, and washed his hands before the multitude, saying, I am innocent of the blood of this just person; see ye to it.

25.   Then answered all the people, and said, His blood be on us, and on our children.

Two differing stages of man's evolution are portrayed in this episode in the life story of Jesus. Throughout, the central figure is in marked contrast to most of the other people in the account, since Jesus personifies perfection while many others, including Peter, Judas, Pilate and the multitude, portray the man in whom various imperfections still exist. Until the Christlike life, the perfect life, is entered, many and various imperfections remain to be outgrown.

Pilate in these verses exemplifies this method of teaching, since against his own better judgment he succumbs to the cries and threats of the multitude and delivers Jesus over to them. His action of washing his hands may possibly be interpreted either as publicly exhibiting his own doubts and even disagreement or closing his mind to the remorse which normally should follow a deliberately sinful act.

Pilate was himself virtually responsible for all the subsequent treatment of Jesus, including his Crucifixion. Even he may possibly have at least begun to repent—as did Peter and Judas—for later he refused to change the wording of the inscription which he wrote and which was to be placed over the head of the crucified Christ.

> Matt. 27:26.   Then released he Barabbas unto them: and when he had scourged Jesus, he delivered him to be crucified.

The gospel story does indeed stand on its own merits as a great epic and is thus customarily read. It is, however, far more than that, since, transcending time, it also and very perfectly reveals the many facets, stages of development, and ways in which these become manifest in everyman as he treads his pathway to perfection or Christhood. On that path the falls are many as are also the heroisms, but because man is essentially an unfolding, imperishable and eternal spiritual being all dangers and obstacles are overcome and the goal of ascended adeptship is attained.

The scourging of Jesus at the order of Pilate may be interpreted as portraying the sufferings of repentance and remorse in the case of an imperfect man, while as part of the experiences of the initiate approaching adeptship, they mark the beginning of the sufferings sometimes referred to as *the Passion*. Why, it may be asked, should one so near to the highest human attainment be called upon thus to suffer? It is in order that every last debt to mankind and to nature in every aspect be utterly and completely paid; for the law of cause and effect demands and must receive its just due.

A more precise interpretation of each of the indignities and sufferings which are said to have been penally inflicted upon Jesus also reveals by means of allegory and symbol certain deeply interior experiences which are inevadable until the necessity for them is transcended. The Adept is fully conscious, not only of the unity of all life, but of the fact that no faintest film actually divides or separates him as a person from that life. The natural egoism characteristic of unredeemed man must be outgrown, and so with suffering the skin of the body—an apt symbol of an enclosing separateness—must be broken. The scourging of the naked body would indicate the beginning of a general emancipation from the illusion of self-separateness.

> Matt. 27:27.   Then the soldiers of the governor took Jesus into the common hall, and gathered unto him the whole band of soldiers.
>
> 28.   And they stripped him, and put on him a scarlet robe.
>
> 29.   And when they had plaited a crown of thorns, they put it upon his head, and a reed in his right hand: and they bowed the knee before him, and mocked him, saying, Hail, King of the Jews!

The mockery described in these verses portrays only too well—if symbolically rather than actually—the attitude of mind and the means of its expression held by the less wise to those who are wiser than themselves. This, however, is understandable, since the teachings of Jesus (such as the Sermon on the Mount) must have been regarded by the multitude os the unillumined as hopelessly impracticable, while the miscalled miracles were by some promptly scorned as exhibitions by a mere charlatan employed to gain power over the ignorant. The descriptions are nevertheless worthy of close attention, sincecertain classical symbols appear in theh.

The exclusive presence of soldiers, for example, suggests that discipline to which the high initiate must attain. In the sacred language nakedness is used as a symbol to portray the absence of the slightest barrier between man's spiritual source of illumination and his mental preparedness to receive it— free from the slightest interposition of accepted traditional ideas. This full exposure of the mind, and so the brain, to the influence of the God within is said to be essential to the full receipt and attainment of pure wisdom, perfect insight, and complete comprehension. The nakedness of the blind Bartimaeus whose sight was restored by Jesus aptly exemplifies both this condition and the result of its attainment, namely, the absence of blindness and the restoration of sight.

Although the soldiers, accustomed not to think but only to obey orders, intended merely to demean and degrade Jesus who had claimed to be a king, the symbols of royalty with which they adorned him in mockery are enlightening. The multitude of the unillumined are able to discern only red robe, crown of thorns, and reed scepter rather than the attainments of spiritual royalty and a coronation of spirit. The crowd thus sees only mockery and suffering, but the initiated perceive a deep spiritual significance in each of the emblems of kingship.

The red robe is part of the insignia of power, while the crown of thorns which pierced the skin of the head implies the completed attainment of freedom in the realm of the intellect from even the slightest restriction of separated self-existence. This is not reached without both effort and considerable pain as the last vestiges of egotism are transcended. The crown also refers to the opened force-center or chakra on the crown of the head (on Golgotha, the place of the skull).[6] The act of crowning represents the process of the opening of this force-center and consequent assurance of free interplay and communion between the divine and the mortal man. In ancient days when kings were also high initiates of the Greater Mysteries and even incarnations of divinity, this critical force-center was awakened in them by two means. One of these consisted of prolonged contemplation of the Supreme Deity; the other occurred by the action of heirophants of the Mystery rites, who brought certain occult and spiritual forces to bear upon specific parts of the head, notably the crown. The uninitiated merely saw a king or a queen wearing a ureus or crown, but the initiated, being occultly instructed and themselves having similarly attained, saw the manifestation of true spiritual royalty. Thus viewed, the crown of thorns itself and the act of placing it upon the head of Jesus constitute the most deeply spiritual part of the symbolism of the Crucifixion.

The reed scepter as symbol of kingship, correctly understood, demonstrates the greatest of all sources of human power and self-rule, namely, that gentleness with which such power is ever applied when the purpose is to instruct, to inspire, and when necessary to correct. A dual development is thus displayed—veritably a kingly will and a complete mastery over its expression in action.

When of his own choice a man becomes an occult sage, his self-command is so great that he remains unmoved by the antagonism which his greatness evokes and undisturbed by the cruel revelry with which the scorn is accompanied. Before the attainment of adeptship, a certain amount of suffering in payment of debts incurred must be accepted; for then and then only are all bonds finally cast away.

> Matt. 27:30. And they spit upon him, and took the reed, and smote him on the head.
>
> 31. And after that they had mocked him, they took the robe off him, and put his own raiment on him, and led him away to crucify him.

The soldiers personify the narrowly restricted states of mind of those whose thought has become confined in a set and very limited groove. Their scorn is further applied to the intellect of an enlightened one. Every true leader of men, every light-bringer to the human race, passes through such experiences interiorly as the conflict rages between widening vision and expanding comprehension, on the one hand, and the mental habits and bodily appetites, on the other. In such a view, the betrayal, trial, condemnation, scorn, and Crucifixion of Jesus are descriptive of interior experiences through which every Adept has passed in one form or another and through which every man must pass before final deliverance is attained. The Palestine of two thousand years ago and Jerusalem, its capital, are not only places which existed in time and space, but they are symbols of the body, the heart, and the head of every initiate who, Jesus-like, becomes a Master of life and death.

> Matt. 27:32. And as they came out, they found a man of Cyrene, Simon by name: him they compelled to bear his cross.

The incident recorded in this verse is chiefly significant as exemplifying the fact that, however severe and demanding the ordeals of initiation, they are never beyond the capacity of the candidate to endure and to emerge victorious, crowned in fact. Either the spirit of the initiate is sufficiently evolved or, should this not be the case, reasonable aid is provided. Even so, in order to emerge triumphant, the initiate-to-be must demonstrate his power to withstand the ordeal, though some assistance may be accorded him. Simon of Cyrene personifies this principle of compassion amid the sorest trials.

> Matt. 27:33. And when they were come unto a place called Golgotha, that is to say, a place of a skull,

The name of the place where Jesus was crucified provides a key with which the esoteric meaning of his Passion and death may be understood. When this key is fitted into the lock and turned even once, the real location of the great event is revealed, namely, *within* the skull or head of man. The great triumph must be won and the great illumination must occur in the physical organ of consciousness; for it is not the bodily man who is crucified and rises from the dead, but the radiant and enthroned inner Self which, after long ages of evolution, attains to spiritual kingship. The resultant capacities, powers, and wisdom are parts of the riches of the evolving soul rather than of the bodily man. Thus, in this verse the inspired authors of the Gospels provide the seeker for esoteric wisdom within their writings with the necessary hint, clue, or more accurately, the veritable key.

> Matt. 27:34.   They gave him vinegar to drink mingled with gall: and when he had tasted thereof, he would not drink.

If this incident is to be regarded as of greater significance than the action itself implies, then profound insight into the mystic life of man is displayed by the inspired authors. At some stage, during some life of self-emancipation from the delusion of separateness and of the final meeting of the demands of the law, the pain which one endures includes that of a profound bitterness of heart. Not only hands, feet, head, and side must all be pierced, each with its symbolic meaning, but even the interior organ and sense of taste must suffer. This implies that the pains endured penetrate deep into the inner nature of the initiate, so that he or she endures bitterness of heart and mind in a peculiarly poignant way.

Jesus merely tasted the vinegar and gall but did not drink deeply, implying that he had neither psychological nor karmic reason to do so. Though he must taste the bitterness, he had no need to drink it, being free to refuse.

> Matt. 27:35.   And they crucified him, and parted his garments, casting lots: that it might be fulfilled which was spoken by the prophet, They parted my garments amongst them, and upon my vesture did they cast lots.

Three orders of symbology are referred to in this terse description of most dreadful conduct and agonizing suffering. These are the cross itself, garments and parts of the body, and the nails with which hammers must be associated.

Macrocosmically, as heretofore suggested, the Cross is symbolic of the processes of cosmogenesis, the vertical arm representing the positive creative potency or spirit and the horizontal arm the receptive, negative creative potency or matter. At the point of intersection, the Logos—as conceiver, manifester, fashioner, and Life-giver—is as it were "crucified," very severely restricted, upon fructified substance with its four directions of space depicted by the arms of the cross.

While this act of self-sacrifice is voluntary, the loss of timeless freedom, logoic bliss and illimitable power is inevitably suffered—a deprivation which is beyond the capacity of the human mind even remotely to comprehend. If this interpretation may permissibly be carried further, then being nailed to the cross refers to the loss of freedom, the spear wound in the heart to the loss of bliss, and the ironic crown of thorns to the loss of that power which is the kingly crown of every Logos. The body itself is forced to lie prone upon the ground while being nailed to the cross—itself a further and most expressive representation of the great Sacrifice, as the incarnation of divinity is sometimes and very aptly described. The exceedingly painful, enforced prevention of the movement of the feet may permissibly be regarded as a reference to loss of logoic freedom of movement throughout space. While at spiritual levels of consciousness the normal, three-dimensional concept of space, with its divisions and its separated areas, is transcended, the Logos of a solar system is incarnate therein. Thus to some extent the Logos is confined —however voluntarily—to the region of his domain as solar king. The similar prevention of manual movement may well indicate restriction of the action of the will-thought-sound by means of which a universe is emanated, fashioned, and directed in terms of divine activity, a loss of freedom indeed.

While the text in general refers to a spear wound in the side, death may be presumed to have followed the entry of the point of the spear into the heart, ever a symbol of the purely spiritual parts of both Logos and man. The pain of the wound, the effect of incarnation in matter—particularly the densest matter (the wooden cross and the iron nails)—as well as the complete loss of freedom of movement and action may contribute to a diminution of the divine bliss.

A crown of bejeweled gold placed upon the head applies symbolically to joy-giving intellectual enlightenment, while a crown of thorns implies pain-produced restriction and loss of power. Thus the Cross, wounded heart and crown of thorns signify logoic loss of freedom, bliss, and power.

In the usual collection of symbols associated with the Crucifixion of Jesus, the nails are four-sided and with a geometrically shaped head, both oft-used symbols of matter itself and of spirit deeply "driven" into matter. The driving force is represented in such symbology by the hammer, which must have been used throughout the excruciatingly painful procedure. It may be regarded as an emblem of the very will-force of the Logos himself in the fulfillment of his design to suffer a symbolic—and to some extent, actual —crucifixion. Extending this reading, the long, geometrically formed, and sharply pointed nails may symbolize the projected dynamic electrical force by which atoms are formed and the divine design or Archetype is impressed upon matter. The flail, the mace, club, and hammer, associated with actively present divine beings in the symbology of ancient peoples, may all refer both to this power itself and to the manner in which it is employed. Thus viewed, the Crucifixion of Jesus the Christ is regarded as an allegorical description of the Self-incarnation of the immanent Logos in the matter of his universe and of all the sacrifices and restrictions which this must entail. Nevertheless, the Logos is also transcendent above and beyond his universe, and in this aspect of his Being, relatively free of spatial limitations, he experiences the consciousness typical of divine Beings.

The wounded but ever-open heart of the Lord, sometimes called the Sacred Heart, indicates that in both Logos and Adept the heart of all-inclusive love is ever open to the needs, the aspirations, and even the denials and the hatred of the worlds of mind-endowed beings. In a mystical interpretation, the conflict between the inner will of the aspirant and undesirable traits of character and habitual modes of thought, feeling and action inflicts those mystical "wounds" from which Jesus suffered as he trod the way of the Cross from Gethsemane to Golgotha.

The disrobing of Jesus, the "parting" of his garments, and the gambling for the pieces of cloth may be interpreted symbolically. In manifestation the Life of the Logos, personified by Jesus and symbolized by his supposed seamless dress, becomes embodied in innumerable forms, or parted. This apparent division is an illusion since despite the diversity of forms, inorganic and organic, physical and superphysical, the indwelling Life in all of them is one and the same. If such an interpretation is not pushed too far, then the proclaimed gambling may refer to the apparent chance under which nature produces her almost innumerable progeny—the natural forms. Actually, of course, no such gambling nor any uncertainty whatever are associated with the production and development of nature's forms, all of which appear and change according to exact law.

Matt. 27:36.   And sitting down they watched him there;

37.   And set up over his head his accusation written, THIS IS JESUS THE KING OF THE JEWS.

The watchers must be presumed to have included both Roman soldiers and the people of Jerusalem who had followed the procession from the judgment hall to Golgotha. As the act of Crucifixion continued, they sat down to watch the agony of Jesus and to wait for his death. This shows an attitude of mind which sadly is displayed by some members of the human race, though fortunately far from all.

The proclamation quoting the supposed admission of Jesus must be regarded as an expression of the scorn with which his claim was received. Yet in the purely spiritual sense he was a king among his fellow Hebrews, being far more highly evolved than any of them, a man of truly royal stature. In addition, he was descended from the ancient kings, as diverse genealogies indicate. Although neither of these was recognized, nevertheless both substantiated such a claim, although it is extremely unlikely he ever made it.

Matt. 27:38.   Then were there two thieves crucified with him, one on the right hand, and another on the left.

The truly repellent and horrible spectacle of the three bodies hanging in agony upon three crosses on Golgotha too well known, all too familiar, and almost treasured by some Christian hearts. It has been and still is repeated and referred to millions and millions of times by means of crucifixes set up and worn throughout Christendom. Yet the mystical experience which John records in his apocryphal gospel indicates that it was either an illusion or a physical symbol of a spiritual event,[7] as will later be discussed.

The event itself may well be regarded as the attainment by a high initiate of the highest spiritual experience, namely, conscious realization while awake in the body of oneself as a manifestation of the spirit-essence of the universe. The supporting symbology, already partly interpreted, lends weight to such a view and is worthy of close examination.

The great obstacle to self-conscious realization of oneself as part of Deity consists of the uncontrolled intermingling of the concrete with the abstract aspect of the human intelligence. The former is essentially and very usefully analytical, ideally logical, intensely demanding of external evidence and critical of ideas not thus supported. However, the instinctive sense of self-separateness which takes the form of egoism and personal pride can combine with the above-described qualities to rob the human intellect of its capacity for intuitive perception of interior, nonobjective verities. In consequence, as H.P. Blavatsky indicates, "the mind is the great slayer of the Real," and she follows the affirmation with the advice, "Let the disciple slay the slayer."[8] In symbology the mind is also represented as a robber or a thief, and very aptly, for the above-described reasons.

Since one of these thieves scorned and scoffed at Jesus, he may well personify the analytical and unintuitional formal mind. The other thief prayed to be with Jesus in paradise after the death of their bodies, a petition which was granted. If this present delineation is acceptable, then this second thief personifies the abstract human intelligence which is responsive to ideas and flashes of illumination from intuitional and purely spiritual levels. Jesus between the two thieves indicates that state of consciousness in which the formal mind with all its operations and functions is fully and consciously separated from the abstract intellect, so that the former could no more inhibit the interior functions of the latter. In consequence, the purely spiritual, highly intuitional, and indeed royal supramental aspects of man, personified by Jesus on the Cross, could and did become manifest. Thus, it is a state of consciousness and a stage in human evolution which are being allegorically and symbolically portrayed and not the degrading, abhorrent spectacle of the threefold act of inhuman cruelty and sadism. As before mentioned, such a view gains further support by the name of the location at which the scene of horror was enacted, Golgotha, "the place of the skull." It is worthy of note that the physical body had been made helpless and so was unable to achieve purely spiritual self-illumination, self-liberation, and self-coronation.

Matt. 27:39.   And they that passed by reviled him wagging their heads.

40.   And saying, Thou that destroyest the temple, and buildest it in three days, save thyself. If thou be the Son of God, come down from the cross.

While the ignorant challenged Jesus to come down from the cross, the wise saw and knew that on the contrary he ascended above it, having left his body by the egress formed by the opened force-center at the crown of the head.This is the real Resurrection, the tomb later referred to symbolizing the body and the skull wherein normally the center of self-awareness is imprisoned.

The Apocryphal gospel of John, which describes many mystical experiences of the disciple whom Jesus loved, would seem to support a view that the supposed Crucifixion on Golgotha was really a glyph or even an illusion induced in the public mind. By this no doubt he meant the unillumined mind which mistakes the veil of allegory and symbol as reality, being either unable or unwilling to perceive the underlying truths.[9] John writes that, inspired by the Master during the Crucifixion, he went up on to the Mount of Olives and entered a cave.[10] There he saw the Lord who said unto him: "John, unto the multitude below in Jerusalem I am being crucified and pierced with lances and reeds, and gall and vinegar is given me to drink. But unto thee I speak . . ." He then showed John a cross of light as the true Cross and the cross of wood as an illusion, continuing: "Neither am I he that is on the Cross . . . for know thou that I am wholly with the Father, and the Father with me."

Hence, death in the Mysteries is dual; the initiate has both overcome the dread of death and ascended above the lower worlds. He determines to progress and knows that this is the only way. There is pain, a veritable passion of pain, but the consciousness is not restricted to it. Pain becomes a shadowy undertone to the chant of triumph which the Monad-Ego sings.

Matt. 27:41.	Likewise also the chief priests mocking him, with the scribes and elders, said,
42.	He saved others; himself he cannot save. If he be the King of Israel, let him now come down from the cross, and we will believe him.
43.	He trusted in God; let him deliver him now, if he will have him: for he said, I am the Son of God.

The multitude, the soldiers, and the officials who mocked at and challenged Jesus while he was dying on the Cross saw only the complete helplessness to which their actions had reduced a human being who was said to have claimed divine powers. Hence their mockery, which contrasts those who are spiritually unillumined with those passing through the processes of self-illumination and attainment of adeptship. The latter is a spiritual and therefore physically invisible procedure, while to worldly minds it is but an exhibition of ignorance.

The student of the meanings of symbols may well remember that some of these convey more than one idea and may sometimes even seem to contradict one another. The death of Jesus on the Cross, for example, implied a final freedom from the limitations of the body—especially of the brain in the skull—and entry into the exalted state of awareness in which the perfected man perpetually abides. The life heroes of scripture and mythology who are made to suffer figurative deaths portray the killing out from within themselves of qualities and tendencies which blind the intellect to the perception of the light of spirit. Death in such cases—including that of Jesus when so interpreted—is not a defeat but a victory, an allegorical episode on the pathway to a fuller manifestation of divine manhood. The life stories of Peter, Pilate, Thomas, and Judas Iscariot may be similarly interpreted, as also may that of the disciple John whom Jesus loved. It is suggested that Martha, Mary, and Lazarus of Bethany as well as John the Baptist, may similarly be regarded.

The death of an ordinary person not preceded by allegorical description of stages of interior unfoldment refers to a state of spiritual deadness or absence of illumination while using the body in everyday life. When a supposedly deceased person is brought back to life by an Adept, an allegory of the attainment of spiritual awareness is implied. The presence of a Master in the story refers to the realized divine power and presence inherent in the spiritual soul. At a certain stage in the contemplative life, the devotee, symbolically deceased, has now come to life in terms of conscious knowledge of his or her own divinity with its inherent spiritual power, wisdom, and intelligence.

Matt. 27:44. The thieves also, which were crucified with him?cast the same in his teeth.

St. Luke records this incident differently in that, while one of the thieves mocked at Jesus, the other said unto him, "Lord, remember me when thou comest into thy kingdom."[11] It is worthy of note that despite difference in conduct, both thieves died. This perchance refers to the slaying of the power of the mind to obstruct the function of the intuition or Christ-consciousness.

Matt. 27:45. Now from the sixth hour there was darkness over all the land unto the ninth hour.

46. And about the ninth hour Jesus cried with a loud voice, saying, Eli, Eli, lama sabachthani? that is to say, My God, my God, why hast thou forsaken me?

St. Paul evidently did not regard the Nativity and the Crucifixion of Christ as single, isolated events occurring at two particular times, but rather as interior experiences passed through by all men who successfully tread the pathway to spiritual kingship. This view is also implicit in the preceding suggested interpretation of the life of Jesus, and particularly of his Passion and Crucifixion. If this view is accepted, then readers of the life of Christ are metaphorically taken into a temple of the Greater Mysteries and permitted to observe the passage of a candidate therein through the five great initiations which culminate in the attainment of adeptship or allegorical Ascension to the right hand of God. This last exit from the human kingdom of nature and self-liberation from the limitations of purely human existence upon a single planet is foreshadowed in the verses under consideration.

The darkness refers to the condition of mind of all those supposedly present at Golgotha concerning the reality of that which was occurring. For most, if not all, this was the complete humiliation and slow death by crucifixion of a man who had claimed to be king of the Jews and the Son of God upon earth. Since Jesus did not display the powers supposedly possessed by such a person, he became the subject of scorn and mockery. Such people saw only an external event, since, being in darkness, they were unable to perceive the reality which that event concealed. All readers of the gospel story, unless informed or spiritually illumined, are in precisely this position.

The forty-sixth verse offers a ray of light by which the event becomes visible in its transcendent aspects. Two translations of the cry of Jesus when near to death have been suggested, both revealing the states of consciousness through which the initiate passes. The first is that given in this verse and reveals descriptively the fact that during the rite the initiate experiences absolute loneliness in the universe, commencing in Gethsemane for Jesus and reaching its culmination on the Cross. This failure of all external and personal support is followed by a mental darkness during which the realization of his own divinity and his unity with the Logos is completely lost. This suppression, however temporary, of a state of consciousness already attained, namely, unity with the Lord of the universe, may last but a moment or a timeless hour. So great a deprivation evokes a cry of protest from the mind and heart of the initiate who is breaking his final shackles—in effect a protest that the Deity had forsaken him.

This is an essential experience. Only after every external support is withdrawn does the truth burst upon the self-crucified one that he and the eternal Deity are one and the same Being. This discovery is so revolutionary and so transcendent that the initiate can never again lose his attained knowledge, not merely of unity, but even of identity with the universal God. A second translation would apply more appropriately to the exultation of an experience which comes later, with the appropriate cry, "My God, my God, how thou dost glorify me." Thus, the two possible translations are not mutually exclusive, but rather consecutive in time, as indicated.

> Matt. 27:47.   Some of them that stood there, when they heard that, said, This man calleth for Elias.

Objectively regarded, certain verses in the gospel narrative give rise to the question as to the authenticity of the observer, reporter, and recorder of apparently minor incidents such as the one referred to in this verse; for the conversation was carried out among the people present and was therefore quite distinct from the dramatic spectacle itself. However, the faulty hearing of such watchers and their misinterpretation and lack of understanding of the words reportedly uttered by Jesus may be read as indicating the total ignorance of the masses of the people concerning the real significance of the drama being enacted before their eyes, particularly as descripitive of entering the superhuman kingdom.

> Matt. 27:48.   And straightway one of them ran, and took a sponge, and filled it with vinegar, and put it on a reed, and gave him to drink.

Betrayal, defamation, and uttermost loneliness are bitter experiences, and this incident may have been included in the story to symbolize the nature and the depth of suffering through which a man must pass at the final rupture and transcendence of every human limitation, notably that of conscious existence as a separate individuality. Every human attachment which binds must be broken—a bitter experience indeed. The betrayal by Judas, the denial by Peter, and the inability of his disciple and his mother to help him, may all be read as descriptive of this form of suffering, typically portrayed by vinegar to be drunk as the agony of physical death came upon him.

> Matt. 27:49.   The rest said, let be, let us see whether Elias will come to save him.

Here is a further example of the ignorance of unillumined humanity and its complete inability to comprehend, still less to participate in, the profound, accompanying mystical states of consciousness accompanying Crucifixion.

> Matt. 27:50.   Jesus, when he had cried again with a loud voice, yielded up the ghost.

A surcease of the agony, both physical and psychological, comes at last through death, whether actually of the body or figuratively of the consciousness of the mortal man.

Ceremonials of the Mysteries, Greater and Lesser, and the processes of dying, death, and burial, have little or nothing to do with the natural death of the physical body. Rather are they figurative, descriptive of the transition of the sense of personal identity from the limitations of the terrestrial, mortal nature of man to the freedom of his spiritual, immortal Selfhood. Such death implies a letting go, an outgrowing and leaving behind of selfish, personal desires and the self-separateness. The initiate makes a transition from undue concern with the more personal nature in the body—which thus metaphorically dies—to the spiritual Self in its so-called body of perpetual light. The center of awareness is then mystically newborn, having died to and been resurrected from the tomb of the flesh. In his *Georgias,* Plato writes: "For I should not wonder if Euripides spoke the truth when saying: 'Who knows whether to live is not to die, and to die is not to live?' And we are perhaps in reality dead. For I have heard from one of the wise that we are now dead; and that the body is our sepulchre."[12]

This symbolic death may in fact occur in the midst of bodily virility, although in certain allegories it is attained at the mystic thirty-three years of age at which the Christ is assumed to have arrived. Physical life is largely outflowing and eventually ends in physical death. The spiritual life of the inner Self, on the other hand, consists of an inflowing or upwelling from within of an ever-increasing fullness of life. In order to experience the life of the soul, the outer life of the body must metaphorically die.

The experience of death to material interests and resurrection to spiritual consciousness occurs either naturally as a result of normal evolutionary progress or is enforced by an intense effort of an awakened soul. In the Lesser Mysteries, designed to lead gradually and safely toward the experience, the death of the lower self is enacted ceremonially and described allegorically, as in the various Mystery Traditions recounting the deaths of saviors, deities, and heroes. In the Greater Mysteries, designed to produce the actual experience, the candidate is aided externally by the rite of initiation and interiorly by means of the regular practice of yoga. This achievement is only fully possible when a certain stage of Egoic or soul development has been reached at which the personality is literally forced to collaborate with the initiated Ego, by whom it is "slain."

Aspirants attain this gradually by the continual and habitual surrender of the lower self to the higher and the transcendence of personal, possessive desire and the egoistic pride from which it is born. This death is, however, not a single act occurring at one single time. The process continues over many lives until fulfilled at the final initiation—the triumphal coronation of the spirit of man.

Man on the threshold of superhumanity thus ascends the evolutionary ladder which symbolizes the soul's path from the lower nature to the higher, from the terrestrial to the spiritual. This ladder ascends from earth to the sun, from the physical body to the Monad. The upward path, the path of holiness itself, consists of stages or steps of progress—Nativity, Baptism, Transfiguration, Crucifixion, Death. It thus represents the evolution of the higher qualities of human nature and the gradual manifestation of the Dweller in the Innermost, the Monad, through the state of the illumined and initiated Ego of man to adeptship or Christhood. Egoism itself does not and will not last forever; for it is destined to become one of the rungs whereby the initiate mounts the "throne of divine glory" through love of God and love of neighbor or fellowmen.[13]

Mystically, the ladder of evolution, indeed the very path itself, is *within* man, who ascends upon it from ignorance and suffering to knowledge, wisdom, kingship. This ascension culminates in union with the one eternal, universal Life, "like water in water, light in light, and space in space." The crown of thorns has then become the true symbol of royalty. The reed-scepter is an emblem of power, reed-like and easily broken in the eyes of the multitude, but in fact an emblem of spiritual sway over the whole spiritual, intellectual and physical nature of self-liberated man.

> Matt. 27:51. And, behold, the veil of the temple was rent in twain from the top to the bottom; and the earth did quake, and the rocks rent;

The problem of trustworthy historicity is partly solved and an allegorical reading supported by the combined statements in the four Gospels of events said to occur from the moment of arrest in Gethsemane to death on Golgatha. Indeed, the several events included in a total narrative could not have transpired within the limits of the allotted period. A symbolical reading, thus encouraged, provides descriptions of changes in consciousness which are achieved during passage through the fourth great initiatory rite.

Thus read, the veil is seen as a barrier between the spiritual Self and the mind-brain, doubtless protective and fulfilling other functions.[14] This intervening barrier, already almost passed through, now disappears entirely. In consequence, the inner Self has uninhibited access to the mind and through that to the brain, while the initiate in his turn is readily able to know himself as a divine and immortal Son of God and to enjoy free access to supramental levels of awareness.

The earthquake and the rending of stones can be interpreted as the purely physical effects of this communion between the inner and outer. The matter of the brain and nervous system is no longer able to impose a resistance to the full and free play of the spiritual power and life of the immortal Self, thereby profoundly affecting both states of consciousness and physical activities.

> Matt. 27:52. And the graves were opened; and many bodies of the saints which slept arose,
>
> 53. And came out of the graves after his resurrection, and went into the holy city, and appeared unto many.

The above-suggested meanings are supported in this verse, the body itself being a grave in the sense that so many of the attributes and powers of the inherent divinity of man become inactive, buried, during physical and bodily awareness. As the state of perfected manhood is approached this inhibition disappears.

The statement that the saints rose from their graves is susceptible of at least two interpretations. First, the attainment of lofty evolutionary stature by a single individual renders easier—may even bring about—the same attainments in others on the threshold of adeptship, or "saints." Indeed, the spiritual attainments of any one successful aspirant are shared in varying degrees by every other who has reached a stage at which such receptivity becomes possible. A second meaning is that the above experiences are universal, so that every highly developed and illumined initiate has passed through these phases of expansions of consciousness and self-liberation from the grave of the body and bodily life.

Although but briefly described by the Evangelists, this experience of transcendence of all barriers interposed by nature between the God-Self and the mortal body of man is a most exalting, elevating experience. Life at the physical level becomes transformed, while little or no effect is needed for the initiate to enter into unity with his own divine nature at almost any chosen time. However, such a man is not entirely perfect, until a further expansion of consciousness is attained and a fifth initiation conferred.

> Matt. 27:54. Now when the centurion, and they that were with him, watching Jesus, saw the earthquake, and those things that were done, they feared greatly, saying, Truly this was the Son of God.

The soldiers and their commander who carried out the Crucifixion at the order of their superiors, and who watched Jesus upon the cross until he died would naturally be impressed by the described physical phenomena. If, however, the whole account personifies aspects of human nature, then the soldiers represent a high degree of self-discipline and obedience to words of command.

> Matt. 27:55. And many women were there beholding afar off, which followed Jesus from Galilee, ministering unto him:
>
> 56. Among which was Mary Magdalene, and Mary the mother of James and Joses, and the mother of Zebedee's children.

If these verses are read historically, the pathos of the scene is extreme. Indeed, it may well be assumed that, symbology apart, Jesus of Nazareth was personally accompanied on his travels throughout his country by a considerable number of men and women, far more than twelve disciples. Those whom he had admitted to his person and taught by both his words and his life must have revered and loved him. His agony upon the Cross must also have been theirs, especially in the case of his mother and Mary Magdalene. These women may be presumed to have received the body of Jesus, wept over it, prepared it for burial, then later discovered the empty tomb.

> Matt. 27:57. When the even was done, there came a rich man of Arimathaea, named Joseph, who also himself was Jesus' disciple:

434 LIFE OF CHRIST

58. He went to Pilate, and begged the body of Jesus. Then Pilate commanded the body to be delivered.

59. And when Joseph had taken the body, he wrapped it in a clean linen cloth,

60. And laid it in his own new tomb, which he had hewn out of the rock: and he rolled a great stone to the door of the sepulchre, and departed.

While these events were perfectly natural and may thus be read according to custom, they also lend themselves to the interpretations which have more than once been advanced in this book.

In both interpretations Joseph of Arimathaea personifies those archangelic and angelic agents, servants of the One Life, which are intimately associated with and may be said to assist that Life on the pathway of forthgoing. These hosts of the Logos also aid in the manifestation of the Monad at each stage of self-embodiment in matter, and particularly at the densest physical level, the human body.[15] The tomb is thus accurately described as hitherto unused and hewn out of the rock, implying the mineral kingdom and the bony structure of man's body, especially the skull.

The action of Joseph of Arimathaea in rolling a great stone "to the door of the sepulchre" is of great occult significance. At each reincarnation members of the angelic hierarchy assist the unfolding spiritual Self to construct the new bodies and the mechanism of consciousness, so that during waking hours consciousness is imprisoned in the physical body. This is essential in order to fulfill those evolutionary purposes which are dependent upon fully restrictive *physical* experiences. Once incarnated or born into a physical body, consciousness must during waking hours be limited thereto. Just as the bones forming the crown of the head of the newborn babe are not entirely closed but gradually unite, so also a similar enclosure is performed in the superphysical parts of the mechanism of consciousness. In Kabbalistic terms, the angelic hosts associated with the four "lowest" Sephiras—*Netzarch, Hod, Yesod* and *Malkuth*—enclose the projected ray of the Monad-Ego (the supernal Triad) in the encasement of the physical body, this being one part of their function on behalf of man, the microcosm.[16]

The doorway to still lower regions and states of consciousness —*Klippoth*—is also closed against the incarnating human self. Only at certain advanced stages of development and progress on the pathway of return are these two procedures nullified, as those on the threshold of adeptship acquire the power to enter into both spiritual and subphysical awareness and to leave the body at will and enter into other regions of the planets and the universe. Symbolically, in such cases the stone is rolled away from the sepulcher, as will be later described.

Matt. 27:61. And there was Mary Magdalene, and the other Mary, sitting over against the sepulchre.

62. Now the next day, that followed the day of the preparation, the chief priests and Pharisees came together unto Pilate,

63.   Saying, Sir, we remember that that deceiver said, while he was yet alive, After, three days I will rise again.

64.   Command therefore that the sepulchre be made sure until the third day, lest his disciples come by night, and steal him away, and say unto the people, He is risen from the dead: so the last error shall be worse than the first.

65.   Pilate said unto them, Ye have a watch: go your way, make it as sure as ye can.

66.   So they went, and made the sepulchre sure, sealing the stone, and setting a watch.

These actions of the people and of Pilate and the sealing of the sepulchre may be read as allegorical descriptions of the above-described imprisonment of conciousness.

The triplicity of natural polarities and of the triune Logos is also necessarily included in the episode. Pilate, agent of the power of the Roman Empire, and his soldiery personify spiritual Will or God the Father; Jesus the Christ is spiritual Wisdom; and the two Marys represent spiritual Intelligence or God the Holy Ghost. It is worthy of note that the sequence of events is somewhat broken in the sixty-first verse, which indicates that the two Marys were "sitting over against the sepulchre."

The ministry of the angels to man is greatly extended beyond the concept which is normal in exoteric Christian theology. Members of certain orders of angels are intimately concerned, not only with such beneficent acts as guardianship, healing and guiding, but also in the deeply occult procedures of divine and monadic manifestation in and withdrawal from matter. The latter function may be referred to by the Evangelists when they portray the discovery of the emply sepulcher and presence of two angels who relate Jesus is risen from the dead.

While the account of the death and burial of Jesus may also be read as a somewhat simple and staightforward narrative of events, the two supernatural occurrences above referred to cannot be so regarded. Their inclusion in the story renders it susceptible of being interpreted as an allegory revealing far more than the history of physical happenings. This approach is supported by the remarkable aptness of the whole account viewed as revelation of fundamental macrocosmic and microcosmic processes.

NOTES AND REFERENCES

1. Luke 24:13, et. seq.

2. Matt. 7:13-14; Isa. 35:8.

3. See diagram, p.

4. Ptah, creator of the world who put visible forms into existence by means of his heart (thought) and his tongue (by utternace).

5. *Gunas*—see Glossary.

6. *Chakra*—see Glossary.

7. See Hodson, *Hidden Wisdom*, Vol. 2, pp. 42-43.

8. H. P. Blavatsky, *The Voice of the Silence*, (Wheaton: Theosophical Publishing House, 2nd Quest ed.), p. 17.

9. See *The Apocryphal New Testament*, trans. Montague Rhodes James (Oxford: Clarendon Press), pp. 254-256.

10. See Hodson, *Hidden Wisdom*, Vol. 2, pp. 42-43.

11. Luke 23:42.

12. *The Collected Dialogues of Plato*, (Princeton University Press, 1969), p. 275.

13. Mark 12:31.

14. The Veil. For fuller interpretation see Hodson, *Hidden Wisdom*, Vol. 1, pp. 141-3.

15. See Hodson, *The Kingdom of the Gods* and *The Miracle of Birth*.

16. Kabbalah—see Glossary.

Chapter Twenty-Nine

The Resurrection of Jesus, the historicity of which is not here in question, has already and even repeatedly been interpreted. As descriptive of an epoch in the life-period of the Logos and the objective universe, it refers to the end of the processes of involution and the beginning of those of evolution.

In this view, the resurrected Jesus is seen as a personification of the unfolding life principle of the Logos after it has reached and passed through the deepest degrees of dense matter—the mineral, symbolized by the rock tomb.

> Matt. 28:1. In the end of the sabbath, as it began to dawn toward the first day of the week, came Mary Magdalene and the other Mary to see the sepulchre.
>
> 2. And, behold, there was a great earthquake: for the angel of the Lord descended from heaven, and came and rolled back the stone from the door, and sat upon it.
>
> 3. His countenance was like lightning, and his raiment white as snow:

An earthquake is said to have occurred as a phenomenon accompanying the rolling away of the stone which had closed the door of the sepulcher. This may refer to the breaking of the power of matter over spirit, of form over life, and of mineral over the human Monad, as already discussed. Although as yet far removed from the attainment of human individuality and later adeptship, nevertheless this change of direction from involution to evolution constitutes a revolutionary event. The stone rolled away may refer allegorically to major and minor cycles of a divine being manifesting in matter and his voluntary submission to the resultant limitations.

As heretofore suggested, the orders of the angelic hierarchies concerned with the outward and return journeys made by the One Life are of two distinct characters. One of these accepts as its mission the imprisoning procedures, and is therefore susceptible of symbolic representation as dark or even satanic. The archangels and angels of the Resurrection and Ascension are by their contrasting functions appropriately regarded as white, even intensely bright, as of a lightning flash. These are represented in the gospel stories by angels in white garments, as at the two Annunciations—to Zacharius and to Mary.

The fear combined with the gladness which moved the two Marys, along with the doubts of the apostles, indicate the greatness of the phenomenon of change from forthgoing to return. Since the Monads of men participate by means of the projection of monadic life and consciousness into the cosmic processes, it follows that the change of direction profoundly affects both the present and the future of every human Monad. Just as the prodigal son exclaimed, "I will arise," so every man will eventually arise to the phase of his evolution at which the spiritual goal is clearly comprehended. In due course in his physical body the way of the Cross which leads to symbolic Resurrection and Ascension is self-consciously entered upon. Such is one possible interpretation—the microcosmic—of the events recorded in the final chapters of the Four Gospels.

Macrocosmically, as the "upward," or rather "inward," journey of return is pursued, the physical universe, planet by planet, is deserted. The indwelling divine Life is withdrawn from physical matter and "the sepulcher is empty."

Man on the threshold of adeptship passes through this phase in advance of the normal evolutionary time and rhythm. Even though a physical body may be maintained by an Adept, it is no longer a "sepulcher," since man thus exalted enters and departs from it at will. Acquaintances, friends, and disciples who knew an Adept before the attainment of his exalted state become aware of this change in him. Even though the association may be continued after this attainment, the form in which a Master appears is less physical than superphysical. In the Christ story this is indicated allegorically by the discovery of the empty tomb by the two Marys and later by Peter and other disciples.

Since he is no longer restricted by the laws and conditions pertaining to physical matter, the Master can reappear within closed rooms, as did the Christ.

The grave clothes found in the sepulcher where they have been left behind may also imply the death of the power of physical matter, never again able to "bury" the consciousness of the Adept. The swaddling clothes of the Christ child symbolize physical matter with its component rotating atoms which was consciously and deliberately assumed at "birth." This has become as grave clothes at the allegorical death. Together, the empty sepulcher and discarded grave clothes portray the end of the power of physical matter over human consciousness and, in the macroscosmic sense, the end of an epoch.

> Matt. 28:4.   And for fear of him the keepers did shake, and became as dead men.
>
> 5.   And the angel answered and said unto the women, Fear not ye: for I know that ye seek Jesus, which was crucified.

The unconscious state of the guardians of Jesus's tomb also symbolizes the dominance of the threefold spiritual Self of the resurrected one over the mortal bodies. These are deprived of power to imprison, as it were, and so may be regarded as having fainted or fallen asleep.

The women disciples, on the other hand, as a result of their training, were able to commune with the angel of light and learn that their Master had risen from the grave, signifying that their development enabled them to be aware of and learn about the Dweller in the bodies, the immortal One or spiritual Self.

The feminine mind is traditionally regarded as less argumentative and more capable of intuitive perception than that of the male. This is suggested and supported by the fact that the discovery of the empty tomb and the first revelation of the risen Lord were made known to a female rather than to a male disciple. These facts may also imply that the human mind in general is passing into and becoming capable of direct intuitional perception; for this is a receptive, even passive condition of the human intellect, therefore feminine.

Matt. 28:6. He is not here: for he is risen, as he said. Come, see the place where the Lord lay.

7. And go quickly, and tell his disciples that he is risen from the dead; and, behold, he goeth before you into Galilee; there shall ye see him: lo, I have told you.

The whole of the remaining and closing events in the life of Jesus pertain far more to the spiritual level of consciousness than to the physical and purely historical worlds. Galilee thus becomes a symbol from topography for the supernal worlds where parting is unknown, matter no longer binds, and true disciples know their Master in his Masterhood. The instruction to go and inform the disciples of the Resurrection and instruct them to go to Galilee thus resembles an order to ascend in consciousness to a degree of enlightenment where death is unknown and purely physical happenings have little or no influence upon the soul.

Matt. 28:8. And they departed quickly from the sepulchre with fear and great joy; and did run to bring his disciples word.

9. And as they went to tell his disciples, behold, Jesus met them, saying, All Hail. And they came and held him by the feet, and worshipped him.

In obedience, the disciples quickly come into the presence of their Master and experience a spiritual relationship with him, or symbolically "worshipped him." If, however, the whole narrative is read as the story of every human being who triumphs over death and the limitations of mortal vehicles and their environment, then the permanent state of awareness by that time achieved is being described. This is purely spiritual, highly exalted, and from the time of the triumph onward will be the abiding center or dwelling place of the self-emancipated one.

Matt. 28:10. Then said Jesus unto them, Be not afraid: go tell my brethren that they go into Galilee, and there shall they see me.

Addressing the two Marys after his Resurrection, the Master himself utters the call to the disciples to enter the "Galilee" state of consciousness that he and they may be together in that region. Interpreted interiorly, the highly evolved immortal Self personified by Jesus continually exerts a spiritualizing and elevating influence upon the intuitions, mind, emotions, and physical body—all of which are within his influence. Indeed, the whole mortal man is less commanded than naturally brought to spiritual awareness of the Galilee-Self.

Matt. 28:11. Now when they were going, behold, some of the watch came into the city, and shewed unto the chief priests all the things that were done.

12. And when they were assembled with the elders, and had taken counsel, they gave large money unto the soldiers.

13. Saying, Say ye, His disciples came by night, and stole him away while we slept.

14. And if this come to the governor's ears, we will persuade him, and secure you.

15. So they took the money, and did as they were taught: and this saying is commonly reported among the Jews until this day.

Matter and objective form with their power to delude are dramatically portrayed in these verses, just as the true vision of the worlds of spiritual reality are allegorically presented as the relationships between Jesus and his disciples.

The marked contrast between the unillumined, worldly minded men of the world and those who have become self-spiritualized is displayed. Deceitfulness, bribery, self-protection and the misuse of authority at the cost of truth are briefly but clearly described, as are also the pitiful deceptions by means of which men seek to preserve the utterly false position in which they stand. Interiorly, traces of the "old Adam," as it is called, are seen for what they really are, but also as powerless to affect or change the realities which pertain to the spiritual worlds and the existence of the hidden Self of man consciously abiding in them.

We now consider St. John's account of the Resurrection which in many respects is more profound and more truly revealing than the Synoptics of the spiritual as well as the more material life of Jesus, with its cosmic overtones and its underlying mystical revelations.

John 20:11. But Mary stood without at the sepulchre weeping: and as she wept, she stooped down, and looked into the sepulchre,

12. And seeth two angels in white sitting, the one at the head, and the other at the feet, where the body of Jesus had lain.

13. And they say unto her, Woman, why weepest thou? She saith unto them, Because they have taken away my Lord, and I know not where they have laid him.

14. And when she had thus said, she turned herself back, and saw Jesus standing, and knew not that it was Jesus.

15. Jesus saith unto her, Woman, why weepest thou? whom seekest thou? She, supposing him to be the gardener, saith unto him, Sir, if thou have borne him hence, tell me where thou hast laid him, and I will take him away.

16. Jesus saith unto her, Mary. She turned herself, and saith unto him, Rabboni; which is to say, Master.

17. Jesus saith unto her, Touch me not; for I am not yet ascended to my Father: but go to my brethren, and say unto them, I ascend unto my Father, and your Father; and to my God, and your God.

These verses can be read as descriptive of the way from darkness to light and from death to immortality. Many mystics throughout the ages have, with Mary, trodden that interior pathway which leads from earthly sorrow to heavenly joy. Thus read, the empty sepulcher represents the world and the purely worldly life, which the spiritually awakening person eventually finds as an empty tomb indeed. A dead past is also aptly symbolized by the vacant tomb and the discarded grave cloths. In due course, however, this emptiness having been perceived, angelic aid is forthcoming. In one sense the two angels, with their wings closed and seated one at either end of the sepulcher, represent the spiritual will and the intelligence of the threefold divine Self of man, while Jesus, who almost immediately reveals himself as being present, personifies the divine wisdom or interior Christ nature, thereby completing the spiritual triad.

The experiences of Mary and the conversation which follows indicate that the transition from the worldly point of view and attitude toward life can be somewhat gradual. At first, the wisdom and love aspect of the Dweller in the Innermost (Jesus) remains unperceived, or at best falsely interpreted as part of the common everyday experience—a gardener in his garden. Jesus enabled Mary to recognize him by the sound of her own name, meaning, of course, her true nature, her divine Self. Thus, with intuitive perception, spiritually and occultly aroused, she knew and so addressed her Master, the Christ within.

Even so, in this mystical interpretation of the incident the recognition was incomplete as Jesus forbade her to touch him. The limitation, however, must be regarded as being solely on her part, since Jesus himself was the resurrected Christ, the perfected man, even though "he had not yet ascended unto my (his) Father." The incident as described by St. John is also of profound interest to the student of occult science, especially as symbolism already discussed indicates the process of Self-illumination within the brain while awake. Similarly crucifixion or death occurred within the skull or "on Golgotha." Those thus interested may choose to see in the empty sepulcher a symbol of both the hitherto unillumined brain-mind and also its third ventricle, empty of the faculty of full intuitive insight.

The more occult method of attainment includes the awakening and ascent into the head of the triple current of the divine creative Fire (*Kundalini Shakti*). In such a view, the two angels would represent the two oppositely polarized currents of this triple Serpent Fire, while flows along the spinal cord and passes through the hitherto empty sepulcher, awakening therein the qualities and faculties of the Christ nature in man. This experience is necessarily gradual, since undue haste and too sudden an illumination could make of the neophyte a distraught instead of an illumined human being. Hence Jesus's warning to Mary that she should not touch him at the first reunion.

The command to Mary to inform the brethren of the Resurrection and their experiences which followed refer to developments which later transpire. Also discernible are hints of the deeply occult procedures through which the ascended Adept passes when his physical body is allowed to die as far as outer appearances are concerned. Actually, a successsor in the same mold is formed, in the likeness of the old body but no longer subject to the processes of cellular decay and death. This results in unusual longevity for the "new" human form.[1] In this procedure, the transformation and re-formation may well be somewhat gradual, involving a phase at which full physical solidity has not yet been completed. Conceivably, Jesus asks Mary not to touch him because this procedure was incomplete at that time. This last interpretation, if accepted, supports the view that St. John was possessed of a special knowledge and had himself either passed through or had witnessed the re-formation of the physical body of an Adept. St. John, or whoever this author of the fourth Gospel may have been, may thus be thought to have actually witnessed these deeply occult happenings and indeed many others, since he writes in the thirtieth verse, "many other signs truly did Jesus in the presence of his disciples, which are not written in this book."

> John 20:24.   But Thomas, one of the twelve, called Didymus, was not with them when Jesus came.
>
> 25.   The other disciples therefore said unto him, We have seen the Lord. But he said unto them, Except I shall see in his hands the print of nails, and put my finger into the print of the nails, and thrust my hand into his side, I will not believe.
>
> 26.   And after eight days again his disciples were within, and Thomas with them: then came Jesus, the doors being shut, and stood in the midst, and said, Peace be unto you.
>
> 27.   Then saith he to Thomas, Reach hither thy finger, and behold my hands; and reach hither thy hand, and thrust it into my side: and be not faithless, but believing.
>
> 28.   And Thomas answered and said unto him, My Lord and my God.
>
> 29.   Jesus saith unto him, Thomas, because thou hast seen me, thou hast believed: blessed are they that have not seen and yet have believed.

This introduction to the famous narrative familarly referring to the disciple known as "doubting Thomas" is itself of interest. In the mystical interpretation a person in the presence of Jesus indicates a state of illumination in which the Christ nature of man is being experienced and, as in the so-called miracles of healing, the Christ power actively manifests.

In the case of Thomas, this condition had been entered, as "Thomas. . .was not with them when Jesus came." Thus, Thomas demanded demonstrable proof, both visible and tangible, referring to both mental and intuitional assurances.

In occult philosophy the eyes correspond to the intellect and the act of seeing to knowledge gained by the use of the abstract and concrete intelligence. The sense of touch, in its turn, refers to the faculty of direct intuition, insight and perception. While neither of these is fully available to an unillumined man, both form part of the supersensual powers developed by one who is in the uplifted and illumined state of consciousness. Thomas, therefore, demanded this exceedingly intimate and convincing proof that Jesus was indeed the Teacher who had been crucified and was now proclaimed to have risen from the dead. The twenty-fifth verse may be read as descriptive of his determination to know truth direct by both objective and subjective experiences from the evidence of his normal and supernormal sense.

To explain Jesus's entry into the room despite the fact that the door was closed necessitates either a miracle of the passage of matter through matter or interpretation as inner states of consciousness. If the latter view is accepted, then this uplifted state is indicated in the twenty-seventh verse. No secrets are hid, all truth being available in the degree to which the beholder is capable of perception.

A literal reading makes clear that Thomas was not regarded by Jesus as erring in his demand for objective truth, and from this it may be inferred that the reasoning, logical intellect may permissibly be applied to every occult and spiritual revelation. Thomas, then, was both encouraged and permitted to follow the advice of St. Paul to "prove all things; hold fast that which is good."[2]

Since the immortal story is also that of everyman, it may be adduced that the same principle and the same permission are applicable to everyone who embarks sincerely upon the search for directly perceived truth. Thus, not only Thomas, but every seeker for knowledge is advised to make sure of the intellectual ground upon which he stands and walks every step of the way.

The fact is of interest that only on four occasions was physical intimacy with Jesus ever permitted, namely when Mary Magdalene anointed him, when he himself washed his disciples feet, when the disciple John lay on his breast, and when Thomas was allowed to put his fingers in the bodily wounds.[3] Mystically interpreted, the permitted intimacies may be allegorically descriptive of realization of oneness. When the Christ nature in man becomes sufficiently evolved and human consciousness is, in consequence, elevated into an experience of Christ consciousness, the unity of oneself with all other beings is known as a living truth, separateness being reduced to a minimum. In verse twenty-eight the result of this entry into the uplifted state and of the experience of oneness are well described in the apparently ecstatic exclamation of Thomas, "My Lord and my God."

Throughout the Gospels several such direct revelations and personal discoveries are recorded. The first of these consists of the Annunciation to Mary and her humble acceptance born of interior realization of its verity. A further experience came to the shepherds, both when with their flocks and when worshipping before the newborn Christ child who stands for a newly attained spiritual illumination and spiritual perception. A third revelation was received by the Magi, symbolized by their vision of a star and correct interpretation of it as, metaphorically, shining over the newborn Christ in Bethlehem. This was followed by their presence with the holy family. There was also the descent of the Holy Spirit upon Jesus at his Baptism and the opening for him of the heavens and the sounding forth therefrom of the great pronouncement that he was an Avatar. The incidents now being considered—Peter's direct realization, Mary Magdalene's recognition of Jesus in the garden after his Resurrection, and the declaration by Thomas in the upper room in which they met thereafter—all these constitute veiled references to the spiritual illumination which the presence of Jesus produced in those who drew near to him.

A more advanced phase of evolutionary progress and so of intuitive perception are presumably described in verse twenty-nine; for eventually the faculty of spiritual intuitiveness becomes so highly developed that objective demonstration is no longer necessary, implicit insight having been attained.

John 21:1.　　After these things Jesus shewed himself again to the disciples at the sea of Tiberias; and on this wise shewed he himself.

2.　　There were together Simon Peter, and Thomas called Didymus, and Nathanael of Cana in Galilee, and the sons of Zebedee, and two other of his disciples.

3.　　Simon Peter saith unto them, I go a fishing. They say unto him, We also go with thee. They went forth, and entered into a ship immediately; and that night they caught nothing.

4.　　But when the morning was now come, Jesus stood on the shores: but the disciples knew not that it was Jesus.

5.　　Then Jesus saith unto them, Children, have ye any meat? They answered him, No.

6.　　And he said unto them, Cast the net on the right side of the ship, and ye shall find. They cast therefore, and now they were not able to draw it for the multitude of fishes.

While history may here be related, the manner of so doing renders the account susceptible of interpretation as an allegory of the attainment and exercise of spiritual vision. If this approach is used, the fact that the disciples had failed during the night to catch any fish at all symbolically portrays a mental state of unresponsiveness to the wisdom aspect of the higher Self of man—doubtless temporary only, due to the death of Jesus in this case. The absence of Jesus implies an unillumined state of mind in which spiritual intuitiveness, for which the fish is a symbol,[4] is not accessible. This view is supported by the statement that this part of the episode occurred during the night, implying a spiritually darkened state of mind. Thus viewed, the experience through which the disciples passed, from the time when Jesus was led away after his betrayal up to the moment of death upon the Cross, metaphorically describes a condition into which even close disciples can on occasion pass. This experience is characterized by spiritual aridity, lack of vision and inspiration, and even doubt and despair.

The presence of Jesus, on the other hand, is descriptive of a state of consciousness in which spiritual intuitiveness has become active, with the result that the attributes of the Christ nature in man become available in fullness. The fish signifies all that is implied in Christhood, including profound wisdom, compassionate love for all mankind, and the active expression of that love in sacrificial ministrations, even though these are foreknown to endanger life.

Complete spiritual illumination attained by the disciples is implicit in the description of the experiences beside the sea of Galilee and especially in the recognized presence of Jesus and the result of his plying their trade with a miraculous draft—for some of them were fishermen. In general, a sharp distinction is shown in the fruitage of work done, first with a purely material motive and, second, when spiritually guided. It is furthermore revealed that, however successful the processes of trade may be, they may yet be barren and without results when evaluated in terms of altruism, idealism, and spiritual enrichment.

> John 21:7. Therefore that disciple whom Jesus loved saith unto Peter, It is the Lord. Now when Simon Peter heard that it was the Lord, he girt his fisher's coat unto him (for he was naked) and did cast himself into the sea.
>
> 8. And the other disciples came in a little ship (for they were not far from land, but as it were two hundred cubits) dragging the net with fishes.

While these verses may be read in the purely historical sense, the introduction of miraculous events is recognizable as the author's guidance to seek below the surface of the narrative for hidden truths. The miraculous draft of fishes, Peter's action described in the preceding verse, the symbolical meaning of the fish, and the reappearance of Jesus three days and nights after his supposed death and burial, all constitute typical references to a hidden meaning.

While a spiritual teacher is far above the human attribute of favoritism, indications are given throughout the Gospels that John greatly loved his Master and that this evoked a response. This may be regarded as implying in John a naturally spiritual and intuitive state of mind and general character. This is supported by the statement that it was he who was the first to recognize the Master's presence. John displayed the quality of equipoise and harmony, characteristic of a human being at an advanced stage of development, as did Jesus's mother Mary, although when she chided him in the temple, she failed to understand her son's mission.

Peter, who on occasion had displayed a certain emotionalism and had in fact denied his Lord, remained ignorant of the presence of the resurrected Master. Immediately when it became revealed to him, with his customary impulsiveness he left the boat and attempted to move directly across the water to the feet of Jesus. This action might not be unnatural in one who on occasion had displayed the characteristic of a certain impetuosity. Since, however, Peter is presented as a disciple of an adept Teacher and since water is a symbol of the emotions, the episode may well describe attainment of mastery over emotional weaknesses, so that rather than being sources of distress and even danger, conquered and transmuted they become means of progress toward Masterhood, as personified by Jesus on the shore.

In Buddhistic symbolical writings concerning the hastened pathway to Buddhahood, water (referred to as "the stream") is used to describe the specially dedicated mode of life necessary. "The further shore," in its turn, refers to Buddhahood itself, and those who stood thereon personify those who have attained to Buddhahood. Transferred to Christian symbolism, Jesus stands on the shore while the disciples are still moving over the water toward the shore. This is in strict accordance with universally employed allegories and symbols.

> John 21:9.   As soon then as they were come to land, they saw a fire of coals there, and fish laid thereon, and bread.

While not neglecting the possibility of physical action by Jesus, fire lighted by an Adept is descriptive not only of an awakened, fiery aspiration, but also of the Serpent Fire which brings the brain to such a state of heightened responsiveness that spiritual wisdom and intuitiveness become available in the waking state.

> John 21:10.   Jesus saith unto them, Bring of the fish which ye have now caught.
>
> 11.   Simon Peter went up, and drew the net to land full of great fishes, and hundred and fifty and three: and for all there were so many, yet was not the net broken.

The net full of fish is here used as a symbol of the human mind in a condition of interior illumination (Jesus is present) but still retaining normal mentality and discrimination.

The number of fish is actually given, and if the digits are added together according to the methods of the interpretation of numerical symbolism, they total nine. This number regarded as implying both the completion of a major cycle of activity and unfoldment, whether macrocosmic or microcosmic, and preparedness for the opening of its successor, number ten. The visible and physical ministry of Jesus was ended by his bodily death, while his reappearance in a more spiritual form may indicate the opening of a new cycle on a higher round of the ascending evolutionary spiral.

> John 21:12.   Jesus saith unto them, Come and dine. And none of the disciples durst ask him, Who art thou? knowing that it was the Lord.

As at Emmaus—and now on the shores of Galilee, taking food with Jesus transforms a natural procedure into a sacramental meal, bringing with it spiritual vision and understanding. Thus the disciples are said to have known without question that indeed they were in the presence of the risen Lord, with all the psychological and spiritual meanings attributable to such an experience. In the few words of the sentence ". . . Who art thou? knowing that it was the Lord," the totality of mystical experience may be read; for the Lord here refers not only to the risen Jesus, not even to his supernal aspect as

Avatar of the supreme Lord of the universe, but also to the divine Presence within all mankind.

> John 21:13.   Jesus then cometh, and taketh bread, and giveth them, and fish likewise.

The symbols of bread and fish—particularly in their use as food on special occasions—have heretofore been interpreted as signifying those heightened intellectual and spiritual experiences and capacities passed through during a sacramental and therefore mystical "meal." The meal shared at the Master's invitation may also be interpreted as referring, however guardedly, to experiences in consciousness passed through during certain initiatory rites; for the characteristic of such rites is the realized close relation between human and universal spirit as portrayed in the intimacy of a meal.

Viewed historically, this meal together beside the Seal of Galilee, following upon all that had been endured since the betrayal must have been both a very solemn and an inwardly joyful occasion. Prophecies which had seemed to fail were now fulfilled, at least for the disciples.   As one reads these verses describing the reunion of Jesus and his disciples, one may both envisage the scene as an objective event and may also to some extent participate in the spiritual experience allegorically referred to. This is also true of almost every other account of the events in the great drama of the life of Jesus, from Annunciation to Ascension, as so many faithful and devoted Christians have discovered. Indeed the immortal story not only tells of events in Palestine two thousand or more years ago, but in addition portrays the inner life of every true mystic, with its foreshadowings of spiritual experiences, its happinesses, dangers, triumphs, and temporary darknesses, crucifixions, and ascension. This universality gives to every scriptural account of the lives of the saviors of men its enduring quality and power to inspire and uplift those who read it. So it is with that all too brief account of the blessed but awe-filled third reunion of the disciples with their risen Master.

> John 21:14.   This is now the third time that Jesus shewed himself to his disciples, after that he was risen from the dead.

First in an upper room, then in a house, and now in the open air amid nature the disciples were thrice privileged to be in the presence of their risen Lord. The more natural surroundings by the shores of a lake doubtless imply human consciousness in its pure state. Perfect peace and serene happiness were thus entered into by these faithful disciples.

> John 21:15.   So when they had dined, Jesus saith to Simon Peter, Simon, son of Jonas, lovest thou me more than these? He saith unto him, Yea, Lord; thou knowest that I love thee. He saith unto him, Feed my lambs.
>
> 16.   He saith to him again the second time, Simon, son of Jonas, lovest thou me? He saith unto him, Yea, Lord; thou knowest that I love thee. He saith unto him, Feed my sheep.
>
> 17.   He saith unto him the third time, Simon, son of Jonas, lovest thou me? Peter was grieved because he said unto

him the third time, Lovest thou me? And he said unto him, Lord, thou knowest all things; thou knowest that I love thee. Jesus saith unto him, Feed my sheep.

The disciple Peter is here designated the official representative of Jesus the Christ and the transmitter down the ages of his word to mankind. Upon this choice and this mission, divinely inspired as they were, the institution of the papacy has been founded. Peter himself is declared to have died and been buried under the site where the church bearing his name was erected. Ever since then this church has been regarded by the members of one of its denotinations as the physical heart and center of Christendom. A declaration has even been made under papal authority that certain of the bones of St. Peter's body have been unearthed from zeneath the sacred edifice.

Nevertheless. every disciple who, under test (the triple questioning by Jesus) proves himself or herself to be faithful, capable, and worthy similarly and quite naturally is under the obligation to share with mankind the teachings received. The instructions to Peter may therefore be regarded as descriptive of a timeless and completely impersonal duty which devolves upon *all* disciples, particularly initiated ones.

> John 21:18.   Verily, verily, I say unto thee, When thou wast young, thou girdedst thyself, and walkedst whither thou wouldest: but when thou shalt be old, thou shalt stretch forth thy hands, and another shall gird thee, and carry thee whither thou wouldest not.

The apparently abrupt change of subject matter supports the words of the authors—or perhaps the compilers—of this Gospel that the accounts of many events and many sayings are omitted. Hence the description of the different conditions and experiences of man when young and when old seems to be almost without meaning or point. Doubtless, it is but a small part of a longer utterance.

> John 21:19.   This spake he, signifying by what death he should glorify God. And when he had spoken this, he saith unto him, Follow me.

Evidently, however, Jesus was still addressing Peter and drawing him into close intimacy with himself, particularly instructing the disciple to deliver the message Jesus had given and to continue in his steps.

> John 21:20.   Then Peter, turning about, seeth the disciple whom Jesus loved following; which also leaned on his breast at supper, and said, Lord, which is he that betrayeth thee?
>
> 21.   Peter seeing him saith to Jesus, Lord, and what shall this man do?
>
> 22.   Jesus saith unto him, If I will that he tarry till I come, what is that to thee? follow thou me.

Peter evidently still needed—and in these verses is made to receive—a gentle lesson in the impersonality which must characterize the thought and life of a disciple. He is also taught that each man must be free to fulfill his appointed destiny and, ideally, to do so without attempted intrusion by others.

The mission and future of John differ from that of Peter, as is evidenced not only by these words of Jesus, but also by his conduct elsewhere described by the four Evangelists.

John's mystical nature is revealed in the before-mentioned apocryphal document known as *The Act of John* wherein the spirit of Jesus makes known to John the full reality concerning the apparent crucifixion of Jesus's body. Peter, as far as may be deduced, was somewhat more exoteric, even though his defined mission consisted of the deliverance of the teachings of his Master to mankind. Two distinct types of human beings are thus portrayed, as the rest of the twelve also display various human temperaments whenever personal character and conduct are revealed.

John 21:23. Then went this saying abroad among the brethren, that that disciple should not die: yet Jesus said not unto him, He shall not die; but, if I will that he tarry till I come, what is that to thee?

24. This is the disciple which testifieth of these things, and wrote these things: and we know that his testimony is true.

A not unnatural misinterpretation is here referred to and corrected. Jesus was in fact exemplifying a theory, teaching an ideal, rather than prophesying the future of the disciple whom he is said to have loved.

John 21:25. And there are also many other things which Jesus did, the which, if they should be written every one, I suppose that even the world itself could not contain the books that should be written. Amen.

Thus closes the fourth Gospel. As is affirmed in this closing verse, much remained to be said that is not recorded, suggesting indeed that both additional events and occult and philosophic revelations, doubtless of a secret nature, were withheld from the account of the life of Jesus in the Gospel according to St. John.

We now turn to St. Luke's account.

Luke 24:13. And, behold, two of them went that same day to a villabe called Emmaus, which was from Jerusalem about threescore furlongs.

14. And they talked together of all these things which had happened.

15. And it came to pass, that while they communed together and reasoned, Jesus himself drew near, and went with them.

28. And they drew nigh unto the village, whither they went: and he made as though he would have gone further.

29. But they constrained him, saying, Abide with us: for it is toward evening, and the day is far spent. And he went in to tarry with them.

30. And it came to pass, as he sat at meat with them, he took bread, and blessed it, and brake, and gave to them.

31. And their eyes were opened, and they knew him; and he vanished out of their sight.

The historicity of the account of this incident in Mark and Luke may perhaps be regarded as of less importance than its possible mystical significance. While the road (Emmaus) which each human being treads toward the attainment of self-liberation may differ for each individual, according to the stage or phase which is being described, mystical awakening or spiritual illumination is in certain aspects almost as a mathematical constant. It begins in ignorance (the disciples did not know Jesus) and it ends in fully opened vision (the disciples recognized him). Furthermore, just as the visible person of Jesus became invisible at the moment of enlightenment, so also dependence upon outer form is transcended when once the inner light is perceived.

Occurring several times before Jesus's death and after the Resurrection, the consumption of food together is regarded as an acknowledgment of close friendship. The breaking and blessing of bread and its almost sacramental administraion to the two disciples, which instantly brought about the vision of truth, may be interpreted as descriptive of the breaking down of any remaining mental barriers between the mortal and the immortal parts of man. Thereafter these remain in intimate relationship. The formal mind functioning in the brain and the emotional nature normally expressed through the heart (the two disciples) received the benediction of the Dweller in the Innermost, personified by Jesus.

Now that the mortal has become aware of and illumined by the immortal—always a deeply interior experience—there is no longer necessity for, or even value in instruction by words received from the visible teacher. Metaphorically, Jesus vanishes from their sight, indicating this. The two disciples, it may be presumed, would neither forget their experience nor lose the spiritual awareness into which they were elevated.

In the last verses of the Gospel according to St. Matthew, Jesus, reunited with his disciples, petitions them to carry on his mission.

> Matt. 28:16.   Then the eleven disciples went away into Galilee, into a mountain where Jesus had appointed them.

The reunion between Jesus and his disciples after his Resurrection is made to occur upon a mountain, and correctly so in strict accordance with the rules and usages of the symbolical language; for as has been seen, the summits of mountains are symbols for those states of human consciousness at which awareness of spiritual laws and truths become possible. Furthermore, the risen Jesus represents that which can never finally pass away or die, namely, the eternal, divine spirit-essence itself and similarly the eternal spirit of man.

The state of mind in which death seems to bring final departure and disappearance is portrayed by the symbols from topography of level ground and valleys. When man rises in consciousness above the mists of illusion wherein deaths and departures appear to have occurred, then only does he see the reality. There in the clear and pure air of the mountain tops of human consciousness these delusions are transcended and the ever-existent reality becomes known.

Under grave stresses and strenuous endeavors the human mind loses sight of the spiritual Self, the Christ-Self of man, allegorically portrayed as the central figure tf the gospel story. The events from Gethsemane to Gogotha allegorically portray those stresses and their effects. They hold the mind on the planes of earth itself and in the cities of men where illusion rules and reality is temporarily submerged.

Now, as the immortal story draws to a close, elevated states of mind are re-entered, as Master and disciples are symbolically brought together upon the mount.

> Matt. 28:17.   And when they saw him, they worshipped him: but some doubted.

Human nature is skillfully exemplified in this verse, as are more particularly the varying degrees of Self-illumination to which men, even disciples, are able to attain. Illumined ones are fully assured; they never waver, never doubt; for them the vision splendid is continuously experienced and enjoyed. However, the upward way is steep, and the summit is often veiled from the view from the foothills. In consequence, fatigue and the temporarily lost sight of the goal may cause doubts to arise.

> Matt. 28:18.   And Jesus came and spake unto them, saying, All power is given unto me in heaven and in earth.
>
> 19.   Go ye therefore, and teach all nations, baptizing them in the name of the Father, and of the Son, and of the Holy Ghost:
>
> 20.   Teaching them to observe all things whatsoever I have commanded you: and, lo, I am with you always, even unto the end of the world. Amen.

A solution to the problem of doubt is given in the eighteenth verse, even if in a somewhat veiled manner; for the Lord Jesus, now visibly and audibly present before them, personifies the Christ nature in man, that spiritual wisdom from which the faculty of direct, intuitive perception arises. When in doubt, therefore, realization of the inmost spiritual Self—the Christ Presence—should be sought and gained. Thereafter, all doubts will perforce disappear as do clouds of mist before the rising sun. Truth is thus found to be within, and when discovered bestows not only complete assurance upon the seeking mind but also that all-sufficing power whereby the great quest may be continued until its goal is attained.

The following verse continues the revelation; for not only is doubt dispelled and power attained, but the pathway to be followed is made clear. In the words of the Lord, "Go ye therefore, and teach all nations," the high calling of a teacher of spiritual wisdom to mankind becomes the ordained duty of the now wholly convinced and fully impowered disciple of the Lord.

St. Matthew closes his remarkable Gospel by repeating the wonderful promise of the Lord Christ to all mankind, that he will be with them "even unto the end of the world." Again, a mystical significance may be attributed to this promise, namely, that the Christ Indwelling is and ever will be indubitably present in the inner nature of every human being. This reading gains support from the fact that the historical person of Jesus has not been physically present in visible, audible, and tangible form in the world since that time. One is reminded here of the affirmation of St. Paul that, "Christ in you [is] the hope of glory."[5]

The final word of the Gospel, "Amen," may here be regarded, not only as an affirmation or sign of the completion of a prayer, but perhaps also as an utterance of the divine name which bestows ineffable power upon those who know the manner and the intent with which it should be uttered.

> Luke 24:50.   And he led them out as far to Bethany, and he lifted up his hands, and blessed them.
>
> 51.   And it came to pass, while he blessed them, he was parted from them, and carried up into heaven.
>
> 52.   And they worshipped him, and returned to Jerusalem with great joy;
>
> 53.   And were continually in the temple, praising and blessing God. Amen.

Though Christ's continuing presence among men is assured, nevertheless, as St. Luke reports, he ascended beyond the human plane to a deeply spiritual condition in the last of the great events in the epic story of his life—the Ascension. Humanly, the Ascension of Christ refers to the attainment of adeptship by men of every age through either natural evolution or deliberate self-quickening on the pathway to liberation. Cosmically, it applies to the end of an epoch or creative age when the divine spirit-essence-life hitherto indwelling is withdrawn from objective manifestation, particularly at the levels of mental, emotional and physical form. Evolutionary progress is not lost, however, and each Monad reemerges in the condition attained by the close of the preceding cycle. Nor is the withdrawal final as indicated by the promise to remain spiritually at one with the universe and its inhabitants.

The assurance of a return similarly indicates that a new cycle of active manifestation will open as a vehicle for the divine life, doubtless at another and higher level. The "wars and rumors of wars" which are to be the signal for the new incarnation refer to the inevitable opposition of activity and inertia which characterizes the state of substance at the opening of a new cycle.

The supposed onlookers perhaps are those more advanced beings of the closing cycle—Adepts and Archangels—who are sufficiently evolved and spiritually aware to be able to "see" and to comprehend the cosmic procedure. These are the so-called "first fruits of them that slept" who will assist the Logos in the next dispensation.[6]

Thus the great story ends for a time only to be resumed when the new cycle open. Once more "Christ" will be prophesied, announced, and born to follow the same pathway as before but in a sublimated form on a higher round of the evolutionary spiral. With the thought of the transcendent and immanent Deity as the all-compelling power behind the cycles in universe and man, this study of the life story of the Lord Christ is with deep reverence and humility drawn to a close. We may picture Christ, not only as the wondrous teacher and healer of men, which undoubtedly he was, but as one who also searched for—"fished" for, indeed—the particular men and women through whom the more esoteric aspects of the Wisdom Religion could be imparted to humanity after he had physically withdrawn. He set going a very powerful and enduring spiritualizing impulse and influence which the passage of two thousand years has in no way diminished. Holy Communion, the researches of occultists and mystics, and the spiritual experience of Christians to whom he revealed himself as a living being give, I suggest, to his person, life, and presence on earth a very deep additional significance and value. Even the rise of ruthlessly competitive, highly industrialized and almost wholly materialistic nations, has in no way dimmed the light which he lit; for he was far more mighty than any materialists or groups of merchants that could ever arise among men.

REFERENCES AND NOTES

1. See "The Elixir of Life" by G.M., p. 1-20, in *Five Years of Theosophy* (various authors). London: Theosophical Publishing Society, 1910.

2. Thess. 5:21.

3. John 12:3; Matt. 26:6-7; Mark 14:3; John 13:1-20; John 13:25; John 20:27-28.

4. See Hodson, *Hidden Wisdom,* Vol. 1, p. 109.

5. Col. 1:27.

6. I Cor. 15:20.

GLOSSARY

Absolute. The impersonal, supreme, and incognizable principle of the universe. See Parabrahman.

Adept (L.), Adeptus, "He who has obtained." An Initiate of the Fifth Degree in the Greater Mysteries, a Master in the science of esoteric philosphy, a perfected man, an exalted being who has attained complete mastery over his purely human nature and possesses knowledge and power commensurate with lofty evolutionary stature.

Ahamkara (Sk.) The first tendency toward definiteness, regarded as the origin of all manifestation. In man the conception of "I," self-consciousness or self-identity, the illusion of self as a separate existence in contradistinction to the reality of the universal One Self.

Akasa (Sk.) "The subtle, supersensuous, spiritual essence which pervades all space. The primordial substance erroneously identified as ether. . . .It is to ether what spirit is to matter." H.P.Blavatsky: *The Theosophical Glossary.*

Archetype (Gr.) "First-moulded" or stamped. The ideal, abstract, or essential "idea." The divine conceiving from which arises the divine "idea" of the whole universe in time and space; the governing power of creation.

Arhat (Pali). "The worthy." Exoterically, "one worthy of divine honors." Esoterically, an Initiate of the Fourth Degree who has entered the highest Path and is thus emancipated from both self-separation and enforced rebirth.

Astral. The region of the expression of all feelings and desires of the human soul. See also **Kama.**

Atma (Sk.). "The Self." The universal Spirit, the seventh principle in the septenary constitution of man, the Supreme Soul. The Spirit-Essence of the universe. (Paramatman—"the Self Beyond.")

Augoiedes (Gr.). "The self-radiant divine fragment," the Robe of Glory of the Gnostics, and the Karana Sharira, "Causal Body," of Hinduism.

Aura. A subtle, invisible essence or fluid that emanates from human, animal, and even inanimate bodies.

Avatar (Sk.) The doctrine of Divine incarnation, or "descent."

Avatara (Sk.) "Descent." The incarnation of a Deity, especially Vishnu, the Second Aspect of the Hindu Trimurti.

Brahman (Sk.) The impersonal, supreme, and incognizable Principle of the universe, from the essence of which all emanated and into which all return.

Brahma's Day. A period of 4,320,000,000 (Earth) years during which Brahma, having emerged from his golden egg (Hiranyagarbha), creates and fashions the material world (being simply the fertilizing and creative force in nature.) See H.P. Blavatsky: *The Secret Doctrine* (6-vol. ed.), Vol. III, p. 80.

Brahma's Night. A period of equal duration, during which Brahma is said to be asleep.

Buddhi (Sk.) The sixth principle of man, that of intuitive wisdom, vehicle of the seventh, Atma, the supreme Soul in man. Universal Soul.

Causal Body. The immortal body of the reincarnating Ego of man, built of matter of the "higher" levels of the mental world. It is called Causal, because it gathers up within it the results of all experiences, and these act as causes molding future lives and influencing future conduct.

Chain. In occult philosophy a solar system is said to consist of ten Planetary Schemes. Each Scheme is composed of seven Chains of Globes. In terms of time, a Chain consists of the passage of the life-wave seven times around its seven Globes. Each such passage is called a Round, the completion of the seventh ending the life of the Chain. The Globes of a Round are both superphysical and physical, and are arranged in a cyclic pattern, three being on a descending arc, three on an ascending arc, and the middle, or fourth Globe, being the densest of all and the turning point. The period of each of these units, from solar system to Globe, called *Manvantara,* is succeeded by a passive period of equal duration called *Pralaya*. The completion of the activity of the seventh Globe of the seventh Round of the seventh Chain brings to an end the activity of a Planetary Scheme.

Chakra (Sk.) A "wheel" or "disc." A spinning, vortical, funnel-shaped force center with its opening on the surface of the etheric and subtler bodies of man and its stem leading to the superphysical counterparts of the spinal cord and of nerve centers of glands. There are seven main chakras associated severally with the sacrum, the spleen, the solar plexus, the heart, the throat, and the pituitary and pineal glands. Chakras are both organs of superphysical consciousness and conveyors of the life force between the superphysical and physical bodies. See C.W. Leadbeater: *The Chakras.*

Correspondence. See Law of Correspondence.

Cosmocratores.(Gr.). "Builders of the Universe," the World Architects or creative Forces personified.

Devas (Sk.). "Shining Ones," spiritual beings, Planetary Logoi, and the Heirarchies of Archangels and angels.

Dhyan Chohans (Sk.). The "Lords of Contemplation," the divine intelligences charged with the supervision of the Cosmos.

Dhyāni (Sk.). "Expert in Yoga." Also a generic name for spiritual beings, Planetary Logoi, and Hierarchies of Archangels and angels.

Ego. The threefold, immortal, unfolding spiritual Self of man in its vesture of light, the Causal Body.

Fohat (Tib.). "Divine Energy." The constructive force of cosmic electricity.

Gnostics. (Gr.). The philosophers who formulated and taught the Gnosis or knowledge. They flourished in the first three centuries of the Christian era.

Gunas (Sk.). The three qualities or attributes inherent in matter: Rajas —activity, desire; Sattva—harmony, rhythm; Tamas—inertia, stagnation.

Initiate. From the Latin *Initiatus*. The designation of anyone who was received into and had revealed to him the mysteries and secrets of occult philosophy. See Geoffrey Hodson: *The Hidden Wisdom in the Holy Bible,* Vol. I, pp. 216-228.

Initiation. A profound spiritual and psychological regeneration, as a result of which a new "birth," a new beginning, a new life is entered upon.

Kabala (Heb.). From QBLH, "an unwritten or oral tradition." The hidden wisdom of the Hebrew rabbis derived from the secret doctrine of the early Hebrew peoples. See Hodson: *The Kingdom of the Gods,* Part III, Ch. IV.

Kama (Sk.). Desire, feeling, emotion. See **Astral**

Karma (Sk.). "Action, " connoting both the law of action and reaction, cause and effect, and the results of the operation of this law upon individuals and nations. See Hodson: *Reincarnation, Fact or Fallacy?*

Kundalini (Sk.). The coiled-up, universal life principle. A sevenfold, superphysical, occult power in universe and man, represented in Greek symbology as the Caduceus. See Hodson: The Hidden Wisdom in the Holy Bible, Vol. I, pp. 121-128; Hodson: *Lecture Notes of the School of the Wisdom,* Vol. II, Ch. I, Sec. 3: Arthur Avalon (Sir John Woodroffe): *The Serpent Power.*

Law of Correspondence. The harmonious coordination of mutual resonance between the many apparently separate parts of the universe and corresponding parts of the constitution of man. In occult philosophy, all components of both macrocosm and microcosm are interwoven and interactive according to a universal system of vibrational interchange. Inspired allegories may, and indeed should, be understood equally in the macrocosmic and the microcosmic senses.

Logos (Gr.). "The Word," "A divine, spiritual Entity.' The manifested Deity, the outward expression or effect of the ever-concealed

Cause. Thus speech is the Logos of thought, and Logos is correctly translated into Latin as "Verbum" and into English as "Word" in the metaphysical sense.

Logos Doctrine. The universe is first conceived in divine thought, which is the governing power in creation. The creative "Word" expressive of the idea is then "spoken" and the hitherto quiescent seeds of living things germinate and appear from within the ocean of Space, the Great Deep. See Hodson: *Lecture Notes of the School of the Wisdom*, Vol. II, Part. 2, Sec. 2.

Macrocosm. Literally "Great Universe" or Cosmos.

Mantras (Sk.). Verses from the *Vedas* rhythmically arranged so that, when sounded, certain vibrations are generated, producing desired effects upon the physical and superphysical bodies.

Manvantara (Sk.). "Period between Manus." Epoch of creative activity. A period of manifestation. The period of nonmanifestation is called a "Pralaya."

Microcosm. "Little Universe." The reflection in miniature of the macrocosm. Thus the atom may be spoken of as the "microcosm" of the solar system, its electrons moving under the same laws; and man may be termed the "microcosm" of the universe, since he has within himself all the elements of that universe.

Monad (Gr.). "Alone." The divine Spirit in man, the "Dweller in the Innermost," which is said to evolve through the subhuman kingdoms of nature into the human and thence to the stature of the Adept, beyond which extend unlimited evolutionary heights.

Monad-Ego. A dual term used in the work to connote the individualized manifestation of the human Monad as triple Spirit. The divine Spark or Dweller in the Innermost (Monad) which in the course of evolution has attained to self-conscious individuality as man (Ego), and, during life on earth, is embodied in vehicles of mind, emotion, and flesh.

Nirvana (Sk.). "Having life extinguished." Conscious absorption in the One Life of the Cosmos, or absolute consciousness (Buddhism).

Occult Science. "The science of the secrets of nature—physical and psychic, mental and spiritual. . . .In the West, the Kabbalah may be named; in the East, mysticism, magic, and yoga philosophy." H.P. Blavatsky: *The Theosophical Glossary.*

Parabrahman (Sk.). "Beyond Brahmā" The supreme, infinite Brahmā, the Absolute, attributeless, secondless Reality; the impersonal, nameless, universal, and eternal Principle.

Shakti (Sk.). Ability, power, capability, faculty, strength. The outgoing energy of a god is spoken of as his wife, or shakti. Thus, although a deity or a central personage and his consort or wife are presented as two separate people, the latter (wife) actually personifies attributes or powers of the former (husband). In consequence, the supposed pair in reality represent one being.

BIBLIOGRAPHY

Albright, William Foxwell. *Archaeology of Palestine*.

Arnold, Sir Edwin. *The Light of Asia*. Philadelphia: David McKay Co., 1932.

Bates, Ernest Sutherland, ed. Old Testament. In The Bible, King James Version, pp. 3-897. New York: Simon Schuster, 1936.

_____ New Testament. In the Bible, King James Version, pp. 901-1230. New York: Simon Schuster, 1936.

Besant, Annie, trans. *Bhagavad-Gita*. Adyar: Theosophical Publishing House, 1965.

Blavatsky, Helena Petrovna. *The Secret Doctrine,* vv 1-3. London: Theosophical Publishing House, 1921.

_____ *Theosophical Glossary*. New York: Theosophical Publishing House, 1918.

Book of Common Prayer.

Brandon, S.G.F. *Jesus and the Zealots*. Scribners.

_____ Trial of Jesus.

Chatterji, Mohini M., ed. *Five Years of Theosophy*. London: Theosophical Publishing Society, 1910.

_____ *The Crest Jewel of Wisdom* (Vivekachudamani). Adyar: Theosophical Publishing House, 1968.

Franck. *Origeniana*.

Fuller, J.F.C. *The Secret Wisdom of the Qabalah*.

Graves, Robert. *The Greek Myths*, v 2. New York: George Braziller, 1957.

Guaita, den S. *Ay Seuil de Mystiere*.

Heindel, Max. "Lohengrin." *Mysteries of the Great Operas*. London: L.N. Fowler, 1921.

Hodson, Geoffrey. *Brotherhood of Angels and Men*. London: Theosophical Publishing House, 1927.

_____ *Hidden Wisdom in the Holy Bible,* vv 1-3. Wheaton: Theosophical Publishing House, 1971.

_____ *Hidden Wisdom in the Holy Bible,* vv 1-3. Adyar: Theosophical Publishing House, 1963.

_____ *The Kingdom of the Gods*. Adyar: Theosophical Publishing House, 1952.

_____ *Lecture Notes on the School of the Wisdom*. Madras: Theosophical Publishing House, 1955.

_____ *The Miracle of Birth*. London: Theosophical Publishing House, 1929.

_____ *Pathway to Perfection*. Adyar: Theosophical Publishing House, 1954.

_____ *Reincarnation, Fact or Fallacy?* Adyar: Theosophical Publishing House, 1954.

_____ *The Priestly Ideal*.

Humphreys, Christmas, and Benjamin, Elsie, ed. *The Mahatma Letters to A. P. Sinnett*, 3rd. ed. revised. Adyar: Theosophical Publishing House, 1962.

Johnston, Charles. *Yoga-Sutras of Patanjali*. London: John M. Watkins, 1964.

King, C.W. *The Gnostics and their Remains*. London: David Nutt, 1887.

Lao-Tse, King of Taoism.

Leadbeater, Charles Webster. *Man Visible and Invisible*. Adyar: Theosophical Publishing House, 1925.

"Magnificat." In *The Hymn of the Virgin Mary*.

Mead, George Robert Stow. *The Hymn of the Robe of Glory*. London: Theosophical Publishing House, 1908.

_____ *Echoes from the Gnosis*, v 20. London: Theosophical Publishing Society, 1907.

_____ "The Pistis Sophia." In *Fragments of a raith Forgotten*, 3rd. ed., pp. 459-506. London: John M. Watkins, 1931.

Moulton, Richard G., ed. *The Wisdom of Solomon*. New York: Macmillan Co., 1900.

Origen. *De Principiis*.

_____ Selecta. *Psalmos, Patrologica*.

Pancoast, S. *The Kabbalah*. New York. Worthington Publishing Co., 1883.

Pandit, M.P. *The Upanishads*. Madras: Ganesh & Co. (Madras) Private, 1968.

Pentateuch.

Ramanujacharya. *Brahmasutras*. Madras: The Educational Publishing Co., 1965. Rhodes, Montague, trans. Apocryphal New Testament. Clarendon Press. Silesius, Angelus. Poem.

Sinha, Purnendu Marayana. *Study of the Bhagavata Purana*. Adyar: Theosophical Publishing House, 1950.

Sperling, Harry; Simon, Maurice; and Levertoff, Dr. Paul P., ed. *The Zohar*, vv 1-5. London: The Soncino Press, 1933.

St. Clair and Her Order.

Woods, Rev. Dr. Frank. Sermon.

INDEX

AARON, rods, 112.
ACT OF FAITH, 17.
"ACT OF JOHN," 449.
ACTS, 2:42-47, 24.
ADAM, 19.
ADEPT(S), 25, 60, 219; brotherhood, 23, 317; characteristics, 352-3; magic of teaching, 294; power, 97, 99, 195, 197, 199, 229, 301, 313, 364; transcended all limitations, 254; youthful materity, 173.
ADEPT HIERARCHY, guidance 66; protection, 205.
ADEPTSHIP, 16, 93, 178, 391, 401, 429; attaining, 16, 244; way of holiness leads to, 281.
AGELESS WISDOM, deliverers, 180; in all creeds, 66; teachings, 67.
AHAMKARA, 130.
AKASA, 87.
ALBRIGHT, W.F., *The Archaeology of Palestine*, 10.
ALLEGORIES, people in, 39; used by Initiates, 289; Christ's life, 43; Christ's Nativity, 57; Cosmogenesis, processes, 52; Cronos, 64; eating, 87; evolution, quickened, 113; expansion of consciousness, 79; healing, 184; heavenly marriage, 20; Herod's massacring, 64; historical Jesus, 47; illumination, 99; influence of matter on spirit, 415; Initiation, struggles, 65; Initiation, first of five 58; Initiations, physical and superphysical, 58; Initiatory rite, 332; inner life of true mystic, 447; involution and evolution, 375, 400; Jesus and John the Baptist, 39; Joseph and angel, 52, 65; Joseph, husband of Mary, 51; Keys of interpretation, 13-14; King Kansa, 64; Logos, self-incarnation, 425; Mary's pregnancy, 58; palsy healed, 200; pathway to perfection, 421; practice of yoga, 212; process of regeneration, 206; realization of oneness, 443; reasons for 85; "Salt of the earth," 134; spirit into matter, 406; spiritual alchemy, 129; spirituo-mental conflict, 196; story of Jesus, 391; temptations of Jesus, 86, 87; veil, 313; Way of Holiness, 57; Will and creative Fire, 58; language, 185.

AMMONIUS SACCUS, 9, 12.
"ANALOGETICISTS," 12.
ANALOGY, Jesus taught by, 345, 349.
ANGEL OF LIGHT, 439.
ANGELIC HIERARCHIES, two distinct characters, 244-5, 437.
ANGELIC HOSTS, Ministry, 16.
ANGELUS SILESIUS, 54.
ANNUNCIATION, Angel, 31, 33; interpretations, 33.
ANTHROPOMORPHIC DEITY, 120.
APOSTLES' CREED, 17.
APPOLONIUS OF TYANA, 25.
ARHATS, 25.
AQUARIUS, 226.
ARISTOTLE, 9.
ARJUNA, 324.
ARMAGEDDON, 202, 416.
ASCETISM, 167.
ASPIRANT(S), never alone, 95; vulnerable in new life, 346; goal of, 132.
ASTROLOGICAL SYMBOL, Christian era, 226; Judas Iscariot, 226; twelve disciples, 226.
ASTROLOGY, and life of Christ, 225; as a science, 225.
ATMA, 215, 223, 336.
ATMA-BUDDHI, 20.
ATOM, function 193.
ATONEMENT, 54, 171; esoteric meaning, 386; Theosophical view, 20.
AUGOEIDES, 370.
AUM, 55.
AURIC "CLOUDS OF GLORY," 58.
AVATAR(S), 38, 41, 80, 237, 238, 244, 251, 321, 369; functions, 386.
AVIDYA, 219.
BACON, Lord. 25.
BARDESANES, 72.
BASILIDES (Gnostics), 9.
BEATITUDES, 23.
BEELZEBUD, 86.
BETHLEHEM, 21.
BHAGAVAD PURANA, 55.
BIBLE, original text altered, 203, 232; translation, faulty, 406; literal reading, offensive, 241; dubious authenticity, 228.
BLACK MASS, 267.
BLASPHEMY, sin, 267.